THE PHILISTINES AND
THEIR MATERIAL CULTURE

THE
PHILISTINES
AND THEIR
MATERIAL CULTURE

Trude Dothan

NEW HAVEN AND LONDON   YALE UNIVERSITY PRESS

JERUSALEM   ISRAEL EXPLORATION SOCIETY

To Benjamin Mazar, teacher and friend

Designed by Nancy Ovedovitz and set in VIP Palatino type.
Printed in the United States of America by The Murray Printing Co., Westford, Mass.

Library of Congress Cataloging in Publication Data
Dothan, Trude Krakauer.
 The Philistines and their material culture.
 Revised translation of ha-pelishtim ve-tarbutam ha-ḥomrit.
 Bibliography: p.
 Includes index.
 1. Philistines. 2. Palestine—Antiquities.
I. Title.
DS90. D613 1981   933   80-22060
ISBN 0-300-02258-1
10   9   8   7   6   5   4   3   2   1

CONTENTS

70519

PLATES

FIGURES

CHAPTER 4

CHAPTER 5

MAPS

TABLES

PREFACE

The present volume is a revised, expanded, and up-to-date translation of the author's Hebrew work, *The Philistines and Their Material Culture* (Bialik Institute and Israel Exploration Society, Jerusalem, 1967). Since 1967, much has been added to our knowledge by excavation and publication in Palestine and in the other countries connected with the origin and cultural background of the Philistines. We have endeavored to take this new material into consideration, benefiting by the new light it sheds on old problems to strengthen or modify our previous conclusions. The development of archaeological research and techniques, the numerous stratigraphical excavations of Early Iron Age sites in Palestine, and the striking finds from tombs, all enable us to set our stratigraphical, chronological, typological, and comparative study on a firmer basis than was possible before.

Our emphasis is on the initial stages of Philistine culture when its distinctive character, not yet assimilated into other cultures, still reflected its origins. We concentrate on aspects of material culture that are unequivocally related to the Philistines, using the word *Philistine* as a collective term to include all related groups of Sea Peoples who settled in Canaan.

Invaluable discoveries are being made in Israel at the present time, both in the cities of Philistia proper and in the outlying areas far removed from the main sphere of Philistine culture. At the same time, archaeological and epigraphical-historical research connected with Philistine culture is steadily advancing in neighboring Middle Eastern and Aegean countries, and this research will undoubtedly add to our present knowledge of the historical and archaeological background of the Philistines.

The Bible, Egyptian records, and archaeological finds are the three main sources for our knowledge of Philistine origins, cultural background, and history. This study deals primarily with the archaeological evidence of the material culture of the Philistines, and attempts to place it within the chronological and cultural framework of the eastern Mediterranean, against the background, known from textual sources, of the transitional period between the Late Bronze and Early Iron ages. The archaeological evidence, which comes mainly from the rich finds in Palestine, may also help to elucidate the origins, wanderings, and cultural affinities of the Philistines. A study of their material culture is a necessary complement to information gained from historical and textual sources. Biblical and literary sources, both epigraphical and descriptive, are used here as background to archaeology. Stratigraphical finds are the basis for a relative and absolute chronology.

ACKNOWLEDGMENTS

My deepest gratitude is extended to my teachers, colleagues, and friends, in particular to Benjamin Mazar, who gave freely of his advice, encouragement, and knowledge. I am also grateful to those who granted me permission to publish objects from their excavations or from the collections in their charge, especially the Oriental Institute of the University of Chicago and Helene Kantor; the University Museum of Pennsylvania; the Institute of Archaeology, London University and Peter Parr; the Wellcome-Marston Archaeological Expedition and O. Tufnell; the British Museum; the Ashmolean Museum, Oxford, and P. R. S. Moorey; V. Karageorghis, Director of the Department of Antiquities, Cyprus; the Institute of Archaeology, Hebrew University of Jerusalem; the Israel Museum, M. Tadmor and R. Hestrin; the Israel Department of Antiquities; A. Biran; G. Edelstein; M. Kohavi; and a special thanks to A. Mazar, who allowed me to use the material from his doctoral thesis on Tell Qasile, now published in the *Qedem* monograph series: *Excavations at Tell Qasile, Part One. The Philistine Sanctuary: Architecture and Cult Objects* (Jerusalem, 1980). I also wish to thank M. Dayan and T. Kollek for placing their private collections at my disposal and permitting me to photograph the objects.

I am also greatly obliged to Judith Arnold, who drew all the pottery and mounted the plates; to Jean Leger, who drew many of the figures and reconstructions for chapter 4; to Esther Huber, who drew several of the additions to the English edition; to Sorel Zimmerman, who helped in technical matters; and to Gary Lipton, who drafted the chronological chart.

Thanks are due to Ben Meir, whose translation of the Hebrew edition into English served as a basis for this book. I am indebted also to Ruth Rigbi, who provided valuable assistance in the additions to the English text, and to Essa Cindorf and Daniella Saltz, who edited the text.

Special thanks are due to Baruch Brandl for his useful suggestions in the chapters on stratigraphy and chronology and to Ann Killebrew for her invaluable assistance during the final stages of the preparation of the book.

I am most grateful to Joseph Aviram, Director of the Institute of Archaeology of the Hebrew University, whose wise and practical advice contributed greatly toward the publication of this book. I am especially indebted to J. Schweig, who took many of the photographs in this book. The bulk of the new photographs were taken by Z. Radovan, and I am grateful to him for his fine work.

Last but certainly not least, I must express my deepest thanks to my husband, Moshe Dothan, who placed at my disposal the material from the excavations at ʿAfula, Tel Mor, Azor, and Ashdod, and whose advice helped me at every stage of my work.

Jerusalem, 1979   Trude Dothan

ABBREVIATIONS

PERIODICALS

AA *Archäologischer Anzeiger*

AASOR *Annual of the American Schools of Oriental Research*

ADAJ *Annual of the Department of Antiquities of Jordan*

AfO *Archiv für Orientforschung*

AJA *American Journal of Archaeology*

AJBA *Australian Journal of Biblical Archaeology*

Annuario *Annuario della regia scuola archeologica di Atene e delle missioni italiane in oriente*

AOAT *Alter Orient und Altes Testament*

AS *Anatolian Studies*

ʿAtiqot *ʿAtiqot. Journal of the Israel Department of Antiquities*

BA *The Biblical Archaeologist*

BASOR *Bulletin of the American Schools of Oriental Research*

BBSAJ *Bulletin of the British School of Archaeology in Jerusalem*

BCH *Bulletin de Correspondance Hellénique*

BIAL *Bulletin of the Institute of Archaeology, London*

BIES *Bulletin of the Israel Exploration Society* (Hebrew)

BSA *Annual of the British School at Athens*

Eretz-Israel *Eretz-Israel. Annual of the Israel Exploration Society* (Hebrew and English)

Ergon Τὸ Ἔργον τῆς Ἀρχαιολογικῆς Ἑταιρείας κατὰ τὸ ἔτος . . .

GGA *Göttingische Gelehrte Anzeigen*

Glotta *Glotta. Zeitschrift für griechische und lateinische Sprache.*

IEJ *Israel Exploration Journal*

JAOS *Journal of the American Oriental Society*

JBL *Journal of Biblical Literature*

JDAI *Jahrbuch des deutschen Archäologischen Instituts*

JEA *Journal of Egyptian Archaeology*

JHS *Journal of Hellenic Studies*

JKF *Jahrbuch für Kleinasiatische Forschung*

JNES *Journal of Near Eastern Studies*

JPOS *Journal of the Palestine Oriental Society*

LA *Liber Annuus*

MDIAA *Mitteilungen des deutschen Instituts für ägyptische Altertumskunde in Kairo*

MDOG *Mitteilungen der Deutschen Orientalischen Gesellschaft zu Berlin*

MJ *The Museum Journal,* University of Pennsylvania

OA *Acta Instituti Romani Regni Sueciae: Opuscula Archaeologica*

Op.Ath. *Acta Instituti Atheniensis Regni Sueciae: Opuscula Atheniensia*

PEF Ann *Annual of the Palestine Exploration Fund*

PEFQSt *Palestine Exploration Fund, Quarterly Statement*

PEQ *Palestine Exploration Quarterly*

PMB *Palestine Museum Bulletin*

QDAP *Quarterly of the Department of Antiquities in Palestine,* Jerusalem

Qedem *Qedem. Monographs of the Institute of Archaeology. The Hebrew University of Jerusalem*

RB *Revue biblique*

RDAC *Report of the Department of Antiquities Cyprus*

Tel Aviv *Tel Aviv, Journal of the Tel Aviv University Institute of Archaeology*

VT *Vetus Testamentum*

ZDPV *Zeitschrift des Deutschen Palästina-Vereins*

BOOKS AND ARTICLES

Aegean and the Near East S. Weinberg, ed. *The Aegean and the Near East: Studies presented to Hetty Goldman.* New York, 1956.

ʿAfula M. Dothan. "The Excavations at ʿAfula," *ʿAtiqot* 1 (1955): 19–70.

AG I–IV W. M. F. Petrie. *Ancient Gaza,* vols. I–IV. London, 1931–34.

AG V W. M. F. Petrie, E. J. H. Mackay, and M. A.

Murray. *Ancient Gaza,* vol. V, *City of Shepherd Kings.* London, 1952.

Alasia I C. F. A. Schaeffer. *Alasia I. XXᵉ Campagne de Fouilles á Enkomi-Alasia (1969).* Paris, 1971.

Albright, Syria, the Philistines and Phoenicia W. F. Albright. "Syria, the Philistines and Phoenicia," *CAH³,* vol. II, pt. 2, chap. 33, pp. 507–34.

ANEP J. B. Pritchard. *The Ancient Near East in Pictures.* 2nd ed. with suppl. Princeton, 1969.

ANET J. B. Pritchard, ed. *Ancient Near Eastern Texts Relating to the Old Testament.* 3rd ed. with suppl. Princeton, 1969.

Aniba I–II G. Steindorff et al. *Aniba,* vols. I, II. Hamburg, 1935–37.

Anthedon W. M. F. Petrie. *Anthedon Sinai.* London, 1937.

AS I–II E. Grant. *Ain Shems Excavations,* pts. I–II. Haverford, Pa., 1931–1932.

AS III E. Grant. *Rumeileh, being Ain Shems Excavations,* pt. III. Haverford, Pa., 1934.

AS IV–V E. Grant and G. E. Wright. *Ain Shems Excavations,* Pt. IV: *The Pottery;* pt. V: *The Text.* Haverford, Pa., 1938–39.

Ashdod I M. Dothan and D. N. Freedman. "Ashdod I: The First Season of Excavations, 1962." *'Atiqot* 7 (1967).

Ashdod II–III M. Dothan. "Ashdod II–III: The Second and Third Seasons of Excavations, 1963, 1965, Soundings in 1967." *'Atiqot* 9–10 (1971).

Ashkelon J. A. Garstang. "The Fund's Excavation of Askalon," *PEFQSt* (1921): 12–16; Garstang, "The Excavation of Askalon, 1920–1921," *PEFQSt* (1921): 73–75; Garstang, "Askalon Reports. The Philistine Problem," *PEFQSt* (1921): 162–63; Garstang, "The Excavations at Askalon," *PEFQSt* (1922): 112–19; W. J. Phythian-Adams, "Report on the Stratification of Askalon," *PEFQSt* (1923): 60–84.

Azor M. Dothan. "Excavations at Azor, 1960." *IEJ* 11 (1961): 171–75.

BANE G. E. Wright, ed. *The Bible and the Ancient Near East: Essays in Honour of W. F. Albright.* New York, 1961.

Barnett: The Sea Peoples R. D. Barnett. "The Sea Peoples." In *CAH³,* vol. II, chap. 28.

Beth-Zur O. R. Sellers. *The Citadel of Beth-Zur.* Philadelphia, 1933.

B-M F. J. Bliss and R. A. Macalister. *Excavations in Palestine.* London, 1902.

BP I W. M. F. Petrie and O. Tufnell. *Beth Pelet,* vol. I. London, 1930.

BP II E. Macdonald, J. L. Starkey, and L. Harding. *Beth Pelet,* vol. II. London, 1932.

BS E. Grant. *Beth Shemesh.* Haverford, Pa., 1929.

B-SH I A. Rowe. *The Topography and History of Beth-Shan,* vol. I. Philadelphia, 1930.

B-SH II, Part 1 A. Rowe. *The Four Canaanite Temples of Beth-Shan,* vol. II, part 1: *The Temples and Cult Objects.* Philadelphia, 1940.

B-SH II, Part 2 G. M. Fitzgerald. *The Four Canaanite Temples of Beth-Shan,* vol. II, part 2: *The Pottery.* Philadelphia, 1930.

B-SH Cemetery E. Oren. *The Northern Cemetery of Beth Shan.* Leiden, 1973.

B-SH Iron F. James. *The Iron Age at Beth Shan.* Philadelphia, 1966.

CAH³ *Cambridge Ancient History,* rev. 3d ed., vol. II, pt. 1, 1973; vol. II, pt. 2, 1975. Cambridge.

Catling, Bronzework H. W. Catling. *Cypriot Bronzework in the Mycenaean World.* Oxford, 1964.

CMP A. Furumark. *The Chronology of Mycenaean Pottery.* Stockholm, 1941.

CPP J. G. Duncan. *Corpus of Dated Palestinian Pottery.* London, 1930.

CVA Corpus Vasorum Antiquorum.

Deir ʿAlla H. J. Franken. *Excavations at Tell DeirʿAlla,* vol. I. Leiden, 1969.

Deir el-Balaḥ IEJ 22 T. Dothan. "Anthropoid Clay Coffins from a Late Bronze Age Cemetery near Deir el-Balaḥ (Preliminary Report I)." *IEJ* 22 (1972): 65–72.

Deir el-Balaḥ IEJ 23 T. Dothan. "Anthropoid Clay Coffins from a Late Bronze Age Cemetery near Deir el-Balaḥ (Preliminary Report II)." *IEJ* 23 (1973): 129–46.

Deir el-Balaḥ Qedem 10 T. Dothan. *Excavations at the Cemetery of Deir el-Balaḥ.* Qedem 10. Jerusalem, 1979.

Deir el-Medineh G. Nagel. *La Céramique du Nouvel Empire à Deir el Médineh,* tome I. Cairo, 1938.

DMS V. R. d'A. Desborough. *The Last Mycenaeans and their Successors.* Oxford, 1964.

EAEHL *Encyclopedia of Archaeological Excavations in the Holy Land.* Jerusalem, 1975–78.

Enkomi C. F. A. Schaeffer. *Enkomi-Alasia I: Nouvelles missions en Chypre, 1946–1950.* Paris, 1952.

Enkomi Excavations P. Dikaios. *Enkomi Excavations 1948–1958,* vols. I–III. Mainz, 1969.

Fortetsa J. K. Brock. *Fortetsa: Early Greek Tombs near Knossos.* Cambridge, 1957.

Furumark, OA 3 A. Furumark. "The Mycenaean

III C Pottery and Its Relation to Cypriote Fabrics." *OA* 3 (1944): 194–265.

Gardiner, *Onomastica I* A. H. Gardiner. *Ancient Egyptian Onomastica*, vol. I. Oxford, 1947.

Gerar W. M. F. Petrie. *Gerar*. London, 1928.

Gezer R. A. S. Macalister. *The Excavation of Gezer 1902–1905 and 1907–1909*, vols. I–III. London, 1912.

Gezer I (1964–1966) W. G. Dever, H. D. Lance, and G. E. Wright. *Gezer*, vol. I, *Preliminary Report of the 1964–1966 Seasons*. Jerusalem, 1970.

Gezer II (1967–1970) W. G. Dever, H. D. Lance, R. G. Bullard, D. P. Cole, and J. D. Seger. *Gezer*, vol. II, *Reports of 1967–1970 Seasons in Fields I and II*. Jerusalem, 1975.

Gjerstad, *OA 3* E. Gjerstad. "The Initial Date of the Cypriote Iron Age." *OA* 3 (1944): 73–106.

Gurob G. Brunkon and R. Engelbach. *Gurob*. London, 1927.

HIC W. M. F. Petrie and J. G. Duncan. *Hyksos and Israelite Cities*. London, 1906.

HU Hebrew University

Ialysos I–II A. Maiuri. "Jalisos—Scavi della Missione Archeologica Italiana a Rodi (Parte I e II)." *Annuario* 6–7 (1926): 83–256.

Ialysos G. Jacopi. "Nuovi scavi nella necropoli micenea di Jalisso." *Annuario* 13–14 (1933–40): 253–345.

Kitchen, *The Philistines* K. A. Kitchen. "The Philistines." In *Peoples of Old Testament Times*, D. J. Wiseman, ed., pp. 53–78. Oxford, 1973.

Lachish II O. Tufnell et al. *Lachish*, vol. II, *The Fosse Temple*. Oxford, 1940.

Lachish III O. Tufnell et al. *Lachish*, vol. III, *The Iron Age*. London, 1953.

Lachish IV O. Tufnell et al. *Lachish*, vol. IV, *The Bronze Age*. London, 1958.

Malamat, *The Egyptian Decline* A. Malamat. "The Egyptian Decline in Canaan and the Sea Peoples." In *The World History of the Jewish People*, vol. 3, *Judges*, B. Mazar, ed., pp. 23–38, 294–300. Tel Aviv, 1971.

Mazar, *The Philistines* B. Mazar. "The Philistines and the Rise of Israel and Tyre." *Proceedings of the Israel Academy of Sciences and Humanities* 1, no. 7 (1969): 1–22.

Mazar, *The Philistines and Their Wars* B. Mazar. "The Philistines and Their Wars with Israel." In *The World History of the Jewish People*, vol. 3, *Judges*, B. Mazar, ed., pp. 164–79. Tel Aviv, 1971.

Medinet Habu H. H. Nelson et al. *Medinet Habu* I: *Early Historical Records of Ramses III*. Chicago, 1930.

Meg. I R. Lamon and G. M. Shipton. *Megiddo*, vol. I. Chicago, 1939.

Meg. II G. Loud. *Megiddo*, vol. II. Chicago, 1948.

Meg. Cult H. G. May. *Material Remains of the Megiddo Cult*. Chicago, 1935.

Meg. Ivories G. Loud. *The Megiddo Ivories*. Chicago, 1939.

Meg. T. P. L. O. Guy. *Megiddo Tombs*. Chicago, 1938.

MP A. Furumark. *The Mycenaean Pottery: Analysis and Classification*. Stockholm, 1941.

Mycenaeans in the Eastern Mediterranean *Acts of the International Archaeological Symposium, The Mycenaeans in the Eastern Mediterranean*. Nicosia, 1973.

Nasbeh I C. C. McCown. *Tell en-Nasbeh*, vol. I. Berkeley, 1947.

Nasbeh II J. C. Wampler. *Tell en-Nasbeh*, vol. II: *The Pottery*. Berkeley, 1947.

Nouveaux Documents V. Karageorghis. *Nouveaux Documents pour l'étude du Bronze Recent à Chypre*. Paris, 1965.

Perati A–Γ, B S. Iakovidis. *Perati A–Γ*. Athens, 1969–1970 (text in Greek; English summary in vol. B).

Qasile IEJ 1 B. Mazar. "The Excavations at Tell Qasile: Preliminary Report." *IEJ* 1 (1950–1951): 61–76, 125–40.

Qasile IEJ 23 A. Mazar. "Excavations at Tell Qasile, 1971–1972: Preliminary Report." *IEJ* 23 (1973): 65–71.

Rowe A. Rowe. *A Catalogue of Egyptian Scarabs, Scaraboids, Seals and Amulets in the Palestine Archaeological Museum*. Cairo, 1936.

Salamine de Chypre M. Yon. *Salamine de Chypre*, vol. II: *La Tombe T.I. du XIe s.av.J-C*. Paris, 1971.

SAOC 17 G. M. Shipton. *Notes on the Megiddo Pottery of Strata VI–XX*. Studies in Ancient Oriental Civilization no. 17. Chicago, 1939.

SCE IV, Part 1C P. Åström. *The Swedish Cyprus Expedition*, vol. IV, part 1C: *The Late Cypriote Bronze Age. Architecture and Pottery*. Lund, 1972.

SCE IV, Part 1D L. Åström. *The Swedish Cyprus Expedition*, vol. IV, part 1D: *The Late Cypriote Bronze Age. Other Arts and Crafts*. Lund, 1972.

SCE IV, Part 2 E. Gjerstad. *The Swedish Cyprus Expedition*, vol. IV, part 2: *The Cypro-Geometric, Cypro-Archaic and Cypro-Classical Periods*. Stockholm, 1948.

SIMA *Studies in Mediterranean Archaeology*.

Sinda   A. Furumark. "The Excavations at Sinda: Some Historical Results." *Op.Ath.* 6 (1965): 99–116.

Sjöqvist   E. Sjöqvist. *Problems of the Late Cypriote Bronze Age.* Stockholm, 1940.

Snodgrass, Armour   A. M. Snodgrass. *Early Greek Armour and Weapons.* Edinburgh, 1964.

Stubbings   F. H. Stubbings. *Mycenaean Pottery from the Levant.* Cambridge, 1951.

Tanis II   W. M. F. Petrie. *Tanis,* vol. II. London, 1888.

TBM I–III   W. F. Albright. "The Excavations of Tell Beit Mirsim I," *AASOR* 12 (1932); IA, *AASOR* 13 (1933): 55–128; II, *AASOR* 17 (1938); III, *AASOR* 21–22 (1943).

Tel Abu Hawam   R. W. Hamilton. "Excavations at Tell Abu Hawām." *QDAP* 4 (1935): 1–69.

Tel Zeror I–III   K. Ohata, ed. *Tel Zeror,* vols. I–III. Tokyo, 1966, 1967, 1970.

Tools and Weapons   W. M. F. Petrie. *Tools and Weapons.* London, 1917.

Ugaritica II   C. F. A. Schaeffer. *Ugaritica,* vol. II. Paris, 1949.

Ugaritica III   C. F. A. Schaeffer et al. *Ugaritica,* vol. III. Paris, 1956.

Ugaritica V   C. F. A. Schaeffer et al. *Ugaritica,* vol. V. Paris, 1968.

Ugaritica VI   C. F. A. Schaeffer et al. *Ugaritica,* vol. VI. Paris, 1969.

Wresz   W. Wreszinski. *Atlas zur altägyptischen Kulturgeschichte,* vol. 2. Leipzig, 1935.

Yadin, Warfare   Y. Yadin. *The Art of Warfare in Biblical Lands in Light of Archaeological Study.* London, 1963.

Yahudiyeh   E. Naville and F. Griffith. *The Mound of the Jew and the City of Onias, Antiquities of Tell el Yahudiyah.* London, 1887.

1
THE HISTORICAL SOURCES

The Philistines were among the Sea Peoples that first appeared in the eastern Mediterranean in the second half of the thirteenth century B.C., and they emerge from biblical and Egyptian historical accounts as a strong influence on the history and culture of Palestine. At that time the two major powers, Egypt and the Hittites, were politically weak and militarily impotent, and the Sea Peoples exploited the power vacuum thus created in the region by invading areas previously subject to Egyptian and Hittite control. In wave after wave of land and sea assaults they attacked Syria, Palestine, and even Egypt; the last and mightiest wave, in which the Philistines took part, stormed the coast of Palestine at the beginning of the reign of Ramesses III (ca. 1198–1166 B.C.).[1] According to Egyptian sources, Ramesses defeated the invaders after fierce naval and land battles. Subsequently, according to the Egyptian account, Ramesses gave them permission to settle on the southern coastal plain of Palestine. There they developed into an independent political factor of major importance and constituted a threat to the disunited Canaanite city-states.

During the same period the Israelites, who had invaded Palestine from the east, were settling in the hill country. From the middle of the twelfth to the end of the eleventh century, they fought with the Philistines for the cultural and political domination of the country. Both historically and culturally this was the Philistines' most flourishing era.[2] From the early tenth century on, the Philistines steadily declined in importance

until they played no more than a minor part in the history of Palestine. Succumbing to assimilation, they gradually lost their cultural distinctiveness and merged with the Canaanite population.

EGYPTIAN SOURCES

The main nonbiblical sources for the history of the Philistines and the other Sea Peoples are the Egyptian literary and historical records. In the Amarna letters[3] (ca. 1375 B.C.) and in the annals of Ramesses II[4] (ca. 1304–1237 B.C.) one of the Sea Peoples (Sherden) is mentioned as a mercenary force in the Egyptian army. According to the records of Merneptah (ca. 1236–1223 B.C.), the Sea Peoples attempted to invade Egypt in his fifth regnal year as part of a massive attack from the direction of Libya. In this onslaught the Libyans were leagued with confederates from the north described explicitly as "foreigners from the Sea"—the Sherden, Sheklesh, Lukka, Tursha, and Akawasha.[5] The Philistines and the Tjekker are first mentioned as invaders during the reign of Ramesses III. Although we lack relevant information on the first four years of his reign, we know that in the period between his fifth and

1. We have followed the higher chronology for the accession and reign of Ramesses III, i.e., 1198–1166 B.C. R. C. Faulkner, *CAH*[3], vol. II, chap. 23, pp. 241 ff.

2. Mazar, *The Philistines*, pp. 1 ff., and *The Philistines and Their Wars*, pp. 166 ff. For the latest summary, *see* A. Malamat, "Struggle Against the Philistines," in *The History of the Jewish People*, H. H. Ben-Sasson, ed. (Cambridge, Mass., 1976), pp. 80–87.

3. Barnett, *The Sea Peoples*, p. 360; and Gardiner, *Onomastica I*, pp. 194* ff. Albright does not agree to the reading *Sherden* in the text; *see* W. F. Albright, "Some Oriental Glosses on the Homeric Problem," *AJA* 54 (1950): 162 ff.

4. Faulkner, *CAH*[3], vol. II, p. 228. In the second year of the reign of Ramesses II the Sherden are mentioned as pirates raiding the coast of the Delta (Gardiner, *Onomastica I*, p. 194*). These raids seem to have been frequent and continuous, judging by the fact that the number of Sherden prisoners subsequently serving in the Egyptian army was sufficient to furnish a contingent of their own (*ANET*, p. 476).

5. Faulkner, *CAH*[3], vol. II, p. 233; Albright, "Some Oriental Glosses on the Homeric Problem," p. 166; Gardiner, *Onomastica I*, p. 196*; and Malamat, *The Egyptian Decline*, pp. 24 f., 294 f., nn. 6, 7.

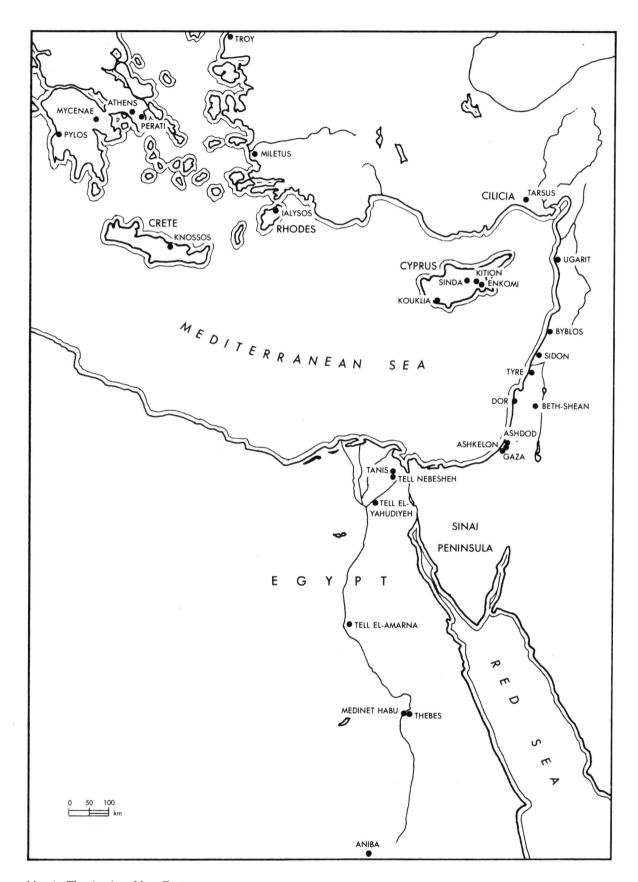

Map 1. The Ancient Near East

eleventh years there were three major wars, the main sources for which are the reliefs and inscriptions in his mortuary temple at Medinet Habu in Thebes. The vivid battle scenes depicted on the walls there are our most precious graphic representation of the Sea Peoples' dress, weaponry, chariotry, naval equipment, and battle tactics (figs. 4, 7). The accompanying inscriptions (if we discount their exaggerated praise of the pharaoh) are also invaluable as records of attacks on the Egyptian frontier by foreigners. This information is supplemented by the Harris Papyrus I,[6] the last part of which refers to political events in the lifetime of the recently deceased Ramesses III. In the Harris Papyrus, Ramesses' wars with the Sea Peoples are described as follows:[7]

> I extended all the frontiers of Egypt and overthrew those who had attacked them from their lands. I slew the Denyen in their islands, while the Tjeker and the Philistines were made ashes. The Sherden and the Weshesh of the Sea were made nonexistent, captured all together and brought in captivity to Egypt like the sands of the shore. I settled them in strongholds, bound in my name. Their military classes were as numerous as hundred-thousands. I assigned portions for them all with clothing and provisions from the treasuries and granaries every year.[8]

Ramesses thus inflicted a decisive defeat on the Sea Peoples, among them the Philistines, and took many captives. Some of these were impressed into military service as part of his troops or as mercenaries in the garrisons located, as a rule, on the borders of the empire. It seems likely, therefore, that Philistine mercenaries were stationed in several Canaanite cities under Egyptian suzerainty.

The Medinet Habu inscriptions[9] give vivid accounts of the wars in the eighth year of Ramesses III and reflect the turmoil in the Levant at that time:

The foreign countries made a conspiracy in their islands. All at once the lands were removed and scattered in the fray. No land could stand before their arms, from Hatti, Kode, Carchemish, Arzawa, and Alashiya on, being cut off at [one time]. A camp [was set up] in one place in Amor. They desolated its people and its land was like that which has never come into being. They were coming forward toward Egypt, while the flame was prepared before them. Their confederation was the Philistines, Tjeker, Shekelesh, Denye[n], and Weshesh, lands united. They laid their hands upon the lands as far as the circuit of the earth, their hearts confident and trusting: "Our plans will succeed!"

After describing his preparations for the battle, how he mustered his military and naval forces, Ramesses relates the results of the conflict:

> Those who reached my frontier, their seed is not, their heart and their soul are finished forever and ever. Those who came forward together on the sea, the full flame was in front of them at the river mouths, while a stockade of lances surrounded them on the shore. They were dragged in, enclosed, and prostrated on the beach, killed, and made into heaps from tail to head. Their ships and their goods were as if fallen into the water.

> . . . The northern countries quivered in their bodies, the Philistines, Tjekk[er, and . . .]. They cut off their [own] land and were coming, their soul finished. They were *teher*-warriors [chariot warriors] on the land; another [group] was on the sea. Those who came on [land were overthrown and killed]. Amon-Re was after them, destroying them. Those who entered the river-mouths were like birds ensnared in the net. . . . Their leaders were carried off and slain. They were cast down and pinioned.[10]

According to the inscription under the land battle scene, the Egyptian army fought the Sea Peoples in the land of Djahi (the Egyptian name for the Phoenician coast and hinterland down to Palestine).[11]

The Onomasticon of Amenope, which dates from the end of the twelfth or beginning of the eleventh century,[12] mentions the areas settled by the Sea

6. The Great Harris Papyrus in the British Museum comes from Thebes and dates from the end of the reign of Ramesses III. It is an important source for the history of the early Twentieth Dynasty. *ANET*, pp. 260–62.

7. Ibid., p. 262.

8. In the extracts we follow the transcription "Tjeker" used in *ANET*, although in the text we adopt the *CAH*'s "Tjekker."

9. *ANET*, pp. 262–63; *see also*, Faulkner, *CAH³*, vol. II, pp. 241–44, who challenges the inscriptions' value as a historical source.

10. *ANET*, pp. 262–63 a–b.

11. Ibid., p. 257, n. 21; p. 260, n. 4.

12. Gardiner, *Onomastica I*, p. 24.

Peoples in Palestine, within the sphere of Egyptian influence. It records a number of peoples, lands, and cities. Three ethnic groups, the Sherden (*srdn*),[13] the Tjekker (*ṭkr*),[14] and the Pelesti (*prst*)—the Philistines[15]—are listed, together with Ashkelon, Ashdod, and Gaza,[16] cities situated in the territory controlled by the Philistines. Although the three ethnic groups cannot be positively identified with the cities mentioned, it can be assumed that the document gives a reasonably accurate picture of the demographic situation on the Palestinian coast at the end of the Twentieth and the beginning of the Twenty-first Dynasty.[17] This Onomasticon, together with the accounts of the Philistines preserved in the Bible and in the Wen Amun tale described below, indicates that Philistine settlement was concentrated on the southern Palestinian coast and that the Tjekker occupied the coastal plain farther to the north. Unfortunately, the location of the Sherden cannot be determined, for no document of the period mentions this contingent of Sea Peoples except for the Medinet Habu reliefs, on which the Sherden are shown fighting side by side with the Philistines against the Egyptians or side by side with the Egyptians.

It is of some importance that the three cities mentioned by Amenope—Ashkelon, Ashdod, and Gaza—though not listed in any geographical order, are all in Philistine territory. No other region mentioned in the Onomasticon is accompanied by a list of cities in such close proximity to each other. The fact that they are emphasized here as a geographical unit may be attributed to the importance of the Philistine territory as an Egyptian line of defense and a means of controlling the commercial routes to the north. It thus seems possible that the Philistines at this time were still nominally under Egyptian rule.

The Wen Amun tale,[18] dating to the middle of the eleventh century B.C. (early in the Twenty-first Dynasty), is the sole reference to the area occupied by the Tjekker, a group of Sea Peoples closely related to the Philistines. Wen Amun, the author of the tale, was a priest of the temple of Amun in Karnak who was sent to Byblos to purchase cedar logs for the construction of Amun's ceremonial barge. He relates that "I reached Dor, a town of Tjeker, and Beder, its prince, had 50 loaves of bread, one jug of wine and one leg of beef brought to me." While in Dor, one of the sailors jumped ship and took refuge in the Tjekkers' port city, taking with him the silver and gold meant for the purchases at Byblos. Wen Amun's pleas to Beder, the Tjekker king, that the thief be apprehended were unavailing, and he finally had to set sail for Byblos to complete his mission. After a long journey and an extended stay in Byblos, Wen Amun discovered that he was being pursued by Beder: "I went [to] the shore of the sea to the place where the timber was lying and I spied eleven ships belonging to the Tjeker coming in from the sea in order to say: 'Arrest him! Don't let a ship of his [go] to the land of Egypt.'"

This account, undoubtedly based on fact, is of great importance because of its references to the Tjekker and to Dor, their capital and, apparently, main port in the Sharon coastal plain. The territory occupied by the Tjekker seems to have extended from south of Tyre to the northern Philistine border. Although the Tjekker king acknowledged Egyptian rule, it is clear that this allegiance was little more than a political fiction, as was most likely the case with the Philistines as well.

Egypt, torn by internal dissension and rival contenders for the throne, during the last days of the Twentieth Dynasty had sunk into a state of weakness bordering on political disintegration. She was incapable of maintaining effective rule over her empire and could not rely upon her military strength to deal with the Tjekker in Dor, Byblos, and Cyprus. The fleet of eleven Tjekker ships sent to Byblos is a fair indication of the naval strength of the Tjekker king.

In the course of his tale, Wen Amun mentions three kings besides Beder: Weret (*wrt*), Mekmer (*mkmr*), and Werket-El (*wrktr*).[19] The last-named appears to have been involved in a commercial treaty with Sidon, to which he provided some fifty merchant ships. If the suggestion that these three were the kings of Ashkelon, Ashdod, and Gaza is correct, it is reasonable to assume that Werket-El was the ruler of Ashkelon, at

13. Ibid., p. 194*, no. 268.
14. Ibid., p. 199*, no. 269.
15. Ibid., p. 200*, no. 270.
16. Ibid., pp. 190*, 191*, nos. 262–64.
17. A. Alt, *Kleine Schriften zur Geschichte des Volkes Israel*, vol. 1 (Munich, 1953), pp. 231 ff.
18. *ANET*, pp. 25–29.

19. Weret (*Wr/lt*), Mekmer (*Mkmr/l*), and Werket-El (*Wr/l ktr/l*) are non-Semitic names which may be Anatolian or Aegean (except for the last name element, "El"); see Mazar, *The Philistines*, p. 3, and *The Philistines and Their Wars*, p. 166; W. F. Albright, *BANE*, p. 359, n. 79, and Albright, *Syria, the Philistines and Phoenicia*, p. 513, n. 4.

that time the largest, richest, and most important of the Philistine cities.[20]

The Wen Amun tale provides a unique picture of the Palestinian coast in the eleventh century B.C., when many autonomous or semiautonomous kingdoms such as that of the Tjekker were entering into commercial or political treaties with one another to engage in, or perhaps to regulate, trade along the coast. The dominion of Egypt had become a dominion in name alone.

The Medinet Habu Reliefs

The triumphal reliefs adorning the mortuary temple of Ramesses III,[21] which depict his naval and land battles against the invading Sea Peoples (their defeat and captivity are shown in detail), provide a rare opportunity to observe the dress and battle tactics, as well as the physical characteristics of the Philistines and other Sea Peoples. They are portrayed as warriors, prisoners of the Egyptian army, and mercenaries or slave troops fighting in the ranks of the Egyptian army. Ramesses' accompanying inscriptions repeatedly speak of using captive troops in his army.[22]

The Sea Peoples are clearly differentiated from other enemies of Egypt. Three groups are immediately distinguishable by their headgear: (a) the Peleset (fig. 1), the Tjekker (fig. 2), and the Denyen (fig. 3) have identical "feathered" headdress; (b) the Sherden wear horned helmets;[23] and (c) the Sheklesh and the Teresh have fillet headbands.

The inscriptions accompanying the prisoner scenes identify the peoples in group (a). The inscription in figure 1 reads, "The vanquished Peleset say: 'Give us

the breath of our nostrils, O King, Son of Amon.'" Since the Peleset, Tjekker, and Denyen (the dominant group) look very much alike, we shall refer to them by the generic term *Philistines* unless the inscriptions state otherwise. Using figure 1, we can identify Philistine warriors in other scenes in which the inscriptions are not so specific, and it is an excellent starting point for a survey of the Philistines' appearance.

The Philistine captives in figure 1 are manacled and stripped of their weapons and armor. They are erect in stature, clean-shaven, and have straight noses that join the forehead in a straight line. The headband of their characteristic "feathered" headdress is decorated with small knobs or a zigzag pattern. Perhaps they have been stripped of their corselets, for they seem to be wearing only a plain shirt or jerkin or, possibly, a smooth, one-piece breastplate like that worn by the Philistine warriors shown in the land battle. There is no sign of the ribbed corselet shown in the naval battle (fig. 7). A wide belt encircles a short, paneled kilt that is decorated with tassels and falls to a point in front.[24]

Another representation of a Philistine captive that bears an identifying inscription is somewhat different.[25] A kneeling, bearded captive (possibly a chief) is wearing a hat that in its details is unlike the "feathered" headdress. Of course, this may be merely a schematic outline representation, like the headgear worn by the Tjekker captive in the same scene.[26] Both the Philistine chief and the Tjekker captive have beards, which are not common among the Philistines shown;[27] beards were, however, apparently characteristic of the Tjekker.

The Relief of the Great Land Battle The relief (fig. 4) depicts the battle fought in Djahi (Phoenicia) between Ramesses III and the Sea Peoples. It is our main source of information for the military organization and battle tactics of the Philistines. The Philistine camp is under Egyptian attack and is composed of three separate

20. Mazar, *The Philistines*, pp. 4–6. For a different interpretation of the names, *see* H. Goedicke, *The Report of Wenamun* (Baltimore, 1975), pp. 32–34. He claims that these names are of Semitic rulers of the harbors between Dor and Byblos, probably Tyre and Sidon.

21. *Medinet Habu*, pls. 32–34, 37, 39–44, 47/C, 49/C–D, 50/A, C, D, 51/C–G, 52.

22. The mercenaries were mainly the Sherden, who are depicted with horned helmets, round shields, and straight swords. They served as a striking force and also as the pharaoh's bodyguard. The depiction of Ramesses III's battle with the Libyans includes an unusual group of Sherden and Philistines, the latter wearing "feather"-topped helmets (Yadin, *Warfare*, pp. 248, 335). *Medinet Habu*, pls. 17, 24, 31, 35.

23. Wainwright was the first to point out the identical headdress worn by the Peleset, Tjekker, and Denyen; *see* his "Some Sea-Peoples," *JEA* 47 (1961): 74.

24. For details of Philistine dress and weapons, *see* the discussion of the naval battle relief below.

25. *Wresz*, p. 160b.

26. Ibid., p. 160.

27. Another bearded "Philistine" appears on one of the glazed tiles depicting foreigners at Ramesses III's palace at Medinet Habu. The bearded "Philistine," who looks like a dignitary, wears a long embroidered robe and a high, "feathered" headdress held by a beaded band. (W. S. Smith, *Ancient Egypt* [Boston: Museum of Fine Arts, 1960], p. 147.)

Fig. 1. Captured Sea Peoples: The Philistines [*Medinet Habu,* pl. 44].

Fig. 2. Captured Sea Peoples: The Tjekker [*Medinet Habu,* pl. 43].

Fig. 3. Captured Sea Peoples: The Denyen [*Medinet Habu,* pl. 44].

units: the noncombatant civilians, the chariotry, and the infantry.

The noncombatants, shown in the center of the upper register, include men, women, and children riding in two-wheeled carts harnessed to teams of four oxen (fig. 5). The bodies of the carts are built of crossed bars of wood or woven reeds and are very similar to transport wagons still in use today in some parts of Turkey.[28] The carts, with their spokeless wheels made of solid circles of wood, appear to be very heavy and slow-moving. The Sea Peoples' civilian population probably transported themselves and their belongings in such carts during their migrations—even onto the field of battle. The armed men in the carts are evidently guards. This picture of the invading Sea Peoples, who had moved down the Syrian coast escorted by a fleet offshore, gives the impression of an invasion with the aim of occupying and settling the lands overrun and not merely staging a large-scale raid.

The chariots of the Philistines (fig. 6) are similar to those of the Egyptians: they are drawn by two horses and have six-spoked wheels.[29] But whereas the bow is part of Egyptian chariot equipment, the Philistine warriors are each armed with a pair of long spears like the infantrymen. It is clear that the Philistine chariot units are employed as mobile infantry for short-range combat to engage in hand-to-hand fighting after the enemy has been stunned by the charge.

The infantry fights in small phalanges of four men each; three are armed with a long, straight sword and a pair of spears, the fourth with only a sword. All carry round shields and wear a plain upper garment—possibly a plain breastplate, which is quite different from the ribbed corselet worn in the naval battle—and the characteristic "feathered" headdress with ornamented bands (see fig. 7).

The Relief of the Great Naval Battle[30]   The Great Naval Battle (fig. 7) took place between contingents of the Sea Peoples and the Egyptian fleet at the entrance to Egypt itself, possibly in the Nile delta.[31] The few ships depicted are no doubt meant to represent a larger fleet.[32] Four Egyptian warships (three on the left and one on the lower right) engage five of the Sea Peoples' ships, two of which are manned by Sherden and three by Philistines.

The Philistine and Egyptian ships have many features in common: sails—here furled—a single mast with a crow's nest, and identical rigging. The most prominent lines in all the ships appear to be brails, the device for shortening sail that here makes its first appearance in recorded history. The new style of hull, the mast with simplified stays and a top, the loose-footed sail possibly fitted with brails—all seem to be features that the Egyptians adopted from other peoples. Where they originally arose is still obscure; the Aegean, Crete, or the Levant are all possibilities.[33] The main difference between the ships of the Egyptians and those of the Philistines is that the latter are shown without oars (except for long stern oars used as rudders). The absence of oars may indicate a different method of navigation (by sails alone), or the artists may have wished to convey that the Philistines were caught by surprise and had no chance to run out their oars. The text accompanying the relief supports the latter explanation. Furthermore, all the Philistine ships have identical prows and sterns terminating in birds' heads, while the Egyptian ships have a prow terminating in a lioness's head with an Asia figure in her jaw and a plain, undecorated stern.

A number of features link the Philistine ships with the Aegean, especially the bird (duck?) figurehead sometimes seen in Aegean representations.[34] The

28. Yadin, *Warfare*, pp. 251, 339.

29. Ibid., pp. 250–51.

30. For a detailed discussion and interpretation of the naval battle, *see* H. H. Nelson, "The Naval Battle Pictured at Medinet Habu," *JNES* 2 (1943): 40–55. For a discussion of the types of ships, *see* L. Casson, *Ships and Seamanship in the Ancient World* (Princeton, 1971), pp. 36–42.

31. Barnett, *The Sea Peoples*, p. 372. A different opinion is expressed by C. F. A. Schaeffer, who places this battle far north of the frontier near Arvad. *See* C. F. A. Schaeffer, "Götter der Nord- und Inselvölker in Zypern," *AfO* 21 (1966): 60.

32. Large fleets were used at this time even by minor rulers such as the king of Ugarit, who, as we know from the archive of Ugarit, had at his disposal 150 ships. (C. Virolleaud, in *Le palais royal d'Ugarit*, vol. V [Paris, 1965], pp. 88–89, no. 62 = RS 18.148; and Malamat, *The Egyptian Decline*, p. 32.)

33. Casson, *Ships and Seamanship in the Ancient World*, p. 38.

34. The closest contemporary parallel to the bird figurehead of the Sea Peoples' ships appears on a Myc. IIIC stirrup jar from Skyros (E. Vermeule, *Greece in the Bronze Age* [Chicago, 1964], pp. 258ff., fig. 43 f.). Another possible parallel is a complete, painted bird shown on a Mycenaean pictorial-style vase from Enkomi, tomb 3 (no. 262). The bird is either a filling motif or a figurehead (Sjöqvist, fig. 20:3). The tradition of bird figureheads continued in Cyprus into the seventh century B.C., as seen in a representation on a Cypro-Archaic

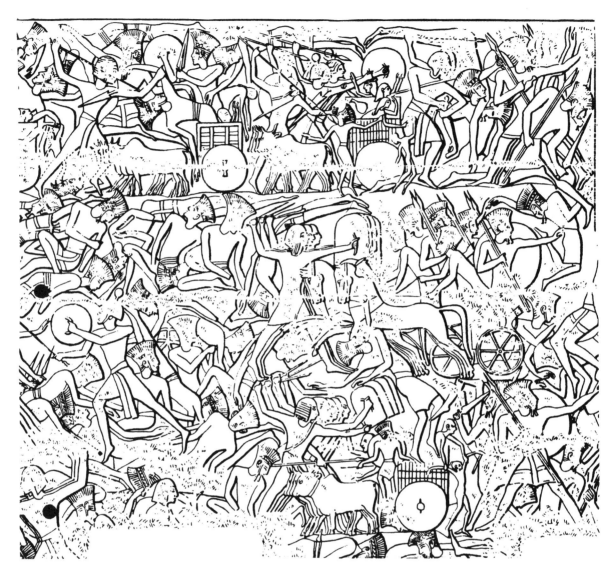

Fig. 4. Land battle between Ramesses III and the Sea Peoples [*Medinet Habu,* pl. 32].

Fig. 5. Wagons harnessed to oxen in the Sea Peoples' camp [details from fig. 4].

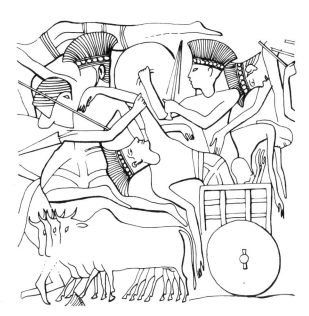

Fig. 6. Sea Peoples' chariot [detail from fig. 4].

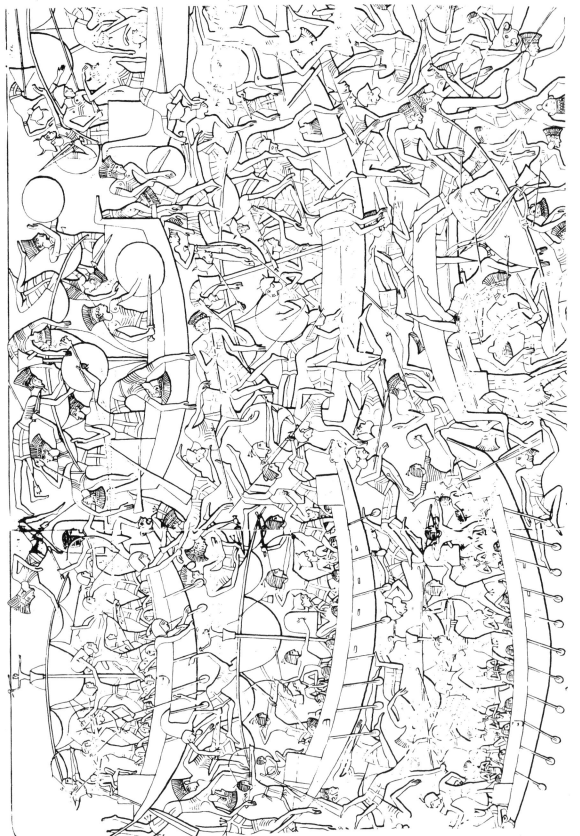

Fig. 7. Naval battle between Ramesses III and the Sea Peoples (including the Philistines) [*Medinet Habu,* pl. 37].

straight profile and angular ends of the Philistine ships are also Aegean in appearance, though the Aegean tradition has so far produced no evidence of double-ended craft. Casson suggests that this innovation might have been the Sea Peoples' own variation on a basically Aegean design.

The relief confirms that the only specifically naval weapon used in this battle was the grappling iron (although the bird figurehead may conceivably have been used as a ram). Thus the sea fight represented at Medinet Habu was only another version of a land fight—one in which ships grappled one another to let their crews have it out on the decks with bow, sword, and pike.[35] The Egyptian assault is supported by archery fire from the shore, putting the Philistines, who lack long-range weapons, at a decided disadvantage. They suffer heavy losses in the melée, and the survivors are taken prisoner.

The two kinds of dress worn by the Sea Peoples are most likely intended to show their mixed origin. The text mentions that the enemy included Peleset, Tjekker, Denyen, Sheklesh, and Weshesh (and possibly other peoples whose names are lost in a lacuna); but the artist has shown only two types of foreigners—one with the "feathered" and the other with the horned headdress. The Philistines wear a short paneled kilt with wide hems and tassels, and ribbed corselets over a shirt. The thin strips of the corselet (which was made of leather or metal) are joined in the middle of the chest and curve either up or down; perhaps they simulate human ribs. The corselet with ribs curving downward is most characteristic of the Sherden warriors. This type of armor is known elsewhere only from two figures of Aegean warriors carved on ivory mirror handles from Cyprus: the Griffin Slayer from Enkomi (pl. 1) and the Lion Slayer from Kouklia. These objects are Mycenaean in character and indicate that Mycenaean

craftsmen were working at Enkomi and Kouklia at the end of the thirteenth and the beginning of the twelfth centuries. The ribbed corselet was, therefore, known in Cyprus toward the end of the Bronze Age and seems to have been worn by warriors of Aegean background.[36]

In the relief the small, round shield held by the Sea Peoples is easily distinguishable from the rectangular Egyptian shield. It is convex and has a handgrip on the inside. In another section of the relief[37] small, round bosses appear on the outer surface; they are probably metal bosses applied to the leather covering of the shield. The small, round shield came into wide use both in the Aegean and in the eastern Mediterranean at the end of the thirteenth and the beginning of the twelfth centuries, superseding the large body shield.[38] That the round shield was related to the Aegean lands and was part of the Sea Peoples' equipment is seen in a domed seal (chap. 5, fig. 14) found at Enkomi under floor III (first part, ca. 1190–1180 B.C.). It belongs to the level attributed to the Sea Peoples[39] and bears an engraving of a warrior with "feathered" headdress crouching behind a large, round shield with fleece covering and a central spiked boss. The shield is larger in proportion to the warrior's body than those shown on the Medinet Habu reliefs, a fact explained by Edith Porada as confirmation of her suggestion that this seal continues the Mycenaean pictorial tradition, in which large body shields were dominant. Hence the large size of the shield (which contrasts with the small, round shields portrayed at Medinet Habu) could be understood as an iconographic tradition and not as a factual representation.[40]

vase: J. L. Myres, *Handbook of the Cesnola Collection of Antiquities from Cyprus* (New York, 1914), p. 97, no. 761; and G. Perrot and C. Chipiez, *Histoire d'Art*, vol. 3, figs. 529–30. For a comprehensive discussion of Mycenaean ships, including the ships of the Sea Peoples, *see* C. Laviosa: "La Marina Micenea," *Annuario* 47–48, n.s. 31–32 (1969–1970): 23–40. Bird representations are characteristic of the Philistine decorative repertoire, and modelled bird heads and bird-shaped vessels are a dominant feature of Philistine cult vessels (*see* chap. 4, fig. 1:1) as well as one of the most distinctive motifs on its painted pottery (*see* chap. 3, figs. 61–62).

35. Casson, *Ships and Seamanship in the Ancient World*, p. 38.

36. The ivory mirror handle showing the Lion Slayer comes from Kouklia, Evreti tomb 8 (Catling, *Bronzework*, p. 51, pl. 1:C). The handle showing the Griffin Slayer is from Enkomi tomb 17 (A. S. Murray and H. B. Walters, *Excavations in Cyprus* [London, 1900], pl. II:872). This corselet is a more flexible type of armor than the one-piece breastplate and recalls the horizontal strips of the metal corselet from Dendra; Catling, *Bronzework*, p. 138.

37. *Wresz*, pls. 113–14.

38. Snodgrass, *Armour*, p. 189.

39. *Enkomi Excavations*, vol. II, app., seals by E. Porada, pp. 801 ff. This domed seal belongs to a group of seals from levels and tomb groups associated with Myc. IIIC pottery in Cyprus and Philistine pottery in Palestine.

40. For a representation of a round shield held by the bronze statue of the god of the ingot found in a sanctuary at Enkomi and dated to the twelfth century, *see* C. F. A. Schaeffer, "Les peuples de la Mer et leurs Sanctuaires à Enkomi-

As to actual finds, the most convincing reconstruction of a bossed shield is the Kaloriziki shield from Cyprus, which was found in the grave of a warrior prince of Aegean origin.[41] In shape it resembles the shields represented on the Warriors' Vase from Mycenae (pl. 2),[42] but it is decorated with round, embossed metal disks and three spiked disks.[43]

The carved ivory figure of the Griffin Slayer (pl. 1) bears a small, round shield very similar to those depicted at Medinet Habu. The relief proves that the small, round shield and body corselet were used by the Sea Peoples, who were following an Aegean tradition. In the Aegean the small shield and corselet replaced the body shield[44] in the thirteenth century B.C., no doubt for the sake of better mobility in battle. The round shield first made its appearance in the eastern Mediterranean at the end of the Bronze Age and the beginning of the Iron Age, as one of the Megiddo Ivories from the stratum VIIA treasury shows (see discussion in chap. 2 and chap. 4, fig. 8).

The Philistine warrior in the relief carries a pair of spears and a large, tapering two-edged sword with a midrib. The same type of sword is also brandished by the Sherden. It is of the cut-and-thrust variety generally referred to as "Naue's Type II." From the thirteenth century onward, this became the principal and almost exclusive cut-and-thrust sword in the eastern Mediterranean. Its ultimate origin is considered to be Central Europe,[45] and it probably reached the eastern Mediterranean via Greece. The appearance of this type of sword in Cyprus is regarded as one of the symptoms of the change in relations between Cyprus and the Aegean that occurred around 1200 B.C., a change brought about by the arrival of Aegean settlers and their distinctive Mycenaean culture.[46] A sword obtained in 1911 at Beit Dagon, near Tel Aviv, is frequently adduced, because of its midrib and size (75 cm. long), as an example of those depicted on the reliefs in Philistine hands.[47] It should be stressed that nothing is known about the original context of this singular sword. The Beit Dagon specimen furthermore has no exact parallels among the Naue's Type II swords. Precisely because of its uniqueness, the utmost caution must be exercised in attempting to date or ethnicize this sword. In fact, it bears a greater resemblance to local Canaanite swords of the Middle Bronze period than to any weapon of Aegean design. Henceforth, references to the Beit Dagon sword in discussions on the ordnance of the Sea Peoples should be used with caution.

The style of headdress provides the essential distinction between the Sherden and the Philistines. The Sherden wear a horned helmet, whereas the Philistines, the Tjekker, and the Denyen wear the "feather" headdress,[48] which is apparently made up of a leather cap and an ornamental headband from which a row of slightly curving strips stand upright to form a kind of diadem. This headdress has been much discussed and variously interpreted as feathers, reeds, leather strips, horsehair, and even a special upswept hairdo held to-

Alasia aux XII–XI S.Av.N.E.," in *Alasia I*, pp. 505–66. This statue is of a warrior-god wearing a thorax, kilt, and horned helmet; his legs are protected by greaves, and he is armed with a small, round shield and a spear. The statue stands on a base in the shape of an ingot. Catling, following Schaeffer (in "A Cypriot Bronze Statuette in the Bomford Collection," *Alasia I*, pp. 15–32), points out the eclectic character of the statue. Iconographically it is a Semitic figure, but it also has Aegean characteristics, e.g., the greaves and possibly the horned helmet. Although these features, together with the round shield, may indicate a connection with the Sea Peoples—specifically the Sherden—positive evidence is still lacking. *See* Barnett, *The Sea Peoples*, p. 368; and C. F. A. Schaeffer, "Götter der Nord- und Inselvölker in Zypern," *AfO* 21 (1966): 61, n. 16.

41. Catling, *Bronzework*, pp. 142 ff., pl. 18 d–e.

42. A. Wace, *Mycenae: An Archaeological History and Guide* (Princeton, 1949), pp. 65 ff., fig. 82:a, b.

43. Metal bosses were fairly widespread in Europe, where they are considered to have originated earlier than in the Mediterranean. G. von Merhart saw them as one of many artifacts introduced into the Aegean by northern warriors during the twelfth century (Catling, *Bronzework*, p. 145, nn. 7, 8). The context in which some of the metal bosses were found proves that they were warlike accoutrements and probably belonged to a shield; V. R. d'A. Desborough, *The Greek Dark Ages* (London, 1972), p. 306.

44. *Enkomi Excavations*, vol. II, app., p. 802, n. 618, and Catling, *Bronzework*, p. 142.

45. Snodgrass, *Armour*, pp. 205 ff.

46. Catling, *Bronzework*, pp. 51, 115–16. *See also* J. Bouzek, "Die Beziehungen zum Vorgeschichtlichen Europa der Neugefundenen Griffzungenschwerter von Enkomi-Alasia, Zypern," in *Alasia I*, pp. 433–48.

47. This sword is now in the British Museum (no. 127137). Barnett, *The Sea Peoples*, p. 368; R. Maxwell-Hyslop, "Daggers and Swords in Western Asia," *Iraq* 8 (1946): 57–59, Type 52. Lorimer sees in the pronounced midrib and great weight a modification of the standard slashing sword designed to meet a formidable foe. H. Lorimer, *Homer and the Monuments* (London, 1950), pp. 264–67; Snodgrass, *Armour*, pp. 93 and 105.

48. J. A. Wainwright, *JEA* 47 (1961): 74 ff.

gether by a band.[49] Whichever interpretation we choose, the "feather" headdress remains the hallmark of the group dominated by the Philistines. It seems certain that the diadem served as both decoration and insignia on the helmet or cap, which fits around the back of the head as a neck guard and is held in place by a strap tied under the chin. The band appears to be a metal diadem decorated in repoussé, with different combinations of plain horizontal strips, rows of round projections, divisions into oblongs, and a kind of plain triglyph division and zigzag pattern. The feather crown is discussed further in connection with the depiction of similar headgear on the anthropoid coffins from Beth-Shean (chap. 5, figs. 11, 12).

It may be that the different diadems and their decorations indicated different military ranks, although a frequency analysis of the appearance of each variant is not decisive. Another possibility is that they are emblems of the tribes or clans into which each group of Sea Peoples was subdivided.[50]

Enkomi has yielded two other depictions of warriors of the Sea Peoples wearing identical headgear; both date from a twelfth-century context. The first is carved on the famous ivory gaming board (chap. 5, fig. 13) and the second on the domed seal described above (chap. 5. fig. 14). The close affinities, typology, and iconography emphasize the Aegean background of both pieces.

Another much-cited parallel is the pictograph of a warrior's head with "feather crown" (pl. 3) impressed on the enigmatic Phaestos Disk (sixteenth century B.C.)[51] This parallel is not conclusive, however, because of the long interval between the disk and the Enkomi and Medinet Habu representations. Furthermore, the origin and meaning of the disk are still an open question.

49. Barnett, *The Sea Peoples*, pp. 372–73; K. Galling, "Die Kopfzier der Philister in den Darstellungen von Medinet Habu," *Ugaritica VI*, pp. 247-65. Galling's "upswept hairdo" interpretation seems unrealistic since the warriors shown wearing the headdress are fully armed for battle, and it is unlikely that they would neglect to wear their protective helmets. *See also* F. Schachermeyr, "Hörnerhelme und Federkronen als Kopfbedeckungen bei den 'Seevölkern' der Ägyptischen Reliefs," ibid., pp. 452 ff.

50. Yadin, *Warfare*, pp. 249, 345.

51. Barnett, *The Sea Peoples*, p. 362; S. Dow, "The Linear Scripts and the Tablets as Historical Documents," *CAH*[3], vol. II, pt. 1, chap. 13, pp. 595-98; and A. Evans, *The Palace of Minos*, vol. 1 (London, 1921), pp. 647 ff., fig. 482.

BIBLICAL SOURCES

Narratives

The biblical sources pertaining to the origin of the Philistines are few and often unclear. The earliest appears in the "Table of Nations" in Genesis 10:14: "And Pathrusim, and Casluhim (out of whom came the Philistim) and Caphtorim." The meaning of this verse seems to be "and Caphtorim—out of whom came the Philistines." According to the table, all these peoples (including the Caphtorim and Philistines) originated in Egypt. Even though the biblical historiographer must have been acquainted with the Philistines and the territory of Philistia, he nonetheless regarded them as having originated in Egypt, probably because the Philistines and other Sea Peoples were first settled in Egypt after their defeat by Ramesses III and served as mercenaries in the Egyptian army.

In other biblical references the Philistines appear as synonymous with or parallel to the Cherethites (that is, Cretans); hence it is clear that they were thought to have a common ethnic origin. Zephaniah equates the land of the Philistines with the nation of the Cherethites (Zeph. 2:5), and for Ezekiel the two names are also synonymous (Ezek. 25:16). The most direct biblical references to Philistine origins are found in Amos 9:7 and Jeremiah 47:4, where the Isle of Caphtor is mentioned as their homeland. Various biblical traditions suggest that the Caphtorim are to be identified with the Cherethites, or at least with some of them. According to one such tradition, the Caphtorim were among the Sea Peoples who settled on the southern Palestinian coast. Thus the biblical sources (with the exception of the "Table of Nations") identified Caphtor with Crete and suggested that the Philistines originated in Caphtor-Crete (see below, p. 21).

The Philistines appear in the patriarchal narratives as inhabitants of the Negev, and their most outstanding figure is Abimelech, "king of the Philistines unto Gerar" (Gen. 26:1). This reference to the Philistines in a much earlier context than the others (which relate to the period following the conquest of Canaan) is usually explained as a simple anachronism. Another view is that the Philistines in the patriarchal stories were people ethnically similar to the Philistines who, known from the books of Judges and Samuel, had settled in the area during the patriarchal period. Most logical, perhaps, is Macalister's suggestion that these early references are not simple anachronisms but

Pl. 1. Ivory mirror handle with Griffin Slayer, Late Cypriot III, Enkomi [British Museum, 97.4-1.872. A. S. Murray, *Excavations in Cyprus* (London, 1900), pl. 2].

Pl. 2. Warriors' Vase, early twelfth century, Mycenae [National Museum, Athens. S. Marinatos, *Crete and Mycenae* (London, 1960), pls. 232–33].

Pl. 3. Phaestos Disk, Middle Minoan III, Crete [Archaeological Museum, Herakleion. S. Marinatos, *Crete and Mycenae* (London, 1960), pls. 72–73].

rather the account of a biblical historiographer who, living during a period of Philistine dominance (twelfth to eleventh centuries) in the area which was the scene of the patriarchal stories, naturally assumed the previous existence and importance of the Philistines in that area.[52]

The first historical reference to the Philistines appears in the Book of Judges. Shamgar ben Anath, a hero of unknown origin, smote the Philistines, thus saving Israel (Judg. 3:31).[53] It is conceivable that the Song of Deborah refers to the unstable situation in northern Palestine that preceded Shamgar's victory over the Philistines: "In the days of Shamgar the son of Anath, in the days of Jael, the highways were unoccupied, and the travellers walked through byways" (Judg. 5:6). This description may also refer to Philistine incursions into Israelite territory, one of which was stemmed by Shamgar ben Anath. It seems, however, that from the beginning of their occupation on the coast of southern Palestine—later called Philistia—until almost the middle of the eleventh century, the Philistines did not expand beyond their own holdings in the southwest or gain control over any tribe but that of Judah (Judg. 15:11).

The earliest biblical stories about the Philistines, the Samson cycle in particular, reflect the territorial conflict between the Philistines and the Israelite tribes of Dan and Judah. The whole of the Samson cycle must indeed be understood against the background of this struggle; the tribe of Dan was fighting for its very existence in the territory allotted to it on the eastern border

of Philistia. Unsuccessful in the struggle, the tribe was forced to abandon its inheritance and move north. Thus the Bible critics are correct in maintaining that Dan's location, at least by the end of the period of the Judges, was in northern Galilee. However, the real conflict during this period was between the tribe of Judah and the Philistines, for the constant Philistine pressure, which is clearly indicated in the Book of Judges, forced Judah to occupy an area much smaller than its original allotment. These confrontations eventually led to open war and to a Philistine expansion the Israelites were powerless to halt until the beginning of the United Monarchy.

Open warfare between the Philistines and Judah began with the battle of Eben-ezer (1 Sam. 4). The Philistines camped at Aphek and arrayed their troops for battle along the slopes of Mount Ephraim. The Israelites were routed in this encounter, and the Philistines captured the Ark of the Lord. Following up their victory, the Philistines advanced inland, took Shiloh (as indicated in Jer. 7:12–14 and Ps. 78:60), and followed the Via Maris northward to capture Megiddo and Beth-Shean. (Philistine control of these two sites is discussed in chap. 2.) The Philistines succeeded in conquering most of the country west of the Jordan River and established garrisons and commanders in the conquered cities (for example, Geba of Benjamin, 1 Sam. 10:5, 13:3). After achieving military and political control of the country, they prohibited the manufacture of any metal implements that could serve a military purpose (1 Sam. 13:19). By their monopoly of metalworking, the Philistines kept the Israelites in a position of economic and, probably, political dependence.

Philistine dominance lasted for several generations, reaching its zenith during the second half of the eleventh century. But the turning point had been foreshadowed in the Philistine defeat recounted in 1 Samuel 7, in which several cities conquered by the Philistines were recaptured by the Israelites. The decisive clash between Israel and the Philistines took place soon after Saul was anointed king of Israel. The resolve to obtain freedom from Philistine domination (the primary motive for the creation of the kingdom) was doubtless also the motivating factor in the organization of a regular army, without which no Israelite victory would have been possible.

The attack began with Jonathan's assault on the Philistine garrison at Geba (in Benjamin). Saul and

52. R. A. S. Macalister, *The Philistines, Their History and Civilization* (London, 1914), p. 39. For another suggestion for the date of this story, *see* W. F. Albright, "A Colony of Cretan Mercenaries on the Coast of the Negeb," *JPOS* 1 (1921): 189; Mazar, *The Philistines and Their Wars*, p. 164; D. N. Freedman, "Early Israelite History in the Light of Early Israelite Poetry," *Unity and Diversity: Essays in the History, Literature and Religion of the Ancient Near East*, H. Goedicke and J. J. M. Roberts, eds. (Baltimore, 1975), pp. 9–10, n. 34; F. M. Cross, *Canaanite Myth and Hebrew Epic: Essays in the History of the Religion of Israel* (Cambridge, Mass., 1973), pp. 124–25; and K. A. Kitchen, "The Philistines," in *Peoples of Old Testament Times*, D. J. Wiseman, ed. (Oxford, 1973), p. 56.

53. A. Malamat, "The Period of the Judges," in *The World History of the Jewish People*, vol. 3, *Judges*, B. Mazar, ed. (Tel Aviv, 1971), p. 137; Mazar, *The Philistines and Their Wars*, p. 172; for a different viewpoint, *see* Y. Aharoni, "New Aspects of the Israelite Occupation in the North," in *Near Eastern Archaeology in the Twentieth Century*, J. A. Sanders, ed. (New York, 1970), pp. 256 ff.

his army gathered at Gilgal near Jericho (1 Sam. 13:4); but because the people were afraid to risk open war with the Philistines, Saul subsequently went to battle at Michmas with a force of only six hundred men. The Philistines dispatched a retaliatory force ("spoilers"), which suffered a major defeat (1 Sam. 14:31).

Another encounter between the Israelites and the Philistines took place in the Elah Valley. The outcome, according to the biblical account, was decided by a duel between the champions, David and Goliath. After Goliath's defeat, the Philistines were pursued "even unto Gath and unto Ekron."

The last battle between Saul and the Philistines was fought on the slopes of Mount Gilboa (1 Sam. 28–31), where Israelite rule was weakest. The Israelites were defeated, Saul and three of his sons were killed, and the Philistines succeeded in capturing the Canaanite cities in the Jezreel Valley. Some of these cities, however, very soon succeeded in freeing themselves from Philistine rule, and others assimilated their captors into the Canaanite population. The Philistines were thus unable to conquer the centers of Israelite occupation in the mountains of Ephraim as they had done after their victory at Eben-ezer.

David's contact with the Philistines began during Saul's reign, when he sought refuge with King Achish of Gath and served him as commander of a troop of mercenaries. When Saul's rule drew to a close, David was dwelling in Ziklag, one of the cities ruled by Achish. During that period, and for the first years of his reign in Hebron, David acted as a Philistine vassal. Only after he had established his rule over the United Monarchy did his conflict with the Philistines begin. In the two battles fought in the valley of Rephaim near Jerusalem, David dealt the Philistines serious blows (2 Sam. 5:18), pursuing them in the second battle "from Geba until thou come to Gezer" (2 Sam. 5:25). These victories freed Judah and the Ephraim Hills from Philistine rule. The biblical narrative relates that "David smote the Philistines, and subdued them; and David took Metheg-ammah [an obscure expression] out of the hand of the Philistines" (2 Sam. 8:1). An alternative version in 1 Chronicles 18:1 states that "David smote the Philistines, and subdued them, and took Gath and her towns out of the hand of the Philistines." Consolidating his victories, David conquered the northern Shephelah (lowlands) and the coastal plain (formerly the tribal portion of Dan), including Dor, the Jezreel Valley, and finally the Beth-Shean Val-

ley. He thus greatly reduced Philistine territory and probably even turned some Philistine cities into Israelite vassal states. The conquered areas are mentioned later in the description of Solomon's administrative division of the country (1 Kings 4).

Borders of Philistia

The territory of the Philistines is described in the Book of Joshua: "This is the land that yet remaineth: all the borders of the Philistines, and all Geshuri, from Sihor, which is before Egypt, even unto the borders of Ekron northward, which is counted to the Canaanite: five lords (*seranim*) of the Philistines; the Gazathites and the Ashdothides, the Eshkalonites, the Gittites, and the Ekronites; also the Avites: From the South . . ." (Josh. 13:2–3) The "borders" are apparently the Philistine territories, which are also referred to at times as kingdoms ruled by the *seranim*. Except for the addition of the Geshuri and the Avites, the area delineated in these verses is essentially an ethno-geographical unit. As the southern border is the Brook of Egypt (Wadi el-Arish) and the Sihor, the eastern branch of the Delta may have been the boundary of the Avites, who inhabited the area south of Gaza (cf. Deut. 2:23). The northeastern extremity of the border is the region north of Ekron (Kh. Muqannaʿ?), the eastern boundary is shared with Judah, and the western border is the Mediterranean Sea.

The territory thus defined coincides with the geographical area occupied by the Philistines for several generations after their arrival in Palestine and before their expansion during the eleventh century. Before the Philistine invasion, this area was considered Canaanite and, according to Israelite tradition, was inhabited (at least partially) by the Anakim (Josh. 11:21). Actually part of the inheritance of Judah (Josh. 15:45–47), it included the territory south of the Ekron-Jabneel line (Josh. 15:11). It seems, therefore, that at that time the northern border of Philistine-held territory did not extend further than Ekron-Jabneel.

Philistine expansion in the eleventh century presumably extended north of the Yarkon River and to the east to engulf large parts of the territory of Judah. Timnah (Tell el-Baṭashi?) is mentioned as a Philistine city in the Samson cycle. Although at the height of their power the Philistines controlled the valleys and cities of Jezreel and Beth-Shean, in actual fact the ethnopolitical entity known as the Philistines never exercised complete control for any considerable period over more than the territory delineated in Joshua 13, together with the coastal region extending north to the Yarkon River and east to the slopes of the Judean Hills.

The Philistine expansion toward the southwest is probably indicated by the term *negeb hakreti* ("the South of the Cherethites," 1 Sam. 30:14), which includes the area under Philistine control from the *haserim* to Gaza.[54]

The Philistine Pentapolis

The land of the Philistines comprised five major cities, the so-called Philistine Pentapolis: Gaza, Ashkelon, Ashdod, Gath, and Ekron were united in a confederation. Three of them, Gaza, Ashkelon, and Ashdod, were well known and important cities even before the Philistine settlement. Situated on what was referred to in the Bible as the "Way to the Land of the Philistines" (Exod. 13:17), they had served at various periods during the Bronze Age as Egyptian strongholds guarding the vital coastal road. The site of ancient Gath has not yet been definitely located, but it was surely in existence before the Philistine occupation. Only Ekron seems to have been founded by the Philistines, as no mention of it appears in any pre-Philistine sources.[55] Our information about the Pentapolis during the early Philistine period is drawn almost entirely from biblical sources.

Gaza   The southernmost of the five cities, Gaza was the capital of the Egyptian province in southern Canaan and served as an administrative and military center for several centuries before the Philistine invasion.[56] In the Samson cycle (Judg. 16), the fortified city of Gaza appears as the principal Philistine center, the place where the *seranim* (Philistine lords) gathered for festivals and sacrifices in the Temple of Dagon. Sam-

son toppled that edifice, killing the three thousand Philistines congregated within.

Ashkelon   Situated north of Gaza on the Mediterranean coast, Ashkelon was an important city-state before the Philistine conquest and was known for its excellent port. It is mentioned in the Samson cycle (for example, Judg. 14:19) less often than Gaza; nonetheless, a later reference to "the markets of Asheklon" (2 Sam. 1:20) attests to the city's status as an important mercantile center.[57] Extra-biblical evidence of Ashkelon's importance includes the tradition recorded by the historian Justin that the king of Ashkelon had defeated the Sidonians one year before the fall of Troy. Since Sidon, and not Tyre, is the major Phoenician power in this tradition, Justin must be referring to events that occurred in the eleventh century—the period of Sidon's dominance in the eastern Mediterranean.[58] Further information on Ashkelon is found on three inscribed plaques of the Megiddo Ivories, which mention Kerker, the female singer in the temple of the Egyptian god Ptah at Ashkelon.[59] The Megiddo treasury also contained an ivory box with the cartouche of Ramesses III, indicating that the Temple of Ptah at Ashkelon was in existence during the reign of that pharaoh (twelfth century). Ashkelon and its king may be hinted at in the Wen Amun tale.[60]

Ashdod   Ashkelon's neighbor to the north was Ashdod, a city whose importance in the Late Bronze Age, especially in the Mediterranean trade, is known to us by documents discovered at Ugarit.[61] The biblical references to Philistine Ashdod come mainly from the account of the capture of the Ark of the Lord. The fact that the Ark was captured at Eben-ezer and then transported all the way to Ashdod clearly indicates that Ashdod was the major Philistine kingdom in the mid-eleventh century. Ashdod's preeminence during this period is further attested to by the fact that the

54. W. F. Albright, "A Colony of Cretan Mercenaries on the Coast of the Negeb," *JPOS* 1 (1921): 187–194. For a discussion of this area, *see* R. Gophna, "Iron Age I Haserim in Southern Philistia," *'Atiqot* 3 (1966): 44–51 (Hebrew).

55. Kh. Muqanna' has been identified by J. Naveh with Ekron and the finds substantiate this identification: Philistine sherds are the oldest remains found in the area (J. Naveh, "Khirbat al-Muqanna'–Ekron, An Archaeological Survey," *IEJ* 8 (1958): 87–100; 165–70. Albright disagreed with this identification; *see* Albright, *Syria, the Philistines and Phoenicia*, p. 509, n. 3.

56. A. Alt, *Kleine Schriften zur Geschichte des Volkes Israel*, vol. 1 (Munich, 1959), pp. 218–19.

57. Mazar, *The Philistines*, pp. 4–6.

58. Mazar, *The Philistines*, p. 5; Malamat, *The Egyptian Decline*, p. 29; H. J. Katzenstein, *The History of Tyre* (Jerusalem, 1973), pp. 59 ff.

59. *Meg. Ivories*, pp. 12–13, pl. 63.

60. Mazar, *The Philistines*, p. 6.

61. *Ashdod I*, pp. 8–9; *Ashdod II-III*, p. 19, n. 13. Astour agrees with the suggested identification of Asdadi with Ashdod and identifies the gentilic with Ashdodites; M. C. Astour, "Ma'hadu, The Harbor of Ugarit," *Journal of the Economic and Social History of the Orient* 13 (1970): 113–27.

men of Ashdod could command that the Ark be sent first to Gath and then to Ekron. According to 1 Samuel 5, one of the two temples of Dagon was at Ashdod. Gaza, Ashkelon, and Ashdod are, of course, the three cities mentioned in the Onomasticon of Amenope.

Gath Considerably less is known about Philistine Gath than about the three cities described above. Its location has not yet been fixed with certainty, although Tell eṣ-Ṣafi has been suggested as its site (see chap. 2, n. 133).[62] Like Ashdod and Gaza, Gath is mentioned in the Bible as a city inhabited by the Anakim prior to the Philistine invasion (Josh. 11:22). Gath's first mention as a Philistine city occurs in the story of the capture of the Ark (1 Sam. 5:8). It appears later as the scene of a battle between the Israelites under David and the sons of the giants (2 Sam. 21:20), the most famous of whom was Goliath. The reference to Achish, "king of Gath" (1 Sam. 27:2), indicates that Philistine rulers held the title of king, at least in the time of David. Gath emerges from the biblical accounts as a city of great importance in Philistia, especially during David's time.

Ekron The northernmost of the Philistine cities, Ekron controlled the territory allotted to the tribe of Dan. Its eastern border, the western limit of the territory of Judah, was the scene of the events recounted in the Samson stories. An interesting detail about the city is preserved in 1 Samuel 17:52, in which it is noted that the men of Israel and Judah pursued the fleeing Philistines "to the gates of Ekron."

Other Philistine Cities In addition to the Pentapolis, two lesser cities are mentioned in the Bible during the early Philistine period as the "towns in the country" (1 Sam. 27:5)—Ziklag and Timna. A third city, Jabneh, is known to have been under Philistine rule in the time of Uzziah (2 Chron. 26). Jabneh has been identified as the much-earlier Jabneel, which before the period of Philistine expansion was situated in the territory of Judah just at the northern border of Philistia.

The role of these smaller cities as secondary, nearly autonomous centers under the control of the capitals of the city-states is exemplified by Ziklag, which was within the kingdom of Gath. Although David resided in Ziklag under the sovereignty of Achish, he was able

to carry out military operations at will without Achish's knowledge. Like the smaller settlements of the Israelite tribes, these smaller Philistine cities are called *ḥaṣerim* ("villages") or *banoth* ("daughters") in the Bible.

With the Philistine conquest and expansion into Israelite territory, certain strategic sites were fortified and manned by a garrison and commander. The account of the battle at Michmas mentions such a garrison at Gibeath-Benjamin; Jonathan's attack on it was the signal for the Israelite revolt against the Philistines in the center of the country. Another Philistine garrison is mentioned at Gibeath-Elohim ("the hill of God," 1 Sam. 10:5), although this may merely be another name for Geba of Benjamin.[63] During David's war with the Philistines a garrison appears to have been stationed at Bethlehem (2 Sam. 23:14: "And the garrison of the Philistines was then in Bethlehem"). Beth-Shean also seems to have been under Philistine rule, although it may not have been inhabited by a Philistine population; after Saul's defeat and death at the foot of Mount Gilboa, his body was "fastened to the wall of Beth-Shean" (1 Sam. 31:10). The same city may have been the site of an earlier garrison established when Beth-Shean was an Egyptian military base under Ramesses III.

Philistine Government

Only a vague, general outline of Philistine governmental and social organization can be gleaned from the few indirect references in the Bible. At the head of each Philistine kingdom (city-state) stood the *seren* (for example, 1 Sam. 5:8, 6:4, 16)—a word that seems to be linguistically related to the Greek τυραννος ("tyrant"), which was itself borrowed by the Greeks from another language, possibly Lydian.[64] The ruler, however, may also have borne the title "king," as did Achish, king of Gath (1 Sam 21:11, 27:2). The extent of the *seren*'s power can be assessed from the account of the meeting of the Philistine rulers in Ashdod during the plague brought about by the capture of the Ark and from the incident of the disagreement between the Philistine "princes" (*sarim*) and Achish about whether David

62. B. Mazar, "Gath and Gittaim," *IEJ* 4 (1954): 227–35.

63. B. Mazar, *Encyclopaedia Biblica*, vol. II, p. 414 (Hebrew); Y. Aharoni, *The Land of the Bible* (London, 1974), p. 254.

64. C. Rabin, "Hittite Words in Hebrew," *Orientalia* 32 (1963): 113–39. On the possibility that *yšby plšt* is equivalent to *sarney pelishtim* in the Song of the Sea (Exod. 15:14), *see* Freedman, "Early Israelite History," pp. 9–10.

could take part in the battle against Saul at Gilboa (1 Sam. 29:4–10). Both show that the Philistine rulers did not possess absolute power over major political or military decisions. There is no direct evidence whether the office of *seren* was an elected or inherited one. The annals of the Assyrian empire suggest that the royal office was hereditary in Philistia, as elsewhere in the ancient Near East. Even so, it seems that the populace retained the power to depose their rulers.[65] Such procedures in the Assyrian period, however, do not necessarily indicate similar practices in earlier periods.

The social organization of the Philistines is generally described as a military aristocracy. This is borne out by the superb military organization, fighting ability, and weaponry that enabled the Philistines to dominate much larger civilian populations. It is clear that for an extended period, until they were assimilated into the indigenous population, the Philistines were the ruling class in the territory they conquered, dominating Canaanites and Israelites alike.

Military Organization

In the military aristocracy of the Philistines, the *seranim*, besides ruling their kingdoms, served as commanders of their own armies. The *sarim* undoubtedly held positions of high military rank. The army was composed of infantry, archers (cf. 1 Sam. 31:3), chariotry, and horsemen (1 Sam. 13). Although the numbers in the 1 Samuel 13 account are obviously exaggerated, it is nonetheless clear that even a very small force of chariots and horsemen could be decisive in a battle fought on the flat, open coastal plain.

The infantry was subdivided into groups of hundreds and thousands (1 Sam. 29:2), and their deployment in battle can be partially reconstructed from the description of the battle at Michmas (1 Sam. 14:15). The main camp of the Philistine attack force was arrayed for battle, and from it the assault companies ("spoilers" in biblical terminology) launched their attacks. Garrisons were established as outposts or security positions in strategic locations, usually to the rear of the attacking force.

The story of David and Goliath related in 1 Samuel 17 has a twofold interest for us: in addition to its presentation of the duel as a type of warfare, it gives a detailed description of Philistine armaments at the beginning of the Davidic period.

When Goliath declares, "Why are ye come out to set your battle in array? Am not I a Philistine and ye servants to Saul? Choose you a man for you, and let him come down to me" (1 Sam. 17:8), he is in fact proposing a contest between himself and a champion of Israel, not a battle between the two armies to decide the military issue.[66] This is made clear when Goliath states the conditions: "If he be able to fight with me, and to kill me, then will we be your servants: But if I prevail against him, and kill him, then shall ye be our servants, and serve us." Thus when David slew his adversary, the effect was immediate: "And when the Philistines saw their champion was dead they fled" (1 Sam. 17:51).

The duel as a method of warfare was known in Canaan long before the arrival of the Philistines. The duel of Sinuhe the Egyptian with the mighty man of Retenu (Twelfth Dynasty) strikingly resembles the contest between David and Goliath. The fact that this type of combat seems to have lapsed and was reintroduced by the Philistines reflects their background in the Aegean world, where the duel was a recognized form of warfare[67] that enabled commanders to secure military decisions without incurring the casualties of full-scale battles.

The detailed description of Goliath's armor and weaponry is the only biblical account of a Philistine warrior in full battle dress: "And he had a helmet of brass upon his head, and he was armed with a coat of mail; and the weight of the coat was five thousand shekels of brass. And he had greaves of brass upon his legs, and a target of brass between his shoulders. And the staff of his spear was like a weaver's beam; and his spear's head weighed six hundred shekels of iron: and one bearing a shield went before him" (1 Sam. 17:5–7).

The Bible compares the shape of the spear (actually a javelin) to a weaver's beam[68] because this type of weapon had not been seen in Israel before and had no Hebrew name. The earliest representation of this javelin with loop occurs on the twelfth-century Warriors' Vase from Mycenae (pl. 2), a fact that clearly implies

65. *ANET*, p. 286 (249–62).

66. Y. Yadin (Sukenik): "Let the young men, I pray thee, arise and play before us," *JPOS* 21 (1948): 114–15.

67. Snodgrass, *Armour*, p. 189; Yadin, *Warfare*, p. 267.

68. The "weaver's beam" is the leash rod of a loom; this block of wood separates the threads of the warp to allow the passage of the threads of the weft. Its main feature was the loops or leashes of cord tied to it. Yadin, *Warfare*, p. 354, and "Goliath's Javelin and the *menor orgim*," *PEQ* (1955): 58–69.

the weapon's Aegean origin and shows that it was already in use at the time of the Sea Peoples' migrations.[69]

Unlike the Philistines in the Medinet Habu reliefs, which depict an earlier period, Goliath of Gath wears a bronze helmet, not a "feathered" headdress. He is clad in a coat of mail instead of a laminated corselet and wears greaves (leg guards),[70] which are not shown in the reliefs. Goliath's javelin, bronze helmet, coat of mail, and bronze greaves, as well as the duel itself, are all known features of Aegean arms and warfare, and indicate clearly the Aegean background of the Philistines. Mycenaean warriors very similarly equipped are vividly depicted on the twelfth-century Warriors' Vase from Mycenae.

Introduction of Iron

It is commonly accepted that the use of iron was introduced into Palestine by the Philistines and that it was one of the factors that enabled them to achieve military superiority. The biblical references are generally interpreted to mean that the Philistines held a monopoly on the importation and forging of iron that was not broken until the reign of Saul. The crucial passage in the Bible on which the literary tradition is based is 1 Samuel 13:19: "Now there was no *smith* found throughout all the land of Israel; for the Philistines said, 'Lest the Hebrews make them swords and spears.' "

The word *iron*, however, does not appear in this passage at all and the word translated as "smith" (*ḥarash*) means simply "craftsman," "artisan," or "maker" unless it is modified to refer to a specific material. Here it is clear that a worker in *metal* is intended and that the Philistines did indeed seek to maintain a military advantage over the Israelites by controlling the production and distribution of metals and the supply of weapons. Whether the weapons were of bronze or iron or both is not, however, explicitly stated. The only place in which the word "iron" (*barzel*) appears in connection with the Philistines is in the description of

Goliath's weaponry: "his spear's head weighed six hundred shekels of iron" (1 Sam. 17:7).

The accumulating archaeological evidence for the appearance of iron in this area in the twelfth–eleventh centuries, as well as the reevaluation of all its facets, including its geopolitical distribution, changes slightly the clear-cut picture that was previously presented in relation to the coming of the Philistines[71] (see discussion and table 1 in chap. 2, pp. 92-93).

Religion

The biblical picture of the Philistine religious organization and beliefs suggests that by the eleventh century the Philistines had begun to assimilate the main elements of Semitic Canaanite beliefs into their own religion. Even the names of their deities are Canaanite. In this context it is important to remember that the worship of these deities was widespread in Canaan before the coming of the Philistines (for example, Dagon and the existence of towns called Beth-Dagon in the territories of Judah and Asher).[72] What is known of Philistine religion and ritual from the Bible evinces no trace of any non-Semitic tradition, except the absence of circumcision. Along with at least part of the Canaanite pantheon, the Philistines probably slowly adopted Canaanite religious beliefs and customs,[73] although elements of their original religion may have been retained in later beliefs and rituals.

The Philistine gods (Judg. 16:23) are only occasionally mentioned in the Bible. The head of the pantheon seems to have been Dagon (1 Chron. 10:10), to whom the temples in Gaza and Ashdod, and possibly one at Beth-Shean, were dedicated. A statue of Dagon, made of clay, stood in the temple at Ashdod (1 Sam. 5:2-4). Another god, Baal-zebub (Baal-zebul), had his oracular temple in Ekron. He is mentioned only in a later source (2 Kings 1:2), but the origin of the name (Baal Zebul was one of the epithets of the Ugaritic Baal) indicates that his cult was probably practiced during early

71. G. E. Wright, "Iron: The Date of its Introduction into Common Use in Palestine," *AJA* 43 (1939): 458-63.

72. The persistence of the Canaanite cult tradition in the Philistine pantheon is exemplified by the Late Bronze Age temple in Ugarit called Beth-Dagon; *Ashdod II–III*, p. 21, n. 22.

73. The eclectic nature of Philistine religion will be discussed in chap. 4. Possible Egyptian affinities are indicated by the existence of a temple dedicated to the Memphite god Ptah at Ashkelon, which is mentioned in *Meg. Ivories*.

69. A typical Aegean javelin had a loop and a cord wound around the shaft so that the weapon could be hurled a greater distance with stability; Yadin, *Warfare*, p. 355.

70. According to recent findings, metal greaves originated in Greece, whence they were brought to Cyprus. Those found in Cyprus are definitely of Aegean origin, as they are unknown in the Near East; Catling, *Bronzework*, pp. 140–41; Snodgrass, *Armour*, pp. 86–88.

Philistine times as well. The goddess Ashtoreth, or Ashtaroth, seems to have had a temple at Beth-Shean (1 Sam. 31:8–13). She was later worshipped as the Aramaic Athtarati, the fish-bodied, human-headed patroness of Ashkelon.[74] Philistine priests appear only once in the Bible, during the captivity of the Ark at Ashdod (1 Sam. 5). The Bible also refers to the Philistine custom of carrying idols into battle (2 Sam. 5:21) and to "Houses of Images," apparently temples where images of the gods were kept.

Among the few specifically Philistine religious beliefs that appear in the Bible are the golden images of mice and golden boils that were sent as a guilt (*asham*) offering to God (1 Sam. 6:4ff.). Others, such as leaping on the threshold of a temple or divining (soothsaying), were also known cult practices among the Israelites and other peoples of the ancient Near East.

There is both agreement and discrepancy between the biblical references and the archaeological finds. The Aegean background (which is not disclosed in the Bible) is especially evident in the earliest twelfth-century examples of cult objects from Ashdod, which emphasize the worship of the Great Mother of the Mycenaean world. Its later replacement by a male Canaanite pantheon may reflect the cultural milieu of the eleventh century.

ORIGINS OF THE PHILISTINES

The problem of determining the origin and homeland of the Philistines has been studied by scholars from the standpoint of three different disciplines: philology, archaeology, and literature (mainly the Greek myths). Because of the fundamental differences between the three approaches, it is hardly surprising that the conclusions they reached are mutually exclusive. Scholars from various disciplines have suggested homelands ranging from Crete to Asia Minor, but no consensus has ever been reached.

The biblical identification of Caphtor with Kriti (Crete) is one of the keys to the puzzle of Philistine origins. If this identity could be verified philologically, there would be no choice but to conclude that Crete and her nearby islands were indeed the Philistines' homeland, or at least the final stop on their great migration to Canaan. Although most scholars tend to agree that Caphtor and Kephtiu are Crete, some inter-

pret the Septuagint's translation of Caphtor as Cilicia to indicate that Caphtor and Kephtiu are the names of a country in southeast Asia Minor, specifically, Cappadocia.[75] This translation, however, may reflect a distortion influenced by Cappadocia's position of importance in the Mediterranean world at the time of the composition of the Septuagint. The Caphtor-Kriti equation, which is borne out by biblical evidence, finds additional support in the written records of three different lands. The Akkadian inscriptions describe Caphtor as a distant land and, in one account, as a land beyond the sea.[76] In the Ugaritic documents, Caphtor designates a country that is almost certainly Crete.[77] Finally the Egyptian word for Crete, *kephtiu*, is very similar linguistically to Caphtor, and its identification with Crete is well supported by archaeological evidence.[78]

The limited but important onomasticon of Philistine words and names presents another area rich in philological and ethnological possibilities. Some of the Sea Peoples' names are known from the el-Amarna tablets and from the annals of Ramesses II, but the most important source is the list of Ramesses III. As mentioned above, Ramesses' list groups the Philis-

74. *Ashdod II–III*, p. 65, n. 223, pl. 21:1; and N. Glueck, *Deities and Dolphins* (Toronto, 1965), p. 382.

75. A Wainwright, "Keftiu," *JEA* 17 (1931): 26–43, and "Caphtor, Keftiu and Cappadocia," *PEFQSt* (1931): 203–16.

76. The geographical name Caphtor-Kaptara is first mentioned in the Mari texts from the reign of Zimrilim. Different objects are described as *Kaptoritum Kaptoaru*. These are merchandise possibly originating in Greece and the Aegean islands. "Kaptara—a country beyond the Upper Sea" is mentioned among the lands allegedly conquered by Sargon of Akkad on a New-Assyrian copy, but the geographical nomenclature unmistakably points to earlier times. A. Malamat, "Campaigns to the Mediterranean by Iahdunlim and Other Early Mesopotamian Rulers," in *Studies in Honor of Benno Landsberger* (Chicago, 1965), pp. 365–73, and, for the Mari reference, "Syro-Palestinian Destinations in a Mari Tin Inventory," *IEJ* 21 (1971): 38 and n. 25.

According to Astour this is a much later amplification of his conquest; Sargon of Akkad himself never claimed to have crossed the Mediterranean. M. C. Astour, "Ugarit and the Aegean," in *Orient and Occident* (Alter Orient und Altes Testament 22), H. A. Hoffner, Jr., ed. (Neukirchen–Vluyn, 1973), pp. 19–20.

77. M. C. Astour, *Hellenosemitica* (Leiden, 1965), pp. 107–10, 137.

78. For the philological and archaeological evidence, *see* J. Vercoutter, *L'Egypte et le monde Égéen préhellénique* (Cairo, 1956), pp. 110 ff. It seems that the Theban topographical list of Amenhotep III published in 1965 by Kitchen indicates clearly the identification of Keftiu with Crete. *See* K. A. Kitchen, *The Philistines*, p. 54.

tines with the Tjekker and the Denyen. It is logical to assume, therefore, that some bond or relationship existed between them. The Egyptians, at the beginning of the twelfth century, had some knowledge of this connection and may in fact have known the last stop-off of the Sea Peoples prior to their invasion of Palestine, if not their land of origin. There are, however, divergent opinions on this question, and the ethno-geographic and linguistic aspects allow an almost unlimited field of speculation.[79]

Some of the main theories regarding the meaning and origin of the names of the Sea Peoples are as follows. The Denyen (*dnyn*; Assyrian, *Danuna*) are associated by some authorities with Cilicia on the basis of the bilingual Phoenician and hieroglyphic Hittite inscription from Karatepe[80] (ninth century B.C.). Others suggest a connection with Cyprus, noting that the island's Assyrian name (*mat*) *Ia-da-na-na* can be interpreted as "the island of the Danuna (Denyen)."[81]

The Tjekker (*tkr*) are considered by some scholars to be the Homeric Sikeloi who occupied the island of Sicily.[82] Others see them as the Homeric τευϰϱοι of Cilicia, who, according to Greek mythology, founded the city of Salamis on Cyprus.[83] The two depictions of Sea People warriors—probably Tjekker—discovered in Enkomi (chapter 5, figs. 13 and 14) near Salamis, assume a special significance in this theory and emphasize the crucial role of Cyprus in the wanderings and settlement of the Sea Peoples.

The Philistines (*plst* = Peleset) are the most controversial of the three groups. The theory that seeks their origin in the Aegean world finds support in the ideogram of the head of a man wearing a "feathered" headdress, which appears on the Phaestos Disk from southern Crete (pl. 3). A more specific proposal identifies the Philistines with the Pelasgians. This is supported by a somewhat doubtful etymology and the Homeric tradition that the Pelasgians were one of the five nations that inhabited Crete.[84] Another theory seeks to connect the Philistines with one of the Illyrian peoples whose name was derived from the place name Palaeste and who were called Palaestini in the Illyrian language.[85]

Two basically conflicting schools of thought exist with regard to the question of Philistine origins and the geographic, historical, and ethnological problems involved. On the one hand Crete, or the Aegean area in general, is held to be the Philistine homeland. The theory of an Illyrian origin agrees with this supposition, for its advocates contend that after migrating from their native Illyria, the Philistines took to the sea and reached the Aegean islands and Crete. The leading proponents of the Aegean theory, while differing on details, concur on the basic assumption that the Tjekker, the Denyen, and the Philistines are tribes of Indo-European origin (Illyrian, Pelasgian, Thraco-Phrygian, etc.).[86] The opposing school maintains an Anatolian origin, locating the Philistine homeland in western Cilicia, more specifically on the banks of the Calycadnus River, where the Philistines and the Tjekker probably dwelt together.[87]

The Philistine words and personal names found in the Bible are another possible key to the enigma of Philistine origins through similarities to other languages, especially those of Asia Minor. The word *seren*, preserved only in the plural, has been the subject of much research and is thought to be a proto–Greek Illyrian or Lydian word that later entered the Greek language. The name Achish, Ἀγχους in the Septuagint and Homer, which closely resembles the name Ikûsu, king of Ekron in the Essarhadon annals, is sometimes compared with Ἀγχίσης (Homer, *Iliad*,

79. The fullest bibliography on the Philistines' origins and language can be found in Barnett, *The Sea Peoples*, bibl. VI; Albright, *Syria, the Philistines and Phoenicia*, bibl. I; Malamat, *The Egyptian Decline*, p. 294 f., nn. 6, 7.

80. R. D. Barnett, "Mopsos," *JHS* 73 (1953): 140–43; idem, *The Sea Peoples*, pp. 363–66.

81. A. Wainwright, "A Teucrian at Salamis in Cyprus," *JHS* 83 (1963): 151. For a brief summary of the possible connection between the tribe of Dan and Danaoi, Danuna, and the Aegean, *see* Y. Yadin, "And Dan, Why Did He Remain in Ships?" *AJBA* 1 (1968): 9–23.

82. Albright, *Syria, the Philistines and Phoenicia*, p. 508; Malamat, *The Egyptian Decline*, p. 33.

83. Wainwright, "A Teucrian at Salamis in Cyprus," *JHS* 83 (1963): 146–51.

84. V. Georgiev, *JFK* 1 (1951): 136 ff.; Albright, *Syria, the Philistines and Phoenicia*, pp. 512–13, n. 9.

85. P. Kretschmer, *Glotta* 30 (1943): 152–54; G. Bonfante, "Who Were the Philistines?" *AJA* 50 (1946): 252 ff.

86. Mazar, *The Philistines and Their Wars*, p. 166, nn. 5, 6; Kitchen, *The Philistines*, pp. 55–56.

87. Keftiu-Kaphtor is identified by Wainwright as a region near the Calycadnus River in western Cilicia; Wainwright, "A Teucrian at Salamis in Cyprus," *JHS* 83 (1963): 149. Albright agrees to the derivation of the Philistines from the general area of southwestern Asia Minor: Albright, *Syria, the Philistines and Phoenicia*, pp. 512–13.

2:819). Ἀγχίσης, in Greek tradition, was related to the Dardanians, one of the Illyrian tribes that later migrated to Asia Minor and Greece.[88] The three Hebrew words kobaʿ ("helmet," "hat"), ʾargaz ("box," "chest," "basket") and pīlegeš ("concubine") are possibly of southwestern Anatolian, Cilician, or Illyrian origin.[89] Opinion is divided on the names Pichol, Goliath, and Ziklag. Goliath is sometimes compared to the Lydian Ἀλυάττης.[90]

Written records and other evidence bearing on the question of Philistine origins are still undergoing intensive philological and historical examination. A new document could throw much light on the picture or even change it completely. The publication of documents recently discovered in the Ugaritic archives is sure to have a marked effect on the subject. So far only a summary of their contents has been published.[91] It is known that the documents include correspondence between the kings of Ugarit and Cyprus at the end of the thirteenth century—just prior to the fall of Cyprus and the Hittite empire, Ugarit, to the invading Sea Peoples. They mention, inter alia, the dispatch of warships to the land of the Luku (Lycians), a tribe of Sea Peoples known from the Merneptah inscriptions. The archives may also contain evidence of a treaty between Egypt and her former enemies and their attempt to unite in time to repel the encroaching Sea Peoples.

Continued progress in historical and philological research will certainly broaden the basis of our understanding of Philistine culture and may even hold the promise of a solution to the question of Philistine origins.

88. For a discussion of the word seren, see Barnett, The Sea Peoples, p. 373; Albright, Syria, The Philistines and Phoenicia, p. 516; for a discussion of the name Achish, see Wainwright, JHS 83 (1963): 151.

89. Mazar, The Philistines and Their Wars, p. 166, n. 5; C. Rabin, "The Origin of the Hebrew Word Pīlegeš," Journal of Jewish Studies 25 (1974): 353–64.

90. Mazar, The Philistines and Their Wars, p. 166; Albright, Syria, the Philistines and Phoenicia, p. 513, n. 8. Also, the three names of the Philistine chieftains mentioned by Wen Amun, Waraktir, Waret, and Makamar, have been interpreted as Luwian; see also W. F. Albright, "The Eastern Mediterranean about 1060 B.C.," in Studies Presented to David Moore Robinson, G. E. Mylonas, ed. (St. Louis, 1951), pp. 228–29.

91. For the documents from the Tablet Oven, one of which (RS 18.148) is of particular importance, see C. Virolleaud, Le palais royal d'Ugarit, vol. 5 (Paris, 1965), pp. 88–89; M. C. Astour, "New Evidence on the Last Days of Ugarit," AJA 69 (1965): 256; and Malamat, The Egyptian Decline, pp. 29–30.

RESEARCH AND ARCHAEOLOGY

The Philistines have always fascinated biblical commentators and historians. The various translations of the name Philistine in the different versions of the Bible reveal that even in early times translators and exegetes were unsure of their identity. The Septuagint, for example, usually translates their name as ἀλλόφυλοι, but it occurs as φυλιστιειμ in the Pentateuch and Joshua. Since the very beginning of biblical exegesis, the name and origins of this enigmatic nation have given rise to speculation.

Encountering the descendants of the Philistines on the coast of southern Palestine, the historian Herodotus, sailors, and travelers from the Persian period onward called them παλαστινοι and their country παλαιστινμ. The use of these names in the works of Josephus Flavius, where they are common translations for Philistines and Philistia and, in some cases, for the entire land of Palestine, indicates the extent to which the names had gained acceptance by Roman times. The emperor Hadrian officially designated the province of Judaea Provincia Palaestina, and by the fourth century A.D. the shortened name Palaestina had become the general term for the whole of Palestine.

Research on the Philistines, although voluminous, was more or less limited to speculation on the biblical sources, and, until the nineteenth century, little could be added to the early theories and interpretations.[92] The discovery and decipherment of the Egyptian inscriptions in the temple of Ramesses III at Medinet Habu, and of other Egyptian documents containing references to the Sea Peoples and the Philistines finally supplemented the Bible with reliable historical records, and scientific study of the Philistines was undertaken. The progress made in ancient Near East studies in the nineteenth century and the application of philology, historical geography, and archaeology to the analysis of the biblical and Egyptian records has made Philistine studies a scholarly discipline in its own right.

J. F. Champollion, the decipherer of the Egyptian hieratic script, was the first to identify the hieroglyphs reading prst with the biblical Philistines. As a result, all Egyptian records containing references to the Philistines were subjected to scrutiny, and a long line

92. For a comprehensive summary of these theories, see Macalister, The Philistines, Their History and Civilization, pp. 1–7.

of scholars from R. Lepsius to A. Gardiner and J. A. Wilson toiled over their decipherment, transcription, and translation.

The discovery and decipherment of the Assyrian records, by contrast, has had almost no influence on research in early Philistine history. The Philistines do indeed appear frequently in Assyrian inscriptions, but only from the ninth century B.C. onward.[93] Thus for all their importance in supplying the background of Philistine history in the days of the Divided Monarchy, the Assyrian historical inscriptions throw no light upon the early period of Philistine history.

Archaeology did not become a major factor in Philistine research until the early part of the twentieth century. Once the principles of stratigraphy had been methodically applied to excavations in Palestine, archaeologists became aware of recurring finds that could be related to the Philistines within limited and well-defined strata, especially in sites situated on the coast and on the inland coastal plain.

The first to recognize affinities between the Philistine and Aegean cultures were the classical archaeologists. Scholars such as F. B. Welch, H. Thiersch, and especially D. Mackenzie[94] grasped the connection between Mycenaean ceramics and the pottery they defined as Philistine, which came exclusively from Early Iron Age strata in sites in Philistia. Mackenzie, who excavated at Beth-Shemesh, and W. J. Phythian-Adams, who dug with J. Garstang at Ashkelon, brought to light Philistine levels rich in material remains. In their publications, both scholars emphasized the Aegean background of the Philistine culture.

A milestone in the study of Philistine history and culture was R. A. S. Macalister's classic work, *The*

Philistines, Their History and Civilization (London, 1914); Macalister incorporated the results of his own excavations at Gezer and presented a thorough compendium of Philistine research and archaeology up to his own time. Important advances in the study of the Philistine material culture were later made when Petrie's excavation at Tell Jemmeh and Tell el-Far'ah, Albright's at Tell Beit Mirsim, and the continuation of Mackenzie's excavations at Beth-Shemesh uncovered the remains of rich Philistine settlements in well-defined strata. Major advances have been made in the last few decades as a result of the stratigraphic excavations of the important sites of Ashdod and Tell Qasile. These discoveries also provided further support for the hypothesis of a connection between Philistine and Aegean cultures—a connection that, as verified by all subsequent studies, will be discussed in the following chapter.

Excavations, soundings, and surveys have all shown that the Philistine culture flourished along the southern Palestinian coast and coastal plain—the territory originally settled by the Philistines. The discovery of archaeological remains of unmistakably Philistine character in sites quite distant from this area has raised the question of how Philistine culture spread beyond the confines of Philistia—through military conquest and territorial expansion, through the establishment of military outposts in areas under Philistine domination but not inhabited by them, or through normal trade and commerce.

Philistine culture (comprising all related remains) is part of a complex whole; but our knowledge of this culture has now advanced to the point where its stratigraphy, typology, and even absolute chronology can be established. Comparative study of the subject has also progressed and is now on a firmer basis as the result of the many new excavations in the Aegean and the Levant and of the formation of a new discipline: Mediterranean studies.

93. H. Tadmor, "Philistia under Assyrian Rule," *BA* 29 (1966): 86–102.

94. See chap. 3, n. 1 below.

2

STRATIGRAPHY AND RELATIVE
CHRONOLOGY OF SITES CONTAINING
REMAINS OF PHILISTINE CULTURE

Although the sites containing remains of Philistine culture are concentrated mainly in the Shephelah, the southern coastal plain, the culture spread beyond that region. Following its traces from south to north, from the strongholds in Philistia proper through the neighboring areas under direct Philistine influence, we shall reach remoter places that were only slightly affected. Sites at which stratigraphic excavations have been conducted and the results published will provide the framework, but unpublished material will also be taken into account. Sites cursorily explored in soundings or surface surveys, as well as illicitly excavated sites (yielding finds, but no stratigraphy), will also be fitted into this framework, enabling us to establish a relative chronology for the beginnings and the diffusion of Philistine culture, from its appearance at the start of the Iron Age to its assimilation and disappearance at the end of the eleventh century B.C.

The collective term *Philistine,* as used here, includes all possible groups of Sea Peoples with a similar cultural background. *Philistine culture* designates the homogeneous assemblage of material culture found primarily in the territory and within the sphere of influence of the Philistines, and which fits into the stratigraphic and chronological framework of Philistine history in Palestine during the Iron Age I, from the twelfth and eleventh centuries B.C. to the conquests of David.

The advent of a new cultural element makes itself felt in many ways. Fortunately for us, the material culture of the Philistines is represented by a combination of archaeological and historical evidence that makes ethnic identification almost certain. In our discussion of the sites we shall treat the stratigraphic problems, the nature of the settlements, their architec-

ture, and burial sites; but above all, we will emphasize the pottery, which is the hallmark and chief indicator of Philistine culture.

The chronological table on pp. 290–91 is based on stratigraphy and on the typological stages in the development of Philistine culture. Although this chapter chiefly concerns Philistine remains and their relative chronology at different sites, we shall also discuss a number of pertinent details of absolute chronology, which are summarized in chapter 6.

TELL EZ-ZUWEYID

The southernmost site at which Philistine pottery has been found, Tell ez-Zuweyid,[1] is south of Raphiah and Wadi el-Arish on the northern Sinai coast. The Philistine pottery comes from levels N and M. The finds from the two levels cannot be clearly distinguished; it is possible that they actually overlap. W. M. F. Petrie, however, stresses that level N was completely destroyed by fire and believes that two occupational levels can be clearly distinguished. Level N is the first to contain architectural remains, even though they are very scanty. Earlier levels are indicated only by Late Bronze Age pottery.[2]

The Philistine ceramic assemblage consists of a Philistine sherd of a Type 1 bowl decorated with a spiral motif,[3] an undecorated sherd of the same type,[4] a rim of a bowl[5] and a body sherd[6] (both decorated with

1. *Anthedon,* pp. 7–9, pls. XIV, XV, XVI.
2. Ibid., pl. XXXIII:23 K6, 23 K18.
3. Ibid., pl. XXXI:32.
4. Ibid., pl. XXXIII:23 U4.
5. Ibid., pl. XXXI:36.
6. Ibid., pl. XXXI:39.

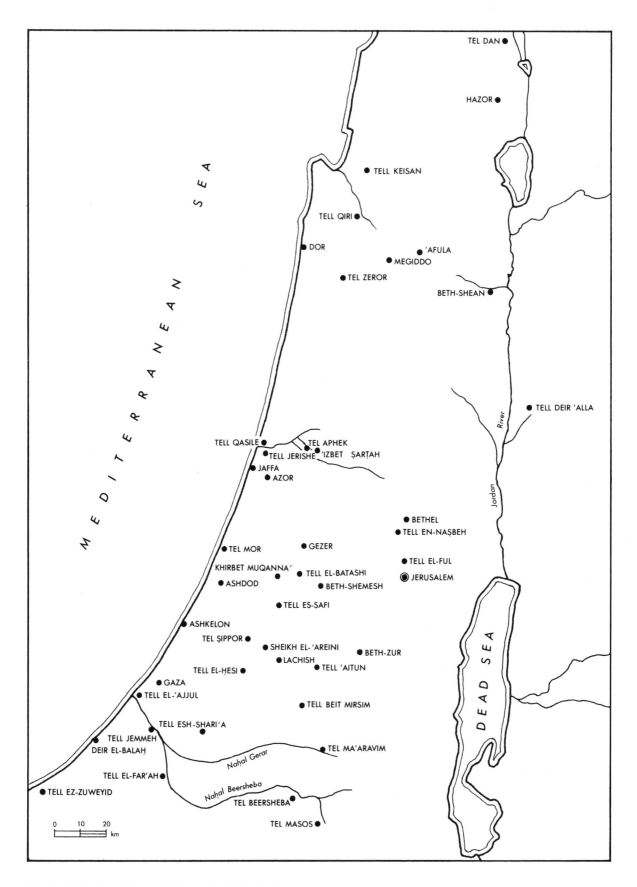

Map 2. Palestine: Principal Sites with Philistine Remains

spiral motifs), and several other ornamental designs that are difficult to identify; all of them are done in such thick black lines that very little of the surface remains bare. The last two sherds are especially important, for they have parallels at Tell Qasile XI.[7]

Besides the Philistine pottery there are a number of non-Philistine pilgrim flasks[8] that reflect the local Late Bronze Age II pottery tradition and are typical of Megiddo VIIB–VIA,[9] several deep carinated bowls[10] characteristic of Qasile XII and especially XI,[11] and, lastly, two rather unusual vessels: an Egyptian jar[12] similar to those found in the Tell el-Farʿah anthropoid burials (chap. 5, fig. 7:14, 15), and a pomegranate-shaped vessel[13] comparable to the pomegranate vases on the kernoi from Gezer and Megiddo, which are dated to the twelfth or eleventh century.

Two body sherds of Cypro-Phoenician Black-on-Red I–II ware allow us to establish the latest chronological limit of level N,[14] for this type of pottery cannot be dated earlier than the tenth century. Thus level N can be chronologically restricted, in general terms, to approximately the same period as Qasile XII–IX and Megiddo from VIIA to VA–IVB—that is, within the period of the second half of the twelfth to the tenth century B.C.[15]

Level M, which Petrie erroneously dated to the period of Ramesses II,[16] produced an upper fragment of a Philistine bowl with a red spiral motif[17] and a similar but undecorated sherd,[18] both of which are probably somewhat later than the Philistine pottery of level N. An approximate date for level M can be determined by a large Cypriot flask of the White Painted I ware, which does not appear in Palestine prior to the second half of the eleventh century. Corroborating evidence comes from a group of Cypriot sherds that includes both White Painted I and Bichrome I–III

ware,[19] which represent the mixture between the pottery of level M and part of level N.

Although meager, these finds indicate a Philistine presence at Tell ez-Zuweyid, or at least its influence at this southern site.

TELL EL-FARʿAH (SOUTH)

Tell el-Farʿah, near Wadi Gaza (Nahal Besor), is generally identified with Sharuhen, one of the chief cities of the Negev and a major Egyptian stronghold. The tombs and occupation levels of the mound provide abundant evidence of Philistine material culture in tomb architecture, anthropoid clay coffins, pottery, weapons, and seals. Both the stratification of the mound and the finds in the tombs enable us to construct a well-founded chronological sequence.

The initial stage and the stratification of Philistine pottery at Tell el-Farʿah can best be traced in the Governor's House (the so-called Residency) at the northern end of the mound. The relatively clear stratigraphy of this building complex, especially in the paved courtyard next to the Residency, reveals the relationship and continuity between the Late Bronze Age and Philistine pottery and supports the division of Philistine pottery into three phases. As we shall show, the pottery assemblages of the three Early Iron Age strata Y, X, and pre-W on the northern end of the mound correspond to these three phases.

The Residency complex consists of three units:

1. The Residency proper,[20] one of the finest structures on the mound, was built around the end of the Late Bronze Age and stood until the eleventh century. The excavators distinguished two levels of Philistine pottery there: level 368–369 contained Phase 1 pottery corresponding primarily to the pottery found in tombs 552 and 542; levels 370–72 contained Phase 2 pottery corresponding to that in tombs 532[21] and 562.

7. Unpublished. Cat. nos. Q. III3171, 3183.
8. *Anthedon*, pl. XXXVIII:85 U3 and 85 L4.
9. *Meg. II*, pl. 67:2.
10. *Anthedon*, pl. XXXIII:23 K16.
11. *Qasile IEJ 1*, fig. 4:6.
12. *Anthedon*, pl. XXXIII:31 K23.
13. Ibid., pl. XXXVIII:74 D3.
14. Ibid., pl. XXXI:27–28.
15. Petrie dated level N to a period before 1275—*see* title ibid., pl. XV—with a possible gap between M and N (*see* ibid., p. 8).
16. Ibid., p. 8, par. 22.
17. Ibid., pl. XXXI:23.
18. Ibid., pl. XXXIII:23 U.

19. Ibid., pl. XXXI:24–26, 29, 30, 34, 37, 38, 40, 41.
20. *BP I*, pp. 17–19, pl. LIV; *BP II*, pp. 28–29, pls. LXVII, LXVIII, LXIX, LXXXIX. The dates proposed by Petrie are too high. They were later corrected by Starkey (*BP II*, pp. 28–29). For other studies, see *CMP*, pp. 117 ff.; *TBM I*, p. 56; *TBM IA*, pp. 94–95; W. F. Albright, *BASOR* 48 (1932): 16–17; and J. Du Plat Taylor, "Late Cypriot III in the Light of Recent Excavations," *PEQ* 88 (1956): 32–33.
21. *BP I*, p. 18. We do not have sufficient information against which to check the ceramic finds of the Residency as proposed by Petrie.

2. The west building, a smaller structure adjoining the Residency on the west, probably housed domestic offices and other palace services. Here Philistine pottery was found in levels 364–70, concentrated in rooms YAA and YEE.[22] Both rooms contained Philistine sherds characteristic of Phase 1.[23] A complete Type 2 krater (see chap. 3, fig. 11:8) with an unusual geometric motif was found in room YAA, and the floors of the building contained a number of scarabs and scaraboids of the late Nineteenth and Twentieth dynasties.[24]

3. The paved courtyard was the area richest in finds and the most important to the stratigraphic sequence of the complex. The open courtyard YX, with its paved surface, adjoins the Residency on the south.[25] As the entire area was leveled before being paved, there is a noticeable difference between the levels of the courtyard (approximately 364) and the Residency proper (approximately 368 and 370–72). Typical Late Bronze II[26] pottery, including some types which date from as late as the twelfth century,[27] was found beneath the courtyard. Above the paving stones, however, the pottery found was predominantly Philistine (levels 364–65) and belonged mainly to Phase 1.[28]

In addition to the Philistine pottery, another group of sherds unlike the local ceramics in ware, workmanship, and decoration was uncovered. They were of thin, well-fired buff ware burnished and decorated in red and black bichrome with geometric motifs of dotted ladders, network, zigzags, and birds.[29] Two other pottery vessels from Tell el-Farʿah apparently also belong to this group. One is a small jug from the Philistine tomb 542,[30] analogous with the Philistine level of the courtyard, and the other is part of the elongated neck of a jug[31] from the area of cemetery 900, which is predominantly Late Bronze Age—although it also contains pieces from as late as the reign of Ramesses IV. This group of pottery was recognized by Petrie as "foreign" to Tell el-Farʿah, while a similarly painted jug

from tomb 1099 at Tell el-ʿAjjul (a disturbed Late Bronze Age group) was described by him as in "a strange style, unique in this place."[32] The same type of sherd was found by Petrie in the debris of Ramesses III's palace at Tell el-Yahudiyeh,[33] and points to a connection between that site and Tell el-Farʿah during the reign of Ramesses III. (This connection is discussed further in chapter 5 in the section on the Tell el-Yahudiyeh.)

According to present evidence, this foreign pottery at Tell el-Farʿah, Tell el-ʿAjjul, and Tell el-Yahudiyeh forms part of the group designated *Midianite*, which has been identified in a dated context in the Hathor temple and nearby sites at Timna,[34] in strata IV–II, which span the Nineteen and Twentieth dynasties. The origins of this very distinctive family of painted pottery are apparently to be sought in Qurayyah in northwest Arabia.[35] It is found in Late Bronze Age as well as twelfth-century contexts, where in two instances—at Tell el-Farʿah—it is associated with Philistine pottery. To Albright, its presence indicated that the Philistines were stationed at this Egyptian fortress as garrison troops sometime between its foundation and its destruction in the latter part of the twelfth or beginning of the eleventh century. In our opinion, however, it is questionable whether the dating of stratum Y and the first appearance of Philistine pottery should be based solely on the cartouche of Seti II (see pl. 1).[36] The cartouche cannot be taken, by itself, as a *terminus post quem* for the advent of Philistine pottery in Palestine, as Furumark and others have done.[37]

22. *BP II*, p. 29, pl. LXIX.

23. Ibid., pls. LXIII:43–45, 47, 50 and LXIV:57.

24. Ibid., p. 28, pl. LXII:20–28, including scarabs found above the pavement of the courtyard.

25. Ibid., pp. 28–29, pls. LXVII:7, 8.

26. Ibid., pls. LXIII:35, 37–42; see plan on pl. LXV.

27. Ibid., pl. LXXXIX, locus ZZG (level 363.10).

28. Ibid., pls. LXIII:46, 49, 51; LXIV:72; LXXXVII:64R1.

29. Ibid., p. 29, pl. LXIII:53–56.

30. *BP I*, pl. XXV; *CPP*, 59 H3.

31. *BP II*, pl. LXIII:52.

32. *AG II*, p. 12, pl. XLI:42 (Type 68M).

33. *HIC*, p. 17, pl. XVII:6, 10, 12, 13. Albright, *TBM I*, p. 58, par. 75, regarded this group of sherds from Tell el-Yahudiyeh as Philistine. Furumark noted the error of this identification in *CMP*, p. 118, n. 1.

34. B. Rothenberg, *Timna* (London, 1972). Temple site: pp. 155–162, figs. 46–47, pl. XXIV; Site 2: p. 109, fig. 32, pls. XXII, 48–52, 54; Site 199: p. 118, fig. 35:1, pl. XXII, 53.

35. P. J. Parr, G. L. Harding, and J. E. Dayton, "Preliminary Survey in N.W. Arabia, 1968," *BIAL* 8–9 (1968–69): 238–39, figs. 15–16.

36. Four fragments of a large, heavy jar were found incised with the name of Seti II in well-carved hieroglyphs. The pieces fit together, although they were found in different parts of the Residency and courtyard; they probably belong to the period of the foundation of the fortress by Seti II. *BP II*, p. 28, pls. LXI, LXIV:74 (YX364 10); and W. F. Albright, *BASOR* 48 (1932): 17; and Albright, *Syria, the Philistines and Phoenicia*, pp. 509–10.

37. *CMP*, p. 121; and Du Plat Taylor, *PEQ* 88 (1956): 32.

At the southern end of the mound, a group of Philistine vessels belonging to Phase 1 was found in building D in levels 387–88.[38]

To sum up, stratum Y (in the northern area of excavation) contained Philistine pottery most characteristic of Phase 1 and the first half of Phase 2. It appears likely that the destruction of the Residency, and stratum Y, took place not long after the close of the twelfth century.

The second phase of Philistine pottery is most clearly represented in the stratum X building complex south of the Residency.[39] Here pottery typical of Phase 2 was found between levels 369 and 372; included were a Type 1 bowl, a Type 2 krater,[40] a Type 8 juglet (see chap. 3, fig. 33:5), and a censer on a tripod base[41] with legs similar to the handle of the Type 14 jug in figure 56:2 of chapter 3.

The final phase of Philistine pottery, characterized by debased Type 1 bowls lacking white slip or decoration,[42] appears in levels 370–71, antedating building complex W.[43] This building level can be dated to the tenth century; it contains typical Cypro-Phoenician Black-on-Red I–II juglets[44] from levels 373–77 of building complex V east of building complex W.[45]

This brief survey demonstrates the stratigraphic continuity of the Iron Age I at Tell el-Far'ah (S). We suggest that the pottery assemblages of the three Early Iron Age strata Y, X, and pre-W in the north end of the mound correspond to the stages of development of Philistine material culture (see comparative chart, pp. 290–91).

The Tombs

Cemeteries 900 and 500[46] are very important for determining both the date of the transition from Late Bronze to Iron I and the beginning of Philistine pottery at Tell el-Far'ah and throughout the area. Cemetery 900 (on the western slope of the tell) was used during Late Bronze II and the beginning of Iron I. Its tombs

contained rich pottery assemblages and numerous Egyptian royal scarabs, which help establish a chronological sequence. A large number of scarabs belong to the period of Ramesses II and Merneptah,[47] a smaller group to Ramesses III,[48] and only two to Ramesses IV.[49] The latter two, being the latest, provide a *terminus post quem* for cemetery 900 as a whole.[50]

Philistine pottery (which is common in cemetery 500) was not discovered in the 900 tombs. The two cemeteries overlap in time, and it seems likely that cemetery 900 continued local Canaanite traditions, whereas cemetery 500 was used by the newly arrived Philistine settlers.

Fragments of a pottery coffin from tomb 935 in cemetery 900 are of the same type as those found in tombs 552 and 562. The latest scarabs in tomb 935 were of Ramesses II, while the pottery indicates a date about 1200 B.C.; by that time Cypriot and Mycenaean imports had ceased.[51] We can observe here a development analogous to that at Beth-Shean, where the anthropoid coffins first appeared in the thirteenth century and were to be taken up by the Philistines in the twelfth and eleventh centuries (see chap. 5).

The Philistine Tombs The Philistine tombs at Tell el-Far'ah are concentrated for the most part in cemetery 500,[52] although there are others scattered about cemeteries 100, 200, 600, and 800.[53] We shall discuss

38. *BP II*, p. 30, pls. LXXV, LXXIX.
39. Ibid., p. 29, pl. LXX.
40. *CPP*, 24 S1, 18 V1; and *BP II*, pl. LXXXVIII:V370.
41. Ibid., pls. LXI:4, LXXXIII:27 T1.
42. E.g., *CPP*, 18 D3, 24 Q; and *BP II*, pl. LXXXIX (WN370.5; WZ371.11).
43. *BP I*, pl. LVI; and *BP II*, p. 29, pl. LXXI.
44. *BP II*, pl. LXXXIX:V373–377, Type 82E.
45. *BP II*, p. 29, pl. LXXI.
46. For discussion of cemeteries 900 and 500, *see* references in no. 20 above and chap. 5, pp. 260–68 below.

47. Scarabs of Ramesses II appeared, inter alia, in tombs 921 (46), 934 (118–25), and 935 (222, 224). The scarabs mentioned contain at least three hieroglyphs (*BP II*, pp. 23–27). Two cartouches of Merneptah were found, one in tomb 980 (ibid., pl. LVII:336) and the other in tomb 914 (ibid., pl. XLVIII:25). Scarab 130 is from tomb 934 and is probably of Seti II.
48. Scarabs of Ramesses III were found in tombs 934 (126–28) and 984 (374) (*BP II*, pp. 24, 26).
49. Scarabs of Ramesses IV were found in tombs 934 (129) and 960 (297) (ibid., pp. 24–26).
50. Two scarabs from tomb 984 were ascribed (by Starkey and not mentioned by Petrie, as Albright stated) to Ramesses VIII (*BP II*, pp. 26, 31; pls. LVI, center row, second from right, LVII:375; Albright did not accept this identification; cf. W. F. Albright, *BASOR* 48 [1932]: 17; *TBM IA*, pp. 94–95).
51. *BP II*, p. 25.
52. The most important tombs containing Philistine pottery, besides the rock-cut chambers, are tombs 503, 507, 523.
53. The following tombs outside cemetery 500 also contained Philistine pottery: in cemetery 100: tombs 103, 126; in cemetery 200: tombs 239, 242, 251, 268; in cemetery 600: tombs 601, 602, 607, 615, 621, 625, 649; in cemetery 800: tombs 828, 839, 851, 859.

here some of the pertinent architectural features of a representative selection of the tombs, as well as their contents, which reflect, inter alia, the development of Philistine pottery through the three phases corresponding, for the most part, to the three habitation levels discussed above.

We shall first consider the five great rock-cut chamber tombs (542, 552, 562, 532, 544), which Petrie called the tombs of the "lords (*seranim*) of the Philistines." Petrie believed that each of these tombs, which are hewn in a row in cemetery 500 northwest of the mound, was used by a single family for several generations. (For the origin of the rock-cut chamber, see chap. 5.). Four contained burial deposits; the fifth and smallest, 544, yielded only a few inconclusive finds and was therefore omitted from Petrie's discussion. Two of them, 552 and 562, contained anthropoid clay coffins (which will be discussed separately in chap. 5). Petrie correctly determined the chronological order of the tombs as 542, 552, 532, and 562; but in assigning absolute dates he relied primarily on the style of the scarabs found in them and, consequently, arrived at an absurdly high chronology—dating them to 1320, 1240, 1130, and 1050 B.C.[54]

Starkey lowered these dates on stylistic grounds and attributed the earliest to the reign of Ramesses IV. He did so after observing that the scarabs by which Petrie had dated the earliest tombs, 542 and 552, continued in use and were sometimes found in the same context as those of Ramesses IV.[55] Albright reached similar conclusions through an analysis of the tombs' ceramic finds; he dated the four tombs to the period from the mid-twelfth century to around 1000 B.C., at the latest.[56]

Furumark accepted these corrections and pointed out that scarabs of Ramesses IV (more accurately, from the period of this pharaoh) were found in tombs 542 and 552.[57] He also accepted Petrie's and Starkey's identification of one scarab in tomb 532 as belonging to Ramesses XI,[58] although Albright's discussion made no mention of it.[59] The debased character of the

scarabs in tomb 562 places the tomb chronologically at the end of the series.

It should be kept in mind, however, that scarabs, while of value in determining a relative chronology, cannot serve as the basis for absolute dates.[60] The ceramic contents of these tombs, on the other hand, especially the Philistine pottery, enable us to establish accurately the internal order of the series and the approximate length of time each tomb was in use.

Tombs 542 and 552 are the earliest of the group, and they resemble one another both in the character of their scarabs and in their ceramic contents. The dissimilarities of their ceramic finds stem primarily from the special nature of tomb 552, which contained an anthropoid coffin burial and the Egyptianizing vessels that tend to accompany such a burial (see chap. 5).

Tomb 542 (fig. 1) is the earliest in the group and the richest in finds. Two burial levels were distinguished by Petrie, even though no clear stylistic development can be traced and the finds are limited to the twelfth century. The general plan of the tomb is similar to that of 552 (see chap. 5, fig. 3), except for some minor differences attributable to the need to accommodate an anthropoid coffin. A stepped dromos leads down to the square opening, which was once sealed by stone slabs. The trapezoidal main burial chamber was formed by cutting into the marl and leaving wide shelves along the walls roofed with roughly hewn arcosolia. "Benches" in the subsidiary chamber are cut in the same way and have partially preserved arcosolia overhead.

Tomb 542 contained a representative assemblage of twelfth-century pottery of the usual local types; the pieces retain a strong resemblance to the Late Bronze Age II ceramic tradition, as well as to typical Phase 1 Philistine pottery. The assemblage as a whole corresponds to and is contemporary with Phase 1 Philistine pottery in the paved courtyard of area YX in stratum Y.

The local Canaanite shapes (a selection is presented in plate 2:1) are as follows: rather deep, rounded bowls; shallow bowls with carinated shoulders and occasional concentric red circles on the inside; carinated chalices on a high trumpet foot, with one unusual deep gobletlike variant having only slight carination; lamps of the large, deep-bowled and rounded-rim

54. *BP I,* pp. 6–9, pls. XIX–XX; for assemblages, *see* esp. pls. XXIII–XXV.
55. *BP II,* p. 31
56. W. F. Albright, *AJA* 36 (1932) : 299–301; *TBM IA,* p. 95.
57. *CMP,* p. 121.
58. *BP II,* p. 31; *BP I,* p. 7, pl. XXII:202; *CMP,* p. 121.
59. Cf. n. 56. B. Brandl has suggested that the scarab be assigned to Ramesses X; *see* his forthcoming article.

60. Tombs 542 and 552 each contained a scarab of Tuthmosis III (*BP I,* pl. XXII:184, 188). The latter was found together with scarabs of the period of Ramesses II (ibid., p. 7, pl. XXII:191, 193, 194).

Pl. 1. Fragments of a large pottery jar with the cartouche of Seti II, Tell el-Farʿah [From the Collection of the Israel Department of Antiquities and Museums, I. 9834. *BP II*, pls. LXI, 1; LXIV, 74].

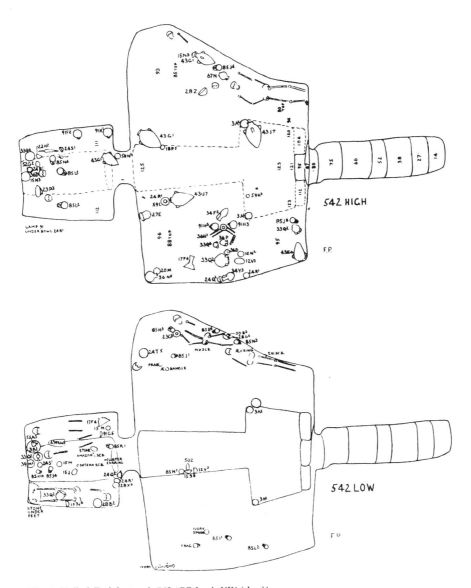

Fig. 1. Tell el-Farʿah, tomb 542 [*BP I*, pl. XIX (dap)].

type, as well as the shallower variant with flat, flaring rim; and pilgrim flasks showing slight variations in shape and decoration, the latter being mainly concentric circles. One example has wheel-spoke decoration and another rather crude example has a lug handle.

The small finds from tomb 542 include a dagger with a bronze handle and an iron blade (pl. 2:2).[61] This weapon is the earliest example of iron at Tell el-Farʿah; the cemetery 900 deposits contained only bronze implements, whereas iron weapons and jewelry appear throughout cemetery 500 in association with Philistine pottery.[62] The dagger's double-edged iron blade was inserted into a bronze handle with a bronze pommel. Three small bronze rings were part of the fittings of the dagger, which was "killed" (snapped in two) in antiquity to prevent its use. A double-edged bronze dagger with a slight midrib on either side was cast in one piece, with a long tang for a handle (pl. 2:2).

Tomb 552 contained Philistine pottery typical of Phase 1 (cf. chap. 5, fig. 7) and local pottery similar to that in tomb 542. Here too the Late Bronze Age II tradition was strong.

Tomb 532 follows in date.[63] Its contents are rather meager, and the pottery types are somewhat less typical than those in the other three tombs. The small amount of Philistine pottery found is difficult to define. It includes a Type 1 bowl (chap. 3, fig. 2:4), which is known to appear in both Phases 1 and 2 of Philistine pottery; a stirrup jar (chap. 3, fig. 17:4) is of equally little value in fixing the date of the tomb, for it is common to both the end of Phase 1 and to Phase 2; and a three-handled jar, a late local imitation of a Mycenaean vessel that is similar to one (Type 5) found at Tell Jemmeh in a stratum bearing Philistine pottery of Phases 1 and 2 (chap. 3, fig. 20). Although the local Iron Age pottery in this tomb has much in common with the ceramic deposits of tombs 542 and 552, the influence of the Late Bronze Age II is here much less pronounced. As we pointed out above, most of the pottery types in tomb 532 are also found in the upper Philistine level of the Residency. Besides the pottery, there were a number of bronze bowls similar to the one found in tomb 562 (chap. 5, fig. 8:21).[64]

The ceramic assemblage of tomb 532 can be dated to the end of the twelfth and begining of the eleventh century. The scarab, which may possibly be assigned to Ramesses X, would accord well with this date (see notes 58, 59).

Tomb 562 (one of the two Philistine tombs containing an anthropoid clay coffin) yielded more typical pottery but very few Philistine vessels. Among the more interesting are a Type 12 jar (chap. 5, fig. 8:20) decorated like those of the second phase of Philistine pottery and a Type 6 jug (chap. 5, fig. 8:19) whose decoration represents a fusion of Philistine and local decorative traditions. Alongside the local ware are the Egyptian types characteristic of anthropoid coffin burials; unlike the Egyptianizing pottery of tomb 552, however, these vessels bear no trace of influence from Late Bronze Age II decoration. Among the small finds were an iron knife (chap. 5, fig. 8:23) and numerous scarabs far more debased than the ones encountered in the previous three tombs. As a whole the tomb deposit points to a date around the end of the twelfth and first half of the eleventh century B.C.

The next tomb in chronological order is 625.[65] It contains Philistine pottery of the end of Phase 2 and the beginning of Phase 3. Although these vessels still retain the typically Philistine white slip, their decorations are in red only and their original motifs have degenerated considerably. Among the finds in this tomb are a krater (chap. 3, fig. 9:2), a Type 6 jug (chap. 3, fig. 27:1), and an iron bracelet.[66]

The final phase of Philistine pottery is represented in tombs 828, 523, and several others. Tomb 828[67] contained a Type 6 jug (chap. 3, fig. 27:3) with decorative motifs that are a debased version of those on a jug from tomb 562 (chap. 3, fig. 27:2). Tomb 523 contained a Type 6 jug[68] whose carinated shape was characteristic of the Phase 3 jugs, and a Type 17 jug (chap. 3, fig. 59:3). The decorative patterns on both jugs consisted of groups of horizontal and vertical lines.

On the basis of finds from Tell el-Farʿah strata Y and

61. Ibid., pls. XXI:90, XXV.
62. G. E. Wright, "Iron: The Date of its Introduction into Common Use in Palestine," *AJA* 43 (1939):459.
63. *BP I*, p. 10, pl. XXII:195–204.
64. Ibid., pl. XXI:93, 93A.

65. Ibid., pl. XXXI:290–92, were incorrectly ascribed by Petrie to tomb 615 while in fact they belong to tomb 625. *CPP* Add. 1655 is also assigned to this tomb. It seems that both drawings are of the same bowl. Nos. 293–94 were incorrectly ascribed to tomb 625 while they actually belong to tomb 125. No. 293 is correctly published in *CPP*, 59 F9. I became aware of this error when examining the Tell el-Farʿah material in the collection of the Archaeological Institute, London.
66. Ibid., pl. XXX:118.
67. Ibid., pl. LXXI.
68. *CPP*, 67P.

X and tombs 552, 542, 532, 625, 815, 506, and 562, A. Furumark divides Philistine pottery into four phases and postulates the absolute chronology of these phases.[69] He uses the cartouche of Seti II from the paved courtyard of area YX as the *terminus post quem* for the first of the four phases, which he dates, with the aid of historical data, to shortly after 1200 B.C. On the basis of the "Ramesses IV scarabs," he assigns tombs 542 and 552 to the second phase. However, as explained above, the Philistine level in the YX courtyard contains pottery contemporary with, and not earlier than, that of tombs 542 and 552; according to our division, it therefore represents the first phase of Philistine pottery. To his third phase, Furumark ascribes tombs 532, 625, and 815, comparing the pottery of these tombs to stratum X of the mound. He bases the *terminus post quem* of Phase 3 on the scarab of Ramesses XI (see n. 59 above for correction to Ramesses X) from tomb 532. However, as we have shown, the ceramic assemblages of tombs 532 and 562 are contemporary with the pottery of the upper Philistine level of the Residency, and, therefore, must antedate stratum X. Moreover, the finds in tomb 625 are not contemporary with those of 532 but are from a later period. Tomb 815, which Furumark ascribes to his Phase 3, does not appear on the area plan of cemetery 800, nor is it mentioned in the list of tombs and their contents. There is, however, an illustration of the decoration of a vessel labeled as coming from tomb 815 on plate LXIII:2 in *BP I*, and Furumark may be referring to this piece. If not, there is apparently an error in the number of this tomb.

Furumark's last phase includes tombs 562 and 506. We discussed tomb 562 above, and tomb 506 is erroneously termed Philistine; the vessel found in the latter and considered by Furumark to be a late type of Philistine jug is in fact a Cypriot "bucchero" jug with incised, rather than painted, decoration.[70]

TELL JEMMEH

Tell Jemmeh (Yurzah?) is situated on the southern bank of Wadi Gaza about ten kilometers south of Gaza. The mound was identified as Gerar by Petrie, who published his excavation report under the title of *Gerar*.[71] Now, however, Mazar's proposal to equate it with Yurzah is accepted by most scholars.[72]

Petrie distinguished six periods of occupation spanning the Late Bronze, Iron, and Persian periods. Petrie's division and dating of the strata are questionable. The strata pertinent to our discussion are JK and GH. They must be reevaluated together with all the published material on the basis of the elevations recorded in his report and in relation to the architectural remains.[73]

A small amount of Philistine pottery was found in levels 176–81 (Petrie's stratum JK).[74] The greatest concentration came from levels 181–83 (Petrie's stratum GH).[75]

Petrie's JK includes at least three different strata, ranging from the Late Bronze Age II to the Iron Age I. The limited quantity of Philistine pottery from levels 176–81 consists primarily of Type 1 bowls[76] and Type 2 kraters.[77] JF is the latest structure in Petrie's JK, and it seems that the Philistine pottery from these levels belongs to an earlier stratum to which we may also relate isolated architectural features, such as the "white wall" below JF and possibly the building JA.

Below this first Philistine occupation is the Late Bronze Age II stratum[78] which, with its typical Cypriot and Mycenaean imports and local painted ware,[79] possibly relates to building JR.[80]

Petrie's GH (levels 180–83) furnished a rich collec-

71. *Gerar*, p. 2, par. 5.
72. B. Maisler (Mazar), "Yurza: The Identification of Tell Jemmeh," *PEQ* (1952): 48–51; and *see also* Y. Aharoni, "The Land of Gerar," *IEJ* 6 (1956): 26–31.
73. See *Gerar*, pp. 3–4; *EAEHL*, pp. 545–48.
74. *Gerar*, pp. 4–5, pl. VI.
75. Ibid., pp. 4, 6, pl. VII.
76. Ibid., pls. LXIII:16, 22; LXIV:46.
77. Ibid., pl. LXIII:14, 15, 19, 20, 32, 39.
78. There is no clear-cut dividing line between the levels with Late Bronze and Iron Age pottery. Each one of Petrie's loci has been separately checked by us, and, though some of the elevations seem to overlap, the stratigraphic sequence as suggested seems to be clear and fits the general picture of the new excavations. No doubt the new excavations will illuminate these complex stratigraphical problems (*see below*, n. 80).
79. Cypriot, *Gerar*, pl. LXIII:3–6, 8–13; Mycenaean, ibid., 7, 29; local Canaanite, ibid., 18, 24, 28, 33, 36, 41; we have attributed the scarab of Tuthmosis III, pl. XIX:20, to this assemblage.
80. Wall JR links up with the Late Bronze Age structure of the new excavations; *see* G. W. Van Beek, "Tell Gamma," *IEJ* 27 (1977): 172–73.

69. *CMP*, p. 121; Furumark, *OA 3* (1944): 260–62.
70. *CPP*, add. 59B; J. Du Plat Taylor, *PEQ* 88 (1956): 35, fig. 2.

tion of Philistine pottery: Type 1 bowls, a large and diversified group of bowl and krater sherds,[81] stirrup jars,[82] a Type 5 jar (chap. 3, fig. 20), a number of body sherds, probably of Type 6 jugs,[83] Type 8 juglets (chap. 3, fig. 33:1), and an amphoriskos with a button base[84] of the same type as those found in the Tell el-Farʿah anthropoid burials (chap. 5, fig. 7:16–18).

It seems that this group of pottery came from below the foundations of the walls of Petrie's GH town and thus must belong to the previous stratum, the one related to building JF, as suggested above.

The Philistine pottery groups from these two suggested strata fit into the general range of Phases 1–2; the limited repertoire of decorative motifs does not allow us to date the division between these strata. Another group, discovered in levels 185–86, consists of descendants of Philistine pottery types. These Phase 3 vessels reflect a regional development attested at other sites in southern Philistia (notably Tell el-Farʿah). The pottery in the group consists of Type 1 bowls and bowls with two horizontal handles (the latter, in contrast to the Type 1 bowls, are carinated and flat);[85] Type 6 jugs lacking the ornamentation characteristic of the last phase of Philistine pottery;[86] and a decorated kernos fragment,[87] similar to one found in Megiddo VI (chap. 4, fig. 3). This group should be associated with buildings H.

There is a marked difference between the Philistine ceramic assemblages of levels 176–81 (pre-building JF), 180–83 (building JF), and 185–86 (buildings H). It is important to note that, precisely at levels 184–85, burnt layers appear in various sections of the city, especially in rooms GT, GX, GY, and GZ in levels 184.7–185.4. The burnt layer spreads northward to point W (187.10) and extends over the slopes of the mound, on the eastern end of which traces of a conflagration are clearly visible in room HB at levels 184.1–184.7 and 184.10–185.2. On the west ridge of the mound, the floors at level 184.11 are also burnt. Petrie pointed to the burnt floors as proof that the fire took place before considerable habitation deposits could accumulate. He used a

scarab of Ramesses III found in level 187 of building FO as the basis for his absolute date for the conflagration of building levels G and H.[88] He therefore dated the destruction to after 1194 B.C. and attributed it to the Philistine conquest.[89] It should be obvious that this scarab, which comes from level 187 but was not found *in situ*, is of no value for dating the destruction of his GH town.

From the above discussion it is clear that this destruction level is later than the levels containing early Philistine pottery and hence must date to a period after Philistine settlement was firmly established. In fact, the conflagration (level 184–85) seems to divide the pottery of Phases 1 and 2 from the later debased Phase 3 pottery.

Iron implements also appear in the second Philistine stratum (levels 181–83) and increase in number throughout the latest Philistine levels (184–87). The furnaces (if, indeed, they are furnaces and not kilns) found on the mound may indicate that Tell Jemmeh was the site of an iron foundry, although Petrie did not mention finding any iron slag. One of the furnaces (in level 185) can perhaps be ascribed to the last phase of Philistine settlement.[90]

Although Petrie assigned several Cypro-Phoenician Black-on-Red juglets to stratum GH,[91] they are not relevant to our discussion because they are only found in open areas of G, which undoubtedly relate to a later stratum.

In the 1975 season, a large two-storied pottery kiln was found clearly associated with Philistine pottery of the twelfth or early eleventh century.[92] No other unequivocal examples of kilns in which Philistine pottery was manufactured are known.

As for the relative chronology of the Philistine levels, the two early Philistine strata can be synchronized with Qasile XII–XI, Megiddo VIIA–VIB, and the main phase of Tell Beit Mirsim B$_2$. The late Philistine

81. *Gerar*, pl. LXIV:6, 56–68, 78–79 (bowls); 42, 44, 45, 51, 52, 54–59, 62–64 (kraters).
82. Ibid., pl. LXIV:82–84.
83. Ibid., pls. LXIII:40; LXIV:50, 65, 70, 76, 81.
84. Ibid., pl. LXIV:49.
85. Ibid., pl. L:23u, 23y, 23t, 24o.
86. Ibid., pl. LVIII:67g, j, l.
87. Ibid., pl. LXIV:88.

88. *Gerar*, p. 4, pl. XIX:26.
89. Ibid., p. 6. Albright and Wright have pointed out that this conflagration cannot be associated with the Philistines. They date the destruction to the middle of the tenth century or to Shishaq's campaign (*TMB I*, p. 74, par. 98; G. E. Wright, "Iron: The Date of its Introduction into Common Use in Palestine," *AJA* 43 [1939]: 460).
90. For the levels of iron implements, *see Gerar*, pls. XXVII–XXVIII. For the furnaces, *see* ibid., pp. 7, 14; pl. VII: GB 185; cf. Wright, *AJA* 43 (1939): 461.
91. *Gerar*, pl. LX:82.
92. Van Beek, *IEJ* 27 (1977): 172–73.

stratum, levels 185–86, has chronological counterparts in Qasile X, Megiddo VIA, and the final phase of Tell Beit Mirsim B₂.

TELL EL-ʿAJJUL

Tell el-ʿAjjul, a prominent Canaanite city in the Bronze Age, is situated about six kilometers southwest of Gaza. Petrie identified it with ancient Gaza. It now seems certain, however, that ancient Gaza, the southernmost city of the Philistine Pentapolis, was located within the modern city of Gaza, at Tell Ḥarube.

At Tell el-ʿAjjul (Beth Eglayim?)[93] most of the mound proper is still unexcavated, and the bulk of the material comes from the extensive cemeteries. The limited excavations revealed no stratum datable to the twelfth or eleventh centuries B.C. The small quantity of pottery dating from this period (mainly from the last phase) comes primarily from the tombs, and the few Philistine vessels come from tombs in cemetery 1000. Tomb 1139 contained a decorated amphoriskos (chap. 3, fig. 18:4), and tomb 1112, a Type 1 bowl and a rude horn-shaped vessel (Type 10)—both undecorated.[94] The meagerness of the finds from the period and the very low proportion of Philistine vessels are among the main reasons for rejecting the identification with ancient Gaza.

GAZA

Tell Ḥarube, which is considered to be the location of ancient Gaza, is about five kilometers from the coast in the northeastern part of the modern city. Although Gaza was allotted to the tribe of Judah (Josh. 15:47; Judg. 1:18), it remained a Canaanite city until the beginning of the twelfth century B.C., when it came into the possession of the Philistines. It was the southernmost city of the Philistine Pentapolis (Josh. 13:3; 1 Sam. 6:17; Jer. 25:20) and contained the famous Philistine temple of Dagon.

In 1922, W. J. Phythian-Adams carried out excavations on the mound. Unfortunately, the limited publication of the excavations[95] is not sufficient to allow an examination of the finds. Only a few soundings were made on the mound. In two of the three unconnected

trenches, the excavators reached a level containing pottery; this level rests upon the remains of a Late Bronze Age II settlement that ended in total destruction. The excavator noted the small amount of Philistine pottery (which he ascribed to the final phase of the Philistine settlement), the absence of the delicate and finely made Philistine ware found at Ashkelon, and the preponderance of kraters decorated with red bands in simple designs.

Only further investigation can provide a final answer to the question of whether Tell Harube is indeed the site of ancient Gaza.

ASHKELON

Ashkelon was one of the cities of the Philistine Pentapolis on the southern coastal plain during the period of Philistine expansion in the twelfth and eleventh centuries B.C. Each city was ruled by a *seren* (Josh. 13:3; 1 Sam. 6:4, 17) supported by a military aristocracy. Ashkelon was of particular economic importance because of its harbor and its location on the Via Maris. In fact, it is the only city in the southern coastal plain situated so close to the sea. The Onomasticon of Amenope, which probably dates from the beginning of the eleventh century B.C., refers to Ashkelon as a Philistine city (along with Ashdod and Gaza). Nonetheless, from the end of the eleventh to the middle of the eighth century B.C., there is no mention of Ashkelon in written records.

Because of its historic importance as a Philistine center, it was chosen by Garstang and Phythian-Adams as the site of an excavation to clarify the origins of Philistine pottery.[96] In the course of the work it became evident that Tell el-Khadra, located on the coast, was the site of the ancient city. To determine the stratigraphy of the mound the excavators dug a number of trial trenches,[97] but the unusually thick deposits of later settlements caused serious difficulties in reaching the ancient levels. (The total height of the accumulation is 13 meters; the Hellenistic level was reached at 5.5 meters, and the Philistine level at 7.5 meters) Only two trenches clearly revealed the early stratigraphy of the site: one is on the northern slope in

93. A. Kempinski suggested identifying Tell el-ʿAjjul with Sharuhen (*IEJ* 24 [1974]: 145–52). See also *EAEHL*, pp. 52–61.

94. *AG II*, pls. XXVIII:26B3, XXXVI:94A.

95. *PEFQSt* (1923): 13, 27 ff.; *EAEHL*, pp. 409–12.

96. *PEFQST* (1920): 97, 145; *Ashkelon*, 1921, pp. 162 ff. For a summary of the problem of Philistine origins and pottery based on the excavations at Ashkelon *see* W. J. Phythian-Adams, *BBSAJ* 3 (1923): 20 ff.; *EAEHL*, pp. 121–27.

97. *Ashkelon*, 1921, pp. 163 ff.

field 163[98] and the other in field 19 at the western base of the mound near the sea.[99] Since the results of its excavation are clearly described and the pottery of the various strata are presented in relative detail, the western trench can serve as the basis for an examination of the Philistine levels at Ashkelon.

The eastern balk of the western trench, summarized below, reveals the stratification from strata V to VII and levels ε to β, together with the ceramic wares characteristic of each stratum, from the Late Bronze Age II to the Hellenistic period.[100]

Period	Level	Stratum	Pottery
Hellenistic	β	VII	Hellenistic
	Burnt Level		
	γ	VII	Philistine
Iron Age I			
	δ	VI	Philistine
	Burnt Level		
Late Bronze Age II	ε	V	Cypriot and Mycenaean imports

Most important is the burnt level separating stratum V (level ε), the Late Bronze Age II city, from stratum VI (levels δ, γ), the Iron Age I settlement. In the Iron Age I stratum, the Mycenaean and Cypriot imports typical of stratum V vanish and are replaced by Philistine pottery. This pottery was concentrated in level δ, the lower of the two levels in stratum VI, while level γ contained relatively little Philistine ware.[101] A purely stratigraphic distinction between the phases of Philistine pottery is rather difficult; it seems, however, that most of the pottery in level δ can be identified as Phase 1, whereas that of level γ belongs primarily to Phase 2. The Phase 1 pottery included a Type 1 bowl (chap. 3, fig. 1:4) and a Type 2 krater (chap. 3, fig. 10:2). Among the sherds that can be related to Phase 1 were a number decorated with artistically drawn bird

motifs[102] and one with the rare fish motif (chap. 3, fig. 64:3). Some of the vessels and sherds of Ashkelon's Phase 1 Philistine pottery are among the earliest Philistine ware found in Palestine, to judge by their excellent workmanship and their closeness to Mycenaean archetypes.

Sherds of a stirrup jar decorated with bands, a Type 6 jug, and a spouted vessel,[103] which come from the upper level (γ) of stratum VI, can all be ascribed to Phase 2. The published material gives no indication of any Phase 3 pottery at Ashkelon; it seems that after Phase 2 Philistine pottery at this site disappeared.

ASHDOD

Ashdod, another of the five cities of the "Lords of the Philistines," stands on the southwestern coast of Canaan on the main military and commercial route to Egypt through Gaza. The mound, which is situated about four kilometers from the coast, extends over an area of about twenty acres and includes an acropolis and a much larger lower city. Excavation has revealed twenty-three strata of settlement. Here, for the first time with the aid of a modern stratified excavation, the Philistine material culture can be studied in one of the principal cities, enabling us to follow its initial development and the transition from the Late Bronze Age (stratum XIV) to the Early Iron Age (stratum XIII). Strata XIII–X, which were uncovered in various areas of the acropolis and which span a period from the close of the thirteenth and beginning of the twelfth century to the end of the eleventh century, are relevant to our discussion.[104] Areas A–B, G, and H[105] present the widest field for our inquiry.

In these areas the latest Late Bronze Age stratum, XIV, was either destroyed and abandoned (areas A–B) or destroyed and newly settled in stratum XIII (areas

98. Ibid., opposite p. 163, schematic figure of the balk.

99. *Ashkelon*, 1922, pp. 118 ff.; 1923, pp. 60 ff.

100. Ibid., 1923, p. 62, fig. 3. One of the difficulties in utilizing the ceramic material published there on pls. I–II (ibid., p. 67) is that many of the vessels are not from the Ashkelon excavations but are whole vessels found elsewhere (*see* ibid., pp. 79 ff.); the excavator has included them to illustrate the types of vessels characteristic of the various phases of the balk.

101. *Ashkelon*, 1923, p. 64, fig. 5; a schematic illustration of the distribution of a number of the ceramic types in levels θ–γ.

102. Ibid., pl. IV:22, 24.

103. Ibid., pl. II:15, 17, 23.

104. *Ashdod I, II–III*; further bibliography: *Ashdod II–III*, p. 17, nn. 1, 3; *EAEHL*, pp. 103–19.

105. M. Dothan, "Relations Between Cyprus and the Philistine Coast in the Late Bronze Age (Tel Mor, Ashdod)," *Praktika*, vol. A (Nicosia, 1972): 51–56, pls. IV–IX; idem, "The Beginnings of the Sea Peoples and of the Philistines at Ashdod" (in press); idem, "Tel Mor, Transition from the Bronze Age to the Iron Age on the Philistine Coast," *Third World Congress of Jewish Studies* (Jerusalem, 1965), pp. 295–97 (Hebrew).

G–H); in the latter case, the rebuilt areas exhibit a new type of architecture. In areas A–B the destruction layer, which is about 85 centimeters thick, is mixed with ashes, indicating that it ended in a conflagration. As very little of stratum XIII was reached in areas A–B, the conclusions on the transition from the Late Bronze to the Early Iron Ages are based mainly on the results of data from areas G and H.

Stratum XIII

Area G   In area G, on the northern perimeter of the acropolis, a huge, fortified Late Bronze Age structure (stratum XIV) was probably situated near a gate. It was abandoned, and the character of the area was completely changed between strata XIV and XIII. In stratum XIII the parallel walls that had formed part of the stratum XIV fortress were destroyed, leaving only the thin inner partition walls. A structure, open to the sky—possibly a "high place"—was uncovered where part of the fortified building had previously stood. The "high place" consisted of a square structure of plastered bricks and a round, stone pillar base (for an idol?). On the surface of the brick structure sherds and bones were found, and the round stone base (which was reused from stratum XIV) showed traces of burning. South of this structure were several small rooms whose thin brick walls had been strengthened with large, dressed stones from stratum XIV. Of special interest is the large amount of charred wood, probably from a kiln, found on the floor of one of these rooms. Twenty-seven pottery vessels were stacked upside down on the floor nearby (pl. 3). The entire area was probably a potter's workshop, and most of the relevant pottery from the lower phase of stratum XIII was found on this floor. It consisted mainly of carinated or bell-shaped bowls, either undecorated or decorated with monochrome red bands. A basket-handled spouted jug was also found (pl. 4). The whole group has close affinities with Myc. IIIC:1 pottery from the Aegean, the eastern Mediterranean, and Cyprus, although, as we shall see, it was locally made (see n. 106 below).

The upper phase of this stratum (XIIIa) differs from the lower phase (XIIIb) only in minor details, such as a higher floor. The change is mainly discernible in the finds: in the upper phase, for the first time, we have a number of typical Philistine sherds (the one or two such sherds found in the lower phase seem to be intrusive).

Area H (fig. 2, pl. 5)   The layer of destruction of the Late Bronze Age stratum XIV was not uniform in depth in this area. In some places the remains were covered with ashes about a meter deep, while in others the stratum XIII foundations were laid directly over the remaining walls of stratum XIV. The plan of the new structures is completely different from that of the few buildings so far excavated from the earlier city. The main feature in stratum XIII is a street about 3.5 meters wide that separates two building complexes. (The street is also the main feature of stratum XII in this area.) As in area G, in some places two phases, XIIIb and XIIIa, can be distinguished.

The relatively scarce finds of this stratum, which are mainly from phase XIIIb, show some continuity with the Canaanite pottery tradition—for example, the four-handled store jar and the bowl with its typical painted-palm motif. The most distinctive group of pottery, however, is the local variant of the Myc. IIIC:1 type, which also appeared in area G; it is mostly undecorated.

Stratum XIIIb (the earlier phase) yielded the first Myc. IIIC:1b pottery (fig. 3). This ware continues into stratum XII, where it appears alongside the typical Philistine bichrome pottery that first appears in stratum XIIIa. Trace-element analysis[106] has shown that both the monochrome Myc. IIIC:1 pottery and the bichrome Philistine pottery were of local manufacture. Even so, there is a clear distinction between the two groups. The Myc. IIIC:1 pottery, in forms, motifs, and color, is a faithful reproduction of the Mycenaean tradition. It is mostly a greenish-buff ware with a fine, hard texture and self-slip. The paint, in shades of black, has a slight lustre and, in some cases, the cracked surface typical of Mycenaean pottery. A less frequent variant is the light-pink ware with a fine dark-brown decoration. Most of the types were bell-shaped bowls and small kraters (fig. 3:1–6, 7–9), although some sherds may have belonged to closed vessels. The decorative motifs on the bowls consist of wavy, scalloped horizontal lines below the rim (fig. 3:1), a feature that is not typically encountered on Philistine bowls but that is well represented in the Mycenaean repertoire. The spiral pattern is prominent on the bell-shaped bowls, both as stemmed (fig. 3:2, 3, 5) and as antithetic stemmed spirals (fig. 3:3). The

---

106. F. Asaro, M. Dothan, and I. Perlman, "An Introductory Study of Mycenaean IIIC:1 Ware from Tell Ashdod," *Archaeometry* 13 (1971): 169–75.

Pl. 2. 1. Objects from tomb 542, Tell el-Farʿah [From the Collection of the Israel Department of Antiquities and Museums].

Pl. 2. 2. Iron and bronze daggers (from pl. 2:1) [From the Collection of the Israel Department of Antiquities and Museums, I. 4339, I. 4340. *BP I*, pls. XXI 90; XXV; XXI 89].

Pl. 3. Assemblage of Philistine pottery *in situ*, Ashdod, stratum XIIIb [*EAEHL*, p. 112].

Pl. 4. Assemblage of Philistine pottery from Ashdod, area G, stratum XIIIb [From the Collection of the Israel Department of Antiquities and Museums].

Pl. 5. Apsidal building, Ashdod, area H, strata XIII–XII [*EAEHL*, p. 109].

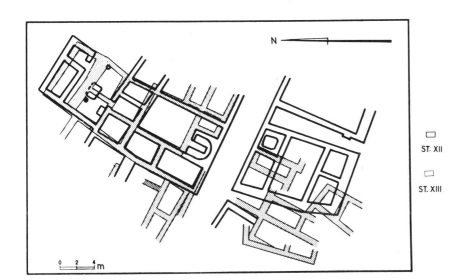

□
ST. XII

□
ST. XIII

Fig. 2. Ashdod, area H, strata XIII–XII [M. Dothan, "Ashdod—Seven Seasons of Excavation," *Qadmoniot* 5 (1972): 7. (Hebrew)].

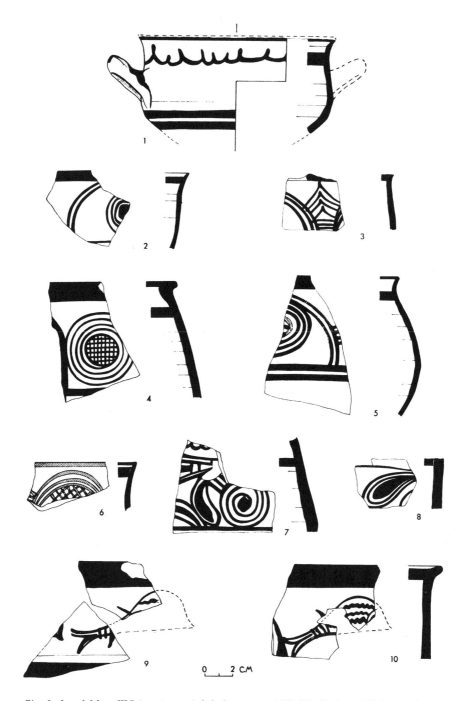

Fig. 3. Local Myc. IIIC:1 pottery, Ashdod, stratum XIII [M. Dothan, "Relations between Cyprus and the Philistine Coast in the Late Bronze Age (Tel Mor, Ashdod)," *Praktika* 1 (1972): fig. 1].

spirals frequently have a net pattern in the center (fig. 3:4, 6)—another feature that is unknown in Philistine pottery but well attested to in Myc. IIIC:1. Also foreign to the Philistine pottery is the vertical zigzag pattern forming part of triglyphs—it too is a typical Mycenaean decoration. The elaborate loops of the spiral decoration appear in different positions (fig. 3:7, 8) and are another clear link with Mycenaean pottery; they have close parallels in the levels ascribed to the Sea Peoples in Cyprus (see chap. 3). Fish motifs occur (fig. 3:9, 10) on two fragments (probably from the same krater), heralding the fish motif depicted on Philistine pottery (chap. 3, fig. 64:1–3).

Birds do not appear on the greenish sherds but only on the reddish monochrome fragments mentioned above. In style they are a link between Mycenaean birds and typical Philistine birds. The dotted filling motif and the dotted lines around the outline of the birds are significant, for they are uncommon in Philistine birds but well represented on the Myc. IIIC:1 version.

The closest parallels to this assemblage are the Myc. IIIC:1 pottery of Cyprus: Sinda level III, Enkomi strata IIIb, IIIa, and the Kouklia (Old Paphos) tombs (see chap. 3, fig. 72). The assemblage presents us with the first glimpse of the prototypes of some Philistine vessels and it was clearly made by potters well versed in Mycenaean pottery techniques, color schemes, and decorative motifs.

Among the small finds was a cylinder seal (pl. 6) with figures seated on either side of signs that may be related to the Cypro-Minoan script.

Stratum XII

Area G In the following stratum (XII) area G underwent a complete change. Stratum XIII seems to have been of short duration, for the inhabitants of stratum XII reused the southern part of the stratum XIV fortress. They widened one of the walls of this building and turned it into the outer city wall. The space between the outer and inner parallel walls was packed with fill and, with the addition of some partition walls, it became a casemate wall. Some of the rooms inside the city served as workshops. In one, a clay larnax was found, together with remains of a kiln, stone vessels, and a big lump of glass. The rooms in this area yielded a large number of Philistine vessels.

Area H (fig. 2, pl. 5) In contrast to area G, the general layout of the buildings of stratum XII in area H is the same as in stratum XIII, and the transition between the strata seems to have been uneventful. The best-preserved building complex is situated north of the street. Its southern part is rectangular and consists of a court with a row of rooms on its west and north sides. The main feature in this part is a quasi-apsidal structure, built above a rectangular substructure. The northern part of the building also contains a court, with a row of rooms to the north and south. Stone bases for two columns, which probably supported the roof, were uncovered here. A rectangular structure (1.80 × 1.30 m.) built of white plastered bricks was attached to one of the column bases.

In stratum XII the local cult seems to have centered around the worship of a female deity, "Ashdoda," who is depicted on a figurine (chap. 4, fig. 9) found near the apsidal structure. Her prototype is to be sought in the Mother Goddess of the Mycenaean world. The worship of this Aegean deity was continued by the Philistine inhabitants of Ashdod.

The finds of strata XII and XI are characterized by impressive quantities of typical Philistine pottery—conclusive evidence that in Philistia proper this was the dominant pottery. Although plain Iron Age I pottery continued to be used for utilitarian purposes, a comparison with sites outside Philistia confirms the overwhelming predominance at Ashdod of Philistine pottery. Most shapes are represented by either complete vessels or sherds, with Type 1 bowls, Type 2 kraters, and Type 6 jugs in the majority. The decoration is bichrome, in most cases on a white slip. The chief decorative motif is the bird, frequently elaborately stylized and often in combination with the entire range of Philistine decoration represented in numerous variations. Many vessels are covered with an overall decoration reminiscent of the Mycenaean Close Style.

Among the other finds from this stratum are jewelry, metal objects (including gold), faience, scarabs, and ivory. Both Aegean and Egyptian influences are exhibited, although Aegean elements predominate, as, for example, in the ivory objects and the gold disc. Some finds strongly emphasize the relations between Ashdod, Cyprus, and the Aegean world. One of these, a stamp seal (pl. 7), bears signs that are tentatively related to the Cypro-Minoan script.

Stratum XI

Area A   In the limited area of the uppermost strata (local 10=XII; local 9=XI) of the Early Iron Age in area A, part of a fortress was discovered. Both of its floors date to the eleventh century B.C. on the basis of the characteristic pottery, including Philistine ware, found on them. This fortress, a walled structure that apparently stood within the city, was built by the Philistines in the twelfth century.

Area G   The buildings of stratum XI differed little from those of stratum XII; only minor destruction was observed. The casemate wall was still in place, with slight alterations, and the floors had been raised. The most significant change is a three-room building, in which two phases were distinguished, extending north of the casemate wall. Between this building and the casemate wall was a narrow street entered through a small opening in the wall. The latest typical Philistine pottery was found in the last phase of stratum XI, as was part of a broken throne with the head of an "Ashdoda."

Area H   The stratum XII city continued almost unchanged in stratum XI, although new houses replaced the destroyed stratum XII buildings. Two phases, a and b, were distinguished. A number of new walls were built in stratum XIa. The main east-west street was preserved, although it was raised, as was the general level of the entire settlement on the slope—by means of a massive fill. A new building technique was introduced in which bricks were set on their narrow side to strengthen walls and to build installations and benches. Stratum XIb was apparently destroyed by an earthquake but was immediately rebuilt. Lacking clear evidence of fire or destruction, it is difficult to establish how stratum XIa was destroyed.

Stratum X

Area A   In area A, Philistine buildings continued in use. The pottery, however, is of the usual Iron Age I types with some intrusive Philistine sherds.

Area G   With the destruction of stratum XI in area G, the plan of the area was radically changed. In stratum X the casemate wall was covered by small houses, and to its north a brick city wall 4.50 meters

wide was built over the buildings erected in stratum XI. In the foundations of this wall was found a hand-burnished bowl of debased Philistine style.

Area H   Most of the buildings of stratum X were built without regard to stratum XI, but it is difficult to obtain a clear picture of them because of the extensive damage caused by erosion and later construction. Nevertheless, some of the stratum XI walls, together with new floors, continued to be used.

There is a conspicuous break in the material culture in this area: Philistine pottery disappears. The dominant pottery is now a red-slipped and hand-burnished ware with black and, sometimes, white decoration. This type is the hallmark of Ashdod pottery from at least the end of the eleventh century.

An extension of area H to the east, where stratum X was well preserved, was excavated in 1969. Only part of the material has been studied so far, but it is clear that the pottery repertoire is identical with that of area H. The outstanding finds of stratum X in this area are the stand with musicians (chap. 4, pl. 33) and a burial containing an Aegean-type iron knife.

Area M   After the destruction of stratum XI in the mid-eleventh century, Ashdod spread outside the acropolis, at first as a small settlement in the lower city (area M, stratum Xb). The main evidence for the expansion is the discovery of several kilns. Later (in stratum Xa) area M was enclosed within a fortified area. Two solid towers stand at the entrance to the gate, which is on the east; and two compartments are joined to each tower in the west. The walls were built mostly of sun-dried bricks, and in several places they are strengthened with stone. The large, well-built gate was destroyed in the first half of the tenth century (judging by the pottery finds), perhaps at the end of the reign of David or during Siamun's expedition in about 960 B.C.

Philistine pottery still appeared in stratum Xb in small quantities together with the earliest hand-burnished red slip ware and also "Ashdod" ware, that is, red-slipped ware decorated with black and white stripes. In stratum Xa these two types of pottery become dominant, and the Philistine pottery disappeared. An extension of the Philistine tradition can be seen in the red-slipped, burnished bowls with vestigial horizontal handles, a typical feature of this period in Philistia.

TEL MOR

The small site of Tel Mor[107] (Tell Kheidar), which lies about one kilometer from the coast near Ashdod, on the north bank of Nahal Lachish, apparently served as a fortified settlement of the inland harbor of Ashdod in the Late Bronze Age. Tel Mor was also one of the fortresses that defended the Via Maris. It was probably founded somewhat later than Ashdod, during the transition between the Middle Bronze and the Late Bronze ages.[108]

This small site, which is only about six dunams in area and rises only seventeen meters above the plain, contains twelve strata of occupation ranging from about 1600 to 130 B.C. The levels relevant to our discussion are strata 6–3.

Above the ruins of the large and almost completely destroyed fortress of stratum 7, which dates to the thirteenth century, a small tower was erected that continued in use through strata 6 and 5. Most of the pottery from this tower is typical of the end of the Late Bronze Age and includes local imitations of Cypriot ware and a large amount of Egyptian-type pottery, strongly indicating the continuation of the Canaanite material culture and the presence of an Egyptian garrison at the end of the thirteenth and beginning of the twelfth century B.C. The destruction of stratum 5 apparently took place in the first half of the twelfth century and resulted in the Philistine occupation of the site. Thus strata 7–5 would fall into a cultural framework of continuous Egyptian domination of this site in Canaan. Despite the total destruction of stratum 7 and the architectural break, material culture continued unaffected. The ethnic change at Tel Mor comes only in stratum 4 (continuing into 3), where we have clear-cut evidence of Philistine occupation.

The Philistine settlement (strata 4 and 3) suggests that there was now no need to protect either the harbor or the coastal road. It consists of an unfortified village of small buildings, courtyards, and silos, all of an agrarian nature. Alongside the typical local Iron Age finds there were Philistine vessels, such as Type 2 kraters and strainer-spout jugs, decorated with fine Philistine white slip and bichrome designs. The stratum 3 settlement was destroyed at the beginning of the tenth century, perhaps by David in one of his campaigns against Philistia or by the Pharaoh Siamun.

TELL BEIT MIRSIM

Because the first clear picture of the ceramic chronology of Palestine is contained in Albright's reports on his excavations at Tell Beit Mirsim, the Philistine pottery found in stratified occupation levels here is of great importance. Stratum B followed the destruction of the Late Bronze Age city (stratum C).[109] During all its three phases (B_1, B_2, B_3) the site was sparsely settled, and in some areas only large silos were uncovered. These were almost the only walled structures that could be dated by their pottery; thus the typological differentiation between the three phases of stratum B was consequently based on the pottery contents of the silos and their relationship to the structures.

The first pre-Philistine settlement, stratum B_1, was poor in architectural and pottery remains and was clearly represented only by a few large silos (for example, silos 14, 24), which were in use between the end of stratum C and the early twelfth century B.C. This Iron Age phase was characterized by pottery of a decadent Late Bronze Age type; there was no Mycenaean or Cypriot ware, nor any Philistine ware.

The Philistine sherds and vessels were concentrated in the levels and loci of stratum B_2, the second Iron Age settlement on the mound, which Albright dated to between 1150 and 1000 B.C.[110] Philistine pottery was found in the building extending over squares SE 12, 22, 13, and 23. Albright contended that this structure was built during B_1 and was based upon a stratum C building of very similar design.[111] The ceramic finds of stratum B_2 are extremely meager and include, in area SE 12 B,[112] some Philistine sherds of Type 1 bowls and Type 2 kraters,[113] and one sherd that may be part of a

---

107. M. Dothan, "Tel Mor" Notes and News, *IEJ* 10 (1960): 123–25; *see also* n. 105 above. *EAEHL*, pp. 889–90.

108. M. Dothan, *IEJ* 23 (1973): 1–17.

109. Stratum B: *TBM I*, pp. 58–59, par. 76; *TBM III*, pp. 8–10, par. 4. Stratum C: a scarab (*TBM I*, p. 52, par. 71, fig. 9) identified by B. Brandl as bearing part of the name of Seti II helps in dating the destruction of stratum C to the very end of the thirteenth century.

110. A full discussion of the problem of Philistine pottery in relation to the absolute date of stratum B appears in *TBM I*, pp. 53–58, par. 73–75; for the date of B_2, see *TBM III*, p. 9, par. 4, pl. 11. See also *EAEHL*, pp. 171–78.

111. *TBM III*, p. 9, par. 4, pl. 11a.

112. *TBM I*, p. 62, par. 82.

113. Ibid., pl. 24:37–40, 42–52.

Type 9 cylindrical bottle.[114] Of importance in determining a more precise date for stratum B_2 is a Type 6 jug (chap. 3, pl. 51) very similar in decoration to jugs of the first phase of Philistine pottery (cf. chap. 3, fig. 23:1–3).

Silo 43,[115] in SE 12 B-3, contained a number of Philistine sherds[116] and an amphoriskos (chap. 3, fig. 18:5) on top of a stone that partially covered the pit. Despite the limited material from this grain pit, it seems that the sherds and pyxis can be ascribed to the end of the twelfth and the first half of the eleventh centuries B.C.—the second phase of Philistine pottery.

An unslipped Type 1 bowl,[117] decorated in red alone, from silo 2 can be ascribed to the last phase of Philistine pottery. Albright dated this silo to the end of the twelfth and the eleventh century. That this silo remained in use for so long is demonstrated by the ceramic evidence: sherds that clearly continue the Late Bronze Age II tradition of ceramic decoration are found together with a hand-burnished ware characteristic of the second half of the eleventh and early tenth centuries B.C.

Lastly, in the eastern cave, a Type 2 krater (chap. 3, fig. 8:3) and Type 6 jug[118] were the only Philistine vessels found. The latter is decorated with a well-executed repeated bird motif characteristic of the early phase of Philistine pottery.

The Philistine pottery in stratum B_2 belongs to Phases 1 and 2; the bowl from silo 2 is the only vessel that can be identified as belonging to Phase 3.

TELL ʿAITUN

Iron Age tombs were uncovered in large numbers in the extensive cemetery of Tell ʿAitun[119] in the Lachish region. Several hundred meters from the mound

proper, a row of Iron Age tombs was hewn into the slope. One of these rock-cut chamber tombs, which was systematically excavated, yielded numerous finds of outstanding quality. This remarkable assemblage of twelfth-century pottery (pl. 8 and figs. 4 and 5) included Philistine bowls, kraters, a strainer-spout jug of extraordinarily fine workmanship (chap. 3, pl. 62 and fig. 29), a Type 9 bottle, and a Type 12 jug. Among the other funerary offerings and personal belongings in the tomb were iron bracelets and bronze artifacts such as vessels, bracelets, and arrowheads, and also conical stone seals—the last associated with the Philistine culture. There is no doubt that many more tombs of the same kind exist here, for the dumps left by the illicit diggers contained both typical Iron Age pottery and Philistine vessels. These tombs were undoubtedly also the source of a number of other objects, such as mourning figurines (chap. 4, fig. 10).

The sequence of the Iron Age tombs at Tell ʿAitun, ranging from the twelfth to the eighth centuries, provides a comprehensive view of the development of tomb architecture.

BETH-ZUR

Remains of Iron Age I at Beth-Zur (Khirbet et-Tubeiqeh),[120] a city in Judah, were found mainly on the north side of the mound. Architectural remains and pottery, including Philistine sherds, have been attributed to this period. Unfortunately it is difficult to clarify the stratigraphic situation of this assemblage, nor is it even certain whether the pottery belongs entirely to one level or to several.

We shall attempt to date the limits of the settlement by means of a brief discussion of the finds, with special attention to fragments of specific chronological value. Among the Philistine sherds is a fragment of a Type 1 bowl[121] of a late debased version and a pyxis[122] identical in shape to an undecorated Philistine amphoriskos from Tell Beit Mirsim B_2 (chap. 3, fig. 18:5). Among the

114. Ibid., pl. 24:41.

115. Ibid., p. 61, par. 81; *TBM III*, p. 9, par. 4.

116. *TBM I*, pl. 26:28–45. Among the sherds in the silo was a neck sherd of a juglet that Albright identified as a Cypro-Phoenician Black-on-Red I. A later examination of the sherd by Albright and Van Beek revealed that it was not an import; cf. *BASOR* 138 (1955): 37, n. 9.

117. *TBM I*, p. 62, par. 82, pl. 50:10; and cf. photo of the vessels found in silo 2, pl. 28:1–16.

118. Ibid., pl. 49:2.

119. Preliminary reports of the ʿAitun excavations have been published so far; *see* Notes and News, *IEJ* 18 (1968): 194–95; G. Edelstein, "A Philistine Jug from ʿAitun," *Qadmoniot* 1 (1968): 100 (Hebrew). A petrographic analysis of the Philistine pottery carried out by G. Edelstein and Y. Glass

indicates that the Philistine vessels were brought from the coastal region—from Philistia proper (G. Edelstein and Y. Glass, "The Origin of Philistine Pottery Based on Petrographic Analysis," in *Excavations and Studies*, Y. Aharoni, ed. [Tel Aviv, 1973], pp. 125–29 [Hebrew]).

120. *Beth-Zur*, p. 37, figs. 29–31, pl. VII; *EAEHL*, pp. 263–67.

121. *Beth-Zur*, fig. 31, upper row, first from left, and pl. VII:12.

122. Ibid., pl. VII:12.

Pl. 6. Cylinder seal with seated figures and signs (script?) between them, Ashdod, area H, stratum XIII [From the Collection of the Israel Department of Antiquities and Museums, 68–1103. M. Dothan, "Ashdod—Seven Seasons of Excavation," *Qadmoniot* 5, no. 1 (1972): 6].

Pl. 7. Stamp seal, Ashdod, area H, stratum XII [From the Collection of the Israel Department of Antiquities and Museums, 68.146].

Pl. 8. Tomb group, Tell ʿAitun [From the Collection of the Israel Department of Antiquities and Museums].

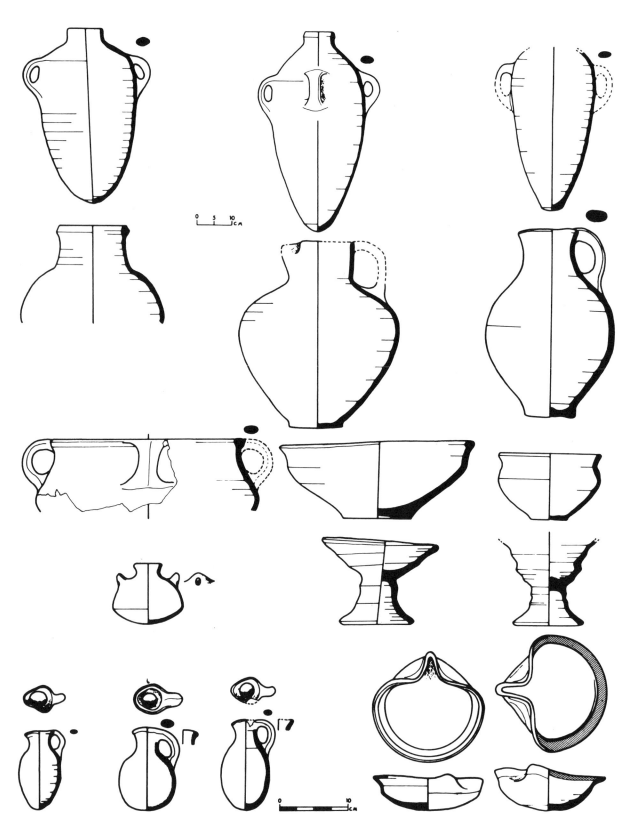

Fig. 4. Pottery assemblage from Philistine tombs, Tell'Aitun [G. Edelstein and Y. Glass, "The Origin of Philistine Pottery Based on Petrographic Analysis," in *Excavation and Studies: Essays in Honour of S. Yeivin*, Y. Aharoni, ed. (Tel Aviv, 1973) (Hebrew), fig. 1].

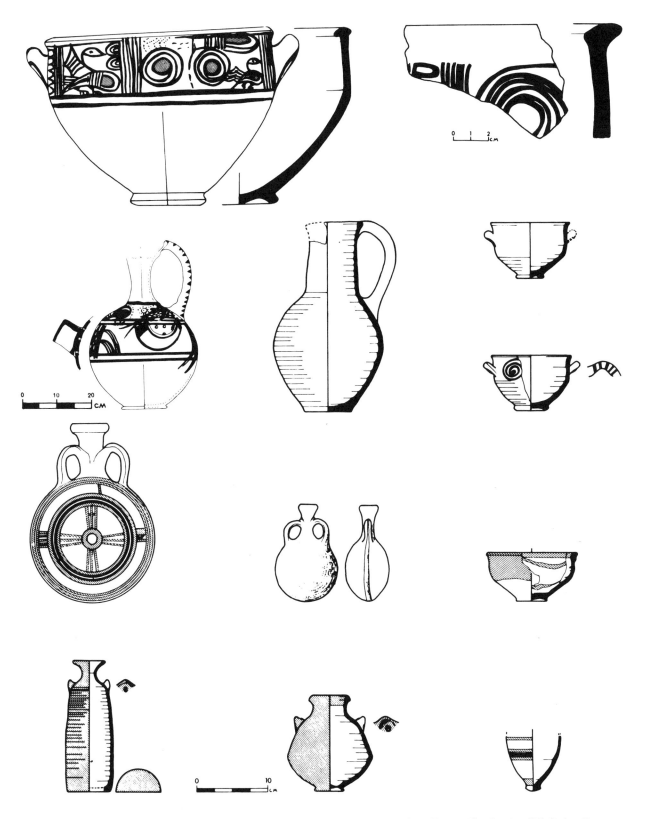

Fig. 5. Pottery assemblage from Philistine tombs, Tell ʿAitun [G. Edelstein and Y. Glass, "The Origin of Philistine Pottery Based on Petrographic Analysis," in *Excavation and Studies: Essays in Honour of S. Yeivin*, Y. Aharoni, ed. (Tel Aviv, 1973) (Hebrew), fig. 2].

published sherds are a number of decorated fragments that Sellers termed Philistine.[123] The non-Philistine pottery includes a group of cooking-pot rims typical of Megiddo VI[124] and a group of chalices[125] of a type also found at Megiddo VI[126] and Tell Qasile X.[127]

Vessels that aid in establishing the lower limit of this Iron Age I level are a dipper juglet[128] with a globular body, high neck, and loop handle pulled from the middle of the neck (it has parallels, inter alia, in Megiddo VA–IVB)[129] and a Cypro-Phoenician Black-on-Red I–II juglet,[130] which also has analogies in Megiddo VA–IVB.[131]

Thus it appears that the habitation level containing this pottery assemblage, which is ascribed to the Iron Age I, is contemporary with Tell Qasile XI–IX, Megiddo VIB and VA–IVB, and Tell Beit Mirsim B_{2-3} (and not with Tel Beit Mirsim B_{1-2}, as originally suggested by the excavators). The Philistine ceramic finds at Beth-Zur are quite meager and atypical and belong to a debased version.

TEL SIPPOR

Tel Sippor is a small mound about half a dunam in area in the heart of the Philistine plain. Excavations on the mound revealed that it was occupied during Middle Bronze I, Late Bronze II, and Iron I.[132] The two top strata (I–II) are dated to the Early Iron Age, and stratum III is attributed to the end of the Late Bronze Age. Strata I–II apparently span the twelfth to the second half of the eleventh centuries B.C.

The finds in stratum III, definitely of the Late Bronze Age, were sealed by the floor of stratum II. The two strata are completely different, but there is no trace of fire between them. The last Canaanite settlement at Tel Ṣippor was apparently small enough to escape the common fate of conflagration at the hands of the Philistines. The nature of the settlement may be inferred from two male figurines found in this level: a

123. Ibid., fig. 31.
124. *Meg. II*, pl. 85:14–16.
125. *Beth-Zur*, pl. VII:1–4.
126. *Meg. II*, pl. 87:5, 6, 9.
127. *Qasile IEJ 1*, fig. 6:3.
128. *Beth-Zur*, pl. VII:11.
129. *Meg. II*, pl. 88:11.
130. *Beth-Zur*, fig. 31.
131. *Meg. II*, pl. 146:20, 21.
132. A. Biran and O. Negbi, "Tel Ṣippor," *IEJ* 16 (1966): 160–73. *EAEHL*, pp. 1111–13.

seated stone deity (?) and a bronze seated figurine. In combination with the unusual smallness of the site, they suggest that Tel Sippor served at the time as a cult place.

Stratum II was built on the ruins of stratum III; the scant architectural remains comprise several mud-brick walls, stone bases that probably supported wooden columns, and a well-made plastered floor. Numerous pits were sunk into the plastered floor; one contained a unique and well-preserved monochrome Philistine krater (chap. 3, pl. 9). A rich and varied assemblage of Philistine pottery was found on the floor and in pits of this level. It includes bell-shaped bowls (fig. 6:1, 2), a strap-handled bowl (fig. 6:3), large kraters with bird decoration, spouted jugs, stirrup jugs and a bull's-head vessel (probably once attached to a ring kernos like those of Ashdod).

There is also no evidence of destruction by fire between stratum II and the overlying stratum I. The architectural remains of stratum I were scanty: a thinly plastered floor, three clay ovens, and four plastered pits. Nonetheless, Iron Age I pottery was found in abundance on the floor and in the pits. Among the hand-burnished vessels, bowls predominate (fig. 6:1–6, 14, 15); two of them (fig. 6:14, 15) have degenerate horizontal handles typical of the last phase of Philistine bowls in the mounds of Philistia, and fit into the regional picture of debased Philistine pottery in this period.

In stratum II (twelfth–mid-eleventh centuries B.C.) the large amount of Philistine ware seems to indicate that a fairly prosperous community with a new population settled on the site. The transition from stratum II to stratum I points to cultural continuity. The debasement and disappearance of Philistine pottery, with which we are familiar in the region, apparently occurred in the second half of the eleventh century B.C., when Tel Ṣippor was abandoned.

The cultic association of the site, which is most clearly seen in the stone and bronze figurines of the Late Bronze Age settlement (stratum III), may have continued into the Philistine settlement of stratum II, where the bull's head from a kernos as well as a pipelike stand (a surface find) may indicate a cult place.

TELL EṢ-ṢAFI

We know of many remarkable Philistine vessels from Tell eṣ-Ṣafi, both from the excavations of Bliss and

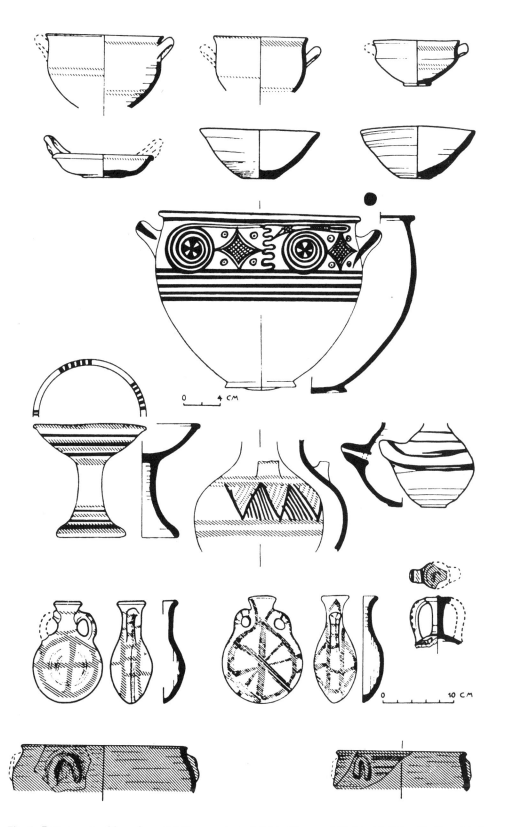

Fig. 6. Pottery assemblage from Tel Ṣippor, strata I–II [A. Biran and O. Negbi, "The Stratigraphical Sequence at Tel Ṣippor," *IEJ* 16 (1966): figs. 5, 6].

Macalister[133] and from private collections. The lack of an adequate published account of the excavations, however, precludes stratigraphic attribution of the various pieces; it is, nonetheless, worthwhile to note the principal finds:

1. A large and diversified group of Type 1 bowls (chap. 3, fig. 3:2).[134]

2. A number of Type 6 jugs[135] (chap. 3, fig. 21:1), most of which should be ascribed to Phase 2. These are among the most beautiful Philistine jugs ever found.

3. A Type 9 bottle (chap. 3, fig. 34:1), which is the sole example of a cylindrical bottle with a bird motif.

4. A lion-headed rhyton (chap. 4, fig. 7), indicating the diversified nature of the eṣ-Ṣafi ceramics.

In addition to the complete vessels, a large group of Philistine sherds[136] displaying most of the motifs in the Philistine decorative repertoire was found.

There can be little doubt that Tell eṣ-Ṣafi was the site of one of the richest, most important Philistine settlements. Additional stratified excavation would undoubtedly shed more light on this mound.

BETH-SHEMESH

According to the Israelite tribal lists (Josh. 19:41), Beth-Shemesh, located in the northeastern Shephelah, was a city of Dan, although other biblical references locate it on the northern boundary of Judah and describe it as a Levitical city (Josh. 21:16). It was an Israelite city in the tenth century B.C., when it is mentioned as being in Solomon's second district (1 Kings 4:9), and it must also have been Israelite earlier, in the time of Samuel, when the Ark was returned to Beth-Shemesh from Philistia (1 Sam. 6:9 ff.).

The first excavations at Beth-Shemesh were conducted in 1911 by D. Mackenzie, who distinguished four strata. The earliest stratum (IV), dating from the Bronze Age, ended with the cessation of Mycenaean and Cypriot imports. The second stratum (III) was characterized by Philistine pottery, which Mackenzie was the first to interpret correctly.[137] The city met its end in a conflagration whose traces were evident in every section of the mound.

The Haverford College Expedition worked at Beth-Shemesh for five seasons between 1921 and 1931 and in 1933.[138]

The Late Bronze Age city of stratum IV (with two phases, IVB and IVA) was destroyed at the end of the thirteenth or beginning of the twelfth century B.C., but it is impossible to identify the attackers. We do not know whether they were Israelites, Philistines, or Egyptians engaged in a military campaign.[139]

The most important evidence for dating the end of stratum IV is the pottery found in silos 530 and 515, for the stratum III walls were built directly above these silos.[140] The pottery represents a transitional phase between Late Bronze II and Iron Age ceramic traditions, but it also contains elements that are typical of stratum IVB alone, sherds found both in strata IVB and III, sherds typical of stratum III alone, and sherds found only in these two silos. The sherds are all rather coarsely made, and the important factors in determining the date of the assemblage are (1) the absence of the Mycenaean and Cypriot imported ware typical of the Late Bronze II strata and (2) the absence of Philistine ware. The pottery of these silos may be contemporary with stratum B_1 of Tell Beit Mirsim.[141] However, if the dating of level B_1 at Tell Beit Mirsim is problematic, it is even more so at Beth-Shemesh, where so little material representative of the period was found.

Large quantities of Philistine pottery were preserved in stratum III within the thick layers of destruction debris.

Before proceeding to a discussion of the Philistine ware, we should note a number of vessels found in the large burial cave, no. 11.[142] This cave was in use from the Early Bronze Age and served as a burial place during the settlements of strata V–III. Its use by the inhabi-

---

133. *B-M,* frontispiece, pp. 89–96, 138, 70, pls. 20, 35, 37–42, 44. For the identification of Tell eṣ-Ṣafi with Gath, *see* A. F. Rainey, "The Identification of Philistine Gath," *Eretz-Israel* 12 (1975): 63*–76*. *See* Kitchen, *The Philistines,* p. 62, for a summary of the different views on the identification of Gath.

134. *B-M,* pl. 35:1–11.

135. Ibid., pls. 20, 44.

136. Ibid., pls. 37–42.

137. D. Mackenzie, "The Excavations at Ain Shems," *PEF Ann* 1 (1911): 84.

138. *BS* and *AS I–V* present the findings in a way that allows the reader to form a picture of the complex stratigraphy and typology of Beth-Shemesh. See also *EAEHL,* pp. 241–53.

139. *AS V,* pp. 12–13, 15, 127–33; G. E. Wright, Review of Books, *JAOS* 70 (1950): 60.

140. *AS V,* pp. 124–25; *AS IV,* pl. XXXII:17–28.

141. *TBM I,* p. 58, par. 76, fig. 10, pl. 26:1–27.

142. *AS V,* pp. 125–26.

tants of stratum III is indicated by a number of Philistine vessels, including Type 1 bowls, Type 2 kraters,[143] and a Type 10 horn-shaped vessel (chap. 3, fig. 40:1). In addition to the Philistine ware, there were a number of Egyptian vessels: a pithos with a high, bulging neck and several amphoriskoi[144] similar to those found in the Tell el-Farʿah anthropoid burial tombs (chap. 5, fig. 7:16–18). Among the small finds are two scarabs of Ramesses III that may belong to this phase of the cave's use[145] and a neck sherd of a Black-on-Red I–II Cypro-Phoenician juglet,[146] which indicates that burial in the cave continued in use in the tenth century.

It is difficult to fix the date of the end of stratum III. The Philistine pottery found here is typical of the twelfth and the first half of the eleventh centuries; there are no examples from the third phase of Philistine pottery. However, as we have already emphasized, this last phase takes different forms in different places. Wright states that "Since we now know that during the second half of the eleventh century fine Philistine pottery ceased to be made, we must infer that the destruction which laid the city waste occurred not later than the early part of the third quarter of the eleventh century." The Philistine ceramic material would be in agreement with Wright's date for the end of stratum III were it not for a number of other vessels that force us to lower the date. These are a Cypro-Phoenician Black-on-Red I–II juglet[147] (which cannot be dated prior to the tenth century), and a number of high-necked juglets with flat button bases[148] (which are not known to appear in any context before the end of the eleventh century).[149] It would appear then that Wright's original suggestion of 1000 B.C. as the date of the destruction of stratum III is correct. Stratum IIA dates from the early tenth century, when Beth-Shemesh was recaptured by David.

It is possible that a group of red-slipped strainer-spout jugs decorated with black bands[150] may belong to the final phase of stratum III. These jugs represent

debased Philistine Types 6 and 16 and are comparable to those found in Megiddo stratum VI.[151]

The evidence of the city's prosperity, together with its geographical location and the quantity of Philistine pottery found, suggests that it was under the political and economic domination of the Philistines despite its Israelite population. The date of the stratum III destruction is still open, as is Wright's assumption that Beth-Shemesh was destroyed with great violence by the Philistines shortly after their destruction of Shiloh and the subsequent removal of the Ark from Beth-Shemesh to Kirjath-Jearim (1 Sam. 1–7:2). As shown above, however, this reconstruction does not fit the ceramic evidence. On the other hand, the assumption that stratum III was continuously inhabited until the very end of the eleventh century agrees well with the ceramic assemblages from both the mound proper and the tomb deposits.

GEZER

Ancient Gezer, located at Tell Jezer (Tell el-Jazari), has yielded an unusual wealth of Philistine pottery of almost every known type. Much of this material, however, is of little value because the first excavator of Gezer, R. A. S. Macalister (1902–09), failed to note the position of most of the finds. Hence it is impossible to construct a stratigraphical sequence of the pottery from the mound itself, and the dating of much of it is based on typological evidence alone. On the other hand, the Philistine pottery found in the tombs and other homogeneous assemblages are of great importance, as they can be dated with greater certainty.

Fortunately, the excavations undertaken by the Hebrew Union College in 1964–73[152] have made it possible to reevaluate and incorporate Macalister's results and have established a firm stratigraphical sequence that clarifies the Philistine period at Gezer (strata XIII–XI). Although detailed discussion of the material must await full publication, the main stratigraphic facts were established by the Hebrew Union College excavation.

The evidence as a whole suggests a partial hiatus in occupation at the very end of the thirteenth and the

143. *BS*, pp. 191:393, 193: 497.
144. Ibid., pp. 173:2, 177:3, 185.
145. D. Mackenzie, *PEF Ann* 2 (1912–13): 61, pl. XXIX A, 1; Rowe, 830; *AS II*, p. 88, pl. LI:42; Rowe, 831.
146. *BS*, p. 187. For the turn of the twelfth century B.C., the scarab of Siptah is important; *see* Rowe, 690.
147. *AS IV*, pl. LXI:39.
148. Ibid., pl. LXI:36.
149. *Meg. II*, pl. 87:16, St. VB.
150. *AS IV*, pl. LX:16, 18, 21, 24, 25.

151. *Meg. II*, pl. 82:2–5.
152. The discussion of the results of the Hebrew Union College excavations is based on *Gezer I (1964–1966)* and *Gezer II (1967–1970)*, esp. pp. 4–5; *EAEHL*, pp. 428–43.

beginning of the twelfth century B.C., which may be designated stratum XIV. It may be a postdestruction level that resulted from the conquest claimed by Pharaoh Merneptah about 1220 B.C. (Among Macalister's finds was an ivory pendant bearing two cartouches of Merneptah.)[153] This would account for the fact that the excavators encountered no real evidence that destruction had accompanied the arrival of the Philistines (or Sea Peoples) in the early twelfth century B.C. By then the site may have already been partly destroyed and deserted.

Gezer was not among the cities captured by Israel during Joshua's conquest. In the twelfth century it was taken over by the Philistines or came under their influence; the evidence for their dominance is the abundance of Philistine pottery found on the site and our present knowledge of Philistine aims and military strategy, as well as the mention of Gezer as a military frontier city in David's wars with the Philistines. The Bible usually speaks of Gezer as a sort of buffer zone between Philistia and Israel; other passages imply that it was in fact the farthest outpost of Philistine influence (2 Sam. 5:25; 1 Chron. 14:16, 20:4). The recent excavations have reinforced the evidence of Philistine presence at Gezer, especially in strata XIII–XI (twelfth and first half of the eleventh century B.C.). In each of the fields of excavation, two or three Philistine phases were revealed, although there are not always clear signs of destruction.

The pottery uncovered is a mixture: local traditions of degenerate Late Bronze Age pottery prevailed until the sudden appearance of Philistine bichrome ware.

In fields II and VI, two ephemeral "post-Philistine, pre-Solomonic" phases were distinguished (strata X–IX). They were marked by a distinctive pottery that is no longer painted but merely treated with an unburnished thin red slip. These levels, wherever they were

investigated, ended in violent destruction attributable to the campaigns of the Egyptian pharaoh who, according to 1 Kings 9:16, "captured Gezer and burned it with fire" before ceding it to Solomon, probably around 950 B.C. (It has been conjectured that the pharaoh was Siamun, of the ill-fated Twenty-first Dynasty.)

We shall first examine the tomb groups (for the cache of ritual objects found by Macalister, see chap. 4, pp. 219–29), then add a short catalogue of Philistine vessels and sherds of uncertain provenance published by him.

Tomb 9

Burial cave 9[154] was used during the Late Bronze Age II, Iron Age I, and the Roman period. The typical Iron Age I pottery found there includes two whole Philistine vessels and a number of Philistine sherds. The vessels are a krater (chap. 3, fig. 11:5) and a stirrup jar (chap. 3, fig. 16:2). A pyxis[155] similar in shape to the typical pyxis (Type 4) may also be considered a Philistine vessel. Among the sherds are a bowl fragment decorated with antithetic spirals (chap. 3, fig. 67:4) and a body sherd displaying a spiral motif.[156] It is not clear whether a fragment of the upper part of a stirrup jar[157] should be classified as Philistine or Mycenaean.

The decorative style of the tomb 9 Philistine pottery displays an artistry, a creative individualism quite unlike the usual Philistine ceramics. This distinctiveness makes it difficult to date the group, however, and relating it to other roughly contemporaneous assemblages is of little help in establishing an accurate date.[158] The high artistic standard, however, may suggest a date somewhere within the first phase of Philistine pottery.

Tomb 58

This tomb[159] was also in use during three different periods—in this case, the Late Bronze Age II, Iron Age I, and the Hellenistic period. A number of Philistine vessels belong to the second phase of the tomb's use: a

153. Rowe, pl. XXXII:66; *Gezer* II, p. 331, fig. 456; *Gezer* I, p. 15. Gezer is rich in Egyptian cartouches of the Twentieth Dynasty ranging from Ramesses III to Ramesses IX. Of the two cartouches of Ramesses III, one comes from the cult cache (chap. 4, fig. 2) and the other from tomb 252 (*Gezer* III, pl. CXXI:20). One scarab of Ramesses IV was found in a Persian assemblage (*Gezer* I, fig. 157). One scarab of Ramesses VIII was uncovered (*Gezer* III, pl. CCVIII:2) and one cartouche of Ramesses IX (*Gezer* III, pl. CXCV:74; and *Gezer* II, p. 250). The latter is a green-enamelled inlay that was originally ascribed to Ramesses X by Macalister and was later assigned to Ramesses IX. *See* Malamat, *The Egyptian Decline*, p. 36, n. 59, and below, discussion in chap. 6.

154. *Gezer* I, p. 308; *Gezer* III, pls. LXX, LXXI.
155. Ibid., III, pls. LXX:6.
156. Ibid., pl. LXXI:23.
157. Ibid., pl. LXXI:22.
158. Ibid., pls. LXX:9, 13; LXXI:15.
159. Ibid., I, pp. 321–25; III, pls. LXXXI, LXXXII, LXXXIII.

small bowl (Type 1),[160] two krater fragments (Type 2) with spiral bichrome motifs, and a Type 7 jug[161] with spout and basket handle. Although the Philistine assemblage in this tomb is quite meager, it can be definitely ascribed to the second phase of Philistine pottery.

Tomb 59

Tomb 59 was first used during the Late Bronze Age II and is of special interest because of its diversified collection of Philistine vessels from Iron Age I.[162] Only a few sherds can be ascribed to Phase 1. These include a krater fragment with a bird motif.[163]

The following vessels (figures in chap. 3) belong to Phase 2: a stirrup jar (fig. 16:4); a strainer-and-spout fragment of a Type 6 jug;[164] four cylindrical bottles (fig. 34:3, 9, 12, 13); three horn-shaped vessels (fig. 40:3);[165] and a juglet with pinched-in girth (fig. 33:4), which may belong to Phase 2 or Phase 3 (compare the Type 8 juglet from Qasile X, fig. 33:6). It should be noted that this tomb group contains a number of examples of two Philistine types that are closely related to Cypriot pottery (cylindrical bottles and horn-shaped vessels), as well as a large group of Type 7 jugs with basket handle and spout,[166] some decorated with horizontal stripes in red or bichrome red and black. A vessel of this type was also found in tomb 58.

A pilgrim's flask[167] and a jug decorated with red and black stripes belong to a group of vessels that are analogous to ones from Qasile X.[168]

A Black-on-Red I–II Cypro-Phoenician sherd[169] and several red and black dipper juglets[170] are typical of the local tenth-century pottery. Probably also from this period is a vessel with a human face molded on its outer surface[171] (chap. 3, fig. 36:5). All of these vessels represent the final phase of burial in the tomb.

We can conclude, on the basis of its pottery, that tomb 59 was in continuous use from the Late Bronze Age II down to the tenth century B.C.

Tomb 84–85

Another tomb containing Philistine pottery, 84–85,[172] was in use from the Late Bronze or Iron Age I–II. A small bowl[173] and a pyxis[174] are the sole vessels that can be identified as Philistine.

Of special interest is a group of cult vessels datable by a cartouche of Ramesses III (see chap. 4 discussion and fig. 2).

The following Philistine vessels lack a clear context and can therefore be dated only on the basis of typological comparisons (all figures are in chap. 3):

Phase 1. Kraters (fig. 1:1, 2), a stirrup jar (fig. 14), a strainer-spout jug (fig. 25:1), various body sherds decorated with bird motifs (fig. 62:25, 28), and other combinations of motifs characteristic of the earliest phase of Philistine pottery.[175]

Phase 2. A stirrup jar (fig. 16:6), a cylindrical bottle (fig. 34:6), and a Type 7 spouted jug with basket handle (fig. 32:1).

A large number of sherds (figures in chap. 3) can be identified only within the wider, more general, framework of Phases 1–2: body sherds,[176] bowls,[177] kraters (fig. 11:1), a pyxis (fig. 18:1), a strainer-spout jug (fig. 25:1), and Type 12 jugs (fig. 47:2, 3). Cup-bearing kraters[178] of the same type as those found at Azor (chap. 4, fig. 14) can also be included in this group. A white-slipped vessel decorated with rows of triangles has been published as a hole-mouth jar.[179] There is a possibility that this is actually the base and lower part of a jar that has been published upside down.

The Philistine ceramic assemblage at Gezer consists primarily of vessels belonging to the first two phases of

160. Ibid., III, pl. LXXXI:4.
161. Ibid., pls. LXXXII:14; LXXXIII:2, 8.
162. Ibid., I, pp. 325–27, figs. 167–171; III, pls. LXXXIV and LXXXV.
163. Ibid., III, pl. LXXXIV:20.
164. Ibid., pl. LXXXV:1.
165. Ibid., I, fig. 171:7; III, pl. LXXXIV:16.
166. Ibid., I, pp. 326–27, fig. 168.
167. Ibid., III, pl. LXXXV:4; *Qasile IEJ 1*, fig. 6:4.
168. *Gezer* III, pl. LXXXV:11; *Qasile IEJ 1*, fig. 5:1.
169. *Gezer* I, fig. 171:6.
170. Ibid., I, Fig. 171:2; III, pl. LXXXIV:10.
171. Ibid., I, p. 329, fig. 169.

172. Ibid.: I, pp. 334–35; III, pls. LXXXVII–LXXIX.
173. Ibid., III, pl. LXXXVIII:14.
174. Ibid., pl. LXXXIX:3.
175. Ibid., pl. CLXVIII:1.
176. Ibid., pls. CLIX:7, 8, 10; CLX:2, 10; CLXV:7, 8; CLXVI:2, 4, 10, 11, 13; CLXVII:14.
177. Ibid., pl. CLVIII:3, 11, 16 (bowls). Bowl no. 3 is unique in its wavy line decoration, which is related to the wavy line Granary Style.
178. Fragments of cup-bearing kraters are in the Gezer Collection in the Archaeological Museum in Istanbul.
179. *Gezer* III, pl. CLXIII:8 (jar).

Philistine pottery, although the last stage is represented by a number of vessels, such as the krater in chapter 3, figure 5:4. One of the most interesting features of this pottery is its evidence that a high degree of artistic ability and an independent style was developed in the Philistine pottery workshop at Gezer.

TELL EN-NASBEH

Tell en-Nasbeh, situated about twelve kilometers north of Jerusalem, is generally identified with biblical Mizpah. The site was first settled at the end of the fourth and at the beginning of the third millennium. It was subsequently abandoned for about 2,000 years, then resettled at the beginning of the Iron Age in the twelfth century. This date is based mainly on the discovery of forty-seven Philistine sherds (and a dozen more possible ones), as well as a large number of sherds typical of the Early Iron Age. The published excavation report attributes this pottery mainly to stratum II.[180] As far as can be determined from the report,[181] the types represented include Type 1 bowls, Type 2 kraters, and Type 6 jugs. All the sherds are slipped, decorated in red and black, and bear motifs such as birds, spirals, concentric semicircles in various combinations, checkered patterns, and stemmed spirals. The latter motif has parallels only at Gezer (chap. 3, fig. 67:4). All the sherds belong to the early phases of Philistine pottery.

BETHEL

The excavations at Beitin—biblical Bethel[182]—which is situated north of Jerusalem, have revealed a flourishing Canaanite settlement occupied almost continuously throughout the Middle and Late Bronze Ages. Toward the end of the thirteenth century the Late Bronze Age settlement burned to the ground.[183] The site was resettled in the Iron Age I, and occupation continued to the end of the Byzantine period. Between the Late Bronze Age and the Iron Age I there is a total cultural break more marked than at any other point in Bethel's long history; it is attributed to the Israelite

conquest. Culturally there is a sharp contrast and deterioration between the flourishing Canaanite Late Bronze Age cities and the Iron Age Israelite settlement. This is reflected in both the architecture and the pottery, which continues to deteriorate throughout the three Iron Age I phases the excavators distinguished there. They correlated these phases with the subdivisions of level B at Tell Beit Mirsim as follows:[184]

Bethel Iron Age I$_1$	Pre-Philistine	TBM B$_1$
Bethel Iron Age I$_2$	Philistine	TBM B$_2$
Bethel Iron Age I$_3$	Post-Philistine	TBM B$_3$

The transition between the Iron Age I$_1$ and I$_2$ is characterized primarily by the introduction of burnishing and the appearance of a number of new pottery shapes, not by Philistine pottery, which is rare at Bethel. Bethel has no record of Philistine occupation or influence, and only a small number of Philistine sherds have been found there. None of these, however, occurred in a stratified context that could be related with the Iron Age I buildings. The published sherds include fragments of a Type 6 jug,[185] among them a shoulder and neck decorated in black and red on a heavy white slip. In the main register, there is a continuous triglyph design of groups of horizontal lines and the "B" pattern, which is similar to one found on a stirrup jar from Beth-Shemesh (chap. 3, fig. 16:5). The shoulder zone is decorated with rows of concentric half-circles.

Three sherds of bowls and kraters were also published. One displays a delicately painted bird with a dotted breast,[186] and is closely related to examples from strata XII and XIII at Ashdod. All the published examples belong to the undebased stage of Philistine pottery.

AZOR

The site is identified with the Azor mentioned in an addition to the Septuagint (Josh. 19:45) as being among the cities of Dan (in the Masoretic text the city is called Yehud). Its name is preserved in the nearby village of Yazur. Although the mound has not yet been

180. *Nasbeh I,* pp. 85–86, 133, 180–83.
181. *Nasbeh II,* pl. 80.
182. J. L. Kelso et al., "The Excavation of Bethel (1934–1960)," *AASOR* 39 (1968): 33–35, 64–66, pl. 38b. See also *EAEHL,* pp. 190–93.
183. Kelso, "Excavation of Bethel," n. 182, pp. 48 ff.

184. Ibid., p. 63.
185. Ibid., pls. 38:15a–b, 59:9.
186. Ibid., pl. 38:13.

excavated, surveys and salvage digs have found traces of occupation from the Chalcolithic period onward, including the Iron Age I. A large number of tombs dating from the Chalcolithic period to the Middle Ages were found in the nearby *kurkar* (sandstone) hills, especially west of the mound. Many of the Iron Age I finds, especially the remarkably fine Philistine assemblages, come from the diggings of amateurs, and therefore can be treated only typologically—not as tomb groups. The finds include a complete range of Philistine pottery, from the earliest types to the later debased, assimilated vessels. The latter include only a scanty sampling of the Tell Qasile X debased kraters (Type 18), even though other types of vessels found are identical with those of Qasile X (for example, the jar in burial 63). The very elaborate decoration of many of the pieces is unique to Azor, which appears to have had a local pottery workshop blessed with talented potters.

The rich Iron Age cemetery located on a *kurkar* hill (area D) next to Tel Azor and east of the Tel Aviv-Jerusalem highway, was excavated by M. Dothan during two seasons (1958, 1960).[187] Forty-five tombs, dating from the twelfth down to the ninth century B.C., were excavated. (The earlier tombs, from the end of the Late Bronze Age, could not be examined as they had been badly damaged by the later Iron Age I burials). Five methods of burial originating in different cultures were represented here. We shall describe the four that date from the twelfth to the end of the eleventh century and thus span the period of Philistine influence.

1. *Plain Burials* A pit was dug in the ground, and the body was laid in it on its back in an east-west position. (This is the most common type of Iron Age I burial at Azor.) Most of these burials can be dated to the twelfth and eleventh centuries by their funerary equipment, which consists chiefly of typical Philistine

pottery. Burial 56[188] is especially interesting. It contained the body of a child seven or eight years old; on its throat lay a unique scarab[189] from the Nineteenth or Twentieth dynasty. An iron bracelet—one of the oldest iron objects from Palestine—was also found in the tomb, showing once again that iron was first used for personal adornment and only later took on utilitarian functions.

2. *Storage-Jar Burial*[190] Two storage jars were cut at the shoulders, joined mouth to mouth (pl. 9), and the body was interred inside. This type of burial is rare in Palestine. An intact example discovered near Kefar Yehoshua dates from the twelfth century and resembles Hittite burials from Alişar Hüyük.[191] As no small finds or diagnostic pottery vessels were found in association with the Azor jar burial, no clear-cut connection with Philistine burial customs can be made.

3. *Brick Tombs* These were built below ground level out of unburnt rectangular bricks laid on their short sides; these were then covered with similar larger bricks, and the whole formed a sort of coffin. The scant pottery found in these burials belongs to the late phase of Philistine ware—that is, the eleventh century B.C. Such tombs are unique in Palestine, although an analogy may be found in the Tel Zeror[192] stone-lined cist tomb of the eleventh century and, even more closely, in a brick-lined cist tomb from the early twelfth century at Tell es-Saidiyeh in Transjordan.[193]

On the basis of the ceramic evidence, it is possible to ascribe the plain burials and possibly the brick tombs to the Philistine presence at Azor in the twelfth and the first half of the eleventh century.

4. *Cremation*[194] This burial (burial 63, pls. 10, 11), consists of a square, stone frame about a meter in height containing a large storage jar and several jugs. The storage jar contained the charred bones of an adult and a child covered with votive vessels, including a

187. *Azor*, pp. 171–75. M. Dothan, "Quelques tombes de l'age du fer ancien à Azor," *Bulletin de la Société d'Anthropologie* 12, XIᵉ série (1961):79–82. The anthropological examination of skulls from the twelfth- and eleventh-century tombs at Azor carried out by Denise Ferembach showed that they are brachycephalic (Alpine or Armenoid). *See* D. Ferembach, "Les restes humains des tombes philistines du cimetière d'Azor," *Bulletin de la Société d'Anthropologie* 12 ibid., pp. 83–91; *see also* M. Dothan, "Preliminary Survey of Azor Excavations," *IEJ* 8 (1958): 272–74; *BIES* 25 (1961): 224–30 (Hebrew); and *EAEHL*, pp. 144, 146–47.

188. *Azor*, pl. 35:1, 4.
189. Ibid., pl. 35:4.
190. Ibid., pl. 35:3.
191. A. Druks, "A 'Hittite' Burial near Kefar Yehoshua," *BIES* 30 (1966):213–20 (Hebrew). Close analogies to this type of burial are found in Anatolia at the end of the Hittite Empire about 1200 B.C.
192. *Tel Zeror II*, pp. 38–41.
193. Pritchard, *Expedition* 6:4 (1964):3–6, and idem, in *The Role of the Phoenicians in the Interaction of Mediterranean Civilization*, W. Ward, ed. (Beirut, 1968), p. 101, fig. 1, grave 101.
194. *Azor*, pl. 35:2.

Pl. 9. Storage-jar burial, Azor [M. Dothan, "Excavations from Azor, 1960," *IEJ* 11 (1961): pl. 35:3].

Pl. 10. Cremation burial, Azor [M. Dothan, "Excavations from Azor, 1960," *IEJ* 11 (1961): pl. 35:2].

Pl. 11. Tomb group from cremation burial, Azor [From the Collection of the Israel Department of Antiquities and Museums, 60-144, 60-552].

well-preserved bronze bowl, and a pottery flask, and a mouthpiece of gold foil. The storage jar and the other pottery found in this grave are identical with that found in stratum X at Tell Qasile,[195] and this type of grave unquestionably belongs to the second half of the eleventh century B.C. This is the earliest example of a cremation burial in Palestine, antedating those at Tell el-Far'ah in the tenth century B.C. and their Phoenician adaptation at Achzib and 'Atlit.[196]

The sudden appearance of cremation at Azor about the middle of the eleventh century marks a definite change in burial methods, and it may be explained by the arrival of a new ethnic element. Cremation was never practiced by the Israelites. To burn a body was, in their eyes, an outrage inflicted only upon criminals or enemies. Although the people of Jabesh-Gilead burnt the bodies of Saul and his sons before burying their bones (1 Sam. 31:12), this seems to have been a departure from tradition; moreover, the parallel passage in 1 Chronicles 10:12 does not mention it.

The origin of cremation is a controversial question. Although in Greece it was formerly attributed to the Dorians who invaded at the beginning of the Dark Ages, it was subsequently seen to be a much older Eastern practice. It made its appearance in Greece as early as the late thirteenth and early twelfth centuries, mainly in association with Levantine trade and the Close Style of Myc. IIIC:1b. The appearance of cremation at the same time as the first iron weapons and in conjunction with Syrian bronze figurines and Syrian and Egyptian seals and scarabs illustrates the intense internationalism of the period of Sea Peoples.[197]

JAFFA

The excavations at ancient Jaffa (el-Qal'a)[198] have so far revealed (in area A) only a very poor occupation level

195. *Qasile IEJ 1*, pl. 26:2.
196. (Tell el-Far'ah) *BP I*, p. 12, pls. XXXIXA and XL:43 K2; (Achzib) *EAEHL*, pp. 26–30; ('Atlit) C. N. Johns, "Excavations at Pilgrims' Castle, 'Atlit (1933): Cremated Burials of Phoenician Origin," *QDAP* 6 (1937): 121–52.
197. E. Vermeule, *Greece in the Bronze Age* (Chicago, 1964), pp. 301–02. For further discussion of the subject, *see* H. L. Lorimer, *Homer and the Monuments* (London, 1950), pp. 103 ff.; *DMS*, p. 71; A. M. Snodgrass, *The Dark Age of Greece* (Edinburgh, 1971), pp. 187 ff., figs. 68, 69; and P. J. Riis, *Hama. Fouilles et recherches 1931–1938. II₃: Les cimetières à crémation* (Copenhagen, 1948), chap. 2, esp. pp. 37–45.
198. J. Kaplan, *Archaeology* 17 (1964):270–76; idem, *BA* 35 (1972): 77–85; idem, in *EAEHL*, pp. 532–41.

of Iron Age I. This level (IIIb) followed the destruction of the flourishing Late Bronze Age city (level IV). In the 1955 season of excavations, a section of a courtyard with a floor of beaten earth and an ash pit containing Philistine sherds of the eleventh century B.C. was assigned to level IIIb. In 1970 the excavations in area A were enlarged and an Iron Age I level was revealed with pits and depressions partly dug into a layer of rubble and clay bricks that had fallen from a nearby structure. The pottery encountered here also included eleventh-century B.C. Philistine ware; it is analogous to that of Qasile stratum XI and indicates that a gap of long duration existed between the destruction of the Late Bronze Age level and the first Philistine settlement at Jaffa. Beneath the Philistine level the foundations of a large structure appeared; it was interpreted by the excavator as a pre-Philistine temple (the so-called Lion Temple) and adjacent citadel. He attributed construction of the temple to the Danuna tribe of the Sea Peoples. However, the chronological evidence and the absence of additional proof refute this assumption.

No occupation level paralleling stratum X at Tell Qasile is represented at Jaffa, and it seems that the main center of population at that time shifted to the Yarkon Basin, where the remains of Tell Qasile and Tell Jerishe point to an era of prosperity and the development of commercial relations with Phoenicia and Egypt.

TELL QASILE

Tell Qasile was founded and developed by the Philistines at the beginning of the Iron Age in the twelfth century B.C. on a *kurkar* ridge on the northern bank of the Yarkon River. Like Tell Jerishe, it is one of many mounds in a chain of ancient towns, villages, and forts whose remains bear witness to continuous occupation and whose cultural development can be followed in this fertile and well-watered region. The uniqueness of Tell Qasile in the pattern of Philistine settlements in the country is that it was a new site chosen by the Philistines; it had never previously been settled. In every other known case except Khirbet Muqanna' (see chap. 6), the Philistines destroyed existing Canaanite towns and settled on the ruins.

The river seems to have been the main factor governing the choice of the site at Tell Qasile. Using the Yarkon waters for irrigation, the Philistine settlers were able to maintain a thriving agriculture. Their success is reflected in the grain pits, silos, presses, and storerooms, and in the store jars for wine and oil, as well as in the great number of farm tools, including flint sickle-blades. Thanks to the river, the city grew into an estuary port in which trade and industry flourished. The archaeological finds include remains of a metal industry and several workshops. The story of the cedars of Lebanon being brough "in rafts by sea to Joppa" in the days of King Solomon (2 Chron. 2:16) and of Zerubbabel, governor of Judah (Ezra 3:7), is very plausible. Indeed, two pieces of burnt wood found on the floor of the stratum X temple at Qasile have been identified as cedar of Lebanon.

Two main series of excavations were carried out at Tell Qasile. The first extended over four seasons, from 1948 to 1951, and concentrated on the southern (area A, residential area and workshops) and western (area B, fortifications) parts of the mound;[199] the second series of campaigns, from 1971 to 1974, was undertaken in the northern part (area C), the site of the temple and the sacred area (fig. 7).[200]

Of the twelve main strata of settlement at Tell Qasile, our discussion centers around strata XII–X, which span a period from the twelfth to the beginning of the tenth centuries. The clear stratigraphic division between these strata provides an excellent starting point for the study of the development of Philistine culture in Iron Age Palestine. Stratum X was the best preserved of the three; it was destroyed by fire, and the city—with its rich assemblages of pottery—was sealed beneath a thick layer of burnt brick and ashes. The earlier strata, XI and XII, were less well preserved and yielded fewer finds.

We shall present here a general description of the settlement according to the areas of excavation, begin-

ning with area A, the southern, residential area of the mound.

Area A

Stratum XII Stratum XII, founded on a *kurkar* knoll, seems to have been the first urban settlement on the site. To judge by the open spaces, it was a planned town, but its population was small. The best preserved architectural remains are Building Q, which consisted of two adjoining structures that continued in use, with changes, into stratum XI.

The pottery assemblages of stratum XII, which are typical of the initial phase of Iron Age I, come from hollows and pits dug into the *kurkar* and from the first habitation layer on the virgin rock. The hallmark of this stratum is the Philistine pottery, which helps to date this initial settlement. Mycenaean and Cypriot imports have disappeared, as has the local elaborately painted Late Bronze Age pottery, but plain household vessels continue the local Canaanite tradition. No complete vessels were found, but the distinguishable shapes include bowls (Type 1), kraters (Type 2), stirrup jars (Type 3) and strainer-spout jugs (Type 6). All the distinctive features of the earliest phase of Philistine pottery are present: the thick white slip, bright bichrome black and red decoration, and decorative motifs in clear delicate lines that sometimes recall the Aegean Close Style (see especially chap. 3, pl. 55). The Philistine bird, elegantly rendered (chap. 3, fig. 61:5; chap. 3, pl. 22), appears combined with a variety of motifs.

Stratum XI There is evidence of increased building activity in this stratum. Substantial remains have come to light, but it is difficult to arrive at a full understanding of their plan because of the large-scale damage caused by the construction of stratum X. Unlike stratum X, the building complexes in this stratum are not arranged in planned units. The method of construction is typical of Iron Age Qasile: foundations of undressed *kurkar* stone are surmounted by mud-brick walls, and occasionally walls are built entirely of mud brick. The best preserved and most interesting is building Q, which partly reuses walls of stratum XII. It was not a residential structure but an industrial plant divided into two main rooms, Q8 and Q9. The large western room, Q8, served as a smelting workshop. It contained two smelting furnaces; the one located on the west side is well preserved. It was elliptical in

199. The first four seasons at Tell Qasile, as well as an additional short dig in 1962–63, were directed by B. Mazar; *see* preliminary reports, *Qasile IEJ 1* and *EAEHL*, pp. 963–68. The writer has also drawn on the unpublished material excavated in these campaigns.

200. The temple complex of Qasile was excavated by A. Mazar and discussed in his doctoral thesis: "The Temples of Tell Qasile. The Excavations and Their Implications for the Study of the Cult and Material Culture in Eretz-Israel during the 12th–10th Centuries B.C.E." The Hebrew University, Jerusalem, 1977 (Hebrew). See also *Qasile IEJ 23*; idem, "A Philistine Temple at Tell Qasile," *BA 36* (1973): 42–48; idem, "The Excavations at Tell Qasile, 1973–74, Preliminary Report," *IEJ 25* (1975): 77–88; and *EAEHL*, pp. 968–75.

shape, measured 1 m. × 0.80 m., and had a brick flue that extended beneath the western wall of the room and turned south. Near the furnace were found two clay crucibles containing some remains of smelted copper (pl. 12). Traces of another furnace and flue were found in the east end of the room. The entire area may have continued to be used for copper smelting into stratum X.

The ceramic assemblage of stratum XI is a continuation of stratum XII. The local domestic Canaanite types continue, but new features make their appearance: for example, the red slip and the irregular burnishing that will characterize the next stratum, X. The Philistine pottery displays some differences in decoration from the preceding stratum (XII). There is a decline in artistry, and the motifs become more repetitive. The lines of the designs are less bright and less carefully drawn, and the bird motif is rarer. The most common types of the Philistine pottery are still Type 1 bowls, Type 2 kraters, Type 3 stirrup jars, and Type 6 jugs. There is also a fragment of a Type 10 horn-shaped vessel and a fragment of a Type 12 vessel.

In summary, the pottery assemblages of strata XII–XI can be correlated with Megiddo VIIA–VIB, Tell Beit Mirsim B$_2$, Beth-Shemesh III, and, in Philistia proper, with Ashdod XIIIa–XI.

Other finds include bronze arrowheads (no iron objects were found in area A in strata XII and XI), a bone graver, spindles, flint sickle blades with traces of bone handles, numerous perforated clay balls (loom weights), and various stone implements such as grindstones and mortars.

Stratum X   The buildings of this stratum (fig. 8, pl. 13) were discovered over the entire excavated area, and it was thus possible to establish both the plans of the buildings and the plan of the quarter as a whole. The layout in area A is exceptionally clear and well defined. The buildings uncovered in the northern complex of the excavated area constitute a complete residential quarter, bounded on three sides by streets and comprising two rows of attached houses accessible only from the streets. The houses were built on an almost uniform ground plan with some individual variations. Most are of the rectangular three-room house type, a variant and probably the archetype of the four-room house typical of the period of the Israelite Monarchy. (At Tell Qasile, we can follow its evolution from strata X to VIII.) The four-room house seems to

have been a local Israelite innovation and was not derived from outside influences.[201] Its compactness and functionality ensured its wide diffusion in the country.

The southern complex differs in character from the northern. The western building, Z, consists of a large unit (fig. 8) divided by two parallel rows of column bases into three spaces of equal width. This was not an ordinary dwelling and may have been used for industrial purposes (continuing the tradition of stratum XI in this area); it is more probable that it is one of the earliest examples of a public storehouse, of a kind well known in Israelite towns of the Iron Age.[202]

In stratum X, preserved beneath the burnt brick and ashes of an extensive conflagration, the Philistine tradition is already on the wane. New elements in both the architecture and the pottery herald the coming Israelite culture. The pottery shows evidence of renewed contacts with the outside world, from which the country had been isolated since the end of the thirteenth century B.C. Some of the vessels (for example, bichrome flasks and jugs, fig. 9:5) attest to sea and land links with the cultural centers on the Mediterranean coast.[203] Others (for example, Egyptian store jars, fig. 9:9) point to renewed trade relations with Egypt.[204]

The local Canaanite pottery traditions continue in both shape and in the striped black and red decoration (fig. 9), but the irregularly burnished red slip that first appeared in stratum XI now becomes dominant. It is decorated with black and sometimes white stripes.

201. Y. Shiloh, "The Four-Room House: Its Situation and Function in the Israelite City," *IEJ* 20 (1970): 180–90; idem, "The Four-Room House: The Israelite Type House?" *Eretz-Israel* 11 (1973): 277–85 (Hebrew).

202. Shiloh, "The Four-Room House: Its Situation and Function," 181 ff., figs. 1, 2.

203. The bichrome globular flasks and jugs are a major problem in Iron Age pottery since they are among the earliest indicators of interconnections and renewed trade relations in the Mediterranean. Three comprehensive discussions concerning the typology, chronology, and diffusion of this group are J. Du Plat Taylor, "The Cypriot and Syrian Pottery from Al-Mina, Syria," *Iraq* 21 (1959): 62–92; J. Birmingham, "The Chronology of Some Early and Middle Iron Age Cypriot Sites," *AJA* 67 (1963): 15–42; and Susannah V. Chapman, "A Catalogue of Iron Age Pottery from the Cemeteries of Khirbet Silm, Joya, Qrayé and Qasmieh of South Lebanon," *Berytus* 21 (1972): 55–194.

204. Parallels to the two Egyptian jars were found at Tell el-Yahudiyeh in Egypt and attributed by Petrie to the Twenty-second Dynasty (*HIC*, pl. XVIIA, 5–6).

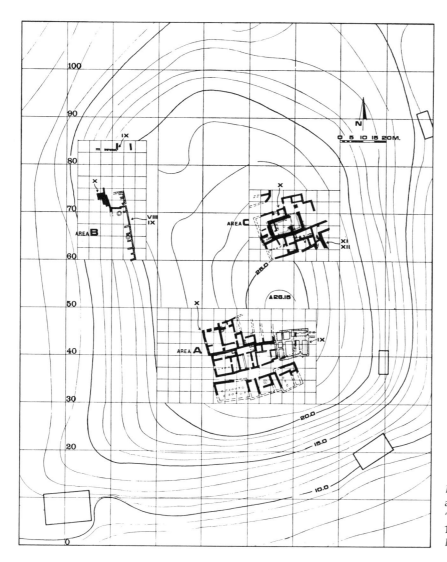

Fig. 7. General plan of excavated areas, Tell Qasile [A. Mazar, "Excavations at Tell Qasile, 1973–1974, Preliminary Report," *IEJ* **25** (1975): fig. 3].

Pl. 12. Clay crucible, Tell Qasile, stratum XI [From the Collection of the Israel Department of Antiquities and Museums, 51.72].

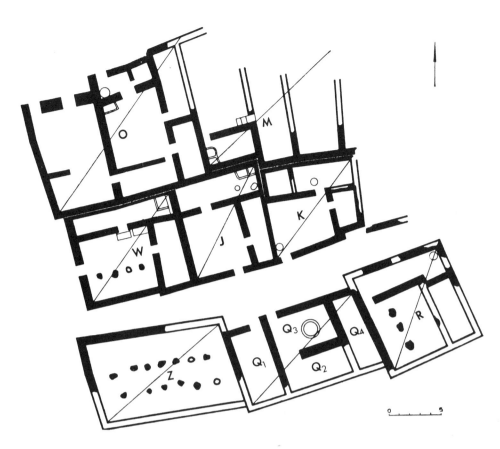

Fig. 8. Plan of southern residential quarter, Tell Qasile, stratum X [B. Mazar, *Canaan and Israel, Historical Essays* (Jerusalem, 1980), p. 161].

Pl. 13. Storerooms, Tell Qasile, stratum X [*Qasile IEJ 1*, pl. 30:C].

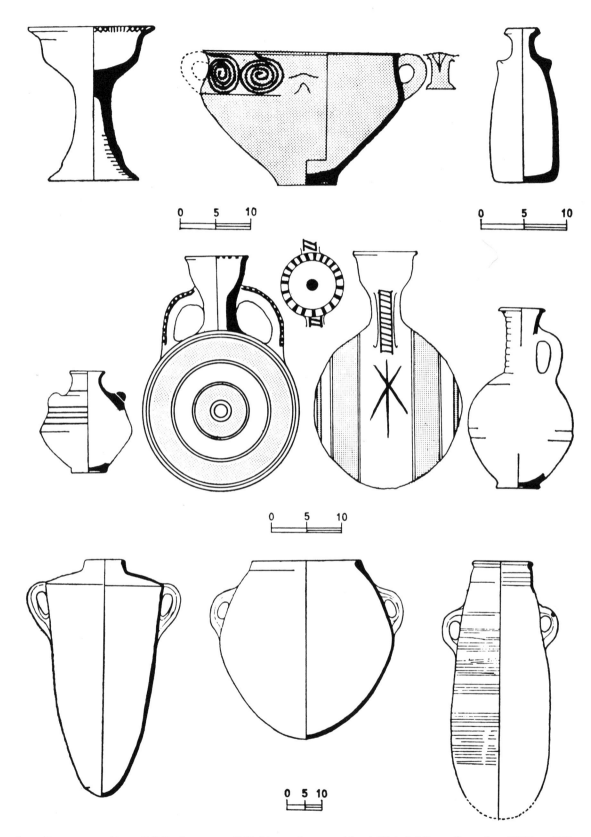

Fig. 9. Pottery assemblage, Tell Qasile, stratum X [B. Mazar, *Canaan and Israel, Historical Essays* (Jerusalem, 1980), p. 163].

The most conspicuous change occurs in the forms and decoration of the Philistine pottery. The white slip and bichrome decoration disappear almost completely, to be replaced here too by the irregularly burnished red slip and black decoration. Some of the distinctive Philistine types of vessels have vanished, others have been debased, and still others have become hybrid. The latter are a blend of Philistine and Canaanite elements, with new characteristics heralding the Israelite pottery style. This transitional style is best exemplified by the kraters of Type 18 shown in chap. 3, fig. 60:1, 3–5. The Philistine element is represented by horizontal handles and by the degenerate spiral pattern; the local tradition can be recognized in the outline of the kraters and in some of the decorative motifs; the new element is the burnished red slip.

The Philistine pottery of stratum X represents the disintegration of the original Philistine ceramic tradition and its assimilation into the local pottery. Reaching its last phase of development in a version peculiar to Tell Qasile, it strikingly exemplifies the evolution of local differences. A comparable development is seen at Tell Jerishe and in stratum VIA at Megiddo (the latter in a modified form), whereas stratum X at Ashdod evolves along quite different lines.

In contrast to strata XII and XI in area A, stratum X yielded several iron objects, such as knives and the blade of a sword. A conical seal engraved with a figure of a man with outstretched hands above the representation of an animal was also found.[205] Another conical seal, attributed to stratum X or XI, belongs to the group of Iron Age I conical seals that are usually associated with Philistine assemblages.[206]

B. Mazar, in his study of the site, designates the whole of stratum X as post-Philistine or pre-Israelite in order to indicate its intermediate position between the last phase of the Philistine period—namely, the second half of the eleventh and the beginning of the tenth century—and the Israelite period (of the United Monarchy)—the tenth century B.C. (stratum IX).

The city of stratum X may have met its end during the campaigns of David (985 B.C.) and his conquest of the coastal cities from the Yarkon to the north. The Israelite settlement of stratum IX was constructed on its ruins.

The Temple and Temple Area (fig. 10; pls. 14, 16)

The three superimposed temples in the northeast part of Tell Qasile[207] (strata XII–X, Early Iron Age, twelfth and eleventh centuries B.C.) are the first unmistakably Philistine temples ever discovered. This area was a well-planned complex of a number of units, and was evidently the cultic center of the Philistine city. In each of the three strata, XII–X, a new temple was erected; and with each new structure the temple was enlarged farther to the east. The western wall, the orientation toward the Mediterranean, and the focal point of the ritual remained unchanged throughout the strata.

The stratigraphical development in the temple compound corresponds to the strata on the southern slopes of the site (area A), as a whole, although further study may reveal additional subdivisions. A number of differences were noted between the pottery assemblages from the temple area and those from the eastern residential quarters; but these differences can be explained by the well-known fact that temple assemblages were handed down from generation to generation and were preserved for use even when new temples were built.

Stratum XII At various places above the *kurkar* bedrock were found traces of the elusive and undefined earliest period of settlement, stratum XIIb. Above this phase the earliest temple building (no. 319) was erected. This was a one-room brick structure measuring 6.4 m. × 6.6 m.; it had plastered benches along the walls and a beaten-lime floor. A plastered brick platform approached by two steps was located at the western end of the building and evidently served as the focal point of the ritual. The entrance to the temple seems to have been in the eastern wall; a *kurkar* slab (1 × 1 m.) found there was probably the threshold.

A unique Philistine vessel was found among the group of pottery vessels on the temple floor under a layer of collapsed bricks. Its neck and handles are those of a flask, but its pinched-in body resembles a Type 8 jug. It bears a bichrome decoration of a geometrized lotus pattern inscribed in a semicircle on a heavy white slip (chap. 3, pl. 39:2). Offering bowls and votive vessels also lay on the temple floor, but no cult vessels are of the type known from the later temples. As

205. *Qasile IEJ 1*, p. 136, pl. 36:C.

206. B. Mazar, "A Philistine Seal from Tell Qasile," *BIES* 31 (1967): 64–67 (Hebrew).

207. *See* n. 200 above.

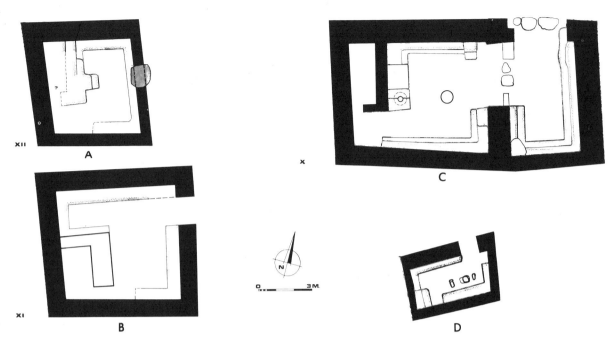

Fig. 10. Schematic plans of temples, Tell Qasile: (A) building 319 (stratum XII); (B) building 200 (stratum XI); (C) building 131 (stratum X); (D) building 300 (strata XI–X) [A. Mazar, "Excavations at Tell Qasile, 1973–1974, Preliminary Report," *IEJ* 25 (1975): fig. 1].

Pl. 14. General view of temple and temple area, Tell Qasile [*EAEHL*, p. 972].

suggested above, these were probably saved for use in the new buildings.

In the spacious courtyard (*temenos*) east of the temple at least two phases were distinguished; layers of ashes contained numerous bones and sherds, including a large quantity of Philistine bichrome decorated ware.

The special finds from this courtyard include an anthropomorphic pottery vessel, a scarab with a chariot scene,[208] and, most significant of all, an ivory knife handle terminating in a suspension ring (pl. 15); the latter bears traces of an iron blade that was fastened to the handle by three bronze rivets. This is the earliest iron implement at Tell Qasile stratum XII and one of the earliest iron knives found anywhere in the country; here it is associated with the initial phase of Philistine settlement. The wide diffusion of knives of this type points to a connection between the Philistine culture and contemporary Aegean and even European cultures. A similar knife, in bronze with an ivory inlaid handle, was discovered at Enkomi, Cyprus, on the floor of a twelfth-century workshop. Schaeffer noted that knives ending in suspension rings are known in the Urnfield culture (twelfth and eleventh centuries B.C.), which ranged from Central Europe to southern Italy and Sicily.[209] Another parallel comes from tomb XV at Ialysos,[210] a Myc. IIIC:1b tomb in which Mycenaean mourning figurines, both freestanding and attached to the rim of a krater (chap. 4, pl. 30), were found. It is striking that the association of mourning figurines and an iron knife occurs in the Myc. III:C1 culture as well as in the Philistine cultural complex.

Stratum XI After the destruction of the stratum XII temple, a new and larger temple (building 200) was built of *kurkar* directly above it. This temple consisted

of a single room, the *cella*, with a plastered floor and brick benches along the walls. The entrance to the temple was in the northern part of the eastern wall. On the southwest side was a corner room over which lay organic material containing an abundance of pottery, cult vessels, and bones. The cult vessels included an anthropomorphic mask, and ivory bird-shaped cosmetic bowl, a conch used as a horn, some heads of terra-cotta animal figurines, beads, and dozens of small votive bowls like the ones found in stratum XII. Red-slipped bowls now appear with the pottery. A new feature in the ceramic repertoire of Palestine is a group of handmade bowls decorated with indentations. These are connected with the so-called Dorian pottery and form another link with Cyprus, the Aegean, and Europe in the twelfth and eleventh centuries B.C.[211]

The focal point of the cult was in the northwest corner of the temple, where the stratum X altar subsequently stood. Some typical Philistine stirrup jars, one of them decorated with the bird pattern, were found in a nearby niche.

The temple of stratum X was evidently merely an enlargement and rebuilding of temple XI on a different plan. No trace of a burnt layer was found on the floor

208. An exact parallel to the scarab comes from area A at Tell Qasile, building L, stratum VIII, *Qasile IEJ 1*, pl. 37:B.

209. C. F. A. Schaeffer, "Ausgrabungen in Enkomi-Alasia," *AfO* 24 (1973): 193–96; V. Karageorghis, "Chronique des fouilles à Chypre en 1970," *BCH* 95 (1971): 376–78, figs. 82a–b. Another feature connecting twelfth-century Enkomi with the European Urnfield culture is the association of these knives with bronze longswords. *See* J. Lagarce, "Quatre Epées de Bronze Provenant d'une Cachette d'Armurier à Enkomi-Alasia," *Ugaritica VI*, pp. 349–68, fig. 2, for four bronze longswords recovered from the Armourer's Well at Enkomi in 1967. Another weapon indicating connections between Philistine, Cypriot, and European cultures is an axe-adze found on the altar of the stratum X temple at Qasile.

210. *Ialysos I–II*, pp. 174–75, fig. 101.

211. S. Hood, "Mycenaean Settlement in Cyprus and the Coming of the Greeks," in *Mycenaeans in the Eastern Mediterranean*, pp. 44–50, fig. 2, pls. VIII, IX. In this comprehensive survey of twelfth-century B.C. handmade pottery designated as "Dorian," Hood makes Cyprus his starting point. In Cyprus, pottery of this type has been found in a Late Cypriot IIIb context. It bears no resemblance to the local ware; an Aegean background had already been suggested by Karageorghis (ibid., p. 46, n. 30). Parallels to the Cypriot vessels can be found among Late Helladic IIIC, sub-Mycenaean, and later handmade wares of the Greek mainland. Troy VIIB also provides analogies for some of the types. Handmade black-burnished ware has since been found at Gordion in an early post-Hittite horizon and dates from the same general period as Troy VIIB—that is, the twelfth century. At Troy and Gordion it is very likely that this type of pottery was being produced by the Phrygians when they first arrived from the Balkans. In Mycenae, handmade burnished vessels with raised decorative bands occur in a deposit assignable to the first phase of LH IIIC ware (ibid., p. 50, n. 51). A vessel of this type was found in a Late Helladic IIIC context at Lefkandi in Euboea (ibid., p. 50, n. 52). The question of the diffusion of the handmade coarse pottery is not yet entirely clear, but its indisputable association with Myc. IIIC ware and its widespread distribution from the Balkans to the eastern Mediterranean coast at Tell Qasile again indicate that there were far more connections with the Balkan area than we previously recognized.

of temple XI, indicating a peaceful transition and no cultural break.

The open courtyard extends west of the temple up to a miniature temple (building 300) adjacent to the western wall of the main temple. Temple 300 encompasses one brick-walled room, the entrance at the eastern end of the northern wall and the altar in the southwest corner of the temple, so that worshippers entering had to turn at a right angle to face the altar. This same bent-axis principle is also found in the temple building of stratum X. The three brick projections along the central axis probably held cult vessels.

Three cylindrical cult stands covered with geometric decoration and with rectangular or oval fenestrations were found in the southwest corner of temple 300. Ritual bowls still stood on two of them. A bowl, which no doubt belonged to the third stand, was found in the porch. Two of the bowls are "bird bowls" with applied molded head, neck, wings, and tail (chap. 4, pl. 10). A group of pottery vessels that lay near the pillars included a globular chalice with faint traces of Philistine decoration; a checkerboard design and a bird can be made out. The globular chalice is a well-known Canaanite shape; many of them were found at Qasile. However, this is the only one known that is decorated in the distinctive style of the Philistine potter. It is badly worn, and it seems likely that it was an heirloom from the previous stratum XII temple.

The miniature temple was destroyed by the collapse of the brick walls and not by fire. The excavator believes it continued in use and remained standing even after the general destruction of stratum X. This is a somewhat unusual phenomenon: no changes in the architecture, no raising of floors, and no traces of the typical pottery of stratum X were found.

Another feature of the courtyard is pit 125. Stratigraphically rather complex, it lies below the altar of stratum X, cuts through the accumulated ash layers above the stratum XII courtyard, and was sealed by the floor of the courtyard of stratum X. It is not clear whether it existed simultaneously with the temple of stratum XI or whether it was dug during the transition from the stratum XI to the stratum X temple. In the latter event, the pit was probably a *favissa*, dug to house a "burial" of cult vessels used in temple 200 of stratum XI.

One of the "buried" objects is an anthropomorphic vessel of a female figure whose nipples serve as spouts (chap. 4, pl. 18); it bears traces of painted decoration. Because of its large size, this vessel is unique among the anthropomorphic vessels known from Palestine. Another important vessel is a pottery lion's head with open mouth and modeled fangs. It is decorated with Philistine designs in red and black paint on a buff slip and belongs to a group of lion-headed rhýta recognized as typical Philistine cult vessels with clear Aegean antecedents (see chap. 4, pl. 17). The abundant collection of pottery vessels in pit 125 also includes two bottles of Type 9 and an elaborately decorated horn-shaped vessel (Type 10). Many of the vessels in this pit already have the red slip that became widespread in stratum X.

Stratum X (fig. 11) The temple (building 131) was based on the previous structure, although it was re-planned and enlarged. The main temple is an elongated building oriented to the west and divided into two main parts: an antechamber and a main hall.

The altar was located directly opposite the central opening of the main hall, so that the visitor had an unobstructed view from the entrance. At the same time, since the entrance to the building was placed at a right angle in the northern wall of the antechamber (on the bent-axis plan), the main hall could not be seen from the outside. It should be noted that the stratum X altar was built directly above the cult installations of both previous temples, although the plan differed from stratum to stratum.

No exact parallels for the temple plan have been found in Palestine, although many features continue the Canaanite tradition and are evidenced in the temples at Lachish[212] and Beth-Shean.[213] Small sanctuaries recently excavated at Mycenae and Phylakopi (on the island of Melos) resemble that of Qasile both in general layout and in details.[214] A thirteenth century B.C. temple from Kition in Cyprus also has similar architectural features[215] and may be further evidence of the Aegean element in Philistine culture.

212. *Lachish II*, chap. 2, pls. LXVII, LXVIII.

213. *B-SH II, Part 1*, chaps. 1–5, esp. pl. XII.

214. W. Taylour, "New Light on Mycenaean Religion," *Antiquity* 44 (1970): 270–80. *See also* G. E. Mylonas, *Mycenae and the Mycenaean Age* (Princeton, 1966), pp. 145–48; Colin Renfrew, "The Mycenaean Sanctuary at Phylakopi," *Antiquity* 52 (1978): 7–14. These temples are significant additions to the very meager and not too definite religious structures known from the Mycenaean world.

215. V. Karageorghis, "Contribution to the Religion of Cyprus in the Thirteenth and Twelfth Centuries B.C.," in *Mycenaeans in the Eastern Mediterranean*, pp. 105–09, fig. 1.

The stratum X temple at Qasile was destroyed by a great conflagration. Two groups of vessels were found on the floor under a thick layer of fallen bricks, wood, and ashes. The first group lay on and around the raised altar and included most of the cult vessels, while the second group was in the small compartment behind the altar that served as a storeroom. The final destruction of the temple can be dated by the first group of vessels (pl. 16), which is identical with the pottery assemblages found in abundance on the floors of houses in stratum X in all the other areas excavated. This destruction corresponds to David's conquest of the town at the beginning of the tenth century B.C.

The second group of finds, from the small storeroom, is somewhat different, for it also contains earlier Philistine pottery types that are characteristic of stratum XI. The range of the deposit suggests it was accumulated over a long period and that the earlier types were heirlooms.

The building was evidently plundered before it was destroyed by fire, for no valuable objects such as jewelry or seals were found—only cult vessels and pottery. Two metal objects were uncovered in temple X. One, a socketed bronze double axe found on the steps of the altar, is identical to two axes found at Megiddo (in strata VIA and VIB).[216] Axes of this type are rare in the Levant and seem to have Aegean prototypes, as Catling observed;[217] Schaeffer proposed an even wider diffusion, tracing the axes to European cultures.[218] The bronze axe found in the Philistine temple at Qasile is an unmistakable indicator of the Sea Peoples' Aegean background.

The second metal object is an iron bracelet found on the floor of the temple; it is of a type known from various Early Iron Age sites (see chart on p. 92). Such bracelets belong to the period of the initial appearance of iron, when the metal was still rare and used mainly for jewelry.

In stratum X the temenos reached its peak of development. To the north the courtyards were surrounded by stone walls; in the southwest courtyard the miniature temple still stood. South of the temple,

standing partly on the foundations of the previous stratum, is a large building (225) that was probably associated with temple functions. In plan it resembles the houses of stratum X in the southern part of the mound, and the rich and varied pottery finds from it are typical of the stratum X repertoire known from those houses. In addition to the usual jugs and kraters, two Egyptian-type jars similar to those discovered in the houses in the south (fig. 9) were found.

A Philistine jug and five stirrup jars, all white slipped with bichrome decoration, were also found in building 225. No other Philistine bichrome pottery, except for the debased black-on-red variant, was discovered in any of the private dwellings excavated in the large, rich building complexes in the eastern part of the mound. We can, therefore, conclude that building 225 was directly connected with the temple service and that the bichrome vessels used in the ritual were preserved from earlier times.

Clearly Tell Qasile was a well-planned city with private dwellings, workshops, and a central temple situated in a sacred area. The peak of its development was reached in stratum X. Whereas the temple shows a continuous evolution from its foundation in stratum XII, no clear conclusions about the development of the private dwellings could be arrived at, and more evidence is needed for our assumption that the beginnings of a well-organized urban settlement can already be discerned in stratum XII. Only in stratum XI do we have more tangible evidence of a planned settlement, which led to the full-fledged city of stratum X. There is no clear evidence of fortifications in stratum XII; in strata XI and X the city was fortified. Strata XII–X form a cultural unit based on Canaanite traditions, together with features of the Philistine culture that appear at the very onset of the settlement.

The earliest settlement can be dated to the first half of the twelfth century B.C. The flourishing city of stratum X, although still Philistine, was already exposed to external influences and contacts and was absorbing the new styles of architecture and pottery that were dominant in the Israelite centers.

TELL JERISHE

Tell Jerishe (Gath Rimmon?) is the largest of the ancient settlements in the Yarkon River valley and is situated near the southern bank.

---

216. O. Negbi, "Origin and Distribution of Early Iron Age Palestinian Bronzeworks," *Tel Aviv* 1 (1974): 168–72. She reassigned Hoard 1739, in which one of the axes was found, to stratum VIA rather than stratum VIB.

217. Catling, *Bronzework,* p. 92.

218. *Enkomi,* pp. 37–67.

Pl. 15. Ivory handle of iron knife, Tell Qasile, stratum XII [A. Mazar, "Excavations at Tell Qasile, 1973–1974: Preliminary Report," *IEJ* 25 (1975): pl. 7:B].

▲ *Pl. 16.* Temple, Tell Qasile, stratum X, locus 134 [*Qasile IEJ* 23, pl. 15:B].

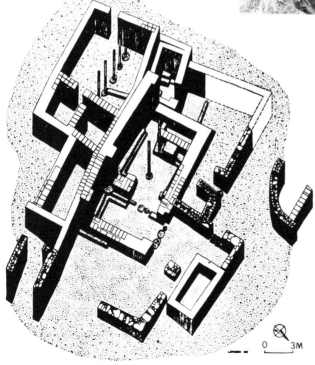

0   3M

Fig. 11. Isometric plan of stratum X temple, Tell Qasile [A. Mazar, "Excavations at Tell Qasile, 1973–1974, Preliminary Report," *IEJ* 25 (1975): fig. 4].

Excavations at Tell Jerishe[219] uncovered only a small portion of the site, but they provided a general outline of the history of the site. It was first settled during the second half of the third millennium B.C. and was inhabited down to the end of the tenth century, when it was finally abandoned. The flourishing Canaanite town of the Late Bronze Age was completely destroyed about 1200 B.C. by either the Israelites or the Sea Peoples; it was rebuilt on a smaller scale and a different plan on the southern part of the mound, which is consequently higher than the rest. The new settlers of the twelfth and eleventh centuries seem to have been Philistines and the history and material culture of Tell Jerishe in this period closely follow the pattern of nearby Tell Qasile. The ceramic development is the same; Tell Jerishe is one of the few sites where the last, debased Qasile X phase of Philistine pottery has been found.

The Philistine city at Tell Jerishe came to an end in an immense conflagration. The thick destruction layer of ashes and burnt brick is identical with the evidence of devastation at stratum X at Tell Qasile. Both destructions can be attributed to David's war against the Philistines.

DOR

The archaeological soundings conducted by Garstang at Tell el-Burj, which is north of Tantura and believed to be the site of ancient Dor, revealed that the town was first settled in the Late Bronze Age. This site was destroyed and then resettled in the Early Iron Age I.[220] The Wen Amun tale mentions the port city of Dor and its ruler Beder, king of the Tjekker—one of the Sea Peoples who invaded Egypt. The pottery from the Iron Age levels consisted of two fragments of Philistine jugs (photos have been published) and one Type 1 small bowl (which is only mentioned). One fragment is a body sherd of a jug (Type 6?) decorated in black and red; its geometric motif is made up of a rhombus and metope filled with alternate red and black net patterns.[221] The second sherd is part of a Type 6 jug decorated only with red stripes.[222] The small bowl[223] is white slipped and decorated with a wavy line and horizontal stripes around the rim. The excavator compared the bowl with a larger Philistine bowl from Ashkelon, but found that the two jug sherds were unlike the pottery commonly associated with the Philistines. The excavator believed the difference to result from the fact that Tjekker material culture was, in his opinion, similar to, but not identical with, that of the Philistines.

It appears, however, that all three vessels are indeed readily identifiable as Philistine pottery of Phase 2 (eleventh century) and are roughly contemporary with the journey of Wen Amun. Moreover, Philistine pottery and that associated with the Tjekker are identical; the contrasts arise only from the fact that there is no evidence of an early phase of Philistine pottery at Dor. Thus, until further excavations are conducted on the site, it will be impossible to determine whether or not there was a twelfth-century settlement there.

TEL ZEROR

Tel Zeror, located in the northern part of the Sharon Valley, is the westernmost of the many ancient sites in this region, most of which lie along the Via Maris.

Two occupational phases of the Iron Age I have been distinguished at the site.[224] The first (stratum XI) dates from the twelfth and early eleventh centuries and followed the destruction of the flourishing Late Bronze Age city with a metal industry (stratum XII); there is evidence of a total break and a deterioration in the culture. There is no evidence of large-scale buildings; only storage pits were discovered in stratum XI. The settlers seem to have lived in an open village in huts and tents—possibly it was an Israelite settlement. This stratum was destroyed by fire.

The subsequent, stratum X, settlement was occupied from the second half of the eleventh to the early tenth century and was concentrated in the northern part of the mound, where a well-built brick fortress was uncovered.[225] The pottery assemblage connected

219. E. L. Sukenik, *QDAP* 4 (1935): 208–09; *EAEHL*, pp. 575–78. The excavation material has not yet been published, but I was afforded the opportunity of examining the catalogs and plans at the Institute of Archaeology of the Hebrew University in Jerusalem.

220. *BBSAJ* 4 (1924): 35–45; *BBSAJ* 7 (1925): 80–82; and *EAEHL*, pp. 334–37.

221. *BBSAJ* 4 (1924): pl. III:1.

222. Ibid., pl. III:6.

223. For the Ashkelon parallel to the bowl, see *BBSAJ* 7 (1925): 80–81; and *Ashkelon, 1923*, p. 71, pl. II:12.

224. The Early Iron Age strata are XI and X (from the Early Iron Age to the first phase of the Late Iron Age) in area AI and stratum X in area AII; *Tel Zeror III*, pp. 3, 13–18.

225. Ibid., pp. 9–10.

with this structure is typical of the eleventh century and includes such vessels as a crude bottle (Type 9)[226] and an open cooking pot with an elongated rim.[227]

The cemetery of Tel Zeror (excavated on a hillock northwest of the mound on the site of a Late Bronze Age necropolis) is most illuminating both in its architectural and its rich funerary offerings. The major features are the multiple burials in stone-built cist tombs and their associated offerings of pottery and bronze vessels, bronze and iron weapons and jewelry, beads, and figurines.[228] This varied assemblage represents a far richer culture than the previous settlement. The pottery exhibits new features; some of them—such as oil lamps with closed nozzles—are unique in Palestinian pottery.[229] Others link the pottery with the Philistine ceramic culture (for example, the strainer-spout jug).[230] The pottery is badly worn and no trace of painted decoration remains, but we can assume that some of the vessels were originally decorated; the surface of the lion-headed rhyton (chap. 4, fig. 6), for example, bears still-discernible traces of typical Philistine decoration.

The vessels typical of Philistine pottery are crude in workmanship and shape, representing the latest, debased phase in the second half of the eleventh century. From this period comes the globular jug with double handle, which was either plain or painted with bichrome decoration.[231] A close parallel is a jug from level VI at Beth-Shean and another from the anthropoid burial in tomb 90.

The material culture represented in strata XI–X attests that the site was occupied by one of the Sea Peoples. The brick fortress may have been a stronghold of the Tjekker, who were settled in nearby Dor.

MEGIDDO

Situated on a low pass in the Carmel range, Megiddo was a great fortress city throughout antiquity; it owed its importance to a strategic position astride the Via Maris and dominating the Plain of Esdraelon.

226. Ibid., pls. XV:2, LX:3.
227. Ibid., pl. LXI:2.
228. *Tel Zeror II*, pp. 35–41; *Tel Zeror III*, pp. 67–74.
229. Ibid., *III*, pl. LX:4.
230. Ibid., *II*, pls. X:8, XLIV lower (tomb V). Tomb V belongs to the late eleventh–early tenth century; for other finds from this burial, *see* ibid., pl. X:3, 6, 11.
231. Ibid., *III*, pls. XV:1, LX:5.

The Early Iron Age is represented at Megiddo by three strata—VIIA, VIB, and VIA—which span a period from the twelfth to the end of the eleventh century b.c. Stratum VIIA, to a large extent, is a continuation of the Late Bronze Age II in its general plan and character. It clearly exhibits the influence of Egyptian culture on the Late Bronze Age city that was for centuries one of the Egypt's strongholds in Canaan.

Following the destruction of stratum VIIA, the city (from the last third of the twelfth to the end of the eleventh century) is represented by strata VIB and VIA. There is a sharp decline in the material culture in stratum VIB, and only in stratum VIA is there a notable renaissance. Stratum VIA was able to withstand the Israelite conquest until the time of David, when it was destroyed by a great fire.

Philistine cultural influence is evident from stratum VIIA to the end of stratum VIA. A detailed discussion of strata VII–VI will enable us to attribute absolute dates in the Iron Age to these strata and to the Philistine pottery found in them.

Stratum VIIA

Stratum VIIA, the first Iron Age stratum, is not adequately represented in the material published by the excavators. The starting point of our analysis will be the date and stratigraphy of building 3073, the "treasury" in the western wing of palace 2041 in the area AA[232] (see fig. 12). The reevaluation of the stratigraphic position of the treasury is of great importance because an ivory pen-box found there bears the cartouche of Ramesses III. The appearance of this pharaoh's name at Megiddo alongside Philistine pottery is highly significant, both for the absolute

232. B. Mazar was the first to recognize that the Late Bronze Age pottery assigned on the Megiddo plates to stratum VIIA actually belongs to stratum VIIB. However, he associated building 3073 with stratum VIIB, relying on the evidence of the Mycenaean sherds. As we shall see, however, these sherds cannot be utilized in determining the date of building 3073. *See* B. Maisler (Mazar), "The Chronology of the Beth-Shean Temples," *BIES* 16 (1951):16, n. 8 (Hebrew). H. Kantor makes the same assumption in her discussion of the date of the Megiddo and Fakhariyah ivories: "The Ivories from Floor 6 of Sounding IX," in C. W. McEwan et al., *Soundings at Tell Fakhariyah* (Chicago, 1958), pp. 63–64. On renewed examination, building 3073's stratigraphy was corrected by the late I. Dunayevsky. The stratigraphic discussion is based also on a checking of plans and material in the Oriental Institute of the University of Chicago.

chronology and for the historical implication of the connection with the Sea Peoples and their settlement in strongholds in Canaan.

In order to clarify the stratigraphy of the area east of the palace, it is necessary to examine the levels of stratum VIII. These show a slight ascent in ground level from east to west.[233] Following the destruction of the palace in stratum VIII, it was rebuilt in stratum VIIB,[234] but on a smaller scale; the entire west wing was never reconstructed. In the rebuilt area, the VIIB floors were cleared down to—or almost down to—the VIII level. Thus, for example, courtyard 2041 is on the same level in stratum VIIB as it was in stratum VIII. Room 3102 to the north was elevated only 30 cm. (from 154.05 m. in VIII to 154.35 m. in VIIB). The collapsed debris in the area of the stratum VIII palace not rebuilt in VIIB, on the other hand, was never cleared away, thus creating a noticeable elevation in VIIB. The east wall of locus 3112 in the complex of small buildings to the west of the stratum VIII palace was based at level 154.20 m., while the east wall of locus 3187, which stands above the 3112 wall in stratum VIIB, is based at 155.85 m.

This same phenomenon is evident in the progression of levels in the west wing of the VIIB palace, where they rise like a series of stairs ascending from the rubble of stratum VIII. In locus 3102 the level is 154.35 m.; in 3103, 154.65 m.; and the ascent continues in the direction of locus 3186, where the levels reach a height of 155.15 m. at the threshold of the locus and 155.05 m. within the locus proper.

An examination of the floor plan of the west wing of the stratum VIIB palace reveals a number of architectural elements that do not form a homogeneous structure. The western end of the palace terminates in a straight wall whose foundations gradually ascend from north to south—from 154.75 m. at the north end, 155.15 m. in the center, to 155.45 m. at the south end. This wall was destroyed by the addition of a completely incongruous structure in L7; it reappears in the floor plan of the VIIA palace and may be assumed to have originated only in stratum VIIA. If this architecturally foreign element is deleted from the VIIB plan, the west wall closed off, and the south end of locus 3186 reconstructed on the model of its north end, the resultant structure is a tripartite building whose three

rooms are arranged in a row and connected by openings placed on the same north-south axis. The entrance to this architectural unit would then be through the south wall of locus 3103. The structural element inconsistent with the VIIB floor plan is, however, perfectly in harmony with the VIIA plan and is actually an organic extension of locus 3073 (see fig. 12).

The analogy between the floor plans of building 3073 in VIIA and building 3186 in VIIB is most interesting. The former has three rooms opening on a north-south axis parallel to that of 3186; it actually appears to be a copy of the earlier building and may conceivably have fulfilled the same function as building 3186 in stratum VIIB. We can thus assume that the original location of at least some of the Megiddo Ivories was in building 3186 of the Late Bronze Age II stratum VIIB. This assumption would also conform with the artistic style of the ivories.[235] After the destruction of building 3186 and the construction of its VIIA counterpart, 3073, the ivories were deposited in this new treasury, possibly with the addition of some new pieces, including the ivory pen-box bearing the cartouche of Ramesses III.[236] Additional evidence for this assumption is provided by one of the Ramesses III scarabs found in locus 1814 in area CC, in a large paved room clearly related to stratum VIIA.[237]

The topographic situation in this area (blocks K, L7, L6) resulting from the destruction of stratum VIII forced the builders of stratum VIIA to drive the foundations of building 3073 deep into the rubble of stratum VIII. At this spot the floor level of 3073 (154.20 cm.) was dug beneath the level of stratum VIII; consequently, pottery from VIIB and even from VIII was brought to the surface of stratum VIIA in the neighborhood of the treasury. This phenomenon will be treated below in our discussion of the ceramic finds from the treasury and its immediate vicinity.

The ceramic finds in the treasury (3073 A–C) are not particularly rich. They include bowls,[238] which occur at Megiddo both in the Late Bronze Age and Iron Age strata, a cup-and-saucer,[239] and the upper part of a krater decorated with motifs characteristic of Late

233. *Meg. II*, fig. 382.
234. Ibid., figs. 383, 384.

235. Kantor, n. 232 above, p. 63.
236. *Meg. Ivories*, pp. 9–12, pl. 62:377.
237. *Meg. II*, p. 154, pl. 152:195. Note the special character of the finds.
238. *Meg. II*, pl. 68:12, 15.
239. Ibid., pl. 70:16.

Bronze Age II painted pottery.[240] However, there was no imported Mycenaean or Cypriot ware in the building. The pottery found in the area north of 3073 is somewhat more diversified: bowls characteristic of Megiddo VIII–VII,[241] a cup-and-saucer,[242] and a biconical jug characteristic of Late Bronze Age II Canaanite pottery.[243] Among the unpublished sherds from this area are Myc. IIIB and Cypriot imported pottery as well as several body sherds of Late Bronze Age II decorated ware.[244]

The published report lists no ceramic finds from locus 3067 (blocks K6–L6), west of the treasury, or from between locus 3073 and the structure that contains locus 3044; the unpublished material, however, includes a fragment of a Myc. IIIB vessel. In locus S=3044 (block K6) three Myc. IIIB sherds were found. As no other finds from this area are mentioned, this locus should apparently be ascribed to stratum VIIB (this locus does not appear in the publications).

Locus 3043, the paved area south of S=3044 in blocks L6–7, contained a rich collection of pottery[245] characteristic of stratum VIIB, and not, as stated by the excavators, of stratum VIIA. Moreover, the unpublished material from the area just south of this locus describes sherds of a krater with a horizontal handle and net-pattern decoration that has parallels in stratum VIIB,[246] a body sherd decorated with a net pattern and an animal stylized in a manner characteristic of local Late Bronze Age II painted pottery, and a body sherd decorated with crossing wavy lines—a recurring motif on decorated pottery of stratum VIIB.[247] These vessels indicate that locus 3043 should be reassigned to stratum VIIB.

Three objects came from the area south of locus 3073: a bowl with a bar handle typical of stratum VIIA,[248] a deep bowl[249] with decoration characteristic of the Late Bronze Age II tradition, and a fragment of a figurine of Astarte.[250] Although three identical Astarte figurines were found in stratum VIII,[251] this fragment is of little value in determining the date of the locus, for it may very well have been kept for an extended period of time. In general the locus seems to fit into strata VIIA–VIIB.

Locus 3185, the antechamber to the treasury, was completely empty of finds, but the vestibule and room leading to the antechamber (locus 3061) contained a wealth of pottery, including a number of vessels characteristic of strata VII–VI.[252] The area directly north of locus 3061 was also rich in easily defined vessels. Especially interesting are an upper fragment of a jar with a high bulging neck[253] (see chap. 5, fig. 7:14, 15) decorated in typical Late Bronze Age II fashion and a large pilgrim flask[254] whose shape and decoration are characteristic of the Late Bronze Age II flasks that persist until the beginning of the Iron Age. Among the unpublished sherds from locus N=3061 were a rim of a Cypriot milk bowl and a fragment of a Mycenaean vessel.

The above brief survey reveals that a large portion of the pottery from the immediate vicinity of the treasury, which was ascribed to stratum VIIA, in fact belongs to stratum VIIB; the reason for this is inherent in the unusual topographic situation of the treasury area.

Besides the Mycenaean pottery uncovered north of the treasury, a number of Myc. IIIB sherds were found in an area of private dwellings in area CC, block S10, locus W=1817.[255] They were assigned to stratum VIIA; but in this area it was very difficult to distinguish between strata VIIB and VIIA. In fact, the same ground plan is used for both strata.

Locus W=1817 is situated west of a section of a destroyed building with no clear floor and no stratigraphic basis for assigning this locus to stratum VIIA. The finds were somewhat unusual and not unlike that of locus 1818 (see below). They included a wall bracket,[256] a cup-and-saucer,[257] an ivory cosmetic dish[258]

240. Ibid., pl. 69:13.
241. Ibid., pl. 68:12, 15, 16.
242. Ibid., pl. 70:16.
243. Ibid., pl. 67:17.
244. In her discussion of the Fakhariyah ivories Kantor cites this group of sherds as one of the proofs that the Megiddo treasury belongs to stratum VIIB (*see* n. 232 above). The excavation report, however, states that these sherds were found in the area north of the treasury and not in the building proper.
245. *Meg. II*, p. 169.
246. Ibid., pl. 66:4.
247. Ibid., pl. 63:8.
248. Ibid., pl. 69:6.
249. Ibid., pl. 69:16.

250. Ibid., pl. 243:16.
251. Ibid., pl. 242:8–10.
252. Ibid., pls. 67:14; 68:12, 16.
253. Ibid., pl. 67:19.
254. Ibid., pl. 70:9.
255. Ibid., pl. 140:7–16, fig. 409.
256. Ibid., pl. 249:2.
257. Ibid., pl. 70:15.
258. Ibid., pl. 200:1.

(with parallels among the treasury ivories),[259] and numerous other vessels of steatite, ivory, and gold.

The Cypriot imported ware ascribed by the excavators to stratum VIIA includes Base-Ring I–II ware and White Slip II milk bowls. Since typologically this pottery cannot belong to VIIA, it is worthwhile to examine the stratigraphic position of these finds to investigate the possibility of reassigning them to stratum VIIB.

One of the Base-Ring vessels ascribed to VIIA is a *bilbil*[260] from area CC, where private dwellings of strata VIIB–VIIA were uncovered. The *bilbil* was found in locus 1818 (block S9), an open area outside the southern boundary of the inhabited area, and is thus not connected with any building whose stratigraphy is certain.[261] Moreover, as we noted above, the distinction between VIIA and VIIB in this area is extremely difficult to draw.

The ceramic assemblage of locus 1818 includes two bowls typical of strata VIII–VIIB, of a type that does not depart from a thirteenth-century context.[262] In addition, there is a group of unusual vessels: a pottery kernos and many vessels in more costly materials (ivory, alabaster, faience, semiprecious stones, and gold). Of special importance is an ivory cosmetic dish[263] whose shape and small bar handle resemble those of the cosmetic dishes found in the treasury.[264] A similar dish was found in locus W=1817. An ivory comb[265] is identical with one found in the treasury.[266] The collection seems to indicate a kind of cache similar in content to the assemblage in locus W=1817, and like that group it belongs wholly to the Late Bronze Age II. It should, therefore, be assigned to stratum VIIB; judging from the *bilbil* from locus 1818, there seems to be no reason to date this locus later than the thirteenth century B.C.

Two Base-Ring II bowls[267] were attributed to stratum VIIA, but this is typologically impossible since this type of vessel is not known to have existed in Canaan after the thirteenth century B.C. Hence it is necessary to reexamine their stratigraphic positions.[268] The first bowl was found in area AA (block K9), in locus S=3158, an open area south of the gate and of silo 3158. No architectural remains from either strata VIIB or VIIA were uncovered here, and the sole artifact (in either strata) was the Base-Ring bowl under discussion. It is clear, therefore, that the excavators ascribed this bowl to stratum VIIA on the basis of erroneous typological considerations and not stratigraphic evidence. It can be reassigned with certainty to VIIB.

The second bowl came from area DD (block K11), locus 5022,[269] a destroyed, unpaved room. The finds in the room are appropriate to stratum VIIB and include a dipper juglet characteristic of Megiddo strata VIIB–VI and a Cypriot milk bowl. It appears that the find is associated with locus 5022, but typologically belongs to locus 5023, the locus defining the same area in stratum VIIB[270] with no related finds of this period.

Two other Cypriot vessels erroneously assigned to VIIA can be placed in VIIB. These are two White Slip II milk bowls; the first,[271] from locus 5022, has been shown (above) to belong to VIIB; the second, from W=1817, area CC,[272] which contained a group of Mycenaean sherds, has also been shown to belong to VIIB.

Our examination has clearly shown that the three Base-Ring vessels and the two milk bowls that the excavators assigned to VIIA belong, in fact, to VIIB.

We have already mentioned that most of the local pottery assigned to VIIA is, like the imported ware, typologically more appropriate to VIIB. The following two sherds also belong in this group:

1. The upper part of a biconical jug[273] found in area CC (block S9), locus 1794. This locus is a room or courtyard adjoining locus 1834 of stratum VIIB. The difficulty in distinguishing between the two phases of stratum VII makes it highly probable that the jug fragment actually belongs to the VIIB locus (1834).[274]

2. A body sherd[275] from block K10, area DD, displaying decorative animal motifs characteristic of the Late Bronze Age II painted pottery. This was the only

259. *Meg. Ivories*, pl. 27.
260. *Meg. II*, pls. 67:20, 139:3.
261. Ibid., fig. 409.
262. Ibid., p. 155, pl. 69:4, 5.
263. Ibid., pl. 200:2.
264. *Meg. Ivories*, pl. 27.
265. *Meg. II*, pl. 201:9.
266. *Meg. Ivories*, pls. 16:108, 109; 17:111; 18:114, 115.
267. *Meg. II*, pl. 69:8, 9.

268. Ibid., p. 175, fig. 384.
269. Ibid., p. 182, fig. 412.
270. Ibid., fig. 411.
271. Ibid., pl. 69:10.
272. Ibid., pl. 140:17.
273. Ibid., pl. 67:18.
274. Ibid., fig. 409.
275. Ibid., pl. 140:18.

sherd in block K10 ascribed to VIIA, all the rest being assigned to stratum VII.[276] The reasons for this are not clear, but there seems to be neither typological nor stratigraphical justification.

Having established the true character of stratum VIIA's ceramic assemblage, we shall now consider the Philistine vessels belonging to this stratum. The publication presents a very deficient picture of the ceramic assemblage. Only one Philistine vessel was published out of a large number of Philistine sherds that can with certainty be ascribed to stratum VIIA.[277] The published vessel is a Type 1 bowl[278] (chap. 3, fig. 2:3) from locus 1799—a paved surface within an area of private dwellings of stratum VIIA[279]—in area CC, block R10.

The unpublished Philistine sherds listed below belong to stratum VIIA and come from the area of private dwellings in area CC.

1. Sherd of a Type 2 krater (pl. 17:4) found on a paved surface in locus 1793.

2. Upper fragment of a Type 6 jug (pl. 18:4) from locus W=1793.

3. Rim of a Type 2 krater (pl. 17:5) from the area south of locus 1824—a small room connected to a badly destroyed building.

4. A body sherd, perhaps of a jug (pl. 17:7).

It is important to note that these sherds can be related with a high degree of certainty to stratum VIIA. They all fall within the range of Phases 1 and 2; some can be definitely assigned to Phase 1 (see especially pls. 17:7 and 18:4).

Another group of Philistine sherds, of which only one was published, is also interesting in this connection. The excavators ascribed the entire group to stratum VII and made no attempt to distinguish between VIIB and VIIA. Thus a reexamination of this group and of the stratigraphic position of each sherd is necessary.

1. The only published sherd is part of a Type 1 bowl[280] found in block K10, area DD, in a section without buildings. The ceramic finds of this section were mixed, but included two milk bowl sherds[281] and fragments of a flask[282] typical of Megiddo VIB–VIA.[283] The assemblage as a whole, therefore, spans strata VIIB to VI, although the Philistine sherd can be related typologically to strata VIIA–VIB.

2. and 3. Two sherds of Type 1 bowls (pl. 17:6, 8) found in locus 2092, area BB, a room of a destroyed building south of temple 2048.[284] No other ceramic finds are mentioned from this room, but the pottery found in an adjacent room is characteristic of strata VIIB–VIIA.[285] Although the two Philistine sherds must be assigned on stratigraphic grounds to stratum VIIA, their decoration and general workmanship point to the second phase of Philistine pottery.

4. A body sherd (pl. 18:2) displaying a spiral motif with a Maltese cross in its center. It is from locus S=2058, south of temple 2048 and north of locus 2092, a location that produced several other Philistine sherds.

5. Sherd of a Type 1 bowl (pl. 18:3) from locus W=2092. This locus and its immediate vicinity also contained a number of other Philistine sherds.

276. Ibid., pl. 141:17, 21–26.
277. A rich collection of Philistine sherds from strata VII–VI is still unpublished. They are at present in the Oriental Institute of the University of Chicago, where they were examined by B. Mazar. I, too, had the opportunity to study these sherds and to check their provenances with the aid of the excavation's field catalogue. It is not clear why these sherds were never included (in sketch, photo, or even in the register of locus material) in the Megiddo excavation reports. Five more Philistine sherds are in the collection of the Israel Department of Antiquities in Jerusalem. Two of the latter, decorated with elaborate metopes, may be part of the same jug or stirrup jar; they come from locus N=5235 in area DD, stratum VI, and are numbered 39.663/12 and 39.663/13. Another sherd, with spiral decoration, comes from the same locus; the fourth, a Type 1 bowl fragment also decorated with a spiral decoration (39.663/9), comes from locus 5234 in square K11. Another Type 1 bowl fragment with spiral decoration was found in locus N=5235. All these pieces were found in the same area as the Philistine bowl (chap. 3, fig. 2:10) from stratum VIB. Loci 5234 and 5235 do not appear in the list of loci in the Megiddo publication, and no objects from them have been published. Also in the collection of the Israel Department of Antiquities is a fragment of a large vessel decorated with concentric rayed semicircles and debased palm motifs. Although not numbered, it probably comes from Megiddo too. The rayed decoration resembles that on the sherd in pl. 17:4 and especially that on the jug from Beth-Shean (fig. 13:6).
278. Meg. II, pls. 69:7; 139:11.
279. Ibid., p. 154, fig. 409.

280. Ibid., pl. 141:26.
281. Ibid., pl. 141:21, 22.
282. Ibid., pl. 141:23–25.
283. Ibid., pl. 80:7.
284. Ibid., fig. 403.
285. Ibid., p. 163.

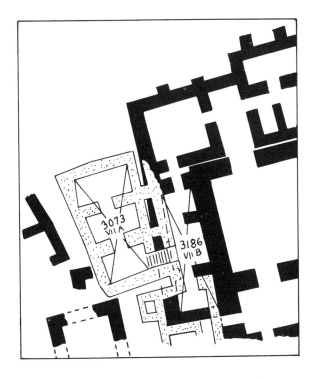

Fig. 12. Suggested plan of the treasury, Megiddo, stratum VIIA [*Meg. II,* fig. 384].

Pl. 17. Philistine sherds, Megiddo [Oriental Institute, Chicago].

1. Body sherd; white slip; black and brown-red decoration. (Area AA; square K8; locus E-2041; stratum VIII–VIIA.)   **2.** Krater, Type 2; white slip; red-purple decoration. (Area AA; square K8; locus E-2086, stratum VIIB.)

3. Body sherd; red decoration. (Area BB; locus 2084 A; stratum VIII–VIIA.)   **4.** Krater, Type 2; white slip; red decoration. (Area CC; square R9; locus 1793; stratum VIIA.)   **5.** Krater, Type 2; white slip; red and gray decoration. (Area CC; square Q9; locus S-1825; stratum VIIA.)

6, 8. Bowl, Type 1; red-brown decoration. (Area BB; square O13; locus 2092; stratum VIIA–VIIB.)

7. Body sherd; white slip; red and dark-brown decoration. (Area CC; square R8; locus N-1805; stratum VIIA.)

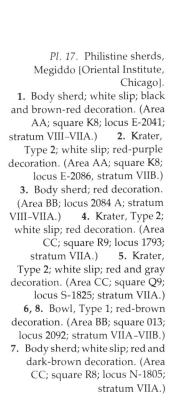

A second group of Philistine sherds requiring reexamination was associated by the excavators with strata VIII–VIIB but actually belongs to stratum VIIA.

1. A Type 2 krater fragment from locus W=5083 (area BB, square M13, north of temple 2048).[286] This locus, related by the excavators to stratum VIII, is merely a corner formed by two walls that cannot be associated with any definitely stratified buildings. The sole finds here are a Cypriot bowl (of the Late Bronze Age strata VIII–VIIB) and a scarab tentatively dated to the Nineteenth and Twentieth dynasties.[287] A single Philistine sherd found in this locus cannot belong to stratum VIII; it was apparently assigned by the excavators on the basis of erroneous typological assumptions.

2. A sherd of a white-slipped Type 1 bowl with a brown spiral decoration[288] was published as belonging to stratum VIIB. Here again it appears that the sherd was erroneously assigned. It was found in locus W=5006 (area DD), an open area with no building remains in stratum VIIB, although it does include a section of the structure 5007 in stratum VIIA.[289] It is, therefore, possible that this Philistine sherd should be associated instead with structure 5007 and, hence, stratum VIIA.

3. and 4. Two unpublished Philistine sherds also related by the excavators to stratum VIIB. (3) The body sherd of a krater (pl. 17:2) from stratum VIIB, locus E=2086, in area AA, an open area with no building remains. The same area in stratum VIIA is identified as locus E=2041 and contained another Philistine sherd (pl. 17:1), apparently from stratum VIIA.[290] (4) A fragment of the strainer and spout of a Type 6 jug (pl. 18:1) from locus N=1843, in area CC, an open area with surrounding buildings belonging to strata VIIB and VIIA.[291]

Lastly, we must mention three Philistine sherds found in block R15, an area on the western slope of the mound that was not described in the publication. Two of the sherds are fragments of a Type 2 krater (pl. 18:5, 6) with decorative motifs carelessly drawn in thin, unsteady lines. One of the sherds bears a Philistine bird

motif—the only example of this motif found in the entire excavation (another such sherd was found in the dump). The third sherd is part of a Type 6 jug (pl. 18:7) very similar in ware and workmanship to another Type 6 fragment found in a clear stratum VIIA context (see pl. 18:4). Although the evidence is not sufficient to determine the stratigraphy of these sherds, typologically they belong to VIIA, not to VIIB.

Our examination of the Philistine pottery of stratum VIIA and the large group of Philistine sherds that may be assigned to it reveals that this stratum already contained Philistine pottery. It is difficult to assign the individual sherds to different phases of Philistine pottery, since most are body sherds from which the type of the complete vessel cannot be deduced. The Philistine pottery of Megiddo VIIA can be compared, for the most part, with that of the early phases of Philistine pottery. From the large quantity of pottery found, it can be inferred that a garrison of Sea Peoples was stationed at Megiddo. This fact, in addition to the other ceramic evidence, indicates that Megiddo VIIA was contemporaneous with Qasile XII. In terms of absolute chronology, the beginning of VIIA can be dated to the reign of Ramesses III by the scarab and the cartouche on the ivory pen-box bearing his name. The end of the stratum can be determined by the latest datable object found—a bronze pedestal incised with the name of Ramesses VI (1156–1148).[292]

Stratum VI

The city of stratum VIB was erected on the ruins of stratum VIIA. It differed considerably from its predecessor, and, judging from its buildings and the meager finds, it could not have been a large settlement. It was founded around 1150 B.C. and experienced its greatest prosperity around 1120 B.C. The city did not last long; it was probably destroyed in the first half of the eleventh century.

The following Philistine vessels can be ascribed with certainty to stratum VIB:

1. A Type 1 bowl from square K11, area DD (chap. 3, fig. 2:10).

2. A body sherd of a jug with a stylized lotus motif from square K11, area DD (chap. 3, fig. 50:6).

3. A sherd of a Type 1 bowl (pl. 19:3).

286. Ibid., pl. 137:11.
287. Ibid., pls. 152:154 and 157:154.
288. Ibid., pl. 138:23.
289. Ibid., fig. 412.
290. Ibid., figs. 384, 385.
291. Ibid., fig. 409.

292. *Meg. II*, pp. 135–36, 156.

Pl. 18. Philistine sherds, Megiddo [Oriental Institute, Chicago].
1. Jug, Type 6; white slip; red-purple and black decoration. (Area CC, square R8; locus N-1843; stratum VIIB.) 2. Body sherd; white slip; black decoration. (Area BB; square 013; locus S-2058; above the fire stratum, stratum VII.) 3. Bowl, Type 1; brown decoration. (Area BB; square 013; locus W-2092; stratum VII.) 4., 5. Two krater sherds, Type 2; white slip; light-black and brown-reddish decoration. (Square R15; east slope. Museum registration No. A13913 a–b. Field catalogue No. 963.) 6. Jug, Type 6; heavy white slip; black-reddish decoration. (Area CC; square W-1793; stratum VIIA. Registration No. 6273.) 7. Jug, Type 6; white slip, black and red-purple decoration. (Square R15; east slope. Museum registration No. 13913. Field catalogue No. 973.

Pl. 19. Philistine sherds, Megiddo [Oriental Institute, Chicago].
1. Krater, Type 17; red slip; black decoration. (Area CC; square R8; locus S-1805. Registration No. p. 6275. According to type—stratum VIA.)
2. Bowl, Type 1; white slip; red-brownish decoration. (Locus N-1789; stratum VL.)
3. Bowl, Type 1; white slip; red-brown decoration. (Area AA; square L7; locus 3031; stratum VIB.)
4. Jug, Type 12, brown clay, gray core; white slip, black and red decoration. (Area AA; square K-L 7-8; locus 3021; stratum VIA.)
5. Krater, Type 1; white slip, dark brown and red decoration. (Area AA; square K8; locus 2073; stratum VIA; Meg. II, pl. 144:23.)
6. Krater, Type 1; perhaps belonging to same bowl as no. 5. Same ware and finish. (Area AA; square R8; locus 2073; stratum VIA.)
7. Body sherd of a globular vessel; white slip, burnished along body; red-brown and black decoration. (Locus 1877. Registration No. A13963.)

Stratum VIB is exceptionally poor in Philistine pottery. This can be explained both in the light of the meager pottery finds of the stratum as a whole and of the difficulty in differentiating between strata VIB and VIA. Remains of VIB were found predominantly in area AA (loci 2159, 2080), but there too the stratum was not easily distinguished. In area DD, square K11, only a small section contained remains of VIB; in areas CC and BB the excavators found it impossible to distinguish between VIB and VIA.[293] We will attempt to reassign a number of sherds that were originally attributed to VIA but belong typologically to VIB. Although there are striking contrasts between strata VIB and VIA, and they share no common architectural features, an unmistakable continuity can be noted in their ceramic finds. Most of the pottery of stratum VIA consists of types known from strata VIIA and VIB; in addition there are several new types, some representing the development and debasement of earlier Philistine pottery and others introducing entirely new pottery shapes into the local repertoire.

We shall first consider the Philistine sherds that were attributed to VIA but are typologically inconsistent with the pottery of that stratum. We shall attempt to ascertain the validity of their stratigraphic identification with VIA and consider the possibility of attributing them to VIB.

The "Orpheus" jug (chap. 3, fig. 28:1), which has white slip and bichrome decoration, is an outstanding example of the debased Philistine pottery of Megiddo VIA. The jug was found in area AA, room 2101, a part of building 2072,[294] the largest public edifice in VIA. B. Mazar believed this building was the residence of the Philistine governor.[295] Because most of the building was paved, its contents could be definitely attributed to VIA. Room 2101, however, was not paved, and it contained scanty and uncharacteristic finds. In stratum VIB,[296] a small structure occupied the area of room 2101, and it seems plausible that the jug may have originated in that building. There is, however, no concrete proof for this assumption. Another possibility is that this jug, being a rare and exceptionally fine vessel—in comparison with the usual pottery of that era—may have been preserved over a long period of time; its quality thus makes it compatible with the special character of building 2072 in which it was found.

Two sherds of Type 1 bowls can be similarly explained. The first[297] is a white-slipped sherd with brown decoration found in locus 5153, area DD. This locus, an unpaved room, also contained a pyxis of local type[298] that on typological grounds can be attributed to VIB. The second sherd[299] is white slipped with red and black decoration and came from locus 5224 in area DD, blocks K11–12. In the whole of area DD, only blocks K11–12 contained building remains that could be related to stratum VIB, and these remains contained Philistine sherds identical to the above two ascribed to VIA. It would seem, then, that these two sherds should be reassigned to VIB[300] on both stratigraphical and typological grounds.

The following unpublished Philistine sherds are ascribed by the excavators to VIA; on typological grounds, we believe that they should be assigned to VIB.

1. Part of a Type 12 jug (pl. 19:4) from locus 3021, area AA.

2. Two sherds of a Type 2 krater (pl. 19:5, 6), from locus 2073, area AA. This is an open area south of building 2072 of stratum VIA. The few finds from this locus seem to be typologically earlier than the assemblages of stratum VIA to which the excavators assigned locus 2073.[301] The published pottery includes a small hemispherical bowl,[302]—a type of vessel running through strata VII–VIA—the upper part of a shallow bowl with rows of suspended triangles[303] (related to Philistine decoration), and two fragments of Philistine kraters of Type 2 (pl. 19:5, 6), whose white slip and style of decoration are strongly indicative of an origin

293. Ibid., p. 22, fig. 385.
294. Ibid., fig. 386, square K9.
295. Mazar, *The Philistines*, p. 10, n. 17.
296. *Meg. II*, p. 37, figs. 83, 386.

297. Ibid., pl. 143:18.
298. Ibid.. pl. 77:7.
299. Ibid., pl. 143:17.
300. During the 1972 Megiddo excavations under the direction of Y. Yadin (*see* Yadin, *BA* 33 [1970]: 66–96), pottery assemblages of stratum VIA were uncovered that, for the most part, repeated the previous picture of the stratum VIA pottery. A unique find is a handleless Type 1 bowl that is decorated with debased spirals yet retains the white slip, which disappeared almost completely in this level. It thus became evident that white-slipped bowls survived into stratum VIA, although only sporadically.
301. *Meg. II*, fig. 386.
302. Ibid., pl. 78:9.
303. Ibid., pl. 79:4.

in stratum VIB. They may be connected with VIB structures[304] underlying locus 2072.

Our reexamination of the Philistine sherds ascribed by the excavators of Megiddo to VIA (or to VI with no attempt at a more precise subdivision) shows clearly that they are typologically alien to the debased Philistine pottery of that stratum and are more characteristic of VIB (Phase 2 of Philistine pottery), to which they should henceforth be assigned.

To sum up our discussion of the Philistine pottery of Phases 1 and 2 at Megiddo,[305] it should be noted that the greatest concentration of Philistine ware is found in stratum VIIA (including unpublished sherds and those erroneously related by the excavators to VIIB or VIII). Most of these sherds can be assigned to Phase 1, although typologically (in general workmanship and decoration) some belong to Phase 2. Only a very few Philistine sherds were originally ascribed to VIB; but we have endeavored to show that a number of other Philistine sherds ascribed to VIA in reality belong to VIB. Most of these are characteristic of the second phase of Philistine pottery.

On the ruins of the city of stratum VIB arose the newly planned, well-built, and densely settled city of stratum VIA. Large and spacious structures were discovered in this stratum; the largest one, building 2072, the so-called governor's residence, was unearthed in area AA. The material culture of stratum VIA, with its unusually rich pottery finds and abundant metal tools, is comparable to that of Tell Qasile X. There are signs of renewed contact with the surrounding lands—for example, in the White Painted I bowl[306] imported from

Cyprus and in the appearance of the Phoenician-type globular flasks and jugs that were also the hallmark of Tell Qasile X.

In stratum VIA the Philistine vessels characteristic of Phases 1 and 2 disappear, to be replaced by a group of vessels representing the assimilation of a number of true Philistine types and the advent of entirely new types. The vessels of this group share several common traits: levigated, well-fired ware, continuous irregular burnishing, bichrome violet-red and black decoration, and motifs such as the spiral, concentric semicircles, triangles, overall net pattern, zigzag pattern, and Maltese cross. In all these motifs, the influence of the Philistine tradition of ceramic decoration is clearly evident.

The vessels of stratum VIA fall into two distinct categories: (1) vessels which in both shape and decoration exhibit a link with the original Philistine tradition; and (2) vessels characteristic of the local Iron Age I pottery types in shape but in decoration revealing a connection with the Philistine tradition. The first category includes:

1. A Type 18 krater (chap. 3, fig. 60:6), which provides clear evidence of the connection between the pottery of Megiddo VIA and Qasile X. The krater comes from locus 3012 in area AA, a locus rich in pottery typical of stratum VIA. The attribution of this locus to stratum VIA is indisputable. Other vessels from this locus are also found in Qasile X: for example, a large carinated bowl,[307] a pilgrim flask of the type common during the Late Bronze Age II,[308] a second flask typical of stratum VIA (with bichrome decoration and a Maltese cross in the center),[309] and, finally, a flask resembling the aforementioned in shape, slip, and decoration that has close parallels in the Phoenician-type bichrome flasks appearing in Qasile X.[310] The Type 18 krater and other vessels found with the flask in this locus clearly demonstrate a close correlation between Megiddo VIA and Qasile X.

2. A krater[311] far removed from the Philistine prototype belongs both in workmanship and decoration

---

304. Ibid., fig. 385.
305. Of significance here is a sherd that cannot be classified with complete certainty as Philistine. It is a body fragment of a white-slipped, burnished, globular vessel (pl. 19:7) decorated in reddish-brown and black with rows of scales with dots. Although the scale motif is known in Philistine pottery, it is not employed as a fill for the entire zone of decoration, as is the case here, nor is it similar to the style of this piece. The closest parallel in ware, general workmanship, and decoration is a sherd from tomb 1101 at Megiddo, dated to the Iron Age I and decorated with elongated triangles formed of scale patterns and bird motifs rendered in a highly naturalistic manner quite unlike any Philistine style. In our opinion, neither sherd is to be considered Philistine; they are nevertheless connected with Aegean culture (*Meg. T.*, pls. 8:1; 87:2).
306. *Meg. II*, pl. 78:20.

307. Ibid., pl. 78:12; *Qasile IEJ 1*, fig. 5:8.
308. *Meg. II*, pl. 80:5; *Qasile IEJ 1*, fig. 6:6.
309. *Meg. II*, pl. 80:3; *Qasile IEJ 1*, fig. 6:4.
310. *Meg. II*, pl. 80:2; *Qasile IEJ 1*, pl. 28:16, 19; *see also* n. 203 above.
311. *Meg. II*, pls. 85:5 and 144:15.

to the last Philistine pottery (Phase 3), characteristic of Megiddo VIA.

3. A Type 1 bowl[312] (designated as belonging to stratum VI, with no subdivision) is important because of its close affinities with a bowl from Beth-Shean VI (figs. 14:2 cf. 13:2).

4. A stirrup jar (chap. 3, fig. 17:6) decorated with a combination of net and triangle patterns. Not far from it were found a cylindrical bottle (chap. 3, fig. 34:5) and a horn-shaped vessel (chap. 3, fig. 40:2) displaying similar decoration.

5. A double pyxis (chap. 3, fig. 18:7) decorated with a combination of concentric semicircles and an overall net pattern.

6. A quadruple pyxis (chap. 3, fig. 18:9) decorated with an overall net pattern.

7. A large group of Type 6 jugs, some of which have retained traces of Philistine decoration (chap. 3, fig. 27:4, 5, 7), while others have lost them completely and are decorated only with vertical lines.

8. The Type 17 jug discussed in chapter 3 (fig. 59:1) should also be ascribed to stratum VI.

Vessels of cultic character, such as the lion-headed rhyton and the group of kernoi discussed in chap. 4, (pls. 2, 5, 14), also belong to this group of stratum VI vessels, although their special character may indicate that they originated in an earlier phase.

The second category of vessels includes:

1. A bowl standing on a base of three loop handles. It is decorated with a triangle motif, net pattern, and Maltese cross—all common Philistine decorations. The excavators note that this bowl is characteristic of Megiddo VIB–VIA.[313]

2. A krater with a base of three loop handles. It is decorated with an overall net pattern (this vessel too is noted as coming from strata VIB–VIA).[314]

3. Pilgrim flasks with a Maltese cross as the central motif. Two variations are found: the flask with a round mouth[315] and the flask with a spoon mouth.[316]

It is interesting that while the vessels of this second category (Philistine decoration on local Palestinian shapes) already appear in stratum VIB alongside pure

Phase 2 Philistine pottery, the vessels of the first category, whose shape and decoration are debased and assimilated Philistine types, are found in VIA alone. These are the vessels of the last phase (Phase 3) of Philistine pottery at Megiddo.

Megiddo VIA was totally destroyed by a fire, whose traces are visible throughout. The thick ash layers, the burnt bricks, and the profusion of buried pottery all parallel Qasile X, which suffered a similar fate. Megiddo VIA was destroyed by David, after he had broken the military supremacy of the Philistines and their hold on the Via Maris.

'AFULA

The Early Iron Age level (stratum III) of 'Afula, which followed the Late Bronze Age occupation known mainly from burials, was uncovered in a strip almost twenty-five meters long in the southwestern part of the mound.[317]

In stratum III the main building is constructed of brick walls on stone foundations and includes some four broad rooms along three sides of a large courtyard. One of the rooms is divided by a row of four columns. Two floors, IIIb and IIIa, could be distinguished in the building at 'Afula. Stratum IIIb contained pottery that continued the local pottery tradition of the Late Bronze Age, together with some Early Iron Age ware; this phase has been dated to the first half of the twelfth century. Stratum IIIa can be dated by the Philistine ware,[318] which appeared with pottery of the previous phase—including storage jars with ridged necks and shallow cooking pots with collar rims—as well as by new types characteristic of the eleventh century.

The Philistine pottery found in this level (only a small percentage of the total, consisting mainly of incomplete vessels and sherds) lacks in both shape and decoration the elegance of the Philistine *floruit* and suggests an eleventh-century date. It included Type I bowls (chap. 3, fig. 1:10, 11) and fragments of Type 6 jugs.[319] A sherd with a rayed half-circle decoration has analogies at Megiddo (pl. 17:4) and points to Cretan prototypes.

The settlement of stratum III (a–b) spans the twelfth

312. Ibid., pls. 85:2 and 144:13.
313. Ibid., pls. 74:10 and 79:4.
314. Ibid., pls. 79:5; 85:6.
315. Ibid., pl. 80:3.
316. Ibid., pls. 74:16; 80:7.

317. 'Afula, pp. 30–35, fig. 3; EAEHL, p. 35.
318. 'Afula, p. 34.
319. Ibid., fig. 15:9, 10. It is also possible that sherds 11 and 16 are part of a Type 6 jug.

and most of the eleventh centuries. Destroyed at the end of the eleventh century, perhaps during the reign of Saul, it apparently remained deserted until the ninth century B.C.

The excavation of the Iron Age I eastern cemetery has provided a collection of Philistine vessels that, on the whole, parallel those from stratum IIIa. The majority belong to the debased phase of Philistine pottery,[320] especially the bowl in figure 1:11 of chapter 3. A jug (chap. 3, fig. 56:2), unique in shape and decoration, cannot be readily classified with any of the phases and styles of Philistine pottery, although it belongs to the monochrome variant of Philistine pottery, which may reflect an early phase.

BETH-SHEAN

Beth-Shean was one of the most important Egyptian strongholds during the Late Bronze Age and Early Iron Age. It is only briefly referred to in the biblical sources, which relate that Israel "did not drive out the inhabitants of Beth-Shean and its villages" (Judg. 1:27; see also Josh. 17:11–12). The Philistines are mentioned in connection with the exposure of the bodies of Saul and his sons on the walls of Beth-Shean—a story that may indicate the presence of a Philistine garrison or settlement there (see chap. 5, pp. 268–76).

Frances James's publication of the very complex Iron Age strata at Beth-Shean has made it possible to reevaluate the structures, stratigraphy, and finds of this period.[321] Level VI, in its main and late phases, contains elements that indicate the cultural and ethnic background of the inhabitants of the town proper and of the corresponding coffin groups of the northern cemetery.[322] This level is characterized by a strong Egyptian influence in both the architecture and the finds, especially in buildings 1500 and 1700, which seem to have been erected in the twelfth century following the destruction of level VII. Doorjambs, lintels, and cornices were found among the large number of well-cut building stones, and Egyptian-type T-shaped doorsills that fit the doorjambs were discovered in situ. More than twenty fragments with hieroglyphs were unearthed. The pottery finds are domestic in nature and include local Canaanite types and many vessels of Egyptian shape.

320. Ibid., fig. 20:7.
321. *B-SH Iron, see* esp. chaps. 2, 13, 14, 16.
322. *B-SH Cemetery*, pp. 146–50.

The lintel of the Egyptian official Ramesses-Weser-Khepesh, bearing the cartouche of Ramesses III, shows that the site was rebuilt under the aegis of that pharaoh. Found beneath locus 1522 of level V, the lintel probably belongs to level VI, since it corresponds in all respects to the Egyptian-type doorjambs. No doubt the statue of Ramesses III found in level V was also originally a feature of level VI; it illustrates the attempt made to Egyptianize Beth-Shean during the reign of Ramesses III.

Frances James suggested that buildings 1500 and 1700 were the headquarters of Ramesses III's "Northern Command" and served the military and administrative staff of the Egyptian garrison stationed at Beth-Shean.

As a whole Beth-Shean VI represents the culmination of the Twentieth Dynasty's Egyptianization of the city. In the preceding period (level VII, Nineteenth Dynasty) Beth-Shean also experienced an intensive Egyptian occupation. The idea that in both periods the city was an Egyptian stronghold is borne out by the coffin burials corresponding to the level VII occupation and continuing down to the end of the level VI occupation. The coffins of the later group contain burials assignable to the Sea Peoples, probably the Philistines who were part of the garrison of Beth-Shean during the Twentieth Dynasty. The pottery finds on the mound proper also indicate Aegean influence and Philistine presence at Beth-Shean, although the scarcity of Philistine pottery is very marked. The pottery types of level VI apparently span a long period, from the beginning of the twelfth century down to the end of the eleventh and beginning of the tenth century; this period is parallel to that of strata VIIA, VIB, and VIA at Megiddo, and there are close analogies between the two assemblages.

Of help in pinpointing the date at which level VI began at Beth-Shean is the Myc. IIIC:1b pottery (pl. 20:1–3) positively identified by Vronwy Hankey.[323] The pottery in question consists of a large stirrup jar (pl. 20:3) from locus 1586 (early level VI)[324] and some

323. V. Hankey, "Late Mycenaean Pottery at Beth Shan," *AJA* 70 (1966): 169–71, pl. 45; idem, "Mycenaean Pottery in the Middle East," *BSA* 62 (1967): 127–28.
324. Hankey, in "Late Mycenaean Pottery," p. 169, mistakenly attributed it to locus 1596. In *B-SH Iron*, pp. 23–24, fig. 49:4, James used this stirrup jar as evidence that Myc. IIIB pottery (as well as Cypriot vessels) was still in use in level VI; at that time the jar had not yet been correctly identified as Myc. IIIC:1.

fragmentary pieces; among the latter, the most distinctively decorated is a body sherd (pl. 20:1) closely related to the locally made Myc. IIIC:1 pottery from Ashdod (fig. 3:7). The appearance of Myc. IIIC:1b pottery at Beth-Shean is additional proof that level VI began at the very beginning of the twelfth century B.C.

The Philistine pottery types found at Beth-Shean are of the debased version typical of the last phase of Philistine pottery (the eleventh century B.C.). One exception is an elaborately decorated sherd (fig. 13:9) that was not well stratified and was assigned to level V.[325] The texture of this sherd, its heavy white slip and red and black elongated triangles all indicate that true Philistine pottery *was* indeed in use at Beth-Shean. The decoration is reminiscent of that of a jar found on the floor of the stratum XII temple at Tell Qasile (chap. 3, pl. 39:2).

A comparison of the pottery shapes from Megiddo and Beth-Shean (figs. 13, 14) shows that their last phases were contemporary. Evidently the two cities were also destroyed at the same time. In Beth-Shean level VI and in stratum VIA at Megiddo, the late Philistine pottery types are as follows: a debased version of the Philistine bell-shaped bowl (fig. 13:1) and a bowl with vestigial handles and red and black decoration (fig. 13:2), which is paralleled only at Megiddo in

stratum VI (fig. 14:2). A variant of Philistine pottery is a rim fragment of a krater (fig. 13:3) with a cream wash and purple decoration with triglyphs and suspended half circles; the latter recur on a krater from stratum VI at Megiddo (fig. 14:3). The strainer-spout jug is represented in late stratum VI (fig. 13:4) with traces of painted decoration; a plain version of this type was also found (fig. 13:5). A unique jug (fig. 13:6) shows a crudely executed decorative motif based on concentric rayed half circles; again, this is related to figure 13:3 as well as to Megiddo figure 14:3 and to the Philistine-derivative pottery from Tell Deir 'Alla. A pilgrim flask with spoon (fig. 13:7) belongs to the group of flasks represented at Megiddo VI (fig. 14:5).

The ceramic material of Megiddo stratum VIA and Beth-Shean late level VI exhibits many common features; early level VI at Beth-Shean with its Myc. IIIC:1b pottery is probably analogous with stratum VIIA at Megiddo, although Myc. IIIC:1 sherds are absent in the latter. The two levels, however, can be considered contemporary on the basis of the presence of cartouches of Ramesses III. Both sites evince Egyptian influence as well as Philistine features.

TEL DAN

Tel Dan (Tell el-Qadi) is situated at the foot of Mount Hermon in northern Israel. The name Dan, well known from the biblical phrase "from Dan to Beersheba," first appears in Genesis 14:14. The city of Dan was originally called Laish, but the tribe of Dan changed the name after its conquest (Judg. 18:29; Josh. 19:47).

The stratigraphic sequence of the beginning of the Iron Age, as it emerges from the excavation on the site, can best be traced in area B.[326] Pits and silos are the dominant feature of the first Iron Age stratum, VI. These were dug into the debris of the latest phase of the Late Bronze Age stratum VII. The pits yielded a representative assemblage of Early Iron pottery, including a complete pithos, fragments of a collar-rim pithos, cooking pots, jars, jugs, and flasks—some of which are decorated with red and black bands. The closest comparison to this assemblage comes from Hazor XII, which, like Dan VI, is a seminomadic set-

325. This was recognized by F. James as the only genuine "Philistine" sherd found at Beth-Shean (*B-SH Iron*, p. 69). In the same area, pottery that can be ascribed to level VI was found in loci 1159 and 1158c. On page 137, in a contradictory remark, James writes that absolutely no decorated "Philistine" ware occurs at Beth-Shean. In addition to the pottery that is presented here in figure 13, several other fragments from level VI may possibly be related to Philistine pottery, although without a firsthand examination, no final conclusion can be reached. These include a sherd bearing traces of red decoration with a row of triangle motifs (*B-SH Iron*, fig. 52:7), the mouth and upper part of a jug reminiscent in outline and stripe decoration of the upper part of a strainer-spout jug (ibid., fig. 52:19), and the upper fragment of a stirrup jar made in thin well-fired, cream-colored ware with a smooth surface (ibid., fig. 54:3). James does not indicate that the last named is a Mycenaean sherd, but we venture to propose that it belongs to either a Philistine stirrup jar or Myc. IIIC:1 vessel. From the same locus (1733) comes a fragment James calls Mycenaean ware; but again its description (thin greenish-buff ware, smooth creamy surface, and black paint) could indicate another Myc. IIIC:1 sherd. These two come from the small houses north of house 1700 and belong to lower level VI, which would make their identification as Myc. IIIC:1 still more acceptable.

326. Excavation results communicated by A. Biran, Notes and News, *IEJ* 26 (1976): 54–55.

Pl. 20. Body fragments (1, 2 dap) and stirrup jar (3) of Myc. IIIC:1 ware, Beth-Shean [From the Collection of the Israel Department of Antiquities and Museums, 32.304, 32.305, 1043. V. Hankey, "Mycenaean Pottery in the Middle East," *BSA* 62 (1967): pl. 29:a–c].

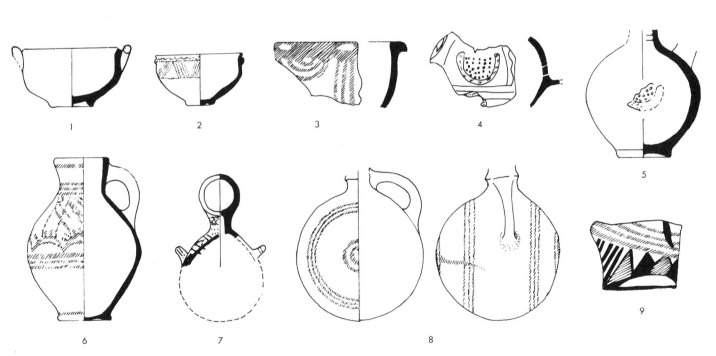

Fig. 13. Selected pottery, Beth-Shean, stratum VI.
1. Small bowl in dark-brown ware with buff surface, loc. 1721 [*B-SH Iron*, fig. 52:21].　　**2.** Small bowl in reddish-brown ware painted in purple and black [*B-SH Iron*, fig. 50:17].　　**3.** Rim fragment of large bowl; gritty, light-brown ware with cream wash and purple paint, loc. 1282 [*B-SH Iron*, fig. 49:15].　　**4.** Strainer-spout jug with light-brown slip and purple paint, loc. 1094 [*B-SH Iron*, fig. 2:4].　　**5.** Strainer-spout jug in red ware, loc. 1198 [*B-SH Iron*, fig. 56:7].　　**6.** Jug in gray ware with purple paint, loc. 1186, stratum VI [*B-SH Iron*, fig. 56:2].　　**7.** Flask in yellow-brown ware with yellowish slip and brown-red paint, loc. 1158 [*B-SH Iron*, fig. 22:18]. Block B-6 (see *B-SH Iron*, p. 68) is assigned to lower level V but in fact belongs to a group of vessels that typologically fit level VI.　　**8.** Globular jug in brown ware with black grits on surface and purple and black paint. East pit in loc. 1588 [*B-SH Iron*, fig. 51:11].　　**9.** Sherd of Philistine ware. Gray fabric with brown wash and purple and black paint, loc. 1167, block B–6 (*B-SH Iron*, p. 69) [*B-SH Iron*, fig. 24:1].

tlement, an initial phase of the process of permanent settlement.

Over the pits and silos of stratum VI were erected the structures of stratum V, which were destroyed by a fire in the mid-eleventh century. The material culture of strata VI and V, which are similar in their pottery repertoire, included the diagnostic collar-rim jars.

The finds relevant to the Philistines were discovered in a large stone-lined pit cut in the eastern section of the Middle Bronze rampart (area Y) during the 1971 season.[327] The pit contained a large store jar and a handleless pithos. In the jar were found animal bones and a number of vessels—cooking pots typical of Iron Age I, two chalices, and fragments of a white-slipped Philistine jug decorated in red with a Philistine bird design. There were also fragments of a large krater with vertical handles; the latter followed the local Canaanite tradition but was decorated with a well-executed Philistine bird and a monochrome geometric design. Near the store jar lay fragments of a typical Philistine stirrup jar. The krater may be of local manufacture and a derivative of Philistine pottery; the other finds are more typical of the pottery of Philistia. This combination may indicate both trade connections and local imitations. The cache can help ascertain the background of the Danite conquest and settlement at Laish, which probably took place in the middle of the twelfth century.

A connection between the tribe of Dan and the Danuna, a tribe of the Sea Peoples not mentioned in the Bible, was suggested by Y. Yadin,[328] who equated the two tribes. The nature of the Tel Dan cache tends to support this proposal and points to the common cultural background of the Sea Peoples.

TELL DEIR ʿALLA

Tell Deir ʿAlla, one of the most prominent mounds in the Jordan Valley, is generally identified with biblical Succoth.[329] Excavations were carried out on the site by H. J. Franken from 1960 on. The transition from the Late Bronze Age to the Iron Age cultures was investigated mainly by stratigraphic and not typological studies. In the publication of the excavation, this aim was more than achieved: the finds were treated *in*

vacuo, and no comparative studies or analysis of other relevant objects were undertaken.

The Early Iron Age settlement is represented by a complicated series of occupation levels spanning the period of the twelfth to the tenth centuries B.C. This occupation succeeds the Late Bronze Age temple complex, which was destroyed by an earthquake and fierce conflagration. This destruction can be dated by a royal cartouche on a broken Egyptian faience vase of Queen Tewosret (1205–1194 B.C., according to the excavator),[330] the wife of Seti II. Confirmation of this date is provided by a Carbon-14 test of one of the burnt roof beams of the latest Late Bronze sanctuary, the end of which coincides with the beginning of the Iron Age occupation, Phase A. It yielded a date of 1180 B.C. ± 60. Another Carbon-14 date of 1190 B.C. ± 50 indicates the end of Phase D. These two dates give a very short life span to Phases A–D. Yet a third Carbon-14 date of 1050 B.C. ± 40[331] is based on a sample from a small ash level in Phase J, one of the late phases of Iron I.

In two rooms east of the main sanctuary, which were destroyed in the fire at the end of the Late Bronze Age, were found the much-discussed clay tablets (pl. 21), which have not yet been deciphered.[332] Because of their similarity to Minoan tablets, they have been associated with the Sea Peoples, but this extremely attractive proposal is difficult to substantiate because the derivative Philistine pottery at Deir ʿAlla was found in the Iron Age I levels following the destruction of the temple complex. During this period there is no evidence of a permanent occupation on the mound. The accumulation consists of a large number of phases made up mainly of open areas with almost no trace of buildings. The remains include furnaces, which probably served for smelting copper (Phase B). The clay end of a blowpipe of a well-known shape found near the furnaces still had a drop of copper attached to the inside of its nozzle. Many tiny metal globules were

327. A. Biran, *BA* 37 (1974): 26–52. Idem, Notes and News, *IEJ* 22 (1972): 165–66; *IEJ* 26 (1976): 205.

328. Y. Yadin, *AJBA* 1 (1968): 9–23.

329. *Deir ʿAlla,* pp. 4–5.

330. Ibid., p. 19. The chronology employed here—1209–1200 B.C.(?)—follows R. Faulkner, *CAH* [3], vol. II, pt. 2, chap. 23, pp. 235–36, 1038.

331. *Deir ʿAlla,* p. 245.

332. H. J. Franken, "Clay Tablets from Deir ʿAlla, Jordan," *VT* 14 (1964): 377 ff. Four inscribed clay tablets were found eight meters east of the Late Bronze Age sanctuary. They belong to the occupational level that was destroyed around 1200 B.C. Albright's suggestion (*CAH* [3], vol. II, pt. 2, chap. 33, p. 510) that they are very early Philistine texts or represent the script of some other Sea People has been refuted; *see* H. J. Franken, *CAH* [3], vol. II, pt. 2, chap. 26 (b), pp. 336–37.

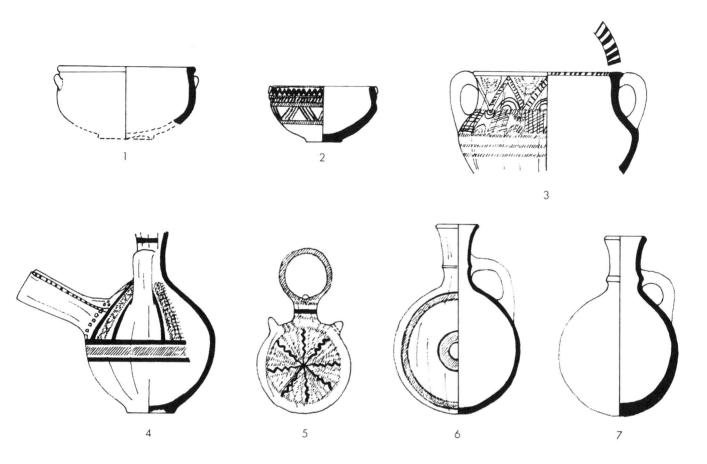

Fig. 14. Selected pottery, Megiddo, stratum VIA.
1. Fragmentary bowl in buff ware; wet-smoothed; loc. 1754, stratum VI [*Meg. II*, pl. 85:1].   **2.** Bowl in pink buff with numerous white grits; wet-smoothed; red and black paint; loc. 1567, stratum VI [*Meg. II*, pl. 85:2].   **3.** Fragmentary krater in fine orange-buff ware; wet-smoothed; red and black paint. Square L8 (northwest corner), stratum VI [*Meg. II*, pl. 85:5].
4. Fragmentary jug in orange-buff ware with some gray grits and a rock; irregular burnish; red and black paint; loc. 5224, stratum VIA [*Meg. II*, pl. 75:22].   **5.** Flask in orange-buff ware; heavily lined; irregular burnish outside; red paint; loc. 2068, stratum VIB–VIA [*Meg. II*, pl. 80:7].   **6.** Globular jug in pink buff with gray-green slip; handle divided by concentric circles; loc. 2070, stratum VIA [*Meg. II*, pl. 80:2].   **7.** Globular jar; buff; well-fired, wet-smoothed; loc. 1735, stratum VI [*Meg. II*, pl. 81:16].

Pl. 21. Clay tablets, Deir ʿAlla [H. J. Franken, "Clay Tablets from Deir ʿAlla, Jordan," *VT* 14 (1964): pl. 1].

also found in the ground in the vicinity. Numerous pits, probably also related to the metal industry, were dug in this period. These finds have led to the assumption that the site was occupied by seminomadic metalworkers who processed copper during the winter months. This occupation has another interesting facet—namely, the derivative Philistine pottery associated with the metal industry. It should be recalled that the Philistines held a monopoly of the metal industry in Palestine until their defeat by David.

Franken presents the "Philistine" pottery under the heading of imported material. He writes:[333] "The only other imported material which is important for dating purposes is the 'Philistine' type material. Some typical shapes and decorated sherds have been found. These are exclusively found in the Phases A–D."

One important example is the decorated jug (chap. 3, fig. 30) from Phase A_2, the first uncontaminated Iron Age phase.[334] From Phase B the derivative Philistine pottery includes body fragments[335] and a large three-legged krater with debased Philistine decoration[336] closely related to examples from Megiddo stratum VI[337] and Beth-Shean level VI.[338] The analogy with Megiddo lies both in the shape of the krater and in the decoration, which is a debased version of Philistine motifs. The similarity to Beth-Shean is in the decoration only. These analogies indicate a date for Phase B later than that suggested by the excavator. The Philistine jug from Phase A_2 is *not* indicative as it is a unique example lacking any close parallels.

ADDITIONAL SITES WITH PHILISTINE REMAINS

As archaeological work continues, additional information on the diffusion of the Philistine material culture is revealed in excavations, soundings, and surveys conducted the length of the country. We will summarize these data and include as well two major sites, Tell el-Ḥesi and Lachish, previously excavated and currently being reexcavated.

Tel Masos (Khirbet el-Meshash)[339]

Located twelve kilometers east of Beersheba, Tel Masos is a widely scattered Iron Age settlement (350 m. × 200 m.) with no traces of a city wall or enclosure. It was investigated in areas A, B, C, F, and H. Three strata were distinguished within the Iron Age settlement: stratum III, on which we shall concentrate, and stratum II span the twelfth to eleventh centuries B.C.; stratum I, which was badly eroded, belongs to the tenth century B.C.

In area A, beneath the houses of stratum II, three buildings of stratum III were unearthed; they are of the three-room house type. They lay over an earlier phase of stratum III (IIIb), which belonged to the first settlement and consisted only of loose beaten-earth floors and ash pits. (Pits of stratum III were also found in area H beneath stratum II buildings.) The pottery of IIIb is the typical extension of the Late Bronze Age tradition but contains none of the distinctive Mycenaean or Cypriot imports or their local imitations. No Philistine pottery was distinguished in stratum IIIb. The excavators date this phase to the last third of the thirteenth century B.C. on the basis of the pottery and a surface find of a scarab.[340] Such a high chronology, however, seems improbable for the pottery assemblage, which should probably be dated to the turn of the century (that is, about 1200 B.C.). This would also fit the pattern noted at other sites (such as Tell Beit Mirsim B_1), where this short-lived pre-Philistine intermediate phase was also found.

Philistine pottery makes its first appearance at Tel Masos in the destruction of the late phase of stratum III (IIIa); it helps date its establishment and the building operations of the settlers to the twelfth century, as the few Philistine sherds include a number that belong

333. *Deir 'Alla*, p. 245.
334. Ibid., fig. 47:4.
335. Ibid., figs. 51:52–64; 52:3, 5.
336. Ibid., fig. 52:4.
337. *Meg. II*, pls. 85:6 (shape) and 85:5 (decoration).
338. *B-SH Iron*, figs. 49:15 and 56:2 (decoration).

339. For the excavation results, *see* A. Kempinski, *EAEHL*, pp. 816–19; idem, Notes and News, *IEJ* 26 (1976): 52–53; idem and V. Fritz, "Excavations at Tel Masos (Khirbet el-Meshâsh), Preliminary Report of the Third Season, 1975," *Tel Aviv* 4 (1977): 136–58.
340. The scarab, found on the surface of area A, depicts a pharaoh striking an enemy. Its date is controversial. The excavators use it as a *terminus ante quem* for the founding of the earliest settlement of stratum III and assign it to the Nineteenth Dynasty (the period of Ramesses II or Seti II). This assignment, however, has been challenged, and a date in the period of Ramesses X has been suggested by B. Brandl in a forthcoming article.

unquestionably to the early phase of Philistine pottery.

Stratum II, spanning nearly the entire eleventh century B.C., is the best preserved. In area H, where a large courtyard house was excavated, two building phases (IIa and IIb) were clearly distinguished; these can help to subdivide this long-lived stratum. The end of stratum II, especially in area H, can be dated with certainty by two rich assemblages from the large courtyard house. Corresponding in certain features with Megiddo VIA and Tell Qasile X, the pottery indicates that the end of stratum II dates to the close of the eleventh or the beginning of the tenth century B.C.

The architecture of stratum II reveals a well-planned town of which the four-room house is a prominent feature. There are also variations of the courtyard house. One excavated in area C corresponds, according to the excavator, to house 1500 of level VI at Beth-Shean.

The identification of the site with the biblical city of Hormah could not be confirmed, but there is no doubt that Tel Masos was an important site in the period of the Judges.

Tel Beersheba[341]

The settlement at Beersheba was founded in the Early Iron Age, early in the period of the Judges, probably at about the same time as Tel Masos. No prior Canaanite city existed on the site. The area outside the gate, mainly around the wall of the fortified Iron Age II city, yielded appreciable remains of three occupation levels of the Iron Age I (strata VIII–VI), which agree roughly with the three occupation levels of Tel Masos (strata III–I). They are preceded by a stage of rock-cut trenches and pits (stratum IX). The earliest stratum containing Philistine sherds (stratum VIII) was reached in the gate area, but no clear picture of this initial settlement can yet be formed.

Tell esh-Shariʿa (Tel Seraʿ)

Tell esh-Shariʿa (Tel Seraʿ) is situated in the northwestern Negev on the north bank of Naḥal Gerar. The site has been tentatively identified with biblical Ziklag,

an identification that has been strengthened by the recent excavations at the site.[342]

The settlements relevant to our discussion are those of strata IX and VIII. Stratum IX, dated to the first half of the twelfth century B.C., has been excavated on a large scale in area A; it contains a massive mud-brick building that may have been a fortified complex which also included some sort of a sanctuary. The rich finds from this building, including a large amount of pottery, are similar to those discovered in the latest Fosse Temple at Lachish. The most important find for purposes of dating is a group of eleven bowls and ostraca with Egyptian hieratic inscriptions of the New Kingdom period. On one of the bowls is inscribed "Year 22," which the excavators suggest is the twenty-second year of Ramesses III. The pottery assemblages of stratum IX contained neither Mycenaean nor Cypriot imports nor Philistine pottery. The excavator has suggested that an early wave of Sea Peoples burned the area around the middle of the twelfth century. The site remained uninhabited until the eleventh century (stratum VIII).

The Early Iron Age city, stratum VIII, was erected above the debris of stratum IX. The main features of this stratum are as follows: (1) buildings of the four-room type (the typical architectural plan of the Israelite houses, which appears here and at other sites, for example, Tel Masos, as early as the eleventh century). This find suggested to the excavator that the four-room house was originally part of the Philistine architectural tradition and was later adopted by the Israelites. (2) Large storage pits containing a thick layer of ash with pottery from the eleventh century and including late Philistine sherds, as well as typical Ashdod pottery of the red-slipped burnished type with black and white decoration, which first appears in the early phase of Ashdod stratum X (see above, p. 42). The absence of Philistine pottery of Phases 1 and 2 is part of the evidence for the gap in occupation between strata IX and VIII.

Tel Maʿaravim

Tel Maʿaravim[343] is a small site (2–3 dunams) on the northern bank of Naḥal Gerar about 1.5 kilometers

341. For the results of the excavation: Y. Aharoni, Notes and News, *IEJ* 23 (1973): 254; *IEJ* 25 (1975): 170; and *IEJ* 27 (1977): 168–69.

342. E. D. Oren in *EAEHL*, pp. 1059–69.
343. E. D. Oren and A. Mazar, Notes and News, *IEJ* 24 (1974): 269–70.

east of Tel Seraʿ. The settlement was probably founded in the fourteenth century B.C. (Phase 4). Overlying it were architectural remains from the thirteenth century (Phase 3). Phase 2, with its badly preserved building remains, yielded late painted Philistine and hand-burnished pottery fragments that point to an eleventh century B.C. date for this phase. The sounding carried out at Tel Maʿaravim uncovered evidence of a "daughter" settlement of the Canaanite and Philistine cities at Tel Seraʿ. Both sites show an occupational gap in the twelfth century B.C.—the period of early Philistine settlement.

Tell el-Ḥesi (Eglon?)

Tell el-Ḥesi, located on the west bank of Wadi Ḥesi twenty-five kilometers northeast of Gaza, was the first site in Palestine to be excavated stratigraphically, initially by Petrie in 1890 and later by Bliss in 1891–1893.[344]

Petrie distinguished a gap in occupation during the period of Judges, between the end of the Late Bronze Age "cities" IVb/IV and "city" V (1000–900 B.C.). Although no trace of buildings from that period was recovered, the pottery drawings presented by Petrie include a bell-shaped krater and a painted fragment that may be Philistine.[345]

Excavations carried out at the site from 1970 to 1975 and 1977[346] have not yet reached this level, if one indeed exists, so that conclusive evidence of an Early Iron Age settlement is still lacking.

In addition to these excavated sites, archaeological surveys of the northern Negev[347] have uncovered Philistine pottery at many other sites, such as Tell Abu Hureira, Tell Maliḥa, Tell Quneitra, and Qubur el-Walaida.[348]

Tell esh-Sheikh Ahmed el-ʿAreini

Tell esh-Sheikh Ahmed el-ʿAreini[349] has been proposed as the location of Gath of the Philistines, the home of Goliath. The results of excavations at the site, however, have made this identification improbable, for only scant Philistine pottery was found there. This pottery was concentrated in one area (area F) in the debris unearthed on the high terrace at the foot of the acropolis. No stratum of occupation could be assigned to the Philistine occupation.

Khirbet Muqannaʿ[350]

Khirbet Muqannaʿ, in the Judean Shephelah, is on the eastern border of the coastal plain. The suggested identification of the site is with Ekron. Khirbet Muqannaʿ was founded by the Philistines and existed until the Persian period. Like Tell Qasile, it was an entirely new settlement, not one built over an earlier Canaanite city. Although the bulk of the Philistine sherds was collected on the northern ridge and in the southwestern corner of the mound, a comprehensive selection of bowls, kraters, stirrup jars, and strainer-spout jugs was also found over all the site.[351] The decoration, in bichrome on a heavy white slip, displays the usual repertoire: bird, spiral, zigzag and chevron, rhombus, Maltese cross, and net pattern. Other Early Iron Age pottery was found with the Philistine pottery, indicating that the site was first settled in the twelfth century B.C.

Lachish

The suggestion of a Philistine presence at Lachish in the first half of the twelfth century will be discussed in chapter 5 (pp. 276–79). The renewed excavations of the site have again focused our attention on two problems: the date of the end of stratum VI and the exis-

344. W. M. F. Petrie, *Tell el Hesy (Lachish)* (London, 1891); F. J. Bliss, *A Mound of Many Cities* (London, 1894).

345. Petrie, *Tell el Hesy*, pl. VIII:128, 181.

346. *EAEHL*, pp. 514–20.

347. A survey of the northern Negev has been undertaken by D. Alon. I thank him for making available to me the results of his extensive study on many of the as yet unexcavated sites of the Early Iron Age I in the northern Negev. An additional survey was undertaken by R. Gophna; *see* R. Gophna, "Sites from the Iron Age between Beer-Sheba and Tell el Farʿa," *BIES* 28 (1964): 236–46 (Hebrew).

348. At Qubur el-Walaida rescue excavations were carried out in 1977; *see* R. Cohen, Notes and News, *IEJ* 28 (1978): 194–95. The earliest settlement, dating to the Late Bronze II, was small and unfortified. During the Early Iron Age, occu-

pation spread out over an area of approximately 10 dunams. Philistine pottery uncovered in the Iron I level includes sherds of typical bichrome pottery of the late twelfth–mid-eleventh centuries. The stratigraphical sequence and ceramic assemblage of Qubur el-Walaida are very similar to those of Deir el-Balaḥ.

349. S. Yeivin, *EAEHL*, pp. 89–97.

350. J. Naveh, "Khirbat al-Muqannaʿ-Ekron, An Archaeological Survey," *IEJ* 8 (1958): 87–100. Albright refutes the possibility of this identification and again suggests the site of ʿAqir, *Syria, the Philistines and Phoenicia*, p. 509, n. 3.

351. Naveh, *IEJ* 8 (1958): fig. 4, pl. 22.

tence of an ephemeral settlement at the beginning of the twelfth century.

The recent excavations have not furnished any clear indications of a separate occupation level immediately following the end of the Late Bronze city. The excavators therefore conjecture that on the tell, at least, stratum VI continued well into the first half of the twelfth century. The Fosse Temple, on the other hand, clearly did not continue after the end of the thirteenth century.[352]

Tel Aphek[353]

The strata at Tel Aphek relevant to our discussion are strata 12–8, located in Area X, which span the period from the end of the Late Bronze Age to the end of the eleventh century B.C.

To stratum X12 of the Late Bronze Age is attributed a *migdol* (fortified residency) on the acropolis, featuring local pottery, including collar-rim jars, as well as Egyptian, Cypriot, and Myc. IIIB imports. The *migdol* also yielded Akkadian, Sumerian, Canaanite, Hittite, and Egyptian inscriptions. A foundation plaque of Ramesses II (not *in situ*) is no doubt also connected with this building, which was covered with debris when it was destroyed in a great fire.

Stratum X11 is not well defined. The pottery, including imported ware, is still in the Late Bronze tradition. The following settlement, stratum X10, was built on a new plan (no remains of which lay above the *migdol*). Large square buildings almost devoid of finds as well as smaller adjoining buildings contained pottery in the Late Bronze tradition, but with virtually no imports. The excavators attributed this stratum to the Sea Peoples on historical evidence alone.

Stratum X10 is followed by the Philistine occupation, which was distinguished in pits—two of them dug into the *migdol* of stratum X12. In the adjacent area, the Philistine settlement superimposed over the buildings of stratum X10 is represented by open areas containing layers of ashes, large pits, and the begin-

nings of walls which may indicate the possibility of buildings of the Philistine period at Aphek (strata X9–8). The Philistine pottery from the pits and floor levels does not appear to belong to the initial phase of Philistine pottery, and may very well date to the second half of the twelfth and early eleventh centuries. A scarab of Ramesses IV from one of the pits dug into the *migdol* indicates that Philistine pottery was already well established during this pharaoh's reign.

ʿIzbet Ṣarṭah[354]

The site of ʿIzbet Ṣarṭah, located on the barren ridge opposite Aphek on the road to Shiloh, may have been the scene of the "battle of Eben-ezer" between the Israelites and Philistines. The founders of the settlement were most likely Ephraimite families who had pushed westward to the edge of the hill country, not daring to move down into the Yarkon basin for fear of the Canaanites and, later, of the Philistines. The site is, in many respects, typical of the earliest Israelite settlements. The excavations have revealed the following history: In the earliest stratum (3), typical local Late Bronze pottery and Myc. IIIb sherds and collar-rim jars were found in stone-lined silos and in a belt of houses encircling the hilltop. The *floruit* of the site is represented by the rebuilt and enlarged stratum 2. The small peripheral houses were reconstructed, and a central four-room house surrounded by stone-lined silos was built. In one of the silos a proto-Canaanite abecedary was found. Stratum 2 contained no imported vessels, but only pottery typical of the Early Iron Age, including collar-rim jars and a large quantity of Philistine ware, the latter forming about 50 percent of the total pottery in this level. The Philistine occupation directly followed the Late Bronze stratum, with no intermediate stage discernible. Stratum 2 was abandoned in the great confrontation between Israel and Philistia, ca. 1050 B.C. The site was resettled for a short time at the beginning of the Monarchy (ca. 1000 B.C.) and subsequently deserted.

Aphek and ʿIzbet Ṣarṭah, only about three kilometers apart, represent totally different transitional phases between the Late Bronze and Iron ages. While at the rich metropolis of Aphek one can distinguish an

352. D. Ussishkin, Notes and News, *IEJ* 24 (1974): 272–73; and *EAEHL*, pp. 750–53.

353. For results of the excavations at Aphek, *see* M. Kochavi, Notes and News, *IEJ* 26 (1976): 51; Notes and News, *IEJ* 27 (1977): 54; and *Aphek-Antipatris; Five Seasons of Excavation at Aphek-Antipatris 1972–1976* (Tel Aviv, 1976), pp. 10–11; idem, "The Archaeological Context of the Aphek Inscriptions," in *Aphek–Antipatris 1974–1977, The Inscriptions*, M. Kochavi et al., eds. (Tel Aviv, 1978), reprint series no. 2, pp. 1–7.

354. M. Kochavi, "An Ostracon of the Period of the Judges from ʿIzbet Ṣarṭah," *Tel Aviv* 4 (1977): 1–13; Notes and News, *IEJ* 28 (1978): 267–68; *Ḥadashot Arkheologiyot* 67–68 (October 1978): 31–32 (Hebrew).

intermediate phase (strata X11–10) between the destruction of the Canaanite city and the coming of the Philistines, at 'Izbet Sartah the Philistine settlement immediately followed the Late Bronze Age settlement (Israelite?), which contained Mycenaean imports. At Aphek there is apparently a stage subsequent to the destruction of the Canaanite city that contains neither imported nor Philistine pottery. The historical event which affected both sites was the battle of Eben-ezer, which is attested at 'Izbet Sartah by the abandonment of stratum 2.

Surveys and soundings conducted in southern Judea and the southwestern coastal plain have revealed Philistine pottery at a number of sites that were significant Philistine settlements: Tell Khuweilifa, Tell Malat, Qatra, Ras Abu Hamid, and Tell el-Batashi. The latter site is currently being excavated more extensively.[355]

Several sites in the north have yielded Philistine pottery in recent years:

Tell Qiri (ha-Zore'a)[356]

Tell Qiri is situated on the eastern Carmel ridge on the slopes leading to the Jezreel Valley. A stratified excavation was begun there in 1975.

The most intensive occupation of the site took place during the Iron Age. Continuous settlements can be traced from the twelfth (or eleventh) through the eighth and seventh centuries B.C. A corner of a building where excavation has only just begun belongs to the earliest phase of the Iron Age. The finds, which included an incense-burner and a Philistine strainer-spout jug, suggest that the building was cultic in character. Other fragments of Philistine bowls and kraters were found in different areas, the whole pattern pointing to a late-twelfth- or early-eleventh-century Philistine influence at the site.

The material culture of the earliest Iron Age stratum is an extension of the Late Bronze Age tradition. This continuation of Canaanite culture and the close affinities with the corresponding strata at Megiddo are not surprising at a site located in the Canaanite heartland between Megiddo and Jokneam.

Tiv'on

In a pit (a tomb?) dug into the Middle Bronze Age I–II occupation level at Tiv'on (locus 36) a number of Philistine sherds were found, including part of a strainer-spout jug that was white-slipped with a plain triglyph decoration.[357]

Hazor

Philistine sherds were found at Hazor on the eastern side of the main road (the lower city) in a salvage dig in 1951. Again, in 1969, a number of fragments of late Philistine types came to light in area A in the Early Iron Age strata.[358]

SUMMARY

Stratigraphic excavations have made possible the establishment of a clear stratigraphic sequence through which we can follow the initial appearance, the flourishing, and the subsequent assimilation of Philistine pottery. The more important sites have also provided the means by which we can study the relative chronology of the Philistine material culture, from its first appearance at the end of the Late Bronze Age II or beginning of the Iron Age I (first quarter of the twelfth century B.C.) to its final assimilation at the beginning of the Iron Age II (the beginning of the tenth century B.C.)

The comparative table on pp. 290–91 presents the major stratified sites containing Philistine remains. The definitive sites for the subdivision and the relative chronology are Ashdod, Tel Mor, Tell el-Far'ah, Tell Qasile, and Tell Beit Mirsim, whose subdivision was

---

355. For Qatra, see J. Kaplan, "Researches in the Gederah-el Mughar Area," BIES 17 (1953): 142 (Hebrew). For Ras Abu Hamid, see B. Mazar, "Gath and Gittaim," IEJ 4 (1954): 234–35, n. 21. The recent excavations under the direction of G. Kelm and A. Mazar at Tel Batash make the identification of Tel Batash with Timnah more plausible; Notes and News, IEJ 27 (1977): 167 f.; IEJ 28 (1978): 195–96.

356. A. Ben-Tor, Notes and News, IEJ 25 (1975): 169; and Notes and News, IEJ 26 (1976): 200–01.

357. I wish to thank A. Raban for bringing these finds, as well as a number of Philistine sherds (krater and bowl fragments) from nearby Tel Risim and Tel Re'ala, to my notice.

358. Two Philistine sherds were found in an unstratified context along with Early Iron Age I pottery; see M. Dothan, "Hazor," Bulletin of the Department of Antiquities of the State of Israel 5–6 (1957): 23–24. The large-scale excavations at Hazor have revealed a few additional unstratified Philistine sherds in the Upper City (area A). Most likely these sherds should be assigned to strata XII or XI. For a discussion of these strata, see Y. Yadin, Hazor, the Schweich Lectures, 1970 (London, 1972), pp. 129–34.

established by excavation. They form the framework into which we have inserted (1) other sites whose excavation did not yield a clear internal division, and (2) tomb groups attributable to the consecutive phases. In addition the chart shows the phases of consolidation, development, and assimilation of Philistine pottery, which will be discussed in chapter 3. The absolute dates given are those of the Egyptian dynasties; finds bearing the names of Ramesses III–X are offered as guides to an absolute chronology.

APPENDIX: DISTRIBUTION OF IRON IN THE TWELFTH AND ELEVENTH CENTURIES B.C. IN PALESTINE

The study of the excavated material from Israel reveals that most iron tools and weapons come from sites that show signs of Philistine occupation or influence (see table 1 below). Several sites, some apparently occupied by the Philistines, have yielded evidence of metalworking, but the installations in question were for the production of copper or bronze rather than iron. Very few iron objects have been found at Israelite or Canaanite sites, perhaps as a result of the rather low level of Israelite material culture in this period as well as the possible Philistine control over the entire metal industry. However, the assumption that the Philistines *introduced* iron production into Canaan, which was generally accepted in the past (see p. 20 above),[359] can now be refuted by the widespread dispersal of iron technology throughout the eastern Mediterranean.

Perhaps the crucial question is, Why did iron production start? Snodgrass was the first to suggest that the adoption of iron in Greece was necessitated by the reduction of trade in other metals.[360] This argument may be applied not only to Greece but also to the entire eastern Mediterranean. J. Waldbaum has further proposed that the copper and/or tin trade was disrupted by the general upheavals and economic chaos at the end of the thirteenth century. The resultant shortage of these metals may have provided an incentive to the development and exploitation of other resources, such as iron.[361]

Iron was known to some extent in the Late Bronze Age, appearing in several areas in the eastern Mediterranean. However, such finds are sporadic, and although the objects are varied, jewelry is predominant, indicating that iron was essentially a luxury product. Iron is not yet prominent immediately after the destruction of the Late Bronze cities, but rather seems to have been only gradually accepted.[362] Relatively small quantities of iron are found in twelfth-century contexts in Canaan, and it is evident that bronze remained the major metal. The use of iron increased during the eleventh century (see table 1), but only in the tenth and ninth centuries did it become the preferred metal.[363]

359. G. E. Wright, "Iron: The Date of its Introduction into Common Use in Palestine," *AJA* 43 (1939): 458–63.

360. A. M. Snodgrass, *The Dark Age of Greece* (Edinburgh, 1971), pp. 217–39.

361. J. C. Waldbaum, *From Bronze to Iron*, SIMA, vol. 54 (Göteborg, 1978), pp. 67–73.

362. This refutes the theory of a Hittite monopoly on iron in twelfth-century contexts; ibid., pp. 20–21, 67–68.

363. Ibid., p. 27.

Table 1. Distribution of Iron*

Site	13th cent.	12th cent.	11th cent.
Har Adir[1]		TI	
• Ha-Zore'a[2]		TA	
• Megiddo[3]	JR	(2)JR,TH,TK	(3)JB,WD,(4)TK,TN,TT
Taanach[4]		TK	
• Beth-Shean[5]		JR,WD,(3)TL,(3+)U	
• Tel Zeror[6]			(5)JB,JR,(3)WD,(5)TK
'Ai[7]		(2)JB,WD(?),(2)WL,WT	(2)TK,TL,TZ,(3)U
Khirbet Raddana[8]		TK,TP,U	
• Tell el-Ful[9]			TP
• Tell Qasile[10]		TK,P	JB,WW,(2)TK,P,(2)U
• Azor[11]		JB	
• Gezer[12]			TK,U
• Beth-Zur[13]			JT
• Beth-Shemesh[14]		TC,TK,TS(2)U	
• Lachish[15]	(1+)U		
• Tell 'Aitun[16]		JR	
• Tel Sera'[17]			TK
• Tell Jemmeh[18]			WA,WD,TK,U
• Tell el-Far'ah (S)[19]		(1+)JB,(1+)JR,WD	(6)JB,(2)JR,(6)TK
• Tell ez-Zuweyid[20]	(2)WA,U	WA,TC	WS,(2)U
Timna[21]	(2)JB,U		

Objects	13th	12th	12th–11th	11th
Jewelry				
JB – Bracelet	2	2+	2	12
JR – Ring	1	5+		3
JT – Toggle Pin				1
Weapons				
WA – Arrowhead	2	1		1
WD – Dagger		2	1?	5
WL – Lance head			2	
WS – Spear head				1
WT – Spear butt		1		
WW – Sword				1
Tools				
TA – Axe		1		
TC – Chisel		1	1	
TH – Hook		1		
TI – Pick		1		
TK– Knife		3	4	20
TL – Nail		3	1	
TN – Needle				1
TP – Ploughshare		1		1
TS – Sickle			1	
TT – Staple				1
TZ – Tweezers			1	
P – Pig Iron		1		1
U – Unidentified or Miscellaneous	3+	4+	5	6
TOTAL	8+	26+	19	54

*This table is largely based on a chart prepared by Y. Baumgarten for an M.A. seminar paper, "Iron and Its Appearance in Palestine," presented at the Institute of Archaeology of the Hebrew University, Jerusalem, in 1975. Also incorporated into the present table is material from Waldbaum's book, n. 361 above, pp. 24–27, 41–42, 59–61, 67–68, as well as new material excavated in Israel after the publication of her book.

• Philistine pottery

–––Exact position within indicated range uncertain

1. Twelfth century B.C.: pick. R. Maddin, J. D. Muhly, and Tamara S. Wheeler, "How the Iron Age Began," *Scientific American* 237 (1977):127–28; a. But compare *Hadashot Arkheologiyot* 59–60 (October 1976): 9–10 (Hebrew), where the excavator dated the beginning of the site to the end of the eleventh century B.C.

2. Twelfth century B.C.: axe (not published).

3. End of the thirteenth century B.C.: ring, M. 3094, tomb 912b, *Meg. T.*, p. 162, pl. 128:19, fig. 176:7.

Twelfth century B.C.: Stratum VIIA: ring, M. 5713, L.N = 1779, *Meg. II*, p. 153; hook, M. 5809, L.N = 1796, *Meg. II*, p. 154. Tomb: ring, × 788, tomb 39, *Meg. T.*, pl. 166:2; knife, × 701, tomb 39, *Meg. T.*, pl. 167:6.

Eleventh century B.C.: Stratum VIA: two bracelets, Y. Yadin, "Megiddo of the Kings of Israel," *BA* 33 (1970): 78. Stratum VI: knife, b141, block K 7, *Meg. II*, p. 145; knife, M. 5656, L. 1729, *Meg. II*, p. 149, pl. 181:58; knife M. 5920, L. 1746, *Meg. II*, p. 151; knife, M. 5661, L.N = 1769, *Meg. II*, p. 152. Needle. M. 5737, L.N = 1732, *Meg. II*, p. 149. Staple, M. 5951, L.S = 1798, *Meg. II*, p. 154. Tombs: dagger, M. 3532, tomb 1101B, *Meg. T.*, p. 162, pl. 87:5, fig. 171:14; bracelet, M. 664, tomb 221B, *Meg. T.*, p. 162, pl. 170:1, fig. 179:6.

4. Twelfth-eleventh centuries B.C.: knife handle, TT 726, loc. 27; see Jane C. Waldbaum, *From Bronze to Iron* (Göteborg, 1978), p. 26, n. 76.

5. Twelfth century B.C.: dagger, 33-9-49, L. 1721, *B-SH Iron*, p. 322; pieces, 31-10-396, L. 1586, and 31-11-247, L. 1585, ibid.; knob, 25-11-9, L. 1060, ibid.; ring (iron?), L. 1778, tomb 90, *B-SH Cemetery*, pp. 115, 119, 229:20, fig. 45:60; three nails, L. 1055, plus L. 2001, *B-SH II, Part 1*, pp. 20, 75, pl. 31:32, 39, 40.

6. Eleventh century B.C.: knife with iron rivets, tomb I, *Tel Zeror II*, p. 40; knife and two bracelets, tomb III, ibid.; knife, bracelet, and two iron daggers, tomb V, ibid.; knife, ring, and two bracelets, tomb VI, *Tel Zeror III*, p. 70, pl. LXII:10; knife, tomb VII, *Tel Zeror III*, p. 70; dagger, tomb VIII, ibid. (We have changed "dagger" to "knife" after Waldbaum, *From Bronze to Iron*, p. 25, n. 71.)

7. Twelfth-eleventh centuries B.C.: two knives, 356 and 1799, J. Marquet-Krause, *Les Fouilles de 'Ay (et-Tell), 1932–1935* (Paris, 1949), pp. 53, 221; dagger or knife, 474, ibid., p. 59, pl. XXXIX; two lance heads, 355 and 2006, ibid., pp. 53, 247, pl. XXXIX; tweezers, 182, ibid., p. 46, pl. XXXIX; nail, 710, ibid., p. 73, pls. XXXIX and LXX; unidentified piece, 1830, ibid., p. 226. From recent excavations: conical spearbutt, 0-70, B-II; unidentified fragment, 0-720, B XVII; two bracelets, 0-757, B and 0-1268 B XXIV; a rod, 0-12, B XXXVII, Waldbaum, *From Bronze to Iron*, p. 25, n. 47.

8. Twelfth century B.C.: knife, 0-1356; tool point (plough?), 0-1750; two "rods" (ingot?), 0-1180, Waldbaum, *From Bronze to Iron*, p. 25, n. 48: *see also*, especially for the date, *Hadashot Arkheologiyot* 43 (1972): 14 (Hebrew).

9. Eleventh century B.C.: plough point, stratum IIA. L. A. Sinclair, "An Archaeological Study of Gibeah (Tell el-Ful)," *AASOR* 34-35 (1954–56): 47, pl. 19a; *BA* 27 (1964): 55, fig. 15.

10. Twelfth century B.C.: stratum XII: knife, 3188 L. 275 (261), *Qasile IEJ 25*, p. 78, pl. 7B; A. Mazar, "The Temples of Tell Qasile" (Ph.D. diss., Hebrew University, Jerusalem, 1977), p. 277; a piece of unworked iron, 2628, L. 221, Mazar, "Temples," p. 230.

Eleventh century B.C.: stratum X: two knives, 599, 3449, *Qasile IEJ 1*, p. 135; sword blade, 3701, ibid.; bracelet, 1981, L. 131, A. Mazar, *Museum Haaretz 1973–74 Yearbook*, p. 61, Mazar, "Temples," p. 229; a piece of unworked iron in building K, stratum XI, Mazar, "Temples," p. 230; two unidentified pieces, 2746 and 3370, ibid.

11. Twelfth century B.C.: bracelet, tomb 56, *Azor*, p. 172.

12. Eleventh century B.C.: knife, tomb 58, *Gezer* III, pl. LXXXIII:29; a rivet in a bronze bucket handle, tomb 58, ibid., pl. LXXXIII:25.

13. Eleventh century B.C.: toggle pin, *Beth-Zur*, p. 84, pl. 44a:9.

14. Twelfth-eleventh centuries B.C.: stratum III, chisel, 33-4-529, *AS III*, p. 49; knife, 33-4-530, ibid., pp. 49, 50; tool fragment, 33-4-514, *AS III*, p. 50; fragment with bronze rivets, *AS II*, p. 34, no. 180; sickle, *AS V*, p. 153.

15. Thirteenth century B.C.: fragments, temple. D. Ussishkin and C. Clamer, *Qadmoniot* 9, no. 4 (1976): 115 (Hebrew).

16. Twelfth century B.C.: ring. G. Edelstein et al., "The Necropolis at Tell ʿAitun," *Qadmoniot* 4, no. 3 (1971): 86–87 (Hebrew).

17. Eleventh century B.C.: knife (not published; Y. Baumgarten's paper).

18. Eleventh century B.C.: arrowhead, from KA 181, *Gerar*, pl. 29:23; knife, from KA 181, *Gerar*, pl. 30:1 (both below buildings G); dagger, from HV 181, *Gerar*, pl. 28:6; fragment, from HL 181, *Gerar*, pl. 27:3 (both can be related to building IF).

19. Twelfth century B.C.: dagger, tomb 542; *BP I*, pl. 21:90; several bracelets, tomb 542, ibid., p. 8; several rings, tomb 552, ibid., p. 8.

Eleventh century B.C.: knife, tomb 562, ibid., pl. 21:96; knife and ring, tomb 237, ibid., pl. 32:172, 173; ring and knife, tomb 220, ibid., pl. 34:185, 189, 190; knife, tomb 523, ibid., pl. 30:132; ring and knife, tomb 615, Philistine pottery, ibid., pl. 30:109, 111; bracelet, tomb 625, Philistine pottery, ibid., pl. 30:118; bracelet, tomb 617, ibid., pl. 30:119; bracelet, tomb 506, ibid., pl. 30:139; bracelet, tomb 859, Philistine pottery, ibid., pl. 71; bracelet, tomb 839, ibid., pl. 71.

20. Thirteenth century (?) B.C.: two arrowheads, level NF 209–204, *Anthedon*, pl. 25:93, 97; a handle, level NF 204, ibid., pl. 25:100.

Twelfth century B.C.: arrowhead, level NF 211; chisel, level NS 215, ibid., pl. 25:98, 99.

Eleventh century B.C.: spearhead, level MF 226; two fragments, levels MX 243 and MD 251, ibid., pls. 25:96 and 50.

21. Thirteenth and twelfth centuries B.C.: site 2, two bracelets, B. Rothenberg, *Timna* (London, 1972), p. 106, fig. 29:10, 11; jewelry from an area outside the temple of Hathor from the end of the Late Bronze Age has been found, ibid., pl. 95; *see also* pp. 177–79 there.

3

PHILISTINE POTTERY

INTRODUCTION

Philistine pottery[1] is a large, homogeneous group of locally made ware painted in black and red usually on a white-slipped background. It is attributed to the Philistines on the basis of typology, stratigraphy, and geographical distribution.

Typologically, Philistine pottery reflects the Sea Peoples' Aegean background, plus certain Cypriot, Egyptian, and local Canaanite elements. Geographically, it is found in the major Philistine cities, follows the spread of Philistine influence through Canaan, and diminishes as one moves away from Philistia (see map 2). Stratigraphically, Philistine vessels appear in strata dated to the first half of the twelfth and the eleventh centuries B.C., a period that corresponds, according to historical and biblical sources, to the arrival

and settlement in Canaan of the Philistines and other Sea Peoples.

Philistine pottery cannot be studied as an isolated phenomenon; chapters 2 and 5 discuss the assemblages accompanying this pottery, which are important for verifying the stratigraphy. In the present chapter, however, we will consider Philistine pottery as an entity and define its distinctive characteristics.

Three main phases, which reflect the crystallization, diffusion, and gradual assimilation of the material culture of the Philistines, can be distinguished in the development of the pottery. Based on stratigraphical and typological distinctions at the key sites discussed in the preceding chapter,[2] these phases will serve as a guide for organizing the great amount of material and

---

1. The first to point out the Aegean background of Philistine pottery was F. B. Welch, "The Influence of the Aegean Civilisation on South Palestine," *PEFQSt* (1900): 342–50. This ware was associated with the Philistines and designated "Philistine pottery" by H. Thiersch, "Die neueren Ausgrabungen in Palästina," *AA* 23 (1908): 378 ff. Mackenzie followed in his footsteps, and in his report on the excavations of Beth-Shemesh, he noted a gap between the disappearance of the Mycenaean and Cypriot imported ware and the advent of Philistine pottery (D. Mackenzie, "The Excavations at Ain Shems," *PEF Ann* 2 [1912–13]: 33–36). In 1920/21, after excavating at Ashkelon with Garstang, Phythian-Adams published "Philistine Origins in the Light of Palestinian Archaeology," *BBSAJ* 3 (1923): 20–27. Among those who opposed the association of this pottery with the Philistines were Père L. H. Vincent and E. Saussey (Vincent, "Chronique," *RB* 31 [1922]: 102 ff.; "Bulletin," ibid. [1926]: 466; and Saussey, "La céramique philistine," *Syria* 5 [1924]: 169–85). A comprehensive survey of Philistine pottery, its association with the Philistines, dissemination, and relative and absolute chronology was published by W. F. Albright in *TBM I*, pp. 53–75. The most thorough examination of this problem so far appears in W. A. Heurtley's article, in which he opposed the use of the term *Philistine* to designate this class of pottery

("The Relationship between 'Philistine' and Mycenaean Pottery," *QDAP* 5 [1936]: 90–110). Despite a fine analysis of the comparative typology of the pottery, he draws conclusions that, in my opinion, are incorrect. The study of Philistine pottery was greatly facilitated and advanced by Furumark's detailed and inclusive analysis of Mycenaean pottery. The clear-cut typological and chronological framework he established permitted easier and more efficient use of the Mycenaean material. Furumark also dealt with the problem of Philistine pottery and concurred with its attribution to the biblical Philistines. In addition, he pointed out the analogy between Philistine pottery and Myc. IIIC:1b ware; *see* Furumark, *MP*, p. 575, and *CMP*, pp. 115–28. The most recent literature on the Philistines is Furumark, *OA 3*, pp. 260–65, and "The Settlement at Ialysos and Aegean History c. 1550–1400 B.C.," *OA* 6 (1950): 243; Trude Dothan, "Archaeological Reflections on the Philistine Problem," *Antiquity and Survival* 2 (1957): 151 ff.; and *DMS*, pp. 209 ff.

2. Unpublished material from the important excavations at Ashdod and Tell Qasile has been taken into account pending the appearance of the forthcoming reports. Incorporated into the text is some of the material from the Tell Qasile temple excavated by A. Mazar. Only those types which add to the Philistine repertoire are included in our discussion.

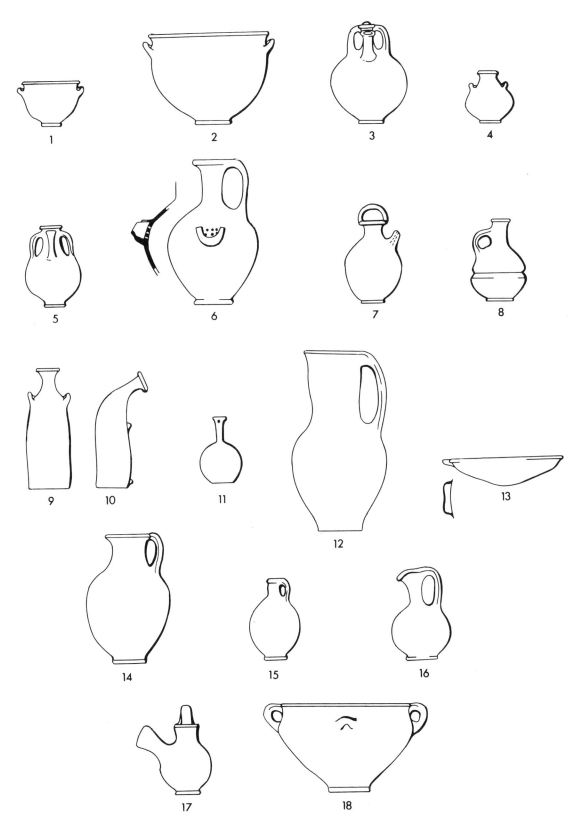

Main types of Philistine pottery.

classifying the many chance discoveries and unstratified finds. In selecting representative examples of the main types of Philistine pottery, we have taken into account both published and unpublished material, spanning the entire range of its rise, zenith, and assimilation. Our intention here is not to present a complete catalogue but rather to illustrate the essential characteristics.

From the excavations at Ashdod we have evidence of a prelude to Philistine pottery. This is the monochrome pottery, which first appears in stratum XIIIb at Ashdod and is a locally produced variant of Myc. IIIC:1 ware. The potters still had firsthand knowledge not only of Mycenaean shapes and decorations but also of Mycenaean methods of working clay, preparing the paint, and firing the vessels. This monochrome ware, which is in all respects identical with Myc. IIIC:1b, seems to overlap the earliest appearance at Ashdod of typical Philistine bichrome pottery and then gradually peters out.

Phase 1: From the beginning to the last quarter of the twelfth century Corresponding to the period of Philistine settlement, this phase represents the rise and *floruit* of the Philistine ceramic culture. The pottery still closely resembles Mycenaean prototypes in shape and decorative motifs, yet it is distinctively Philistine—both in its combination of motifs and in its bichrome red and black decoration on a heavy white slip. The Close Style is in evidence, and the bird motif is common.

Phase 2: From the last quarter of the twelfth to the middle of the eleventh century During this period, although many high-quality vessels continue to be produced, there is a slight overall decline in the general standard and some departure from the Mycenaean prototypes, both in shape and decoration.

Phase 3: From the second half of the eleventh to the beginning of the tenth century In this phase, some types disappear altogether, others are assimilated into local styles, and new hybrid types are created. Regional differences are apparent in special types as well as in complete assemblages. Motifs, often misunderstood, are now far removed from their Mycenaean prototypes. The white-slip and bichrome decoration vanish, often to be replaced by red slip, hand-burnishing and dark-brown decoration—the hallmarks of the local pottery with which it is associated. The distinctiveness of Philistine pottery disappears.

The complex background and culture of the Philistines can best be clarified by a comparative study of the ceramic styles that merged to form their pottery. Four distinct influences can be distinguished: Mycenaean, Cypriot, Egyptian, and local Canaanite. The dominant traits in shape and decoration are Mycenaean.

Philistine pottery can be classifed into six groups, comprising eighteen main types (see pl. 1 and illustration of main types of Philistine pottery). The number of types will doubtless be increased by future excavators. Within each group we shall examine the shape of each type, the general decorative concept, and the motifs and techniques of decoration. A summary and analysis of the motifs and their origins is presented separately at the end of the chapter. We shall attempt to follow the diffusion of each type according to site and context, proceeding geographically in most cases and tracing the background and parallels of each type.

Four of the six groups are classified according to the areas from which their shapes originate. Group I (Types 1–8) is derived from Mycenaean prototypes. Group II (Types 9–11) is derived from Cypriot prototypes. Group III (Type 12) shows Egyptian affinities in shape and decoration. Group IV (Types 13–16) is derived from the local Canaanite repertoire. Group V (Types 17–18) consists of vessels appearing only during the last phase of Philistine pottery. Group VI terra-cottas and vessels of a cultic nature will be treated separately in chapter 4.

In analyzing and comparing the Philistine decorative motifs we shall focus on the areas of origin. The Mycenaean ceramic world is the source of most of the motifs in the Philistine decorative repertoire. Distinct, although less dominant, motifs stem from Egyptian art. Local Canaanite features are interwoven but are rarely prominent.

GROUP I. TYPES 1–8, VESSELS DERIVED FROM MYCENAEAN PROTOTYPES

The eight types of Philistine pottery clearly derived from Mycenaean prototypes are the bowl (Type 1), the krater (Type 2), the stirrup jar (Type 3), the pyxis and the amphoriskos (Type 4), the three-handled jar (Type 5), the strainer-spout jug (Type 6), the jug with basket handle and spout (Type 7), and the juglet with pinched-in girth (Type 8). The last vessel is included in

Pl. 1. Group of Philistine pottery [From the Collection of the Israel Department of Antiquities and Museums].
1. See fig. 3:1. **2.** No figure. **3.** See fig. 6. **4.** See fig. 17:2 and pl. 31. **5.** See fig. 14. **6.** See chap. **2**, fig. 29 ('Aitun). **7.** See pl. 73:5.
8. See pl. 81:1. **9.** See fig. 48.

this group even though it is not a direct derivation of Mycenaean pottery types.

Type 1. Bowl (figs. 1–4, pls. 2–7)

The bowl (Type 1) and the krater (Type 2) are the most common Philistine ceramic types, and are found in abundance on every site containing Philistine pottery. They are almost identical in outline but differ in size (the bowl being the smaller); they also differ in rim shape and in elaboration of decoration.

The bowls are predominantly bell-shaped, to use A. Furumark's term for their Mycenaean equivalents (fig. 1:1–10), and have a rounded, everted rim, rounded and sometimes slightly carinated shoulders, and a small ring base (fig. 1:1–3) or flat disk base (fig. 1:4). A debased version of the bell shape is found in shallower and somewhat more coarsely made bowls (fig. 1:11, 12).

Two horizontal loop handles attached at the shoulder just below the rim are characteristic of the bowl. Three stages of functional degeneration can be distinguished in their variations.

1. Functional handles arching outward from the body of the bowl (fig. 1:2–4, 6–7).
2. Semifunctional handles protruding only slightly (fig. 1:1, 8–10). This is the most common type.
3. Vestigial handles, so degenerate that they are decorative rather than functional (figs. 1:11, 2:12).

A great variety can be distinguished in the ware. The Ashdod material is a good illustration of its earliest features: delicately made bowls of light-greenish ware occur together with well-levigated and well-fired reddish ware. Both these early variants are, as a rule, self-slipped and decorated in monochrome—the greenish bowls usually in black paint, the reddish ones in different shades of red (chap. 2, fig. 3).

The bowls that we can follow through the second half of the twelfth and the eleventh centuries are often coated on the outside with a white slip. The later examples are less delicate; their main decoration is in dark brown, with an occasional lower band in red. Undecorated bowls, both slipped and plain (fig. 1:1–3), are regularly found in the same context as decorated ware.

The decorative patterns appearing on Type 1 bowls fall into three groups.

1. Plain bands around the outside of the bowl (fig. 1:4–12) with an occasional concentric-circle pattern inside the bowl (fig. 1:6, 11).
2. A pair of spirals, usually looped, facing the same direction and separated by curtailed triglyphs of wiggly and vertical lines (fig. 2:1–6). This asymmetrical design, the most common of the Philistine ornamental motifs, is derived from a Mycenaean symmetrical, antithetic spiral pattern. The antithetic spiral, however, appears only rarely in the Philistine repertoire (see fig. 2:7). Another infrequent variation of the spiral motif is the repeated single spiral (fig. 2:10).
3. Less common decorations include the antithetic tongue motif (fig. 3:1), the antithetic tongue motif terminating in spirals (fig. 3:2), and the bird motif (fig. 4). The red accents in some of these examples are seldom seen in bowls of this type.

A brief survey of the major sites and archaeological contexts in which Type 1 bowls have been found can help to elucidate their development.

Tell el-Far'ah This site yielded a large number of both plain and decorated bowls. An example of the former, covered with a white slip, is shown in figure 5:1. Its large size and splaying rim places it between the bowl (Type 1) and the krater (Type 2). It was found in tomb 542 (from the second half of the twelfth century). The bowl in figure 1:3 is a smaller variant from the same tomb. A similar bowl came from tomb 839, which is unfortunately too poor in content to be dated accurately.

Horizontal-band decorations appear on bowls from tomb 542 (fig. 1:9) and tomb 126 (fig. 1:12).[3] The second bowl lacks the graceful profile of the original bell-shaped vessel and is probably later than the first; the contents of tomb 126 cannot, however, be dated more closely than sometime during the eleventh century.

Bowls with a spiral pattern are numerous and very characteristic of the group. Figure 2:7 (pl. 2) from tomb 542 (second half of the twelfth century) is a rare example of the authentic spiral motif. A bowl from tomb 532 (fig. 2:4) and similar bowls from tombs 602 (fig. 2:8)[4]

---

3. *BP I*, pl. LXVIII. Tomb 126 yielded a carinated bowl decorated with concentric circles in the interior (*CPP*, 23 A2). This type of bowl is also found at Tell Qasile XI (*Qasile IEJ 1*, fig. 4:6).

4. The only other vessel found in tomb 602 was a pithos (*CPP*, 43 J) typical of Iron Age I pottery (*BP I*, pl. LXX).

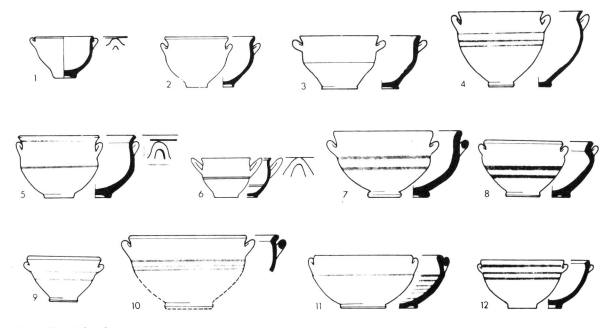

Fig. 1. Type 1 bowls.
1. White slip, Tell Qasile, stratum XI [*Qasile IE] 1*, fig. 4:7]. **2.** Beth-Shemesh [*BS*, p. 209:18]. **3.** White slip, Tell el-Far'ah, tomb 839, tomb 542 [*CPP*, 27 B1]. **4.** White slip, Ashkelon [*PMB* 4, pl. I:6]. **5.** Beth-Shean, tomb 210 [*B-SH Cemetery*, fig. 47:7]. **6.** White slip, Tell Qasile, stratum XI [Q. II 4533]. **7.** White slip, Beth-Shemesh [*AS II*, pl. XXXIII:18]. **8.** White slip, Beth-Shemesh, stratum III [*AS II*, pl. XXXIII:19; *AS IV*, pl. XXXVI:9]. **9.** Tell el-Far'ah, tomb 542 [*BP I*, pl. XXV; *CPP*, 24 S1]. **10.** 'Afula, stratum IIIA ['*Afula*, fig. 15:2]. **11.** 'Afula, East Cemetery ['*Afula*, fig. 20:3]. **12.** White slip, Tell el-Far'ah, tomb 126 [*CPP*, 18 A].

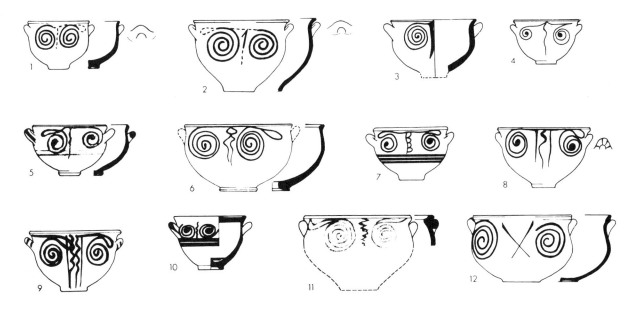

Fig. 2. Type 1 bowls.
1. White slip, Tell Qasile, stratum XI [*Qasile IE] 1*, fig. 4:9]. **2.** White slip, Tell Qasile, stratum XII [Q. II 8109]. **3.** White slip, Megiddo, stratum VIIA [*Meg. II*, pls. 69:7, 139:11]. **4.** Tell el-Far'ah, tomb 532 [*BP I*, pl. XXII:195; *CPP*, Add. 27 D3]. **5.** White slip, Beth-Shemesh [*AS II*, pl. XXXIII:17]. **6.** Tell Qasile, stratum XI [Q. IV 1050/27]. **7.** Tell el-Far'ah, tomb 542 [*BP I*, pl. XXV; *CPP*, 27 D4]. **8.** Tell el-Far'ah, tomb 602 [*BP I*, pl. XXXI:295; *CPP*, Add. 27 D5]. **9.** Tell el-Far'ah, tomb 239 [*BP I*, pl. XXXI:296]. **10.** White slip, Megiddo, stratum VIB [*Meg. II*, pls. 74:9, 142:7]. **11.** White slip, 'Afula, stratum IIA ['*Afula*, fig. 15:1]. **12.** Tell Qasile, stratum XI [Q. II 2904].

Fig. 3. Type 1 bowls.
1. White slip, Ashkelon [*PMB* 4, pl. I:3].   2. White slip, Tell eṣ-Ṣafi [*B-M*, pl. 35:11].

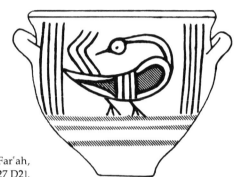

Fig. 4. Type 1 bowl, Tell el-Farʿah,
tomb 542 [*BP I*, pl. XXV; *CPP*, 27 D2].

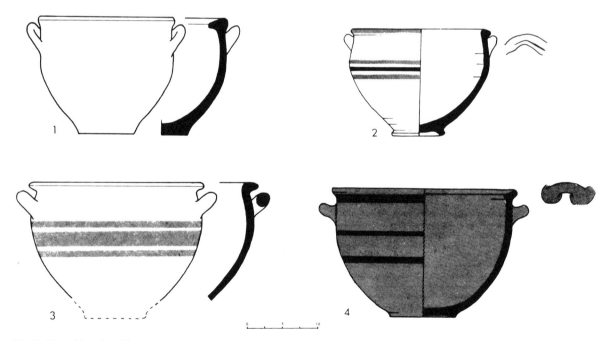

Fig. 5. Type 2 bowl and kraters.
1. White slip, Tell el-Farʿah, tomb 542 [*CPP*, 29 Q].   2. Azor.   3. White slip, Megiddo [*Meg. I*, pls. 31:155, 62:155].
4. Red slip, Gezer [HU no. 243].

Fig. 6. Type **2** krater, white slip, Azor.

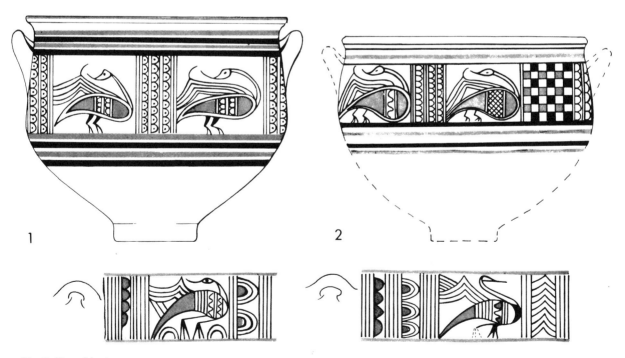

1   2

Fig. 7. Type **2** kraters.
1. White slip, Gezer [*Gezer* III, pl. CLXIII:3].   **2.** White slip, Gezer [*Gezer* III, pl. CLXIII:1].   **3.** White slip, Tell el-Far'ah,
DJ387 [*BP II,* pl. LXXV:1].

and 239 (fig. 2:9)[5] and locus EJ 385[6] can all be dated to the first half of the eleventh century. Figure 2:9 (pl. 2:4) exhibits a more complex attempt at a triglyph motif. Figure 4 (pl. 2:5) from tomb 542 is the unique bowl decorated with the bird motif mentioned above.

Ashkelon Two bowls from Ashkelon are outstanding in their workmanship and heavy white slip. One (fig. 1:4) is decorated with horizontal lines; the other one, mentioned above (fig. 3:1, pl. 3), bears an exceptional bichrome anithetic tongue motif. The closest parallels to the latter are to be seen in the Myc. IIIC:1b ware from Sinda and Enkomi, Cyprus (pl. 4).[7]

Tell eṣ-Ṣafi Aside from a number of Philistine bowls with the standard spiral decoration, Tell eṣ-Ṣafi has yielded an interesting variant of the decorated bichrome bowl from Ashkelon. Whereas the latter retains close links with its Mycenaean prototypes, the decoration on the Tell eṣ-Ṣafi bowl (fig. 3:2), which is made of delicate greenish ware and warped in firing, already shows the characteristic touch of the Philistine potter.

Tell Beit Mirsim Stratum B₂[8] at Tell Beit Mirsim contained white-slipped sherds with spiral patterns. Silo no. 2, whose contents date it to the end of the eleventh and beginning of the tenth centuries,[9] yielded an unslipped bowl decorated with a horizontal band divided into metopes of alternating net motifs. The choice of motifs and the workmanship of this bowl, together with the late context, definitely place it in the debased stage of Philistine ceramic development.

Beth-Shemesh Stratum III at Beth-Shemesh contained numerous bowls of various types: plain (fig. 1:2), banded (fig. 1:7, 8),[10] and decorated with spiral patterns (fig. 2:5). Since stratum III is not stratigraphi-

cally subdivided, no typological development can be traced.

Gezer The Philistine bowls found at Gezer include undecorated ware from tomb 84–85,[11] a sherd of a bowl with horizontal bands from tomb 59,[12] and bowls decorated with double spiral patterns from an undefined context.[13] Especially noteworthy is a bowl[14] with a horizontal wavy-line pattern; this is the only known example of such a motif in Philistine pottery, but it is very common on bowls in Myc. IIIC:1 pottery of the Granary style.[15]

Tell Qasile Type 1 bowls were found in both strata XII and XI, but the greatest concentration came from the latter stratum. They included white-slipped bowls and bowls decorated in monochrome red or dark brown. Bichrome decoration was rare. An example of the plain ware can be seen in figure 1:1 and in an exceptionally well-made bowl (fig. 1:6) with very thin sides and horizontal bands both inside and out that recalls the Myc. IIIC:1 bowls from stratum XIII at Ashdod (chap. 2, pl. 4). The most common type of decoration on the bowls from Qasile is, again, the double spiral motif (fig. 2:1, 2, 6).

One unusual bowl exhibited a rather broad rim ridged on the outside, vestigial handles, and bright-red spirals separated by crossed lines (fig. 2:12). This bowl appears to be a forerunner of the post-Philistine kraters of Type 18 (see fig. 60:3, 4, 5 below), which are characteristic of stratum X. A bowl (fig. 60:1) from stratum X is very similar, in its red slip and debased decoration, to the Type 18 kraters.

Azor The Philistine cemetery at Azor yielded numerous examples of the Type 1 bowl in all its variations. Notable are the carinated and round-bodied bowls that appear together with Philistine pottery (similar bowls have been found, for example, at Tell el-Farʿah, tomb 542).[16] These bowls are often covered with a white slip and decorated with red or bichrome concentric patterns, usually on their inner surface. The carinated bowls (pl. 5) are a fusion of the typical Late

---

5. On the basis of the other vessels uncovered in the tomb, especially the bowl *CPP,* 20 B, the tomb was dated to the eleventh century b.c. (*BP I,* pl. LXVIII).

6. The relationship between the findspot and the adjacent wall (*BP II,* pl. LXXXIII) indicates that the bowl belongs to the Philistine building D (ibid., pl. LXXIX).

7. *Sinda,* p. 107, pl. I (end of period II); *Enkomi Excavations,* vol. IIIa, pl. 94:28 (level IIIA).

8. *TBM I,* p. 62, par. 82, pls. 24:37–40, 42–45.

9. Ibid., pp. 62–63, par. 82–83, pl. 50:10.

10. Other bowls of this type were found at Beth-Shemesh, stratum III (*AS IV,* pl. LXII:2–4; *BS,* p. 191:393, tomb 11).

11. *Gezer* III, pl. LXXXVIII:14.

12. Ibid., pl. LXXXIV:13.

13. *Gezer* II, p. 181; III, pl. CLVIII:11, 16.

14. *Gezer* II, p. 181; III, pl. CLVIII:3.

15. *MP,* p. 374, fig. 65, motif 53:10.

16. *CPP,* 20 M, 24 R4.

Pl. 2. Group of Type 1 bowls [From the Collection of the Israel Department of Antiquities and Museums].
1. No figure.   **2.** See chap. 2, fig. 8:7.   **3.** See fig. 2:5.   **4.** See fig. 2:9.   **5.** See fig. 4.

Pl. 3. Type 1 bowl in fig. 3:1 [From the Collection of the Israel Department of Antiquities and Museums, B. 646].

Pl. 4. Bowl, Myc. IIIC:lb, Sinda [*Sinda*, pl. I].

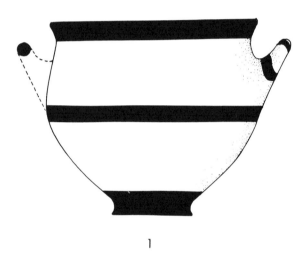

1

2

3

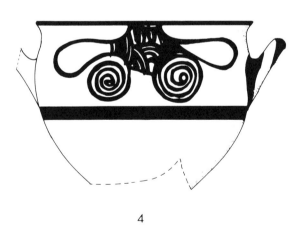

4

Bronze Age Palestinian carinated ware and Iron Age I pottery. The Philistine ceramic influence is evident in the white slip, the horizontal loop handles, and the band decoration. The round-bodied bowls (another example comes from Tell Jerishe; pl. 6) seem to have been borrowed directly from the Mycenaean ceramic repertoire, for this type is particularly characteristic of the Myc. IIIC:1 (LC IIIA) style in Cyprus.[17]

Megiddo Strata VIIA and VIB at Megiddo contained a number of examples of Type 1 bowls.[18] Figure 2:3, from stratum VIIA, represents the ordinary type with double spiral motif. The bowl in figure 2:10, from stratum VIB, in its delicate workmanship, interior decoration, and black-splashed handles is still very close to the Mycenaean prototypes. The repeated single-spiral design alternating with vertical wavy lines on the outside does not appear on small Philistine bowls, although it is known from decorated kraters (see fig. 9:1). On the other hand, the single-spiral decoration does appear alone on the bell-shaped bowls of Myc. IIIC:1, and this may be reflected on the present bowl.

The degenerate type of Philistine bowl, with its shallower outline and vestigial handles, was found in stratum VI. One example from this stratum stands apart, although in style and workmanship it fits into the general picture of the debased Philistine pottery of Megiddo VIA (smooth surface, brick-red and dull-brown decoration).[19] Its decoration consists of a horizontal zigzag line above a series of parallel slanted lines that form another horizontal zigzag pattern. An identical bowl bearing the same tiny vestigial handles comes from Beth-Shean VI (chap. 2, fig. 13:2).

Beth-Shean Apart from the above-mentioned debased example, only two Type 1 bowls are known so far from Beth-Shean. One, which has unusually high loop handles rising above the rim of the bowl (chap. 2, fig. 13:1) comes from upper level VI. The other, a more delicate bowl (fig. 1:5), was found in the anthropoid burial in tomb 221 in the Northern Cemetery.[20]

'Afula Level IIIA at 'Afula has yielded bowls of Type 1, among them an example decorated with horizontal bands (fig. 1:10) and another (fig. 2:11) that approaches the kraters of Type 2 in both shape and antithetic winged-spiral patterns. The flat, slightly carinated bowl (fig. 1:11) was uncovered in the east cemetery, and reflects a later phase.

Ashdod A cache of stacked bowls found in the lowest Philistine level at Ashdod (stratum XIII, area G) is of great importance for understanding the preliminary stages of Philistine pottery. (See description of this ware in the introductory section of this chapter.) This cache consisted of bell-shaped and carinated bowls (chap. 2, pl. 4) with horizontal loop handles. They are closely related to the Mycenaean strap-handle bowls,[21] which were not, however, incorporated into the Philistine repertoire and are confined mainly to Ashdod. The bell-shaped bowls still closely resemble their Mycenaean prototypes, both in the very pronounced profile and the one-color decoration without slip. Although one of the more elaborate decorations does appear in this specific cache, a large number of the fragmentary bell-shaped bowls from stratum XIII (in area G and, mainly, area H) are decorated with typical Myc. IIIC:1 motifs, such as the horizontal wavy line below the rim (chap. 2, fig. 3:1) and the spiral decoration (chap. 2, fig. 3:2, 4–8).

These bowls exhibit certain peculiarities that do not appear in the bichrome Philistine decoration—for example, the cross-hatched center of the spirals (chap. 2, fig. 3:4) and the stemmed spirals (chap. 2, fig. 3:5), which are rare on Philistine bowls but a common feature on Myc. IIIC:1 bowls. This group resembles Myc. IIIC:1 bowls from the mainland, but the closest parallels to the group as a whole come from the twelfth- to the early eleventh-century strata in Cyprus (see below, pp. 216–17). In the subsequent strata, XII–XI, the bell-shaped bowl with the antithetic spiral decoration is dominant, while in stratum X the red slip is the prevailing feature.

Thanks to the Ashdod material, we can now, for the first time, follow the evolution of the Type 1 bowls, starting with their earliest appearance in stratum XIIIb, where they still retain all the characteristics of their Mycenaean contemporaries. Subsequently, the

17. Furumark, *OA 3*, pp. 223 ff., fig. 10:6.
18. Philistine bowl sherds from strata VIII and VIIB at Megiddo were published, but their ascription to these strata is erroneous: *see* chap. 2 above, p. 76; *Meg. II*, pls. 137:11, 138:23.
19. *Meg. II*, pl. 85:2.
20. *B-SH Cemetery*, tomb 221, pp. 112, 130, fig. 47:7.

21. *See*, for example, *Perati B*, pp. 225 (fig. 88:832), 444.

different variants occur side by side: thick, coarsely made bowls together with finer, more delicate ones; slipped together with unslipped; and decorated with undecorated.

With the passage of time, the Philistine bowls grew coarser and shallower, gradually losing the rounded bell shape of the originals. On the decorated bowls, the last stage in this process of degeneration is represented by several examples (fig. 60:1, 2) of red-slip ware decorated with degenerate spirals.

The assimilation of the horizontal loop handles into Palestinian pottery can be observed on bowls down to the end of the tenth century. It is especially evident in the group of red-slipped bowls from Tell el-Far'ah;[22] their sole Philistine characteristic is the horizontal handle. All the other features of these bowls are new; in fact, they foreshadow the ceramic styles of Palestinian pottery in the Iron Age II.

The bell-shaped bowl from which Type 1 is derived is one of the commonest types in the Mycenaean ceramic repertoire. It is found as far back as the Myc. IIIA:2 period and continues unchanged down to Myc. IIIC:1b.[23] No clear Mycenaean bowls of this type have as yet been found in a Late Bronze Age context in Palestine, either as imports or as local imitations.[24] It was, thus, an entirely new pottery type when it made its initial appearance at Ashdod, introduced into Palestine by Philistine potters who drew their inspiration from Myc. IIIC:1 prototypes (pl. 7). It subsequently became one of the most common and popular shapes of Philistine pottery.

22. *CPP*, 18 E, G. These bowls have straight sides, carination toward the belly, and a ring base. The area between the rim and the keel of the carination is decorated with horizontal, incised lines. These bowls are red slipped and usually burnished.

23. *MP*, p. 49, fig. 14:284, 285; *Perati B*, pp. 219–22, 444, figs. 84, 85:1032, 837, 462. For Cypriot parallels, *see* F. G. Maier, "Excavations at Kouklia (Palaepaphos), Seasons 1967," *RDAC* (1968): 90–93; and idem, "The Cemeteries of Old Paphos," *Archaeologia viva* 2 (1969): 119, photo 114. For Myc. IIIC:1b bell-shaped bowls at Enkomi and their connections with the Philistine type, see *Enkomi Excavations*, vol. II, pp. 487–89; vol. IIIa, pls. 74:4, 5, 8, 9 and 94:28.

24. One bell-shaped bowl at 'Aitun comes from an unpublished Late Bronze Age tomb (excavated by V. Tzaferis). Although this tomb seems undisturbed and no late intrusion is recognizable, a Philistine tomb nearby suggests that this bowl is indeed intrusive.

Type 2. Krater (figs. 5–13, pls. 8–25)

Similar to the bowl in shape, but much larger, the krater is generally characterized by a deep, rounded body, although carinated examples also exist (for example, fig. 8:4). The thickened rim may be inverted, everted, or both, and it usually slopes inward. The ring base, either high or flattened, is the most common, but kraters with a disk base are also found. The kraters' two horizontal loop handles vary in postion from horizontal to nearly vertical; in a few instances they are struck straight on to the sides, but the commonest type slants up more or less diagonally. The ware is well fired, retains a dark core, and ranges in color from reddish brown to gray. The white slip usually applied to the exterior of the vessel extends over the rim as well.

Although some of the kraters are undecorated (fig. 5:1) or have plain stripes (fig. 5:2–4), the majority display more complex decorative patterns on a wide band encircling the upper part of the vessel. There are four basic arrangements.

1. *Metopes.* The decorated zone is divided into metopes by triglyphs consisting of various combinations of vertical lines and collateral semicircles, wavy lines, or concentric half-circles. The size of the metopes varies and their arrangement on each face of the band is not always symmetrical in relation to the handles. Two types of motifs are employed in the metopes: (a) the bird, repeated in all the metopes of the band (fig. 7:2) or alternating with geometric motifs such as triangles, spirals, or checkers (figs. 6, 7:1, 8:1); (b) geometric motifs alone, consisting of spirals, semicircles, rhombuses, triangles, checkers, and chevrons (figs. 8:2–5; 9).

2. *Composite.* Individual geometric motifs haphazardly placed around the entire zone of decoration. This is the least common of the four arrangements. The best example is shown in figure 10:4.

3. *Freestanding facial.* Antithetic spirals or spirals facing in the same direction, with solid or Maltese-cross fillings and divided by a variety of curtailed triglyph motifs (fig. 10:1–3).

4. *Repeated units.* Spirals, usually winged, with the addition of one of the more common geometric motifs, such as the rhomboid or wavy line (fig. 11:1–4). Three uncommon motifs also included in this category are the running spiral (fig. 11:5–6), the composite zigzag

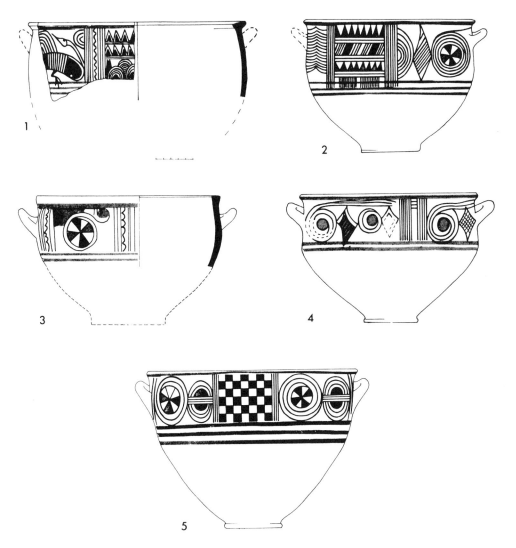

Fig. 8. Type 2 kraters.
1. White slip, Azor.   **2.** White slip, Azor.   **3.** White slip, Tell Beit Mirsim, East Cave [*TBM I*, pl. 49:5].   **4.** White slip, Tell el-Far'ah [*BP I*, pls. XXIII:2, XXIV; *CPP*, 26 B2].   **5.** Gezer [*Gezer III*, pl. CLVIII:1].

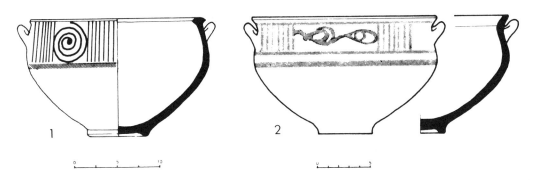

Fig. 9. Type 2 kraters.
1. White slip, Tell Qasile, stratum XII [*Qasile IEJ 1*, fig. 4:2].   **2.** White slip, Tell el-Far'ah, tomb 625 [*BP I*, pl. XXXI:290].

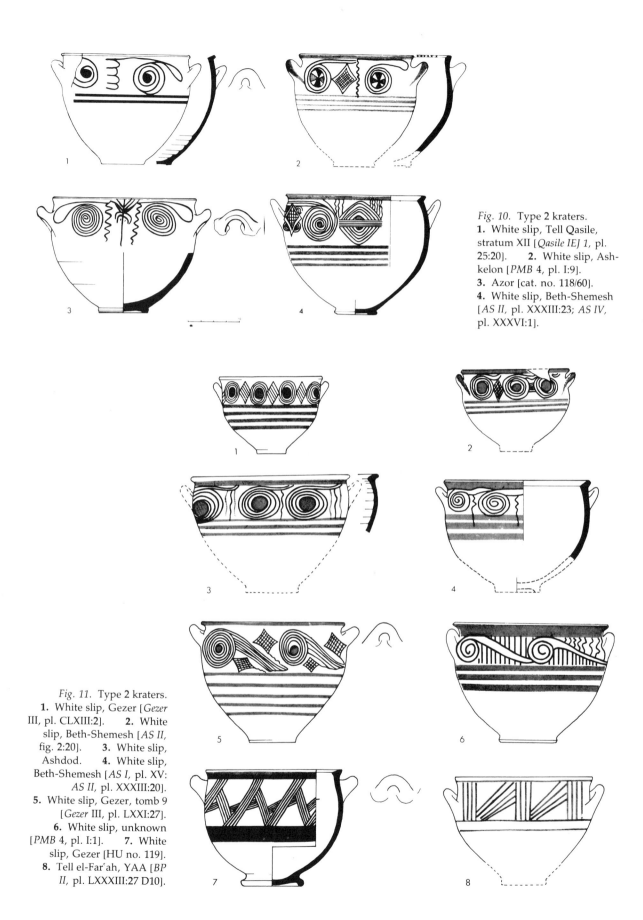

Fig. 10. Type 2 kraters.
1. White slip, Tell Qasile, stratum XII [Qasile IEJ 1, pl. 25:20]. 2. White slip, Ashkelon [PMB 4, pl. I:9]. 3. Azor [cat. no. 118/60]. 4. White slip, Beth-Shemesh [AS II, pl. XXXIII:23; AS IV, pl. XXXVI:1].

Fig. 11. Type 2 kraters.
1. White slip, Gezer [Gezer III, pl. CLXIII:2]. 2. White slip, Beth-Shemesh [AS II, fig. 2:20]. 3. White slip, Ashdod. 4. White slip, Beth-Shemesh [AS I, pl. XV: AS II, pl. XXXIII:20]. 5. White slip, Gezer, tomb 9 [Gezer III, pl. LXXI:27]. 6. White slip, unknown [PMB 4, pl. I:1]. 7. White slip, Gezer [HU no. 119]. 8. Tell el-Farʿah, YAA [BP II, pl. LXXXIII:27 D10].

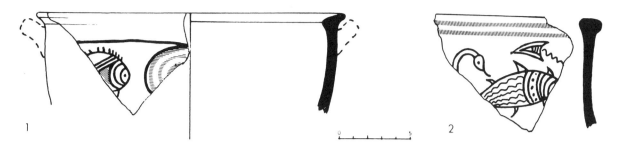

Fig. 12. Type **2** kraters.
1. Azor. **2.** Tell el-Far'ah, YX 364'10" [*BP II*, pl. LXIII:46].

Fig. 13. Type **2** krater [*Sinda*, pl. II (dap); decoration of krater, *Sinda*, fig. 6].

Pl. 8. Type **2** krater in fig. 10:2 [From the Collection of the Israel Department of Antiquities and Museums, B. 645].

Pl. 9. Type **2** krater, Tell Sippor [From the Collection of the Israel Department of Antiquities and Museums, 63-1597].

Pl. 11. Type **2** krater in fig. 8:2 [Weisenfreund Collection].

Pl. 10. Type **2** krater, Beth-Shemesh (and detail) [From the Collection of the Israel Department of Antiquities and Museums, I. 57. *BS,* p. 193].

Pl. 12. Type **2** krater in fig. 10:3 [From the Collection of the Israel Department of Antiquities and Museums, 63-1034].

Pl. 13. Type **2** krater in fig. 6 (and details) [From the Collection of the Israel Department of Antiquities and Museums, 64-360].

Pl. 15. Type 2 krater in fig. 11:7 [Institute of Archaeology, The Hebrew University of Jerusalem, 119].

Pl. 14. Type 2 krater in fig. 11:6 (two views) [From the Collection of the Israel Department of Antiquities and Museums, B. 119].

Pl. 16. Type 2 krater, Azor [Weisenfreund Collection].

Pl. 17. Type 2 krater in fig. 5:2 [From the Collection of the Israel Department of Antiquities and Museums, 60-554].

Pl. 18. Type 2 krater in fig. 5:4 [Institute of Archaeology, The Hebrew University of Jerusalem, 243].

Pl. 19. Type 2 krater fragment in fig. 7:2.

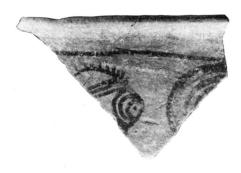

Pl. 23. Type 2 krater fragment in fig. 12:1 [Weisenfreund Collection].

Pl. 20. Type 2 krater fragment in fig. 62:25 [From the Collection of the Israel Department of Antiquities and Museums, P. 1197].

Pl. 24. Krater, Myc. IIIC:1b, in fig. 13 [*Sinda*, fig. 3].

Pl. 21. Type 2 krater fragment [From the Collection of the Israel Department of Antiquities and Museums, P. 1213. F. Bliss and R. A. S. Macalister, *Excavations in Palestine* (London, 1902), frontispiece, pl. 41].

Pl. 22. Type 2 krater fragment in fig. 61:5 [From the Collection of the Israel Department of Antiquities and Museums, 51-64, 51-65].

Pl. 25. Krater, Myc. IIIC:1b, Sinda [*Sinda*, fig. 3].

pattern (fig. 11:7) and its debased version (fig. 11:8), and the repeated triglyph pattern (pl. 16).

We have selected a number of sites where kraters of particular importance and interest have been found. By means of the stylistic or typological aspects of these vessels and their place in stratigraphic contexts we can trace the development of the Philistine krater from its first appearance to its gradual debasement and assimilation into the native pottery.

Ashdod Among the group of krater fragments from stratum XIII at Ashdod, the lowest Philistine level, two types can be distinguished: one of greenish clay with brown-black decoration; the other, of reddish clay, with dark brick-red or brownish decoration. Laboratory tests of the clay have shown that these krater sherds, like the Type 1 bowls, seem to be of local clay; they nonetheless show a close adherence to Mycenaean methods in throwing and firing and in the blending and consistency of the paint. These sherds stand apart from the standard Philistine types by being very close to Myc IIIC:1 prototypes in their flattened rim, one-color scheme, and decoration. Down to the smallest detail, the decoration retains all the Myc. IIIC:1 traits: row of suspended half-circles (chap. 2, fig. 3:1), the spirals with cross-hatched centers (chap. 2, fig. 3:4), spirals with elaborate loops (chap. 2, fig. 3:7, 13), the triglyph motif with zigzag pattern, and especially the fish (chap. 2, fig. 3:9, 10) and bird motifs. All are very close to Myc. IIIC:1b examples (see fig. 72 below). Concurrently and subsequently, in stratum XIII and through strata XII and XI, the bichrome decoration appears at Ashdod in a great range and variety of motifs and exhibits many unusual adaptations that are, so far as is known, unique to Ashdod.

Tell el-Farʿah. The kraters at Tell el Farʿah include three examples with the metope arrangement. The first vessel is of excellent workmanship and displays a wealth of decorative motifs. Birds, facing both forward and backward, are depicted in each of the metopes (fig. 7:3). It is unusual to find both of these two basic variations of the bird motif on the same vessel. This krater belongs to the earliest phase—the *floruit*—of Philistine ceramic art. It comes from stratum D, level 387, at the south end of the mound, where a large number of early Philistine vessels were found. The carinated body and monotonous decoration of the

second krater (fig. 8:4) indicate that it belongs to a later phase of Philistine pottery. The third example (fig. 11:8) comes from room YAA in the west wing of the Residency. Its simple geometric motif may be a debased version of the composite zigzag motif on the Gezer krater shown in figure 11:7.

A krater belonging to the last phase of Philistine pottery was found in tomb 625[25] (the tomb that contained the strainer-spout jug of fig. 27:1). This krater (fig. 9:2) is very similar in concept to a krater from Qasile XII (fig. 9:1). The basic decorative motifs are identical, but the design on the Farʿah krater is clearly a debased version of the original spiral motif as it appears on the Qasile vessel.

A fragment of a krater (fig. 12:2) decorated with the rare combination of bird and fish is closely akin to Mycenaean representations (see fig. 64:5 below). Stratigraphically, it was found above the courtyard (YX 364.10) and belongs to Phase 1 of Philistine pottery.

Ashkelon A krater from Ashkelon (fig. 10:2, pl. 8) is adorned with an unusually fine pair of antithetic spirals with a Maltese cross and a net-filled rhombus.

Tell Beit Mirsim A krater from stratum B₂ at Tell Beit Mirsim (fig. 8:3) has a decorative band divided into metopes, in the center of each of which is a spiral with a Maltese cross.

Tel Ṣippor Similar in concept to the Ashkelon krater, but belonging to the greenish one-color group (as found in Ashdod) is a complete krater from the twelfth-century-B.C. level at Tel Ṣippor (pl. 9).[26] It is close to Myc. IIIC:1 in shape (with a very flat rim and good proportions) and in the meticulous execution of its one-color patterns on a greenish background. However, the Maltese crosses that fill the concentric circles are a feature of true Philistine pottery that almost never appears in Mycenaean ware.

Beth-Shemesh Three kraters from stratum III[27] at Beth-Shemesh merit attention. One (fig. 10:4) displays

25. Regarding the correct attribution of the tomb's contents, *see* chap. 2, p. 32, n. 65, above.

26. A. Biran and O. Negbi, *IEJ* 16 (1966): 163, fig. 6:7, pls. 19A and 21A.

27. Krater fragments that in the published photographs

a composite and unusual random arrangement of rhombuses, winged spirals, and concentric semicircles in its decorative band. Another (fig. 11:4), with its single winged-spiral motif recurring around the entire band, is an example of a repeated unit arrangement. The third krater (fig. 11:2)[28] and another (pl. 10) from tomb 1, both very closely resemble the krater shown in fig. 11:1, except that the spiral motifs of the krater in the photo are separated by groups of horizontal lines joining concentric semicircles on one face, while the other face has a metope arrangement incorporating a very unusual stylization of the bird and spiral, in which the spiral merges with a bird's tail and wing.

In addition to the whole vessels, a large number of krater sherds were found in stratum III;[29] one of them (fig. 61:23) also incorporates the spiral into the bird pattern.

Gezer Most of the kraters from Gezer have a metope arrangement of birds (fig. 7:1–2; pls. 19, 21) or geometric patterns (fig. 8:5).

Three kraters display a repeated-unit arrangement. Figure 11:1 has a spiral and rhombus motif, while figure 11:5, which comes from tomb 9, is highly stylized. Its decorative unit is typical of the Gezer potter and is composed of a multiple-stem spiral and rhombus with a wavy stem (compare fig. 25:1). A krater of unknown origin (fig. 11:6, pl. 14) is decorated with a similarly arranged running spiral against a background of stripes on one face and a slapdash rendition with only one running spiral on the other face.

A large krater (fig. 11:7, pl. 15) bears a unique composite zigzag design. Another exceptionally large krater is decorated with horizontal stripes and may have been part of an oil press.[30] Typical of the last phase of Philistine pottery is the red slip (fig. 5:4, pl. 18).

Tell Qasile A large number of krater sherds came from strata XII and XI at Tell Qasile.[31] Most were

coated with a white slip and decorated in bichrome red and black. It should be noted that the bird motif was found almost exclusively in stratum XII; only one example came from stratum XI. The motifs on several of the stratum XII sherds are painted with the deft, flowing strokes of a skilled hand (fig. 61:5, pl. 22). Another sherd displays unusual stylization of its bird motif (fig. 62:31), which appears together with a winged spiral in a metopically divided band. There is also a rare sherd of brown clay with a geometrized bird motif (fig. 62:30) painted in yellowish colors.

Two other stratum XII kraters worthy of mention here are figure 9:1, which has simple but uncommon decoration (see debased version on the Tell el-Farʿah krater, fig. 9:2), and figure 10:1, whose double-spiral facial motif is closest to that of the Ashkelon krater in figure 10:2.

In strata XII, XI, and X at Tell Qasile we can witness the Philistine krater's gradual degeneration and assimilation into the local ceramic tradition. The result was the emergence of a new pottery type—the "subPhilistine" krater (Type 18).

Azor The excavation of the Philistine cemetery at Azor has brought to light a large number of kraters, the majority of which can be divided into three groups.

1. *Vessels probably produced in the same workshop and perhaps even decorated by the same artist.* They are characterized by an abundance of motifs executed in fine close-set lines very reminiscent of the Mycenaean Close Style. To this group belongs figure 6 (pl. 13), probably the finest example of a Philistine krater known. Both faces on its decorated band are carefully divided into three metopes. The middle metope of each face is square and contains a looped spiral with a Maltese-cross filling. The loop of the spiral is elaborated with lines and chevrons to resemble the body of a stylized bird. Concentric semicircles are added at the corners of the metopes. The birds in the remaining four metopes are identical in every detail, except that one bird's head faces forward, while the other three are turned backward (see also fig. 7:3 for this unusual combination of birds facing forward and backward on the same vessel).

Only two metopes have been preserved on the krater in figure 8:1. One metope contains a bird very similar to those in figure 6; the other is divided into two horizontal rows of triangles and one row of composite concentric semicircles. The krater in figure 8:2, in de-

are seen to belong to Type 2 were found in stratum IVB. Wright believes that these vessels have no connection with Philistine pottery but should be considered local imitations of the Myc. IIIB kraters (*AS V*, p. 121).

28. *AS III*, p. 79, fig. 2:20. Room 315 I, in which the krater was found, contained a number of other Philistine sherds.

29. Cf. esp. *AS IV*, pl. XXXVI:2–5.

30. *Gezer* II, p. 66, fig. 260; p. 181, fig. 341.

31. *Qasile IEJ 1*, p. 127, fig. 4:1, pl. 25:1, 2.

sign and arrangement, is almost identical with the one in figure 8:1, but it bears geometric motifs alone (cf. pl. 11).

One krater (fig. 10:3, pl. 12) is rather unusual in that its antithetic spirals are very close to the original Mycenaean prototype, while its triglyph consists of a stylized palm—a motif otherwise unknown in Philistine ceramics but common in the local ceramic tradition. One of the few examples of the fish motif in the entire Philistine repertoire can be seen in figure 12:1 (pl. 23).

2. *Vessels decorated only with geometric motifs, either in metope arrangements or in repeated units such as the composite triglyph in plate 16. The workmanship is somewhat crude and is clearly inferior to that of the first group.*

3. *Kraters decorated solely with stripes (fig. 5:2, pl. 17).*

Megiddo A number of Philistine krater sherds were included in the unpublished material from Megiddo. Two white-slipped sherds with red and black decoration belong to stratum VIIA. One sherd (chap. 2, pl. 18:6) is decorated with a winged spiral, and the other (chap. 2, pl. 17:5) shows only the remnants of alternating red and black vertical lines.

Two fragments of a krater (chap. 2, pl. 19:5, 6) from an unclear context, although they are typologically very similar to sherds from stratum VII, display an interesting arrangement of geometric motifs somewhat similar to the Azor kraters (fig. 8:1, 2).

Stratum VIA contained "sub-Philistine" kraters typical of Tell Qasile X (see also Type 18 below) and an unstratified krater (fig. 5:3) decorated with horizontal stripes very similar in shape to one from Gezer (fig. 5:4).

The krater with two horizontal handles is known to have been in Palestine from Late Bronze II on, sometimes as a possible imported vessel[32] but predominantly as a local imitation. The largest collection of locally made kraters of this type comes from the Megiddo Late Bronze II tombs[33] and from stratum VIIB on the mound.[34]

The Philistine kraters bear little resemblance to the local imitations of the Mycenaean vessel, either in shape or decoration, and their divergence from the local ware is marked. Their affinities with the original Mycenaean krater, on the other hand, are all the more conspicuous. The prototype of the Philistine krater is the Mycenaean Type 282 krater, which is found in Myc. IIIB but is more characteristic of Myc. IIIC:1.[35] The similarity between the two is evident in shape (the carinated body and lip), in the range and combination of decorative motifs, in the metope arrangement, and in the style of the decoration, which is much the same as the Mycenaean Close Style of the Argolid.[36] The closest published parallels to the Philistine kraters are the Myc. IIIC:1b kraters from Sinda (fig. 13, pls. 24 and 25) and Enkomi, which are related to the monochrome variant from Ashdod (chap. 2, fig. 3:7).

For all its indebtedness to a Mycenaean prototype, the Philistine krater nevertheless reflects the uniqueness and individuality of Philistine pottery: the potters took Mycenaean motifs and fashioned them into a new and distinctively Philistine style.

Type 3. Stirrup Jar (figs. 14–17, pls. 26–35)

The stirrup (or false-necked) jar is distinguished mainly by the solid (hence false) neck and disk top. The disk is part of the neck and usually has a knob projecting above its rim which resembles a stopper. In a later variant, this disk top is slightly concave (pl. 30). The only actual opening is a funnel-like spout on the shoulder of the jar. The most common type of spout rises vertically, or nearly so, to approximately the height of the neck (fig. 17:2–5). Two debased variants are the short spout (fig. 16:2), which reaches to about half the height of the neck, and the splaying spout (fig. 17:6), which extends well above the top of the neck. Two loop handles, either oval or, more often, flattened in section, extend from the rim to the shoulders. The body is globular (fig. 16:3), squat (fig. 17:3), or piriform (fig. 16:2) and stands on a ring base. The Philistine stirrup jar is small in comparison to its Mycenaean prototype, with an overall height that ranges from ten to eighteen centimeters.

The method employed in the manufacture of the

32. There is one possible example from Megiddo; *Meg. T.,* tomb 912B, pls. 34:9, 124:8.

33. Ibid., p. 157, tomb 877, pl. 13:24; tomb 911, pl. 31:4; tomb 912, pl. 35:30.

34. *Meg. II,* pls. 66:4, 70:2, 72:3.

35. *MP,* p. 50, figs. 13:281, 14:282.

36. *Sinda,* pp. 108 ff.; *Enkomi Excavations,* vol. I, p. 285, vol. IIIa, pls. 78:11; 81:12, 13 (belonging to levels IIIA–B).

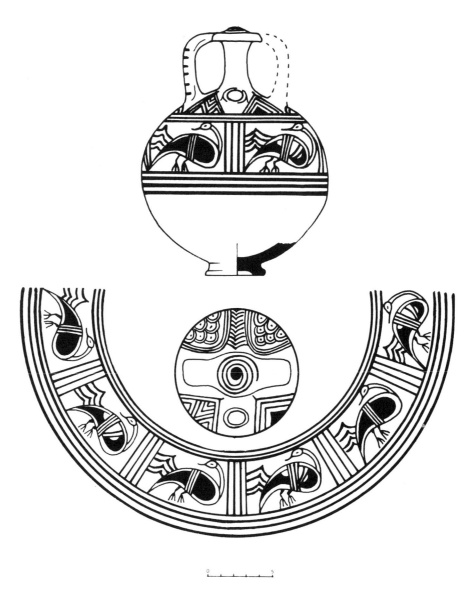

Fig. 14. Type 3 stirrup jar, white slip, Gezer [*Gezer* II, fig. 339; *PMB* 4, pl. II:5].

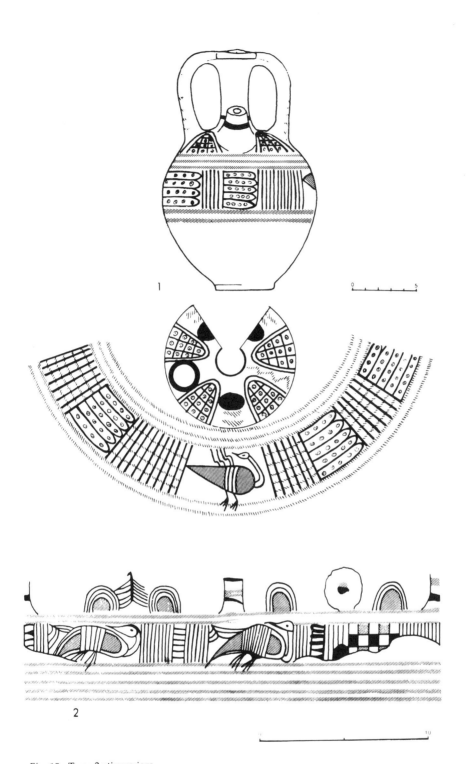

Fig. 15. Type 3 stirrup jars.
1. White slip, Azor.   **2.** Tell el-Farʿah [*BP I,* pl. LXIII:1].

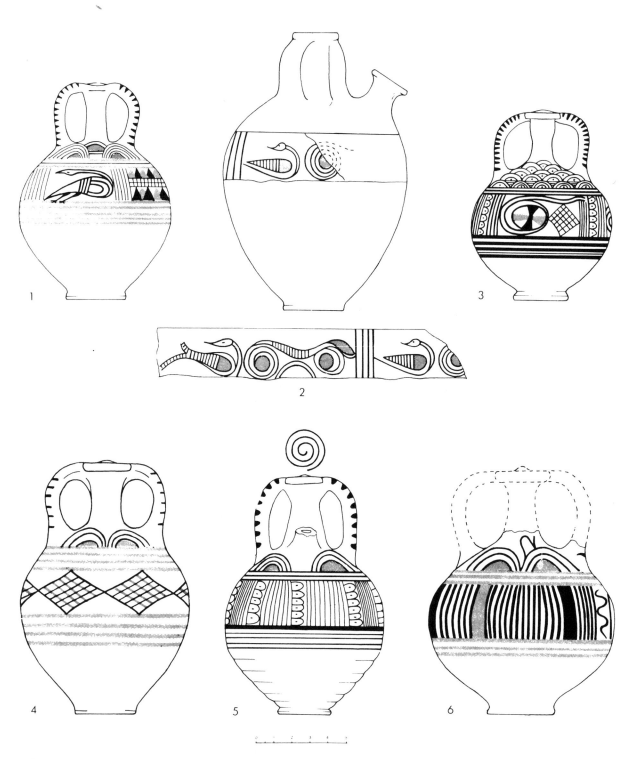

Fig. 16. Type 3 stirrup jars.

1. Beth-Shemesh, stratum III [*AS III,* fig. **2**:19; *AS IV,* pl. XXXVIII:20].   **2.** White slip, Gezer, tomb 9 [*Gezer* III, pl. LXX:14].
3. Beth-Shemesh, stratum III [*AS III,* fig. **2**:17; *AS IV,* pl. XXXVIII:21].   **4.** Gezer, tomb 59 [*Gezer* III, pl. LXXXV:7].
5. White slip, Beth-Shemesh, stratum III [*AS III,* fig. **2**:15].   **6.** White slip, Gezer (?) [*PMB* 4, pl. II:7].

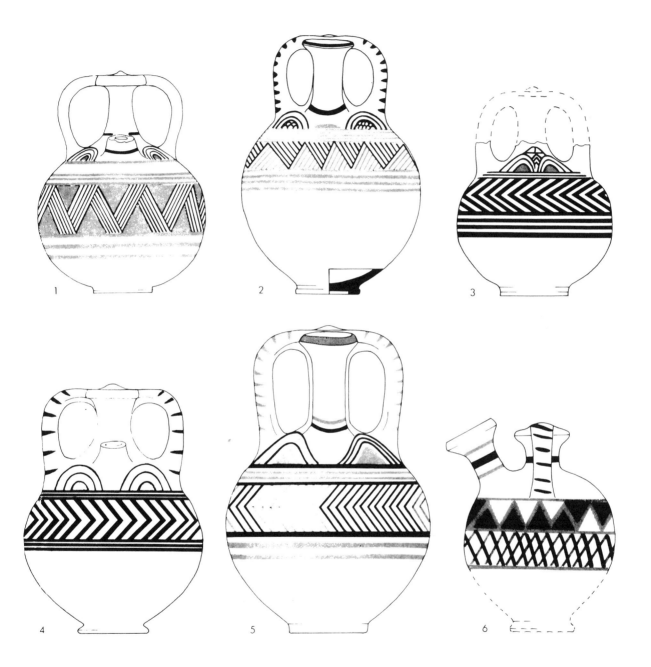

Fig. 17. Type 3 stirrup jars.
1. White slip, Tell el-Farʿah, YX365 [*BP II*, pls. LXIV:72, LXXXVII:64R']. **2.** White slip, Azor. **3.** Beth-Shemesh, stratum III [*AS IV*, pl. LX:15]. **4.** Tell el-Farʿah, tomb 532 [*BP I*, pl. XXII:199]. **5.** White slip, Azor. **6.** Light buff slip, burnished, Megiddo, stratum VI [*Meg. II*, pls. 86:12, 144:19].

Pl. 26. Group of Type 3 stirrup jars [From the Collection of the Israel Department of Antiquities and Museums, 68-1033, 33.1855, and Private Collection].
1. See fig. 15:1.   **2.** No figure.   **3.** See fig. 16:1.

Pl. 27. Type 3 stirrup jar in fig. 17:1
[Ashmolean Museum].

Pl. 28. Group of Type 3 stirrup jars [From the Collection of the Israel Department of Antiquities and Museums, 33.1835, I. 10510, 33.1854].
1. See fig. 16:5.   **2.** No figure.   **3.** See fig. 16:3.

Pl. 33. Stirrup jar, Myc. IIIC:1b, Ialysos
[*Ialysos*, pl. XXIV].

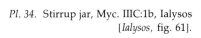

Pl. 34. Stirrup jar, Myc. IIIC:1b, Ialysos
[*Ialysos*, fig. 61].

Pl. 35. Stirrup jar, Myc. IIIC:1b, Ialysos
[*Ialysos*, fig. 40].

Philistine jar differed somewhat from the Mycenaean technique. Like its Mycenaean counterpart, the false neck is wheel-thrown and inserted into the top of the jar; but it widens out at the bottom into a broad, flat, string-cut base, which must have been inserted into a much larger hole that was then smoothed out. Both the spout, which is inserted into the shoulder, and the handles, which are attached to the outside, follow the Mycenaean tradition.

The ware is usually well levigated and ranges from pale-greenish hues through light-red and light-buff clay. Most jars are covered with a white slip, although some are self-slipped and decorated in bichrome red and black—the black being used to outline the central motifs, while the red is used as filling to accentuate individual features. The top disk is decorated with a spiral, the spout has a painted band around its lip, and the handles are decorated with horizontal stripes of one or two alternating colors.

In the early monochrome style represented by the Gezer jar (see fig. 14) the body is divided into two registers of decoration:

1. *The upper register.* The handles and the spout separate the upper register of the jar into three sections. To create a symmetrical arrangement, a dividing motif is painted opposite the spout, thus producing four decorative units with elaborate "triangle" patterns. A variation and slight degeneration of the triangle pattern is the substitution of four concentric semicircles with different filling motifs; the concentric semicircle is, in fact, the most common decorative motif on Philistine stirrup jars (fig. 16:4–6). On some debased examples, the upper register is left plain (fig. 17:6).

2. *The lower register.* This register, the main focus of decoration, is a broad band around the belly of the jar bearing one of the following two decorations:
(a) division into a series of metopes containing bird motifs (fig. 14), geometric motifs (fig. 16:3), or a combination of both (figs. 15:2, 16:1);
(b) an undivided arrangement of continuous geometric motifs such as the composite zigzag (fig. 17:1–2) or chevrons (fig. 17:3–5) or repeated motifs such as the rhombus (fig. 16:4) or triglyphs (fig. 16:5–6).

Although a great many stirrup jars have been found, few are intact. Most of these come from Beth-Shemesh, Tell el-Farʿah, Gezer, Azor, and Ashdod.

Beth-Shemesh A number of well preserved and exceptionally well made stirrup jars come from Beth-Shemesh stratum III. The decorative arrangements on the lower register fit the two categories mentioned above.

DIVISION INTO METOPES Figure 16:3 (pl. 28:3)[37] displays a winged spiral and a rhombus motif in each of the two (front and back) metopes on its register. An elaborate, dotted, continuous scale pattern fills the upper register. Figure 16:1 has wingless birds with heads turned back alternating with double decks of red and black triangles along its lower register (cf. also fig. 8:1, 2). The workmanship and decorative style of both these jars place them in the first phase of Philistine pottery.

CONTINUOUS MOTIF The jar in plate 28:2 is decorated with a continuous zigzag pattern formed by groups of parallel lines arranged in alternating diagonals with red filling in the angles between them. This design is known in the Myc IIIC:1 period and is especially common on stirrup jars (fig. 71:7, pl. 35).[38] A sub-Mycenaean variation of this pattern is found, for example, on a stirrup jar from Cyprus.[39] The decoration on the Beth-Shemesh jar is identical to that of a stirrup jar from Tell el-Farʿah (fig. 17:1, pl. 27) that is dated to the mid-twelfth century B.C. The date of the Farʿah jar and the closeness of the zigzag pattern to its Mycenaean prototype point to the same date for the Beth-Shemesh stirrup jar. Both these jars are excellent examples of the adaptation—by means of a few minor alterations—of a purely Mycenaean vessel and motif to a Philistine ceramic type.

Like the vessel described above, the stirrup jar in plate 35 has a very similar, although not quite identical, counterpart at Tell el-Farʿah (fig. 17:4). This Farʿah jar, from tomb 532, is dated by its context to the end of the twelfth and beginning of the eleventh centuries, and the Beth-Shemesh jar can be assigned to approximately the same period. The main decorative motif on the former is a belt of horizontal chevrons in the lower register, a design frequently used as a primary motif on Myc. IIIC:1 stirrup jars (fig. 71:1, pl. 35). The chevron motif on the Beth-Shemesh jar is clearly Mycenaean in origin, which fits its date at the end of the first phase of Philistine pottery.

37. *AS V*, p. 127.
38. *MP*, p. 388.
39. Gjerstad, *OA 3*, p. 92, fig. 5:5.

The jar in figure 16:5 (pl. 28:1) is decorated with a repeated motif consisting of groups of vertical lines separated by single rows of collateral, dotted semicircles. This design often serves as a triglyph but seldom as the dominant motif. Similar use of a triglyph motif is found on a stirrup jar from Azor (fig. 15:2). The shape and derivative way of rendering the triglyph motif may indicate a later stage in Philistine ceramics than the two previous jars from Beth-Shemesh.

The Beth-Shemesh stirrup jars cannot be fitted into a clearer archaeological context nor a more narrowly defined substratification within the rather broad stratum III. Only on the basis of typological evidence (the nature of the decorative motifs and their relative proximity to the Mycenaean prototypes) and by stylistic comparisons (with the two stirrup jars from datable contexts at Tell el-Far'ah) can the first two Beth-Shemesh jars be dated to between the second quarter of the twelfth and the first half of the eleventh century B.C., and the third jar to the end of that period.

Tell el-Far'ah Two of the stirrup jars found at Tell el-Far'ah are of special importance because they are counterparts of the Beth-Shemesh jars described above. The jar shown in plate 31 (comparable to the Beth-Shemesh examples in pl. 28:2) comes from the YX courtyard and dates to the second third of the twelfth century B.C. The second jar, shown in figure 17:4 (compare the Beth-Shemesh jar, fig. 17:3), comes from tomb 532 (the end of the twelfth and beginning of the eleventh century).

Evidence of artistic talent is conspicuously lacking on a third stirrup jar from Tell el-Far'ah (fig. 15:2), for the potter seems to have been unable to successfully adapt the standard bird motif to fit a rectangular metope.

Gezer A diversified group of stirrup jars was uncovered at Gezer. Here, too, the decorative arangement conforms to either the metope or the continuous geometric pattern.

DIVISION INTO METOPES One of the best examples (fig. 14, pl. 32) displays on each of the metopes of the band a bird with its head turned back. This vessel is very close to the original Mycenaean style in its globular shape and one-color scheme; and the elaborate triangle pattern in the upper register above the metope band is typical of Myc. IIIC:1 stirrup jars.[40]

40. *MP*, pp. 174, 210, 407 ff.

A jar from tomb 9 (fig. 16:2) is exceptional in both its elongated shape and stylized decoration. The decorative elements are limited to the central band and consist of the unique combination of a double spiral and bird motifs in a single, long, narrow metope. The wingless birds are less naturalistic and more decorative. The feet have vanished, and the body, streamlined and stylized, ends in one case in a fish tail. Also unusual is the manner in which the stylized lines of the bird's body are repeated in the design connecting the two spirals. The overall workmanship and extreme stylization show a high level of artistry. The uncommon nature of the Philistine pottery group from tomb 9 has already been discussed (cf. chap. 2 and chap. 4, fig. 1); we pointed out that the character of this tomb group is not the result of a development or degeneration from an early prototype but must be attributed to the skill of the Gezer potter, who modified and stylized ordinary Philistine motifs to suit his own taste. On the basis of the Philistine sherds found in the same tomb,[41] we have suggested that this stirrup jar should be dated to the first phase of Philistine pottery.

CONTINUOUS MOTIF The stirrup jar in figure 16:4 comes from tomb 59, the Philistine contents of which are dated to the first half of the eleventh century. Its central band is decorated with a series of net-filled rhomboids.

Figure 16:6 illustrates the complete debasement of the triglyph as a central motif on stirrup jars.[42] This use of the triglyph was noted in the description of figure 16:5 (above), in which the original character of the motif has been at least partly retained. In the Gezer example, on the other hand, the origin of the triglyph pattern—groups of close-set vertical lines separated by single wavy lines and areas of red and black—is not immediately discernible.

Azor The complete stirrup jars discovered in the Philistine cemetery at Azor illustrate the diversity of Philistine decoration. The simplest are several small, plain, white-slipped jars decorated only with horizontal red lines.

A more unusual jar (fig. 15:1) has as its main decora-

41. *Gezer* III, pl. LXXI:21, 23.
42. Ibid., pl. CLXXIX:15; *PMB* 4 (1927): pl. II:7. The vessel is published among the Hellenistic vessels at Gezer and in *PMB* it appears with no indication of the location at which it was uncovered; in fact, both references are to the same stirrup jar.

tive motif a curious and novel version of the collateral semicircle and vertical triglyph repeated around the band (for example, fig. 16:5, pl. 28:1). The semicircles are elongated and contain a row of four dots instead of the usual one. The vertical lines are crossed with horizontal red lines to form a bichrome net pattern that is used again as a filling for the semicircles in the handle zone. A single bird motif occupies the metope below one of the handles. The bird is poorly executed, its body and wings badly drawn and confused—it is a far cry from the usual outstanding quality of Philistine ceramic art at Azor. This jar probably belongs to a late phase of Philistine pottery at Azor.

Two stirrup jars with continuous geometric motifs (fig. 17:2, 5, pls. 29, 31) are decorated with an unusual feature: a band of horizontal chevrons in alternate groups of red and black. The jar in figure 17:2 (pl. 31) is the work of a meticulous hand. Concentric semicircles with a scale-pattern filling occupy the handle area of the jar. The lower register contains a composite zigzag motif with the upper groups of lines in black and the lower in red. This type of motif is known in the Myc. IIIC:1 ceramic tradition and is especially common on stirrup jars (fig. 71:4, pl. 35).

Megiddo Figure 17:6 (pl. 30) shows the debased stirrup jar of Megiddo VI. In workmanship and decoration, it belongs to the debased Philistine pottery peculiar to stratum VIA at Megiddo. Unlike most Philistine stirrup jars, the neck is short, the top disk is concave, and the spout, rising above the neck, terminates in a splaying rim. The handle area is plain, and the lower register is divided into two, the upper band being filled with asymmetrically colored triangles and the lower with a continuous net pattern. An identical design is found on a basket-handle and strainer-spout jug (fig. 59:1, Type 17) from the same Megiddo VIA ceramic group.

The stirrup jar is one of the most common Mycenaean imports in the Levant. It first appeared as a Myc. IIIA vessel during the fourteenth century, was widely distributed as a Myc. IIIB import in the thirteenth century,[43] and ceased to be imported almost entirely at the end of the century. The Mycenaean stirrup jar was incorporated into the Canaanite pottery tradition, and local imitations, which were most numerous in the thirteenth century, continued to appear until the eleventh century B.C.[44]

The Philistine stirrup jar, however, is not an imitation of the local Palestinian vessel, and the similarities between the two are in fact due to their common prototype—the Mycenaean stirrup jar. The decorative motifs of the Philistine jar are clearly borrowed directly from Myc. IIIC:1 jars of Types 175–76 and their closest parallels can be found in stirrup jars from Perati, Rhodes, and Cyprus,[45] and also from Beth-Shean (chap. 2, pl. 20).[46]

Although the metope arrangement characteristic of Philistine stirrup jar decoration does appear in Myc. III:C1 pottery, it is not very common. An especially striking example of a Mycenaean metope arrangement is the stirrup jar from Ialysos shown in plate 33. Most of its decorative motifs are also found on the Philistine stirrup jars, where they appear, however, in different arrangements on the decorative zones. The stirrup jars in plates 34 and 35 display a repeated geometric decoration. Being artistically limited, they show less divergence from their Mycenaean origin. The same is true of the elaborate triangles on the handle zone of the Gezer jar in figure 14.

The most outstanding features of Philistine stirrup jars as a whole are their close kinship to their Mycenaean prototypes and the emergence of a new decorative style based entirely on Mycenaean motifs but arranged in new and different ways.

Type 4. Amphoriskos and Pyxis (figs. 18–19, pls. 36–45)

This type of vessel originally included only the squat pyxis and some fragments that seemed to be variants of it. New discoveries, however, have shown that these fragments belong to a separate group of round-bodied amphoriskoi. Because of their close affinities, we have included both groups of vessels under Type 4.

Amphoriskos The amphoriskos (fig. 18:4, 5) has a globular body, tall cylindrical neck, ring base, and two horizontal handles on the shoulders. The pyxis and

43. Stubbings, pp. 69, 81–87.

44. *CPP*, 64 K1, K2, K4, M, P.

45. The Philistine stirrup jars have no ventilation hole in their shoulders as do the Mycenaean jars of the last phase of the IIIC:1 period; cf. *DMS*, p. 211.

46. V. Hankey, "Late Mycenaean Pottery at Beth-Shean", *AJA* 70 (1966): 169–71, pl. 45; idem, "Mycenaean Pottery in the Middle East," *BSA* 62 (1967): 128, pl. 29:b, c, d.

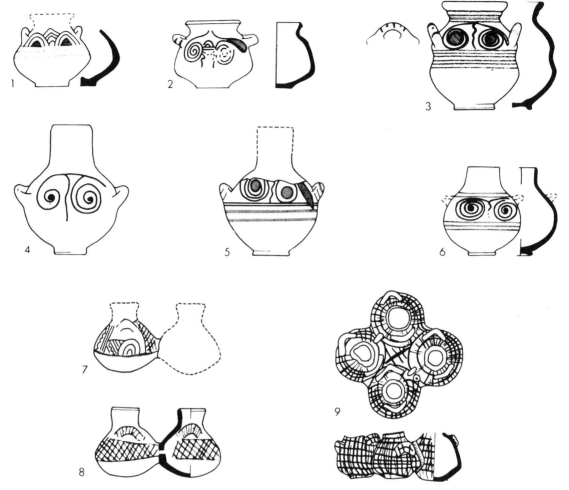

Fig. 18. Type 4 pyxides and amphoriskoi.
1. White slip, Gezer [*PMB* 4, pl. II:3; *Gezer* III, pl. CLXIII:5].   **2.** Tell Qasile, stratum XI [Q. IV 1052/1].   **3.** White slip, unknown.   **4.** Tell el-ʿAjjul, cemetery 1000, tomb 1139 [*AG II*, pl. XXXIV:55 T15].   **5.** White slip, Tell Beit Mirsim, B₂ [*TBM I*, pl. 51:18].   **6.** White slip, Tell Qasile, stratum XI [Q. IV 1051/1].   **7.** Burnished, Megiddo, stratum VI [No. P5830].   **8.** Burnished, Megiddo, stratum VIIA [*Meg. II*, pl. 68:8].   **9.** Burnished, Megiddo, stratum VIA [*Meg. II*, pl. 77:8].

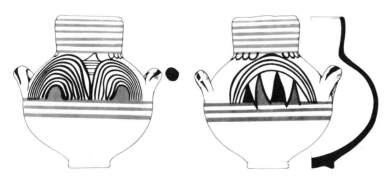

Fig. 19. Amphoriskos, Azor (?) [MW.9.4768].

Pl. 40. Pyxis, Myc. IIIC:1b, Ialysos [*Ialysos,* fig. 4].

Pl. 36. Type 4 pyxis in fig. 18:2 [From the Collection of the Israel Department of Antiquities and Museums, 1052/1].

Pl. 37. Type 4 pyxis in fig. 18:3 [T. Kollek Collection].

Pl. 38. Type 4 pyxis [Weisenfreund Collection].

Pl. 39.1. Type 4 amphoriskos in fig. 19 (Azor?) [Museum Ha'aretz, MHP 4768].

Pl. 39.2. Type 4 pyxis jar, Tell Qasile, stratum XII [A. Mazar, "Excavations at Tell Qasile, 1973–1974: Preliminary Report," *IEJ* 25 (1975): pl. 7:A].

Pl. 41. Type 4 pyxis in fig. 18:7 [Oriental Institute, Chicago, A 28141].

Pl. 42. Type 4 double pyxis, Mycenaean, Ialysos [British Museum, BM Cat. A 959].

Pl. 43. Type 4 quadruple pyxis in fig. 18:9 (two views) [From the Collection of the Israel Department of Antiquities and Museums, 39.583].

Pl. 44. Quadruple pyxis, Mycenaean [British Museum, BM Cat. A 1004].

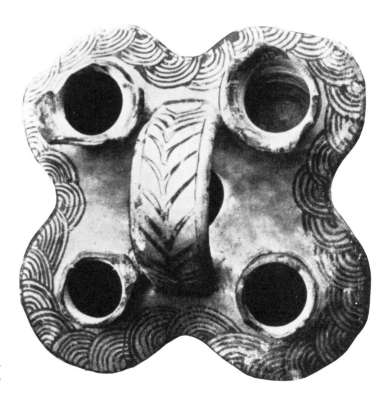

Pl. 45. Quadruple pyxis, Ialysos [*Ialysos*, fig. 83].

amphoriskos are both covered with a white slip, and their ornamental repertoire is limited mainly to the double spiral or stripe and line patterns. We shall first describe a number of amphoriskoi.

Two amphoriskoi were found at Tell el-'Ajjul in the vicinity of cemetery 1000 (not from any specific tomb) and in tomb 1139, whose meager contents were rather uncharacteristic and difficult to date (fig. 18:4).

One example of an amphoriskos was found in stratum B₂ at Tell Beit Mirsim (fig. 18:5).[47]

The group of amphoriskoi has been enlarged by a new example of unknown provenance, probably from Azor (fig. 19, pl. 38:1). It is of the tall-necked globular type and its main decoration is an arcade containing elongated triangles in alternate red and black. This is an unusual composition but a somewhat similar design can be seen on a Philistine sherd from Beth-Shean.

Although the amphoriskos was a popular Mycenaean vessel in the Late Bronze Age, it was not imported into Canaan. Nor was the shape of the amphoriskos common in the local pottery. Most eastern examples date to the twelfth and eleventh centuries. The Philistine amphoriskos was derived from the Myc. IIIC:1 variant well known in the central and eastern Mediterranean. Close parallels to the Philistine amphoriskoi were found in Rhodes (pl. 40)[48] and Cyprus, where the form appears both as a Myc. IIIC:1 vessel and as a local Cypriot product during the Late Cypriot III and Cypro-Geometric periods.[49]

Pyxis The pyxis is one of the less common Philistine pottery types; infrequent examples have been found at only a small number of sites, although they have increased in quantity with additions from new excavations and sporadic finds. The pyxis is either biconical in shape (fig. 18:1), with carination at the shoulder and belly (fig. 18:2, 9), or squat (fig. 18:7, 8). The base is either flattened or rounded. The neck is short with a splayed rim (fig. 18:2), and two horizontal loop handles are attached at the shoulder.

Examples of the pyxides found at various sites are described below.

A biconical pyxis from Gezer (fig. 18:1) is the only example so far known of a pyxis decorated with a pair of concentric half-circles joined by chevrons.

A box-shaped pyxis (fig. 18:2, pl. 36) and a globular pyxis (fig. 18:6)—both with double spiral decoration—were found in stratum XI at Tell Qasile.

A number of composite pyxides (two or four individual pyxides joined together near the base or at the middle of the body) were found at Megiddo.

A squat double pyxis with a rounded base, irregular burnish, and bichrome red and black decoration (fig. 18:8) was assigned by the excavators to stratum VIIA. Another double vessel (fig. 18:7, pl. 41) is identical in shape and workmanship but has a slightly different decoration. In finish and decoration both vessels belong to the debased group of Philistine pottery peculiar to stratum VI at Megiddo and should probably be assigned to this stratum. Further evidence for this conclusion is an undecorated double pyxis identical in shape with the above two and found in stratum VIB.[50]

A quadruple pyxis—four separate pyxides joined by a broken basket handle (fig. 18:9, pl. 43)—was found in stratum VIA. The four vessels are all irregularly burnished and decorated in red with an overall net pattern that was probably once a solid checkerboard design. They stood on a pedestal base (of which only the broken stem has survived).

A unique variant is a pyxis of unknown provenance (fig. 18:3, pl. 37) with a pinched-in girth faintly reminiscent of the slight inward curve of Mycenaean pyxides of the Late Bronze Age. A similarly shaped vessel, a local Late Bronze Age II imitation of a Mycenaean pyxis, is known from Lachish;[51] a parallel closer in date, with apparently the same antecedents, comes from Azor (pl. 38). The pinched-in body is a characteristic feature of the Type 8 juglets, which, however, seem to have had a different history and to have followed a totally different course of development. Our example seems to be a hybrid owing some-

47. *TBM I*, p. 61, par. 80.
48. *MP*, p. 38, fig. 9:59, 61, 64.
49. Gjerstad, *OA 3*, p. 78, fig. 1:7–11; Furumark, *OA 3*, p. 245, fig. 12:A:C; B:4.

50. *Meg. II*, pl. 73:13.
51. *Lachish IV*, pl. 82:920, tomb 4013.

thing to both the pyxides and the Type 8 juglets. Another variant is the jar with pinched-in girth found on the floor of the stratum XII temple at Tell Qasile (pl. 39:2).

The pyxis first appeared in Palestine during the Late Bronze Age I as a Mycenaean import. The predominant pyxis types during this period were the squat, boxlike vessels with convex bases (Myc. Types 94–96);[52] the base-ring pyxis (Myc. Type 97) apparently never reached Palestine,[53] although a base ring is found in some local variations. Almost every Mycenaean import gave rise to local imitations, but the pyxis, more than any other, became solidly entrenched in the local Palestinian pottery tradition during the Late Bronze Age II; it continued to appear as a local pottery type even after the cessation of Mycenaean imports. Its development can be followed until the ninth and eighth centuries B.C., over a period in which it underwent alterations in shape, design, and decoration under the influence of local ceramic trends.

Despite the fact that relatively few Philistine pyxides have been found, a number of variations in its basic design can be observed.

1. *The biconical pyxis with a flat ring base.* This is the most common pyxoid shape, especially during the twelfth to tenth centuries. It is now, however, a typical Mycenaean shape and seems to be a hybrid of two Mycenaean types: 96 (a pyxis with sloping sides widening toward the bottom into a convex base) and 97 (the base-ring pyxis).[54]

2. *The squat pyxis.* This pyxis, with its rounded base, is a later development of an original Mycenaean type (96) imported into Palestine during the Late Bronze Age II. Thereafter, it became firmly rooted in the local Palestinian ceramic repertoire and continues to appear down to the ninth century B.C.

3. *The composite pyxis.* No examples of this kind are known in Palestine, either as Mycenaean imports or as local imitations, earlier than those from Megiddo. There are, however, excellent examples of double, triple, and quadruple pyxides in the Myc. IIIB–C:1 ceramic repertoire, and the Ialysos and Perati cemeteries have provided some especially close parallels to the double pyxis (pl. 42) and the quadruple

pyxis (pls. 44, 45),[55] which, however, lack the high pedestal of which traces survive on the Megiddo vessel. Cyprus has also provided some close parallels.[56] Thus the composite vessels seem to be a new type that arrived in Palestine only with the new wave of Philistine pottery.

The local imitations of the pyxides continued into the Iron Age, and the majority of the shapes used by the Philistine potters were probably borrowed from these imitations, to which they added their own decoration. The pinched-in-body pyxis and the composite (quadruple or double) pyxis, however, must be considered as purely Philistine innovations in Palestine based on Myc. IIIC:1 prototypes from Greece, Rhodes, and Cyprus. The same applies to the amphoriskos.

Even though Philistine pyxides and amphoriskoi are not numerous, they nevertheless convey the combination of influences typical of Philistine pottery as a whole: a basic, predominant Mycenaean element, together with unusual and even unique additions.

Type 5. The Three-handled Jar (fig. 20)

Only one example of the Type 5 jar is known in Palestine. It comes from room HJ, level 181 in the Philistine level of building H at Tell Jemmeh.[57]

The jar is very small (only 6 cm high) and has three loop handles extending from the top of the neck just below the rim to the shoulder. It is covered with a white slip and bears red and black decoration (divided like that of the types 3 and 6 jars) consisting of an upper register with concentric semicircles between the handles and a lower register of parallel zigzag lines above a row of red triangles.

The closest parallel to this decorative pattern is found on a strainer-spout jug from Megiddo VI (cf. fig. 27:7). The zigzag lines and triangle motif can be considered as a later degeneration of the composite zigzag motif of the early Philistine vessels (fig. 17:1).

Although the three handles are rare in the Palestinian ceramic tradition, they are one of the most dis-

52. *MP*, p. 44, fig. 12:94–96.
53. Ibid., fig. 12:97.
54. *See* nn. 52, 53 above.

55. *MP*, pp. 69, 641, fig. 20:325; *Ialysos*, figs. 18, 28, 30, 83 (fig. 18 is our pl. 42; fig. 83 is our pl. 45).
56. E.g., a triple pyxis of LC III Proto–White Painted ware (V. Karageorghis, *CVA*, Private Collections, vol. 1 [1965], pl. 35:1–3).
57. *Gerar*, p. 23, pl. LXIV:48, HJ, 181; *see* chap. 2, p. 34, above.

tinctive traits of Mycenaean ware, on which they appear as either vertical or horizontal loop handles. The vertical handles are usually restricted to the shoulders of the vessel; more rarely, they extend from the rim to the shoulder. They do not, however, extend from the neck to the shoulder, as do the handles on the Philistine jar from Tell Jemmeh.

The Mycenaean vessel closest in shape to the Tell Jemmeh jar is the Type 151 jar, with its narrow, elongated neck. Vessels of this type are most common during the Myc. IIIA:2 and have been found at Enkomi, Ugarit, and Ialysos;[58] they are so far unknown among the Mycenaean imported ware of Palestine in the Late Bronze Age II. Thus, the three-handled jar from Tell Jemmeh adds to the corpus of Philistine pottery a new ceramic type whose origin lies undoubtedly in the Mycenaean world.

Two other three-handled jars should be considered in this connection. One comes from the Philistine tomb 532 at Tell el-Far'ah (cf. chap. 2, p. 32), and the other was discovered at Tell Jemmeh, in room JC, level 178 (a level containing Philistine pottery).[59] Both are local imitations of the Myc. IIIB Type 38 jar,[60] found in Palestine during the Late Bronze Age as imported ware and local imitations.[61] Although neither of the two can be identified as Philistine pottery on the basis of their design or decoration, they were both discovered in purely Philistine contexts; the one from Tell Jemmeh lay very close to the spot where the Philistine three-handled jar was discovered.

Type 6. Strainer-Spout Jug (figs. 21–31, pls. 46–67a)

The strainer-spout jug, or Philistine "beer jug," is one of the best-known Philistine pottery types. Its body is rounded and sometimes displays a slight carination (fig. 21:2). The neck is tall and narrow with a wide upward-splaying rim. The jug has one wide, flat loop handle extending from the lip to the shoulder. The trough-shaped spout is broad and tilts upward. The ware covers a wide range from greenish-white, well-levigated, well-fired clay to a cruder reddish, slightly gritty ware. Most jugs are covered with a white slip,

and bichrome decoration predominates. The ornamental motifs are outstanding in their profusion and diversity.

The decoration on the spout usually consists of either parallel lines (fig. 21:1) or a group of short lines accentuating only the side and rim (fig. 27:1). The handle is painted with horizontal or vertical lines, and the body decoration is very similar to that of the stirrup jar—both in syntactical arrangement and in the combinations of motifs used. The upper half of the body is divided into two horizontal bands. The upper register (the handle zone) exhibits the same motifs found on the handle zone of the stirrup jar: various combinations of concentric semicircles with the addition of other simple geometric patterns. As in Type 3, there are several examples of a bird motif in the upper band.

The main register (the spout zone) displays three distinct decorative arrangements: (1) the metope arrangement (alternating bird and geometric motifs—figs. 22–23—or geometric motifs alone—fig. 24); (2) the repeated composite motif (fig. 25); and (3) the overall net pattern (fig. 26).

Tell el-Far'ah The jugs from Tell el-Far'ah are of special importance because they were discovered in clear and well-defined archaeological contexts which are detable in terms of absolute chronology. A number of white-slipped bichrome jugs belong to the first phase of Philistine pottery. In this group the metope arrangement predominates, with birds, spirals, rhomboids, and checkered patterns providing the decorative motifs. Two of these jugs were found in tombs 552 (chap. 5, fig. 7:20) and 542 (fig. 23:3), and two others (fig. 23:1, 2) come from the vicinity of building D at the south end of the mound, where the elegant krater described above (fig. 7:3) was also found.

Two of the jugs, on the basis of their style, apparently represent a transition between Phases 1 and 2. The first (fig. 21:2) is from tomb 859, whose contents were too meager to allow an accurate dating. The jug's decoration consists of two pairs of antithetic spirals facing the same direction with a rhomboid net pattern between them. The two pairs of spirals flank a uniquely stylized bird whose head is depicted as a separate decorative element severed from its body. The stylization of the body and wings reveals both a lack of artistic ability and an unfamiliarity with the nature of the original motif. The long triglyph next to the spout is the sole survivor of the original metope arrangement. The second jug (fig. 26:1, pl. 52) was the

58. Stubbings, p. 35, n. 4; ibid., p. 62, fig. 17, pls. II:6, VIII:12.

59. *Gerar*, pl. LVII 55t; *CPP*, 55 V2.

60. *MP*, pp. 24–25, fig. 4.

61. *See*, for example, *Lachish IV*, pls. 82:940–44 and 83:945–46.

0   1   2   3   4   5

Fig. 20. Type 5 three-handled jar, white slip, Tell Jemmeh, level HJ 181 [*Gerar*, pl. LXIV:48].

1

Fig. 21.1. Type 6 strainer-spout jug. White slip, Tell eṣ-Ṣafi [*B-M*, pls. 20:3, 44; *PMB* 4, pl. II:8].

Fig. 21.2. Type 6 strainer-spout jug. White slip, Tell el-Farʿah, tomb 859 [*BP I*, pl. XXIII:8; *CPP*, 67 D6].

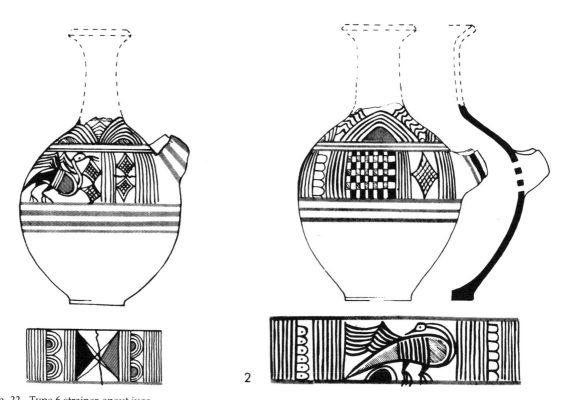

Fig. 22. Type 6 strainer-spout jugs.
1. White slip, Beth-Shemesh, stratum III [*AS III*, fig. 2:16, pl. XXI].   **2.** White slip, Beth-Shemesh [D. Mackenzie, "The Excavations at Ain Shems," *PEF Ann* **2**, frontispiece; *PMB* **4**, pl. II:1].

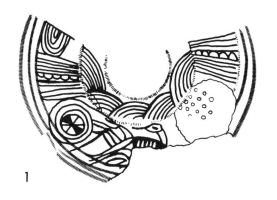

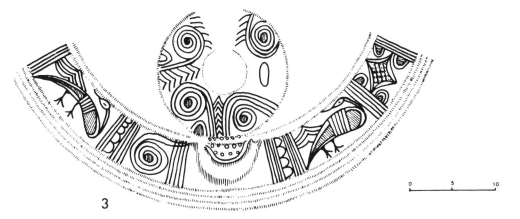

Fig. 23. Type 6 strainer-spout jugs.
1. White slip, Tell el-Farʿah, DJ 388 [*BP II*, pl. LXXV:3]. **2.** White slip, Tell el-Farʿah, DC 387.7 [*BP II*, pl. LXXV:2]. **3.** White slip, Tell el-Farʿah, tomb 542 [*BP I*, pl. XXIII:3].

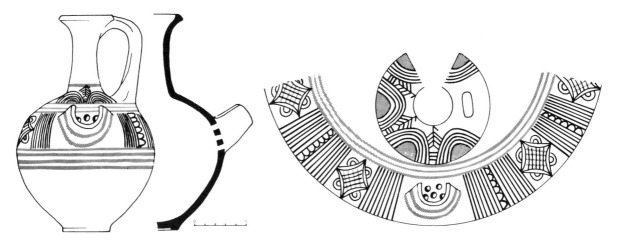

Fig. 24. Type 6 strainer-spout jug, white slip, Azor.

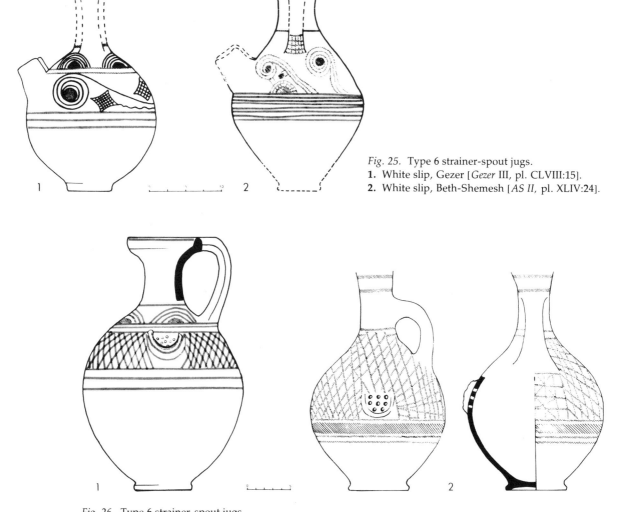

Fig. 25. Type 6 strainer-spout jugs.
1. White slip, Gezer [*Gezer* III, pl. CLVIII:15].
2. White slip, Beth-Shemesh [*AS II*, pl. XLIV:24].

Fig. 26. Type 6 strainer-spout jugs.
1. White slip, Tell el-Farʿah, tomb 601 [CPP, 67 D2]. **2.** Megiddo [G. Schumacher, *Tell el-Mutesellim*, vol. 2, pl. XXXVIII:f].

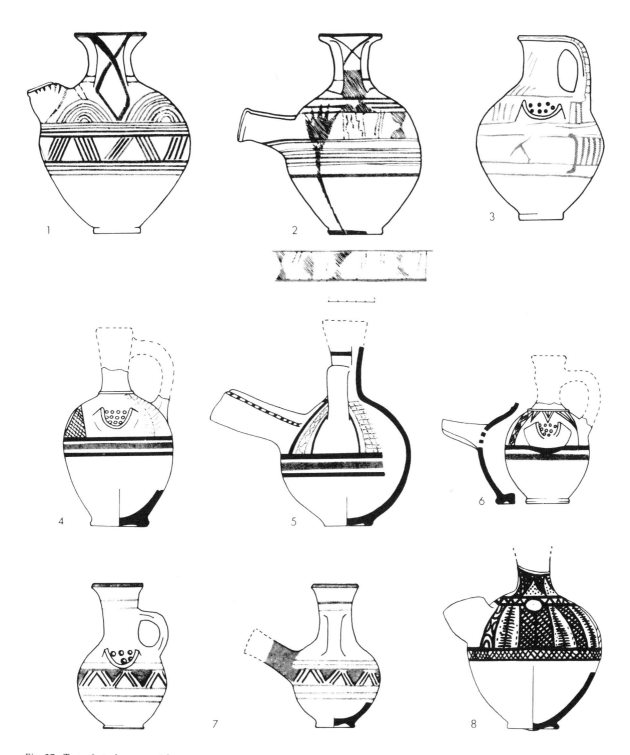

Fig. 27. Type 6 strainer-spout jugs.
1. White slip, Tell el-Farʿah, tomb 625 [*CPP*, 67 D4].   **2.** Tell el-Farʿah, tomb 542, tomb 562 [*CPP*, Add. 67 N].   **3.** Tell el-Farʿah, tomb 828 [*CPP*, 67 Q].   **4.** Burnished, Megiddo, stratum VIA [*Meg. II*, pl. 75:23].   **5.** Burnished, Megiddo, stratum VIA [*Meg. II*, pls. 75:22, 142:19].   **6.** Burnished, Megiddo, tomb 1101B [*Meg. T.*, pls. 8:12, 87:4].   **7.** Burnished, Megiddo, stratum VI [No. 1403].   **8.** Burnished, Megiddo, tomb 29 [*Meg. T.*, pl. 68:8].

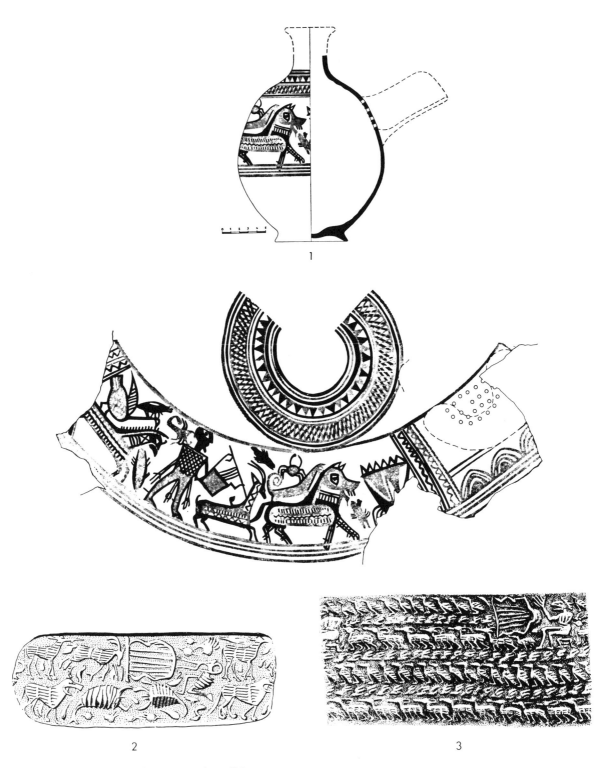

Fig. 28. Strainer-spout jug decoration and parallels.
1. Type 6 jug, white slip, Megiddo, stratum VIA [*Meg. II,* pl. 76:1]. **2.** Cylinder-seal impression, Tarsus [H. Goldman, *Excavations at Gözlü Kule: Tarsus,* vol. 2 (Princeton, 1956), figs. 394:35, 400:35]. **3.** Cylinder-seal impression from Mardin in southern Turkey [J. Rimmer, *Ancient Musical Instruments of Western Asia* (London, 1969), fig. 6, pl. VIII].

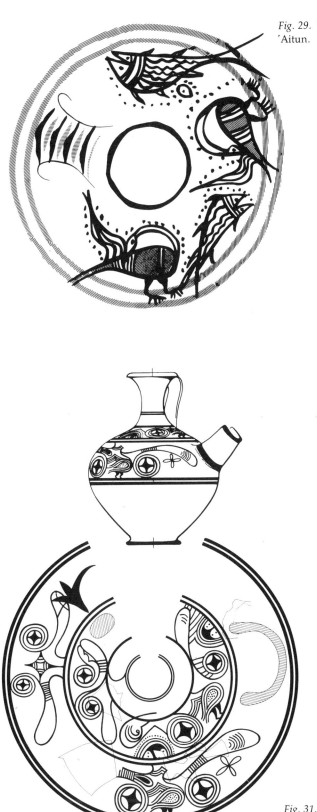

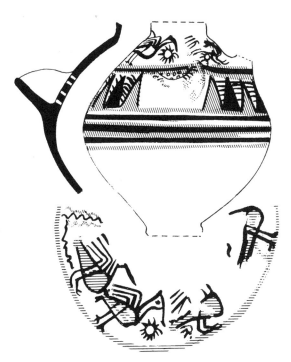

Fig. 29. Type 6 strainer-spout jug, Tell ʿAitun.

Fig. 30. Type 6 strainer-spout jug, Deir ʿAlla, phase A [*Deir ʿAlla*, fig. 47:4].

Fig. 31. Type 6 strainer-spout jug, Sinda, level III [*Sinda*, pl. II (dap), fig. 6].

Pl. 46. Type 6 strainer-spout jug in fig. 22:1 [University Museum, Pennsylvania].

Pl. 47. Type 6 strainer-spout jug, Ashdod [Israel Museum, 68/32/1].

Pl. 48 Type 6 strainer-spout jug in fig. 21:1 [From the Collection of the Israel Department of Antiquities and Museums, V. 505].

Pl. 49. Type 6 strainer-spout jug in fig. 22:2 (two views) [From the Collection of the Israel Department of Antiquities and Museums, V. 504].

Pl. 50. Type 6 strainer-spout jug in fig. 22:1 [University Museum, Pennsylvania].

Pl. 51. Type 6 strainer-spout jug fragments, Tell Beit Mirsim B₂ [From the Collection of the Israel Department of Antiquities and Museums, I. 8980. *TBM I,* pl. 23].

Pl. 52. Type 6 strainer-spout jug in fig. 26:1 [From the Collection of the Israel Department of Antiquities and Museums, V. 1935].

Pl. 53. Type 6 strainer-spout jug in fig. 24 [Weisenfreund Collection].

Pl. 55. Type 6 strainer-spout jug fragments, Tell Qasile, stratum XII [Q III 5642].

Pl. 54. Type 6 strainer-spout jug, Azor [Private Collection].

Pl. 56. Type 6 strainer-spout jug in fig. 27:1 [Institute of Archaeology, London].

Pl. 57. Type 6 strainer-spout jug in fig. 27:2 [Institute of Archaeology, London].

Pl. 58. Type 6 strainer-spout jug in fig. 27:3 [Institute of Archaeology, London].

Pl. 59. Type 6 strainer-spout jug, Tell el-Farʿah, tomb 636 [Institute of Archaeology, London].

Pl. 60. Type 6 strainer-spout jug in fig. 27:7 (two views) [The Oriental Institute, Chicago].

Pl. 61. Type 6 strainer-spout jug in fig. 28:1 (mirror image at right) [From the Collection of the Israel Department of Antiquities and Museums, 36.1921].

Pl. 62. Type 6 strainer-spout jug in fig. 29 (three views and detail) [From the Collection of the Israel Department of Antiquities and Museums, 69–99].

Pl. 63. Strainer-spout jug, Myc. IIIC:1b, Ialysos [*Ialysos*, fig. 41].

Pl. 64. Strainer-spout jug, Myc. IIIC:1b, Ialysos [*Ialysos*, fig. 62].

Pl. 65. Strainer-spout jug in fig. 31 [*Sinda*, fig. 3, courtesy of A. Furumark].

Pl. 66. Strainer-spout jug, Myc. IIIC:1b, Sinda, level III [*Sinda*, fig. 3, courtesy of A. Furumark].

Pl. 67. Strainer-spout jug from Kouklia (dap) [F. Maier, "The Cemeteries of Old Paphos," *Archaeologia viva* 2 (1969), no. 115].

Pl. 67a. Jug, Cyprus.

only piece of pottery found in tomb 601,[62] although a similar jug was found in tomb 268, which can be dated to the eleventh century B.C.[63] In shape and workmanship it has clear affinities with the Phase 1 jugs described above (figures 21–22), although the overall net pattern on its main band is unusual in the Phase 1 repertoire of decorative motifs. A late degeneration of this motif appears on the jug in figure 26:2 from Megiddo, which can be typologically included with the Megiddo VI group of late debased Philistine ware.

Three jugs belonging to Phase 2 are shown in figure 27:1–3. They are shorter and have squat necks and slightly splaying rims. Only one of them has a white slip. The decoration is in red alone. The first (fig. 27:1, pl. 56) comes from tomb 625, where the debased Philistine krater (fig. 9:2) was also found. The upper of its two horizontal bands is much wider than usual. It extends over the shoulder of the vessel from the base of the neck to just below the base of the spout. The decoration is the usual concentric semicircles, but they are not linked by any secondary geometric motif. The lower main band bears a continuous composite zigzag pattern.

The jug from tomb 562 (fig. 27:2, pl. 57) is even further removed from the original Philistine strainer-spout jug both in its carinated shape and its decoration. The decorative motifs are derived not from the Philistine repertoire, but from the local ceramic tradition.[64] In our survey of the Egyptian vessels in the Far'ah tombs (see pp. 263–68), we have noted the phenomenon of Egyptian pottery forms ornamented with typically Palestinian motifs. This Philistine jug seems to have undergone a similar process; it should thus not be considered a debasement in form and decoration of the original Philistine type, but rather a modification and intentional adaptation of the Philistine shape to the local decorative tradition. This would explain its appearance in an archaeological context that cannot be dated to later than the beginning of the eleventh century.

Three jugs, decorated only in red and lacking the white slip, belong to the third phase of Philistine pottery. One (fig. 27:3, pl. 58) comes from tomb 828 and dates to around the end of the eleventh century B.C. Its painted decoration is in no way related to the Philistine decorative tradition, and it probably represents a complete debasement of a local or Philistine decoration. The second jug, from tomb 636 (pl. 59) and dating from the second half of the eleventh to the beginning of the tenth century,[65] is identical in shape with the jug in plate 57 but is decorated with red and white stripes. In this combination of colors it closely resembles a number of vessels from Tell Qasile X.[66] The third jar belonging to the last phase of Philistine pottery comes from tomb 523,[67] where the Type 17 strainer-spout and basket-handle jug (fig. 59:3) was found.

It should be noted that the shape and decoration of the jugs in Phase 2, and especially in Phase 3, are peculiar to Tell el-Far'ah; this later development may have been limited to Far'ah alone. We will discuss these jugs and comparable ones from Megiddo below.

Beth-Shemesh One of the finest examples of a Philistine strainer-spout jug (fig. 22:1, pl. 46) was found in stratum III at Beth-Shemesh in a silo in room 487, which also contained a number of Philistine potsherds.[68] The main band of the jug is divided into metopes, which vary in size. The distinction between metope and triglyph is not always clear. The motif in one metope, a bird facing forward, was executed with the light swift stroke of a true artist. The space between the bird and the triglyph is filled with two rhomboids, one atop the other, and this same design appears again in one of the triglyphs. The other metope contains a geometric motif: a square divided by diagonals into four triangles (pl. 50). The varied nature of the motifs and their high artistic quality date this jug to the *floruit* of Phase 1. (A similar jug was found at Ashdod; see pl. 47.) Another strainer-spout jug from Beth-Shemesh (fig. 22:2, pl. 49) was not found in a stratigraphic context;[69] it is very similar in arrangement to the above jug, although there is greater precision in the design.

A third jug from Beth-Shemesh (fig. 25:2) differs strikingly from the other two. It is slightly carinated and unslipped, and its decoration—in red alone rather than the characteristic bichrome—consists of a combination of unusual motifs executed in unsteady lines.

62. In addition to this jug, scarabs and seals were found in tomb 601 (*BP I*, pl. XXXI:287, 288).

63. Ibid., pl. LXVIII.

64. For the combinations of motifs, cf. *Meg. II*, pls. 63:3, 64:4.

65. *BP I*, pl. LXX.

66. *Qasile IEJ 1*, pl. 26:4.

67. *CPP*, 67P.

68. *AS III*, p. 35, map 3.

69. D. Mackenzie, "The Excavations at Ain Shems," *PEF Ann* 1 (1911):84.

The usual division of the decoration into handle and spout zones is absent; instead, a single broad band fills the entire upper part of the vessel. The decorative motif is repeated, but with a different spiral on a composite wavering stem with an unusual rayed concentric semicircle below it. This jug should undoubtedly be placed in the second phase of Philistine pottery and can be compared in general decorative motifs and carinated shape with the jug from Tell el-Far'ah (fig. 27:1).

A red-slipped jug with brown stripes[70] belongs to the last phase of Philistine pottery.

Tell eṣ-Ṣafi The strainer-spout jug from Tell eṣ-Ṣafi (fig. 21:1, pl. 48) is similar in the character and artistic standard of the decoration to the two Phase 1 jugs from Beth-Shemesh. The unique feature of this vessel is that the figures and geometric motifs are outlined in black and the usual red filling is omitted.

Tell Beit Mirsim The upper part of a white-slipped jug decorated in bichrome (pl. 51)[71] was found in Tell Beit Mirsim B₂. The main band is divided into metopes, one of which displays a bird motif similar to those on the jugs in figures 21 and 22. The Tell Beit Mirsim jug is, however, inferior in the quality of its design.

A second jug from the east cave[72] is unslipped and decorated in red alone. Each of its metopes contained a bird motif. As on the kraters from Azor and Tell el-Far'ah shown in figures 6 and 7:3, the birds face forward and back. This vessel's general style and decoration recall a krater sherd from Megiddo (chap. 2, pl. 18:5,6).

Gezer A strainer-spout jug from Gezer[73] can be assigned, on stylistic grounds, to the first phase of Philistine pottery. Its upper zone contains the usual concentric semicircle motif, and its main band is divided into metopes with alternating bird and rhomboid motifs. A second jug (fig. 25:1) is decorated with a variation of the spiral and rhombus motif on a wavy stem in a repeated-unit arrangement around the main band. This motif, in several variations, was apparently a favorite of the Gezer potter discussed above (fig. 11:5).

Azor A white-slipped jug with bichrome decoration (fig. 24, pl. 53) was found in the Philistine cemetery at Azor. Its main band is divided into metopes, with a rhombus motif in each metope. Its elegant shape, design, white slip, bichrome decoration, and fine workmanship all indicate that despite the rather repetitive geometric designs it belongs to the early, not degenerate, Azor ceramic group.

A number of squat jugs more simply decorated with horizontal stripes were also found here. Some (for example, pl. 54) were covered with a white slip; others had the red slip characteristic of the last phase of Philistine pottery.

Tell Qasile A fragment of the upper section of a white-slipped strainer-spout jug (pl. 55) from Qasile XII is of great importance because its bichrome decoration—geometric motifs in a crowded pattern that fills all the available space in the decorative zone—is very reminiscent of the Mycenaean Close Style. The combination of motifs is unusual, ranging from filling motifs of suspended half-circles with attached wavy lines to the large cross-hatched triangle filling the space below the winged spiral. The suspended half-circles also appear at the top.

Only a few examples of strainer-spout jugs were found in stratum XI, most of them being white slipped and decorated in bichrome. A red-slipped jug with black stripes found in stratum X exemplifies the stratum's combination of new local features and Philistine features.

Megiddo None of the published strainer-spout jugs from Megiddo can be assigned to the first or the second phases of Philistine pottery; but three white-slipped fragments with bichrome decoration (chap. 2, pl. 18:4, 7) are among the unpublished sherds that clearly belong to these phases. Two of them are definitely from stratum VIIA and thus are early. There is also a large group of strainer-spout jugs from stratum VIA and from contemporary tombs that represent the last phase of Philistine pottery (figs. 26:2, 27:4–8, pl. 60). Their loop handles (where they survive) extend from the middle of the neck to the shoulder (instead of from the lip to the shoulder as is typical of Philistine jugs). These jugs are irregularly burnished and decorated in bichrome red and brown; but original Philistine motifs—such as concentric semicircles (fig. 27:8), zigzag lines (fig. 27:7), rhomboid designs (fig. 27:6), and overall net patterns (fig. 26:2)—are still employed.

70. *AS IV*, pl. LX:25, st. III.
71. *TBM I*, p. 62, par. 82, pl. 23:1.
72. Ibid., p. 62, par. 82.
73. *Gezer* II, pp. 178, 181; III, pl. CLXIII:7.

The bronze hoard of building 1739, stratum VI, includes a restored strainer-spout jug—the only metal example of this type of vessel.[74]

The strainer-spout jug shown in figure 28:1 (pl. 61) is unique in almost every aspect of its decoration. It is ascribed to stratum VIA[75] (area AA, building 2072, the so-called Residency). The jug is divided into a wide central band with two narrow bands above it. The uppermost, and narrowest, band contains overlapping and intersecting red and black semicircular arcs that create an effect of continuous red, black, and white triangles. This is possibly an adaptation of a Myc. IIIB–C motif that is a geometrization of the papyrus-flower motif.[76] The middle band is filled with an overall net pattern in red and black, which is characteristic of the Megiddo VI Philistine pottery. The strainer spout is bounded by triglyphs in the area of the main band, and below the spout is a row of concentric semicircles. The decorative enclosure of the spout in a metope on an otherwise continuous band is unusual, especially with the emphasis on the enclosure provided by the semicircles.

The main frieze depicts a processional scene arranged in three "superimposed" rows. The bottom row contains the main figures: a lyre player, standing erect, who occupies the full height of the band, a lion, a gazelle, a horse, a tree, and, as filling motifs, two fish. The second row contains a dog, a lyre, and a bird, all neatly fitted into the vacant areas above the main figures. The upper row, above the heads of the main and secondary figures, is occupied by two fish, a crab and a scorpion, surprisingly well integrated with the other figures.

The technique of the composition is basically Philistine. The outlines and important details of the figures are in black, with the filling in red and black. The bodies of the lion, antelope, and horse are decorated in geometric patterns. It is interesting that this same decorative technique is found on the Philistine

zoomorphic vessels (chap. 4, fig. 1:1–6). Some sort of reciprocal influence undoubtedly existed between the animals of the Megiddo jug and the Philistine zoomorphic vessels.

We will examine each figure in the procession individually and attempt to draw parallels wherever possible and to trace the source of the specific motifs.

THE LYRE PLAYER. The entire black-headed figure is somewhat grotesque, with its stiff stance, head and legs in profile, trapezoidal cross-hatched chest *en face*, and sticklike black arms holding the lyre. The musician's head, with the exception of his one eye, is solid black. His nose is long, his mouth protruding, and his beard (if indeed it is a beard) juts downward. The player seems to be wearing a costume that has a crisscross pattern on the chest. His hips and legs are outlined in black and filled in with solid red. Two bands (ribbons? belts?) hang down on either side of his waist, and two more are suspended between his legs.

Human figures on Philistine pottery are uncommon, but the few known examples follow the same principle of schematization: two triangles are joined at their apexes to form the torso, to which the head and limbs are attached. The lyre player on the Megiddo jug, although more realistically drawn, reflects the same stylistic principle. The closest parallels to the player in style and detail are three figures on a fragment of a zoomorphic vessel—perhaps part of a kernos—from Megiddo VIIA.[77] Like the lyre player, the kernos figures have bands falling from their waists and between their legs, and it is therefore quite possible that the Megiddo musician merely reflects the local iconographic tradition.

The lyre's sound box is square, and its two arms are asymmetrical, the taller one curving inward at the top and the shorter one bent outward at a right angle. Four strings are stretched from the sound box to the oblique crossbar that joins the two arms. The slant of the crossbar enables the musician to tune his instrument by simply moving the string up or down the bar. Lyres of this type seem to have originated in north Syria.[78] A similar lyre appears on a plaque of the Megiddo Ivories from stratum VIIA (chap. 4, fig. 8:1).

THE GAZELLE. This is a very common depiction in

74. *Meg. II*, pl. 190:6; *B-SH Cemetery*, p. 107, tomb 221 A–C, fig. 47:24.

75. *Meg. II*, pl. 76:1. This vessel was originally thought to belong to Type 6. Our examination of the vessel at the Israel Department of Antiquities, however, revealed no signs of a handle on the body. It was, therefore, probably a strainer-spout jug with a basket handle similar to two decorated with geometrical bichrome decoration found in stratum X at Qasile. *See* discussion of Type 17, p. 194.

76. *MP*, fig. 33, motif 11:16; fig. 58, motif 43:g–s.

77. *Meg. II*, pl. 247:7.

78. E. Porada, in "A Lyre Player from Tarsus and his Relations," *Aegean and the Near East*, pp. 204 ff., figs. a–k.

Late Bronze Age II pottery decoration. The graceful and naturalistic gazelle on the Megiddo jug, however, is far superior to any such animal known from local pottery and is very similar to the Myc. IIIC:1 gazelle motif.[79] Both the Mycenaean and Megiddo animals are naturalistically rendered in outline, whereas the body decoration is geometrically stylized.

THE LION. Although the identification of this animal is not absolutely certain, the proportions of the body, the relatively large head, accentuated jaws and teeth, and the curled tail which projects from behind the gazelle's back all suggest that it was in fact the artist's intention to draw a lion. No parallels can be found in either local or Mycenaean cultures.

THE DOG. Representations of dogs are unknown in the Palestinian pottery tradition, but similar stylized dogs with upward-curling spiral tails, either seated upon or pouncing on another animal, are quite common in almost identical Myc. IIIB hunting scenes from Mycenae, Tiryns, and Cyprus.[80] The dog on the Megiddo jug should not, however, be considered the result of direct influence, but rather the later stage of an artistic tradition whose intermediate phases are as yet unknown.[81]

THE HORSE. This animal also does not occur in the local ceramic decoration. Although its very common Mycenaean counterpart is rendered in an entirely different stylistic technique, one Myc. IIIC:1 vessel does display a horse motif in which the body area is decorated with geometric designs that recall the decoration on this horse.[82]

THE BIRD. With its barely discernible net pattern filling an ovoid body, the bird on the Megiddo jug is quite unlike the standard stylized Philistine bird, whose leaf-shaped body is generally filled with a triglyph motif. The tail is a separate element attached to the body rather than a flowing continuation of the body lines as it is in the Philistine bird motifs. The wing, too, is different, and both wing and tail are filled with a stripe pattern quite alien to the Philistine tradi-

tion. The Megiddo bird is actually much closer to the bird motifs on local Late Bronze II pottery.[83]

THE FISH. Of the four fish on the Megiddo jug, two are solid black, with no attempt made to render details, and the other two are red with black outlines and fins. Fish are not common on Philistine pottery decoration, and the ones we know do not resemble the fish on the Megiddo jug. Like the bird, the fish is a continuation of a motif occurring on local Late Bronze II pottery.[84]

THE CRAB. Drawings of crabs are found on the local Late Bronze II pottery. A crab appears as the sole decorative motif below the handle of a jug from tomb 912D at Megiddo;[85] its body is solid black with no outline, and it is rendered much more naturalistically than the crab on this jug.

THE SCORPION. This motif does not occur in the Canaanite pottery tradition, but it is not uncommon in the Mycenaean. A similar depiction of the scorpion appears on a Myc. IIIC:1b stirrup jar, one of a group characteristic of Rhodes and Crete. The usual decoration on these stirrup jars consists of an octopus with birds, fish, crabs, scorpions, and gazelles painted between its tentacles [86]

THE "TREE." The object toward which the procession is marching resembles a schematized palm, a dominant motif in the local tradition of decorated pottery from the Late Bronze Age to the Iron Age I. The principal similarity lies in the three lines suspended from both sides of the tree, which also appear on the stylized palms in Palestinian pottery. The chalice-shaped body that comprises the main portion of the tree, however, is very different from the Palestinian palms and more closely resembles a lotus calyx (cf. fig. 51:7). Depictions of a lyre player alongside a "sacred tree" are known from various sources both in the ancient Near East and in the Aegean world.

The motifs of the Megiddo jug—both individually and in combination as the ornamentation on one vessel—have parallels in the local pottery tradition as well as in the Myc. IIIC:1b. The uniqueness of the scene as a whole, however, lies in the fact that it is rendered not in heraldic fashion, as was common in

79. *MP*, fig. 29, motifs 6:9–10.
80. Ibid., fig. 31, motif 8:3; Stubbings, p. 38, fig. 7; A. Akerstrom, "Some Pictorial Vase Representations from the Mainland in Late Helladic Times," *Op.Ath.* 1 (1953): 19 ff., figs. 5–8.
81. The monumental stele of Beth-Shean shows a dog (?) attacking a lion: *B-SH I*, frontispiece; City Level IX, p. 16.
82. *MP*, fig. 26, motif 2:9.

83. *Meg. T.*, pl. 134; *Meg. II*, pls. 69:13, 72:3.
84. For example, *Lachish II*, pl. XLVIIB:238.
85. *Meg. T.*, pl. 134.
86. *MP*, fig. 49, motif 21:28; *DMS*, pp. 12 ff., pl. 6.

the local tradition, but as a narrative picture, with all the separate components facing in the same direction. Decorative compositions, which Furumark terms "processional scenes,"[87] do appear in the Myc. IIIC:1; but aside from the shared general conception there is no relationship whatsoever between such Mycenaean compositions and the scene on the Megiddo jug. Indeed, the closest parallels to the Megiddo scene are found on a cylinder seal from Tarsus (fig. 28:2) dating from between the mid-fourteenth century and the appearance of the Sea Peoples[88] and another from Mardin in southern Turkey (fig. 28:3).

On the Tarsus seal a lyre player faces a group of animals: two scorpions, a lion, a horse, and an antelope, arranged before him in two horizontal registers, with birds and fish employed as background fill. H. Goldman has already pointed out the similarity between the scenes on the Tarsus seal and the Megiddo jug and suggests that both are narrative depictions of the Orpheus legend.[89] The Tarsus seal lacks the "sacred tree" of the Megiddo jug. Without entering into the problem of the symbolic significance of this motif, it should be noted that scenes in which the stylized palm tree appears with a lyre player beside it are generally considered ritual ones and that the tree may be seen as the "Tree of Life."[90]

Judging from the type, shape, artistic technique, and some of the motifs, the Megiddo jug is definitely a Philistine vessel, although the influence of the local Palestinian and Myc. IIIC:1 ceramic decorative traditions—especially of the Myc. IIIC:1 cuttlefish

compositions on stirrup jars—is obvious. The Aegean character of a number of the figures in the frieze lends credence to the suggestion that the scene is a depiction of the Orpheus legend. In all events, it must be based on some well-known theme.

A later development of the figurative pictorial composition somewhat comparable to the Megiddo jug is the Hubbard painted amphora from Cyprus. A number of scenes, probably of cultic significance, are depicted on it, and one scene includes a lyre player.[91]

B. Mazar[92] has challenged Goldman's suggestion that the Tarsus seal and the Megiddo jug frieze both depict Orpheus playing to the animals. On the Megiddo jug the animals do not face the lyre player; furthermore, it is not at all certain that the painter has portrayed them as listening to the music. Mazar remarked that Orpheus is unknown in Greek art and literature prior to the sixth century B.C., although the late traditions doubtless imply an early origin. Conversely, scenes taken from everyday life, from mythology, and from epic poems are not foreign to Canaan and her neighbors in the Early Iron Age, as is vividly shown by the ivories found in the Megiddo VIIA treasury (chap. 4, fig. 8:1). Among these is a victory scene showing a lyre player playing before his master. The painter of the frieze on the Megiddo jug may, therefore, have depicted a familiar scene: a lyre player celebrating in song the animals and tree represented. The immediate association, says Mazar, is with the wisdom and the songs of King Solomon, as described in 1 Kings 5:13: "He spoke of trees . . . he spoke also of beasts, and of fowl, and of creeping things, and of fishes."

Fables and riddles were very popular throughout the ancient world. We can recall the riddles posed by Samson at the feast of the Philistines (Judg. 14:10 ff.). The narrator of a fable usually accompanied his words with music. Mazar's intriguing suggestion would, therefore, certainly correspond with the atmosphere at the time of the United Monarchy. Moreover, depic-

87. *MP*, p. 449.

88. H. Goldman, *Excavations at Gözlü Kule: Tarsus*, vol. 2 (Princeton, 1956), pp. 235–36, figs. 344:35 and 400:35. Another cylinder seal, brought to my attention by B. Brandl, is very close in style (fig. 28:3), date, and geographical provenance to the Tarsus cylinder seal probably found at Mardin in southeast Turkey. *See* J. Rimmer, *Ancient Musical Instruments of Western Asia*, Department of Western Asiatic Antiquities, The British Museum (London, 1969), pp. 27–28, fig. 6, pl. VIII; the plate depicts a lyre player surrounded by rows of birds and horned animals. The parallel is very close in the depiction of the bird-faced man, the horizontal position of the lyre, and the stylization of the animals. These two seals are the only ones of their kind known to exist and may reflect the same mythological background as the Orpheus jug.

89. In the preliminary publication it was dated to about 1000 B.C. (H. Goldman, "Excavations at Gözlü Kule, Tarsus, 1935," *AJA* 39 [1935]: 537, fig. 21).

90. Porada, "A Lyre Player from Tarsus and his Relations," in *Aegean and the Near East*, p. 199, figs. 2, 5, 12.

91. P. Dikaios, "An Iron Age Painted Amphora in the Cyprus Museum," *BSA* 37 (1936–1937): 56 ff., pls. 7, 8, 8b. Another representation of a Cypriot lyre player is found on a kalathos from the cemetery of Old Paphos. The lyre player here holds a sword. The vessel is dated to the first half of the eleventh century B.C. (Proto-White Painted ware) (F. G. Maier, "The Cemeteries of Old Paphos," *Archaeologia viva* 2 [1969]: photo 116).

92. B. Mazar, *Canaan and Israel, Historical Essays* (Jerusalem, 1974), pp. 174–82 (Hebrew).

tions of musicians from the Philistine period have come to light in Palestine in recent years. The most impressive example is the Ashdod pottery "musicians' stand" from a late Philistine stratum (chap. 4, pl. 33).

Other important additions to the corpus are provided by two remarkable jugs from Tell ʿAitun and Tell Deir ʿAlla. Both have the same unusual pictorial arrangement on the upper register. The Tell ʿAitun jug is far superior in all respects to the Tell Deir ʿAlla jug, which is a clumsy piece of work, even though it is extremely important because of its geographical location and the implications thereof.

Tell ʿAitun (fig. 29, pl. 62) The twelfth-century rock-cut chamber tomb at Tell ʿAitun yielded one of the most original and elaborate of Philistine jars. It is distinguished by high artisitic merit and an unusual stylization and distribution of its decorative motifs. The upper register, usually reserved for geometric designs, is here decorated with an alternating bird-and-fish scene that includes a single stylized sea anemone.[93] The upper contours of the fish and birds are outlined with a row of dots, and the entire composition has a Nilotic character.

The main register is decorated with a metope arrangement. Two of the metopes contain ordinary geometric motifs—a checkered pattern and an elaborate rhombus with dotted circles. An abbreviated Nilotic scene consisting of a fish and a plant fills the metope to the right of the handle. The plant in this scene is stylized on the pattern of antithetic tongues suspended beneath the handle of the jug and recurs as an isolated decoration in the metope to the left of the strainer spout. In the metope between the two geometric motifs a solitary bird is depicted, and facing it is a vertical zigzag pattern, possibly representing water. The most unusual motif appears below the handle of the jug. It consists of double antithetic tongues with a center fill of semicircles ending in a tasseled papyrus pattern.

The following aspects of the decoration should be noted:

1. The ʿAitun and Deir ʿAlla jugs (figs. 29, 30) are the only two examples of Philistine vessels in which pictorial representations appear in the upper register. This placement of pictorial motifs, on the other hand, is common on Myc. IIIC:1 stirrup jars (pl. 33).

2. The antithetic tongue motif is well attested in both Philistine and Mycenaean pottery (cf. fig. 67:5–10), but its modification here into a double-tongue pattern suspended upside down below the jug's handle and extending beyond the lower limit of the register is unparalleled in either tradition.

3. The birds on the ʿAitun jug are all depicted in typical Philistine fashion: the head and neck thrown back sharply into a high arch extending down to the end of the beak; the leaf-shaped body divided by groups of parallel lines; and the double tail. The wings, however, are quite unlike those of other Philistine birds (cf. figs. 61, 62). They are drawn at the far end of the body as a rhythmical series of wavy lines rising flamelike into a point, whereas the usual Philistine wing is depicted by parallel wavy lines that do not converge. The shape of the ʿAitun wings is merely a variation of the antithetic tongue motif described above, and although no parallels for this stylization are known in Philistine pottery, it very closely resembles Myc. IIIC representations (cf. fig. 63:8).

4. The fish is one of the rarest of Philistine motifs. The ʿAitun jar adds a new dimension to the repertoire of fish motifs (cf. figs. 12:1, 2). Its unusual features include the exaggerated arch of the bodies and the problematic representation of the heads. There seems to be no satisfactory explanation for the double head, but the following suggestions may be ventured:

(a) If the whole is considered as one fish, the dot below the open jaw may merely have been added as a nonrepresentational addition to the dots outlining the whole scene.

(b) The artist may have attempted an abridged portrayal of two fish swimming side by side. The two bodies are drawn as one, and only the heads are depicted separately, giving the effect of one head seen *en face* or one head above the other. This method of multiple representations in an abridged form is well attested in Mycenaean iconography; striking examples are the Mycenaean "chariot kraters" on which a team of horses is stylized in exactly the same manner.[94]

5. The use of dots to outline an individual motif or a complete scene is rare in Philistine decoration, and the only other examples known are an antithetic tongue

93. *MP*, fig. 53, motif 27:31 IIIC:1.

94. Ibid., p. 247.

motif on a bowl from Ashkelon (fig. 3:1) and, from the Ashdod excavations, numerous dotted outline pieces of monochrome ware from the earliest phase of Philistine pottery. Dotted outlines are quite common, however, on Myc. IIIC:1 vessels, as seen on a "beer jug" from Sinda, period III (fig. 31) and, especially, on the Octopus-style stirrup jars.[95]

The Nilotic scene of birds, fish, and sea anemone in a stylized papyrus thicket is strongly reminiscent of the Myc. IIIC Close Style, especially as it appears on the elaborate cuttlefish stirrup jars of this phase. The resemblance between the ʿAitun jug and the Mycenaean examples is also evident in the arrangement and general character of the decoration. But in beauty, freedom, and unity, the ʿAitun potter's motifs are unique.

Tell Deir ʿAlla (fig. 30) This jug comes from phase A at Tell Deir ʿAlla, whose beginning was dated by Carbon-14 tests to 1180 B.C. ± 60.[96] The jug is squat and ungainly in shape. The upper register contains a partly preserved "procession" of birds in a free field, with rayed circles used as filling motifs. (The latter are perhaps sea urchins; see the dotted circles on the ʿAitun jug, fig. 29, pl. 62.) The birds are a crude variant of the well-known Philistine motif; they retain the basic stylization of a raised, chevron-shaped wing, a body divided by triglyph, and a head thrown back or facing forward. The elongated triangle pattern, alternately red and black, in the central band, and the background filled with transverse stripes have close affinities with the geometrized lotus pattern (see fig. 50:1, 2) common in Philistine decoration. The general effect is that of a variation on the Philistine theme, linking Deir ʿAlla, however tenuously, with the Philistine material culture. This link is supported by other "Philistine" sherds from Deir ʿAlla (as described in chap. 2).

In summary then, what is known of the origin of the strainer-spout jug? It first appears in Palestine as a Philistine vessel that has no direct connections with any earlier ceramic tradition. According to Furumark, the strainer spout itself—on a different type of vessel—can be traced back to local Canaanite pottery and the strainer-spout jug is not a Mycenaean shape.

In his opinion the Mycenaean potter borrowed it from Syro-Palestinian prototypes, and he cites several Palestinian parallels. Although his examples undoubtedly have strainer spouts, typologically they do not belong to our Philistine Type 6 strainer-spout jug.[97] Nor is this type of jug very common in Mycenaean pottery. It is known in the Levant mainly from Myc IIIC:1b pottery, but it makes sporadic appearances on the Greek mainland as, for example, in the cemetery at Perati, at Naxos, and in the Dodecanese,[98] where examples are found in the cemetery of Ialysos on Rhodes (pls. 63, 64). The jugs from Rhodes are decorated with sparse filling motifs in the metope style, and plate 64 has an alternating bird-and-spiral motif.

The closest parallels come from Cyprus. The earliest is probably the globular jug with strainer spout decorated in the Cypriot Rude Style (second half of the thirteenth century B.C.) found in the cemetery of Old Paphos[99] (pl. 67). Like the complete specimens from Sinda (fig. 31) and Enkomi, this jug shares several similarities in shape with the Philistine jugs of the pure early period: tall narrow neck, splaying rim, and broad ribbonlike handle.

Level III at Sinda has produced two elaborately decorated examples (fig. 31, pls. 65–66). The complete jug (fig. 31) has two zones of decoration, both of which contain compositions of looped spirals and highly stylized birds with dotted filling motifs. The center of the spirals bears inward-curving rhomboids, which may be related to the Maltese cross appearing as a filling motif in Philistine pottery. The other strainer-spout jug from Sinda (only the upper part has survived) is decorated in a style similar to the elaborate Close Style tradition of the Argolid.[100] The strainer-spout zone repeats the stemmed spiral motif.

Schaeffer's excavations at Enkomi, building 18, floor V[101] yielded an elaborately decorated jug. The motifs

97. Furumark, *OA 3*, pp. 236 ff.
98. *Perati B*, p. 446; *Perati Γ*, pls. 21:553, 78:474, 102:280. The jug in the last plate has a rope handle reminiscent of the handle of the strainer-spout jug from tomb 221A at Beth-Shean. Iakovidis, in his discussion of the Perati vessels, states that they are imitations of Late Helladic IIIB–IIIC prototypes from Naxos and the Dodecanese and points out that this shape was adopted by the Philistine potter.
99. Maier, "The Cemeteries of Old Paphos," pp. 118, 123:115.
100. *Sinda*, p. 107.
101. *Enkomi*, pp. 270 ff., 303 ff. (especially p. 307), fig. 91.

95. *DMS*, frontispiece.
96. *Deir ʿAlla*, fig. 47:4, pl. XIV.

are again reminiscent of the Argolid Close Style and recall those on the complete jug from Sinda and those on another jug from Cyprus (provenance unknown, pl. 67a). The light-on-dark design and several other features of the decoration resemble a Myc. IIIC:1 pyxis from Lefkandi in Euboea; it is decorated in the "fantastic" style typical of this site.[102]

Later and cruder variants of the strainer-spout jug were also found by Schaeffer at Enkomi.[103] They are more elongated in shape, and, in contrast to the earlier sophisticated decoration described above, they are decorated with spirals and plain geometric designs. These jugs show close affinities to the debased Philistine jugs of the eleventh century B.C., which are far removed from their Mycenaean precursor. This group of jugs branched off in a direction different from that of the Proto–White Painted contemporary group in Cyprus,[104] which in shape and decoration is closer to the more elegant early version.

P. Dikaios's excavations at Enkomi produced well-stratified examples of strainer-spout jugs, one of which, from the early phase of level IIIA, early twelfth century B.C., is of great importance.[105] Its decoration, which shows links with Philistine pottery, consists, in the upper zone, of an elaborate scheme of stemmed spirals recalling the Argolid Close Style and incorporating a bird as well as a sea anemone (a similar combination appears on the Deir ʿAlla jug, fig. 30). The shoulder zone is decorated with spirals and birds. This jug closely resembles Philistine examples, but, again, with a difference in the composition of the decoration. Elaborate motifs appear in the upper register as well as in the lower (main) register—a feature uncommon on Philistine jugs (apart from the isolated examples from Tell ʿAitun and Tell Deir ʿAlla; figs. 29, 30). The jug

from Enkomi is very important, since it serves as a link between Philistine pottery and parallel examples in Cyprus. As a well-stratified vessel dating to the initial phase of the twelfth century B.C., it may perhaps be considered the closest prototype of the Philistine strainer-spout jugs.

It is our view that the Type 6 jug evolved not from a local Canaanite shape, as suggested by Furumark, but from the Myc. IIIC:1b strainer-spout jugs. Although widely diffused throughout the Aegean, it is not a common type and was apparently concentrated in the central Aegean, in the Dodecanese, and in Cyprus. It has particularly close affinities with the Cypriot and Rhodian examples of Myc. IIIC:1b; but this type of vessel became primarily and characteristically Philistine—the celebrated Philistine "beer-jug." Additional support for our theory of the Mycenaean antecedents of this vessel is provided by a fragment of a Myc. IIIC:1b strainer-spout jug from Ashdod.

As in Cyprus, where strainer-spout jugs continue to appear throughout the periods of Proto–White Painted down to Cypro-Geometric I–II,[106] so too in Palestine, the strainer-spout jug was incorporated into the local ceramic repertoire, where it is found in several variations and adaptations throughout the Iron Age.

Type 7. Jug with Basket Handle and Spout ("Feeding Bottle") (fig. 32, pls. 68, 69)

This jug, which is commonly known as a "feeding bottle," is one of the rarer types in the Philistine ceramic repertoire. Only one of the few vessels of this kind discovered displays a definite Philistine decoration (fig. 32:1). The others, although they bear the typical white slip, are decorated only with horizontal red stripes. Most of the jugs have rounded shoulders (fig. 32:1–3); the biconical shape is rare (fig. 32:4). Some examples have a double basket handle, and, except for one example from Ashdod, the spout is usually short.

Gezer A jug decorated with two separate spirals (fig. 32:1) was found in an unclear context at Gezer. A second jug of this type, decorated with red and black stripes and found in tomb 58,[107] should be assigned to

---

Floor V belongs to a phase immediately preceding the final destruction of building 18, dated by Schaeffer to 1225–1175 B.C.

102. V.R.d'A. Desborough, *The Greek Dark Ages* (London, 1972), p. 32, pl. 1:C.

103. Only one example of this group has been published: E. Coche de la Ferté, *Essai de Classification de la Céramique Mycénienne d'Enkomi* (Paris, 1951), p. 31, pl. V:6.

104. Furumark, *OA 3*, pp. 236 ff., fig. 10:16; Gjerstad, *OA 3*, p. 80, fig. 2:14.

105. *Enkomi Excavations*, vol. I, p. 269, vol. III, pl. 75:43–44. Additional fragments of strainer-spout jugs come from levels IIIA–C: from area I, level IIIB (pl. 79:17); area I, level IIIC (pl. 84:20). Mycenaean and derivative styles in area III, level IIIC (pl. 85:18); area I, room 44 on floor VI (pl. 88:10); and area I, room 43, between floors IV and III (pl. 99:44).

106. Gjerstad, *OA 3*, fig. 2:14 (Proto–White Painted), 15, 16 (Cypro-Geometric I); *SCE IV*, Part 2, figs. IV:15, VIII:18, XIII:19, XVI:9.

107. *Gezer* III, pl. LXXXIII:2; *CPP*, 64 E3.

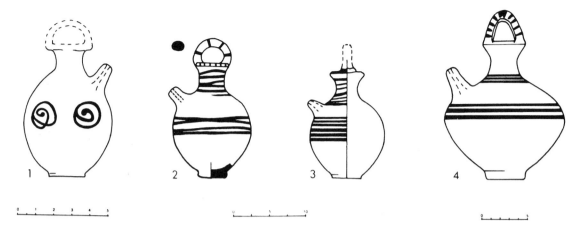

Fig. 32. Type 7 jugs with basket handle and spout ("feeding bottle").
1. Gezer [*Gezer* III, pl. CLXIX:20]. **2.** White slip, Tell Qasile [*Qasile IEJ 1*, fig. 4:3]. **3.** White slip, Beth-Shemesh [HU V491]. **4.** White slip, Azor.

Pl. 68. Type 7 jug with basket handle in fig. 32:4 [Private collection].

Pl. 69. Type 7 jug with basket handle in fig. 32:3 [Institute of Archaeology, The Hebrew University of Jerusalem, 23].

the Philistine phase of the tomb. Another Type 7 jug, altogether lacking ornamentation, comes from tomb 7. Although this tomb was in use mainly during the Late Bronze Age II, it also contained a number of Early Iron Age vessels.[108]

Tell el-Farʿah A number of undecorated jugs of this type were found in the Philistine tomb 513,[109] and one jug came from the vicinity of the Philistine cemetery 500.[110]

Beth-Shemesh The jug from Beth-Shemesh (fig. 32:3, pl. 69) is coated with a very thick white slip and decorated with close-set horizontal red bands. Another jug of the same type was ascribed to stratum IVB.[111]

Azor A jug with an unusual biconical shape was unearthed in the Philistine cemetery at Azor (fig. 32:4, pl. 68).

Tell Qasile A white-slipped jug with red stripes (fig. 32:2) was found in stratum XI at Tell Qasile.

Ashdod Ashdod has yielded many fragments of this type of jug, as well as one complete vessel found with the large group of bowls in the earliest Philistine stratum, XIII, in area G (chap. 2, pl. 4). In ware and shape this jug shows close affinities with Mycenaean prototypes and is the earliest of its series in the country.

The "feeding bottle" made its first appearance in Palestine with the Ashdod examples at the start of the twelfth century B.C. and was subsequently incorporated into the Philistine repertoire. Its geographic distribution was restricted to the major Philistine centers. The vessel, which is characteristic of a Mycenaean ceramic tradition, extends as far back as the Myc.

IIIA:1 and continues until the end of the Myc. IIIC:1. It was widely distributed—from the mainland, through the Dodecanese,[112] to Cyprus[113] and Philistia. It is also one of the most common pottery types in the Late Cypriot IIIA–B[114] and continues into Cypro-Geometric I–III.[115]

In our opinion the Type 7 Philistine "feeding bottle" was derived from Mycenaean ceramic shapes. This assumption is strengthened by the Ashdod jug, which has all the ingredients of its Mycenaean prototypes. The absence in this group of some of the more elaborate Philistine decorative motifs can perhaps be explained by the corresponding plain decorative style prevalent among Mycenaean vessels of this type.

The fusion of the characteristic features of the Type 6 (strainer-spout) and Type 7 (basket-handle) vessels resulted in the appearance, mainly during the last phase of Philistine pottery, of the Type 17 jug with a basket handle and troughlike strainer spout. A unique example of this type, of elegant shape and elaborate decoration, was uncovered in stratum X of the Philistine temple at Tell Qasile, indicating that this hybrid shape was not confined to late debased variants (see below, p. 194).

Type 8. Juglet with Pinched Body (fig. 33, pls. 70–72)

Type 8 is a small juglet (10–15 cm. in height) with a round mouth, slightly outward-splaying rim, ring base, and loop handle extending from the middle of the neck to the shoulder (fig. 33:1–3, 6). One exception (fig. 33:4) has a trefoil rim and a double loop handle drawn from the rim to the shoulder. The distinguishing characteristic of this type is its pinched-in girth. These vessels have been found in small numbers at Tell Jemmeh, Tell el-Farʿah, Tell Qasile, and Gezer. They are all decorated in red on a white slip or on plain ware, and only two juglets (fig. 33:1, 2) carry typically Philistine decoration.

---

108. *Gezer* III, pls. LXIV:10, LXVIII:2.

109. *CPP*, 67 F4. A small Philistine bowl was also found in tomb 513; cf. *CPP*, 18 V1. *BP I*, pl. LXIX.

110. *CPP*, 67 F2.

111. *AS IV*, pl. LVI:6. The spout is broken.

112. *MP*, pp. 28, 34, 83, figs. 5:159, 6:160; *CMP*, p. 24:45; *Perati B*, pp. 241–44, figs. 101, 102, 447; *Ialysos I–II*, tomb XX E XXI, fig. 63; ibid., tomb XXXII, fig. 102; ibid., tomb XXXVIII, fig. 117; *Ialysos*, tomb LXI, fig. 4; ibid., tomb LXX, fig. 28; and ibid., tomb LXXII, fig. 34.

113. The source of the Mycenaean variant of the "feeding-bottle" in Cyprus is a matter of debate between Sjöqvist and Furumark. The former considers it to be derived from Mycenaean prototypes (*see* Sjöqvist, p. 74), while the latter contends that no Mycenaean prototype exists in the Levanto-Mycenaean sphere of influence and that the "feeding-bottle" itself bears no resemblance to the original Mycenaean vessel in shape (*see* Furumark, *OA 3*, p. 236).

114. Furumark, *OA 3*, p. 235, fig. 10:I$_1$, I$_2$.

115. *SCE IV, Part 2*, figs. IV:18, 19, XIII:21, XVI:10, XIX:14, 15, XXIII:9–11, XXV:22, XXVII:23 and XXXIX:11–12.

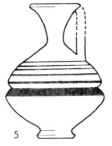

Fig. 33. Type 8 juglets with pinched body.
1. White slip, Tell Jemmeh, building HN 182 [*Gerar*, pl. LXIV:53]. **2.** Tell el-Farʿah, tomb 607 [*CPP*, 59 J1]. **3.** Tell el-Farʿah, tomb 503 [*CPP*, 59 J2]. **4.** Gezer, tomb 59 [*Gezer* I, fig. 171:1]. **5.** Tell el-Farʿah, XT 370.3 [*CPP*, 59 J3]. **6.** Burnished, Tell Qasile, stratum X [*Qasile IEJ 1*, fig. 5:7].

Pl. 71. Type 8 juglet with pinched body in fig. 33:6.

Pl. 70. Type 8 juglet with pinched body in fig. 33:1 [Institute of Archaeology, London].

Pl. 72. Juglet with pinched body, Cyprus [Cesnola Collection, Metropolitan Museum, 74.51.414].

Tell Jemmeh A juglet (fig. 33:1, pl. 70),[116] decorated with horizontal stripes and concentric semicircles, was included in a Philistine assemblage from Tell Jemmeh.

Tell el-Far'ah Four Type 8 juglets were discovered at Tell el-Far'ah; only one of them (fig. 33:2) displays definite Philistine motifs—in this case concentric semicircles connected by chevron patterns. This juglet comes from tomb 607, which cannot be dated with certainty.

The decoration on the other three consists only of horizontal-stripe patterns that cannot, on stylistic grounds, identify the vessels as Philistine. One juglet (fig. 33:5) was found in a locus containing a great many Philistine sherds.[117] Another, incomplete, came from tomb 617,[118] and the last (fig. 33:3) was the only object found in tomb 503.

Tell Qasile and Gezer The juglet from Qasile stratum X (fig. 33:6, pl. 71) is the latest example of this type of vessel. The juglet from tomb 59 at Gezer (fig. 33:4) may possibly date from the same period.

Unlike Types 1–7, which stem directly from clear Mycenaean prototypes, the Type 8 pinched-in juglet has only partial and at best indirect parallels. Several local imitations of Mycenaean pyxides dating to Late Bronze Age (pl. 38) and a later derivation of a Philistine pyxis (pl. 37) are examples of vessels with a pinched girth found in Palestine that are associated with Mycenaean shapes. A unique vessel (pl. 39:2) found on the floor of the stratum XII temple at Tell Qasile also belongs to this group. It is a small, two-handled jar with a pinched body, elaborately decorated

on a white slip with black and red elongated triangles inscribed in a semicircle; its decoration is similar to that on the Philistine sherd from Beth-Shean; (see chap. 2, fig. 13:9). The jar is hybrid in shape; the neck and two handles are like those of pilgrim flasks, while the pinched-in body belongs to our Type 8. This well-stratified jar is proof that vessels with this shape indeed existed in the first half of the twelfth century—that is, in the early phase of Philistine pottery.

Juglets with pinched-in girths have isolated parallels in widely dispersed areas from Anatolia[119] and Syria (Tell Atchana-Alalakh, level IV)[120] to Cyprus (pl. 72). The Alalakh example is very like the base-ring *bilbils* in shape, while the example from Cyprus is related to the "Syrian" jugs. The resemblance of these juglets to the Philistine ones is evident in the round mouth, slightly everted rim, handle extending from neck to shoulder, and pinched-in girth. The proportions of the vessels, however, are different: in the Philistine juglet the neck is shorter and its ring-base wider and flatter (adapted, as it were, to the norm of contemporary Palestinian pottery). There is also a basic dissimilarity in ware and decoration.

Despite the many points of comparison between the Philistine, Cypriot, Syrian, and perhaps also the Anatolian juglets, the intermediate stages, of importance in determining the exact source from which the Philistine potter drew his inspiration, are still obscure.

Similar juglets have been found at the sub-Mycenaean cemetery (eleventh century B.C.) at Salamis, Cyprus,[121] and in the Proto-Geometric tomb X (850–820 B.C.) at Fortetsa near Knossos.[122] The Fortetsa juglets bear a very close resemblance to the Philistine vessels and demonstrate the same two variations of shape encountered in the Philistine Type 8 group. One type of juglet has a round mouth and a handle extending from the middle of the neck; another type is a trefoil-mouth juglet with the handle pulled from the lip. A third variation of a pinched-in juglet, found in

116. *Gerar*, p. 23.

117. *CPP*, 59 J3. XT 370.3.

118. This vessel is at present in the Archaeological Institute, London, no. E VII48/3. It is of the same type as the tomb 607 juglet, *CPP*, 59 J1. Tomb 617 also contained a black juglet decorated with incised decorations (*CPP*, 59 F8), which is related to *CPP*, 59 B and bucchero jugs (*CPP*, 59 E1, 2; F1, 2, 3). All these jugs are from Tell el-Far'ah—cemeteries 100, 200, 500, and 600—and date to the end of the eleventh and early tenth centuries B.C. For a discussion of this group, *see* J. Du Plat Taylor, *PEQ* 88 (1956): 33, 34, fig. 2:5–8. In *BP I*, pl. LXX (tomb 607), 51 J1 is mistakenly recorded for 59 J1. In *BP I*, 59 J1 is also recorded for tomb 617. Only in *CPP* is 59 J1 recorded for tomb 607. The Tell Jemmeh and Tell el-Far'ah juglets have a close parallel in an eleventh-century assemblage at Tell Keisan (J. Briend, "Chronique archéologique: Tell Keisan," *RB* 83 [1976]: pl. XV).

119. A similar juglet has been published from Boğazköy, but its place of discovery is unknown. No such juglets were found in the actual excavations. K. Bittel, *Boğazköy: Die Kleinfunde der Grabungen, 1906–1912*, vol. 1, *Funde Hethitischer Zeit* (Leipzig, 1937), p. 44, pl. 28:2.

120. C. L. Woolley, *Alalakh* (Oxford, 1955), pp. 358, 399, pl. CXXVI:ATP/38/155.

121. C. G. Styrenius, "The Vases from the Submycenaean Cemetery of Salamis," *Op.Ath.* 4 (1962): 112, pl. IV, 3617. For a discussion of the date of these tombs, cf. *DMS*, pp. 18 ff.

122. *Fortetsa*, pl. 34:432, 513, tomb X.

tomb X at Fortetsa, has an additional loop handle joining the two sections of the body.[123]

It is difficult to determine whether these later juglets from Salamis and Fortetsa are a continuation of a local ceramic tradition, whose beginnings and early development are simply unknown at present, or whether they resulted from Eastern stylistic influence on the Aegean world[124] (see discussion of types 9 and 10 below).

The Type 8 juglet was introduced into Palestine by Philistine potters, and it first appeared in purely Philistine contexts during the second half of the twelfth century. It is one of the rarer types in the Philistine repertoire, and it failed to gain a foothold in the Palestinian ceramic tradition before disappearing completely by the beginning of the tenth century. During the last stage of its existence, the Type 8 juglet lost all traces of its original Philistine character and its design and decoration were adapted to the local contemporary ceramic style.

GROUP II. TYPES 9–11, VESSELS RELATED TO CYPRIOT CERAMIC TYPES

Three pottery types can be included in this group: the cylindrical bottle (Type 9), the horn-shaped vessel (Type 10), and the gourd-shaped jar (Type 11). The last vessel, while not in itself a clearly defined type, has nevertheless been included here since it appears to be typologically related to types 9 and 10 and to a Cypriot prototype.

Type 9. Cylindrical Bottle (figs. 34–39, pls. 73–78)

The cylindrical bottles (elongated, squat, bulging, straight, or concave) all display an outward splaying rim, a narrow, sometimes ridged neck (fig. 34:8, 16), and a sloped (fig. 34:1–7, 9–14) or occasionally carinated (fig. 34:15) shoulder. They have horizontal loop handles (fig. 34:1, 2) or pierced lug handles (fig. 34:4), and their base, though predominantly flat (fig. 34:2, 4, 7–9), is sometimes a disk (fig. 34:12) or ring-base (fig. 34:16). The ware is mainly reddish-buff and is usually well fired.

The ornamentation is either in black and red or red alone on a white slip (fig. 34:1–14). Other decorative techniques employed are burnishing on a self-slipped

123. Ibid., pls. 36:537, 149:537, tomb X.
124. Ibid., p. 218.

surface (fig. 34:16) or on a red slip (fig. 35:4) and incised horizontal lines (fig. 34:16), occasionally incombination with painted horizontal lines (fig. 34:15). The decoration is usually plain geometric forms, but there is one example of the bird design (fig. 34:1).

Cylindrical bottles first appeared in Palestine[125] in the twelfth century B.C., vanishing before the end of the tenth century. They have been found at Tell el-Far'ah, Ashdod, Gezer, Beth-Shemesh, Tell eṣ-Ṣafi, Azor, Tell Qasile, Tell Jerishe, Megiddo, and Tel Zeror.

Tell el-Far'ah Five cylindrical bottles have been published from Tell el-Far'ah. Only one of them (fig. 34:2) has the white slip, bichrome decoration, and motifs (in this case, concentric semicircles) characteristics of Philistine pottery. The bottle was found in a clear Philistine context that should be ascribed to the second phase of Philistine pottery.

The decoration of the second bottle (fig. 34:8), which is unslipped, is a combination of debased Philistine motifs (horizontal stripes and concentric semicircles below the handles) and common Canaanite motifs (straight and wavy vertical lines). It was discovered in the vicinity of cemetery 500, in which most of the Philistine tombs at Far'ah were found.

The third bottle (fig. 34:15), which narrows sharply from the belly to the raised base, is somewhat atypical in shape; it is incised with horizontal ribbing on the shoulder. The few accompanying finds in tomb 507, where this bottle was found, were equally unusual and difficult to define. A similar bottle came from locus DF, level 390 in building D at the south end of the mound, a level that contained a large number of Philistine vessels characteristic of the second half of the twelfth and beginning of the eleventh century.[126]

125. A vessel similar in shape to the Type 9 cylindrical bottles was found at Tell Abu Hawam, stratum V, G 5, 60, in a clear Late Bronze Age context; *Tell Abu Hawam*, p. 42, pl. XVI:256. The bottle is incomplete. Two handles, now missing, seem to have originally extended immediately below the shoulder of the bottle. Hamilton remarked that it was not clear how the bottle should be restored; in our view it should be reconstructed along the lines of the Type 9 bottles. Its ware and finish strongly resemble Plain White Cypriot ware and thus provide a further link with Cyprus. The closest Plain White I parallel to the Tell Abu Hawam bottle comes from an eleventh-century B.C. tomb at Salamis and seems to be a later development of this type (*Salamine de Chypre*, pl. 24:73).
126. *CPP*, 66 W2; *BP II*, p. 30, pl. LXXIX.

Fig. 34. Type 9 cylindrical bottles.
1. White slip, Tell eṣ-Ṣafi [*PMB* 4, pl. II:4; *B-M*, pl. 42:163].   **2.** White slip, Tell el-Farʿah, TY 374 [*CPP*, Add. 75 P3,
TY].   **3.** Gezer, tomb 59 [*Gezer* III, pl. LXXXV:2; *CPP*, 66 X2].   **4.** White slip, Azor.   **5.** Burnished, Megiddo, stratum
VIA [No. S10, Loc. 1769, P6341].   **6.** Gezer [*Gezer* III, pl. CLXVI:14].   **7.** White slip, Gezer, ritual vessel [*Gezer* II, fig.
390:3].   **8.** Tell el-Farʿah, cemetery 500 [*CPP*, 66 Z].   **9.** Gezer, tomb 59 [*Gezer* III, pl. LXXXV:6; *CPP*, 66
X5].   **10.** Megiddo, stratum VII [*Meg. II,* pl. 71:15].   **11.** White slip, Beth-Shemesh, stratum III [*AS IV,* pl.
XXXVI:22].   **12.** Gezer, tomb 59 [*Gezer* III, pl. LXXXV:8; *CPP*, 66 W6].   **13.** Gezer, tomb 59 [*Gezer* III, pl. LXXXV:5; *CPP*, 66
W4].   **14.** Azor.   **15.** Burnished, Tell el-Farʿah, tomb 507, DF 390 [*CPP*, 66 W2].   **16.** Burnished, Tell el-Farʿah, tomb 649
[*CPP*, 66 Y].

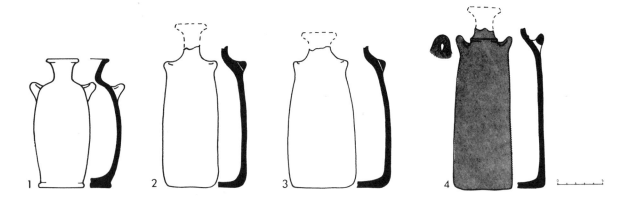

Fig. 35. Type 9 cylindrical bottles.
1. White slip, traces of red decoration, Beth-Shemesh [*AS II*, pl. XLIV:1]. **2.** Megiddo [P5799]. **3.** Red slip, burnished, Tell Qasile, stratum X [Q. 6997]. **4.** Red slip, burnished, Megiddo, stratum VIB [*Meg. II*, pls. 73:9, 142:3].

Fig. 36. Proto–White Painted cylindrical bottles from Cyprus.
1. [*Salamine de Chypre*, pl. 24:78] **2.** [*Salamine de Chypre*, pl. 24:77] **3.** Lapithos, tomb 503 lower, LC IIIB [Gjerstad, *OA 3*, fig. 2:5]. **4.** [*Salamine de Chypre*, pl. 24:74] **5.** Head of bottle from Gezer, tomb 59 [*Gezer* I, fig. 169].

Fig. 37. White Painted I cylindrical bottles from Cyprus [*SCE IV*, *Part 2*, fig. V:2–6].

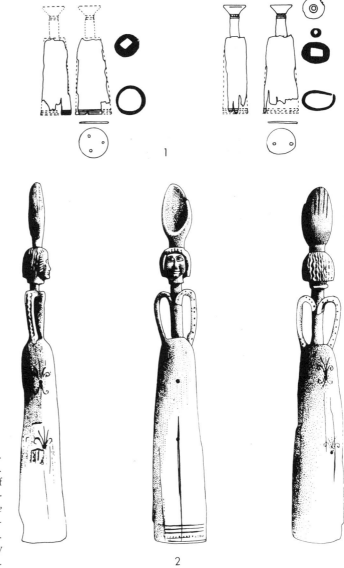

1

Fig. 38. Ivory cylindrical bottles.
1. Tell es-Saidiyeh, grave 101 [J. B. Pritchard, "New Evidence on the Role of the Sea Peoples in Canaan at the Beginning of the Iron Age," in *The Role of the Phoenicians in the Interaction of Mediterranean Civilizations*, W. Ward, ed., pl. XXXVIII. (Beirut, 1968)]. **2.** Ivory cosmetic bottle [*Lachish II*, pl. XV].

2

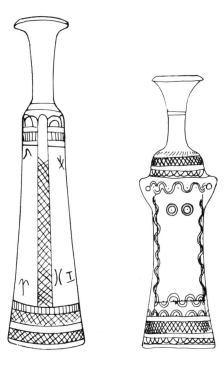

Fig. 39. Alabaster cylindrical bottles from Cyprus.
1. [V. and S. Karageorghis, "Some Inscribed Iron-Age Vases from Cyprus," *AJA* 60 (1956): illus. 1]. **2.** [P. Dikaios, "Alabaster Bottle-Shaped Rhyton," *RDAC* 2 (1934): pl. VI:4].

Pl. 73. Type 9 cylindrical bottles [Private Collection and the Israel Museum].
1. See fig. 34:14. **2.** Azor. No figure. **3.** See fig. 34:7. **4.** No figure. **5.** See fig. 34:4.

Pl. 74. Type 9 cylindrical bottle in fig. 34:1 [From the Collection of the Israel Department of Antiquities and Museums, P. 1219].

Pl. 75. Type 9 cylindrical bottle, Ashdod [From the Collection of the Israel Department of Antiquities and Museums].

Pl. 76. Type 9 cylindrical bottle in fig. 35:4 [Oriental Institute, Chicago].

Pl. 77. Type 9 cylindrical bottle in fig. 34:5 [Oriental Institute, Chicago, A 28108].

Pl. 78. Proto–White Painted bottle, Cyprus [Cesnola Collection, Metropolitan Museum, 74-51-1051].

The fifth bottle (fig. 34:16) also has an uncommon shape. It has a ring base, and its tall, narrow body gradually tapers at the top into a sloping shoulder. The bottle is burnished and decorated with groups of incised horizontal lines. It was found in tomb 649, which is dated to the second half of the eleventh century.[127]

The cylindrical bottle first appears at Far'ah as a Philistine vessel in a Philistine context, but it gradually loses its Philistine character and disappears by the end of the eleventh century.

Ashdod Stratum XII at Ashdod yielded another version of the bottle (pl. 75), this one with tapering sides and a herringbone-and-triangle decoration. It resembles the Azor bottle (fig. 34:4) but is squatter and less elegant.

Gezer A large collection of cylindrical bottles, most of them concentrated in tomb 59, comes from Gezer. Four decorated bottles of this tomb group have been published, along with a number of undecorated ones. Of these four, two have a simple horizontal-stripe pattern (fig. 34:12, 13) and the other two have more complex bichrome decorations (fig. 34:3, 9). Like the bottle from Tell el-Far'ah (fig. 34:8), the one in figure 34:9 is an interesting adaptation of typical local decorative motifs, for it combines horizontal stripes with straight and wavy vertical lines. Figure 34:3 shows an overall horizontal-stripe decoration broken by a single, elaborate zigzag band. The head of the anthropomorphic vessel from tomb 59 (fig. 36:5) can be reconstructed as a bottle of the type found in tomb 1 at Salamis (fig. 36:4).

A handmade miniature bottle, no doubt a votive vessel (fig. 34:7, pl. 73:3), was found in the cache of Philistine ritual vessels (see chap. 4, fig. 1:4), which should be dated within the twelfth century. This bottle is covered with a thick white slip and is crudely decorated in brick-red with a debased metope and zigzag pattern and almost unrecognizable semicircles on the neck.

The base and lower part of a vessel (fig. 34:6), which may have been a cylindrical bottle, was found at Gezer. The convex base and vertical rows of geometric decorations, however, suggest that, unlike the bottles, this vessel was not intended to stand upright.

Beth-Shemesh A bottle (fig. 34:11) was discovered at Beth-Shemesh in stratum III, where part of another

cylindrical bottle with red slip and white decoration was also found.[128] Another bottle (fig. 35:1), with white slip, a shaved surface, and traces of red decoration, probably also belongs to stratum III.

Tell eṣ-Ṣafi The decoration of this cylindrical bottle (fig. 34:1, pl. 74) was decisive in identifying this entire cla.3 of vessels as Philistine pottery.[129] Its decorative motifs are purely and unmistakably Philistine: concentric semicircles on the shoulder of the vessel and metopes on the body, each metope containing a debased version of the Philistine bird with head turned back. An unusual petallike decoration is partially preserved around the neck.

Tell Qasile A cylindrical bottle (fig. 35:3) from stratum X at Tell Qasile has the red slip and burnish characteristic of the stratum X pottery. Like the bottle from Beth-Shemesh (fig. 35:1), its surface is lightly shaved in long vertical strokes.[130]

Tell Jerishe Several cylindrical bottles were found at Tell Jerishe[131] in contexts comparable to strata XII–X at Tell Qasile.

Azor The Philistine cemetery at Azor has yielded a large group of cylindrical bottles, of which one decorated example is outstanding (fig. 34:4, pl. 73:5). Its body is decorated with two broad horizontal bands, the upper one containing a row of alternately red and black elongated triangles (cf. fig. 50:3), and the lower one displaying a row of short, broad triangles with bichrome net fill. In both shape and decoration this bottle has especially close affinities with the Cypriot cylindrical bottles and seems to be a creation of the Azor potter's workshop that produced other beautifully made Philistine vessels.

127. *BP I*, pl. LXX.

128. *AS IV*, pl. XXXVI:22, 34; *AS V*, p. 128. Wright stated that fragment 34 is not Philistine and probably dates to the twelfth century. However, this fragment, with its red slip and white paint, corresponds with pottery types of the second half of the eleventh century and the early part of the tenth century (Qasile X, Ashdod X) and should thus be considered one of the later types of this group.
129. *B-M*, pl. 42:163; *PMB* 4 (1927): pl. II:4. W. A. Heurtley erroneously cited these two illustrations as different vessels in "The Relationship between 'Philistine' and Mycenaean Pottery," *QDAP* 5 (1936): figs. 11:11, 12:2.
130. A number of bottles, both decorated and red slipped, come from the Philistine temple (strata XI–X) at Tell Qasile.
131. Unpublished. Cat. no. 288, provenance AII.

Of the debased version, we have selected two examples. One (pl. 73:2) is covered with a red-burnished slip and an overall net pattern, while the other (fig. 34:14, pl. 73:1) is squat in shape and decorated with horizontal stripes.

Megiddo Cylindrical bottles were also found at Megiddo in strata VII to VI. One example (fig. 34:10), ascribed to stratum VII, is the upper part of a bottle decorated with two curious patterns that are rather difficult to identify. Another bottle from strata VII–VIB[132] bears remains of a red slip and brown stripes.

A bottle found in strata VII–VIB (fig. 35:4, pl. 76) is a crude handmade specimen covered with a dull red slip and burnished in long vertical strokes. It is similar in shape to the bottle shown in figure 35:2, whose stratigraphy is unknown.

The lower part of a bottle (fig. 34:5, pl. 77) comes from stratum VIA. Its decorative motifs identify it as one of the group of debased Philistine pottery characteristic of Megiddo VIA.

Tel Zeror In locus 139 of stratum X at Tel Zeror (second half of the eleventh to the mid-tenth century)[133] a squat, badly worn cylindrical bottle was uncovered. Any decoration on this, as on the rest of the vessels of this group, had long since disappeared (see chap. 4, fig. 6, the lion-shaped rhyton, where traces of decoration remain). The Tel Zeror bottle is important because it provides further evidence linking the Tel Zeror Iron Age material with the Philistine pottery repertoire.

Apart from a single appearance at Tell Abu Hawam, the cylindrical bottle is first known as a Philistine vessel. It is most common at the end of the twelfth and during the eleventh centuries and disappears completely by the beginning of the tenth century. Parallels to the Philistine bottles come from Cyprus, where they first occur in the Late Cypriot IIIB period as Proto–White Painted (fig. 36:1, 3, pl. 78) and its Proto–White Painted Bichrome variation (fig. 36:2)[134] and continue

into the Cypro-Geometric I–II period as White Painted I and Bichrome I–II vessels.[135]

The Cypriot and Philistine bottles have many features in common: cylindrical bodies widening or tapering toward the base, outward-splaying rims, and a ridge sometimes encircling the neck (on the Cypriot vessels the ridge usually occurs in the middle of the neck and is more prominent); the pierced horizontal lug handles or horizontal loop handles of the Philistine bottles have exact Cypriot counterparts. Some of the Cypriot bottles bear a loop handle not found on the Philistine examples.

There is a striking similarity between the Cypriot and Philistine decorations in both division and details: the Philistine cross-hatching, elaborate zigzag bands, and row of triangles have exact parallels in Cyprus (fig. 37). Although most of the Cypriot examples occur in the White-Painted monochrome variant, the bichrome examples are even closer to bichrome Philistine pottery.

The nature of the connection between the Philistine and Cypriot bottles and between the Cypriot bottles and their Aegean counterparts has been widely discussed.[136] Differences of opinion exist as to the origin

---

Cyprus after the second destruction in Greece about 1150 B.C. It was produced in Cyprus by newly arrived refugees and shows clear affinities and a fusion with Myc. IIIC:lc and sub-Minoan pottery, as well as Phoenician influence (as seen in some of the shapes and in the bichrome ware). The basic studies of the Proto–White Painted pottery in Cyprus include Gjerstad, *OA 3*, pp. 73–106, and Furumark, *OA 3*, pp. 194–265. For an up-to-date summary and bibliography, *see* P. Åström, *SCE IV, Part 1D*, pp. 750–51.

No Proto–White Painted bottles from stratified excavations have been published. The late P. Dikaios informed me that bottles of this type were found in his excavation at Enkomi in a stratum ascribed to the twelfth century B.C., but no examples are given in his final published report. M. Lagarce of the French mission at Enkomi reported at the Sheffield Colloquium in 1972 the finding of such a bottle at Enkomi in a late-twelfth-century context.

All the early published examples come from tomb groups of the eleventh century, with a possible extension into the twelfth; e.g., Kouklia (V. Karageorghis, "An Early XIth Century B.C. Tomb from Palaepaphos," *RDAC* [1967]: fig. 9, dated to around 1100 B.C.); Kaloriziki (J. L. Benson, *The Necropolis of Kaloriziki*, SIMA, vol. 36 [Göteborg, 1973], p. 76, pl. 19:164, 165); and Salamis (*Salamine de Chypre*, pp. 37–41, pl. 24).

135. *SCE IV, Part 2*, p. 49, figs. V:2–6 (White Painted I), VIII:23, XVI:12 (Bichrome I–II).

136. The relationship between the Philistine and Cypriot bottles has been examined by Furumark (*CMP*, pp. 124 ff.),

---

132. *Meg. II*, pl. 71:14, locus 2048. This fragment comes from the last phase of Temple 2048, which is dated by the excavator to stratum VIIA. A reexamination of the finds ascribed to this phase of the temple shows that a number of vessels seem to be more closely related to the assemblage of stratum VI; e.g., ibid., pls. 71:7, 72:9.

133. *Tel Zeror III*, p. 11, pls. XV:2, LX:3.

134. The Proto–White Painted ware probably appeared in

of the vessel and the date of its appearance; the disagreements stem from the fact that in Cyprus the bottles were not found in well-stratified excavations but mainly in tomb groups. The Canaanite material has been misinterpreted in some cases, and not all of it was available to scholars for use in corroborating their datings of the Cypriot cylindrical bottles.

Our examination of the Canaanite material has led us to the conclusion that the cylindrical bottle appeared in the first half of the twelfth century B.C. as a fully developed ceramic type and shows no signs of having been derived from either the Mycenaean pyxis or any local vessel. Its closest parallels, as we have seen, are the Cypriot bottles, which may have been created through a fusion of Mycenaean and native Cypriot ceramic types. The main stumbling block in the assumption that the Philistine vessel is a development of a bottle that originated in Cyprus—an assumption that seems very likely to us—is the later appearance of the Cypriot vessel. This problem of chronology could perhaps be solved if in Cyprus the vessel were found to coincide with the initial appearance of the Proto-White Painted ware around 1150 B.C. This question, however, will be resolved only by future excavations.

Similar bottles have been found in the Aegean, in Karphi on Crete,[137] and in the sub-Mycenaean cemeteries at Athens.[138] The bottles are definitely not native to Greece, and they indicate the beginning of an Oriental-Cypriot influence on the West. An example of this fluctuating influence has been encountered above (in Type 8) and will be met again in Type 10.

The prototypes of these pottery bottles are to be sought in the precious ointment bottles of ivory (fig. 38)[139] and alabaster (fig. 39),[140] which will be discussed in greater detail in connection with the horn-shaped vessel, Type 10.

Type 10. Horn-shaped Vessel (figs. 40–43, pls. 79–82)

The horn-shaped vessel appears to be the twin of the cylindrical bottle in shape, decoration, and function, and the two types are frequently found together.

An elongated cylindrical body tapering to a narrow curved neck gives the vessel its name. Its rim splays outward, and its base is usually slightly convex, unsuitable for standing. Its two pierced horizontal lug handles are attached in a line on the inner curvature of the body—one at the base and one on the body just below the crook of the neck. Its curved base and pierced handles indicate that the vessel was sus-

---

who cited the cylindrical bottle as evidence for his correlation between Myc. IIIC:2 and Cypro-Geometric I pottery. In his opinion, the vessel originated in Myc. IIIC:1; he thus used it as the basis for dating the Cypro-Geometric period as prior to 1100 B.C. He based his chronology on two assumptions: first, that the cylindrical bottle in Palestine is a local imitation of a Cypro-Geometric bottle; secondly, and erroneously, that the cylindrical bottle does not appear in Palestine before 1100 B.C. (primarily on the evidence of Gezer tomb 59). Gjerstad, in *OA 3*, pp. 96 ff., opposed these two assumptions, noting that both the origin of the cylindrical bottle and the date of its first appearance are in dispute and that the date of its appearance in Palestine is also unclear. J. Du Plat Taylor, *PEQ* 88 (1956): 35 ff., attempted to show the influence of the Cypriot Proto-White Painted bottle on the appearance of the bottles in Palestine, but failed to take the chronological difficulties into account.

137. The Karphi example has been mentioned by Desborough as a link between Crete and Cyprus (*DMS*, pp. 27 ff., 172 ff.). *See also* M. Seiradaki, "Pottery from Karphi," *BSA* 55 (1960): pl. 11B. The site is dated by the excavators to ca. 1100–900 B.C.

138. For a discussion, see *DMS*, pp. 27 ff., pl. 16 c–d. One comes from a late sub-Mycenaean tomb and another from a grave that is transitional to Proto-Geometric.

139. Two ivory vessels were found at Tell es-Saidiyeh in grave 101, which dates to ca. 1200 B.C. (J. B. Pritchard in *The Role of the Phoenicians in the Interaction of Mediterranean Civilization* [Beirut, 1968], p. 102, fig. 2:6, 7). These "bottles" are published upside-down. When turned around, they resemble in shape the bottles under discussion. A late development of the ivory ointment bottle can be seen in the Nimrud ivories of the ninth century B.C. (R. D. Barnett, *A Catalogue of the Nimrud Ivories* [London, 1957], pp. 94, 199, pl. LVIII, S. 106). This alabastron is drilled with four small, vertical holes to hold a small handle, perhaps of wood or metal, of the same type as those that appear on our pottery bottles. Barnett mentions a bronze vase of this shape also found at Nimrud. A variant of the alabastron is the woman-flask, of which a well-known example comes from the Fosse Temple at Lachish (*Lachish II*, pl. XV).

140. Two alabaster bottles are known from Cyprus; both are dated by V. Karageorghis to the Cypro-Geometric I period (V. and J. Karageorghis, "Some Inscribed Iron-Age Vases from Cyprus," *AJA* 60 [1956]: 353–54). One of them was published by P. Dikaios in *RDAC* 2 (1934): 16, pl. VI:4. This vessel probably comes from the Iron Age necropolis near Gysos in the Famagusta district. The elongated body with two pierced handles is incised with hatching, concentric circles, and concentric semicircles. The second bottle (*AJA* 60, p. 353:7, ill. 1) resembles the first in outline but no handles are indicated. The incised decoration of cross-hatchings and concentric semicircles indicates a connection with the earlier Proto-White ware. It has been suggested that the incised signs are a later addition. *See* J. Karageorghis, "The Inscriptions," *AJA* 60 (1956): 356.

Fig. 40. Type 10 horn-shaped vessels.
1. Beth-Shemesh, tomb 11 [*BS*, pls. 167:3, 193:501].
2. Burnished, Megiddo, stratum VI (?) [*Meg. II*, pl. 84:13 (mentioned as III, pl. LXXXV:3]. **4.** White slip, Tell Qasile, strata XII–XI [Q. II 2358].

Fig. 42. Proto–White Painted horn-shaped vessels from Cyprus. **1.** Horn-shaped vessel, 19 cm. long, Kouklia, tomb 9 [V. Karageorghis, "An Early XIth Century B.C. Tomb from Palaeopaphos," *RDAC* (1967): fig. 9:20]. **2.** Horn-shaped vessel, 18.5 cm. long, Kouklia, tomb 9 [V. Karageorghis, "An Early XIth Century B.C. Tomb from Palaeopaphos," *RDAC* (1967): fig. 9:21].

Fig. 41. Type 10 horn-shaped vessel, burnished.

Fig. 43. Ivory cosmetic vessels.
1. Ivory vessel with female head, Megiddo, stratum VIII [*Meg. II*, pl. 202 (dap)]. **2.** Horn-shaped vessel with female head from a wall painting in the tomb of Sebekheten at Thebes, tomb 63 [*Lachish II*, pl. XV (dap)].

Pl. 79. Type 10 horn-shaped vessel in fig. 40:1 (mirror image at right) [From the Collection of the Israel Department of Antiquities and Museums, 63–466].

Pl. 80. Type 10 horn-shaped vessel in fig. 40:2 [Oriental Institute, Chicago, A 28010].

1   2

Pl. 81. Type 10 horn-shaped vessels [Dayan Collection].
1. See pl. 1:8.   2. See fig. 41.

Pl. 82. Alabaster horn-shaped vessel, Deir el-Balaḥ (two views) [Israel Museum, 69.87.423].

pended or carried on a cord. The ware is usually light buff and well fired, and the decoration is confined to geometric patterns in bichrome red and black, or red alone, on a white slip or plain surface.

Although the number of horn-shaped vessels found in Palestine is not large, they seem to have enjoyed a wide geographical distribution, having been found at Tell el-ʿAjjul, Beth-Shemesh, Gezer, Azor, Tell Qasile, and Megiddo.

Tell el-ʿAjjul   Tomb 1112 at Tell el-ʿAjjul contained one horn-shaped vessel as well as a Type 1 Philistine bowl.[141] Unlike most Type 10 vessels, the one from ʿAjjul is a crude, handmade product that lacks all slip or ornamentation, aside from what may be horizontal lines.

Beth-Shemesh   A complete horn-shaped vessel (fig. 40:1, pl. 79) comes from tomb 11 at Beth-Shemesh. It has been assigned to the Philistine period of this tomb by analogy with other horn-shaped vessels (see chap. 2, p. 51).

Gezer   Three horn-shaped vessels were found in tomb 59 at Gezer. One (fig. 40:3) bears typical Philistine motifs—rhombuses and chevrons in alternate metopes. The other two consist of a fragment of a base and part of a neck.[142]

Tell Qasile   Two fragments of horn-shaped vessels were found in Qasile XI, a base (fig. 40:4) and a neck.[143] Both were covered with a white slip and decorated with a bichrome pattern of horizontal stripes.

Azor   The Azor cemetery has yielded a number of horn-shaped vessels,[144] one of which is exceptionally well made (pl. 81:1). In its very slightly curved shape,

carinated shoulder, tall and narrow neck, and wide rim, it is a clear variant of the bottles. The light buff, self-slipped clay is decorated in black and red designs that were meticulously executed, with a geometric pattern divided into zones by horizontal lines. The decorative scheme consists of an overall net pattern and a continuous triglyph motif of chevrons and horizontal lines. The whole composition, although purely geometric, is typically Philistine.

Of unknown provenance (it was purchased in Nablus) is a very elegant bottle (fig. 41, pl. 81:2); its horn shape is accentuated by the curve of the narrow neck and splaying rim. It is made of well-levigated and well-fired buff clay and is burnished lengthwise. It bears a debased geometric pattern executed in a slipshod manner. This vessel recalls the bottle from Megiddo (fig. 40:2, pl. 80) in both ware and finish.

Megiddo   The base of a horn-shaped vessel (fig. 40:2, pl. 80) with bichrome decoration on a burnished surface was found in Megiddo stratum VI. The style of its decorative motifs places it in the group of debased Philistine pottery of Megiddo VI.

The horn-shaped vessel is unknown in Palestinian pottery prior to its appearance in Philistine contexts. Cyprus contains its closest parallels: Cypriot Proto–White Painted and White Painted I–II (fig. 42)[145] and Plain White III ware of the Late Cypriot III and Cypro-Geometric periods.[146] Even though it is not the most common of Cypriot pottery types and the course of its development is still obscure, J. A. Daniel and E. Gjerstad nonetheless identify it as an original Cypriot vessel.[147]

The horn-shaped vessels from Cyprus and Canaan have almost identical shapes and handles (although a variant from Cyprus with one loop handle on its inner curvature is not known in Canaan) as well as close

141. *AG II,* pls. XXVIII:26 B3, XXXVI:94 A.

142. *Gezer I,* fig. 171:7; *Gezer III,* pl. LXXXIV:16.

143. Cat. no. Q II 2358 is a base from which a pierced handle is pulled; cat. no. Q II 2442 is a neck fragment. An elaborately decorated horn-shaped vessel comes from the temple area locus 125, intermediate between XI–X strata.

144. One vessel (SS 179 68.32.10) with a missing rim is rather crude in ware and finish. Except for the area between the handles, the body is completely covered with an overall net pattern in red and black. A complete specimen has a red slip and burnished surface, recalling the finish of the Type 9 bottle from Megiddo VIB (fig. 35:4 above).

145. J. F. Daniel, "Two Late Cypriot III Tombs at Kourion," *AJA* 41 (1937): 68 ff., pl. II:44. Daniel ascribes this vessel to a pottery group that he calls "Cypriot Wheel-Made Pottery in the Cypriote Tradition." *See also* V. Karageorghis, "An Early XIth Century B.C. Tomb from Palaepaphos," *RDAC* (1967): 20, 21, fig. 9:20, 21.

146. *SCE IV, Part 2,* p. 49, fig. V:13 (White Painted I); p. 86, fig. XIV:5 (White Painted II), and fig. XXVII:25–26 (Plain White III ware).

147. Ibid., p. 284, n. 20.

affinities in their decorative techniques and motifs. Consequently, an Egyptian origin for this vessel in pottery does not seem probable,[148] and its development appears to be a clear example of Cypriot-Philistine interaction that is part of a more complex general situation. The later development of this vessel in the Aegean world can be observed in the Geometric period assemblages at Exochi, Ialysos, and Vroulia on the island of Rhodes.[149]

The horn-shaped vessels and straight-sided bottles are both variations on a single type (probably an ointment container) produced in pottery as well as in the more costly ivory and alabaster (pl. 82).[150] The ultimate origin of the shape is no doubt the ivory tusk. There are well-known ivory cosmetic bottles, both horn-shaped from the Late Bronze treasure hoard at Megiddo (fig. 43:1)[151] and straight-sided from the Lachish temple (fig. 38:2). In Egypt the horn-shaped bottle has been found *in corpore,* and it is also depicted in wall paintings (fig. 43:2).[152] The vessels appear earlier in precious materials than in pottery and have a wider diffusion. The Philistine and Cypriot pottery bottles and horn-shaped vessels, undoubtedly cheaper copies, are so much alike in shape and decoration that they obviously form a single group. In both places they represent a new shape in the local ceramic repertoire. (In Cyprus the horn-shaped vessel, variously stylized, has a long tradition but no clear antecedent.)

Two related problems remain unresolved: (1) the ultimate source of the pottery bottles and horn-shaped vessels as a pottery type and (2) the date of their appearance. A number of opposing solutions have been proposed for these much-debated questions; even so, all that can be definitely stated at present is that (1) the Cypriot and Philistine vessels are closely related, and (2) the Philistine vessels were already known in the twelfth century B.C., although clear evidence of the first appearance of their Cypriot counterparts is still lacking. The origin of these vessels is still not known, but it is indisputable that in Palestine they appear in Philistine contexts as Philistine vessels.

Type 11. Gourd-shaped Jar (fig. 44, pl. 83)

Two identical gourd-shaped jars come from the Philistine cemetery of Azor. They have a long narrow neck, splaying rim, globular body, flattened base, and a neck pierced by two holes below the rim (apparently for a carrying-rope). The jars are white-slipped and are covered with close-set black and red horizontal stripes in alternating groups. Several radial lines, alternately red and black, are painted upward from the base. Because of their finish and paint, as well as certain features of shape and decoration that have affinities with typical Philistine vessels—especially from Azor—these two jars are considered part of the Philistine pottery repertoire. The neck is identical in shape and decoration with some of the bottles and horn-shaped vessels of types 9 and 10 (fig. 34:4, pl. 73:5), and the decorated base is exactly like the base of a Type 13 bowl (see pl. 90). All the vessels of this group were probably produced in the same workshop.

The shape of the vessels is foreign to Canaanite pottery and rare in Mycenaean pottery.[153] In outline they are reminiscent of the gourd-shaped Cypriot vessels, although no exact contemporary parallels are known. These vessels are further proof of our assumption of the variety and distinctive quality of the Philistine pottery from Azor, which remains our sole source of such shapes.

Since they are unique, we have classified these jars as a separate type having analogies with types 9 and 10; they may also be related to Cypriot pottery.

GROUP III. TYPE 12, JUG WITH EGYPTIAN AFFINITIES (FIGS. 45–53, PLS. 84–89)

This jug shows Egyptian influence both in form and decoration. It has an exceptionally tall, sometimes

148. R. Amiran, "The Arm-shaped Vessel and Its Family," *JNES* 21 (1962): 161–74.

149. K. Friis Johansen, "Exochi, ein frührodisches Gräberfeld," *Acta Archaeologica* 28 (1957): 19; *Ialysos I–II,* p. 307, fig. 204; and K. F. Kinch, *Vroulia* (Berlin, 1914), pls. 34:2, 5 and 41:15, 2.

150. The one alabaster example known to us from Canaan probably originated from the Deir el-Balah cemetery. This vessel is composed of three separate parts: a mouthpiece, a curved body, and a disk base. On the inner curvature of the base is a small pierced handle, but there is no trace of another handle. For examples in other materials such as faience and wood, *see* the detailed study of Amiran, "The Arm-shaped Vessel and Its Family," *JNES* 21 (1962): 166 ff., figs. 2, 3.

151. *Meg. II,* pl. 202, stratum VIII, locus 3100.

152. E.g., Syrian tributary carrying a horn-shaped vessel in the Tomb of Sebekhetep at Thebes, ca. 1450 B.C. (*Lachish II,* pl. XV).

153. A close parallel comes from a Myc. III:B tomb at Ephesus (M. J. Mellink, "Archaeology in Asia Minor," *AJA* 68 [1964]: 157 ff., pl. 50:13).

bulging neck with close-set wheel marks inside, an everted and mildly splaying rim, and a wide, flat loop handle extending from the rim to the shoulder. Its body is rounded and narrows toward a flat base, an unusual feature in Philistine ceramics. The ware is well fired, of reddish or greenish color, and is covered with a thick white slip.

The jug is decorated in black and red and displays a wealth of motifs rendered, in most cases, with unusual skill and artistry. There are two separate zones of decoration—one on the neck and the other on the shoulder. The neck decoration (the distinctive feature) consists of: (a) a lotus flower as a central motif, flanked by either spirals (fig. 50:1) or birds (fig. 50:2); (b) a series of alternating black and red elongated triangles (fig. 50:3); or (c) a stylized plant motif (fig. 47:3). The wide shoulder band (sometimes divided into two horizontal registers) displays typical Philistine motifs in metope arrangements (figs. 45, 46:1, 47:1, 48) or repeated composite geometric patterns (figs. 46:2, 47:2, 3).

Type 12 jugs have been found thus far at Tell el-Farʿah, Ashdod, Beth-Shemesh, Gezer, Azor, Tell Qasile, and Tell ʿAitun.

Tell el-Farʿah   The largest concentration of Type 12 jugs comes from tombs 242, 542, 552, 562, and 851 at Tell el-Farʿah. Three jugs can be attributed to the earliest phase of Philistine pottery.

The first (fig. 45, pl. 84) is from tomb 542. Its outstanding feature is the tall, slender neck decorated with a stylized lotus motif outlined in black. The leaves of the calyx are black, while the upper half of the petals is solid red and the lower half is accentuated with horizontal black lines. Three spirals curve gracefully down from the outer leaves on either side of the calyx. The decorated band on the shoulder of the jug is divided into metopes containing a checkered pattern, bird, and rhomboid motifs.

The lotus motif with spirals has a debased parallel in a Philistine vessel from Megiddo VIB (fig. 50:6), but the Megiddo potter was rather wanting in artistic skill; moreover, he was apparently unfamiliar with the original motif.

A second, identical jug was found in tomb 242, which is dated by its ceramic contents to about the same period as tomb 542.[154] The last of the early jugs

(fig. 46:1, pl. 85), from tomb 552, is similar to the first two in its tall neck, metope arrangement, and decorative motifs on the shoulder band. The decoration on the neck, however, consists of a row of elongated red and black triangles.

A jug from tomb 562 (fig. 46:2) and a similar jar from tomb 851[155] (which is contemporary with tomb 562)[156] belong to the second phase of Philistine pottery. Their tall necks bulge slightly in the middle and are decorated with a row of elongated triangles. Their shoulder bands exhibit a row of concentric semicircles joined by chevrons. A jug that is identical in decoration but has a shorter neck was found in tomb 841.[157] It, too, should be ascribed to the second phase of Philistine pottery.

Ashdod   Stratum XII at Ashdod has yielded a jug with a row of elongated triangles around the neck interspaced with horizontal lines. The lines represent the lotus calyx, as they also do on the Tell el-Farʿah jug (fig. 45) and the Azor jug (fig. 48). This composite design forms a link between the lotus pattern and the row of elongated triangles. The body of the jug has two bands of decoration which are crudely reminiscent of the decoration on the Beth-Shemesh jug (fig. 47:1). Besides this almost complete example, numerous sherds of the same type were found in strata XIII–XI at Ashdod.

Beth-Shemesh   An excellent example of a Type 12 jug was found in stratum III at Beth-Shemesh (fig. 47:1, pl. 86).[158] Its very tall and elegant neck is decorated with elongated triangles painted black. The shoulder band consists of two horizontal registers: the upper and wider one is divided into metopes containing alternating scale-pattern and rhomboid motifs; and the lower displays a horizontal chevron pattern.

Gezer   Two Type 12 jugs from Gezer have been published. One (fig. 47:2) is decorated on the neck with a row of elongated triangles and on the shoulder band with a repeated unit arrangement of the composite running spiral and rhombus motifs. Identical plant

154. *CPP*, 34 Y3; *BP I*, pl. LXVIII.

155. *CPP*, 34 Y4.
156. An Egyptian jug similar to the one in tomb 562 (*CPP*, 41 F) was also found in tomb 851 (*CPP*, 41 S) (cf. chap. 5, fig. 8:18 below).
157. *CPP*, 34 Y6. The contents of tomb 841 do not appear in the cemetery 800 registers.
158. *AS V*, p. 128.

Fig. 44. Type 11 jar, white slip, Azor.

Pl. 83. Type 11 gourd-shaped jars in fig. 44 [From the Collection of the Israel Department of Antiquities and Museums, 63-446, 63-490].

Fig. 45. Type 12 jug, white slip, Tell el-Farʻah, tomb 542 [*BP I*, pl. XXIII:4; *CPP*, 34 Y3].

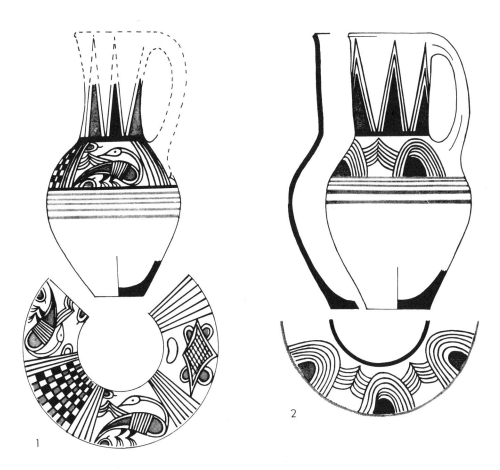

Fig. 46. Type 12 jugs.
1. White slip, Tell el-Farʿah, tomb 552.   **2. White slip, Tell el-Farʿah, tomb 562.**

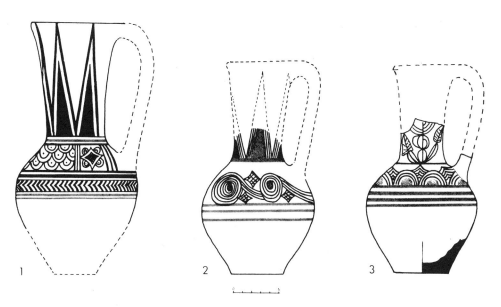

Fig. 47. Type 12 jugs.
1. White slip, Beth-Shemesh, stratum III [*AS I,* pl. XIII; *AS II,* pl. XLII:9].   **2.** Gezer [*Gezer* III, pl. CLXIII:4].   **3.** Gezer [*Gezer* III, pl. CLX:1; *PMB 4,* pl. II:6].

Fig. 48. Type 12 jug, white slip, Azor.

Fig. 49. Type 12 jug, white slip,
Tell-ʿAitun (?).

Fig. 50. Lotus flower pattern in Philistine decoration.
1. See fig. 45. **2.** See fig. 48. **3.** See fig. 46:2. **4.** See fig. 54:1. **5.** See fig. 54:2. **6.** Megiddo, stratum VIB [*Meg. II*, pl. 142:12]. **7.** See fig. 28:1. **8.** See fig. 27:2.

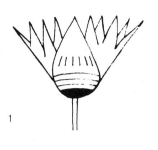 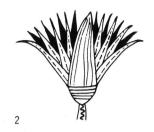 

1   2   3

 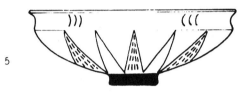

4   5

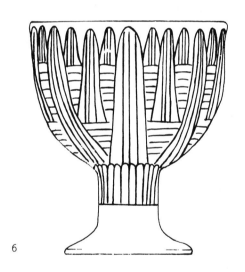 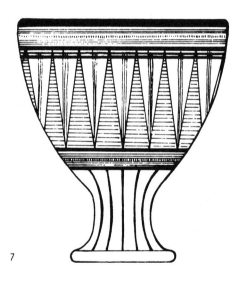

6   7

Fig. 51. Lotus pattern in Egyptian decoration.
1. Faience bowl, detail [W. Krönig, "Ägyptische Fayence Schalen des Neuen Reiches," *MDIAA* 5 (1934): fig. 20].   **2.** Faience bowl, detail [Krönig, "Ägyptische Fayence," pl. XXVI:a].   **3.** Faience bowl, detail [Krönig, "Ägyptische Fayence," fig. 12].
   4. Faience bowl [*Deir el-Medineh*, pl. III:IV, 1057:3].   **5.** Faience bowl [Krönig, "Ägyptische Fayence," fig. 19].   **6.** Faience goblet (*Gurob,* pl. XVII:8].   **7.** Faience goblet [*Deir el-Medineh,* fig. 167, pl. XVII:XXV D.M. 22, 22b].

Fig. 52. Alabaster "lotus" goblet, Deir el-Balah, tomb 118 [*Deir el-Balah Qedem 10*, ill. 145].

Fig. 53. Chalices.
1. Tell el-Farʿah, tomb 213 [*CPP*, 17 K6].   **2.** Tell el-Farʿah, tomb 229, tomb 202 [*CPP*, 17 K7].   **3.** Tell el-Farʿah, tomb 228 [*CPP*, 17 L2].

Pl. 84. Type 12 jug with Egyptian affinities in fig. 45 (and detail) [From the Collection of the Israel Department of Antiquities and Museums, I. 4276].

Pl. 85. Type 12 jug with Egyptian affinities in fig. 46:1 (detail) [Institute of Archaeology, London].

Pl. 86. Type 12 jug with Egyptian affinities in fig. 47:1 [From the Collection of the Israel Department of Antiquities and Museums, I. 8650].

Pl. 87. Type 12 jug with Egyptian affinities in fig. 47:3 [From the Collection of
the Israel Department of Antiquities and
Museums, V. 492].

Pl. 88. Type 12 jug with Egyptian affinities in fig. 48 (two views and details) [From the Collection of the Israel Department of
Antiquities and Museums, 63–450].

Pl. 89. Type 12 jugs with Egyptian affinities [From the Collection of the Israel Department of Antiquities and Museums].
1. See fig. 45.   **2.** Azor. No figure.   **3.** See fig. 48.   **4.** See fig. 49.

motifs (a stylized palm tree?) are depicted on either side of the neck of the second jug (fig. 47:3, pl. 87). A row of concentric semicircles joined by chevrons appears in the shoulder band. Both jugs demonstrate the distinctive style of the Gezer potter.

Azor The finest example of a Type 12 jug, and perhaps the most richly decorated vessel in the entire Philistine pottery repertoire, is the jug shown in figure 48 (pl. 88); it is from the Philistine cemetery at Azor. The jug is exceptional in the delicacy and precision of its dense ornamentation and in the wealth and variety of its decorative motifs. The neck is decorated with a stylized lotus similar to the one on the neck of the Tell el-Farʿah jug (fig. 45); but, instead of spirals, a bird is depicted on either side of the flower. The birds point in the same direction with their necks curved and their heads forward (one bird faces the lotus, the other faces away from it), creating an asymmetrical heraldic device. The upper part of the body of the jug is divided into two horizontal registers, both of which are arranged in metopes. The upper and wider of the two registers contains geometric designs, whereas the lower displays alternating rhomboids, nets, and birds with their heads turned back.

A large number of sherds of Type 12 jugs were uncovered at Azor, indicating that this type of vessel was common there.

Tell Qasile A few sherds, which can be identified as neck fragments of Type 12 jugs, were found in strata XII–XI at Tell Qasile.[159]

Tell ʿAitun The Philistine tomb in the cemetery at Tell ʿAitun (chap. 2, fig. 5:4) yielded a jug of Type 12. It is of greenish ware and bears traces of a white slip and red horizontal stripes, but no remains of any other decoration.

A complete vessel (fig. 49, pl. 89:4) acquired in the Hebron area and probably originating from the Tell ʿAitun cemetery presents a new variation on the Type 12 jug. Its body is biconical, similar in shape to the ʿAfula jug (fig. 56:2), and its neck is ridged and decorated with the usual elongated triangles. The body decoration is divided into two registers, the upper containing a row of concentric semicircles and the lower divided into metopes with simple geometric motifs

consisting of groups of straight lines and double triangles. This jug from ʿAitun evidently belongs to Phase 2 of Philistine pottery.

Decorative Motifs Related to Egyptian Styles The distinctive characteristic of the Type 12 jug—the high and sometimes slightly bulging neck with lotus or triangle decoration—is foreign to local Canaanite pottery, but it is one of the most common features of Egyptian pottery. This sort of neck is also found on imported Egyptian pottery in Palestine and on local imitations of Egyptian ware (chap. 5, fig. 7:14, 15).

The two types of designs decorating the necks of the Type 12 jugs are (1) the stylized lotus and (2) the row of elongated triangles. Neither occurs in the decorative repertoire of the local Canaanite ceramic traditions. In the following discussion, we will attempt to identify the source of these two motifs, trace their dispersion, and analyze the connection between them.

The lotus flower, as depicted on the Tell el-Farʿah and Azor jugs (fig. 50:1, 2), is a Philistine adaptation of a motif prevalent throughout Egyptian art. Whereas the Philstines distinguished between the leaves and petals by rendering them alternately in red and black, the Egyptians employed either different colors (fig. 51:2) or a fill with hatching or dots (fig. 51:3, 4). In both techniques, horizontal lines, probably representing the calyx (fig. 51:6), filled the lower portions of the petals. Even the typically Philistine additions, spirals and birds, may possibly be patterned on Egyptian motifs, for the spirals curving down on either side of the lotus in figure 45 are similar to those on the Egyptian lily (which at times can barely be distinguished from the lotus, as the two often appear as a hybrid design [fig. 51:3]). The heraldic arrangement of birds on either side of the lotus also has parallels—albeit uncommon ones—in Egyptian lotus designs.[160]

From the beginning of the Middle Bronze Age II the Egyptian lotus motif is found in Canaan on imported Egyptian ware, especially on faience[161] and alabaster vessels (fig. 52).[162] We can follow its development

159. Unpublished Q II 2780, Q II 2120.

160. E.g., *Gurob,* pl. XX:1.

161. For a discussion of the lotus motif and its stylization on faience vessels, *see* W. Krönig, "Ägyptische Fayence Schalen des Neuen Reiches," *MDIAA* 5 (1934): 144 ff.; *Gezer* II, p. 337, vol. III, pl. CCXI:13, 16; *BP I,* pl. VI:18; *TBM I,* pp. 29 ff., fig. 4; and *Lachish II,* p. 63, pls. XIV, XXI:55, XXII:55, XXIII:64, 67, 74, XXXVI:102.

162. *Meg. II,* pls. 260:29–30, 261:29–30. *Deir el-Balaḥ IEJ 22,* p. 70; *Deir el-Balaḥ IEJ 23,* p. 36, pl. 44:B. The lotus motif is a

down to its various representations on the Megiddo Ivories[163] (end of the thirteenth to beginning of the twelfth century B.C.).

On local Canaanite ware the lotus motif appears only sporadically. One example, from Tell el-ʿAjjul, consists of an Egyptian-type jar decorated in red and black with two horizontal rows of alternating lotus leaves and petals and, between them, a "lotus chain" of flowers and buds. Petrie pointed out that the decoration was copied from an Egyptian design of the Eighteenth Dynasty. He judged that it was of local workmanship by the reversal of the "lotus chain," which points upward instead of downward as in the usual Egyptian depictions. The same feature is found on a Philistine Type 12 jug.[164]

The first locally manufactured ware bearing the lotus decoration is the group of Type 12 Philistine jugs under discussion. A contemporary but somewhat different adaptation is found on the Type 13 Philistine bowls (see fig. 54:1, 2), where a stylized lotus rosette (see fig. 54) or a geometrized one (see fig. 55) appears on the interior of the bowls.

An isolated group of chalices from cemetery 200 at Tell el-Farʿah provides additional examples of the lotus motif on native Palestinian ware (tenth century B.C.). Some of the chalices display a lotus chain (fig. 53:1, 2), while others are decorated with rows of alternating red and black triangles (fig. 53:3) that are really stylized lotus petals.

An incense stand from Gezer,[165] which combines the triangles and lotuses of the Farʿah chalices, provides an example of geometric and naturalistic lotus motifs on the same vessel. It is decorated with a row of alternately red and black elongated triangles and a row of plastic leaves. This same combination of plastic and painted motifs appears on a stone censer from Megiddo, whose decoration includes a lotus chain.[166]

The row of red and black elongated triangles (fig. 50:3) is the second and more frequent of the two motifs depicted on the neck of the Type 12 jugs. This is, in

effect, a complete geometrization of the original lotus flower motif—the black triangles representing the leaves, and the red, the petals. The high neck with triangles represents the flower's calyx, as in the Egyptian lotus goblets (fig. 51:7). The group of bowls and goblets shown in figure 51:4–7 illustrates the process by which the stylization of the lotus in Egyptian art evolved from naturalism to complete geometrization.

The faience bowl in figure 51:4 is a very interesting example of a common Egyptian artistic concept—namely, the combination of two different degrees of stylization on the same vessel. The lotus flower decorating the interior of the bowl is rendered naturalistically (with only slight stylization); the exterior of the bowl displays the same basic motif geometrically stylized (cf. Type 13), although it still preserves much of the lotus's natural appearance. The lotus motif in figure 51:5, on the other hand, is completely geometrized, and the leaves and petals are differentiated by the use of dotted and blank triangles. The same effect is achieved by the use of colors in the triangle motifs on the Philistine Type 12 jugs.

The two different methods of representing lotus motifs can be observed on the goblets (figs. 51:6, 7 and 52), whose shape and decoration in themselves imitate the shape of the lotus flower. The stylized motif in figure 51:6 preserves the natural curvature of the lotus petals, while the horizontal lines at the base of the petals is a common featue on naturalistic depictions of the lotus. In figure 51:7, on the other hand, the lotus is completely transformed into elongated triangles, and no attempt is made to retain or stylistically represent any natural details. Similar combinations on the same vessel are found on the Tell el-ʿAjjul jar, on the alabaster jugs from Megiddo and Deir el-Balaḥ (fig. 52), and on the faience jug from Lachish, all of which have an Egyptian background.

In the Philistine examples of lotus motifs, the two methods of stylization appear side by side within this homogeneous group of vessels—the stylized but still recognizable lotus alongside completely geometrical elongated triangles. The triangles depicted on the necks of the Philistine Type 12 jugs are a complete geometrization of the lotus motif. The only semblances of naturalism in this design are the elongated shape of the triangles (which may also be due to the shape of the jugs' necks), the emphasis on this elongation created by the addition of lines running parallel to the sides of the triangles, and the use of alternating

---

prominent feature on the lids of the anthropoid coffins from Deir el-Balaḥ; *see* chap. 5, pl. 4 below.

163. *Meg. Ivories*, pls. 4:2a, b, 8:27–31, 32:160a–c, and 39:175.

164. *AG III*, p. 13, pl. XLIV:77. The jar was found in a rubbish pit of unclear date.

165. *Gezer* II, p. 336, fig. 460.

166. *Meg. Cult*, p. 21, fig. 6.

colors to distinguish between the leaves and the petals of the flower.

The elongated red and black triangles appear in different combinations in the Philistine decorative repertoire (see, for example, figs. 19, 34:4). The rows of alternate red and black triangles decorating some of the chalices (fig. 53:3) in the Tell el-Farʿah cemetery 200 group are another variation, though more remote, of the geometrization of the lotus motif, as seen in other examples from this cemetery (fig. 53:1, 2).

Finally, the censers from Megiddo and Gezer provide additional evidence that the elongated triangle motif is a geometrization of the lotus motif. The lotus chain is depicted on the basin of the Megiddo censer and is encircled by two rows of plastic lotus leaves. The Gezer censer is similarly decorated with plastic leaves, but instead of a lotus chain it has rows of alternate red and black elongated triangles arranged exactly like those on the Farʿah chalices.

As to the origin of the lotus motifs depicted on the Type 12 Philistine jugs, the lotus, as we have seen, is essentially an Egyptian motif that entered Canaan at the beginning of the Middle Bronze Age II. Appearing only sporadically in Canaanite art, it became part of Phoenician decoration. Did the Philistine potter take his Type 12 lotus decoration from the local Canaanite tradition or did he copy it from the original Egyptian motif?

The lotus is not a common motif in Late Bronze II or Iron I local ceramic decoration, and its geometrization, as it appears on the Philistine Type 12 jugs, is totally unknown on Canaanite pottery or on other finds from this period. However, they are very common in Egyptian art, both prior to and during the period in which the Type 12 jug made its appearance in Canaan. The method by which the Philistine potter stylized his lotus motifs into geometric shapes is, moreover, a direct adaptation of Egyptian stylizing techniques. It is reasonable to conclude, therefore, that the Philistine motifs were taken from Egyptian prototypes and were adapted to suit the peculiar artistic taste and requirements of the Philistine potter.

The specifically Philistine elements in these adaptations of the Egyptian motif are the lotus's role as the sole decorative motif on the necks of the Type 12 jars, its upright position (unlike the downward position in Egyptian representation), the addition of typically Philistine birds and spirals, and the decorative geometrization of the motif into elongated triangles patterned on the examples of the Egyptian lotus goblets.

A further indication of the close link between the Type 12 jug and the Egyptian ceramic tradition is the tall, sometimes slightly bulging neck, occasionally decorated with lotus petals. Lotus petals and the elongated triangles imitating the lotus flower are characteristic of Egyptian pottery.

The Type 12 jug never became common in the general Philistine ceramic repertoire. Geographically, its distribution was limited, and chronologically it was relatively short-lived—from the first half of the twelfth to the middle of the eleventh century B.C. Its importance lies primarily in the fact that it is the only Philistine vessel that exhibits both in shape and decoration clear Egyptian influences. In this connection, it is illuminating to recall that the Type 12 jug is associated with the anthropoid coffin tombs of Tell el-Farʿah, where it was found in a pottery assemblage containing numerous imitations of purely Egyptian pottery types (see chap. 5, fig. 7).

The Type 12 jug is an outstanding example of the eclectic nature of Philistine pottery: it is Egyptian in shape and decoration of the neck, Aegean in the decorative motifs on the main band, and Canaanite in the shape of the body. All three elements are synthesized into a single pottery type.

GROUP IV. TYPES 13–16, VESSELS DERIVED FROM CANAANITE TYPES

This group includes four types of vessels whose shapes are a continuation of, or very similar to, several local pottery types. Although the total number of vessels in each category is small, the unmistakable Philistine decoration on pottery that is clearly Canaanite in shape can be explained only as the result of the Philistine potter's application of his own motifs to well-established local pottery types.

Type 13. Small Bowl with Bar Handle (figs. 54–55, pls. 90–92)

These small bowls (diameter approximately 7–14 cm.) are shallow vessels; most of them have a flattened base, though some have a ring base. A single bar handle is attached to the rim. The bowls are decorated in red and black on a white slip with alternating red and black lines on the rim, and a lotus rosette, dif-

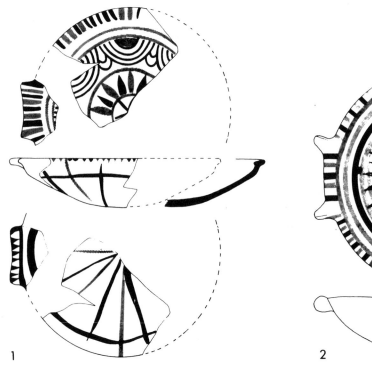

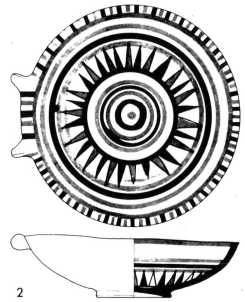

Fig. 54. Type 13 bowls.
1. White slip, Azor [*Azor*, pl. 35:5].   **2.** White slip, Azor.

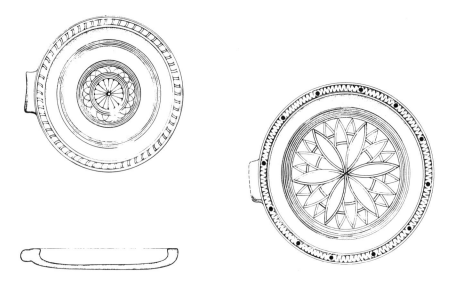

Fig. 55. Ivory bowls from the treasury, Megiddo, stratum VIIA [*Meg. Ivories*, pls. 27:147, 29:151].

Pl. 90. Type 13 small bowl with bar handle in figs. 54:1 and 50:4 (two views) [From the Collection of the Israel Department of Antiquities and Museums, 60-555].

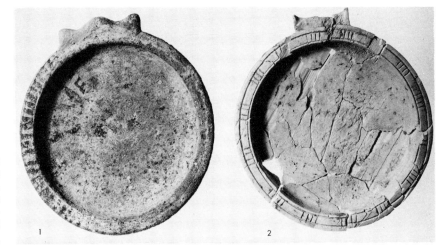

Pl. 91. Small bowls with bar handles. **1.** Azor(?) [Private Collection]. **2.** Ivory Bowl, Tell el-Farʿah, tomb 984 [From the Collection of the Israel Department of Antiquities and Museums. *BP II*, pl. LVI].

Pl. 92. Type 13 small bowl with bar handle in figs. 54:2 and 50:5 [Israel Museum, 68.32.5].

ferently stylized, on the interior. Only a few examples have been found: one from strata XII–X at Tell Qasile,[167] three complete bowls from the Philistine cemetery at Azor, and several from Ashdod (strata XII–XI).

Azor The first of the three bowls from Azor (fig. 54:1, pl. 90)[168] is shallow, with a flat, slanted rim flaring inward and out, and a rounded base slightly flattened at the center. The exterior of the bowl is decorated with a horizontal stripe below the rim and alternating red and black lines radiating from the base. The shape and decoration of the base are identical with that of the gourd-shaped vessel from Azor (see fig. 44 above). Groups of red and black stripes decorate the rim of the bowl and extend over the bar handle as well. A lotus rosette surrounded by a band of inverted concentric semicircles adorns the inside of the bowl.

The second bowl (pl. 91:1) is a miniature version of the first (it is about 9.5 cm. in diameter). A poorly preserved lotus-rosette decoration covers the interior.

The third bowl (fig. 54:2, pl. 92) is deeper, with a flat rim, concave disk base, and "horned" bar handle. On the interior the lotus-rosette motif of the other two bowls is geometrized in the form of concentric circles.

The three Azor bowls are examples of the stylistic phenomenon discussed above: the same motif (here the lotus rosette) variously stylized appears on vessels of the same type or group. The motif on the first bowl, although schematized, retains some of the natural rounded shape of the lotus leaves, while the second bowl bears an Egyptian motif that found its way into Phoenician and Greek art.[169]

The origin of the Type 13 bowl is somewhat difficult to determine. Similarly shaped pottery bowls—both with rounded bases and ring bases and one bar handle—are known in Canaan during the Late Bronze Age and Iron I, but their affinity does not extend beyond the shape of the bowls and their handles. None of the Canaanite examples display analogous decorative motifs, although some Iron Age examples have a white slip and bichrome decoration.[170] Bowls similar

in shape and type of handle are also found in other materials; for example, identical wooden bowls from Gurob (Egypt),[171] a bronze bowl from Aniba (Nubia),[172] and Egyptian faience bowls (fig. 51:4,5),[173] which resemble the Type 1 bowl both in shape and decorative motifs. The closest parallel to the Azor bowls appears in the Megiddo treasury (stratum VIIA, fig. 55). Small bowls found among the Megiddo Ivories show close affinities with the Philistine bowl in diameter, shape, bar handle, and the lotus-rosette motif (cf. an example from Tell el-Far'ah, tomb 984, in pl. 91:2). Chronologically, the close connection between them is quite acceptable.

In both shape and decoration, the Type 13 bowls reflect a combination of elements from diverse sources. The shape of the Type 13 bowl with base is found in the Late Bronze Age and Early Iron Age pottery of Canaan. The lotus rosette is an Egyptian motif adorning bowls of faience, alabaster, and other materials, and it also appears on imported Egyptian ware in Canaan. The Megiddo ivory bowls, however, whose decorative motifs are the "Phoenician expression" of Egyptian motifs, are most closely akin in every aspect of shape and decoration to the Type 13 Philistine bowls, especially the shallow flattened ones; they may possibly have inspired the Philistine type. Since some of these bowls exactly fit into the mouth of some of the Type 12 jugs, they may also have been used as lids, in which case the two types were even more closely linked.

Type 14. Jugs (fig. 56, pl. 93)

Two jugs have been classed in this category. The first, from stratum III at Beth-Shemesh (fig. 56:1), has a round mouth, flanged rim, broad, flat neck, flat loop handle extending from the lip to the shoulder, and a rounded body on a ring base. It is covered with a white slip and decorated with a band of concentric, brown and brick-red semicircles around the shoulders. This

167. Stratum XII, unpublished Q 4864.
168. *Azor*, p. 173, pl. 35:5.
169. Barnett, *A Catalogue of the Nimrud Ivories*, p. 64.
170. *See*, e.g., from the Late Bronze Age II, *Lachish II*, from temples II–III, pl. XLIII B:158, 160, 164; *Meg. II*, pls. 72:4, 78:8, 9, strata VII–VIA); Iron Age examples are *Gezer* II, p. 208; *Gezer* III, pl. CLXXIII:4 (white-slipped bichrome and stylized

palm tree); and *Beth-Shemesh*, PAM 10549 (not published) (white slip and red and black decoration). A similar bowl with a center motif of the Maltese cross comes from Enkomi, area I, ashlar building 623, pit A under floor III (*Enkomi Excavations*, vol. IIIa, pl. 97:3).
171. *Gurob*, pl. XVIII:49, groups of Ramesses II.
172. *Aniba II*, p. 148:591, pl. 98:2, 4.
173. *Meg. II*, pl. 191:7, stratum VII; Krönig, *MDIAA 5* (1934), p. 144 (faience).

decoration is repeated on the neck. With the exception of the Type 12 jugs, this is the only example of a Philistine vessel with a decorated neck. The shape of the jug was evidently borrowed from a local ceramic type common in the Iron Age I,[174] but it is also closely related to the Philistine Type 6 vessel. This jug never became a popular vessel in the Philistine ceramic repertoire. The example from Beth-Shemesh dates from the eleventh century.

The second jug (fig. 56:2, pl. 93) was found at ʿAfula in tomb 2, which is contemporary with stratum III on the mound.[175] Its body is biconical, continuing a local tradition of the Late Bronze Age[176] that is rarely found in Iron Age contexts.[177] The only other example in Philistine pottery is the Type 12 jug (fig. 49). The jug's triple handle with a twisted middle coil seems to be an imitation of handles known on bronze vessels.[178] The ʿAfula handle has close parallels on other pottery vessels: a handle from a Philistine context at Tell Jemmeh,[179] a pilgrim flask handle dated to Iron I from ʿAi,[180] and a tripod stand from a Philistine context at Tell el-Farʿah,[181] each of whose three legs is an exact copy of the handle of the ʿAfula jug and of the strainer-spout jug from the anthropoid burial at Beth-Shean.[182]

The jug's decoration consists of an upper register of concentric semicircles separated by vertical wavy lines, and a lower band of horizontal stripes above and below a single horizontal wavy line broken at intervals by short vertical wavy lines. The concentric-semicircle motif is quite common on Philistine jugs and stirrup jars (see figs. 16, 21:1, 22:1, 2 above). The horizontal wavy line, however, is very rare in Philistine ceramic decoration (see, for example, fig. 58:2), but is typical of Myc. IIIC:1 pottery.[183] The brushstroke shading of red employed in the jug's ornamentation also closely recalls a Mycenaean brush technique.

174. E.g., *Meg. II*, pl. 73:1.
175. *ʿAfula*, pp. 48, 51.
176. E.g. (Late Bronze Age), *Meg. II*, pls. 48:11, 57:8; *Lachish IV*, pl. 76:721.
177. E.g., *Meg. II*, pls. 67:11, 75:5, 12.
178. Catling, *Bronzework*, pl. 30:a, c. This unique type of handle may be an imitation of bronze vessels, especially the Cypriot tripod type.
179. *Gerar*, pl. LXIV:89.
180. J. Marquet-Krause, *Les Fouilles d'Ay (et-Tell)* (Paris, 1949), p. 219, pl. LXXVI:1786.
181. *BP II*, p. 29, pl. LXXXIII:27 T 1.
182. *B-SH Cemetery*, p. 107, fig. 47B:24, tomb 221 A–C.
183. *MP*, p. 371, fig. 65, motif 53:15.

This jug, therefore, represents a singular combination: a Canaanite pottery shape suggesting metal prototypes, coming from a Philistine context, and bearing decorative elements characteristic of both Philistine and Myc. IIIC:1 pottery. This unique amalgamation of three ceramic traditions was not subsequently continued.

Type 15. Juglets (fig. 57)

The juglets included within Type 15 have a round mouth, narrow, sometimes bulging neck, small loop handle attached to the lip and shoulder, rounded body, and flat or disk base. They are covered with a white slip and decorated either in bichrome red and black or in red alone. The decoration of concentric semicircles links them with Philistine pottery. A juglet from Beth-Shemesh (fig. 57:2) has been included here, even though its rim and handle are missing and its neck is wider than that of the other examples of this group.

Tell el-Farʿah A Type 15 juglet decorated with a debased concentric-semicircle motif (fig. 57:1) was found in Tell el-Farʿah in tomb 552. A number of similar juglets, also covered with a white slip but decorated in red with horizontal stripes, were uncovered in tombs 552 and 532.[184]

Lachish An identical juglet comes from tomb 570 at Lachish (see chap. 5, fig. 16:11), the tomb in which the anthropoid clay coffins were discovered. This juglet is coated with a thick white slip and decorated with red and black horizontal stripes. In ware, slip, and decoration, it resembles Philistine pottery.

The Type 15 juglets comprise the following two groups: (1) juglets displaying the characteristic white slip and decorative motifs of Philistine pottery; and (2) juglets identical in shape and white slip with those of the first group but lacking the typical Philistine decorative motifs. These latter juglets are classified as Philistine on the basis of their shape, white slip, bichrome decoration, and the fact that they were found for the most part in Philistine contexts.

Juglets of this shape are known in Canaan as early as the Late Bronze Age and apparently continue into the twelfth century B.C.[185] Close variants, especially of the

184. *CPP*, 59 N1, 2; 65 D2, 4.
185. *Lachish IV*, p. 304, pl. 76:722, 723, 726.

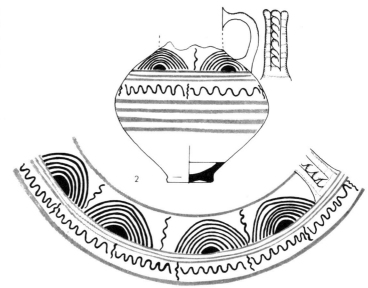

Fig. 56. Type 14 jugs.
1. White slip, Beth-Shemesh, stratum III [*AS I*, pl. XV:1106; *AS II*, pl. XLII:4].
2. ʿAfula, tomb 2 [ʿ*Afula*, fig. 20:2, pl. V:2].

Pl. 93. Type 14 jug in fig. 56:2 [From the Collection of the Israel Department of Antiquities and Museums].

Tell el-Far'ah juglet (fig. 57:1), include a number of vessels ranging in date from the late thirteenth to the twelfth century;[186] these are outstanding in their very well levigated clay, heavy white slip and meticulous stripe decoration. Although Canaanite in shape, it is possible that this group is an Egyptian adaptation of a Canaanite vessel (chap. 5, fig. 18:11).

Myc. IIIC:1 juglets, on the other hand, continue into the sub-Mycenaean tradition of the Aegean as well as into the Proto-White Painted pottery of Cyprus.[187] The Aegean examples show close affinities with the Tell el-Far'ah juglet, but it is difficult to establish a connection between the Mycenaean and Philistine juglets since neither exhibits enough typical features to provide a basis for such a connection. It appears, therefore, that the Philistine potter who produced the Type 15 juglet used, with only minor alterations, a local ceramic type that was in existence in Canaan from Late Bronze II until Iron I. The Egyptian variant may also be regarded as a possible prototype of the Philistine adaptation, especially in view of the bulging neck—a typical feature of Egyptian vessels. The Type 15 juglet can thus be defined as an adaptation of a vessel with a local tradition, Egyptian affinities, and possible Aegean influences (decoration), and which appears only sporadically as a clear-cut Philistine type.

Type 16. Trefoil-mouth Juglets (fig. 58, pl. 94)

The juglets designated as Type 16 are characterized by a trefoil mouth, narrow neck, globular body, ring base, loop handle extending from lip to shoulder, and bichrome decoration on a white slip. The juglet from Ashkelon (fig. 58:1) is decorated with plain horizontal black and red stripes. A second juglet (fig. 58:2, pl. 94) comes from the Philistine cemetery at Azor. It has an unusually high neck and a widened trefoil mouth. The decoration is in two horizontal bands: the upper contains a row of concentric semicircles with red filling, and the lower a single wavy line. As mentioned above (Type 14, fig. 56:2), the horizontal wavy-line motif is rare in Philistine pottery, but common in Myc. IIIC:1 vessels.

Juglets of this type are known in the local Canaanite repertoire of the Late Bronze Age.[188] Parallels to this Type 16 juglet, especially to the Azor juglet, can also be found in the Mycenaean oinochoe, which appeared in the Aegean and on the Greek mainland in Myc. IIIC:1 and continued to the sub-Mycenaean.[189] In Cyprus a similar type occurs in the Proto-White Painted and White Painted I groups.[190] It is among the juglets of the Proto-Geometric period from the Fortetsa cemetery in Crete[191] that we find vessels most closely resembling the Azor juglet in both shape and decorative technique. A similar manifestation of Eastern stylistic influence, which was observed in Types 8 and 10, may also be present here.

As with the Type 15 vessels, here too a direct relation between the Philistine and Mycenaean juglets is difficult to prove, for the Philistine vessels show a clear continuation of a local pottery type. Yet, at the same time, they (especially fig. 58:2) can be very convincingly connected with the Mycenaean tradition; they even continue into the later phases of the sub-Mycenaean and Proto-Geometric pottery, thereby bridging a gap in mainland Mycenaean ceramic history.

GROUP V. TYPES 17–18, TYPES APPEARING IN THE LAST PHASE OF PHILISTINE POTTERY

Types 17 and 18 appear during the last, debased phase of Philistine pottery. They are the result of the gradual fusion of the earlier Philistine characteristics and local ceramic traits.

Type 17. Jug with Strainer Spout and Basket Handle (fig. 59, pl. 95)

Type 17 represents a fusion of the distinctive features of Type 6 (the strainer-spout jug) and Type 7 (the spouted basket-handle jug). Burnishing or red slip has, in most cases, replaced the typical Philistine white slip. A few of the jugs are decorated in the Philistine tradition.

---

186. A complete juglet of this type comes from tomb 116 at Deir el-Balah; see Deir el-Balah IEJ 22, p. 68 (Deir el-Balah Qedem 10, p. 38, ill. 86).

187. MP, fig. 6:123. A large group of Myc. IIIC:1 juglets was found at Perati (Perati B, pp. 244, 246 ff., figs. 100, 105). For the sub-Mycenaean juglets, see DMS, p. 13, pl. 15a, c. For Cypriot parallels, see Gjerstad, OA 3, fig. 5:8, 11.

188. Lachish IV, pl. 76:720. The juglet is white slipped and decorated in black and red. It was found in tomb 216, which is dated to 1400–1300 B.C.

189. Perati B, p. 446, fig. 99; DMS, p. 13, pl. 14:b.

190. Salamine de Chypre, p. 33, pl. 23:67, 68.

191. Fortetsa, p. 156:621

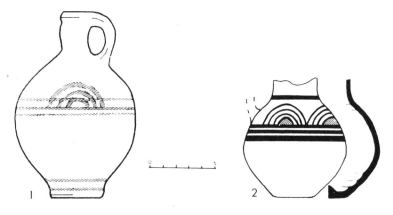

Fig. 57. Type 15 juglets.
1. White slip, Tell el-Farʿah, tomb 552 [*CPP*, 59 T]. **2.** Beth-Shemesh, stratum III [*AS III*, fig. 2:12, pl. XXII:2].

Fig. 58.1. Type 16 trefoil-mouth juglet. White slip, Ashkelon [*PMB* 4, pl. III:8].

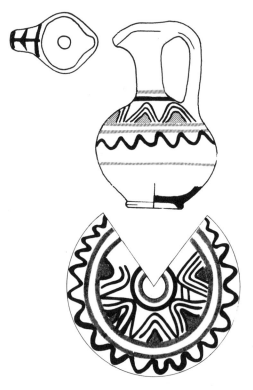

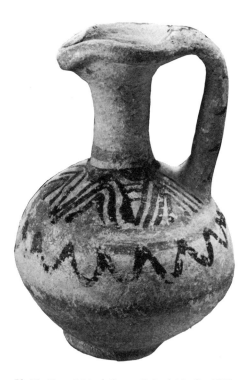

Fig. 58.2. Type 16 trefoil-mouth juglet, Azor.

Pl. 94. Type 16 trefoil-mouth juglet in fig. 58:2 [Private Collection].

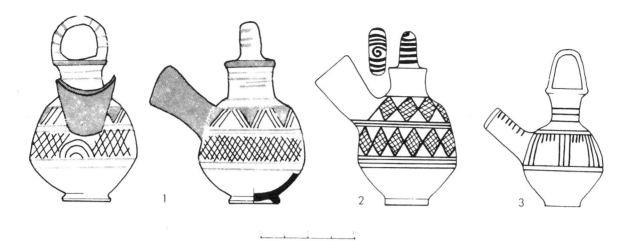

Fig. 59. Type 17 jugs with strainer spout and basket handle.
1. Burnished, Megiddo [No. 1404].   **2.** Megiddo, tomb 37 [*Meg. T.*, pls. 39:6, 136:13].   **3.** Tell el-Farʻah, tomb 523 [*CPP*, 67 E3].

Pl. 95. Type 17 jug with strainer spout and basket handle in fig. 59:1 (two views) [Oriental Institute, Chicago].

Tell Qasile   In the storeroom of the Philistine temple (locus 188, early stratum X) a unique example of this type of jug was found. Its elegant outline and elaborate bichrome decoration on a heavy white slip are still in the Philistine tradition; this hybrid shape may have had an earlier development of which no clear trace has survived.[192] Additional examples of Type 17 from the same locus are typical, in their debased shape and decoration, of the last phase of Philistine pottery.

Megiddo   The Megiddo group of debased Philistine pottery includes two Type 17 jugs (fig. 59:1, 2; pl. 95) decorated in the Philistine tradition with geometric motifs: a row of triangles, a net pattern, concentric semicircles, and rows of rhombuses. A number of other Type 17 jugs ascribed to stratum VI either lack decoration or burnish or else bear only plain red or alternating red and black bichrome stripes.[193]

The jug from tomb 37 (fig. 59:2), with its two horizontal rows of net-filled rhombuses, is clearly a continuation of the Philistine decorative tradition and belongs to the Early Iron Age phase of this very long-lived tomb group. The "Orpheus" jug may belong to Type 17 (see p. 150 and fig. 28:1 above).

Tell el-Farʿah   Several Type 17 jugs were found at Tell el-Farʿah. All can be dated to the end of the eleventh or early in the tenth century B.C. One jug, from tomb 523 (fig. 59:3),[194] is carinated; its decoration illustrates the complete deterioration of the Philistine metope arrangement. Two other jugs come from cemetery 100.[195] Both have rounded bodies and one, which was found in tomb 105 together with a debased Philistine bowl and a Cypriot bucchero jug, is covered with a red slip and is irregularly burnished. Both the

debased Philistine variation of this type and its adaptation into the red-slipped, burnished, and undecorated Iron Age group are found at Tell el-Farʿah.

Tell Jemmeh   A Type 17 jug with a high neck was uncovered at Tell Jemmeh. It dates to the end of the eleventh or the beginning of the tenth century B.C.[196]

Beth-Shemesh   A high-necked jug similar to the Tell Jemmeh vessel was found in stratum III at Beth-Shemesh.[197] It is covered with a red slip and decorated in brown. Another red-slipped jug from this stratum is carinated and decorated in brown and white.[198] The mouths of both vessels were sealed.

In shape, design, and decoration, the Type 17 jug displays the influences of both the local Canaanite and the Philistine ceramic traditions. The combination of the basket handle and strainer spout appears in Canaan in Middle Bronze II,[199] and is widespread during Late Bronze II.[200] In these periods, however, the vessels to which the handle and spout are attached are open, their shapes bearing no resemblance to the closed Philistine jug.

This combination of features was not noted in any Aegean vessel, but a late development of the type, an identically shaped White Painted jug dating to the Cypro-Geometric I period, was found in Cyprus.[201] Here again there may have been reciprocal influences during the evolution of the vessel.

The example from the Philistine temple at Tell Qasile indicates that a hybrid Type 17 also appeared infrequently during the zenith of Philistine pottery. Type 17 was common mainly in the last phase, when the Philistine pottery types became assimilated into the local ceramic styles and acquired such typical Iron Age characteristics as red slip, burnishing, and dark-brown decoration. Type 17 vanished completely toward the end of the tenth century B.C.

192. Locus 188 yielded a rich collection of pottery. As already stressed in chap. 2, the assemblage in this storeroom included Philistine pottery vessels that were earlier than those found in the temple proper (*see* p. 67).

193. *Meg. II*, pl. 82:1–4.

194. Only one other vessel was found in tomb 523: *CPP, 67 P*. This is a Type 6 strainer-spout jug similar in outline to the Type 17 jug and decorated in the same debased fashion.

195. *CPP, 67 E2*. The provenance of this jug with double basket handle is in the area of cemetery 100. The second jug, from tomb 105 (*CPP, 67 E1*), was found together with a bowl (*CPP, 18 D7*) and a bucchero jug (*CPP, 59 F3*). For further discussion of this group, *see* J. Du Plat Taylor, "Late Cypriot III in the Light of Recent Excavations," *PEQ* 88 (1956): 33–34.

196. *CPP, 67 D8*. This jug was the only find in room GA, level 183.

197. *AS IV*, pl. LX:18.

198. Ibid., pl. LX:16. Another jug from Beth-Shemesh is ascribed to stratum IVB, but it may possibly belong to stratum III, since the locus in which it was found was disturbed (*AS IV*, pl. LVI:5).

199. E.g., *Meg. II*, pl. 51:10.

200. Ibid., pl. 63:7, 8.

201. *SCE IV, Part 2*, fig. IV:16.

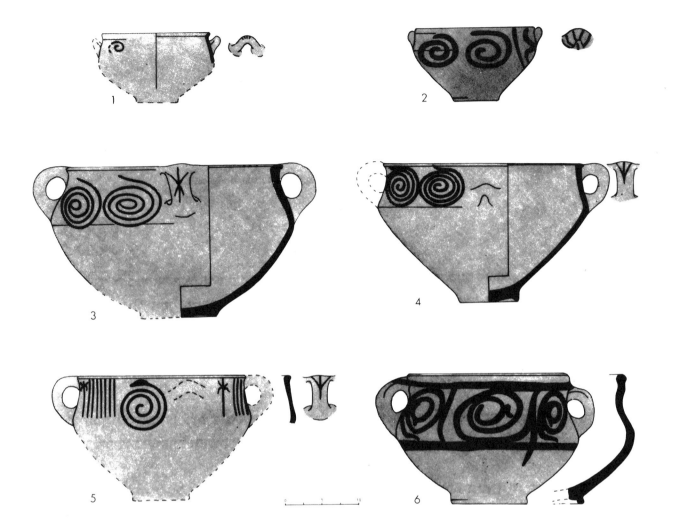

Fig. 60. Type 18 bowls and kraters.
1. Red slip, burnished, Tell Qasile, stratum X [Q. II 1681]. **2.** Red slip, Tell Jerishe [HU, t152]. **3.** Red slip, burnished, Tell Qasile, stratum X [Q. III 8401]. **4.** Red slip, burnished, Tell Qasile, stratum X [Q. III 2555]. **5.** Reddish-gray slip, Tell Qasile, stratum X [Q. II 5189, Q. II 5325]. **6.** Light-red slip, Megiddo, stratum VIA [*Meg. II*, pls. 78:19, 143:5].

Pl. 97. Type 18 krater in fig. 60:6 [Oriental Institute, Chicago].

2

Pl. 96. Type 18 kraters. **1.** See fig. 60:3 [Q II 2861]. **2.** See fig. 60:4 [From the Collection of the Israel Department of Antiquities and Museums, 51–78].

Pl. 98. Type 18 krater, Megiddo, stratum VIA [Oriental Institute, Chicago. *Meg. II*, pl. 144:15].

Pl. 99. Type 18 krater in fig. 60:2 [Institute of Archaeology, The Hebrew University of Jerusalem, 152].

Type 18. Kraters (fig. 60, pls. 96–99)

The final phase of Philistine pottery is typified by a group of deep kraters found only at Tell Qasile, Tell Jerishe,[202] and Megiddo. Their stratigraphy and archaeological contexts place them between the second half of the eleventh and beginning of the tenth century B.C. (that is, within the chronological limits of the last phase of Philistine pottery).

Tell Qasile The largest and most representative group comes from stratum X at Tell Qasile (fig. 60:1, 3–5, pl. 96). The other ceramic evidence from this stratum demonstrates that this period witnessed the merging of the Philistine ceramic tradition—in workmanship, individual decorative motifs, and exclusive pottery types—with the local pottery repertoire. The hybrid kraters preserve remnants of Philistine features and decoration.[203]

The kraters are made of a predominantly brown ware, medium to well fired, with black or white grits. They are covered with a red slip, are sometimes irregularly burnished and decorated in dark brown. They have a carinated shoulder and flanged rim. The ring base is most common, but occasional disk bases are found. The kraters are provided with four handles. Some have four vertical loop handles extending from the rim to the shoulder (fig. 60:3), and others have two vertical loop handles (fig. 60:1, 2) or two vestigial horizontal handles (fig. 60:1, 2) that have lost their original function and are merely the last traces of a once characteristic Philistine element.

Groups of short stripes decorate the rims of the kraters, while the branch motif (three converging lines—a common motif on Canaanite pottery from the Late Bronze Age onward) appears on the vertical handles. The horizontal handles are decorated with rows of short vertical lines. The main band of decoration, which is no longer delineated by horizontal stripes as in the early (Type 2) kraters, is divided facially into four zones at the handles. Two spirals—debased versions of the original Philistine spiral motif—are depicted on each face.

The krater in figure 60:5 is exceptional in its irregular reddish-gray slip and the seemingly haphazard conglomeration of motifs on its central band; it appears to be a lingering remnant of the Philistine metope arrangement. The spirals are somewhat reminiscent of the original Philistine looped spirals. The other motif on the band, however, the stylized tree, is a direct descendant of the Canaanite decorative tradition.

Megiddo The krater (figure 60:6, pl. 97) from stratum VIA at Megiddo differs slightly from the Qasile group, both in shape and decoration. It has a thickened rim with a low ridge beneath it; the shoulder is rounded and has only two vertical handles. Its decorative band, delineated above and below by horizontal stripes, is divided by vertical lines into metopes. Each metope contains an inverted spiral.

This vessel is quite similar both in shape and decoration to the group of kraters characteristic of Megiddo strata VIIB–VI[204] and of contemporary Late Bronze and Iron I tombs,[205] but it exhibits one major difference—the distinctive spiral motif that links this vessel with the Qasile Type 18 kraters.

Another Megiddo krater (pl. 98) is ascribed to stratum VI. In style, workmanship, decorative motifs, and bichrome decoration, it belongs to the Megiddo VI group of debased Philistine ware. It shows clear affinities with the Deir 'Alla version of Philistine pottery.

The small bowls from Tell Qasile (fig. 60:1) and Tell Jerishe (fig. 60:2, pl. 99) are identical in ware, slip, and decoration to the Type 18 kraters, although in shape they are essentially a continuation of the Type 1 bowl.

The Type 18 krater's appearance is limited to the second half of the eleventh and the beginning of the tenth century. It is found solely at Tell Qasile stratum X and Megiddo stratum VIA, where Philistine pottery has for the most part already disappeared.

These kraters are the product of three separate ceramic trends:

1. Philistine, seen in the horizontal handles and spiral motif;
2. Local, seen in the shape of the krater and the decorative palm and branch motifs;
3. A new element, which ushers in the ceramic style of the last stages of Iron I and Iron II and is characterized by red slip and burnishing.

---

202. The kraters were not published, but I had the opportunity to examine sketches of them in the field catalogue.
203. *Qasile IEJ 1*, p. 134, fig. 6:8, pl. 26:5.

204. *Meg. II*, pls. 66:3, 69:14, 78:18.
205. *Meg. T.*, pls. 32:22, 23; 73:3.

Type 18 kraters are the most striking example of a Philistine pottery type created through the fusion of old and new, local and foreign ceramic styles.

THE DECORATION OF PHILISTINE POTTERY

The sources of the motifs appearing in the decoration of Philistine pottery provide an additional point of departure for the examination of its cultural background. In our discussion thus far, we have dwelt at length with three main subjects: (1) the zones of decoration in relation to the shape of the vessel; (2) the division of the zones; and (3) the repertoire of motifs and their stylization. Although a vessel and its decoration should be considered as an integral unit, we shall describe the motifs separately, according to their origin, in order to establish and trace the origin and development of each motif.

Three main groups of Philistine motifs can be differentiated:

1. Mycenaean in origin (including those common to Mycenaean and Canaanite decoration).
2. Egyptian in origin (discussed in full above in the description of the Type 12 jug and the Type 13 bowl).
3. Local Canaanite.

Motifs of Mycenaean Origin

Philistine decorative motifs were derived primarily from the Mycenaean repertoire. Comparative charts[206] showing each motif with its Mycenaean prototypes are presented in the first column of figs. 64–71. The decorative motifs selected here include the bird, fish, spirals, antithetic tongue, concentric semicircles, scale pattern, wavy horizontal line, lozenges, chevrons, zigzags and triangles, checkered patterns, net patterns, and triglyphs.

The Bird (figs. 61, 62) The bird motif with outspread wing and turned-back head is one of the hallmarks of Philistine ceramic decoration. It is characteristic of the first and second phases and almost totally absent in

206. In the discussion of Philistine motifs taken from the Mycenaean decorative repertoire, we have utilized Furumark's studies (*MP, CMP*). The designation of chronological periods appearing in our illustration captions is based on Furumark's division of Myc. IIIC:1 into two subphases, early and late (*CMP*, p. 125). We have used his division into three subphases only with regard to Rhodes and Cyprus (cf. Furumark, *OA 3*, pp. 196, 262–63).

the third. This motif is first encountered in the monochrome bird on the Ashdod stratum XIII variant of Myc. IIIC:1b (chap. 2, fig. 3:11), which already includes most of the features of the bichrome Philistine bird, although some details of the monochrome version do not continue in later examples. The bird appears most commonly on kraters (Type 2), stirrup jars (Type 3), strainer-spout jugs (Type 6), and the Type 12 jug. Isolated examples are known on bowls (Type 1, fig. 61:19) and bottles (Type 9, fig. 62:26), and one is also found on a lid (fig. 62:29).

The outline and individual details of the bird's body are most often drawn in black, with red used only for filling. The bird usually appears as the single central motif within a metope in the main register and either reappears in each metope (fig. 14), alternates with other motifs (fig. 48) or is limited to a single metope in the band (fig. 16:1). An unusual placement of the bird in a free-field composition in the upper register is found on the strainer-spout jugs from Deir ʿAlla (fig. 30), and ʿAitun (fig. 29). The bird is usually accommodated to the shape of the metope and fills the major part of the frame. The auxiliary motifs filling the background are either concentric semicircles or rhombuses. On the ʿAitun jug and on sherds from Ashdod we find dotted lines following the outline of the bird. This is a well-known feature of the Myc. IIIC:1 style,[207] especially from the Dodecanese and Crete, and is another important link between the Philistine bird motif and its Mycenaean and Minoan counterparts.

The bird is usually the sole figurative motif. More elaborate representations include one or more additional birds (fig. 62:28, 29) or a fish (fig. 64:2), which in the ʿAitun jug is part of a Nilotic scene. The heraldic arrangement of two birds on either side of a lotus (fig. 48) is a unique example of a self-contained decorative unit freely adapted to the neck of a jug.

Figures 61 and 62 present a selection of bird motifs from Philistine pottery arranged according to variations in the shape of the body and stylization of details. The bird is depicted in two positions:

1. Head turned back while the beak seems to preen the wing feathers (fig. 61:2, 3, 5, 6, 8–15, 18, 19, 21). The neck joins the body at a point low on the breast, a position most suitable for fitting within the confines of a metope.

207. *DMS*, pp. 6–7, frontispiece; M. Seiradaki, "Pottery from Karphi," *BSA* 55 (1960): 31, 37, fig. 25g.

2. Head facing forward (fig. 61:1, 4, 7, 16, 17, 20, 22–24). Here the neck is arched back and joined to the body high up on the breast or back so that the bird remains inside the metope. Occasionally, birds are depicted in both positions on the same vessel (fig. 61:3, 4, 17).

The bird's head is oval in shape. The eye is a dot and the elongated beak is almost always a single line. Rarely, crossed lines are added inside the bird's head (figs. 61:20, 62:31). Another uncommon feature is a wavy line suspended from the bottom of the head (fig. 61:23, 24).

The body is leaf-shaped, the rounded breast almost semicircular, and the tail tapers off into a downward-curving triangle. In several examples the tail curves upward (fig. 61:19), is level with the body (fig. 62:30), or terminates in a fishtail (fig. 62:34). The body (except in figure 61:13) is divided vertically by a triglyph consisting of:

1. straight and wavy lines (figs. 61:1–4, 23, 62:25)
2. straight lines and collateral semicircles (fig. 61:5–7)
3. straight lines enclosing a net pattern (fig. 61:8)
4. straight lines alone (figs. 61:9–12, 14–22, 62:26–29, 31, 32)

In some cases these lines fill the entire back portion of the bird (fig. 62:33–34) and even the entire body (fig. 62:30).

This use of the triglyph to create an internal division of the body results in a more or less semicircular breast that is almost always emphasized by the addition of one or more concentric semicircles and a triangular tail, also accentuated by additional lines.

On some of the monochrome Ashdod birds, the filling motifs are dots, a technique also found on Myc. IIIC:1b bird representations from Enkomi (fig. 72:5, 6).[208]

The bird's legs are usually three toed. On a few somewhat debased examples, the legs are rendered schematically by a zigzag line (fig. 62:26); sometimes they are omitted and only the feet or toes are drawn (fig. 61:20). There are also a number of examples of birds depicted altogether without legs (figs. 61:6, 62:34), which is probably an intentional stylization. One sherd from Ashdod shows a three-legged bird

and another elaborately depicts a four-legged bird (fig. 62:36). The latter may perhaps be understood as a conventional representation of two birds whose bodies and wings have merged, only their feet remaining separate.[209]

In most cases the bird is depicted with one wing raised, but in one example a bird is clearly portrayed with both wings (fig. 61:16). The wing is represented by a chevron pattern with curved sides and an acute apex (fig. 61:1–16, 21, 22), which is sometimes accentuated by a spur (fig. 61:2, 6, 8). In a few examples (fig. 61:17, 18) the apex is not acute, and the sides of the chevrons meet at an obtuse angle. This style is peculiar to the Azor potter. As a rule the lines forming the wings are left open and do not converge. The bird on the 'Aitun jug has an unusual wing that rises flamelike to a closed point (fig. 29). Figures 62:25–30, 33 illustrate a degeneration of the wing motif and a lack of familiarity with the manner in which it was originally depicted.

In only a few isolated examples are birds depicted with tail feathers (figs. 61:1, 62:29, 30).

One peculiarly Philistine trait is the addition of a spiral, either as an accompanying motif next to the wing (fig. 61:22) or as a transmutation of the end of the wing (fig. 61:21, 23).[210] The design on a krater from Beth-Shemesh (fig. 11:2) is an even greater abstraction: the potter shaped the end of the spiral to resemble the tail of a bird, adding the usual wing-feather motif above. A small number of wingless birds (fig. 62:28, 29, 31, 32, 34) appear along with the more common winged forms.

There are many poorly drawn, artistically weak Philistine birds that differ considerably from the original motif (cf. fig. 62:25, 26). In addition, there are birds whose departures from the original are the result of intentional schematization rather than debasement or incompetence (fig. 62:34, 35). An interesting, but unsuccessful, attempt can be seen in figure 62:33. The bird (a lame duck indeed) no longer stands as the central theme of the metope but has been relegated to an intermediate position between two spirals. Its head is disconnected from its body, and—thus decapitated—

208. *Enkomi Excavations*, vol. I, p. 286; vol. IIIa, pls. 81:26, 33, 37.

209. *Ashdod II–III*, fig. 7:13, area A; another fragment of a four-legged bird. Compare the stylization of the fish on the 'Aitun jug (fig. 29) with the stylization of the pair of horses in Mycenaean art (*MP*, p. 243, motif 2).

210. The fish terminating in a spiral loop is found in Myc. IIIC:1 decorations (*MP*, fig. 48, motif 20:13).

it becomes a separate decorative element (a phenomenon also known in the Myc. IIIC:1 pottery).[211] Its wing has been broken into a few disconnected lines that barely define something of the original shape. The body of the bird, at least in shape, is faithful to that of its predecessors; but the vertical lines of the triglyph, instead of dividing it in two, merely fill in the rear end. The artist's failure to stylize the Philistine bird into a new and unified motif is a result of both lack of skill and the fact that he has lost touch with the original concept.

A stirrup jar from Gezer (fig. 62:34) represents a further stage in the schematization of the bird into a decorative design of an entirely different character. The feet have disappeared completely, and the wings and body have been stylized into an almost plantlike motif. The stylized body, ending in a fish tail,[212] is then repeated in the design used to join the two spirals. The entire composition is unique, reflecting the skill and imagination of an artist, and the unusual character of the Philistine pottery from Gezer.

The final step in the total geometrization of the bird can be seen in figure 62:35. Were it not for the intermediate stages apparent in figure 62:33, 34, it would indeed be difficult to grasp the connection between these geometric motifs and the Philistine bird. The elongated figure in figure 62:35, however, must certainly be interpreted as a representation of a bird's body. The geometric motifs alongside it, moreover, are among those that frequently accompany the original bird motif.

The bird as stylized by the Philistines is totally unlike the bird motifs found on local Canaanite painted pottery of the Late Bronze Age, nor does it resemble the few isolated examples known from the Iron Age I. The only bird on a typical Philistine vessel that fits stylistically into the local tradition is one at the end of the procession on the "Orpheus" jug from Megiddo (fig. 28:1).

It is perfectly clear that the Philistine bird motif was taken from the Minoan and Mycenaean traditions (fig. 63). Parallels between the two exist in the shape of the bodies (fig. 63:2), in the division by triglyphs (fig. 63:12), in the curve of the long neck and the head—sometimes turned back (fig. 63:2, 3)—and in the wavy line suspended from the head (fig. 63:1). The chevronlike stylization of the wing is extremely rare in Mycenaean bird motifs,[213] however, although an isolated example from Perati (fig. 63:11) hints at the close connection between this site and Philistine cultural traits.

Often the freehand drawing, stylization, and composition of the Philistine bird show remarkable artistic merit. The Philistine potter was well versed in Minoan and Mycenaean styles, and he fused them into a unique decorative motif that at times was far superior in its abstraction to the original.

J. L. Benson[214] has made a very valuable contribution to the discussion of the bird motif by classifying the pertinent material and tracing its development. Nevertheless, owing to insufficient data and a lack of firsthand knowledge, he arrived at untenable conclusions. He apparently failed to realize the wide range of the bird motif in Philistine pottery, its high artistic level, and its close affinities with Mycenaean antecedents. The homogeneity of the bird motif led Benson to assume that the style was the creation of one man or of one workshop dominated by a single artisan whose work was carried on by his son. To them he attributed the production of Philistine pottery from its initial appearance down to the eleventh century B.C. This theory (anticipated by W. A. Heurtley) was taken up by Desborough,[215] who carried it one stage further in suggesting that a potter had made his way from Cyprus to Philistia (perhaps as a result of the second period of destruction of that island) and that it was he who had introduced a type of Mycenaean pottery that immediately became fashionable throughout Philistia.

This theory dissociates the appearance of Philistine pottery in Canaan from the arrival and settlement of the Philistines and is contradicted by a large accumulation of material, all of which points clearly to a close connection between the two.

The bird motif in Canaan first appears in the local monochrome Myc. IIIC:1b at Ashdod, which, as we

---

211. *MP*, p. 254, fig. 71, motif 73:6.

212. For the Minoan prototype of the fish tail ending of the bird's body, see *MP*, fig. 31, motif 7:35, and for the Myc. IIIB Late Eastern type, ibid., fig. 31, motif 7:38. For further bibliography, *see* J. L. Benson, "A Problem in Orientalizing Cretan Birds: Mycenaean or Philistine Prototypes?" *JNES* 20 (1961): 83.

213. Ibid., p. 82. He suggests the possibility that the chevronlike stylization of the wing is inspired by the chevron motif connecting semicircles, which is common in Philistine pottery.

214. Ibid., pp. 82 ff.

215. *DMS*, pp. 212 ff.

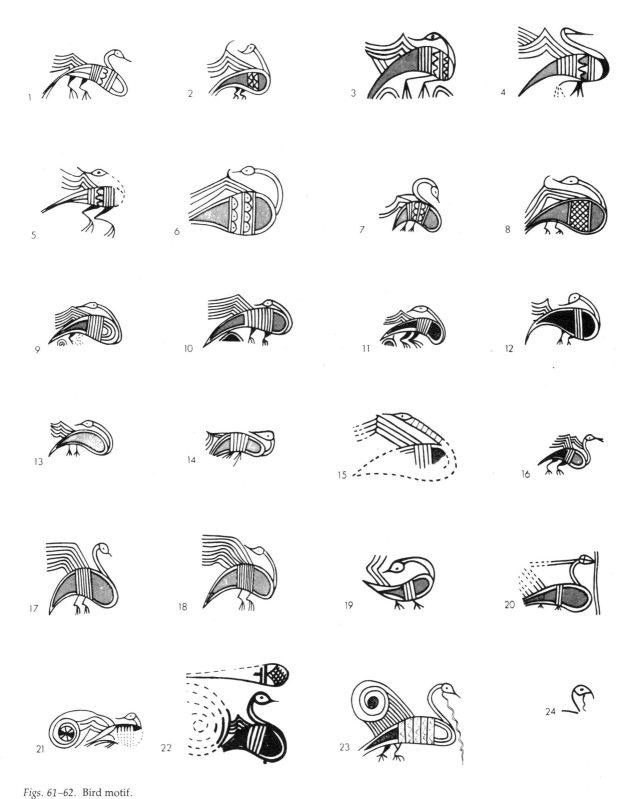

Figs. 61–62. Bird motif.

1. See fig. 21:1. **2.** See fig. 7:2. **3.** See fig. 7:3. **4.** See fig. 7:3. **5.** See pl. 22. **6.** [*Gezer* III, pl. CLXIII:7] **7.** See fig. 48.
8. See fig. 7:1. **9.** See fig. 23:2. **10.** See fig. 22:2. **11.** See fig. 46:1. **12.** See fig. 14:1. **13.** See fig. 48. **14.** See fig.
15:3. **15.** [*Gezer* III, pl. CLXVIII:9] **16.** See fig. 22:1. **17.** See fig. 6. **18.** See fig. 6. **19.** See fig. 4. **20.** [*Gezer* III, pl.
CLXVIII:8] **21.** See fig. 23:1. **22.** Krater [*Ashdod II–III*, fig. 2:9]. **23.** [*BS*, p. 213] **24.** [*Gezer* III, pl. CLXVII:15]

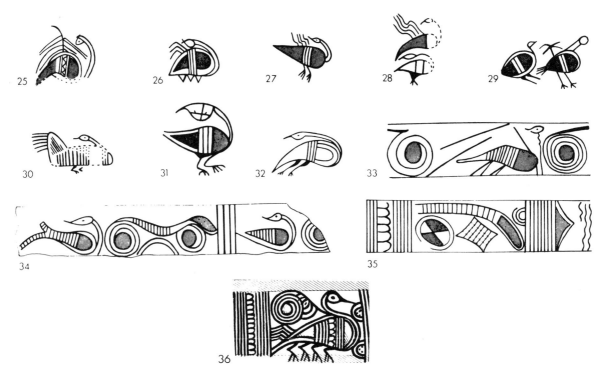

Figs. 61–62. Bird motif (*continued*).

25. [*Gezer* III, pl. CLX:4]. **26.** See fig. 34:1. **27.** See fig. 15:2. **28.** *Gezer* III, pl. CLXVI:6] **29.** See chap. 4, fig. 1:3.
30. Tell Qasile, stratum XII [*Qasile IEJ 1*, pl. 25:2]. **31.** Tell Qasile, stratum XII [*Qasile IEJ 1*, fig. 4:1]. **32.** See fig. 16:1.
33. See fig. 21:2. **34.** See fig. 16:2. **35.** [*BP I*, pl. XXIII:6] **36.** Ashdod, stratum XII.

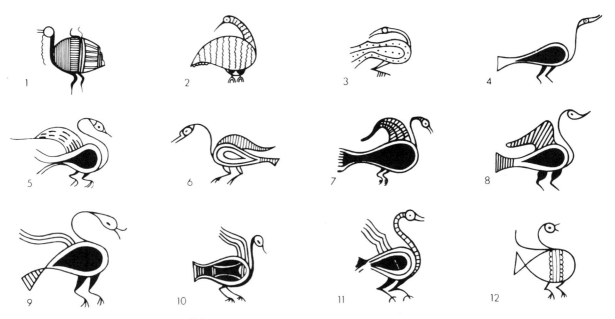

Fig. 63. Bird motif, Mycenaean parallels.

1. [*MP*, fig. 29, mot. 7,h; Myc. III] **2.** [*MP*, fig. 30, mot. 7,17; Myc. IIIB] **3.** [*MP*, fig. 31, mot. 7,39; Myc. IIIC:1] **4.** [*MP*, fig. 31, mot. 7,42; Myc. IIIC:1] **5.** [*Ialysos*, pl. XXI; Myc. IIIC:1] **6.** [*Ialysos*, pl. XXIV; Myc. IIIC:1] **7.** [*MP*, fig. 31, mot. 7,40; Myc. IIIC:1] **8.** [*MP*, fig. 31, mot. 7,41; Myc. IIIC:1] **9.** [*Ialysos*, pl. XXV; Myc. IIIC:1] **10.** [*MP*, fig. 31, mot. 7,43; Myc. IIIC:1] **11.** [*Perati A–Γ*, vol. B, p. 187, no. 569; Myc. IIIC:1] **12.** [*MP*, fig. 31, mot. 7,q; Myc. IIIB:2]

have seen, is close to contemporary Mycenaean prototypes. Furthermore, close parallels to the stylization of the Philistine bird can be traced to other areas of Mycenaean culture: the Greek mainland (especially the Myc. IIIC cemetery of Perati)[216] and the Dodecanese with its development of the Octopus Style—the counterpart of the Argive Close Style.[217] Crete shows some very similar features, both in stylization and in the composition of the bird motif,[218] while Cyprus is the closest link, both stylistically and geographically,[219] with Philistia.

The bird motif is thus a sensitive indicator of the background of the Philistines. It shows clear affinities with the mainland home of the Mycenaean style, together with elements absorbed during the Philistines' meandering through the Aegean isles. It is interesting that parallels have been found at Crete, as Cretan affinities to Philistine pottery are usually rather elusive. The final, Cypriot manifestation may indicate the last stop of this group of Sea Peoples on their way to Canaan.

The Fish (fig. 64) The fish was thought to be rare among Philistine decorative motifs, and until the discovery of the ʿAitun jug (fig. 29) and the Ashdod krater sherds (chap. 2, fig. 3:9, 10), only a few examples, all quite diverse in stylization and composition, were known (fig. 64:1–3).

The fish on the "Orpheus" jug (fig. 28:1) from Megiddo have no distinctive Philistine features. Their unsophisticated execution is much closer to the local, indigenous tradition of painted pottery than to that of the Philistines. Other fish designs, however, are all far more lifelike and are closely related to the fish and dolphin series in Minoan and Mycenaean compositions (fig. 64:4, 5).

The Philistine fish motifs known include:

1. The earliest in the series of fish representations and the closest to their Mycenaean derivatives are the krater sherds from Ashdod (chap. 2, fig. 3:9, 10). On one of these kraters we can reconstruct two leaping dolphinlike fish drawn in outline and filled with wavy lines. Close parallels to this composition and stylization appear on a Myc. IIIC:1b vessel from Enkomi (fig.

72:7),[220] on which a row of fish are similarly but less elegantly depicted. The Ashdod fish were inspired by Myc. IIIC:1 examples.[221] The same stylization is seen on the elaborate pictorial scene on the stirrup jar of Perati (fig. 64:5).

2. In figure 64:1 (see pl. 23) the head and gills are rendered by a series of concentric semicircles (as in fig. 64:2, 3), the fins are depicted by a row of sawtooth strokes along the back, and the body is painted red. The style, the bichrome coloring, and the combination of the fish with a spiral all show clearly that it has been incorporated into the Philistine compositional approach.

3. Again, in figure 64:3, the head is emphasized by concentric semicircles and the center of the body is solidly filled, very much as it is in the Mycenaean parallel in figure 64:4. However, there is an additional floral motif emerging from the fish's mouth, a very common feature in Egyptian fish representations (fig. 64:6).

4. Figure 64:2 is part of a pictorial scene composed of a fish, a bird, and a stylized papyrus plant. Since the fish's head is worn off, it is impossible to ascertain whether the papyrus is part of a Nilotic background or whether it issues from the fish's mouth. As in the previous two examples, the head is indicated by concentric semicircles. The gills here are a single dotted line, and horizontal wavy lines fill the body. An almost exact parallel to this composition and stylization is seen on a Myc. IIIC:1b sherd from Enkomi (fig. 72:6) showing a bird attacking a fish.[222] These wavy lines, as well as the combination of a bird and papyrus, point to a compositional link with the ʿAitun jug, the most complete and elaborate composition of a Nilotic scene.

5. The unique features of the fish on the ʿAitun jug are the high arched body and the problematic representation of the double head, which may be a stylization of two merging fish or a representation of a fish shown *en face*, as is perhaps also the case in one of the Perati examples.[223] The ʿAitun jug demonstrates that fish motifs occur either as part of a standard Nilotic scene of birds, fish, and sea anemone or in an abridged scene in which only the fish and stylized plant are shown. The closest analogies to the ʿAitun jug are rep-

216. *Perati B*, pp. 148 ff., fig. 23, p. 436.
217. *DMS*, pp. 7 ff.
218. *See* nn. 207, 212 above.
219. *Enkomi Excavations*, vol. I, pp. 286 ff.; vol. IIIa, pl. 81:26–28, 30–38, level III B.

220. Ibid., vol. I, p. 286; vol. IIIa, pl. 81:29, level III B.
221. *MP*, Fig. 48, motif 20:12.
222. *Enkomi Excavations*, vol. I, p. 286; vol. IIIa, pl. 81:26, level III B.
223. *Perati B*, pp. 140–42, fig. 21, p. 435.

resentations on the Myc. IIIC:1 elaborate cuttlefish stirrup jars, where we find very similar depictions of birds, fish (fig. 64:5), and sea anemone, as well as accompaniments such as dotted lines.

The Philistine fish motifs have close analogies in Myc. IIIC:1 pottery (fig. 64:5). The Mycenaean motifs were derived from Late Minoan III prototypes, in which they often appeared as part of a more elaborate Nilotic scene with sea-anemone and papyrus derivatives—a cycle well known in the Minoan repertoire.[224]

We can trace the fish motif in Philistine pottery from the early Ashdod krater sherds, which are still part of the Myc. IIIC:1b decorative tradition, through its subsequent variations in Philistine pottery, into which it was never fully incorporated.

The Spiral (figs. 65–67) The spiral is the most common of the Philistine motifs and appears either as a primary or secondary motif on the vast majority of Philistine pottery (Types 1–4, 6, 7, 12, 18). It is employed in the design in four ways:

1. As a single spiral repeated around the entire decorative band (fig. 65:2, 3, 5, 6)
2. As a decorative unit composed of two spirals in an undelineated field (fig. 66:2–7)
3. As a decorative unit within a metope (fig. 66:19)
4. In conjunction with other decorative motifs (cf. figs. 45, 61:21, 23)

The center of the spiral is often filled with red paint. One of the most characteristic traits of Philistine pottery decoration is a spiral with a Maltese-cross center. The cross usually has two red arms and two black arms, but in some examples only the outline of the cross is indicated (fig. 67:2, 4).

The spiral with the Maltese-cross center is rare in Mycenaean pottery decoration and only abbreviated variants are known (fig. 72:3). The material from Enkomi indicates that the motif was known to the Mycenaean potter in Cyprus; and, by means of the different examples discovered at Enkomi, we can trace the evolution of the Maltese cross and its use as a filling for spirals and concentric circles. It continued in use and became popular in the Cypro-Geometric period.[225] Different versions of the Maltese cross as a

central filling for spirals include a two-armed variant[226] and a four-petalled light rosette depicted against a dark background—which stands out as a Maltese cross brought into the foreground as the main motif.[227] The one example of a geometrized Maltese cross on the interior of a bowl[228] (which most closely resembles the Maltese cross on the Philistine pottery) shows links with the later development of this design in the Cypro-Geometric period.

Although the Maltese cross is known in the Canaanite bichrome pottery group as early as the sixteenth century B.C., we have found no connecting link between this group and the Philistine examples. The Maltese cross was probably adopted by the Philistine potter as part of the Mycenaean repertoire, to reappear in the twelfth century as an integral part of the Philistine repertoire. This process, however, is still by no means clear.

The Maltese cross also appears on local Canaanite pottery of the Iron Age from the eleventh century onward, on vessels that are not Philistine but were influenced by Philistine decoration. This phenomenon is especially striking in a group of vessels from Megiddo VIA and Qasile stratum X (chap. 4, pl. 4).

A hitherto-unknown filling motif of the spiral is the net pattern, which is found on monochrome krater fragments from stratum XIII at Ashdod (chap. 2, fig. 3:4, 6). It provides a clear link between the monochrome group and the Myc. IIIC:1b pottery (figs. 65:7, 72:4).[229] This motif was not taken over into bichrome Philistine pottery.

There are seven main variations of the spiral theme: running spiral, stemmed spiral, winged spiral, "antithetic" spirals, antithetic stemmed spirals, spiral compounds, and debased spirals.

THE RUNNING SPIRAL (FIG. 65:1–5) The running spiral is fairly rare in Philistine decoration. All the known examples are confined to the main band of decoration. Figure 65:2 shows a band spiral that has close parallels with Myc. IIIC:1 motifs (fig. 65:1). The line spiral (fig. 65:4) is very common in Mycenaean decoration, where (like its Philistine counterpart) it is used with stemmed

224. *MP*, pp. 193–95.
225. *SCE IV, Part 2*, pp. 50–51; *Salamine de Chypre*, p. 94, pls. 30:115, 31:116, 135.
226. *Enkomi Excavations*, vol. II, pp. 848–49; vol. IIIa, pl. 78:23, 32, level III B.
227. Ibid., vol. II, pp. 846, 849; vol. IIIa, pls. 71:26, level III A; 81:13–14, level III B.
228. Ibid., vol. I, p. 317; vol. IIIa, pl. 97:3, level II B.
229. Ibid., vol. IIIa, pl. 71:23, level III A; *MP*, fig. 63, motif 51:8–10, Myc. IIIB–IIIC.

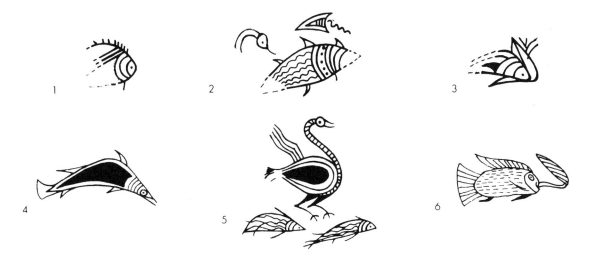

Fig. 64. Fish motif.
1. See fig. 12:1. **2.** See fig. 12:2. **3.** Ashkelon [*PMB* 4, pl. I:5]. **4.** [*MP*, fig. 48, mot. 20,9; Myc. IIIC:1] **5.** Stirrup jar, Myc. IIIC:1 [*Perati A–Γ*, vol. B, p. 187, no. 569]. **6.** [W. Krönig, "Ägyptische Fayence Schalen des Neuen Reiches," *MDIAA* 5 (1934): fig. 20]

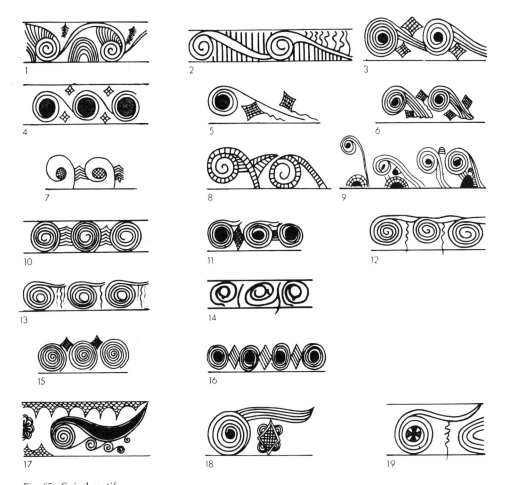

Fig. 65. Spiral motif.
1. [*MP*, fig. 60, mot. 46,37; Myc. IIIC:1] **2.** See fig. 11:6. **3.** See fig. 47:2. **4.** [*MP*, fig. 72, mot. 73,16; Myc. IIIB] **5.** See fig. 25:1. **6.** See fig. 11:5. **7.** [*MP*, fig. 63, mot. 51,9; Myc. IIIB–C:1] **8.** [*Gezer* III, pl. CLXVI:10] **9.** See fig. 25:2. **10.** [*MP*, fig. 65, mot. 52,2; Myc. IIIC:1 early] **11.** See fig. 11:2. **12.** See fig. 11:4. **13.** See fig. 11:3. **14.** See fig. 60:6. **15.** [*DMS*, pl. 8; Myc. IIIC] **16.** See fig. 11:1. **17.** [*MP*, fig. 68, mot. 62,36; Myc. IIIC:1] **18.** Ain Shems, stratum III [*AS IV*, pl. XXXVI:1]. **19.** See fig. 21:1.

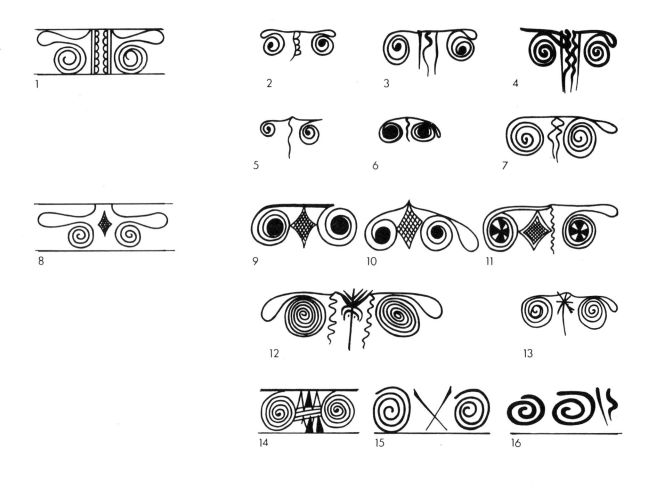

Fig. 66. Antithetic spiral motif.
1. [*MP*, fig. 62, mot. 50,4; Myc. IIIB]   **2.** See fig. 2:7.   **3.** See fig. 2:8.   **4.** See fig. 2:9.   **5.** See fig. 2:4.   **6.** See fig. 18:3.
7. See fig. 2:6.   **8.** [*MP*, fig. 63, mot. 50,27; Myc. IIIB–C:1]   **9.** See fig. 21:2.   **10.** [*BP II*, pl. LXIII:47]   **11.** See fig. 10:2.
12. See fig. 10:3.   **13.** Krater, Tell Qasile, stratum XI.   **14.** Krater, Tell Qasile, stratum XI.   **15.** See fig. 2:12.   **16.** See
fig. 60:2.   **17.** Myc. IIIC:1 late, "close style" [*MP*, fig. 62, mot. 50,18].   **18.** Krater, Ashdod.   **19.** See fig. 6.   **20.** See pl. 9.

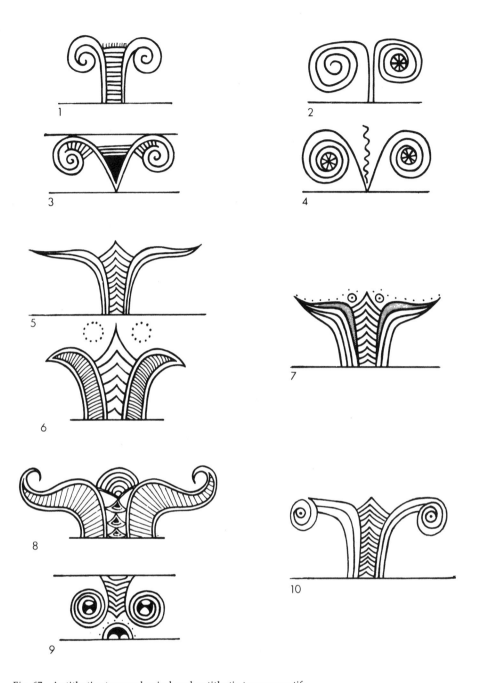

Fig. 67. Antithetic stemmed spiral and antithetic tongue motifs.
1. [*MP*, fig. 63, mot. 51,17; Myc. IIIC:1 early] **2.** Megiddo (*see above*, chap. 2, pl. 17:6). **3.** [*MP*, fig. 63, mot. 51,20; Myc. IIIC:1 late] **4.** Gezer, tomb 9 [*Gezer* III, pl. LXXI:21]. **5.** See pl. 4. **6.** [*MP*, fig. 47, mot. 19,44; Myc. IIIC:1 early] **7.** See fig. 3:1. **8.** [*MP*, fig. 47, mot. 19,45; Myc. IIIC:1 late] **9.** [*MP*, fig. 63, mot. 51,26; Myc. IIIC:1 early] **10.** See fig. 3:2.

lozenge motifs (fig. 65:5). A Philistine variation of the running spiral is seen in figure 65:3. The composite band connecting the spirals is made up of four parallel lines.

THE STEMMED SPIRAL (FIG. 65:6–9) The stemmed spiral appears as a repeated unit (fig. 65:6, 8, 9) or an antithetic motif (fig. 67:2, 4). The examples of stemmed spirals illustrated here display a number of stylistic variations. Figure 65:8 is a barred version of the running band spiral (fig. 65:2); a leaflike element is the sole connection between the spirals. Figure 65:6 is another version of the multiple-stemmed running spiral seen in figure 65:3. Lozenges are used as filling motifs between the spirals, but the addition of wavy stems suggests a lozengelike plant. The multiple-stemmed spiral has especially close parallels with the Myc. IIIC:1b Close Style pottery from Sinda[230] (fig. 13). A variant of the multiple-stemmed spiral from Sinda, with the looped addition, is paralleled on a monochrome krater from Ashdod (chap. 2, fig. 3:7).

Figure 65:9 shows a group of swaying, stemmed spirals accompanied by concentric semicircles. It is faintly reminiscent in composition of the Mycenaean band spiral in figure 65:1.

THE WINGED SPIRAL (FIG. 65:11–13, 17–19) The winged spiral appears either (1) in a repeated-unit arrangement (fig. 65:11–13) or (2) as the central motif in a metope (fig. 65:18, 19).

In the repeated-unit arrangement the winged spiral is accompanied by lozenges (fig. 65:11) or dividing wavy lines (fig. 65:12, 13). A Type 18 krater from Megiddo displays a debased upside-down version of the winged spiral (fig. 65:14). Mycenaean pottery provides no exact parallels for the Philistine winged-spiral series, but the spiral-and-chevron combination known in Myc. IIIC:1 (fig. 65:10) may have had some influence on the Philistine motif. The repeated, closed spiral-and-lozenge series (fig. 65:16), for example, closely resembles the Myc. IIIC:1 motif in figure 65:15.

The winged spiral as the primary motif in a metope (fig. 65:18, 19), appears with auxiliary motifs such as the lozenge wavy line, concentric semicircles, and bird. The winged spiral is not found in Mycenaean decoration as a motif in its own right but always in a compound motif of two antithetic spirals (fig. 65:17). Hence the Philistine winged spiral may be either an abridgment of the original Mycenaean motif or a re-

duction of the Philistine repeated-unit arrangement to one unit.

"ANTITHETIC" SPIRALS (FIG. 66) The "antithetic" spiral is one of the most common of the Philistine motifs and appears predominantly on bowls, kraters, and pyxides and on the lion-headed rhyton from Qasile (chap. 4, pl. 17). The Mycenaean prototype (fig. 66:1, 8) is invariably arranged in an heraldic pattern, while the Philistine spirals almost always face the same way (fig. 66:3–7, 9–11, 13). We shall use the term *antithetic* for convenience, even though only a few examples of the Philistine variation of this motif (fig. 66:2, 12) are faithful to the symmetrical arrangement of their Mycenaean prototypes.

The two antithetic spirals are separated by different geometric motifs. On bowls, these are generally simple groups of straight and wavy lines (fig. 66:2, 7), while the kraters have more complex motifs—a lozenge (fig. 66:9–11), a stylized palm (fig. 66:12, 13), or groups of triangles (fig. 66:14). The final degeneration of the antithetic spiral motif appears on bowls from the last phase of Philistine pottery (fig. 66:16).

Half of the motif—one spiral and one loop—sometimes serves as an independent decorative element (fig. 66:18, 19). The loop terminating the spiral is decorated with concentric semicircles, chevrons, or rows of vertical lines. Only one example of such loop decoration is known on a complete antithetic spiral unit (fig. 66:20)—on a krater from Tel Ṣippor. Similar decorative designs on the end loops of antithetic spirals appear in Mycenaean Close Style pottery (fig. 66:17, pl. 25) and on a krater fragment from stratum XIII at Ashdod (chap. 2, fig. 3:7).

ANTITHETIC STEMMED SPIRALS (FIG. 67:1–4) Despite the abundance of antithetic spirals in Philistine ceramic decoration, the stemmed variant of this motif is very rare. Antithetic stemmed spirals appear either on parallel stems (fig. 67:2) or on stems that curl outward from a V (fig. 67:4). Both have very close parallels in Myc. IIIC:1 motifs (fig. 67:1, 3).

SPIRAL COMPOUNDS Besides the five basic variations described above, the spiral is also used in combination with and attached to such other motifs as the bird (fig. 61:21, 23), lotus (fig. 45), and antithetic tongue motifs (fig. 67:10). These composite motifs are peculiar to Philistine pottery.

DEBASED SPIRALS The spiral motif appears in the last phase of Philistine pottery on the Type 18 kraters (fig. 60) from Tell Qasile stratum X and Megiddo

230. *Sinda*, p. 107, pl. II; *see also* pl. 25, this chapter.

stratum VIA. It resembles the Mycenaean debased spiral motifs found in the Myc. IIIC:1 period.[231]

The Antithetic Tongue Motif (fig. 67:5–10) The antithetic tongue motif is rare in Philistine pottery. The two examples presented here (fig. 67:7, 10) are the sole motif in facial arrangements appearing on Type 1 bowls (fig. 3). Figure 67:7 is very close to its Mycenaean prototype both in general conception and in specific details such as the vertical chevrons between the two tongues, the two small circles above the chevron, and the accompanying dot pattern. The similarity between this motif and the Myc. IIIC:1b antithetic tongue motifs, for example from Sinda (fig. 67:5, pl. 4), is especially striking. Figure 67:10 is further removed from its Mycenaean prototpye. The addition of spirals (significantly nonheraldic here) to the ends of the tongue is a typical Philistine variant, although examples of antithetic tongues terminating in spirals are known in Mycenaean decoration (fig. 67:8, 9). The Mycenaean motif belongs to the group of hybrid motifs created through the combination of floral and vestigial octopus designs.

The antithetic double-tongue motif suspended upside-down beneath the handle of the ʿAitun jug (pl. 62) is a unique variant of the standard Philistine motif. Here the basic tongue theme recurs in different guises: we can recognize its influence in the plant motifs (both alone and as part of an abridged Nilotic composition) and in the shape of the bird's wings. This pervading theme lends harmony and unity to the jug.

The Concentric Semicircles Motif (figs. 68, 69) Concentric semicircles are a dominant and recurring motif on vessels of Types 2–6, 8, 9, 12–16. They appear on various zones of decoration and in numerous combinations. In most cases the inner semicircle is solid red. Six main groups of semicircle motifs can be differentiated.

1. Concentric semicircles arranged in a row (fig. 68:2), occasionally with secondary motifs (a wavy line, etc.) between them (fig. 68:3).

2. Concentric semicircles in a row or in pairs that are joined by another row of smaller concentric semicircles (fig. 68:11) or by chevrons (fig. 68:5–6, 8–9). The apices of the connecting chevron patterns sometimes terminate in an elongated stroke or spur (fig. 68:8). One

example (fig. 68:13), of concentric semicircles arranged in an overall pattern, has obvious affinities with the scale pattern.

Groups 1 and 2 are most commonly applied to the handle areas of Types 3, 6, and 12 vessels. They are also employed in a continuous arrangement on the main decorative band, especially on Types 12, 14, and 16 vessels of the second phase of Philistine pottery.

3. Concentric semicircles on either side of a triglyph (fig. 69:2–4). This rather uncommon motif on Philistine pottery has parallels in the Myc. IIIC:1 repertoire (fig. 69:1), which was influenced by the Minoan-Mycenaean triglyph and half-rosette motif.

4. A pair of concentric semicircles arranged antithetically as the sole motif in a metope (fig. 69:6, 8, 10, 11). Like its Mycenaean prototypes (fig. 69:5, 7, 9), this arrangement is stylized in numerous ways— sometimes the background, sometimes the motif is accentuated in solid color. Two examples (fig. 69:8, 12) have a wiggly line superimposed on, but not part of, the pattern, whereas in two others (fig. 69:10 and especially fig. 69:11), the line has become an integral part of the pattern. We can also follow the gradual transformation of the semicircles into triangles; figure 69:12, for example, seems to be a geometrized development of figure 69:11.

5. Concentric semicircles employed as background fill in metopes when the main motif is, for example, a bird (fig. 61:3). When the main motif is a rhombus, the semicircles are often attached to its sides, creating a new pattern (fig. 70:7). Concentric semicircles also appear as a variation of the collateral-semicircle design on triglyph motifs (fig. 7:3).

6. Concentric canopied semicircles (fig. 69:15, 16). Hitherto rare in the Philistine repertoire, some additional examples of this distinctive motif were found at Ashdod. It is well known in Myc. IIIB and continues into Myc. IIIC:1 (fig. 69:13, 14). The concentric canopied semicircle pattern in different outlines seems to have been a combination of the stylized "papyrus" motif with concentric semicircles.[232]

All the concentric semicircle arrangements described above have clear prototypes in Mycenaean decoration. However, as Furumark points out, it was only during the Myc. IIIC:1 period that they evolved from secondary or auxiliary motifs into primary de-

231. *MP*, fig. 63, motif 51:27.

232. *Enkomi Excavations*, vol. II, pp. 848–49, pls. 308:228 (early level III B), 309:268, 275 (destruction of level III B); *MP*, p. 346, motif 43.

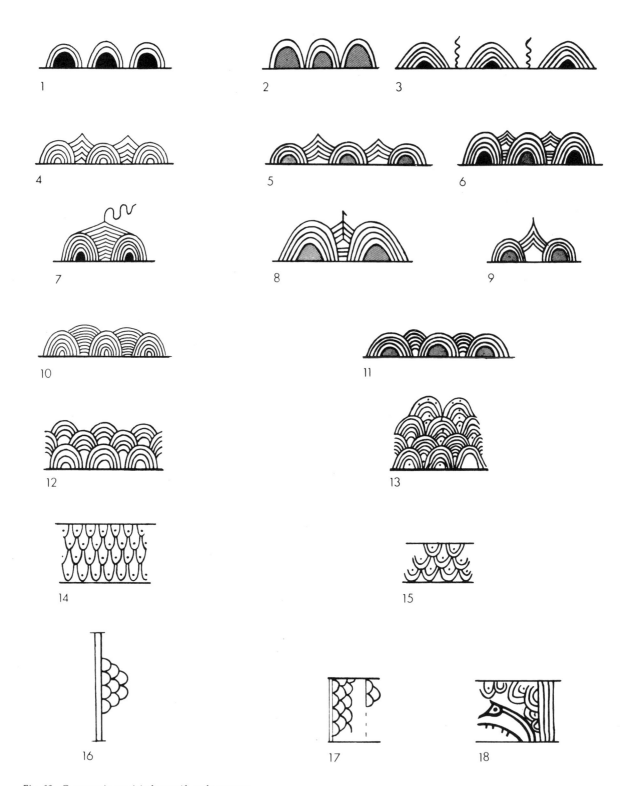

Fig. 68. Concentric semicircle motif, scale pattern.
1. [*MP*, fig. 58, mot. 43,24; Myc. IIIC]   **2.** [*Gezer* III, pl. CLIX:7]   **3.** See fig. 56:2.   **4.** [*MP*, fig. 58, mot. 43,32; Myc. IIIC:1]
5. See fig. 47:3.   **6.** [*BP II*, pl. LXIII:43]   **7.** [*MP*, fig. 58, mot. 43,33; Myc IIIC:1]   **8.** See fig. 24.   **9.** See fig. 21:2.
10. [*MP*, fig. 58, mot. 43,34; Myc. IIIC:1–2]   **11.** See pl. 46.   **12.** [*MP*, fig. 58, mot. 43,35; Myc. IIIC:1]   **13.** Megiddo (*see above*, chap. 2, pl. 19:7).   **14.** [*MP*, fig. 70, mot. 70,2; Myc. IIIA:1]   **15.** See fig. 47:1.   **16.** [*MP*, fig. 57, mot. 42,24; Myc. IIIB–C:1]   **17.** [*B-M*, pl. 40:122]   **18.** [*BP II*, pl. LXIII:49]

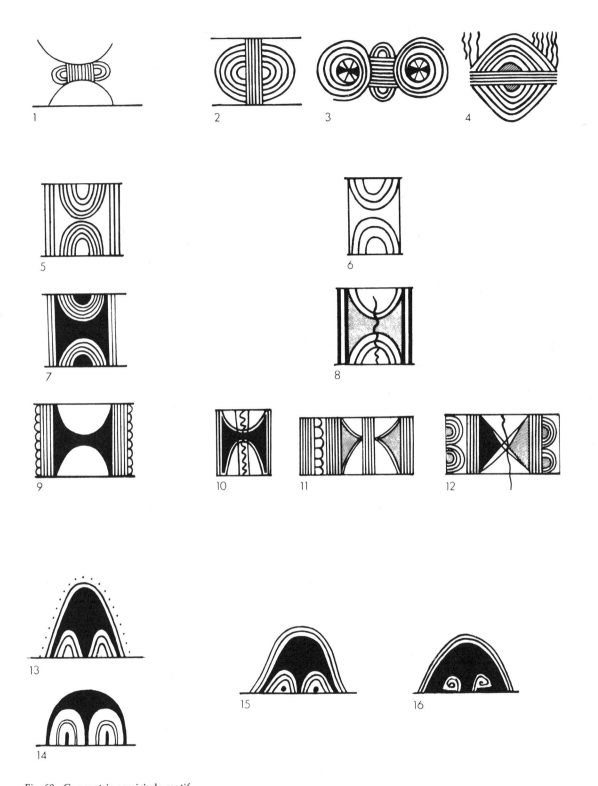

Fig. 69. Concentric semicircle motif.
1. [*MP*, fig. 58, mot. 43,46; Myc. IIIC:1]   **2.** Ashkelon, surface find.   **3.** [*B-M*, pl. 40:114]   **4.** See fig. 10:4.   **5.** [*MP*, fig. 58, mot. 43,38; Myc. IIIC:1]   **6.** Megiddo, stratum VI [*Meg. II*, pl. 85:5].   **7.** [*MP*, fig. 58, mot. 43,40; Myc. IIIC:1 late]   **8.** [*Gezer* III, pl. CLXV:10]   **9.** [*MP*, fig. 58, mot. 43,39; Myc. IIIC:1]   **10.** [*Gezer* III, pl. CLXVII:7]   **11.** [*B-M*, pl. 42:159]   **12.** See fig. 22:1.   **13.** [*MP*, fig. 58, mot. 43,w; Myc. IIIC:1 late]   **14.** [*MP*, fig. 58, mot. 43,q; Myc. IIIC:1]   **15.** Jar, Ashdod.   **16.** [*Gezer* III, pl. CLXVII:6]

corative themes depicted in numerous combinations and variations.[233]

The Scale Pattern (fig. 68:14–18) The scale pattern has numerous uses on Philistine pottery; it appears suspended downward as a metope fill (fig. 68:15), pointing upward as the fill in the "triangles" on the shoulders of stirrup jars (figs. 14, 15:1), decorating the handle area (fig. 16:3), aligned vertically with triglyphs (fig. 68:17), or as background fill (fig. 68:18). These variations all have their respective counterparts in Myc. IIIB–C ceramic decoration (fig. 68:14, 16). Dots are often added in the center of the scales for emphasis, and the scale outlines are often doubled, tripled, or even quadrupled. Dots in this context are quite rare in Mycenaean pottery, although they do occur as early as the Myc. IIIA repertoire (fig. 68:14).

The Wavy Horizontal Line There are two main variants of the wavy horizontal line appearing on Philistine pottery. (1) The deep, wavy horizontal line is very rare in Philistine ceramic decoration as a primary motif, but two examples are known: figure 56:2 and a cruder version, figure 58:2. This motif appears in the main decorative band of Mycenaean vessels during Myc. IIIC:1; Furumark interprets it as a stylized representation of octopus tentacles.[234] (2) The shallow horizontal wavy line appears on the monochrome bowls from Ashdod. It is a crude version of the festoonlike joined semicircles that appear on some of the Ashdod bowls (chap. 2, fig. 3:7), which are typical of Myc. IIIC:1b bell-shaped bowls; for a parallel see figure 72:1.[235]

The multiple horizontal wavy lines typical of Myc. III:1c Granary Class have not yet been encountered on Philistine vessels, except for one example from Gezer (see p. 53, above). Their absence proves that this class of pottery neither reached Canaan nor influenced Philistine pottery. Evidently, the second wave of Achaeans, who brought it to Cyprus, never arrived in Canaan.

The Lozenge (fig. 70) The lozenge or rhombus, often with curved sides and double outline (fig. 70:4), is common in Philistine ceramic art. It appears in diverse combinations and arrangements and is usually cross-hatched (fig. 70:2, 6, 7). Concentric semicircles are often attached to the sides of the lozenge (fig. 70:7) and are occasionally used to accentuate the inner corners (fig. 70:4). The lozenge is used in the following ways:

1. As the primary motif in a metope (fig. 70:2, 4). In most of these cases concentric semicircles are added to the sides of the metope (fig. 70:6) or to the lozenge itself (fig. 70:7).
2. As a continuous motif in a horizontal band (fig. 70:13).
3. As a connective between spirals (fig. 66:9–11).
4. As an auxiliary motif, often with winged spirals (fig. 65:18), multiple-stemmed spirals (fig. 70:15), or bird motifs (fig. 22:2).
5. As an auxiliary motif with spirals mounted on a wavy stem (fig. 70:17). The stemmed rhombus is very rare. The few examples known in Philistine pottery all come from Gezer (figs. 25:1, 70:17).

The Myc. IIIB–C tradition provides clear parallels and prototypes for all but two of the lozenge versions discussed above: figure 70:7, the lozenge with concentric semicircles attached to its sides, is a purely Philistine innovation; and figure 70:9, which has four dotted circles around the lozenge, has only a partial parallel in Mycenaean decoration (fig. 70:8).

Lozenge motifs continue to appear until the last phase of Philistine pottery, where they occur as a continuous band (fig. 27:6) or as a filling pattern (fig. 59:2).

Chevrons (fig. 71) Chevrons are used in a variety of ways: in horizontal or vertical bands, in combination with other motifs, or singly. They most often appear:

1. Connecting concentric semicircles (fig. 68:5, 6, 8, 9)
2. Connecting antithetic tongues (fig. 67:7, 10)
3. As a triglyph fill (figs. 7:3, 40:3, 48)
4. As a fill for the loop of a winged spiral (fig. 66:19, 20)
5. As a primary motif in a horizontal band, generally on stirrup jars (fig. 71:2, 3).

As a connective or auxiliary element the chevron is quite common in Mycenaean pottery decoration, but as a primary motif (in a horizontal band) it appears predominantly during the Myc. IIIC:1 period (as in fig. 34 above). The Mycenaean chevron closely resembles the Philistine, except for the two-color scheme in some Philistine examples (fig. 71:3). Uniquely Philis-

233. *MP*, p. 344.
234. Ibid., fig. 65, motif 53:15.
235. E.g., *Enkomi Excavations*, vol. I, p. 318; vol. IIIa, pl. 97:19. E. French, "Pottery from Late Helladic III B1 Destruction Contexts at Mycenae," *BSA* 62 (1967): 149–93.

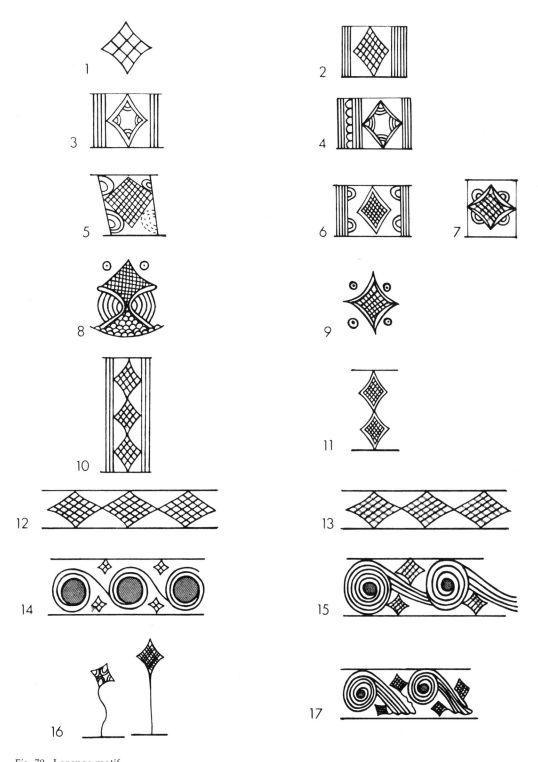

Fig. 70. Lozenge motif.
1. [*MP*, fig. 71, mot. 73,y; Myc. IIIC:1]   **2.** See fig. 22:2.   **3.** [*MP*, fig. 72, mot. 73,15; Myc. IIIC:1 early]
4. [*Gezer* III, pl. CLXVI:13]   **5.** [*Enkomi*, Ceramique, pl. IV:12]   **6.** [*BP I*, pl. XXIII:3]   **7.** See fig. 24.   **8.** [*MP*,
fig. 72, mot. 73,10; Myc. IIIC:1]   **9.** See pl. 9.   **10.** [*MP*, fig. 72, mot. 75,27; Myc. IIIB]   **11.** See fig. 22:1.
12. [*Sinda*, pl. I; Myc. IIIC:1b]   **13.** See fig. 16:4.   **14.** [*MP*, fig. 72, mot. 73,16; Myc. IIIB]   **15.** See fig. 47:2.
16. [*MP*, fig. 71, mot. 73,8–9; Myc. IIIB]   **17.** See fig. 11:5.

tine, however, is the chevron in the bird motif modified to represent the bird's stylized wing (fig. 61:1–4). Here, as in its more conventional uses (cf. fig. 67:9), the chevron at times has a spur at the apex (figs. 61:2, 6, 68:8). Variants of this feature appear in Mycenaean pottery (fig. 68:7).

The Zigzag and Triangle Motifs (fig. 71:4–9) The simple vertical zigzag pattern used as a filling motif for triglyphs appears predominantly on the monochrome Ashdod kraters of stratum XIII. This zigzag pattern is painted by means of short strokes in a special technique not employed in the later development of Philistine pottery but evident in the Myc. IIIB–C:1 ware (fig. 72:2).[236]

Elaborate zigzags, on the other hand, are used in a number of ways:

1. As a continuous horizontal pattern forming hatched triangles, usually on the main decorative band of the vessel (fig. 71:5).

2. In a pattern similar to 1, but with the small inner triangles filled with solid color (fig. 71:8, 9).

Both designs 1 and 2 are closely related to the Myc. IIIC:1 motifs. They generally appear as the main decoration on stirrup jars (fig. 71:4, 6, 7).

3. As a vertical hatched triangle pattern filling a metope (fig. 48, upper register) analogous to the Close Style decoration.[237]

4. In the last stages of Philistine pottery, in continuous rows of parallel zigzag lines (fig. 27:1), with either the upper (fig. 27) or lower row of triangles (fig. 20) filled with solid color.

The latter may be related to the various elongated triangle motifs mentioned above (see p. 215 below) in connection with the geometrized lotus leaves. An interesting combination and adaptation of the triangle motif inscribed in concentric semicircles appears on a number of examples of Philistine pottery (e.g., pl. 39). This motif is very close in concept to the "canopied" triangles that evolved in Mycenaean pottery from Minoan prototypes and is indicative of the eclectic character of Philistine pottery. The "canopied" triangles motif is paralleled by the "elaborate" triangle, which appears frequently in Philistine pottery on the shoulder zone of stirrup jars (fig. 14).[238]

Checkerboard Pattern The checkerboard pattern is very common in Philistine pottery; it was used from the very beginning of Phase 1 as a fill for metopes (cf. figs. 7:1, 23:2) along with other motifs of clear Mycenaean origin. Checks are known in the local Late Bronze Age Canaanite decorative tradition, but they are rare on Iron Age I Canaanite pottery[239] and apparently reappear with the advent of Philistine pottery. The Philistine checkerboard motif was probably incorporated from the Mycenaean repertoire, in which it was similarly employed as a metope fill during the Myc. IIIB and IIIC:1 (pl. 33).[240]

The Net Pattern The oblique net pattern is used as an overall pattern (fig. 26:1, 2) as a fill for metopes (fig. 48), for lozenges (fig. 70:2, 6, 7), or for the triglyph dividing the body of a bird (fig. 61:8). It appears in the earliest phase of Philistine pottery, continues into the second, but it is most prevalent in the last phase, as exemplified by the Megiddo VIA group (figs. 17:6, 18: 7, 8). It is quite common in Myc. IIIB–C:1 decoration,[241] where it appears in the same variations and fulfills the same function as the Philistine pattern.

The right angle (or square) net pattern is a variant of the oblique and is very rare in the Philistine repertoire. It occurs in the debased decoration of a stirrup jar (fig. 15:1), as part of the triglyph motif on the main band, and as the fill in the triangles of the handle area on the quadruple pyxides in figure 18:9.

Triglyph Motifs Paneled patterns are a standard Philistine concept. Thus far we have concentrated on the motifs found within the metopes. We shall now turn to the individual motifs of which the dividing triglyphs are composed.

The basic triglyph element is the vertical line, to which may be added:

1. vertical wavy lines (fig. 8:3)

2. collateral semicircles (fig. 7:1)

3. collateral dotted semicircles (fig. 7:2). The addition of the dot is a purely Philistine innovation.

4. elongated semicircles containing a number of dots (fig. 15:1).

5. concentric semicircles (fig. 7:3)

6. chevrons (fig. 7:3)

236. *MP*, p. 387, fig. 67, motif 61:3.
237. Ibid., fig. 58, motif 43:44.
238. Ibid., p. 408; Gjerstad, *OA 3*, pp. 92–94, fig. 7; Furumark, *OA 3*, pp. 250–52, fig. 13.

239. E.g., *Meg. T.*, pl. 134; A. Druks, "A 'Hittite' Burial near Kefar Yehoshua," *BIES* 30 (1966): 215 (Hebrew).
240. *MP*, fig. 67, motif 56:2.
241. Ibid., fig. 67, motif 57:2.

7. a vertical zigzag pattern, as found on early Philistine kraters from Ashdod.

A complete triglyph motif can also serve as the principal element in a decorative band. Figure 16:5 shows a series of identical triglyph motifs that form a repeated-unit arrangement in which the unit is the triglyph itself. Similarly, in figure 48 the upper register of the shoulder band is decorated with a series of triglyphs consisting of various geometric motifs, some of which also appear as primary motifs (such as the checker or elaborate zigzag patterns). There is not always a clear distinction between dividing triglyphs and the fill ornaments of the metopes.

Although it is true that a paneled arrangement of decorative motifs and some of the simpler components of Philistine triglyphs (for example, straight and wavy lines) are known in local Late Bronze and Early Iron painted pottery, the origin of the more elaborate Philistine panel style and of the main motifs in the metopes and triglyphs must be sought, as we have seen, in the Myc. IIIB–C tradition (see fig. 72).[242]

Egyptianizing Motifs

The Philistine motifs originating in Egyptian art (the lotus in its various stylistic representations) have been dealt with above in full in our discussions of Types 12 and 13. We shall therefore confine ourselves here to a summary of the principal ways of rendering the lotus flower (figs. 50–52) on Philistine ceramics and their relation to various other motifs possibly influenced by the geometrization of the lotus.

The lotus on the neck of the Type 12 jug is either (1) depicted naturalistically, thus preserving the original shape and character of the flower (fig. 50:1, 2); or (2) geometrized into a series of elongated triangles (fig. 50:3). The lotus-rosette on the interior of the Type 13 bowls is either (1) stylized but still preserving the rounded shape of the leaves (fig. 50:4); or (2) completely geometrized, with the leaves and petals depicted as elongated triangles (fig. 50:5).

The rows of elongated red and black triangles appearing on the Type 9 cylindrical bottle (fig. 34:4), in the metopes of Types 1 and 3 vessels (figs. 8:1, 2, 16:1), and on the Ashdod figurine (chap. 4, fig. 9) may also be derivatives of the geometrized lotus flower. The same may be true of the more unusual variant of triangles filling canopied semicircles. Rows of trian-

gles seem to be a more prominent feature than was previously realized. Besides the commoner elongated variation, plain rows of triangles also occur, sometimes even without the distinctive alternate red and black filling. Rows of triangles, in most of our examples, may derive from the geometrized lotus pattern. They are not a common feature in Mycenaean pottery, but are well represented in its later developments, for example, in the Proto-White Painted pottery of Cyprus (cf. fig. 36).

Motifs Derived from Canaanite Ceramic Decoration

The local tradition of pottery decoration exerted little influence on the Philistine repertoire. The motifs common to both Canaanite and Mycenaean decorative traditions (the checkerboard pattern, net pattern, and triglyph motif) discussed above should be considered part of the overall pervasive Mycenaean influence.

Only one motif in the Philistine pottery decoration can be attributed with absolute certainty to the local Canaanite decorative tradition: the date palm. The palm first appears on a Philistine krater from Azor as a central motif between two antithetic spirals (fig. 66:12). In its general composition and especially in certain details (for example, the wavy lines suspended from either side and the "date clusters" hanging from the bottom of the lowest branch), this example follows the Canaanite Late Bronze II tradition of stylized palms at its finest and bears no resemblance to the debased version of the motif as it appears on Iron I local ware (cf. chap. 5, fig. 7:15). It is in the debased form that the palm motif appears on Philistine Type 18 kraters (fig. 60:5)—another example of the degree to which the last phase of Philistine pottery became assimilated into the local ceramic tradition.

Another aspect of Philistine decoration that may be correlated with the local Late Bronze Age tradition is the use of bichrome decoration on a white background. This technique may be related to the Syro-Palestinian tradition, in which the outline of the motif is drawn in black and the filling or internal details in red. This technique may also have links with Cypriot White Painted ware. Bichrome decoration is almost unknown in Mycenaean pottery, although isolated examples from the mainland (Mycenae) have been found.[243] The monochrome trend of Mycenaean deco-

---

242. Ibid., pp. 416 ff., fig. 72, motif 75.

243. Benson, "A Problem in Orientalizing Cretan Birds," p. 81.

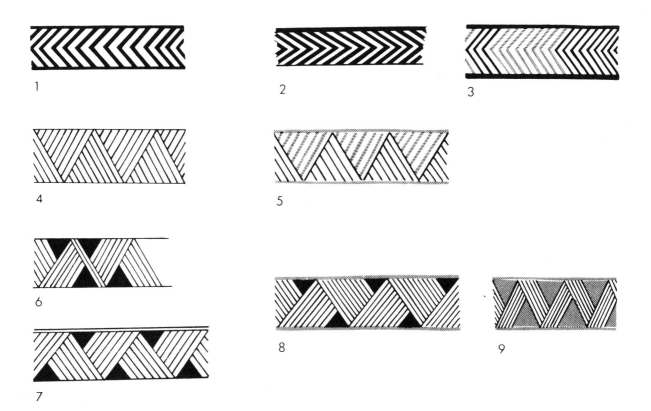

Fig. 71. Chevron, zigzag, and triangle motifs.
1. [*MP*, fig. 67, mot. 58,33; Myc. IIIA2–C:1] 2. See fig. 17:3. 3. See fig. 17:5. 4. [Furumark, *OA 3*, p. 92; fig. 5:4] 5. See fig. 17:2. 6. [*Ialysos*, fig. 74, tomb LXXXV, 3] 7. [Furumark, *OA 3*, p. 92; fig. 5:5] 8. Stirrup jar, Ashdod C 160/11. 9. See fig. 17:1.

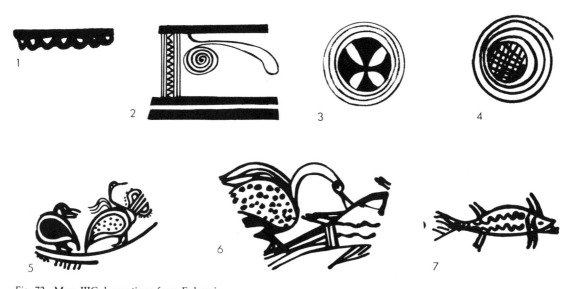

Fig. 72. Myc. IIIC decorations from Enkomi.
1. Suspended half-circles [*Enkomi Excavations*, vol. II, pl. 307:154]. 2. Zigzag [Ibid., vol. II, pls. 307:165, 306:120].
3. Maltese cross [Ibid., vol. II, pl. 309:265]. 4. Spirals with crosshatching [Ibid., vol. IIIa, pl. 71:23]. 5. Dotted bird [Ibid., vol. II, pl. 309:282]. 6. Bird attacking fish [Ibid., vol. II, pl. 309:277]. 7. Row of fish [Ibid., vol. II, pl. 309:280].

ration is reflected in the earliest appearance of Philistine pottery at Ashdod, but shortly afterward the bichrome, Oriental trend becomes predominant, only to fade out again in the final phase.

SUMMARY

Of the four different sources of influence distinguishable in the shapes and decoration of Philistine pottery—Mycenaean, Cypriot, Egyptian, and local Canaanite—the dominant influence is that of the Mycenaean as it was derived from the Aegean repertoire. Types 1, 2, 3, 6, and 7 already appear in Myc. IIIC:1 monochrome ware from Ashdod and Beth-Shean and herald the first phase of Philistine pottery. The types showing Cypriot affinities are somewhat rarer, being confined mainly to Phase 2 (Types 9–11), with only faint traces in Phase 1. Although rare in Cyprus itself before the end of the eleventh century B.C., these shapes are typologically native to that land, where they have a very long history. Egyptian influence is evident in Type 12 of Group III, which seems to be restricted to Phases 1 and 2, although the elongated-triangle motif persists in a degenerate form on diverse types of Philistine pottery. The local Canaanite ceramic tradition is more difficult to specify. It includes Types 13–16; Type 13 is an exceptional vessel, and Types 14, 15, and 16 appear only sporadically. To these should be added several nonhomogeneous local vessels bearing Philistine decoration (for example, the pilgrim flask), which, although growing in number, are not yet sufficiently numerous to constitute a well-defined group. The variability of these types is characteristic of the last phase of Philistine pottery.

The evolution of the decoration of Philistine pottery can be traced from its initial appearance on the monochrome ware, which has so far been identified with certainty only at Ashdod and Beth-Shean; there it is still a faithful rendering of the original Myc. IIIC:1 version in shape, monochrome paint, and decorative motifs. Its closest links are with the less elaborate decoration of Myc. IIIC:1b, as found in its original homeland, the Argolid. Examples are known from Mycenae, Pylos and Perati, from Rhodes, Tarsus in Cicilia, and especially from Cyprus—at Enkomi, Sinda, and Kouklia. Only at a few sites is the more elaborate Close Style of Myc. IIIC:1b found. Here too, its strongest connection is with Cyprus, where this style is one of the manifestations of the culture of the incoming Achaeans and Sea Peoples.

Most of the motifs appearing on the "classical" Philistine pottery were borrowed from the elaborate Close Style repertoire of Myc. IIIC:1b. The new elements are the way in which they were modified and the bichrome decoration. This is the pottery that is the hallmark of Philistine culture. Made by potters well versed in the Mycenaean tradition, the vessels are nevertheless no mere copies. The artistic style of Philistine pottery is unique. On Types 12 and 13 we find Egyptian decorative motifs, and, although the influence of local Canaanite decorative tradition on Philistine pottery (aside from the white slip and bichrome decoration) is only faintly perceptible, it becomes more apparent in the last phase of Philistine pottery.

It appears that Philistine pottery was one of the local ramifications that developed after the collapse of the Myc. IIIB pottery *koine* style of the Late Bronze Age. It can be stated with confidence that this pottery was not the product of a people coming directly from their country of origin with a homogeneous tradition but rather reflects the cultural influences picked up along the way in the long, slow, meandering migration from their Aegean homeland.

Philistine pottery is confined mainly to the area of Philistine settlement known from written sources. Excavations and surveys have shown that it had penetrated farther afield, but in doing so it diminished proportionally in quantity. The appearance of Philistine pottery in areas far removed from Philistine settlement should probably be understood as the result of political or commercial activities.

In a number of sites Philistine pottery appears in a clear stratigraphic context that provides the basis for our threefold division of the pottery. This stratigraphical-typological division should not be taken as a rigorous guide but only as the framework for our study of the development of the pottery. Phase 1 directly follows the Late Bronze II strata or occurs after a brief appearance of the local version of Myc. IIIC:1b pottery, or after an intermediate Iron IA Canaanite or Israelite stratum. Phase 3 represents the period of the disintegration of Philistine pottery, when it became assimilated into the local ceramic tradition (and developed regional differences). Pottery of this phase appears in strata belonging to the close of the eleventh century B.C.

The association of Philistine pottery with the Philistines is based on the Aegean background of the pottery and of the people (as reflected in the Bible and Egyptian sources) and on the fact that this pottery appears almost exclusively in areas settled by the Philistines and other Sea Peoples and is found in the strata corresponding in time to references to them in the historical sources.

Since Philistine pottery is related in its earliest stages to Myc. IIIC:1b pottery, and the end of this phase of Mycenaean pottery is based primarily on the date of the appearance of Philistine pottery in Canaan, it will be necessary to determine the length of time that passed between the end of the Myc. IIIB and the first appearance of Philistine pottery (which, as mentioned above, must be related, for typological and stratigraphic reasons, to an advanced stage of the Myc. IIIC:1b period). Stratigraphic finds from Canaanite sites indicate with a high degree of certainty that the end of the Myc. IIIB falls around the last third of the thirteenth century B.C. This date has been lowered to about 1200 B.C. by the finds from Tell Deir ʿAlla (see p. 84 above). It is improbable that much time could have elapsed between the end of Myc. IIIB and the beginning of Philistine pottery, for the latter bears so close a resemblance in shape and decoration to the former. Philistine pottery in Canaan should not, therefore, be fixed much later than one or two generations after the end of the Myc. IIIB. Its suggested date in the early twelfth century is also in accord with what is known of the period from historical sources.

The end of the Mycenaean Empire and the destruction by the Sea Peoples of civilizations on the coast of the eastern Mediterranean basin cannot predate the end of the thirteenth century. Desborough's summary[244] of the historical events of this period seems acceptable, and is reinforced by Dikaios's monumental work on Enkomi. The latter supports the correlation between the arrival and settlement of the Sea Peoples in Cyprus and on the southern coast of Canaan. All the available sources indicate that the conquest (or settlement) of the Philistines must have taken place around 1190 B.C. Desborough utilized all the historical sources, with the exception of the most recently discovered texts from the archives of Ugarit (which mention events that would seem to indicate the possibility of an earlier invasion of Sea Peoples into Syria). These early invasions, however, can in no way be associated with the Philistines and hence cannot alter Desborough's conclusions regarding the beginning of Philistine pottery.

Desborough, following Benson, has attempted to explain Philistine pottery as the work of a single potter and dates its appearance about fifteen years after the Philistine settlement. But all the evidence indicates that the Philistines began producing their unique pottery immediately after their settlement in Palestine (the prelude of the monochrome ware may indicate an earlier wave of Sea Peoples). The appearance of this pottery cannot be dissociated from the appearance of the Philistines themselves.

The basis for the absolute chronology of the second phase of Philistine pottery is provided by the scarab of Ramesses X in tomb 532 at Tel el-Farʿah. The finds from this tomb belong to the second phase of Philistine pottery and represent the era of Philistine expansion from the end of the twelfth to the middle of the eleventh century B.C.

The third and last phase of Philistine pottery corresponds to Israelite ascendancy over Philistia during the time of David. The biblical account of the decline of Philistine power accords with a decrease of Philistine finds in excavations and, especially, with the disappearance of the pottery's distinctively Philistine traits and its complete assimilation into the local pottery around the end of the eleventh and the beginning of the tenth century B.C.

244. *DMS*, pp. 209–14.

4

CULT AND CULT VESSELS

INTRODUCTION

In addition to the types of Philistine pottery discussed in the preceding chapters were found terra-cotta vessels and figurines that are unmistakably cultic.[1] Group VI, which is continually enriched by new finds from the eastern Mediterranean and the Aegean world, illustrates the link between the Mycenaean and Philistine cultures. The Philistine craftsmen who fashioned these vessels interwove the legacy of their Aegean traditions with strands from Egypt and Canaan, added ideas of their own, and thus created vessels that were truly innovative.

The excavations at Ashdod[2] and Tell Qasile[3] have opened new insights on the Philistine cult, cultic architecture, and cultic and funerary vessels. They have also helped to confirm the nature and attribution of many sporadic finds that in the past could only tentatively be attributed to the Philistine cult. The finds at Ashdod and Qasile also enable us to reappraise the contents of the Gezer cache and to add essential details lacking in the excavation report. The three sites of Gezer, Ashdod, and Qasile have all yielded vessels

that are definitely cultic, in context as well as in character.

Our discussion of the Philistine cult objects in this chapter will be mainly typological. It will include, inter alia, ring kernoi, kernos bowls, zoomorphic vessels, rhyta, cup-bearing kraters, and terra-cotta figurines, all of which can be related to Philistine culture in workmanship, decoration, and context. The Gezer cache will be treated as a separate group. Of the Ashdod and Qasile assemblages, only pertinent examples will be described at length, since the assemblages as a whole have been discussed in context in chapter 2.

THE GEZER CACHE

R. A. S. Macalister's publication of this cache of objects (fig. 1, pl. 1),[4] makes it impossible to relate it to any architectural remains. The *terminus a quo* of the cache is provided by a fragment of an Egyptian faience vase bearing the cartouche of Ramesses III (fig. 2).[5] The shapes, technique (white slip and bichrome decoration), and decorative motifs of the vessels are all clearly Philistine. The cache appears to be an early assemblage of Philistine cultic vessels and figurines. We have selected a number of these objects, which are of interest in themselves and can serve as a starting point for a discussion of the principal types.

---

1. A paper was presented on this topic ("Terracotta Figurines and Cult Vessels") by the author at the First Congress of Mycenaean Studies in Rome. *See* Atti e Memorie del 1° Congresso Internazionale di Micenologia, Rome 1967/68.

2. *Ashdod II–III*, pp. 20–21; R. Hachlili in ibid., pp. 125–35; M. Dothan, "The Musicians of Ashdod," *Archaeology* 23 (1970): 301–11.

3. For discussion of the site, *see* chap. 2, pp. 57–69. Our remarks on Tell Qasile are based on firsthand knowledge of the material and on the preliminary excavation reports: A. Mazar, *Qasile IEJ 23*; idem, "Excavations at Tell Qasile, 1973–1974 (Preliminary Report)," *IEJ* 25 (1975): 77–88; idem, *EAEHL*, pp. 963–75. A detailed discussion of the cultic vessels appears in A. Mazar's Ph.D. thesis for the Hebrew University of Jerusalem, which is to be published in a forthcoming volume of *Qedem*. I thank A. Mazar for putting the finds from the temple complex at my disposal.

4. *Gezer* II, pp. 235–39. This group of vessels was found at the southern end of trench 29, above the inner city wall and the southern gate (dated to the Middle Bronze Age).

5. The publication erroneously ascribes the cartouche to Ramesses II. In the first report of this find, however, it was correctly ascribed to Ramesses III. R. A. S. Macalister, *PEFQSt* (1908): 111, fig. 8. Furumark, in *CMP*, p. 121, ascribed this group to the final phase of Philistine pottery—Phase 4, according to his divisions. In the light of our discussion, this suggestion does not seem feasible.

Fig. 1. Group of ritual vessels, Gezer.
1. Zoomorphic vessel [*Gezer* II, fig. 389]. **2.** Figurine [*Gezer* II, fig. 271]. **3.** Lid [*Gezer* II, fig. 390:5]. **4.** Miniature bottle, white slip [*Gezer* II, fig. 390:3]. **5.** Kernos bowl [*Gezer* II, fig. 390:2]. **6.** Kernos [*Gezer* II, fig. 390:1].

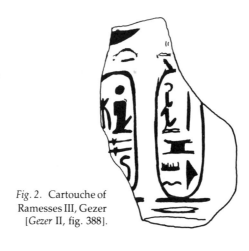

Fig. 2. Cartouche of
Ramesses III, Gezer
[*Gezer* II, fig. 388].

Pl. 1. The Gezer cache in fig. 1 [From the Collection of the Israel Department of Antiquities and Museums].
1. See fig. 1:1.   **2.** See fig. 1:6.   **3.** See fig. 1:3.   **4.** See fig. 1:4.

Pl. 2. Ring kernos, Megiddo, stratum VI, in fig. 3 [Oriental Institute, Chicago, P. 2282. *Meg. Cult,* pl. XVI].

Pl. 3. Pilgrim flask, Megiddo, stratum VI [From the Collection of the Israel Department of Antiquities and Museums, 36.1999. G. M. Shipton, "Notes on the Megiddo Pottery of Strata VI–XX," *Studies in Ancient Civilization,* no. 17 (Chicago, 1939), pl. 1:14, chart VI, 32].

Cylindrical Bottle

This handmade, miniature cylindrical votive bottle (fig. 1:4, pl. 1:4) is covered with a heavy white slip and decorated in red. It is the only miniature votive example of its kind known and points to the special character of the cache. It is also the earliest well-dated example of a typical Philistine bottle of Type 9, if the cartouche of Ramesses III is taken as absolute dating evidence.

Lid

A narrow, uniquely shaped rectangular lid (fig. 1:3, pl. 1:3)[6] bears all the hallmarks of Philistine decoration. One end is damaged; on the other, unbroken end is a small round projection that probably served as a hinge to fit into a socket on the box itself. The lid is white slipped and decorated in bichrome: black for outlining the motifs and red and black for the filling. The decoration consists of different arrangements and combinations of triangles and combinations of triangles and rows of squares with dotted centers. In the panel closest to the hinge are two clumsily painted birds (the artist's lack of understanding being especially apparent in the rendering of the wing and tail of one of the birds). Two birds side by side in a metope is unusual, although another example from Gezer shows two birds, one above the other (chap. 3, fig. 62:28), and examples of both these combinations have been found at Ashdod.

This lid may have belonged to a "cult" box similar to those found in the Beth-Shean sanctuaries.[7] Decorated boxes with lids are known from the Aegean—for example, the lid of the clay model of a small shrine from Crete of the Sub-Minoan period (ca. 1100–1000 B.C.).[8]

Ring Kernoi

Of several kernos fragments found,[9] the best preserved is part of a ring kernos to which are attached a miniature bird and a pomegranate (fig. 1:6, pl. 1:2). The pomegranate is red slipped, and the bird's back is decorated with a red and black checkerboard and two triangles that follow the contours of the tail. The wing feathers are indicated by red lines. These Gezer fragments are the earliest well-dated and clearly Philistine examples of the elaborate kernoi, on the hollow rings of which were attached small receptacles shaped like minature vases, birds, pomegranates, and bull protomes with spouts facing outwards. Each of the attached vessels was connected to the hollow ring, so that any liquid poured into one vessel would circulate and could be poured out again through the bull protome. The bull protome, birds (doves?), pomegranates, and vases are all common symbols in the fertility cult, representing the fertility of the earth and its creatures. It can safely be assumed that these kernoi were used in ritual libations.

Stratum VI at Megiddo has provided the most complete example of a ring kernos (fig. 3, pl. 2),[10] which is decorated in Philistine style and dated to the eleventh century B.C. The ring supports a bull's head (not, as suggested by the excavator, a gazelle) flanked by two miniature amphorae for liquids, two pomegranates, and two doves drinking from a miniature bowl very like the Philistine Type 1 bowls.[11] The birds on these kernoi are similar to those on the Gezer kernos, but in workmanship and decoration—radial lines and a Maltese cross in the center—they resemble the Megiddo VI pilgrim flasks (pl. 3).[12]

Other fragments of kernoi were found in Megiddo VI. The kernos shown in plate 4 is doubtless a fragment of one of the elaborate examples discussed above. The miniature vase in plate 5 was probably also part of a kernos. It is burnished and decorated in black and red with a net pattern, groups of straight and wavy vertical lines, and a concentric semicircle motif. It is typical of the debased Philistine pottery of Megiddo VIA.

The abundant material from Ashdod[13] enables us to follow the development of this type of kernos in Palestine. The origin, distribution, and use of the kernos, which has a long and varied history in the Aegean and Near East, has been discussed in connection with finds

---

6. *Gezer* II, p. 238. A fragment of this lid was published separately (*Gezer* III, pl. CLXVI:7).

7. *B-SH II, Part 1*, p. 67; box and box lids: pl. XXII:13–16, levels VI–VII temple.

8. S. Marinatos, *Crete and Mycenae* (London, 1960), p. 154, pls. 138–39.

9. *Gezer* II, pp. 236–37.

10. *Meg. Cult.*, pp. 17–18, pl. XVI (no. 2282).

11. *See* ibid., pl. XVI (no. 3303), for a small cup (bowl), which also belongs to this kernos and is similar in shape to the bowl under discussion.

12. *Meg. II*, pl. 74:16; the range of the type is strata VIB–VIA.

13. *Ashdod II–III*, p. 132, figs. 66:9–13, 67–71.

Pl. 4. Fragment of a ring kernos, Megiddo (three views) [From the Collection of the Israel Department of Antiquities and Museums, 36.1967. *Meg. Cult,* pl. XVI].

Pl. 5. Miniature vase belonging to a ring kernos, Megiddo, stratum VIA [Oriental Institute, Chicago, P. 6363].

from Megiddo and Beth-Shean (pl. 6).[14] We will limit our observations here to the fact that the Philistine kernos is related to the kernoi of the last phase of Mycenaean culture, of which the finest example is the so-called Boston kernos (pl. 7). Although its provenance is uncertain, it probably originated in Cyprus, where these kernoi are most numerous and continue to appear down to the Cypro-Geometric period I–II.[15]

Kernos Bowls

A bull-headed spout (fig. 1:5) from the Gezer cache probably belonged to a kernos bowl similar to the one found at Beth-Shemesh in stratum III (fig. 4, pl. 8),[16] which is the only known example that has typical Philistine decoration. The Beth-Shemesh bowl is white slipped and decorated with red and black lines and a red spiral on the outside. In technique and decoration it belongs to Philistine pottery. The Gezer fragment should be reconstructed on the same lines.

The Beth-Shemesh bowl consists of a tubular rim to which two hollow bull's heads are attached. Apart from broken horns, the figures and the bowl itself are in excellent condition. One of the bull's heads points outward and obviously served as a spout. The other slants downward and inward, as if drinking from the bottom of the bowl. If one were to suck at the spout (the bull facing outward), any liquid in the bowl would be drawn up into the mouth of the other (drinking) bull, along the tubular rim, and out through the spout.

The Ashdod excavations[17] have revealed kernos bowl fragments as well as large number of bull's heads, which should be restored along the lines of the Beth-Shemesh bowl. Another complete, although crude, example comes from the twelfth century level at Deir 'Alla,[18] and another, oblong in shape, from the temple of stratum X at Tell Qasile.

Various types of kernos bowls appeared sporadically in Canaan from the Late Bronze Age down to the eighth century B.C., although most of the examples are from the Iron Age I.[19] Very elaborate examples are found in Cyprus in the Proto-White Painted pottery of Late Cypriot IIIB and in the White Painted I–II pottery of the Cypro-Geometric period.[20] The Mycenaean variant of a ring-rim vessel is Furumark's type 199:14—a rhyton with a hollow ring around the upper part[21]—which is a different category of vessel.

The Philistine kernos was probably based on local prototypes, for in Iron I it appears alongside kernos bowls of clearly local manufacture.

Fragment of a Plain Bowl with a Pomegranate-Shaped Vessel Attached to its Rim

This vessel is mentioned only by Macalister, who published neither drawing nor photograph of it. No complete vessel of this type is known.[22]

The pomegranate as a separate vessel, no doubt symbolizing fertility, is found in Canaan from the Middle Bronze Age onward. In the Middle Bronze Age tombs at Jericho, wooden pomegranates were discovered, and glass ones of Egyptian type are known from Cyprus.[23] The much cheaper pottery version is found in Canaan at, inter alia, Tell ez-Zuweyid (see discussion in chap. 2), Ashdod, stratum XI, and in the stratum X temple at Tell Qasile.

Zoomorphic Bird-Shaped Vessel (fig. 1:1, pl. 1:1)

The bird—possibly a duck—is made of light-yellow ware coated with white slip and decorated in black and red. The wings are outspread and the legs are folded under and attached along their entire length to the lower side of the body. On the back is a pierced handle

14. *Meg. Cult*, pp. 17–18; *B-SH II, Part 1*, pp. 51 f. An article on kernoi and kernos bowls is in preparation by the writer.

15. *SCE IV, Part 2*, p. 238, figs. VII:12, XV:2; L. D. Caskey, "Recent Acquisitions of the Museum of Fine Arts, Boston," *AJA* 40 (1936): 312, fig. 10. For a comprehensive discussion of kernoi in Cyprus and a bibliography on the subject, *see* A. Pieridou, "Κυπριακα Τελετουργικα Αγγεια," *RDAC* (1971): 18–26, pls. VII–XI. Furumark believes the ultimate origin of the kernos is in the East (*MP*, pp. 69–70, fig. 20:197).

16. *AS I*, pl. XI; *AS III*, p. 38, pl. B.

17. *Ashdod II–III*, p. 111, fig. 58:29, 30. Among the still unpublished fragments of bulls' heads dating to the twelfth and eleventh centuries at Ashdod some decidedly show signs of belonging to ring kernoi.

18. H. J. Franken, "Iron Age Jordan Village," *Illustrated London News* (May 1965): 27, fig. 4.

19. Trude Dothan, forthcoming; see n. 14.

20. Pieridou, "Κυπριακα Τελετουργικα Αγγεια."

21. *MP*, p. 69.

22. *Gezer* II, p. 237 (4). A recently discovered bowl with pomegranate inside comes from Tel Halif, dating to the Iron Age. See Notes and News, *IEJ* 28 (1978): 121, pl. 24:b.

23. *Enkomi*, p. 211, pl. XL (tomb 5, Late Cypriot III). For wooden pomegranate discovered at Jericho, *see* K. Kenyon, *Jericho I* (London, 1960), p. 390, fig. 158:6, pl. XVII:1.

Pl. 6. Ring kernos, Beth-Shean [From the Collection of the Israel Department of Antiquities and Museums, P. 1810. *B-SH II, Part 1*, pls. XX:21; LXA:3].

Pl. 7. The "Boston kernos" [Courtesy Museum of Fine Arts, Boston, 35-735].

Pl. 8. Kernos bowl, Beth-Shemesh, stratum III, in fig. 4 [From the Collection of the Israel Department of Antiquities and Museums, I. 8655. *AS I*, pl. XI].

Fig. 3. Kernos, Megiddo, stratum VI [*Meg. Cult*, pl. XVI, p 2282].

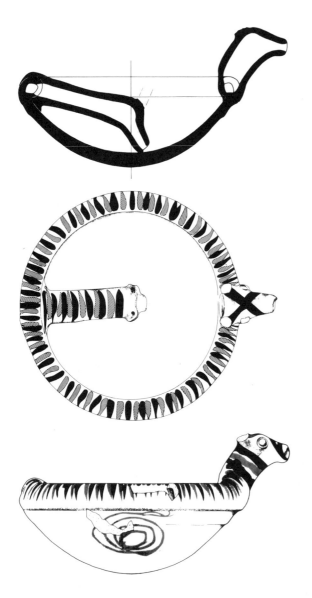

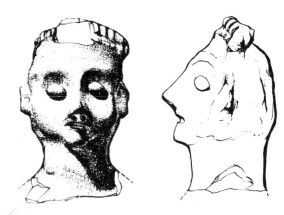

Fig. 5. Head of terra-cotta figurine, Tell eṣ-Ṣafi.

Pl. 12. Head of figurine, Tell eṣ-Ṣafi, in fig. 5 [From the Collection of the Israel Department of Antiquities and Museums, 64-362].

Fig. 4. Kernos bowl, Beth-Shemesh [*AS I*, pl. XI; *AS III*, p. 38, pl. B].

and under each wing a perforation. These very unusual features and the fact that the beak has no opening suggest that the bird was hung by a cord passed through the holes and that it was not used for libation. Wavy lines are painted along the bird's back and the wings are outlined in black. A patch of red and black decoration on the breast is akin to the Philistine dotted-scale pattern.[24]

Such a freestanding, hollow bird vessel is very rare in Palestine in this period, although hollow birds form a standard part of the kernos. Bird or duck vases from Cyprus and the Aegean, dating from ca. 1125–1050 B.C., have been discussed by Desborough,[25] who deals with their typology, distribution, and antecedents in the Aegean world. He writes: "The bird may not be one of the most common Mycenaean vase shapes, but it is thoroughly characteristic, found everywhere where there were Mycenaeans and in use from LH IIB to LH IIIC." The Cyprus vases are of two main types: Type I has a bird's head and spout and a handle on the back; Type II has a spout instead of a bird's head and also bears a handle. Our Gezer bird matches Type I. Some of the Type II examples are horn-shaped vessels with zoomorphic features. The vases are often decorated with geometric designs that echo Mycenaean motifs and are not always related to body shape.

According to Desborough, the bird vase (both types) was designed for pouring wine or water. Since it has been found in tombs, settlements, and sanctuaries, he suggests that it was used in various contexts and not specifically as a ritual vase or for burial offerings. He believes that the idea of a wine or water pourer of this distinctive type was introduced by some enterprising potter and that the fashion caught on.

At Gezer we find both ring kernoi with birds and pomegranates attached and a bird and a pomegranate as vessels in their own right. In both cases they were used in cultic rituals. (The Gezer bird was found in a cache of ritual vessels, and the accompanying kernoi are indisputably cultic.) Like the Tell Qasile pomegra-

nates, the Gezer bird has holes and was probably hung up in the temple or cult place.

The bird motif in terra-cotta vessels became increasingly prominent in cult vessels related to the Philistines. Solid birds' heads (perhaps ducks) detached from their original vessels have been found in the Philistine strata at Ashdod (pl. 9),[26] while in the Tell Qasile temple complex (stratum XI–X) bird-headed bowls (pl. 10), which were placed on high stands (pl. 11), are among the most outstanding features.[27] Although the bird has a long history and is well attested in the local Canaanite repertoire, its recurrence in different facets of Philistine culture is striking: various types of terra-cotta vessels are formed in the likeness of birds; painted birds are a distinctive feature of Philistine pottery; and the ships of the Sea Peoples depicted at Medinet Habu have bird figureheads (chap. 1, fig. 7). The bird is almost the emblem of the Philistines.

Upper Part of a Male Pottery Figurine (fig. 1:2)

The figurine is coated with a thick white slip, and the details of its face and features are accentuated in red and black. The eyes are applied pellets delineated by black circles, and the eyebrows are a single horizontal line. The nose is molded and accentuated with a red line, and the moustache and beard are painted in black. A short vertical black line represents the protruding tongue. A large round hole in the figurine's chest may have been intended to admit a peg (although it is also possible that the figurine was itself part of the handle of another vessel). The function of two smaller holes, one in the back and one beneath the chin, is not clear. Macalister suggested that their purpose was to allow steam to escape during firing.

The figurine is clothed in a flat cap (a sort of tam-o'-shanter) or coronet with a braided edge and six ribbons streaming down behind; a crenellated necklace or ruffled collar; and a garment indicated by strokes of color on the shoulders. This figurine is unique in ancient

24. *Ialysos I–II*, p. 170, fig. 98. The same scale pattern on the breast appears on a zoomorphic vessel from tomb XII and is ascribed to the sub-Mycenaean period. A bird-shaped vessel was found in a LH IIIC tomb, no. 15, *Ialysos I–II*, p. 173, figs. 99, 100.

25. V. R. d'A. Desborough, "Bird Vases," Κρητικα Χρονικα, (1972), pp. 245–77. *See also* Pieridou, "Κυπριακα Πλαστικα Αγγεια," *RDAC* (1970): 92–102, pls. XIII–XVII.

26. *Ashdod I*, p. 110, figs. 35:1, 2; 47:2.

27. Bird's heads of the same type were found in level VI at Beth-Shean (*B-SH II, Part 1*, pl. XX:11–18). Bowls were found in locus 1740 in stratum VI at Megiddo (*Meg. II*, pl. 85:7), Tel eṣ-Ṣafi (*B-M*, pl. 47), and at Deir el-Medineh (*Deir el-Medineh*, pp. 172–76) from the New Kingdom. Bird-shaped cosmetic bowls are common vessels, but they differ in size and function from those under discussion. For bird-headed bowls placed on cultic stands at Tel Qasile, see *EAEHL*, pp. 971, 975.

Pl. 9. Bird head, Ashdod [From the Collection of the Israel Department of Antiquities and Museums, 62-454].

Pl. 10. Bird-headed bowl, Tell Qasile, strata XI–X (two views) [A. Mazar, "Excavations at Tell Qasile, 1973–1974, Preliminary Report," *IEJ* 25 (1975): pl. 7:D].

Pl. 11. Cult stands with bird-headed bowls and top view of bowl on middle stand, Tell Qasile [A. Mazar, "Excavations at Tell Qasile, 1973–1974, Preliminary Report," *IEJ* 25 (1975): pl. 7:E].

Near Eastern terra-cotta sculpture, but Mycenaean terra-cottas, once again, provide parallels—especially a perforated human figurine from Asine on the Greek mainland.[28]

The shape of the Gezer figurine's head and cap can be compared with the head of a figurine found in a Philistine context at Tell eṣ-Ṣafi (fig. 5, pl. 12). The headgear of the latter is represented by two stripes of clay applied to the top of the head and incised with short vertical strokes.

The group of cult objects contained in the Gezer cache has enriched the Philistine ceramic repertoire with a number of new types, in addition to the absolute date supplied by the cartouche of Ramesses III.

PHILISTINE CULT OBJECTS

Lion-Headed Rhyta

Five lion-headed rhyta bearing all the hallmarks of the Philistine decorative style have so far been uncovered in Palestine at Tel Zeror, Tell eṣ-Ṣafi, Megiddo, Tell Jerishe, and Tell Qasile. They are one-handled drinking or libation cups that have no opening in the mouth (an unusual feature for this type of vessel). Stylistically, these rhyta can be divided into two groups:

Group A. The rhyta from Zeror, Megiddo, and Ṣafi (figs. 6, 7, pls. 13, 14, 15) have closed mouths and naturalistic, delicately rendered features.

Group B. The less naturalistic, cruder rhyta from Jerishe and Qasile (pls. 16, 17) have open jaws showing tongue and fangs, bulging eyes and cheeks, flattened noses, and upturned muzzles.

The rhyta in both groups are decorated with painted designs that accentuate the features (red and black on a whitish slip) and filling ornaments that do not convey the surface texture of a real animal but correspond to the planes of the face.

Group A

TEL ZEROR (FIG. 6, PL. 13) The Tel Zeror rhyton comes from the Iron Age I cemetery,[29] which con-

tained derivative Philistine pottery whose decoration has been weathered by time.

The rhyton is of reddish clay and, although it too is badly worn, traces of paint remain on the lower part of the head. It was no doubt originally painted all over—probably in a geometric pattern. Fine checkerboard patterns and rows of collateral semicircles (?) are painted in black, while faint remains of black dots suggest whiskers (see Tell eṣ-Ṣafi, below).

The rhyton, which was almost complete when found, is shown restored in figure 6. The cup is proportionately shorter than that of the complete Qasile example (pl. 17) and matches the different shapes and lengths of rhyta depicted on the Egyptian wall painting of the Eighteenth-Dynasty tombs at Thebes (fig. 8:2).

Tel Zeror was probably settled or influenced by the Tjekker, a branch of the Sea Peoples known from the Wen Amun letter to have been established at Dor. The rhyton is Zeror's clearest link with Philistine culture (besides the few quasi-Philistine vessels mentioned above); and it is stylistically very like the rhyton from Ṣafi in Philistia proper and the one from Megiddo, where Philistine influence was strong.

MEGIDDO (PL. 14) The stratigraphy of the Megiddo rhyton is unclear,[30] even though stylistically it seems to belong to stratum VI (chap. 2, p. 80). The upper part of the head, with the ears, eyes, and part of the nose, has survived and allows us to assign the rhyton to Group A. The lower part should probably be restored along the lines of the rhyta from Ṣafi and Zeror. A handle extending from the right temple evidently was attached to the lost rim, as in the Zeror and Qasile examples. The modeling is artistic, and the facial features are accentuated in red in a highly realistic manner, while the rest of the head is densely covered with geometric motifs in red and black. The top of the skull above the forehead is divided into three parallel zones: a net pattern covers the middle zone and is repeated beneath the eyes, and elongated triangles (geometrized lotus pattern) occupy the zones on either side. The forehead is decorated with combinations of triangles, alternately red filled and dotted, and the bridge of the nose bears a chevron pattern. Such motifs, espe-

28. O. Frödin and A. W. Persson, *Asine, Results of the Swedish Excavations 1922–1930* (Stockholm, 1938), p. 308 and fig. 211.

29. *Tel Zeror III*, p. 72, pl. LIX:6.

30. A 13533, the rhyton, was not found in a stratified context and not published by the excavator. It was identified by B. Mazar during his examination of the excavation material stored in the Oriental Institute of the University of Chicago.

Pl. 13 Lion-headed rhyton, Tell Zeror, in fig. 6 (two views) [From the Collection of the Israel Department of Antiquities and Museums, 67-386].

Pl. 14. Lion-headed rhyton, Megiddo [Oriental Institute, Chicago, A 13533].

Pl. 15. Lion-headed rhyton, Tell eṣ-Ṣafi, in fig. 7 (two views) [Israel Museum, 69.9.121].

cially the net pattern, are characteristic of Megiddo VI Philistine pottery; and the filling of the surface with geometric patterns recalls the decoration of the bodies of animals on the "Orpheus" jug (chap. 3, fig. 28:1).

TELL EŞ-ŞAFI (FIG. 7, PL. 15) The Tell eş-Şafi rhyton was found together with Philistine pottery,[31] but not in a systematic excavation. It closely resembles the Megiddo and Zeror rhyta in the modeling of its facial features and is basically similar in decoration, although less detailed. The forehead is decorated with a bichrome chevron-and-horizontal-line motif. Dots decorating the area below the eyes and the upper part of the muzzle perhaps represent the lion's whiskers, as they do on the rhyton from Tel Zeror.

Group B

TELL JERISHE (PL. 16) A fragment of a lion-headed rhyton was uncovered in the Iron Age I strata at Tell Jerishe.[32] The eyes protrude, the jaws are open, and the tongue hangs out. Originally there were probably fangs modeled in appliqué, as in the Qasile example. The facial features and other details are painted in brown and red, but these are now almost worn away. The cheeks, the bridge of the nose, and the eyes are boldly outlined, and the cheeks are covered with a net pattern that reappears beneath the chin. The features, design, workmanship, and style of decoration correspond to those of the Qasile rhyton, but are inferior to it.

TELL QASILE (PL. 17) The Qasile rhyton,[33] the most complete example yet found, comes from the pit (*favissa*) north of the temple, which belongs to the phase just antedating the construction of the temple of stratum X. The pit contained a remarkable collection of pottery vessels, of which the most outstanding was a large anthropomorphic female figurine (pl. 18). The ceramic assemblage as a whole fits the repertoire of stratum XI, although some elements herald stratum X. There seems to be no doubt that the whole assemblage is a collection of discarded or intentionally buried vessels and cult objects originally belonging to the stratum XI temple.

In addition to the geometric patterns common to the other rhyta, the Qasile rhyton displays the typical

Philistine spiral motif—a hallmark of Philistine pottery. This motif confirms our earlier suggestion that this group of rhyta belongs to the Philistine repertoire; the context at Qasile proves its cultic significance beyond doubt. Thus, all five rhyta must clearly be classified as Philistine (with that at Tel Zeror possibly seen as a "Tjekker" variant)—adding a new and unique type to the previously known cult vessels.

Our Philistine pottery rhyta seem to be the last echo of a long Mycenaean-Minoan tradition of animal-headed rhyta. They can be traced back to the shaft graves of Mycenae (where the famous lion-headed gold rhyton was found) and to the stone examples of Crete from the Late Minoan Ib central treasury at Knossos.[34] These were doubtless the prototypes of the animal-headed rhyta depicted in the Eighteenth Dynasty tombs of high functionaries at Thebes, Egypt (fig. 8:2). Processional scenes painted in these tombs show the "Keftiu," probably envoys from Crete or the Aegean islands, bearing precious gifts to the Egyptian functionaries. Many of the vessels carried by the envoys are animal-headed rhyta, and the lion-headed ones are clearly Aegean in origin.[35] They were no doubt fashioned of precious metal.

From a later period (thirteenth to early twelfth century B.C.) comes an ivory plaque from the treasury at Megiddo VIIA (fig. 8:1) on which are incised two rhyta, one lion headed and the other gazelle headed, borne on a table between two servants. Megiddo thus yields an unusual combination: both a depiction of a lion-headed rhyton and the rhyton itself.

The Philistine pottery rhyta seem to have had the same raison d'être as those of the Mycenaeans: an inexpensive substitute for silver, gold, and stone. They were part of the widely distributed *koine* of Myc. IIIB.[36] The majority, decorated in the style of Mycenaean pottery, were found in Cyprus and at Ugarit. Yet among all these animal-headed rhyta there is not a single example of a lion's head in Mycenaean ware and decoration, although plain examples are known from Thera

31. The rhyton is in the Israel Museum.

32. The rhyton fragment is in the Hebrew University collection, no. T332. No clearly associated object can be traced in the unpublished Tell Jerishe material.

33. Reg. no. 2256, locus 125, stratum XI.

34. A. Evans, *The Palace of Minos*, vol. II (London, 1928), pp. 826–31, figs. 541–45, 549.

35. H. J. Kantor, *The Aegean and the Orient in the Second Millennium B.C.* (Bloomington, 1947), p. 47, n. 125, pl. IX:M, N, O. For a discussion of the ethnic origins of the tribute bearers, *see* A. Furumark, "The Settlement of Ialysos and Aegean History c. 1550–1400 B.C.," *OA* 6 (1950): 232 ff.

36. *Nouveaux Documents*, pp. 224–30, pls. XXI–XXII.

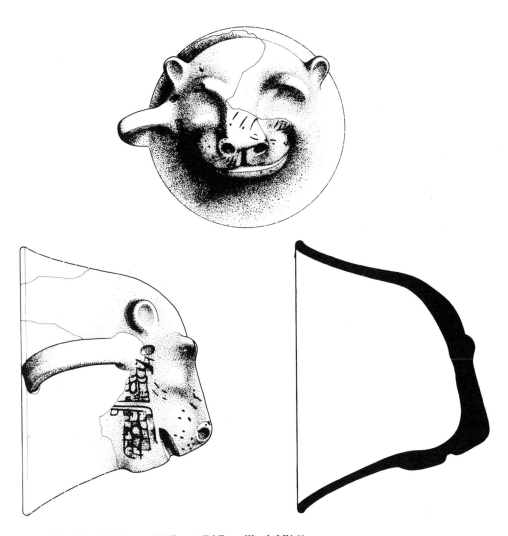

Fig. 6. Lion-headed rhyton, Tel Zeror [*Tel Zeror III*, pl. LIX:6].

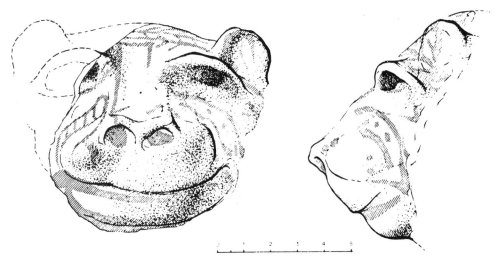

Fig. 7. Lion-headed rhyton, white slip, Tell eṣ-Ṣafi.

Pl. 16. Lion-headed rhyton, Tell Jerishe (two views) [Institute of Archaeology, The Hebrew University of Jerusalem, 332].

Pl. 17. Lion-headed rhyton, Tell Qasile [From the Collection of the Israel Department of Antiquities and Museums, 76-451. *Qasile IEJ 23*, pl. 18:B].

Fig. 8. Plaque and rhyta.
1. Ivory plaque, Megiddo, stratum VIIA [*Meg. Ivories*, pl. 4:2b].   2. Lion-headed rhyta depicted in Egyptian tomb paintings [H. Kantor, *The Aegean and the Orient in the Second Millennium B.C.*, pl. IX: M, N, O].

and Ugarit.[37] No animal-headed rhyta have so far been found in Myc. IIIC pottery. Thus the group of Philistine lion-headed rhyta evidently continues the Myc. IIIB zoomorphic rhyton tradition and fills a gap in the corpus of animal-headed pottery rhyta.

Terra-cotta Female Figurines

Sites containing Philistine materials have yielded an increasingly large group of terra-cotta female figurines, the richest and best stratified coming from the excavations at Ashdod. All of them show a stylization of the head closely resembling the Mycenaean terra-cotta figurines—a long neck, small birdlike head with spreading *polos*, projecting, pinched nose, and eyes (and sometimes ears) formed of appliqued pellets. None of these features appears in local Canaanite terra-cotta figurines of the Late Bronze or Early Iron Ages; as we shall see, they are clearly derived from Mycenaean prototypes.

Although for the most part only the heads were found (pl. 19:1), enough examples of complete figurines have been collected to enable us to distinguish two main categories: (1) seated figurines, and (2) standing figurines in various attitudes.

Seated Figurines (fig. 9, pl. 19:2) A unique, complete example of a seated figurine 17 cm. in height and nicknamed "Ashdoda," comes from the floor of a twelfth-century B.C. house in the Philistine stratum XII at Ashdod.[38] Its discovery enables us to restore the numerous heads (pl. 19:1), four- and three-legged seats, and fragmentary bodies found earlier at Ashdod. It is clear that the Ashdoda is not an isolated find but belongs to a well-defined group that began at Ashdod in the twelfth century B.C. and remained in existence there down to the eighth century. The Ash-

doda is a solid, handmade figurine with an upright back, very long, slender neck, plano-concave, spreading *polos* headdress, projecting pinched nose, and appliqued eyes and ears. Her body merges into a four-legged throne or couch (perhaps used as an offering table) and forms a schematic whole in which the flat armless torso with molded breasts forms the back of the couch. The surface of the figurine is covered with a heavy white slip decorated in red and black with typical Philistine elongated triangles and black horizontal bands. Two small black triangles on the back of the head may represent hair. The breasts, which are outlined in black, have a black-painted necklace and pendant suspended between them.

The Ashdoda was found near the unusual apsidal structure of stratum XII that was very likely a cult place. The persistence of this figurine into the eighth century strengthens its cultic identification, since a large number of broken specimens of similar type were found near an obvious cult-place of the eighth century in area D.

The Ashdoda figurine is most likely a schematic representation of a female deity and throne. It is evidently a variant of the Mycenaean female figurine seated on a throne, and sometimes holding a child, which is well known throughout the Greek mainland, Rhodes, and Cyprus. The Mycenaean figurines, usually found in graves, are thought to represent a mother goddess. In the Mycenaean versions the type of throne and the rendering of the goddess vary. Some figurines can be detached from their thrones (pl. 20) others are molded as one piece with the throne but still retain a recognizably human form (pl. 21:1, 2); still others are shaped as part of the throne itself. (A Late Cypriote adaptation of this concept in Base-Ring ware can be seen in plate 22.) The Ashdoda is a transmutation of this last type of Mycenaean figurine, schematically modeled so that the head and breasts are organically part of the throne. The head, the general form, the throne, and the legs are Mycenaean concepts that were borrowed and adapted to the Philistine style in design and color.

It may be that the Ashdoda group is the missing link between the earlier Mycenaean figurines and their later development in Greece, as are the Archaic Boeotian figures.[39]

The Ashdoda and the broken heads and thrones of

---

37. C. F. A. Schaeffer, "La Neuvième Campagne de Fouilles à Ras Shamra-Ugarit (Printemps 1937)," *Syria* 19 (1938): 194, pl. XIX:1; S. Marinatos, *Treasures of Thera* (Athens, 1972), pl. 35.

38. *Ashdod I*, pp. 110–11, 137–39, figs. 35:3, 43:5; *Ashdod II–III*, pl. LXXXII, fig. 91:1. For a discussion of the cultic significance of the Ashdoda, see *Ashdod II–III*, pp. 20–21; for a comprehensive discussion of this type and its parallels, see *Ashdod II–III*, pp. 129–30. An interesting variant of the seated female figurine with a vestigial chair (and two supports) is known in local Cypriot base-ring ware from the thirteenth century B.C. (*SCE IV, Part ID*, fig. 70:5). The idea may be similar but stylistically the Ashdoda belongs to a different world—the Mycenaean.

39. *See* R. A. Higgins, *Greek Terracottas* (London, 1967), pp. 45–46, pl. 19 a.b. for sixth-century B.C. Boeotian figurines.

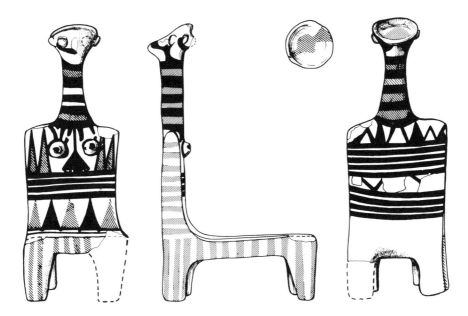

Fig. 9. "Ashdoda" figurine [*Ashdod II–III*, fig. 91:1].

Pl. 18. Anthropomorphic female vessel, Tell Qasile [From the Collection of the Israel Department of Antiquities and Museums, 76-453. *Qasile IEJ 23*, pl. 17:B].

Pl. 19. **1.** Heads of female figurines. **2.** ''Ashdoda'' in fig. 9 [From the Collection of the Israel Department of Antiquities and Museums, 68.1139, 68-1094].

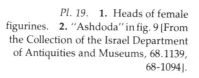

similar figurines are among the most significant cultic finds of the early Philistine period (twelfth century) because they demonstrate the Aegean cultural background of the Philistines. Other than the Canaanite deities known from biblical sources (Dagon, Baal Zebub [Zebul], and Ashtoreth), Ashdoda is the first archaeological evidence of a deity among the Philistines. Thus it is evident that, at least in the twelfth century, the Philistines were still worshipping a goddess whose prototype was Mycenaean.

Mourning and Other Standing Figurines Standing female figurines have been found at Azor (fig. 12:2, pls. 25, 27), Tell Jemmeh (fig. 12:1, pl. 26), Tell Jerishe, and Ashdod; two come from the Lachish region, probably from Tell ʿAitun (they are hereafter referred to as the ʿAitun examples [fig. 10 A and B, pls. 23, 24]). All are from Philistine contexts, and at Azor they were found with the cup-bearing kraters described below. Except for those of the ʿAitun examples, all the features are rendered similarly. Stylistically, they closely resemble the well-known Mycenaean terra-cotta figurines and show no links with Canaanite tradition.

The ʿAitun examples, which are Aegean in inspiration, stand apart as a separate group.[40] They are the only figurines attached to a krater that have both arms preserved and raised to the head in a mourning gesture. In them may perhaps be found the key to the posture and meaning of all the figurines. They are assumed to have come from the twelfth- to eleventh-century B.C. cemetery of Tell ʿAitun, where some of the tombs contained Philistine pottery.

Each of the almost identical figurines (fig. 10, A and B) mounted on the rim of a krater represents a mourning woman. Part of the rim of the krater remains attached to the bottom of figurine A, while the base of figurine B retains the negative impression of an identical rim. It can be assumed that both figurines were originally mounted on the same krater (see proposed reconstruction, fig. 11:1). The fragmentary rim of the krater to which figurine A was attached bears faint traces of a white slip and a red band painted below the rim on the outside. The fragment belongs to a krater of Type 2, of which several examples were found in the tombs of Tell ʿAitun (see chap. 2, fig. 5:18, 19). The right side of figurine A is slightly damaged, and from the knees downward it is broken off in a way that shows that it was separately made and mounted (the same method of construction is clearly seen in figurine B). Both figurines face sideways along the rim of the krater.

They are handmade, roughly but naturalistically rendered in the round, with a combination of appliqué modeling and incision. The face is broad, with a small pointed chin. The eyes and nose are accentuated, the mouth faintly indicated by a thin incision. The hair is arranged in a straight fringe across the forehead and falls down behind in two long thick plaits that reach the rim of the krater and follow it as far as the break. The way the hair is drawn back at the nape and the incision marks show that the plaits follow the flowing line of the garment, their length deliberately exaggerated for a more elegant silhouette.

The figures wear a long garment open down the front to reveal the naked body. Below the knees (figurine B) the garment blends into the curves along the rim of the krater. The raised arms seem to continue the line of the garment, and the potter evidently meant to show a long-sleeved dress. The hands are laid on the head, the right hand (the fingers schematically rendered by incisions) resting on the left.

The naturalistic style of these figurines recalls the so-called Astarte plaques common in Canaan in the Late Bronze Age and continuing into the Early Iron Age.[41] However, a combination of several unusual features distinguishes our figurines from the ordinary run of Canaanite terra-cotta female figurines: the modeling in the round, the garment and coiffure, the position of the hands, and the mounting on the krater rim. The last two elements have Aegean parallels in a group of deep bowls—*lekanai*—with mourning figures mounted on their rims. These Mycenaean lekanai (apparently reflections of an earlier form of a well-attested funeral practice observed in Greece during the historic period) were found in the Mycenaean cemeteries at Perati and at Ialysos in Rhodes. Incomplete examples come from Iolkos in Thessaly, from Naxos, Crete, and Cyprus. Perati was founded on the east coast of Attica

---

40. These two figurines have been published by the writer: Trude Dothan, "A Female Mourner Figurine from the Lachish Region," *Eretz-Israel* 9 (1969): 42–46 (Hebrew); idem, "Another Mourning Woman Figurine from the Lachish Region," *Eretz-Israel* 11 (1973): 120–21 (Hebrew). The pottery analysis by neutron activation, carried out by I. Perlman, shows that figurine A was made at Tell ʿAitun and matches the locally made ware.

41. J. B. Pritchard, *Palestinian Figurines in Relation to Certain Goddesses Known Through Literature* (New Haven, 1943).

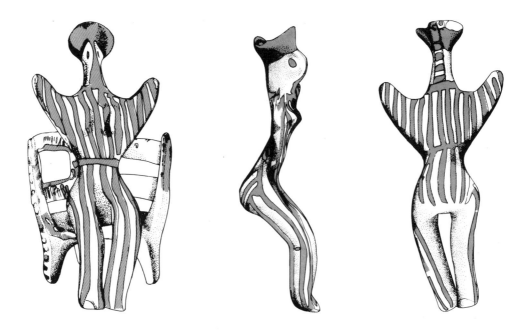

Pl. 20. Seated Mycenaean figurine (dap) [G. E. Mylonas, "Seated and Multiple Mycenaean Figurines in the National Museum of Athens, Greece," in *Aegean and the Near East,* pl. XIII].

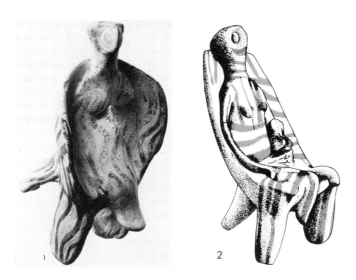

Pl. 21. **1.** Seated Mycenaean figurine [Nir David Museum, 337]. **2.** Seated Mycenaean figurine with child (dap) [G. E. Mylonas, "Seated and Multiple Mycenaean Figurines in the National Museum of Athens, Greece," in *Aegean and the Near East,* pl. XV:7].

Pl. 22. Seated figurine, Katydata, Cyprus [Cyprus Museum, Nicosia, A 39. H. Buchholz and V. Karageorghis, *Prehistoric Greece and Cyprus, An Archaeological Handbook* (London, 1973), no. 1727].

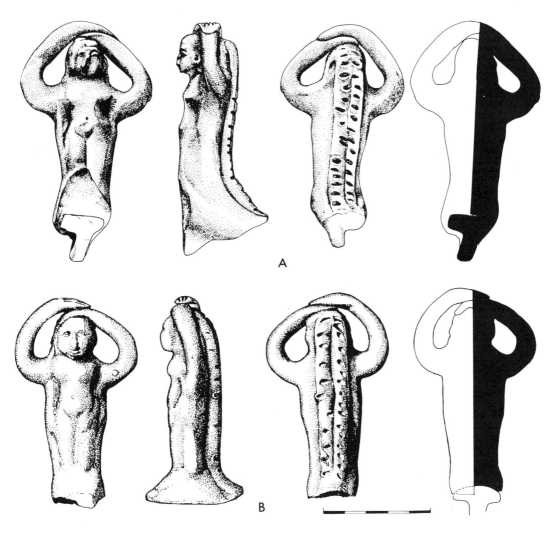

Fig. 10. Mourning figurines, Tell ʿAitun [T. Dothan, "Another Mourning-Woman Figurine from the Lachish Region," *Eretz-Israel* 11 (1973): figs. 1–2 (Hebrew)].

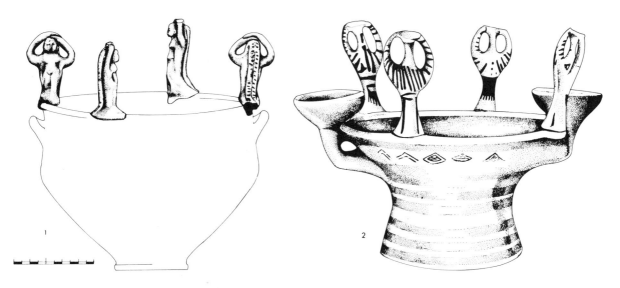

Fig. 11. Krater and lekane with mourning figurines.
1. Suggested reconstruction of Philistine krater with mourning figurines [Ibid., fig. 3].   **2.** Lekane with mourning figurines, Perati [S. P. E. Iakovidis, "A Mycenaean Mourning Custom," *AJA* 70 (1966): pl. 15:4 (dap)].

Pl. 23. Mourning figurine, Tell ʿAitun, in fig. 10A (three views) [Israel Museum, 68.32.3].

Pl. 24. Mourning figurine, Tell ʿAitun, in fig. 10B (three views) [Dayan Collection].

Pl. 25. Mourning figurine, Azor, in fig. 12:2 [From the Collection of the Israel Department of Antiquities and Museums, 64-361].

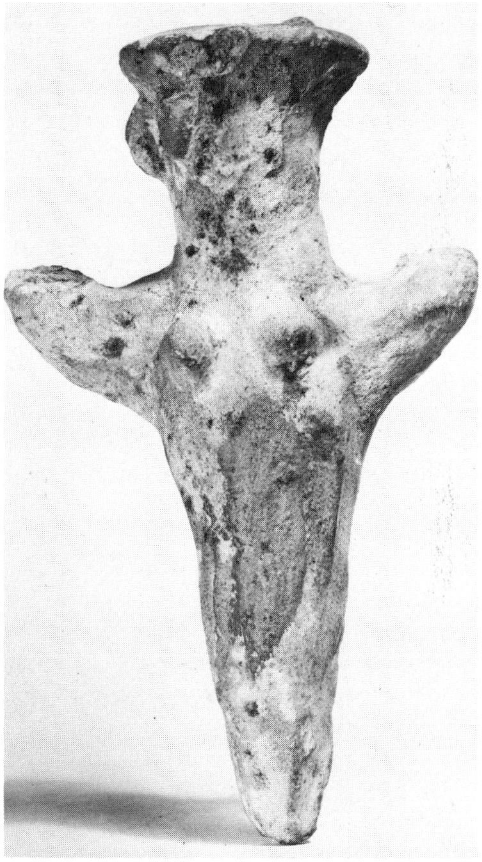

Pl. 26. Mourning figurine, Tell Jemmeh, in fig. 12:1 [British Museum].

Pl. 27. Mourning figurine, Azor [Weisenfreund Collection].

at the end of the thirteenth century B.C. by settlers moving to the shore after the destruction of the great Mycenaean centers and their palaces. According to S. P. E. Iakovidis' dating, burial in the Perati cemetery began just after the reign of Ramesses II and lasted for about three generations. The very varied finds indicate that this harbor town still had contact with the centers in Argolid and had also developed strong trade links with the Aegean Isles and the eastern Mediterranean.

The kraters were found in rock-cut chamber tombs approached through a long, narrow, sloping dromos. This style of tomb architecture is common throughout the Mycenaean empire, and it influenced the architecture of the Philistine tombs at Tell el-Far'ah.

Two variants of the lekane found at Perati have been distinguished. One (no. 65, tomb 5) has a concave profile, splaying base, and two horizontal loop handles (fig. 11:2, pl. 28).[42] From the center of each handle an upright cylindrical stem rises to support a small, shallow, rounded cup that adheres to the rim of the lekane at the point of its junction with the stem. Four small triangular projections symmetrically arranged between the handles jut out horizontally from the rim. They are perforated through the center; holes with the same diameter were also bored deep into the bases of four solid clay figurines found near the lekane. The figurines were originally attached to the rim of the lekane by pegs the same size as the holes and long enough to be driven into the figurine's foot and through the hole; the rims thus kept the figurine in position between the handles and the cups. The second variant is simpler (no. 820 from tomb 3a). It is a lekane with two horizontal handles and three mourning figurines attached to the krater rim in the same fashion.

The schematic style of the figurines from Perati places them among the large group of Mycenaean terra-cotta figurines of women standing in different attitudes. There are many such figurines, but a limited number of attitudes. The bird-headed figurine with broad-brimmed polos headdress is the most common. The torso is flat, the bosom indicated by paint or appliqué, and the garments by painted lines. The lower part of the body is a simple cylindrical column, widening at the base. Sometimes these figurines hold a child in their arms, sometimes they are seated on a sort of throne (see above), but usually they are free-

standing. These Mycenaean figurines have been classified by Furumark into three groups: ψ, φ, and τ.[43] Such figurines were common throughout the Mycenaean empire in tombs, cult places, and levels of settlement from the thirteenth century B.C. on. (Myc. IIIB). The τ and ψ types continued into the twelfth century B.C. (Myc. IIIC). We do not, however, know exactly what they signified nor what their purpose was. Most authorities consider them votive figurines whose diverse functions can only be guessed (blessing goddess, mother goddess, sacred nurse).[44] In our figurines, however, the hands express pain, grief, and despair, in the classic gestures of women mourners depicted in ancient art: they clutch their heads, tear their hair, and scratch their faces.

Mourning figurines are rare in the Mycenaean repertoire, but have been found sporadically in widely scattered parts of the Mycenaean world. Two groups can be distinguished: one of freestanding figurines and the other of figurines attached to a vessel, temporarily or permanently.

Three figurines from the Mycenaean cemetery at Ialysos in Rhodes belong to the freestanding group. They come from Myc. IIIC:1 rock-cut tombs nos. XV and XXXI.[45] The same tombs yielded another figurine holding her hands to her breast and lekane vases with figurines attached to the rim. Two more figurines of the freestanding type, found in the cemetery at Kamini in Naxos (fig. 12:5),[46] are poorer in workmanship than those from Perati and Ialysos. Only the modeling of their faces departs from the usual Mycenaean figurine style.

Mourning figurines with a deep perforation in the base (indicating the same mounting technique as at Perati) have recently been found both in Thessaly and in Crete. One figurine was uncovered at Iolkos,[47] the main Mycenaean center in Thessaly, in a twelfth-century B.C. context, and a group of three figurines was

42. S. P. E. Iakovidis, "A Mycenaean Mourning Custom," AJA 70 (1966): 43–50, pl. 16:7; Perati Γ, pls. 177, 178.

43. CMP, pp. 86–89.

44. Of the publications dealing with Mycenaean figurines, we have made use mainly of the following: F. F. Jones, "Three Mycenaean Figurines," in Aegean and the Near East, pp. 122 ff.; G. E. Mylonas, "Seated and Multiple Mycenaean Figurines in the National Museum of Athens, Greece," ibid., pp. 110 ff.; K. Nicolau, "Mycenaean Terracotta Figurines in the Cyprus Museum," Op.Ath. 5 (1965): 47 ff.

45. Ialysos I–II, pp. 172–75, nos. 15–17, fig. 99; p. 181, no. 59.

46. Ergon 1960, "Naxos," (1961): 190–91, fig. 216.

47. Ergon 1960, "Iolkos," (1961): 60, fig. 72.

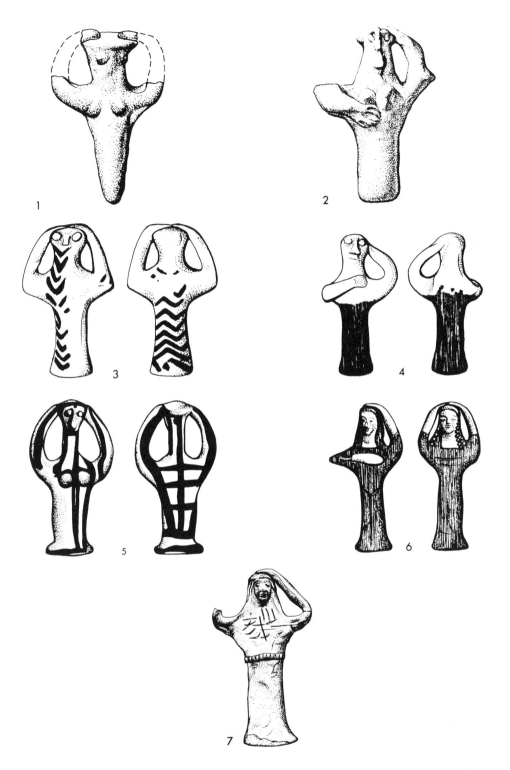

Fig. 12. Mourning figurines.
1. Tell Jemmeh.   **2.** Azor.   **3,4.** East Crete [H. E. Schmid in *Festschrift Karl Schefold* (Bern, 1967), pl. 58:2c, a (dap)].   **5.** Naxos ["Naxos," *Ergon* 1960 (1961), figs. 216, 217].   **6.** Athens, Keramaikos [G. Karo, *An Attic Cemetery* (Philadelphia, 1943), pl. 16].   **7.** Rhodes, Kamiros [R. A. Higgins, *Catalogue of Terracottas in the Department of Greek and Roman Antiquities, British Museum*, vol. I (London, 1954), pl. 2].

discovered in a tomb in eastern Crete (fig. 12:3, 4).[48] We may assume that they were all originally mounted on the rim of a lekane, like the Perati figurines. The crude attempted naturalism of the faces (in appliqué and incision), the bullet heads, geometric zigzag decoration, and overall paint—all suggest a later date than those described above, approaching the style of the Sub-Minoan period.

In this group of figurines two different gestures of grief and lamentation are seen side by side. Two of the figurines stand in the most common attitude of mourning, with both hands clasping their heads (fig. 12:3), while the third figurine holds one hand to her breast and the other to her head (fig. 12:4). Both gestures occur in representations of mourning women, and express different stages of the same act.

Another Cretan example is a kernos from the cemetery of Kourtes dating from the Late Minoan III.[49] On the hollow ring of the kernos stand three amphoriskoi and three figurines in Mycenaean figurine style. Two display the variations we have mentioned, but the third grasps with both hands the handle of the amphoriskos by her side. Some scholars have explained these attitudes as movements in a dance, but in the light of the whole assemblage of finds they seem far more likely to be the gestures of a woman mourner. These two gestures were the standard concept of mourning women and can be followed down into Greek Geometric and Archaic art. An example is the group of figurines from the Athens Kerameikos, which were mounted on amphorae of the early Attic period (seventh century B.C.; fig. 12:6).[50] They are naturalistically rendered, even to the painted blood streaming from the cheeks and forehead. Another figurine of a mourning woman from the same period was discovered in the cemetery of Kamiros in Rhodes (fig. 12:7).[51] Her hands (broken) clasp her head, her

hair is in disarray, and the deep scratches on her chest and cheeks are filled with red. In addition to their traditional attitude of mourning, all these figurines emphasize in vivid detail the mourner's hair tearing, face scratching, and violent breast beating.

We shall now return to the finds from the Myc. IIIC:1 period, and to the second variant, namely, figurines permanently attached to the rims of lekane vases, found in tombs XV and XXI at Ialysos (pls. 29, 30).[52] The figurines on the lekane are of the τ and φ types. Only one of them is of a mourning woman in the classic attitude with one hand to her head and the other to her breast (pl. 30). We have no means of interpreting the attitudes of the remaining figurines, but in this context they apparently also served the cult of the dead. In subject and conception the figurines are very close to the paintings of mourning women on the pottery larnakes (sarcophagi) found in the cemetery near Tanagra in eastern Boeotia. Larnakes appear for the first time on the Greek mainland in Myc. IIIC:1 (about 1200 B.C.),[53] and were surely influenced by Cretan culture, in which this type of burial was practiced from the Middle Minoan period. The figurative scenes and their subjects, on the other hand, are wholly foreign to the spirit of Minoan iconography: they originated in the pottery-painting traditions of Mycenae. The artistic skill and sophistication of the drawings show them to be no first fumbling attempts, but rather the fruits of tradition and knowledge. They evidently reflect a hitherto unknown aspect of Mycenaean art connected with the cult of the dead.

The discovery of the figurines enables us to reinterpret the various depictions on pottery, such as the scenes of mourning on the chariot kraters or the female mourners on the warrior krater from Mycenae,[54] and to recognize their connection with burial customs and the cult of the dead. On the larnakes mourning women are depicted wearing long dresses and flat hats (fig. 13). Their hands clutch their heads in the classic gesture of mourning. The iconographic connection between these drawings and the mourning figurines is

48. H. E. Schmid, "Frühgriechische Terrakotten aus Kreta," in *Gestalt und Geschichte, Festschrift Karl Schefold* (Bern, 1967), pp. 168 ff., pl. 58:2a–c.

49. St. Xanthudidis, "Cretan Kernoi," *BSA* 12 (1905): 9 ff., fig. 3.

50. G. Karo, *An Attic Cemetery* (Philadelphia, 1943), p. 14, pl. 16.

51. R. A. Higgins, *Catalogue of Terracottas in the Department of Greek and Roman Antiquities*, vol. 1 (London: British Museum, 1954), pl. 2:14. Another figurine (pl. 1:6) from Kamiros, from the beginning of the seventh century B.C., is holding her hands on her head one above the other, like the figurines from ʿAitun.

52. *Ialysos I–II*, pp. 140–45, figs. 63, 65N31 (tomb XXI); pp. 172–75, figs. 99, 101N13 (tomb XV). Tomb XV contains a varied collection of pottery vessels including a bird vase (see p. 227). Of special interest is a bronze knife with a circular handle (ibid., fig. 101N26). This knife is an exact parallel of knives from Tell Qasile and Enkomi (*see* chap. 2, n. 209).

53. E. T. Vermeule, "Painted Mycenaean Larnakes," *JHS* 85 (1965): 123 ff.

54. Ibid., p. 143.

Pl. 28. Lekane with mourning figurines, Perati, in fig. 11:2 [National Museum, Athens].

Pl. 29. Lekane with mourning figurines, Ialysos [British Museum, cat. no. A 950].

Pl. 30. Lekane with mourning figurines (dap), Ialysos [*Ialysos I–II*, fig. 101].

obvious in the long dresses, polos, and the position of the hands.

Together the two groups convey the eclectic nature of Mycenaean culture at the end of the empire and the new influences that were working on it. The mourning motif (as on the larnakes and terra-cotta figurines) crystallized into a standard depiction of mourning women in the cult of the dead. This version continued, with slight inconographic changes, until the end of the Archaic period.[55]

Having traced the representations of mourning women in the Aegean world, we may now reconsider their background and origin. The Philistine and Mycenaean figurines have in common the gesture of the hands and the mounting on the krater rim. The difference between them is in style: the naturalism of our figurines is utterly unlike the schematization of the Mycenaean figurines, although their attitude and style of dress resemble those in representations of mourning women on the larnakes and the warrior krater from Mycenae. The assumption that the *Philistine* figurines belong to the Aegean tradition is strengthened by comparison with a group of female figurines found at Tell Jemmeh, Ashdod, Azor, and Tell Jerishe in twelfth- to eleventh-century B.C. levels of settlement and Philistine tombs. Some of these figurines are even decorated with typical Philistine ceramic patterns. In design and workmanship they are very close to the Mycenaean figures; there are striking similarities in the schematization of the face, the conical polos headgear, the broad neck continuing the line of the face, and the torso with appliqué breasts. The lower part of the body is cylindrical or conical, and here too a long dress covering the legs seems to be indicated. Surviving bands of color here and there show details of the garment. The arms of the figurines are in most cases broken, but some were found whole or were restorable. We will discuss two of these figurines, since the position of their hands is the same as in the mourning gesture of the Mycenaean female figurines.

A mourning figurine (fig. 12:2, pl. 25) was found in the Philistine cemetery at Azor (another, similar one, broken, also comes from Azor—pl. 27). One hand is on the head and the other is below the breast. The fingers are shown by incision, as in the figurines from 'Aitun and those on the Kourtes kernos. The body is cylindrical and the base, which is broken, seems to have been

55. Cf. n. 42 above.

attached to a pot; it was probably mounted on the rim of a krater, like the Lachish and Aegean examples.

Another figurine was found at Tell Jemmeh (fig. 12:1, pl. 26). Its raised arms are broken at the elbow, but, as the hands resting on the head are preserved, there is no doubt that this is a mourner clutching her head.[56] The conical figurine has a small flat base and does not seem to have been freestanding.

Stylistically, both figurines fit the Mycenaean mourner-figurine group, although they are cruder and closer to the Naxos figurine in the appliqué facial details (fig. 12:5). The elements common to these and the Mycenaean figurines allow us to assume that the Philistine examples are descended from a Mycenaean prototype.

A further connection between the lekanai from Perati and the Philistine mourning women figurines can be seen in a group of Philistine kraters found in the Azor cemetery (fig. 14, pls. 31, 32).[57] These held small cups (apparently four in number) that were attached to the rim of the vessel. The cups are perforated on the interior, and the perforation extends down to the solid rim of the krater. On one krater fragment, the remains of a broken accessory next to the cups can be noted. Judging from the whole weight of the evidence, particularly the 'Aitun figurines, these kraters, like the Perati and Ialysos ones (fig. 11:2, pls. 28–30), bore mourning women figurines and cups mounted alternately on the rim, as suggested in the reconstruction in fig. 11:1.

Mourning figurines and cup-bearing kraters are closely linked with the burial customs and cult of the dead observed in the Aegean world at the end of the Mycenaean period. Most of the mourning figurines were found near the coast (Perati, Naxos, Crete, Rhodes, Cyprus, Philistia), the logical meeting place of foreign ideas and new customs. This was a period of reciprocal influence between the Aegean isles, Crete, Cyprus, the Levant, and Anatolia, and the Mycenaean culture in its last flowering. The latter culture was brought to the eastern Mediterranean basin by the Sea Peoples. Such interfusion can explain the appearance

56. The figurine is in the British Museum, where I examined it and made the sketch included here by kind permission of R. D. Barnett, Keeper of the Western Asiatic Department.

57. Another resemblance to Perati is the deep hole in each small attached bowl that is like the holes in the lekanai rims and the figurines' bases. Were those bowls intended for the same purpose? Were figurines or other objects placed in them? No such holes have so far been found in the figurines from Azor. Only further discoveries will solve this problem.

Fig. 13. Painted mourning figurines on larnakes, Tanagra [S. P. E. Iakovidis, "A Mycenaean Mourning Custom," *AJA* 70 (1966): ills. 1, 4].

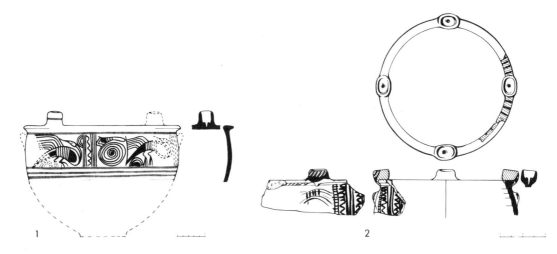

Fig. 14. Kraters bearing cups, Azor.

Pl. 31. Philistine krater with small cups attached to rim, in fig. 14:1 [Weisenfreund Collection].

Pl. 32. Philistine krater with small cups attached to rim, in fig. 14:2 [Weisenfreund Collection].

in Philistine sites of mourning women figurines and cup-bearing kraters.

While noting the classic representation and wide currency of mourning women in the Aegean world, which spread even as far as Palestine, we must bear in mind that the custom of women mourners (and its expression in literature and iconography) was equally well known in the ancient Near East.[58] However, the combination of all the elements discussed here points to a common religious and ritual background for the Palestinian and Mycenaean mourning figurines.

Pottery Ritual Stands

A late extension of the Philistine cult vessels is a pottery ritual stand—the stand with musicians from Ashdod (pl. 33).[59] The stand was discovered in area H/K in stratum X, which follows the destruction of the Philistine city of stratum XI, probably toward the end of the eleventh century B.C. This destruction brought with it a complete change in the building plan of the new city (stratum X) as well as in the remains of its material culture. However, some Philistine elements—several of them evident in the stand—do survive. Near the findspot of the stand were other vessels that seem to suggest a cult character for the area.

The stand consists of a deep carinated bowl attached to a high cylindrical body. Above the base three arch-like openings are cut out of the body of the stand, and five figures of musicians are placed around the stand. Four of them are modeled in the round and stand in rectangular windowlike openings; they are attached by peglike lower parts of their bodies. The heads of the figurines are disproportionately large and have bulging eyes and exaggeratedly large noses. The fifth and central figure is distinctive because of its large dimensions and different style of workmanship. It is formed by a combined technique in which the outline of the figure is cut out and the individual features are applied. The cut-out technique of the main figurine has its closest analogy in the cult stand found on the

bama ("high place") of the stratum X temple at Tell Qasile (see chap. 2, p. 66)—another Philistine affinity.

Each of the figures plays a musical instrument—cymbals, double pipe, tambourine, and a string instrument that is probably the lyre. Above the row of musicians is a procession of three animals (quadrupeds) rendered by incisions and low relief. The stand still bears traces of white slip, and the bowl is decorated with a red-and-black lattice pattern. The pattern, the white wash, and the bichrome decoration suggest an affinity with and a continuation of Philistine decoration. The stand should thus be dated—by its stratigraphical context, shape, and decoration—to the end of the Iron Age I.

The Iron Age has yielded an impressive group of ritual stands, some with modeled and incised representations of human and animal figures; the most notable finds are from Megiddo, Beth-Shean, and, most recently, the temple at Tell Qasile (pl. 34). The Ashdod stand, however, is the only one displaying a modeled group of musicians even though drawings, reliefs, and sculptures of musicians are quite common in the ancient Near East and the Aegean. Individual musicians are known from Megiddo VI, which yielded the "Orpheus" jug (chap. 3, fig. 28:1) with its drawing of a musician playing a stringed instrument (possibly a lyre); and from Megiddo IV comes a woman playing a double pipe—she is sculptured on the foot of a bronze lampstand.[60] The closest comparison to our figurines, however, is the pottery figurine of a lyre player (pl. 35) found near a cult place in the lower city of Ashdod and dated to the eighth century B.C.

The Ashdod stand, with its group of musicians, may have been used for libation and was almost certainly related to a cult place. The musicians represented were probably part of a Philistine cult, their role being similar to that of the "Levites which were the singers" in the temple of Jerusalem (2 Chron. 5:12–13). Another biblical passage that may throw light upon the scene represented in the Ashdod stand is 1 Samuel 10:5: "After that thou shalt come to the hill of God, where is the garrison of the Philistines; and it shall come to pass, when thou are come thither to the city, that thou shalt meet a company of prophets coming down from the

58. For a depiction of mourning women, *see*, e.g., a relief of the Nineteenth Dynasty from Egypt, *ANEP*, no. 638. On the sarcophagus of Ahiram, King of Byblos, are carved mourning women; the upper parts of their bodies are naked and two of them hold their hands on their heads (*ANEP*, no. 459) in the manner of the mourning figurines discussed above.

59. Cf. n. 2 above.

60. G. Schumacher, *Tell el Mutesellim*, vol. 1 (Leipzig, 1908), pp. 85 ff., fig. 117; C. Watzinger, *Tell el Mutesellim*, vol. 2 (Leipzig, 1929), pp. 27 ff., fig. 20; and Catling, *Bronzework*, pp. 212–13, pl. 37:e.

Pl. 33. Stand with musicians, Ashdod (three views) [From the Collection of the Israel Department of Antiquities and Museums, 68-1182. M.Dothan, "The Musicians of Ashdod," *Archaeology* 23 (1970): 310].

Pl. 34. Cult stand, Tell Qasile [From the Collection of the Israel Department of Antiquities and Museums, 76-58. *Qasile IEJ 23*, pl. 16:A].

Pl. 35. Lyre player, Ashdod [From the Collection of the Israel Department of Antiquities and Museums, 63-92. *Ashdod II–III*, pl. LV:1].

high place with a psaltery, and a tabret, and a pipe, and a harp, before them; and they shall prophesy."

SUMMARY

The cult vessels from Ashdod and Gezer, dating from the initial stage of the Sea Peoples' settlement in Philistia, reflect the Aegean background of the Philistines at a time when they were still closely linked with their Aegean homeland. The Ashdoda and mourning figurines, rhyta, kernoi, and bird-shaped vessels all exemplify this phase. At the other extreme, the cult vessels from strata XI–X at Tell Qasile express the assimilation of different influences and the almost total departure from Aegean sources. Whereas some of the Qasile cult vessels continue ideas and techniques of the earlier period (in some cases they are doubtless heirlooms from the older temples), others are innovations and inventions of the local potter, made to accommodate the Qasile cult. The latter vessels incorporate the new stylistic features of the period: red-burnished slip and black—and sometimes white—painted decoration.

The cult vessels clearly illustrate the evolution of the Philistine culture, whose Aegean base was gradually "diluted" by local cultural and religious influence. Moreover, these vessels provide some knowledge of the art of the Early Iron Age, of which no monumental examples have been found and only few small objects.

Philistine cult buildings and temples are now more clearly understood in the light of the discoveries at Tell Qasile and the earlier phase at Ashdod. At Ashdod, the open-air high place (area G) belonging to level XIII included a brick altar and a stone base on which the statue of a god may once have stood. In area H, the apsidal building (part of the northern complex) associated with the Ashdoda figurine may also have been of cultic significance. The remarkable persistence of certain features of the cult is seen in the. eighth-century levels in area D, where the large concentration of these objects attests to the assimilation of the Ashdodites into their local environment. Although they continued to imitate vessels from the Philistine cult tradition, from the ninth to the early seventh centuries they produced predominantly male figures instead of the female figures common in the early phase.

The temples at Tell Qasile show a fusion of architectural styles whose principal elements (see chap. 2, p. 66) are related to those of the well-known Canaanite temples at Lachish and Beth-Shean. Even though very little is known of cult architecture in the Aegean world and its offshoots in the Mediterranean, clear analogies with the Philistine temples may be found in the newly excavated Late Cypriot III temples at Kition in Cyprus, the temple in the citadel of Mycenae, and the newest discovery, the shrines at Phylakopi on Melos (see chap. 2, p. 66).

A further noteworthy analogy with the temple at Mycenae is in the deities represented. The female anthropomorphic figurine from the *favissa* in the Tell Qasile temple, which no doubt represents one of the goddesses worshipped in the temple, resembles, in style and essence, the female figurines from the temple complex at Mycenae. The female deity seems to have been the focus of the cult, although at Qasile the Egyptian-style plaque from temple X, which depicts both male and female silhouettes, suggests the existence of dual worship.

Of the few biblical references to Philistine temples (see pp. 20–21), the verse describing the temple in Gaza torn down by Samson should be noted: "And Samson took hold of the two middle pillars upon which the house stood, and on which it was borne up, of the one with his right hand, and of the other with his left" (Judges 16:20). The temple at Gaza seems to have been of the same type as that at Qasile, for there too two wooden pillars were an essential component of its construction.

The objects connected with the cult of the dead (mourning figurines and figurines standing on kraters) also indicate the Aegean background of the Philistine cult, as will be shown in chapter 5.

5

BURIAL CUSTOMS

Burial customs are generally a sensitive indicator of cultural affinities, and those of the Philistines show the same fusion of Aegean background with Egyptian and local Canaanite elements that distinguishes every other aspect of their culture.

As yet no burial grounds in any of the main Philistine cities, such as Ashdod, have been explored; nonetheless, the cemeteries that can be related to Philistine culture on the basis of tomb contents show great diversity in the manner of interment. In some cases, the Philistines perpetuated the indigenous funerary customs and tomb architecture; in others, they employed foreign modes of burial.[1]

Two contemporary and interrelated features of Philistine burial customs—both of which are borrowed from foreign traditions—are anthropoid clay coffins and rock-cut chamber tombs. The anthropoid coffins are of Egyptian origin, while the rock-cut chamber tombs and some of the associated objects (for example, Philistine pottery) are of Mycenaean origin.

ANTHROPOID BURIALS IN CANAAN

Burial in anthropoid clay coffins in Canaan can be traced from its beginnings in the Late Bronze Age at Deir el-Balaḥ through its appearance at other sites in Canaan and Philistia—specifically, at Tell el-Farʿah, Beth-Shean, Tell Midras (pl. 15), and Lachish, where evidence of this burial practice ranges from the thirteenth to the eleventh centuries B.C. (map 3).[2] We shall

present here a survey of the development of anthropoid coffin burial in Canaan[3] and examine the manner in which the Philistines adapted an originally Egyptian custom; at the same time we shall seek to throw light on another aspect of Philistine settlement in Canaan.

We shall begin our discussion with the cemetery of Deir el-Balaḥ, the earliest in the series. Excavations conducted there by the writer have furnished us with firsthand knowledge of the mode of burial and the associated finds.

Deir el-Balaḥ

The burial ground of Deir el-Balaḥ, south of Gaza, has yielded an outstanding harvest of some forty complete coffins (for example, pl. 2) as well as rich assemblages of funerary objects. These include bronze, faience, and alabaster vessels, Ushabti figurines (pl. 1:9), scarabs, gold jewelry, semiprecious stone beads,

---

1. An as yet isolated example of a completely new mode of burial was found in the cemetery of Azor, where the sudden appearance of cremation about the middle of the eleventh century B.C. may be explained by the arrival of a new ethnic element. This is the earliest Iron Age cremation burial in Palestine and may reflect an Aegean background (*see* chap. 2, p. 75 above).

2. A face mask belonging to a coffin lid from Tell Midras, near Beth-Shean, was found on the surface together with

Late Bronze and Early Iron Age pottery; see N. Tzori, "Archaeological News in Israel," in *Bulletin of the Department of Antiquities of the State of Israel* 4 (1953): 4–5, pl. Ia (Hebrew). A later, tenth to seventh century B.C. extension of this burial custom—not to be dealt with here—comes from three sites in Transjordan—Saḥâb: W. F. Albright, "An Anthropoid Clay Coffin from Saḥâb in Transjordan," *AJA* 36 (1932): 295–306; Amman: J. B. Pritchard, *ANEP supp.* (Princeton, 1969), p. 381:853; and Dibon: ibid., p. 381:851–52, and F. V. Winnet and W. L. Reed, "The Excavations at Dibon (Dhîbân) in Moab, Part II: The Second Campaign, 1952," *AASOR* 36–37 (1964): 58–60.

3. We suggested in "Archaeological Reflections on the Philistine Problem," *Antiquity and Survival* 2, no. 2/3 (1957): 151–64 and in the Hebrew version of *The Philistines and Their Material Culture* (Jerusalem, 1967) that this burial custom began in Canaan with the coming of the Philistines. However, Oren's discussion (*B-SH Cemetery*, pp. 139–50) and the results of our excavations at Deir el-Balaḥ (*Deir el-Balaḥ Qedem 10*, pp. 98–104) prove that there was an early phase of this type of burial in the Late Bronze Age.

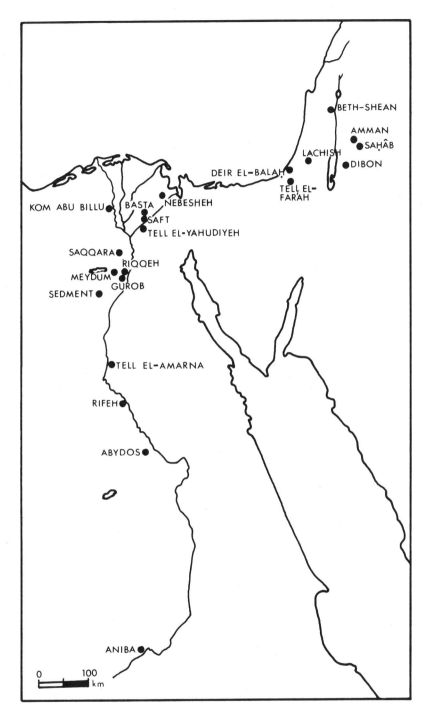

Map 3. Distribution of Main Sites with Anthropoid Coffins

burial stelae, and a large collection of Late Bronze Age pottery—Mycenaean, Cypriot, Egyptian, and local Canaanite—that comes mainly from the thirteenth century B.C.,[4] with probable extensions into the fourteenth and twelfth centuries.

The method of burial and the disposition of the funerary gifts are known from the three burials (tombs 114, 116, and 118) that were uncovered in the course of systematic archaeological excavations (tomb 118; pl. 5:1–2).[5] Unfortunately the vast majority of coffins and many of the other finds were clandestinely unearthed before our work began.

The tombs were constructed on a simple plan. Rectangular graves about 3.25 m. long, 1.70 m. wide, and 1.70 m. deep were roughly cut into the marl following the outline of the coffin. Near the head and alongside the coffin were placed store jars and other large vessels (of Canaanite, Egyptian, Mycenaean, and Cypriot origin [pl. 1:7, 8]). A similar typical Late Bronze Age assemblage of small pottery vessels was found inside the coffin (pl. 1:1–6).

Two or three skeletons were found inside each coffin. There was no evidence of mummification (pl. 5:2). The coffins contained offerings of small pottery vessels as well as more precious gifts of alabaster and bronze. There were also rich finds of gold and carnelian jewelry (pl. 1), pendants, rings, and scarabs—all bearing the stamp of Egyptian influence. The scarabs and seals aid in dating the assemblages to the thirteenth century B.C., the period of Ramesses II.

The following discussion of the typology and iconography of the coffins is based on the complete assemblage from Deir el-Balah.

The Coffins The cylindrical clay coffins range in height from 1.60 m. to 2 m. and have a circumference

of about 1.70 m. to 2.20 m. They taper toward a rounded or square-shaped flat base that in some cases bulges to accommodate the feet (pl. 2). The upper part of the coffin is covered by a removable lid on which the facial features, arms, and hands of the deceased are modeled in high relief. The lids are from 0.40 m. to 0.90 m. high and from 0.50 m. to 0.80 m. wide. They extend only as far as the face or bust and do not extend down to the base (as in the stone or wooden prototypes or the later development of pottery coffins).

The coffins were built up by the coil technique, which was often used in forming large vessels. The lid was cut out of the leather-hard clay before firing so that it fits the opening. In some coffins, a row of small, round holes was pierced along the back, and a round aperture at the top of the "head" rose to a molded pithos-like rim (as in fig. 1);[6] others have a round hole cut out (pl. 4), and still others are completely closed at the top (pl. 3:1–4). The rows of small holes were probably for draining the effluvia of the corpse, while the round aperture has been tentatively explained as a *Seelenloch,* an opening through which the soul could escape.[7]

As all the coffins are very large and brittle, they would have been difficult to transport and were thus locally made, as has also been proven by analysis of their clay.[8] The practice of firing the coffins in an open fire at a low temperature would account for their sometimes friable and mottled material. There is no doubt, however, that far greater care was devoted to the firing and finish of the lids, many of which may have been fired or refired separately at a higher temperature.

Two main groups of coffins can be differentiated on the basis of shape and outline.

Group A. (pl. 3) This group represents a new variant in Canaan and is dominant at Deir el-Balah. The coffins are mummy shaped, and the head and shoulders are delineated in various proportions and silhouettes. The shape follows the traditional outline of Egyptian anthropoid coffins; although in Egypt they are seldom

4. *Deir el Balah IEJ 23,* pp. 129–46 (a discussion of the coffins and associated finds in private collections and museums); I. Perlman, F. Asaro, and Trude Dothan, "Provenance of the Deir el-Balah Coffins," *IEJ* 23 (1973): 147–51.

5. The final report of the writer's excavations at Deir el-Balah, with full documentation of the background of the anthropoid burial customs and comparative Canaanite and Egyptian material in the associated assemblages, appears in *Deir el-Balah Qedem 10.* A study of the coffins and finds dispersed in various museums and private collections is in preparation by the author and B. Brandl. The scarabs of the latter group will be published by R. Giveon of Tel Aviv University, who kindly put at my disposal information on their range and dating. Egyptian-type funerary stelae are being studied by R. Ventura.

6. An interesting coffin of this type without any facial features comes from Tell el-Yahudiyeh in Egypt (see later discussion in this chapter). This coffin is described by Petrie as a debased version of the anthropoid painted coffins. The accompanying offerings range in date from the Nineteenth to the Twenty-third dynasties; see *HIC,* p. 17, pl. XVIIA:4.

7. *B-SH I,* p. 39; *Aniba II,* p. 72.

8. I. Perlman et al., *IEJ* 23 (1973): 147–51.

encountered in pottery, they are well known in wood, cartonnage (molded linen and plaster), and stone.

Group B. (pls. 4, 5) In this type the head and shoulders are not indicated. Only five examples of this group are found at Deir el-Balah, although it is the dominant shape in pottery coffins from Egypt. In Canaan these coffins are confined to Tell el-Far῾ah, Beth-Shean, and Lachish.

Iconography of the Lids The coffin lids differ greatly in style, technique, shape, and workmanship, but two basic iconographic approaches can be distinguished. For convenience we shall designate them as naturalistic and grotesque. At Deir el-Balah the naturalistic type is dominant.

The basic distinguishing feature of the naturalistic lids (pls. 3, 5) is the clearly marked outline of the face, which in some cases is very nearly like sculpture in the round. The face mask, which is smaller or larger than life size, was usually modeled separately and then applied to the lid; then the ears, wig, lotus flower, and beard were added in appliqué. Other details were indented, incised, or painted.

In the grotesque lids (pl. 4), the eyes, eyebrows, nose, mouth, ears, and beard were applied separately to the surface of the lid, and no facial outline was delineated. The lid *is* the face—a fact that gives a somewhat bizarre and caricaturelike effect to the whole (see below, Beth-Shean and Tell el-Far῾ah).

The coffins from Deir el-Balah display a wider spectrum of types and more varied levels of execution than any group of pottery coffins known from Egypt—the home of anthropoid burial—or from Canaan. The more elaborate lids follow Egyptian iconographic canons and are faithful to their more costly prototypes in wood, cartonnage, and stone. Other lids show different degrees of deviation from the original concept, with resulting misinterpretations and debasing of original traits. All the coffins were made locally, some by trained craftsmen well versed in Egyptian tradition, others by potters lacking tradition and skill. Despite all the differences in style, technique, shape, and workmanship, it seems from the three excavated tombs that coffins of diverse types can be contemporaneous and do not necessarily reflect chronological differences.

The cemetery as a whole reflects the cosmopolitan character of the period, although Egyptian elements are predominant in the stelae and small finds, and in the actual practice of burial in anthropoid coffins. Since Deir el-Balah is situated in the heart of the terri-

tory that was under Egyptian control in the Late Bronze Age, the strong Egyptian flavor of the site can easily be understood.

Our subsequent excavations in the 1977–78 seasons revealed a planned settlement of the thirteenth century B.C. buried beneath the sand dunes at the same level as the cemetery. Associated with the two buildings uncovered are ovens and ash-filled pits rich in pottery. On the floors of these brick buildings were found domestic pottery vessels, local painted vessels of the period, and sherds of imported Cypriot and Mycenaean wares. The large quantity of Egyptian-type vessels found all over the area is striking. The unusually large number of stone implements found may point to industrial activities carried out at the site.

The connection between this settlement and the contemporary burials in the cemetery is clear from the pottery assemblages found in each area. However, we do not yet have decisive evidence as to whether this settlement was the dwelling place of those buried in the cemetery or whether it was an artisans' village connected with it.

A previously unknown feature of the site is the newly discovered Philistine occupation, consisting primarily of pits dug into the Late Bronze settlement. These pits contain a high proportion of Philistine pottery compared to the amount of accompanying household wares. The latter are typical of early Iron I, though Egyptian types known from the Late Bronze period (for example, V-shaped bowls, "flower pots," and drop-shaped vessels) are still prominent.

A preliminary study of the stratigraphy and finds suggests that the Philistine occupation had two phases, the first belonging to the late twelfth and first half of the eleventh centuries B.C. and the second belonging to the second half of the eleventh century and beginning of the tenth. Occupation during the tenth century is indicated by surface finds in the excavated area and in the surrounding areas surveyed. Byzantine sherds represent the last phase of settlement before the site was covered by sand dunes.

The discovery of Philistine occupation at Deir el-Balah necessitates a new examination of the finds from the cemetery. Are there any burials of the Iron Age paralleling the Philistine occupation? Further study of the clandestinely excavated material in museums and private collections, and renewed stratigraphic excavations in the area of the cemetery will provide more conclusive evidence.

Pl. 1. Egyptian (**1, 4, 7**), Mycenaean (**3, 6, 8**), and Cypriot vessels, local (**5**), local imitation (**2**), and Ushabti figurine (**9**), Deir el-Balaḥ [Private Collection. *Deir el-Balaḥ IEJ 23*, pls. 43, 44:C, D]. *Below:* Assemblage of jewelry, Deir el-Balaḥ [T. Kollek Collection. *Deir el-Balaḥ IEJ 23*, pl. 45:A, B].

Pl. 2. Group of anthropoid clay coffins, Deir el-Balaḥ [Dayan Collection].

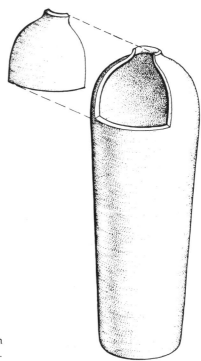

Fig. 1. Clay coffin, Tell el-Yahudiyeh
[*HIC*, pl. XVII, A:4].

Pl. 3. Group A coffin lids, Deir el-Balaḥ [Israel Museum, 71.10.216 and Dayan Collection. *Deir el-Balaḥ IEJ* 23, pls. 34:a; 35:a; 37:A, B].

Pl. 4. Group B coffin lid, Deir el-Balaḥ [Israel Museum,
71.10.217 and Dayan Collection. *Deir el-Balaḥ IEJ 23,* pls. 40,
41].

Pl. 5. Anthropoid coffin from tomb 118 *in situ,* Deir el-Balaḥ (two views, closed and open) [*Deir el-Balaḥ Qedem 10,* ills. 115,
136].

The Philistine settlement dug into the ruins of a typical Egyptianizing site of the thirteenth century seems to confirm the suggested pattern of Philistine settlements on Canaanite sites controlled by Egyptians. After Ramesses III defeated the Sea Peoples (among them the Philistines), he conscripted some of them into the Egyptian army and settled them in Egyptian strongholds in Canaan, such as Tell el-Far'ah and Beth-Shean. It is possible that the cemetery of Deir el-Balaḥ will also fit into the pattern of these two sites where anthropoid pottery coffins were used first for burials of Egyptians or Egyptianized Canaanites and later for Philistines settled in their midst.

Tell el-Far'ah

A fragmentary coffin without a lid was found in the rock-cut chamber tomb 935 in cemetery 900 (chap. 2, n. 51). This tomb is dated by scarabs of Ramesses II to the thirteenth century B.C. and thus parallels the main phase of the Deir el-Balaḥ burials. Cemetery 900 spans the thirteenth and early twelfth centuries, and the latest scarabs in it are of Ramesses IV with a possible extension to Ramesses VIII (see chap. 2, p. 29). The burials contained no Philistine pottery, in contrast to cemetery 500, where this was the dominant feature in the corresponding period.

Two complete anthropoid coffins were found in cemetery 500 (fig. 2) in tombs 552 and 562 (figs. 3, 4, 5, 6), two of the five large, rock-cut chamber tombs[9] that are outstanding in their architectural features, size, and abundance of Philistine pottery. The large rectangular tombs with stepped dromoi reflect Mycenaean burial architecture, which was, as Jane Waldbaum has convincingly argued,[10] disseminated throughout the Mycenaean sphere of influence. We agree with her conclusions as to the Aegean origin of cemetery 500; but we do not accept her attribution of an Aegean derivation to the Late Bronze Age II chamber tombs from cemetery 900 and her interpretation of both cemeteries as products of a group of people from the Aegean. As for cemetery 900, which is similar in style to the Philis-

tine tombs, she claims that there was no continuous architectural development on the site and that cemeteries 500 and 900 arose from two separate phases of one general movement that characterized the latter part of the Bronze Age in the eastern Mediterranean.

We accept Waldbaum's parallels with Mycenae and the Mycenaean world; this affiliation is crucial in tracing the origin of the Philistines before their arrival in Canaan. On the other hand, we question her interpretation of the chamber tombs in cemetery 900; for in order to prove the absence of any native prototype of rectangular chambers in Canaan in the Late Bronze Age, she attributes cemetery 900 to "some enclave of refugees or mercenary Mycenaeans," doing so on the sole basis of a "small quantity of such [Mycenaean] pottery in the tombs." This suggestion, which would link the appearance of rectangular rock-cut tombs with an early wave of Sea Peoples, does not seem feasible to us, since the tombs and the Mycenaean material contained in them are of a type known in other thirteenth century B.C. sites in Canaan. Tomb 935, in which the coffin was found, is a clear continuation of the bilobate chamber tombs originating in the Middle Bronze Age. It thus belongs to a different line of development—a local one. However, the reservation—expressed by S. Loffreda[11] and W. H. Stiebing[12]—concerning the Mycenaean influence on the establishment of the five large rock-cut chamber tombs cannot be dismissed. Waldbaum's arguments for the Mycenaean antece-

11. S. Loffreda, "Typological Sequence of Iron Age Rock-Cut Tombs in Palestine," *LA* 18 (1968): 282–87 summarizes the development of the chamber tomb and emphasizes the importance of Tell el-Far'ah as a type site for the study of the evolution of rock-cut chamber tombs from the Late Bronze to the Iron Age, with special emphasis on the origin of the Philistine chamber tombs from Tell el-Far'ah. In his view, the Philistine tomb represents the end of a long, homogeneous tradition of funerary architecture, and he suggests that its evolution toward the bench tomb was speeded up under some foreign—possibly Cypriot—stimulus.

12. W. H. Stiebing, Jr., "Another Look at the Origins of the Philistine Tombs at Tell el-Far'ah (S)," *AJA* 74 (1970): 139–43. Unaware of Loffreda's basic study, Stiebing attempts to prove that this type of tomb is not a new phenomenon but has a long local history. He goes too far, however, in his rejection of the association of the cemetery 500 chamber tombs with the arrival of the Philistines; nor does he take into account the special character of the five tombs under discussion, although he is correct in considering the cemetery 900 group as a local development and not as another proof of an earlier wave of Sea Peoples.

9. For a detailed discussion of the chronology of the tombs in cemetery 500, *see* chap. 2, pp. 29–33. W. F. Albright was the first to treat the entire problem of the anthropoid coffins in their regional setting within the context of the relevant Tell el-Far'ah tombs. *See* his "An Anthropoid Clay Coffin from Sahâb in Trans-Jordan," *AJA* 36 (1932): 299–301.

10. J. C. Waldbaum, "Philistine Tombs at Tell Fara and their Aegean Prototypes," *AJA* 70 (1966): 331–40.

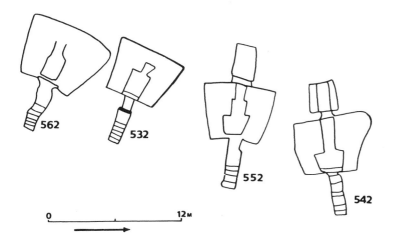

0   12 M

Fig. 2. Plan of cemetery 500, Tell el-Farʿah [*BP I*, pl. LXIV].

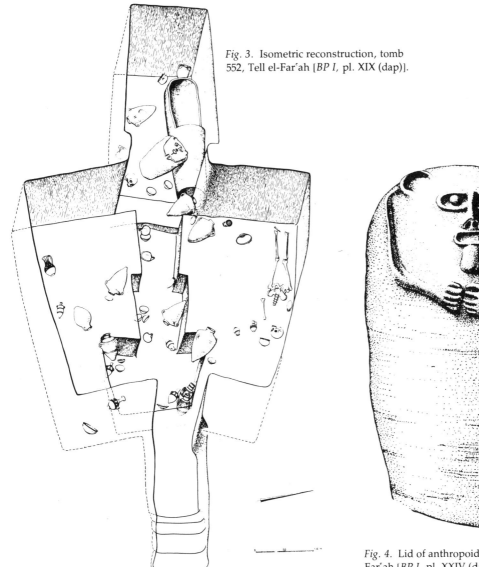

Fig. 3. Isometric reconstruction, tomb 552, Tell el-Farʿah [*BP I*, pl. XIX (dap)].

Fig. 4. Lid of anthropoid coffin, tomb 552, Tell el-Farʿah [*BP I*, pl. XXIV (dap)].

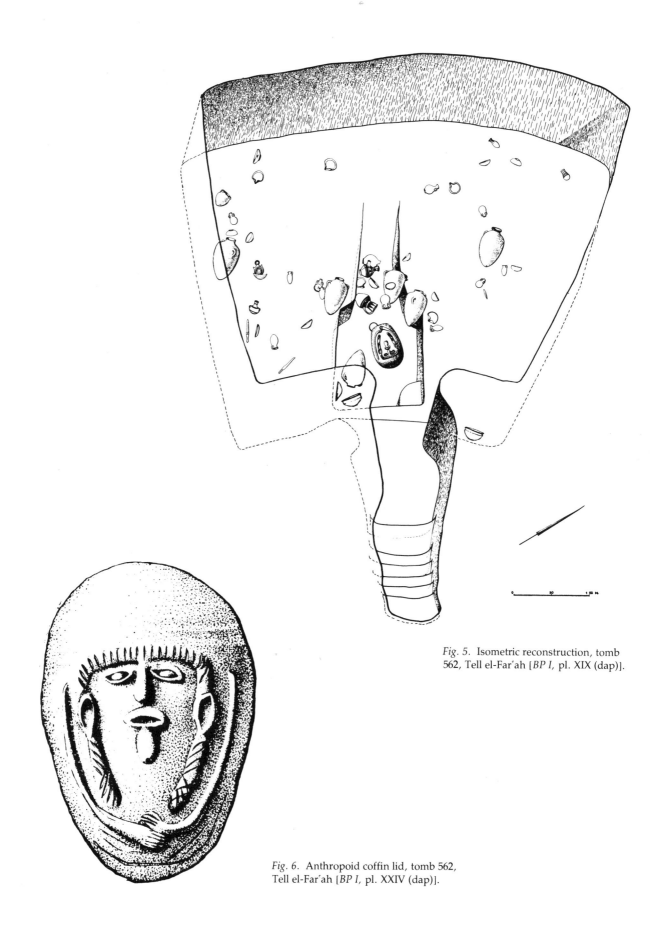

Fig. 5. Isometric reconstruction, tomb 562, Tell el-Farʿah [*BP I*, pl. XIX (dap)].

Fig. 6. Anthropoid coffin lid, tomb 562, Tell el-Farʿah [*BP I*, pl. XXIV (dap)].

dents of cemetery 500 seem to be correct, and we can conclude that although rock-cut chamber tombs are known in Canaan from the Middle Bronze Age onward, the tombs in cemetery 500 are exceptional in both plan and size and are the result of foreign stimuli of Aegean origin.

In tomb 562 the lid of the coffin had been thrown into the entrance of the chamber, and the coffin itself was lying on the left shelf (not shown by Petrie in his plan of the tomb [fig. 5]). In tomb 552 the coffin lay in its original position in the antechamber (fig. 3) although the lid had been removed, no doubt in antiquity by grave robbers searching for jewelry and other precious objects that had been placed in the coffin with the dead, as our excavations of undisturbed coffin burials at Deir el-Balaḥ showed.

The Tell el-Farʿah coffins are of the Group B type, with no delineation of shoulders or opening at the top. The lids, ineptly modeled in the grotesque style with an Osiris beard, are far removed from the deliberate exaggeration of the Beth-Shean grotesque lids (see pls. 20, 21 below).

The lid from tomb 552 (fig. 4, pl. 6) bears no trace of a wig. The ears are placed high on the head and are more animallike than human. The sticklike arms, with clenched hands meeting below the stylized Osiris beard, frame the crude features of the face. The lid from tomb 562 (fig. 6, pl. 8) shows a debased version of a wig made in a combination of appliqué and deep incisions with oval ears incorporated. The sticklike arms with overlapping hands follow the curving line of the wig and frame the face. An unusual feature is a round indentation at the base of the Osiris beard.

Tombs 552 and 562 contain homogeneous assemblages (figs. 7, 8, pls. 7, 9) spanning a period from the twelfth century to the first half of the eleventh century B.C. Tomb 562 is the later tomb, as is attested by the debased character of its Philistine pottery (see chap. 2, p. 32). The pottery of these two tombs combines four different ceramic traditions:

1. Pottery characteristic of the local Canaanite tradition, which continues into the Early Iron Age (figs. 7:1–13, 8:1–4, 6–15).

2. A representative group of Philistine vessels, including Egyptianizing long-necked jugs (figs. 7:19–21, 8:5, 16, 19, 20).

3. Vessels showing reciprocal Canaanite-Egyptian influence (fig. 7:14–18).

4. A group of locally made vessels imitating Egyptian pottery forms (fig. 8:17, 18).

Groups 3 and 4 are of special importance for the study of the ceramic repertoire connected with anthropoid burials in both Canaan and Egypt.

Among the more striking examples of reciprocal Canaanite-Egyptian influence (group 3) from tomb 552 are two identical jars (fig. 7:14, 15), which follow the decorative tradition of local Late Bronze Canaanite potters. The Egyptianizing element in these jars is the high, bulging neck, while the vessel itself was surely derived from the Canaanite jar, which was adopted by the Egyptians (fig. 18:14) and reappeared in Canaan as an Egyptian import[13] (at, for example, Deir el-Balaḥ) in association with anthropoid coffin burials. A similar process can be traced in the group of amphoriskoi (fig. 7:16–18), which are distinguished by high, bulging necks and button bases. These three examples represent a late evolutionary stage and a degeneration of the type, which is known in Canaan at the end of the thirteenth century B.C.[14] Parallels have been found at two sites in Egypt—Gurob[15] and Tell el-Yahudiyeh—as well as at Aniba in Nubia. In the last two sites they appear in conjunction with anthropoid burials (figs. 18:4, 19:6).

Although as a pottery vessel this type is rare in Egypt, its Egyptian origin may be postulated on the basis of its frequent appearance in the large collection of Egyptian glass amphoriskoi known in Egypt during the Eighteenth Dynasty[16] and found in Canaan as imports in the Late Bronze Age.[17] It may therefore be conjectured that the pottery amphoriskoi are imitations of the glass ones. This is further evidenced by the unique button base common in glassware as a result of glass-working techniques. The main significance of these amphoriskoi lies in their appearance in an-

13. V. Grace, "The Canaanite Jar," in *Aegean and the Near East,* pp. 80–109, pls. IX–XII.

14. Examples of this type of amphoriskos are known from Tell Jemmeh: *Gerar,* pl. LXIV:49; Tell Zakariyah: E. T. Richmond, "Selected Types of Iron Age and Hellenistic Pottery," *PMB* 4 (1927): pl. III:1; and Beth-Shemesh: *BS,* tomb 1, pl. 177:3.

15. *Gurob,* pls. XXVII:13, XXVIII, Type 48D from tomb 473.

16. *See,* for example, P. Fossing, *Glass Vessels Before Glass Blowing* (Copenhagen, 1940), p. 11; F. Neuburg, *Glass in Antiquity* (London, 1949), pls. II:3, VII:19.

17. *Lachish II,* pl. XXIV:77, 80, 83.

Pl. 6. Anthropoid clay coffin lid, Tell el-Farʿah, tomb 552, in fig. 4 [From the Collection of the Israel Department of Antiquities and Museums, I. 5662].

Pl. 7. Pottery assemblage, Tell el-Farʿah, in fig. 7 [Institute of Archaeology, London].
1. See fig. 7:4.   **2.** See fig. 7:19.   **3.** See fig. 7:3.   **4.** See fig. 7:10.   **5.** See fig. 7:13.   **6.** See fig. 7:20.   **7.** See fig. 7:15.   **8.** See fig. 7:7.   **9.** See fig. 7:18.   **10.** See fig. 7:2.

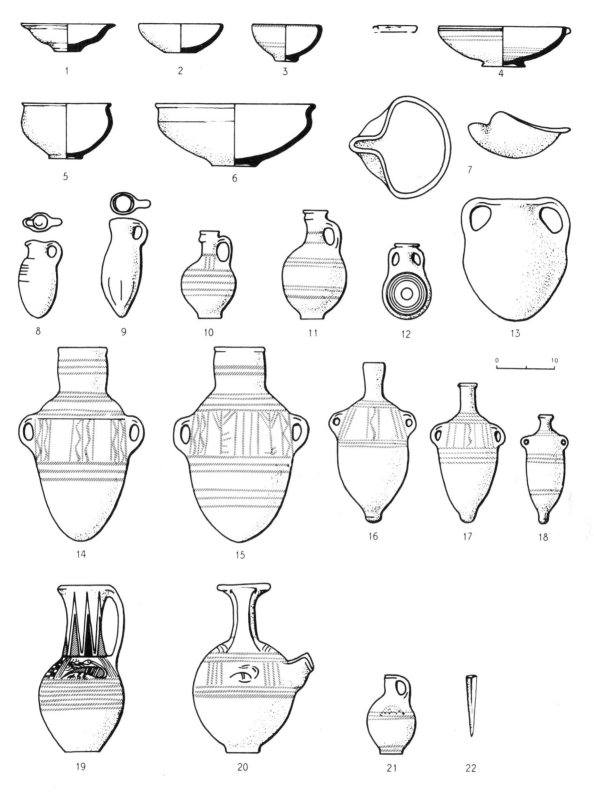

Fig. 7. Assemblage from tomb 552, Tell el-Farʿah [drawn from *CPP*].

1. [3 A2]   **2.** [12 V3]   **3.** [15 N2]   **4.** [20 P]   **5.** [28 X2]   **6.** [23 J14]   **7.** [91 J5]   **8.** [50 N2]   **9.** [50 G2]   **10.** [65 D2]   **11.** [65 D4]   **12.** [85 H12]   **13.** [33 Q5]   **14.** [44 R1]   **15.** [44 R2]   **16.** [55 W4]   **17.** [55 W6]   **18.** [55 W8]   **19.** [34 Y4]   **20.** [Add. 67 D5]   **21.** [59 T]   **22.** [*BP I*, pl. XXI:92]

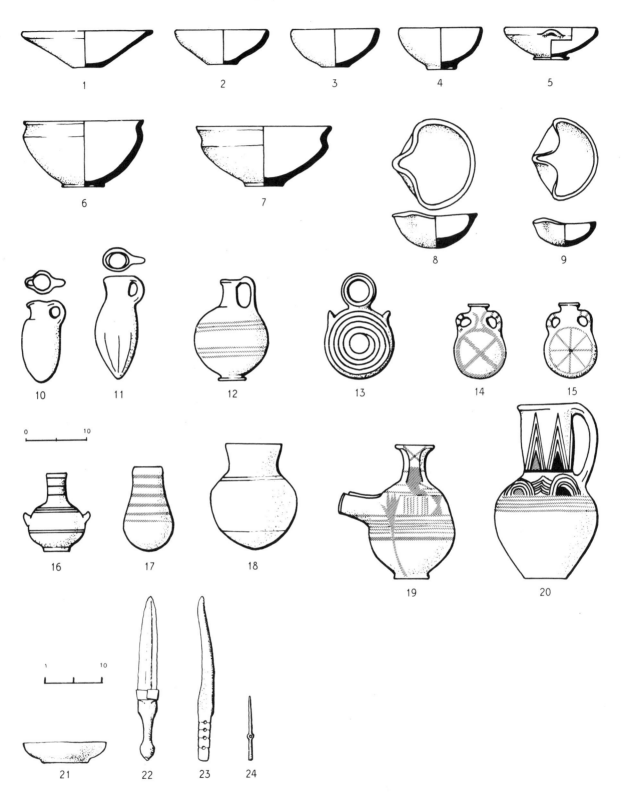

Fig. 8. Assemblage from tomb 562, Tell el-Farʿah [drawn from *CPP*].
1. [6 F]   **2.** [12 T]   **3.** [12 V3]   **4.** [22 E1]   **5.** [24 04]   **6.** [24 D3]   **7.** [23 K3]   **8.** [91 C3]   **9.** [91 F1]   **10.** [50 N2]   **11.** [50 F]   **12.** [59 N1]   **13.** [85 08]   14. [85 H17]   **15.** [85 N6]   **16.** [55 T8]   **17.** [75 N2]   **18.** [41 F]   **19.** [Add. 67N]   **20.** [34 Y4]   **21.** [*BP I*, pl. XXI:97]   **22.** [*BP I*, pl. XXI:94]   **23.** [*BP I*, pl. XXI:96]   **24.** [*BP I*, pl. XXI:95]

Pl. 8. Anthropoid clay coffin lid, Tell el-Far'ah, tomb 562, in fig. 6.

Pl. 9. Pottery assemblage, Tell el-Far'ah, in fig. 8 [Institute of Archaeology, London].
1. See fig. 8:8.   **2.** See fig. 8:17.   **3.** See fig. 8:19.
4. See fig. 8:20.   **5.** See fig. 8:15.   **6.** See fig. 8:14.
7. See fig. 8:7.   **8.** See fig. 8:13.

thropoid burials of Canaanite, Egyptian, and Nubian types and in their Egyptian and Canaanite features.

Purely Egyptian in form (group 4) are the handleless vessels (fig. 8:17, 18) from tomb 562. One (no. 17) is a drop-shaped, hole-mouth jar decorated with red stripes; the other (no. 18) is a necked globular jar. Both shapes are typical of Egyptian pottery, in which tradition they have a long history (figs. 18:1, 17, 19:4, 5). The Deir-el Balaḥ cemetery has yielded a large number of vessels like these, some of which are Egyptian imports, while others are local imitations (pl. 1:2). In the Iron Age, only isolated examples appear in Canaan, the latest coming from Tell Qasile stratum X (see chap. 2, fig. 9).

In addition to the wealth of pottery in these tombs, there are also bronze and iron objects (bronze: figs. 7:22, 8:21, 24; iron: fig. 8:22, 23); the latter represent some of the earliest appearances of iron in Philistine assemblages.

At Tell el-Farʿah, we see that the practice of burial in anthropoid coffins first appeared in the thirteenth century B.C. in tomb 935. Tombs 552 and 562 indicate that in certain cases anthropoid coffins were adopted by the Philistines, although they did not become common, as the proportionately greater number of Philistine tombs containing plain burials attest.

Tombs 552 and 562, although they were disturbed by robbers in antiquity, contained no intrusive burials and no trace of any finds earlier than the twelfth century. There is therefore no concrete proof for the suggestion that the coffins are intrusive and represent an early phase in the use of these tombs. There is no question that the coffins in these tombs must be related to the Iron Age.[18]

Beth-Shean

About fifty anthropoid coffins were discovered in eleven funeral deposits in the Northern Cemetery of Beth-Shean.[19] They can be dated by the associated finds to the period ranging from the thirteenth to the eleventh centuries B.C. Only two coffins could be reconstructed. The others were found smashed and scattered all over the area of tombs and intermixed with bones and funerary offerings. The coffins had been laid in disused Early Bronze Age IV tombs and were badly damaged by later Roman and Byzantine burials. Hence it was impossible to attribute skeletal remains or grave goods to specific sarcophagi, although some of the assemblages of the tomb groups could be restored.

All the coffins are of the cylindrical slipper-shaped type, and in outline belong to Group B (undelineated shoulders). The majority of the lids are naturalistic (pls. 11–14); five are of the grotesque type (pls. 16–21). Here the contrast between the naturalistic and the grotesque lids is much sharper than at Deir el-Balaḥ.

The naturalistic lids first appeared at Beth-Shean in the thirteenth century and continued into the Iron Age (twelfth and eleventh centuries). They have analogies at Deir el-Balaḥ, but are much more limited stylistically. Rather surprisingly, the Beth-Shean lids show no clear representations of the Osiris beard that is so common on the coffin groups of Deir el-Balaḥ, Tell el-Farʿah, and Lachish.

Of the five coffins with grotesque lids, one comes from tomb 66 and four from tomb 90 (figs. 9, 10, pls. 16, 19).[20] The facial features of all five are boldly stylized and naively exaggerated, probably the result of intentional stylization rather than artistic ineptitude (as at Tell el-Farʿah). The high-ridged nose is applied, the mouth is a horizontal deep groove, and the chin is only faintly indicated. The sticklike arms and hands, beginning near the top of the head, are bent at the elbows, and the hands have outstretched fingers touching below the mouth. Incised grooves near the wrists and above the elbows may represent bracelets (fig. 11:1, 3).

The distinctive feature of this group of lids is the appliqué headdress, which consists of plain horizontal bands, rows of knobs, zigzag patterns, and vertical fluting. These patterns are arranged differently on each lid. Five variations are found:

---

18. E. Oren in his discussion has suggested that the tombs were disturbed and that, consequently, an association between the anthropoid coffins and the Philistine pottery contained in them cannot be proven. See *B-SH Cemetery*, esp. p. 141 and the discussion below.

19. The report of the Northern Cemetery of Beth-Shean by E. Oren provides a full picture of the anthropoid coffins and the associated finds (*see* n. 3 above). We have based our conclusions on his study, as well as on our examination of the material itself in the University Museum at Philadelphia (with the kind permission of J. B. Pritchard).

20. Both tombs are chamber tombs and show (albeit somewhat unclearly) architectural affinities with the Aegean rock-cut chamber tombs at Tell el-Farʿah. We cannot press the suggestion that the change in funerary architecture here is connected with the arrival of the Philistines; however, there is a possibility that the tombs were dug anew to make room for the anthropoid sarcophagi.

Pl. 10. Naturalistic anthropoid coffin lids, Beth-Shean [University Museum, Pennsylvania. F. W. James, "Beth Shan," *Expedition* 3 (1961): 34].

Pl. 11. Coffin lid from tomb 66c, Beth-Shean [From the Collection of the Israel Department of Antiquities and Museums, P. 3337].

Pl. 12. Coffin *in situ* from tomb 66c, Beth-Shean [*B-SH Cemetery,* fig. 63:2].

Pl. 15. Naturalistic anthropoid coffin lid,
Tell Midras [From the Collection of the Is-
rael Department of Antiquities and
Museums, 51-138].

Pl. 13. Naturalistic anthropoid coffin lid,
Beth-Shean [*B-SH I*, pl. 39:1].

Pl. 14. Naturalistic anthropoid coffin lids, Beth-Shean [From the Collection of the Israel Department of Antiquities and
Museums, P. 1722, P. 1721].

Pl. 17. Anthropoid coffin, tomb 66,
Beth-Shean (two views) [From the Col-
lection of the Israel Department of
Antiquities and Museums, P. 1433-4.
B-SH I, pl. 37].

Pl. 16. Anthropoid coffin *in situ*, tomb 66,
Beth-Shean [*B-SH Cemetery*, fig. 62:2].

Pl. 18. Grotesque coffin lid, tomb 66, Beth-Shean (two views) [From the Collection of the Israel Department of Antiquities and Museums, P. 1434].

Pl. 19. Anthropoid coffins *in situ*, tomb 90, Beth-Shean [*B-SH Cemetery*, fig. 62:1].

Pl. 20. Grotesque coffin lid, tomb 90, Beth-Shean [From the Collection of the Israel Department of Antiquities and Museums, P. 1431].

Pl. 21. Grotesque coffin lid, tomb 90, Beth-Shean (two views) [*B-SH I*, pl. 38:3, 4].

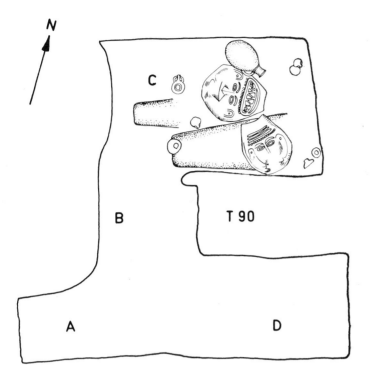

N

C

B

T 90

A

D

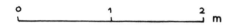

o   1   2
                           m

Fig. 9. Plan of tomb 90, Beth-Shean
[*B-SH Cemetery,* fig. 9].

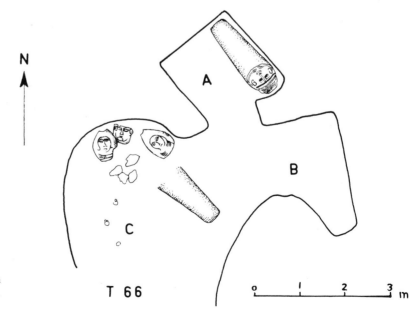

N

A

B

C

T 66

o   1   2   3
                        m

Fig. 10. Plan of tomb 66, Beth-Shean
[*B-SH Cemetery,* fig. 12].

1. Plain horizontal band between rows of knobs, crowned by vertical fluting, representing feathers, reeds, or leather strips standing up from the ornamental band (fig. 11:2, pl. 18).

2. Three plain bands with two rows of knobs (fig. 12:2).

3. A row of knobs between plain bands crowned by a diademlike zigzag pattern (fig. 11:3, pl. 21).

4. A single row of knobs beneath two plain horizontal bands (fig. 11:1, pl. 20).

5. A single row of knobs beneath three plain horizontal bands (fig. 12:1).

This unique headgear (for which no analogies have been found on anthropoid coffins in Canaan or Egypt) may be identical with the feathered cap worn by the Peleset, Tjekker, and Denyen depicted on the wall reliefs of Ramesses III at Medinet Habu in Egypt (see fig. 11:4–6 and chap. 1, figs. 1–3).[21] Confirmation for this proposal can be seen in the most complete representation, on the lid from tomb 66 (fig. 11:2), where the vertical bands are an exact stylized depiction of the circle of feathers, reeds, leather strips, or whatever standing upright from the ornamental band.

The Sea Peoples portrayed at Medinet Habu wear a cap that fits around the back of the head as a neck guard and is held in place by a strap tied under the chin. It is decorated with an ornamental band, probably a metal diadem,[22] from which a circle of feathers, reeds, or leather strips projects. The diadems of the Sea Peoples bear combinations of plain horizontal strips, rows of knobs, and zigzag patterns—all of which are represented on the Beth-Shean coffin lids. The specific Beth-Shean combination of zigzag and knobs does not appear at Medinet Habu, and certain Medinet Habu variations, such as the horizontal or slanting rectangle motifs, do not appear at Beth-Shean. It is possible that these different combinations were insignia of military rank or designated membership in a particular tribe or clan (see chap. 1, n. 50).

Two other depictions of warriors with headgear very similar to the Medinet Habu representations (see

chap. 1, p. 13) were found at Enkomi. Both can be dated to the first half of the twelfth century B.C. The first (fig. 13), part of a hunting scene carved in relief on an ivory game box, shows a bearded arms bearer wearing a feather headdress identical to those in the Medinet Habu scenes. The second (fig. 14), which was engraved on a conical stone seal found in the occupation level of the Sea Peoples, depicts a kneeling, bearded soldier bearing a round shield with a spiked boss in the center and wearing a feather crown. In both depictions, the headband is a single row of knobs identical with the Beth-Shean and Medinet Habu bands. Both the seal and the game box should probably be attributed to the settlement of the Sea Peoples (perhaps the Tjekker) who arrived in Cyprus in the early twelfth century B.C.

The headgear provides decisive evidence that the bodies buried in the grotesque coffins at Beth-Shean were Sea Peoples, most likely Philistines. There seems no reason to identify them with any other group of Sea Peoples, such as the Denyen,[23] since both the biblical and the archaeological evidence support their identification as Philistines. The Bible (1 Sam. 31:8–13; 1 Chron. 10:9–12) relates that Beth-Shean was occupied by the Philistines, and that the bodies of Saul and his sons were displayed on its walls after their defeat at the battle of Gilboa in the last quarter of the eleventh century B.C.

The archaeological evidence also dates these coffins to the period of Saul; the fullest representation of the headdress, as we have seen, comes from a clear Iron Age context in tomb 66 (fig. 10). Along with other finds a debased Philistine strainer-spout jug helps to date tomb 66 to the second half of the eleventh and the beginning of the tenth century, when Philistine pottery was already on the wane (see chap. 2, fig. 13:4— late level VI on the mound). The other four grotesque coffins were found in tomb 90, which, although first used in the Late Bronze Age, is predominantly Iron Age in date. That these coffins were deposited in the Iron Age, in the second half of the eleventh century B.C., is clear from a photograph (pl. 19) showing two of the grotesque coffins *in situ*; a globular Iron Age flask

---

21. Ranke was the first to draw attention to the resemblance between the headgear on the coffin lids of Beth-Shean and the headgear of some of the Sea Peoples on Egyptian monuments (as noted in Pritchard, *Palestinian Figurines in Relation to Certain Goddesses Known Through Literature* [New Haven, 1943], p. 39).

22. For gold diadems, *see*, e.g., *Meg. II*, pl. 227:5; *AG III*, pls. XIV:6, XV.

23. As suggested by Oren in *B-SH Cemetery*, pp. 138, 149. He does not take into account the pure Iron Age context of tomb 66, nor the predominantly Iron Age context of tomb 90 and the association of Iron Age pottery with the grotesque lids. He accepts the identification of this group with the Sea Peoples, but disregards the most obvious candidate of this group, the Philistines.

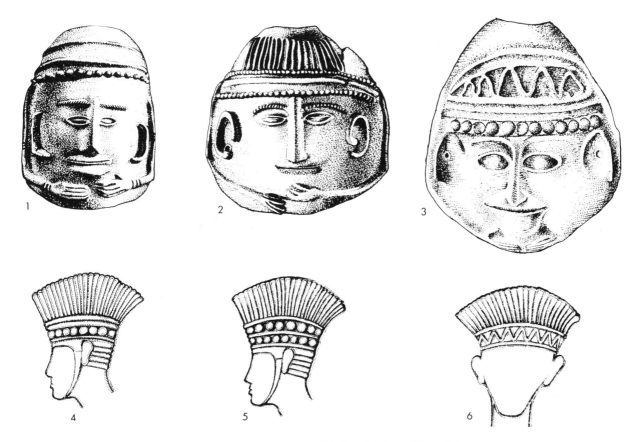

Fig. 11. Anthropoid coffin lids from tombs 90 and 66 and parallels from Medinet Habu reliefs.
1. [*B-SH Cemetery*, fig. 52:2, tomb 90C]   2. [*B-SH Cemetery*, fig. 53:4, tomb 66]   3. [*B-SH Cemetery*, fig. 52:3, tomb 90C]   4–6. Detail from depiction of Sea Peoples (see chap. 1, fig. 7).

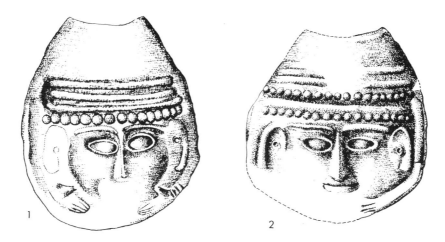

Fig. 12. Anthropoid coffin lids from tomb 90, Beth-Shean.   1. [*B-SH Cemetery*, fig. 52:1, tomb 90C]   2. [*B-SH Cemetery*, fig. 52:4, tomb 90]

lies in its original position beside the lid of one of them. The flask is typical of the second half of the eleventh century and has close analogies at Tell Qasile stratum X, Beth-Shean late level VI, and Megiddo stratum VIA (see chap. 2, figs. 9, 13, 14).

There remains the problem of the scarcity of Philistine pottery at Beth-Shean. From Frances James's publication of the Iron Age material it is evident that Philistine pottery, though scanty, did exist at Beth-Shean and that by late level VI (second half of the eleventh century, corresponding to the grotesque coffins), it had already degenerated and been assimilated into the local ware. The pottery would seem to fit the date indicated by the biblical references to Beth-Shean, as well as the Canaanite-Philistine stratum VI at Megiddo and stratum X at Tell Qasile, both of which were probably destroyed by David.

It is now evident that the custom of burial in anthropoid coffins began at Beth-Shean during level VII on the mound, in the thirteenth century B.C., *before* Philistine settlement in Canaan; thus its first appearance there cannot be attributed to them, as was previously assumed. The custom was probably introduced by Egyptian officials or mercenaries stationed in Beth-Shean when it was an Egyptian stronghold. The grotesque coffins show that, as at Tell el-Farʿah, this type of burial was taken over by the Philistines and continued through level VI to the beginning of the tenth century B.C.

Lachish

Two anthropoid clay coffins came from a disturbed tomb (no. 570) that (with the adjacent tomb 571) was cut into the side of the Middle Bronze fosse.[24] The coffins have crudely modeled lids in the naturalistic style (fig. 15, pls. 22, 23). One bears a painted hieroglyphic inscription (fig. 15, pl. 24) and crude depictions of the Egyptian deities Isis and Nephthys. Egyptologists have concluded that the inscription is a row of pseudo-Egyptian hieroglyphs written by an unskilled scribe who was trying to copy the ancient formulae.[25] This is the sole Canaanite example of an inscribed cof-

fin, although painted decoration occurs at Deir el-Balaḥ. Despite the great similarity between the assemblages of tombs 570 and 571, a number of crucial differences compel us to date tomb 571 somewhat earlier than tomb 570. Most of the ceramic contents of the former correspond to Fosse Temple III, whereas contents of the latter (fig. 16), although they still preserve something of the Late Bronze ceramic tradition, have none of the typical features of this period that are found in tomb 571.

Tomb 570 appears to correspond to a habitation level following the destruction of stratum VI and Fosse Temple III. It may belong to an elusive and more limited occupation level of the twelfth century.[26] Evidence for the existence of such a level includes, inter alia, numerous pits whose ceramic contents recall Tell Beit Mirsim stratum B_1,[27] a number of tombs later than level VI and Fosse Temple III,[28] a scarab of Ramesses III,[29] and the Philistine sherds from cave 4034, pit B,[30] which give the latest extension of this phase. Thus the Lachish tomb overlaps the final phase of the Deir el-Balaḥ tombs, is contemporary with some of the Beth-Shean tombs, and precedes the Tell el-Farʿah Philistine tombs. This sequence would agree with the assumption that the destruction of the Late Canaanite

24. C. H. Inge, "Excavations at Tell ed-Duweir," *PEQ* 70 (1938): 246–47, pl. XXII. L. Hennequin, "Trois Sarcophages anthropoïdes en poterie trouvés à Tell Douweir (Palestine)," in *Mélanges Syriens offerts à Monsieur René Dussaud*, vol. 2 (Paris, 1939), pp. 965 ff. *Lachish III*, p. 219, pl. 126; *Lachish IV*, pp. 36, 66, 68, 131–32, 248–50, pls. 45:1–3, 46.

25. *Lachish IV*, pp. 131–32.

26. Trude Dothan, Review of Olga Tufnell, *Lachish IV*, *IEJ* 10 (1960): 62–63.

27. *Lachish II*, p. 23; *Lachish III*, p. 52.

28. *Lachish IV*, pp. 66, 68.

29. The scarab (*Lachish IV*, p. 126, pl. 39:388) was found in a dump east of the palace fort (locus J15, *Lachish IV*, p. 132; *Lachish III*, pl. 115) and was assigned by the excavator to the last phase of level VI. In examining the description of its location, the writer discovered that the picture that evolves is extremely unclear (see *Lachish III*, pp. 46, 51 and *Lachish IV*, pp. 37, 98, 132). In the same area were found a scarab of Ramesses II (*Lachish III*, p. 51; *Lachish IV*, pp. 98, 126, 132, pls. 39, 40, no. 389), fragments of a Late Minoan octopus vase and a Mycenaean chariot krater (*Lachish IV*, pp. 132, 213–14, pl. 83:949, 951), and also four bowl fragments bearing hieratic inscriptions (*Lachish IV*, pl. 44:3–6). The most important of them is no. 3, which mentions the fourth year of a ruler. Suggestions for the pharaoh in question range from Merneptah to as late as the period of Ramesses IV (*Lachish IV*, pp. 37, 133).

An additional fragment of a hieratic inscription was discovered in the foundation fill of palace A. According to M. Gilula it dates to the thirteenth and twelfth centuries B.C., mentioning the regnal year 10 to 19, but the king's name is missing. D. Ussishkin, Notes and News, *IEJ* 24 (1974): 272; idem, "Excavations at Tel Lachish, 1973–1977, Preliminary Report," *Tel Aviv* 5 (1978): 92.

30. *Lachish III*, pl. 128; *Lachish IV*, pp. 291–93, pl. 8:6.

Fig. 13. Warrior of the Sea Peoples on an ivory game box, Enkomi [A. S. Murray and H. B. Walters, *Excavations in Cyprus* (London, 1900), pl. I, fig. 19].

Fig. 14. Warrior of the Sea Peoples on a conical seal, Enkomi [*Enkomi Excavations*, vol. IIIa, frontispiece].

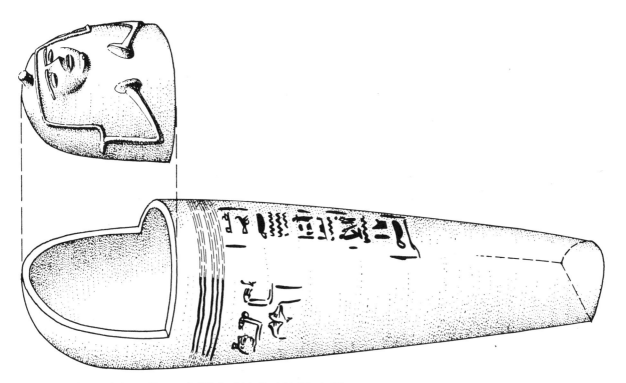

Fig. 15. Anthropoid clay coffin, tomb 570, Lachish [*Lachish IV*, pl. 46].

Pl. 22. Anthropoid coffin lid, tomb 570, Lachish (two views) [Institute of Archaeology, London].

Pl. 23. Anthropoid coffin lid, tomb 570, Lachish [Institute of Archaeology, London].

Pl. 24. Anthropoid coffin with hiero-glyphic inscription, Lachish [From the Collection of the Israel Department of Antiquities and Museums, 38.767].

city (level VI) dates to Ramesses III[31] and that the coffins should be attributed to officers in the Egyptian garrison.

ANTHROPOID BURIALS IN EGYPT

The custom of burial in anthropoid coffins originated in Egypt.[32] Anthropoid coffins and mummy cases first came into use in the Middle Kingdom during the Twelfth Dynasty. The typical mummy of this period, wrapped in heavy bandaging and wearing a mask (sometimes gilded), was the basic form on which the later coffins were modeled. This burial custom continued into the New Kingdom. Mummiform coffins were made of wood or cartonnage. Stone sarcophagi were, as a rule, used only in royal burials. In burials of the rich and aristocratic, the mummy was encased in several coffins, one inside the other.

During the New Kingdom, burial customs that were formerly restricted to the upper classes extended into other levels of society. The mummy cases and coffins were combined, and the features (and, in many cases, the crossed hands) of the deceased were shown on wooden or pottery anthropoid coffins.

Although the published material from Egypt on anthropoid pottery coffins is incomplete, it seems that their use was not very widespread. In the New Kingdom it was concentrated primarily in the Delta area[33] and in Nubia (especially Aniba, fig. 19).[34]

At Kom Abu Billu, a Delta site about 70 km. northwest of Cairo[35] that has recently been explored, the assemblages connected with the burials were pillaged in ancient times—as at most Egyptian sites. Enough remained, however, to demonstrate the wealth of the burial gifts. The pottery published is a combination of Mycenaean, Cypriot, and local Egyptian. There are necklaces of carnelian lotus beads, cosmetic articles such as a bronze mirror, and a wide range of royal scarabs bearing the names of Thutmose I, Thutmose III, Amenhotep II, Seti I, and Ramesses II. The entire assemblage is very like that found at Deir el-Balaḥ (which apparently covers the same period) and at other contemporary sites in the Delta and in Nubia.

In the publication of the finds from Egypt, pottery anthropoid coffins are regarded as burials for the poor who could not afford expensive mummy cases or embalming. Yet it appears from the Egyptian evidence that pottery coffins were also used as mummy cases. Steindorff[36] claims that such coffins were meant to hold mummified bodies, but he fails to mention whether any such bodies were found. Engelbach[37] states with certainty that the Nineteenth Dynasty pottery coffins from Riqqeh contained mummified bodies, and he regarded this fact, as well as the high quality of the amulets found with the bodies, as evidence that burial in these coffins was by no means confined to the lower classes and the poor, as had been generally assumed. It should be remembered that during every period in ancient Egypt, simple coffins were also employed; made of wooden planks, rough mats, or large pottery jars, they provided the very poor with the shelter essential for their life after death.

Deir el-Balaḥ conforms well with the total complex of Egyptian burials of the Eighteenth and Nineteenth dynasties, as seen in the published Egyptian material and the finds in museums and collections. The outstanding features of Deir el-Balaḥ burials are the great

---

31. A cartouche of Ramesses III on a bronze sheet is part of a metal hoard, probably belonging to stratum VI; the hoard was unearthed beneath the Iron Age city gate of stratum IV. This find again raises the problem of the date of the destruction of stratum VI. Further discussion must await the publication of the stratigraphic position of this find and the final reading of the cartouche.

32. For a general discussion, *see*: W. C. Hayes, *The Scepter of Egypt* (New York, 1968), pt. 1, pp. 303–12; pt. 2, pp. 29–31, 69–71, 221–23, 414–20. *See also* I. E. S. Edwards, *A General Guide to the Egyptian Collection of the British Museum* (London, 1971), pp. 148 ff.

33. Albright, *AJA* 36 (1932): 301–06; Trude Dothan (*see* nn. 3, 4 above); *B-SH Cemetery*, pp. 142–46.

34. For the most important site in Nubia, see *Aniba II*, pp. 72 ff., pls. 39d–e, 40: 1–3. Here anthropoid clay-coffin burials of the Nineteenth and Twentieth dynasties were uncovered, together with the eclectic assemblages of local Egyptian (*see here* fig. 19:3–5, 7, 8), Cypriot, Mycenaean (fig. 19:10), and Canaanite vessels (*see here* fig. 19:11, 12).

35. J. Leclant, "Fouilles et travaux en Egypte et au Soudan

1969–1970 (6. Kôm Abû Billou)," *Orientalia* 40 (1971): 227–28, pls. XX:4, XXIV:11; S. Farid, "Preliminary Report on the Excavations of the Antiquities Department at Kôm Abû Billou," *Annales du service des antiquités de l'Egypte*, 61 (1973): 21–26, pls. I–XII.

36. *Aniba II*, p. 72.

37. R. Engelbach, *Riqqeh and Memphis, vol. VI* (London, 1915), p. 18. Mummified bodies in anthropoid clay coffins were also discovered at Asfûnul-Matâ'neh; *see* H. S. K. Bakry, "Asfûnul-Matâ'neh Sondages," *Annales du service des antiquités de l'Egypte* 61 (1973): 1 ff. Except for those at Deir el-Balaḥ, the Palestinian coffin burials have yielded no skeletons in coffins and no traces of mummification; thus the problem remains unresolved.

diversity of the coffins, the large proportion of mummy-shaped specimens, and the relatively high artistic level. The Deir el-Balaḥ coffins are not paralleled in Egypt, and they are also far superior to the usual level of contemporary burials in Canaan. The intact burials at Deir el-Balaḥ illustrate how some of the Egyptian burials must have looked before they were looted in antiquity. Such burials may have been associated with a certain class of officials, military or administrative, both in Egypt and in Canaan.

From the Twentieth Dynasty in Egypt (the period relevant to our discussion) we find at Tell el-Yahudiyeh and Nebesheh clear evidence of assemblages that were partly foreign to Egypt but analogous to those at Tell el-Farʿah (S) and Beth-Shean.

Tell el-Yahudiyeh

Tombs containing anthropoid clay coffins were discovered in eight tumuli in a desert cemetery within sight of the mound at Tell el-Yahudiyeh.[38] This group of coffins is discussed in detail in F. Griffith's report published in 1890. His excellent presentation of the scene and the finds and his dating of the assemblage to the Twentieth Dynasty have stood the test of time and remain unchallenged. Not so E. Naville's report of the site in the very same volume, which misconstrues the evidence and attributes the burials to the Hellenistic or Roman period.

Most of the tombs at Tell el-Yahudiyeh had been plundered in antiquity. Only pottery and a few bronze pieces survived, so that the original arrangement cannot be reconstructed with certainty. The coffins were roughly oriented to the west and laid on raised heaps of basalt blocks or on the sandy desert floor. The body with its personal adornments was placed in the coffin, which was enclosed with a single row of bricks. A simple brick arch was built overhead for protection and small vases and bronze vessels were inserted in it; larger funerary vessels (pl. 25) were arranged around the grave. The whole was then covered with sand and stone slabs to form a tumulus. The eight tumuli at Tell el-Yahudiyeh vary in size according to the number of burials within.

The slipper-shaped coffins have the usual round hole pierced at the head and foot. A number were plain (though covered with whitish slip), but most were painted (on the front half only) in a tricolor

scheme of red, yellow, and black (as at Deir el-Balaḥ); sometimes blue was added. The pattern, badly preserved, appeared to imitate the bands of mummy cartonnage. There were traces of hieroglyphic inscriptions intended to represent a common formula with the name of the deceased and depictions of deities connected with the cult of the dead.

The faces on the coffin lids are all of the masklike naturalistic type, molded separately and applied to the lid. Some include more details, such as the Osiris beard (fig. 17:2). Others show either a clearly depicted wig (fig. 17:2) very similar to the Deir el-Balaḥ convention or only the vague outline of the wig (pl. 26). Stylized ears are shown on all lids, although their position varies. Some lids display sticklike arms and crossed hands (fig. 17:1, pl. 27); others show hands and wrists in the usual formalized convention (fig. 17:2; see also pls. 11–13 from Beth-Shean and fig. 19:1, 2 from Aniba). In concept and general character, these anthropoid lids are very close the naturalistic lids from Beth-Shean, Tell el-Farʿah, Lachish, and Deir el-Balaḥ.

The pottery assemblages (fig. 18) from the Tell el-Yahudiyeh tumuli show affinities with Egyptian, Aegean, and Canaanite ceramic types. Mycenaean and Cypriot imports are conspicuously absent, however, and only debased derivatives of the former are found. The general horizon is a step later than the Deir el-Balaḥ assemblages. Many of the pottery types are the same, but this is not of significance because Egyptian pottery styles are generally long-lived. The assemblage partially overlaps that of the Philistine rock-cut chamber tombs at Tell el-Farʿah dating from the twelfth to the beginning of the eleventh century. This date is supported by the scarabs found in the Yahudiyeh tumuli: one of Seth-Nakht (Ramesses III's father), two of Ramesses III, and one bearing the pronomen of Ramesses VI.[39]

We differentiate four groups at Tell el-Yahudiyeh, each of which has counterparts at Tell el-Farʿah. The typical Egyptian forms include (1) wide handleless jars (fig. 18:1; cf. Farʿah tomb 562, fig. 8:18) and (2) cylindrical handleless jars (fig. 18:2, 17; cf. Farʿah tomb 562, fig. 8:17). Reciprocal Canaanite-Egyptian forms include (3) pithoi with high bulging necks (fig. 18:14–16; cf. Farʿah tomb 552, fig. 7:14, 15) and (4) amphoriskoi with tall necks and but-

38. *Yahudiyeh*, pp. 15–17, 42–48, pls. 12, 13, XIV, XV.

39. Ibid., pp. 42–47, pls. XV:a, tumulus IV:2 (Ramesses III), XVI:1 (Ramesses VI).

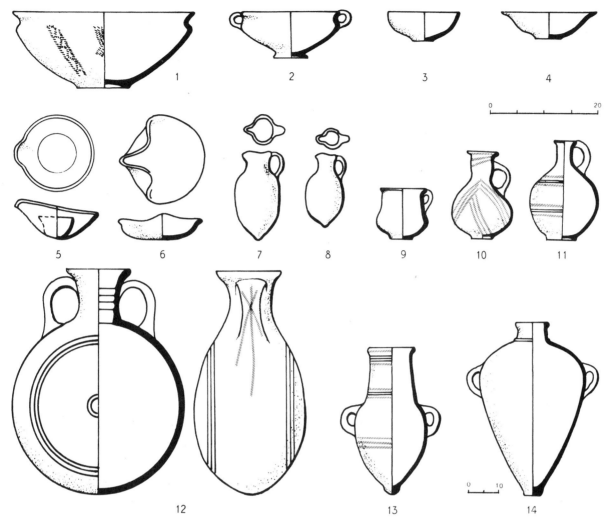

Fig. 16. Selected pottery, tomb 570, Lachish [*Lachish IV*].
1. [Pl. 69:555]   **2.** [Pl. 69:581]   **3.** [Pl. 71:LII:48]   **4.** [Pl. 72:LII:91]   **5.** [Pl. 72:626]   **6.** [Pl. 73:665]   **7.** [Pl. 78:787]   **8.** [Pl. 78:788]   **9.** [Pl. 84:967]   **10.** [Pl. 82:901]   **11.** [Pl. 76:725]   **12.** [Pl. 84:958]   **13.** [Pl. 85:985]   **14.** [Pl. 87:1018]

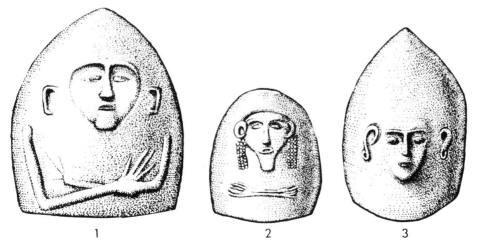

Fig. 17. Anthropoid coffin lids, Tell el-Yahudiyeh [*Yahudiyeh*].
1. [Pl. XIV:1]   **2.** [Pl. XIV:2]   **3.** [Pl. XIII:1]

Pl. 25. Anthropoid coffin *in situ* (open), Tell el-Yahudiyeh [*Yahudiyeh*, pl. XIII:3].

Pl. 26. Anthropoid coffin lid, Tell el-Yahudiyeh [British Museum].

Pl. 27. Anthropoid coffin *in situ*, Tell el-Yahudiyeh [*Yahudiyeh*, pl. XIII:1].

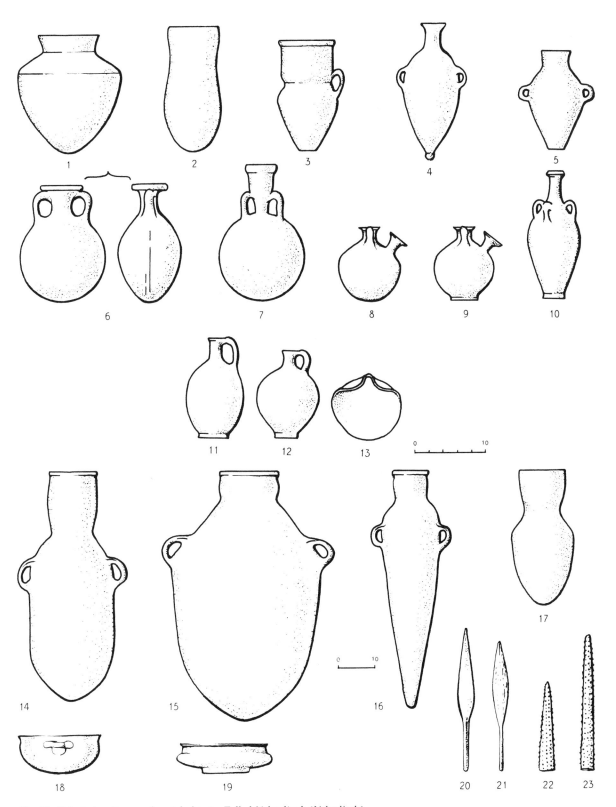

Fig. 18. Selected pottery and metal objects, Tell el-Yahudiyeh [*Yahudiyeh*].
1. [Pl. XV:5]   **2.** [Pl. XV:4]   **3.** [Pl. XV:10]   **4.** [Pl. XV:12]   **5.** [Pl. XV:6]   **6.** [Pl. XV:13]   **7.** [Pl. XV:14]   **8.** [Pl. XV:15]   **9.** [Pl. XIII:3]   **10.** [Pl. XV:11]   **11.** [Pl. XV:8]   **12.** [Pl. XV:9]   **13.** [Pl. XV:3]   **14.** [Pl. XIV:5]   **15.** [Pl. XIV:3]   **16.** [Pl. XIV:8]   **17.** [Pl. XIV:7]   **18.** [Pl. XV:16]   **19.** [Pl. XV:17]   **20.** [Pl. XV:22]   **21.** [Pl. XV:23]   **22.** [Pl. XV:21]   **23.** [Pl. XV:20]

ton bases (fig. 18:4; cf. Far'ah tomb 552, fig. 7:16–18). Juglets (fig. 18:11, 12) were borrowed by the Egyptians and appear in the Egyptian repertoire, although not as a common feature. The Egyptian elongated variant (fig. 18:11) also appears as an import in Canaan. The juglet in figure 18:12 bears all the hallmarks of the Canaanite jug and has many parallels in the local Canaanite Iron Age repertoire (for example, fig. 8:12 from Far'ah tomb 562).

Oil lamps with pinched spouts are rare in the Egyptian ceramic repertoire, and those found are identical to Canaanite prototypes (see, for example, the lamp in fig. 19:11 from the anthropoid burial at Aniba). Another link with Canaan is seen in the white-slipped handled cups with high bulging necks (fig. 18:3). This is an Egyptian form, well known in both pottery and stone, that had a long life span during the New Empire period in Egypt. Palestinian examples span Late Bronze II and the Early Iron Age.[40]

The Aegean character of the assemblage is evident only in local late imitations of Mycenaean stirrup jars with rounded or flat bases—these are sometimes decorated with red stripes (fig. 18:8, 9) and are very similar to the Beth-Shean stirrup jars[41]—and in the three-handled jars (fig. 18:10) of the type found in a Philistine tomb at Tell el-Far'ah (tomb 532).[42]

In addition to pottery, the Tell el-Yahudiyeh tombs contained a number of bronze bowls (fig. 18:18, 19), arrowheads, and bronze scrapers (fig. 18:20–23). An iron implement in the disturbed upper layer of tumulus V was probably not part of the original burial deposits, but intrusive.

The close similarity between the assemblage in the Tell el-Yahudiyeh anthropoid coffin burials and that of Tell el-Far'ah is immediately apparent, for both contain composite groups of Egyptian, Aegean, and Canaanite pottery types that show the same modes of adaption; moreover, they date to approximately the same period—the twelfth century B.C.

Tell Nebesheh

The second group of Egyptian anthropoid pottery coffins comes from Tell Nebesheh (fig. 20) in the northeast section of the Delta.[43] The excavator, Sir Flinders Petrie, dated these tombs between the eighth and fifth centuries B.C. and ascribed them to a Cypriot mercenary colony. A reexamination of the finds, however, makes it clear that Petrie's original assumptions were mistaken and his dates wrong. The tombs must without a doubt be dated to the period from the second half or perhaps even the beginning of the eleventh century to the beginning of the tenth century B.C.

The tombs containing the anthropoid coffins are of the single square-chamber type typical of that period in Egypt. So far only one of the anthropoid lids (pl. 28) has been published. The modeling of the bearded face, arms, and hands is very crude and is closest in concept to the coffins from Beth-Shean (Group B) and Tell el-Far'ah.

The ceramic assemblage at Nebesheh includes both Egyptian local ware and non-Egyptian pottery (for example, the jug in fig. 20:17)—typical Canaanite tradition from the middle of the twelfth to the beginning of the tenth century B.C.[44] The bulk of the ceramic finds, however, consists of flasks (fig. 20:12–14) and globular bichrome jugs (fig. 20:15, 16). The jugs, burnished and covered with a yellowish-cream slip and decorated with concentric red-and-black stripes, belong to a large family of pottery known as Phoenician Bichrome ware, whose distribution throughout the eastern Mediterranean included Cyprus and Egypt, and which can be dated, on the basis of stratified finds in Palestine, to the eleventh and tenth centuries B.C.[45]

Of special importance is the large number of forked spear butts (fig. 20:5–10) that are similar to the one found in a Beth-Shean anthropoid burial (pl. 29).[46]

The pottery of the Nebesheh anthropoid burial tombs indicates a date between the eleventh and the tenth centuries B.C.—somewhat later than the dates of the other anthropoid burials we have discussed. Nonetheless, the eclectic nature of the ceramic assemblage is still very clear, for it contains Egyptian and

40. *Deir el-Balaḥ Qedem 10*, p. 13, ills. 24, 29.
41. Cf. the Iron Age anthropoid coffin burial in tomb 66 from Beth-Shean; *B-SH Cemetery*, pp. 112–13, fig. 42b:23–24.
42. *CPP*, 55 V; *see also* chap. 3, Type 5, above.
43. *Tanis II*, pp. 20 ff., pls. I, II, XVI.

44. Parallels to the figure 20:17 jug in Palestine are found, for example, in Philistine tomb 242 at Tell el-Far'ah (*CPP*, 39 H2). Other jugs of this type are known from Tell Qasile, stratum X (*Qasile IEJ 1*, pl. 28:1) and Megiddo, stratum VI (*Meg. II*, pl. 75:10).
45. Cf. bichrome jugs from Qasile, stratum XI (*Qasile IEJ 1*, pl. 28:16, 19) and Megiddo stratum VIA (*Meg. II*, pl. 80:2, 86:1).
46. A spear butt of this type comes from tomb 90 at Beth-Shean; *B-SH Cemetery*, pp. 118 ff., fig. 45:5. *See* the writer's article, "Forked Spear Butts in Palestine and Egypt," *IEJ* 26 (1976): 20–34.

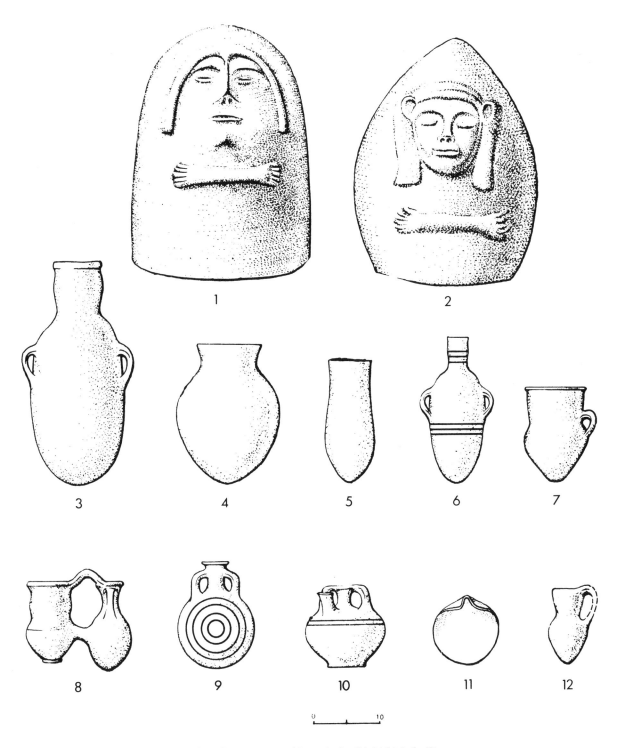

Fig. 19. Anthropoid coffin lids and selected pottery assemblage, Aniba (Nubia) [*Aniba II*].
1. [Pl. 39e]   **2.** [Pl. 39d]   **3.** [Pl. 80:34b,2]   **4.** [Pl. 75:19,4]   **5.** [Pl. 75:19,5]   **6.** [Pl. 87:49,8]   **7.** [Pl. 81:36a,4]
8. [Pl. 85:44a,4]   **9.** [Pl. 85:44b,5]   **10.** [Pl. 86:46a,4]   **11.** [Pl. 77:24,1,2,3]   **12.** [Pl. 81:36a,3]

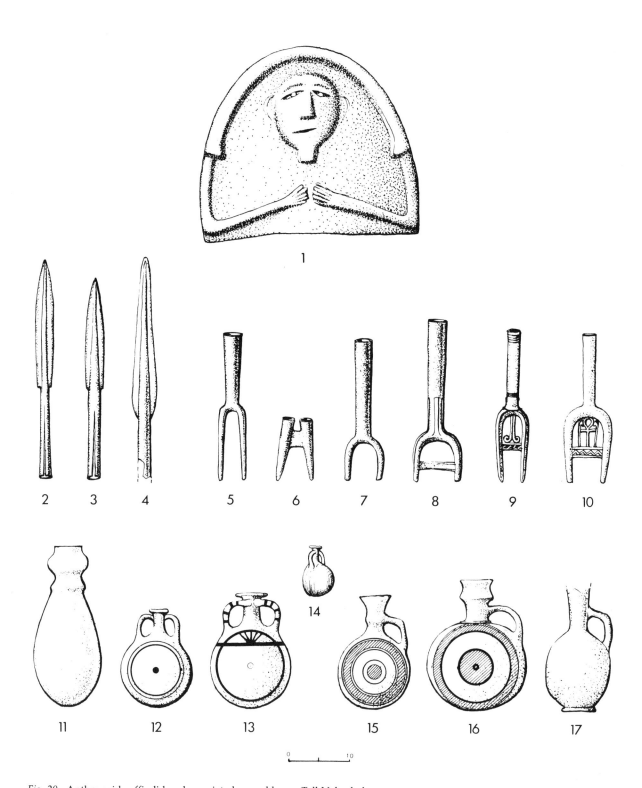

Fig. 20. Anthropoid coffin lid and associated assemblages, Tell Nebesheh.
1. [*Tanis II*, pl. I:17] **2–9.** [*Tanis II*, pl. III] **10.** [*Tools and Weapons*, pl. XL:186 (dap)] **11–17.** [*Tanis II*, pl. III]

Pl. 28. Anthropoid coffin lid, Tell Nebesheh, in fig. 20:1 [Department of Antiquities, Ashmolean Museum].

Pl. 29. Spear butt, Beth-Shean [From the Collection of the Israel Department of Antiquities and Museums. *B-SH Cemetery,* fig. 45:5].

Aegean ware, together with Phoenician pottery that most likely reached Egypt from Canaan and has not been found in any other anthropoid burial in Egypt. It seems noteworthy that anthropoid coffin burials in Egypt are generally associated with foreign ceramic elements. This may indicate that non-Egyptians were also buried in these coffins.

SUMMARY

As we have seen in our survey of anthropoid coffins, the earliest appearance in Canaan of this custom is attested at Deir el-Balaḥ in the late fourteenth century B.C. The thirteenth-century phase at Deir el-Balaḥ overlaps the early group of anthropoid burials at Beth-Shean. Tomb 935 at Tell el-Farʿah also belongs to this phase, while tomb 570 at Lachish may extend to the end of the thirteenth century. The Philistine tombs from the twelfth and eleventh centuries from Tell el-Farʿah and the Beth-Shean coffins with the grotesque lids that exhibit the distinctive headgear of the Sea Peoples prove that the custom of anthropoid burial was adopted by the Philistines.

The burials at Deir el-Balaḥ and Tell el-Farʿah display the same patterns and stages of development as those at Beth-Shean. Two chronological groups are distinguishable:

Early Group (Thirteenth Century B.C.)

These burials should probably be attributed to Egyptian officials or garrison troops stationed in Egyptian strongholds in Canaan. Anthropoid pottery coffins in Egypt—the home of this custom—were not used by the very rich, but they were also not used by the poor,

as shown by the occasional mummified body and the rich burial gifts. The largely looted remains in the tombs still show a mixture of Mycenaean, Cypriot, and Canaanite pottery types of the fourteenth and thirteenth centuries B.C., as well as native Egyptian tomb furniture. This combination, which is typical of the cosmopolitan Late Bronze Age in the eastern Mediterranean, is often strikingly associated with anthropoid burials of the period and reflects a more than casual link between the cultural backgrounds of those buried in Egypt and Canaan.

Later Group (Twelfth and Eleventh Centuries B.C.)

The predominance in Egypt of foreign (that is, non-Egyptian) elements becomes apparent in the twelfth- and eleventh-century burials and assemblages at Tell el-Yahudiyeh, which parallel those of Tell el-Farʿah, and in the Nebesheh assemblages, which are related to the later group at Beth-Shean. In Canaan this later group consists of the grotesque coffins from Beth-Shean and the burials and Philistine assemblages in the rock-cut chamber tombs at Tell el-Farʿah. These show that the custom of burial in anthropoid coffins was adopted by the Sea Peoples—the Philistines—who were first settled as mercenaries in Egyptian strongholds in Canaan by Ramesses III after he had defeated them about 1190 B.C. in the battles depicted on the walls of his temple at Medinet Habu.

The Philistines incorporated this burial custom of their Egyptian predecessors and counterparts in these strongholds. This facet of Philistine settlement in Canaan, where the Philistines first served as Egyptian mercenaries, can also explain the appearance of other Egyptian features in the Philistine culture.

6
ABSOLUTE CHRONOLOGY AND CONCLUSIONS

The turbulent events which occurred at the end of the thirteenth century and beginning of the twelfth changed the history of Canaan and ushered in a new era. It was a period that witnessed the collapse of the Hittite Empire, the end of the Canaanite city-states, the decline of Egyptian political and military power in Asia, the arrival and settlement of the Israelite tribes, and the appearance of Sea Peoples, mainly the Philistines, on the coast of Canaan.

The complexity of a period of dislocation, while characteristic of intermediate periods in general, is particularly well illustrated in Canaan during the transition from the Late Bronze to the Iron Age, for here the various cultural and ethnic elements coexisted and overlapped. In order to bring the events of this unstable period into focus, one must try to define and distinguish these different components.

At some sites, certain facets of the local Canaanite culture continued into the Early Iron Age, indicating the persistence of a local Canaanite population. Egyptian presence and influence can be discerned, and this continued at some sites into the second half of the twelfth century. The unsettled state of affairs of this period is further highlighted by the sudden interruption of sea trade; the importation of Cypriot and Mycenaean vessels, which epitomized the cosmopolitan *koine* of the Late Bronze Age in the region, ceased. The diffusion of the Israelites is evident in the character and geosociological pattern of their new settlements. Finally, the Philistines added new and eclectic elements to this cultural mélange.

DATING THE COMING OF THE SEA PEOPLES AND THE PHILISTINES

In dealing with the absolute chronology of the Philistines, we have only a few dates at our disposal. The most significant one is the year 1190 B.C., the eighth year of Ramesses III, when the deeds of the Philistines are related for the first time on the reliefs at Medinet Habu. Does this mean that the Sea Peoples first appeared in Canaan in 1190? Or should we assume their presence in Canaan before the eighth year of Ramesses III? As Egyptian rule steadily weakened toward the end of the Nineteenth Dynasty,[1] there was general instability in Canaan. Some of the other Sea Peoples mentioned together with the Philistines in the Medinet Habu reliefs also appear in earlier Egyptian documents, and several such groups may be concealed in the Bible under the generic name of Philistines.[2]

We must therefore search for other data, events, and documents to help establish early Philistine chronology within the historical framework of the ancient Near East and the Aegean. One such event occurred in the fifth year of Pharaoh Merneptah (1231 B.C.), when he defeated a coalition of Libyans and Sea Peoples. The "Peoples of the Sea" who advanced on the Delta with their families and possessions[3] must have been part of a great movement of invasion and migration very similar to that of the Sea Peoples in the eighth year of Ramesses III (when the Philistines are explicitly mentioned). Although we do not know if the Sea Peoples had already reached Canaan in the time of Merneptah, the general thrust of their movements from then on seems to have been toward Syria, Canaan, and Egypt.

1. For the latest appraisal and bibliography, *see* Faulkner, *CAH³*, vol. II, pt. 2, chap. 23, pp. 232–39; and Malamat, *The Egyptian Decline*, pp. 23–38.
2. F. M. Cross, Jr., *Canaanite Myth and Hebrew Epic: Essays in the History of the Religion of Israel* (Cambridge, Mass., 1973), pp. 124–25.
3. See chap. 1, n. 5 above.

Vertical side labels (Historical Data column): PHILISTINE EXPANSION; PHILISTINE SETTLEMENT AND CONSOLIDATION; Israelite settlement; PERIOD OF THE JUDGES.

HISTORICAL DATA	EGYPT RULER	DYN	GREECE AND THE EASTERN MEDITERRANEAN	PHASES OF PHILISTINE CULTURE	DATES	TELL EL FAR'AH (S) CITY	CEMETERIES	DEIR EL-BALAH	TELL JEMMEH	TEL SERA'
	Siamon 945 ↑									
David's wars with the Philistines			Proto Geometric		— 975 —	W-V		2	Buildings G / 187	VII
					— 1000 —					
The battle of Gilboa / Saul		XXI	Myc. IIIC:2 (Submyc.)	Philistine III	— 1025 —	371 ↑ (Pre W) ↓ 370	T.828 / T.523		186 / Buildings H ↓	
The battle of Eben-ezer					— 1050 —		T.625		185 / 184 Burnt layer	VIII
					— 1075 —	372 372				183
Wen Amun	Ramesses XI 1113–1085		Myc. IIIC:1c	Philistine II	— 1085 —	X ↕ Residency	T.562	Philistine pits / 3	Building JF	
	Ramesses X 1121–1113				— 1100 —					
					— 1125 —	369 370	Ram. X T.532		181 ↑	↓ 180
	Ramesses VIII 1147–1140 / Ramesses VI 1156–1148 / Ramesses IV 1166–1160	XX		Philistine I	— 1150 —	Court-yard YX / 365 Residency	Ram. VIII?		Pre building JF	
	Ramesses III 1198–1166 / 8th year				— 1175 —	364 / 368	Ram. IV / Ram. IV / T.552 T.542		176	
			Myc. IIIC:1b (Myc.IIIC:1a)	"Sea People" Monochrome	— 1190 —	Z	Ram. III / Ram. III			IX
	Tewosret 1209–1200 / Seti II 1216–1210				— 1200 —	Seti II ▲	Seti II?	Cemetery and Settlement	Building JR	
	Merneptah 1236–1223	XIX	Myc. IIIB		— 1225 —			4		X
						T.934 / T.960 / T.984		T.114 / T.116 / T.118		

LEGEND: ● Scarab   ▲ Object   ■ Monumental

Table 2. Comparative Chart of Sites with Philistine Remains

In establishing the date of the appearance of the Sea Peoples in Canaan, we must take into account the destruction of Ugarit. A sword bearing the cartouche of Merneptah fixes the date of the last burnt layer at Ugarit after his accession in 1236.[4] With this destruction, the last Mycenaean pottery (IIIB) at Ugarit vanished.[5] The testimony of the Hittite documents and of the Ugaritic kiln tablets from the last days of the city tends to support the view that the victory over Ugarit by the "hordes of the enemy" (most likely the Sea Peoples, although they are not mentioned by name)

4. C. F. A. Schaeffer, "A Bronze Sword from Ugarit with Cartouche of Mineptah (Ras Shamra, Syria)," *Antiquity* 29 (1955): 226–29; idem, *Ugaritica III*, pp. 169 ff., pl. VIII, figs. 123, 124.

5. For evidence of the exceptionally rich assemblages of Myc. IIIB pottery at Ugarit, *see* Stubbings, pp. 71–75; *Ugaritica II*, chap. 4; V. Hankey, "Mycenaean Pottery in the

Middle East," *BSA* 62 (1967): 112–13. For the possible appearance of Mycenaean IIIC pottery at Ugarit, *see* J. Courtois, "Sur divers groupes de vases mycéniens en Méditerranée Orientale," in *Mycenaeans in the Eastern Mediterranean*, pp. 137–65. V. Hankey ("A Late Bronze Age Temple at Amman. I. The Aegean Pottery," *Levant* 6 [1974]: 132–33, n. 16), quotes Furumark, who disputes the appearance of pottery later than Myc. IIIB. If Courtois's thesis is accepted, the Myc. IIIC pottery could be attributed to squatters living at Ugarit after the razing of the Late Bronze Age city. The de-

TEL SIPPOR	ASHDOD	TEL MOR	TELL QASILE	APHEK	IZBET SARTAH	TEL MASOS	TELL BEIT MIRSIM	LACHISH	BETH SHEMESH	GEZER Tombs Strata	TELL ZEROR	MEGIDDO	BETH SHEAN Levels Cemetery	AFULA	TEL DAN	TELL DEIR ʿALLA	DATES
		2	IX	X7 Silos	I	I	B3	V	IIa	IX		VB	V				— 975
	Xa										X		Late VI		IV		— 1000
I	Xb		X							X		VIA	T.66 T.90			Phase D	— 1025
						II	Silo 2										— 1050
										XI T.58-59					V	POTTERY	— 1075
II	XI	3	XI	X8	II		B2		III		XI	VIB	VI	IIIa	?		— 1100
						Ram.X? ●	Silo 43								Pits VI		— 1125
	XII	4	XII	X9 Pits Ram.IV		IIIa	East Cave	Cave 4013	T(II)	XII T.9 / XIII		Ram.VI ▲				"PHILISTINE"	— 1150
	XIIIa	5		Ram.IV ●		IIIb	Silo 43	Ram.III ●▲	Ram.III	Cult cache Ram.III ▲		VIIA Ram.III ▲●	Ram.III Early VI ■		IIIb	Phase A	— 1175
	XIIIb	6		X10			B1	T.570	Silos 530 515	XIV					?	Temple Tewosret ▲	— 1200
III	XIV	7		X11	III	Seti II C ●	(B1)	VI	IV	XV	XIII	VIIB	VII	IV	VII	Myc. IIIB Tablets	— 1225

took place during the final years of the weakened Nineteenth Dynasty.[6] On the other hand, a faience vase bearing the name of Queen Tewosret (1209–1200 B.C.) found, together with some Myc. IIIB pottery, in the destruction level of the Late Bronze II stratum at Deir ʿAlla, gives us a *terminus ad quem* for this pottery and a *terminus post quem* for one of the suggested early waves of Sea Peoples who destroyed or settled the

struction of stratum V at Tell Abu Hawam should probably also be dated to the last quarter of the thirteenth century B.C. The Myc. IIIB pottery from the end of this stratum is not later than that from Ugarit. Tell Abu Hawam was undoubtedly one of the chief harbors on the Canaanite coast and would have been an easy target for the Sea Peoples. The city may have been destroyed by an early wave of Sea Peoples who did not rebuild it. Certainly it was never settled by the Philistines. Though a long gap is postulated between strata V and IV, a small squatter settlement of short duration—judging by the

discovery of pottery similar to Myc. IIIC—may have existed on the site. The still unresolved stratigraphical problems of Tell Abu Hawam and the related finds are illustrated by a group of pottery vessels, which are probably intrusive from stratum IV, assigned to stratum V. *See* R. W. Hamilton, "Excavations at Tell Abu Hawām," *QDAP* 4 (1935): 41, vessels nos. 248–52. No. 256, a bottle comparable to our Type 9, is either the earliest of the series or is intrusive and belongs to the Proto–White Painted Cypriot ware (*see* chap. 3, n. 125 above).

Syro-Palestinian coast and some strategic inland towns. The evidence from Ugarit and Deir ʿAlla, though isolated, bears witness to the final appearance of Myc. IIIB pottery at the very end of the thirteenth century B.C.[7] This fact is significant, for it enables us to date with greater accuracy the earliest Myc. IIIC:1 pottery in the eastern Mediterranean, because it appears stratigraphically immediately after the disappearance of Mycenaean IIIB pottery. Its bearers were undoubtedly the Sea Peoples. For evidence of the emergence of this type of pottery, which is closely akin to Philistine

ware, we must turn to nearby Cyprus, where it was clearly observed in quantity and in stratigraphical context.

The Mycenaean culture dominant in the Aegean and parts of Asia Minor and the eastern Mediterranean world during the fourteenth and thirteenth centuries B.C. was destroyed by a series of catastrophes. On the mainland, southern and central Greece were devastated, Mycenae itself was attacked, and Troy was razed. The exact causes of these destructions are unknown, but scholars most frequently attribute them to invasions and natural disasters.[8] The catastrophes marked the end of the Myc. IIIB palaces with their characteristic architecture, advanced standards of art and craftsmanship, and literate and highly sophisticated culture. Mycenaean culture was a homogeneous one, of which the Myc. IIIB pottery is now the single most easily distinguishable element. When the Mycenaeans fled from their homeland, they took these ceramic skills with them. At many sites, this new type of pottery, Myc. IIIC, indicates that immigrants from the Aegean settled there and revived Mycenaean culture. The main Mycenaean destructions seem to parallel the disasters inflicted by the great waves of Sea Peoples on the Hittite Empire and the Syrian coast at this time. These raids are better documented than the early settlements, and the identity of the main groups of attackers is known from Egyptian, Ugaritic, and Hittite sources.

It is generally agreed that toward the end of the thirteenth century B.C., Cyprus was invaded by a people who put an end to the Late Cypriot II culture with its Myc. IIIB pottery. They are thought to have been Aegeans, probably Achaeans fleeing from their homeland.[9] The impact of this invasion is most clearly

For the stratigraphy and reevaluation of the site, *see* Hamilton, ibid., pp. 1–69, esp. his stratigraphic and chronological conclusions, pp. 66–67. Hamilton suggested that Tell Abu Hawam was settled from 1400 until 925 B.C. Stratum V was destroyed by Merneptah, and the following stratum (IVA, B) was partially destroyed around 1196 B.C. in raids from the sea. This chronology has been challenged by B. Mazar ("The Stratification of Tell Abū Huwâm on the Bay of Acre," *BASOR* 124 [1951]: 21–25), followed by E. Anati (in *EAEHL*, pp. 9–12). *See also* G. W. Van Beek, "The Date of Tell Abu Huwam, Stratum III," *BASOR* 138 (1955): 34–38. Mazar suggested that there was a gap between the end of stratum V and the resettlement of stratum IVA in the mid-eleventh century B.C. He based this assumption on the complete lack of twelfth and early eleventh century B.C. material and on close analogies of the finds with those of Tell Qasile X and Megiddo VIA.

As to the possibility of a phase containing Myc. IIIC pottery, *see* Hankey, "Mycenaean Pottery in the Middle East," pp. 123–25. J. Balensi, who is working on the Tell Abu Hawam materials, has encountered a number of Myc. IIIC fragments; they are not, however, from stratified contexts.

6. The tablets were published by C. Virolleaud, *Le palais royal d'Ugarit*, vol. V (Paris, 1965), pp. 81 ff., 180 ff.; and by J. Nougayrol, *Ugaritica V*, pp. 79 ff. For a discussion and additional bibliography, *see* Malamat, *The Egyptian Decline*, pp. 30–32; M. Astour, "New Evidence on the Last Days of Ugarit," *AJA* 69 (1965): 253–58. For Schaeffer's view of the end of Ugarit, which he attributes to the time of Ramesses III, see *Ugaritica V*, pp. 666ff. *See also* M. S. Drower, *CAH*[3], vol. II, pt. 2, chap. 21, p. 147.

In addition to the Ugaritic documents, contemporary Hittite tablets found at Hattuša describe the last days of the Hittite Empire and the destruction by the Sea Peoples. *See* H. Otten, "Neue Quellen Zum Ausklang des Hethitischen Reiches," *MDOG* 94 (1963): 1 ff.; E. O. Forrer, "Der Untergang des Hatti-Reiches," *Ugaritica VI*, pp. 207 ff.; Drower, *CAH*[3], vol. II, pt. 2, chap. 21, pp. 145–48.

7. *See* chap. 2, p. 84 for an analysis of the Deir ʿAlla Mycenaean pottery, which seems to be early Myc. IIIB; *see also*, Hankey, "Mycenaean Pottery in the Middle East," pp. 131–34; idem, "A Late Bronze Age Temple at Amman," p. 133. She suggests that the Mycenaean stirrup jars at Deir ʿAlla may have been heirlooms kept in the sanctuary.

8. Numerous hypotheses have been advanced to explain the end of the Mycenaean supremacy, among them invasions, drought, a volcanic eruption, social revolution, internal struggles, and economic collapse. For a comprehensive bibliography, see *SCE IV, Part 1D*, p. 776, nn. 7–9, p. 777, nn. 1–6; V. R. d'A. Desborough, *CAH*[3], vol. II, pt. 2, chap. 36:I; P. Betancourt, "The End of the Greek Bronze Age," *Antiquity* 50 (1976): 40–47.

9. Several views regarding the destruction and resettlement of Cyprus at the end of the thirteenth century can be summarized as follows. According to H. W. Catling, many of the Mycenaean homelands were struck by disaster at the end of the thirteenth century, and settlements of refugees were established. At least one group of refugees fled to Cyprus, where they settled at a number of sites. These refugees included many craftsmen highly skilled in ivory, bronzework,

seen at Enkomi, where the Late Cypriot IIC town was laid waste and a new city with ashlar buildings was erected. The dominant element in the decorated pottery of this new level (IIIA) is Myc. IIIC:1 ware, which continued an Argolid tradition.[10] After a very short period, Enkomi was again destroyed—this time apparently during the Sea Peoples' invasion of Cyprus, which took place before they were defeated by Ramesses III in his eighth year.[11] One of these two invasions is referred to in the last correspondence between the king of Ugarit (Ammurapi) and the ruler of Alashiya.[12]

In the first phase of the new city erected after that invasion (Enkomi level IIIB 1st), Myc. IIIC:1b continued to be dominant.[13] Hence the initial appearance of this pottery can be dated no later than around 1190 B.C. In the next phase of level IIIB of Enkomi, the pottery features Myc. IIIC:1c and the "Granary" Style.[14] It seems therefore that Myc. IIIC:1b was used in level IIIB at Enkomi by the Sea Peoples.[15] Few other artifacts show specific traits of the Sea Peoples. Exceptions are the domed seal with the depiction of a warrior of the Sea Peoples, which was found in the destruction level of the previous city,[16] and, to a lesser degree, the ivory

box found in a tomb.[17] Otherwise, the Sea Peoples seem to have blended easily with the "Achaean" invaders, to whom they were apparently closely related.

The beginnings of Myc. IIIC:1 pottery in Cyprus and of Myc. IIIC pottery in Palestine must be considered in the light of the same chronological data. The latest Myc. IIIB pottery at Enkomi level IIC is very similar to that found in the last destruction level of Ugarit.[18] The close relationship between Ugarit and Cyprus, not only geographically but also in trade and other matters, implies that the disasters that struck them occurred at almost the same time.[19]

A stratigraphical sequence similar to that found at Enkomi was also revealed at other relevant sites such as Kition,[20] Sinda,[21] and Kouklia,[22] where the destruction of the Late Cypriot IIC strata by either Achaeans or Sea Peoples was followed by the introduction of Myc. IIIC:1 pottery. The synchronism between these

and gem-cutting (see *CAH*[3], vol. II, pt. 2, chap. 22:XI, XII, pp. 207-13. P. Dikaios suggests that among those who destroyed level IIB (LC II) at Enkomi about 1230 B.C. was a large number of Mycenaeans who had fled after the fall of Mycenae and other towns on the mainland. The raiders may have recruited others on their way to the island. The Karnak inscriptions, for example, have preserved the history of Merneptah's Libyan campaign against the raiders, and among the latter are mentioned the Akawasha (*Enkomi Excavations*, vol. II, pp. 484-87, 513-14, 528-29). Desborough argues from the evidence of Enkomi, Sinda, and Kition that with the breakup of the central power on the Greek mainland, there was a massive and probably aggressive movement to Cyprus (Desborough, *CAH*[3], vol. II, pt. 2, chap. 36, pp. 659-60).

10. *Enkomi Excavations*, vol. II, pp. 487, 518-21.

11. Ibid., pp. 487-89, 522-23; *Enkomi*, p. 38. Several tombs uncovered in the excavations of 1934 and 1946-50 were dated to the twelfth century B.C. by scarabs of Ramesses III found in some of them (V. E. G. Kenna, *Corpus of Cypriote Antiquities*, vol. 3, *Catalogue of the Cypriote Seals of the Bronze Age in the British Museum* [Göteborg, 1971], p. 34, pl. XXX:111).

12. *Ugaritica V*, pp. 83-88 (letters between the kings of Alashiya and Ugarit, nos. 22-24).

13. *Enkomi Excavations*, vol. II, pp. 489, 525-26.

14. Ibid., pp. 490-91, 529.

15. Ibid., p. 529.

16. *See* chap. 1, p. 13, chap. 5, p. 274, fig. 14. *Enkomi Excavations*, vol. II, p. 488. The destruction of level IIIA can be dated around 1190 B.C. and attributed to the Sea Peoples, like

the destruction of Sinda II. This receives confirmation from the discovery of the "Philistine" seal under the floor of rooms 9 and 10 (originally the southernmost part of the megaron of the Ashlar Building). This floor was laid after the destruction of level IIIA. The layer which yielded the seal also contained a scarab (ibid., vol. I, p. 196; vol. IIIa, pl. 95:1[182]) attributed to the beginning of the reign of Ramesses II. Particular scarabs often were used over a long period. The "Philistine" seal is of decisive chronological importance because it bears a striking resemblance to the warriors of the Sea Peoples depicted at Medinet Habu (1190 B.C.). Since the seal belongs to the Ashlar Building, which was rebuilt after the destruction that ended level IIIA, it can serve both to date the end of that level and as a *terminus post quem* for its rebuilding as level IIIB.

17. See chap. 1, p. 13; chap. 5, p. 274, fig. 13. For the identification of the warrior as a Tjekker, *see* J. A. Wainwright, "A Teucrian at Salamis in Cyprus," *JHS* 83 (1963): 146-51.

18. Hankey, "A Late Bronze Age Temple at Amman," p. 133.

19. *Ugaritica V*, pp. 83-88. For a discussion, *see* Astour, "New Evidence on the Last Days of Ugarit."

20. For the most recent discussion and bibliography, *see* Karageorghis, *Kition: Mycenaean and Phoenician* (London: British Academy, 1973), pp. 10-11, 19, 27. The end of the first phase at Kition, which coincides with the end of LC II (last quarter of the thirteenth century B.C.), is explained by Karageorghis in the light of R. Carpenter's theory that the decline of Mycenaean civilization was the outcome of a long drought. This theory has not been accepted by Schaeffer for the end of Ugarit (*see* R. Carpenter, *Discontinuity in Greek Civilization* [Cambridge, 1966]; *Ugaritica V*, pp. 760 ff.).

21. *Sinda*.

22. F. G. Maier, "Evidence for Mycenaean Settlement at Old Paphos," in *Mycenaeans in the Eastern Mediterranean*, pp. 68-78.

sites and others in Cyprus[23] where the same phenomenon has been observed is not always exact, and these destruction levels have not been noted everywhere. The one fact on which most scholars agree is that it was the Sea Peoples who were responsible for one of these destructions and that they took place before the eighth year of Ramesses III.

Myc. IIIC:1 pottery has been published from only two sites in Canaan, but there are hints of a wider distribution (e.g., Tell Abu Hawam, Tell Keisan, Ashkelon and Tel ʿAkko). At Beth-Shean it appears in early level VI after the disappearance of Myc. IIIB pottery in level VII. Both the statue of Ramesses III and the lintel of one of his officials, though found in level V, should be assigned to the later stage of early level VI. Thus the earliest stage of this level to which the Myc. IIIC:1b pottery could belong would have to be a brief period between the destruction of level VII and the flourishing Egyptian city of Ramesses III.

At Ashdod, the last stratum containing Myc. IIIB pottery is stratum XIV. Myc. IIIC:1b pottery held sway for a very short time in stratum XIIIb, for the typical bichrome Philistine pottery initially appeared with Myc. IIIC:1b pottery on a higher floor of this stratum (XIIIa). If we accept that Myc. IIIB was still extant ca. 1209 B.C., this period of Myc. IIIC:1b must have lasted only from the very end of the thirteenth century to ca. 1190.

The end of the Myc. IIIB pottery has been observed at several sites. At Tell el-Farʿah (S), its final appearance occurs in a level prior to or contemporary with the time of Seti II, that is, the end of the thirteenth century. The transition from Làte Bronze to Iron I associated with the cessation of Cypriot and Mycenaean imports can be observed in tombs 934, 960 and 984. The scarabs found in these tombs, ranging from Ramesses II to IV, and possibly even to Ramesses VIII, indicate a long period of usage. But it should be noted that, although these tombs were robbed in antiquity, the associated pottery assemblages, which lack both Mycenaean and Cypriot imports, can be dated from the end of the thirteenth to the beginning of the twelfth century B.C. Paralleling these tombs of the "900" cemetery are the Philistine tombs 542 and 552 in the "500" cemetery, a fact which demonstrates that the Egyptian-Canaanite

elements of the Late Bronze Age continued and coexisted side by side with the incoming Philistines.

At Gezer the last appearance of Myc. IIIB pottery occurs in stratum XV; it is then completely absent from the very short and enigmatic stratum XIV (which may perhaps be assigned to the first wave of Sea Peoples). A cache of cultic vessels contained Philistine pottery and a cartouche of Ramesses III. This cache should be correlated with stratum XIII.

At Beth-Shemesh the last traces of Mycenaean pottery are found in stratum IVB. There is no Philistine presence in the intermediate pits, which probably correspond to stratum B_1 at Tell Beit Mirsim. Chronologically, the Philistine appearance in stratum III should be connected with the two scarabs of Ramesses III found in a corresponding tomb.

At Lachish, recent excavations have raised new questions regarding the end of the Late Bronze Age, for they indicate that stratum VI, which contained Myc. IIIB pottery, continued without a break down to the period of Ramesses III. According to another interpretation, a limited settlement—most probably an Egyptian garrison—associated with the period of Ramesses III followed the destruction of stratum VI and Fosse Temple III.

At Megiddo imported Myc. IIIB pottery came to an end with the destruction of stratum VIIB. Philistine pottery began in stratum VIIA, where two cartouches of Ramesses III were found—one on an ivory pencase and the other on a scarab.

At Deir ʿAlla, a *terminus ad quem* for the latest appearance of Myc. IIIB pottery is supplied by the cartouche of Queen Tewosret; some scholars consider the Mycenaean pottery associated with this cartouche to be heirlooms, but this is a most unlikely possibility. After the complete destruction (by earthquake?) of the stratum containing Myc. IIIB pottery and inscribed tablets, a new type of pottery was encountered; it is closely related to the Philistine both in shape and decoration. This new stratum (A) must date sometime after 1200 B.C. The Carbon-14 date for this stratum is 1180 B.C. ± 60 and hence is of no help in refining the dating.

The absolute chronology of the first stage of Philistines in Canaan (which may include other Sea Peoples) seems to be clear. The Late Bronze Age cultures both in Cyprus and on the Syro-Palestinian coast disappeared in the late thirteenth century, followed by the emergence of the culture of the Sea Peoples; the beginning of Myc. IIIC:1 must be related to the end of this

---

23. For the pattern of destruction and resettlement, see *DMS*, pp. 198 ff.; *SCE IV, Part 1D*, pp. 777 ff.; Catling, *CAH³*, vol. II, pt. 2, chap. 22(b), pp. 209–12.

period. This hypothesis is supported by the ever-growing documentary evidence that at least one wave of Sea Peoples invaded Syria and Palestine before the great onslaughts in the fifth and eighth years of Ramesses III. The first stage has so far been better observed in Cyprus than in Canaan.

The next stage in Canaan, which is definitely Philistine in character, emerges about 1190 B.C. The relatively large number of scarabs bearing cartouches of Ramesses III[24] in the strata and burials containing Philistine pottery testifies to the wide diffusion of this culture both in Philistia proper and in the strategically situated cities of Canaan.

Of the subsequent stage of the first phase of Philistine culture we possess far less data. Scarabs of Ramesses IV associated with Philistine pottery were found at Tell el-Farʿah (S) (tombs 542 and 552), Tell eṣ-Ṣafi, and Aphek. From the period of Ramesses VI we have the bronze stand bearing his cartouche from Megiddo VIIA. The latter is the last appearance of the name of an Egyptian pharaoh in the northern part of the country. This fits well into the overall picture of the duration of the Egyptian presence in Canaan, as already attested at Timna and Serabit el-Khadem.

For the second phase of Philistine culture, only one well-stratified scarab is known—that of Ramesses X from tomb 532 at Tell el-Farʿah (S). This agrees well with the weakening Egyptian position in Canaan, which culminates at the end of the Twentieth Dynasty in the historical situation as known from the Wen Amun tale.

THE PROCESS OF PHILISTINE SETTLEMENT

The earliest settlement of Sea Peoples is indicated by a single decisive factor: the appearance of Myc. IIIC:1b pottery following the destruction of a flourishing Canaanite city. Stylistically and stratigraphically, Myc. IIIC:1b pottery somewhat precedes and heralds mainstream Philistine pottery.

This phenomenon occurs in stratum XIIIb at Ashdod, which comes immediately after the destruction of the last Canaanite town (stratum XIV); in plan and material culture, the town of stratum XIIIb differs completely from its predecessor. The only other city presenting a similar picture is Beth-Shean, where the initial phase of level VI, which follows the destruction of the Late Bronze city (level VII), also contains Myc. IIIC:1b pottery.

Evidence of this early Sea People settlement has so far been found only at these two sites, but it may in time also be uncovered in other towns situated along the coast or at other strategic locations. While it is not certain whether these first settlers should be called Philistines, it is clear that their culture was very close to the subsequent classical Philistine culture.

Roughly contemporary with this early Sea People settlement, a short and elusive phase immediately following the Bronze Age destruction level has been discerned at a number of sites. This phase, first defined by Albright at Tell Beit Mirsim (stratum B₁), was attributed by him to the incoming Israelites. Bethel ("Iron I") and Beth-Shemesh (stratum IVA) show the same phenomenon following the destructions of their respective Late Bronze cities. However, it should be stressed that this phenomenon is diverse in nature and varies from site to site. At Aphek (stratum X10), Jaffa ("Lion's Temple"), ʿAfula (stratum IIIb), and Gezer (stratum XIV), this phase has been attributed to the influence of the Sea Peoples, while at such sites as Tel Mor (strata 6 and 5) and Tell Shariʿa (stratum IX), a renewed Egyptian presence is postulated.

The first settlements which can definitely be attributed to the Philistines were primarily, though not exclusively, concentrated along the southern coast and in the Shephelah. This region had a natural strategic and commercial importance, for through it passed the Via Maris to and from Egypt. The Philistines came into an area that was already populated, although these extant sites varied in material culture, function, and size. The stratigraphic analysis and study of the Philistine settlement and its material culture together with the information from the Bible enable us to perceive a

---

24. Besides the scarabs of Ramesses III found in the strata and in tombs with Philistine pottery, several others were uncovered either unstratified or in sites not associated with Philistine finds (e.g., see, for Tell Jemmeh, p. 34). Very indicative of Ramesses III's authority and the scope of his occupation of Canaan is his use of the copper mines and the neighboring trade routes in the ʿArabah. Cartouches of Ramesses III were found in the temple of Hathor at Timna; see B. Rothenberg, *Timna* (London, 1972), p. 163, fig. 49. A rock

stele on a cliff north of the shrine and about 20 m. above it bore two cartouches of Ramesses III; see R. Ventura, "An Egyptian Rock Stela in Timna," *Tel Aviv* 1 (1974): 60–63. A large double cartouche of Ramesses III was discovered inscribed on a rock at nearby Naḥal Roded, which extends from Sinai into the Negev (Rothenberg, *Timna*, p. 201, fig. 62).

pattern of developing Philistine settlement (which may hold true for other groups of Sea Peoples as well).

The main wave of Philistine settlers and the major impact of their culture occurred in the stage of settlement that came in the aftermath of their defeat at the hands of Ramesses III. This period also seems to have been the formative stage of the Philistine entity in an area which included Philistia proper, from the northwestern Negev to the Yarkon River and from the sea to the western slopes of Judea, with the addition of some towns newly founded by the Philistines. In this period, the borders were more or less stabilized, and the Pentapolis, centering around the coastal cities of Gaza, Ashkelon, and Ashdod (mainly the city of stratum XII), was organized; Ekron and Gath joined probably at a somewhat later stage.

The presence of Egyptian influence and strongholds must be regarded as an important factor in the process of Philistine settlement. The Philistines occupied some of these sites primarily as mercenaries. While Deir el-Balaḥ, Tel Mor, and Tell el-Farʿah (S) in Philistia proper, Lachish and Gezer (stratum XIII) on the borders of Philistia, Beth-Shean (in the later phase of early level VI), and Megiddo (stratum VIIA) all vary in character, function, and chronological range, their common denominator is a continued Egyptian presence incorporating the new ethnic element.

At several sites in Philistia proper, such as Ashkelon, Tell Jemmeh, Tel Ṣippor, and Tell Jerishe, it seems that Philistine settlement directly followed the destruction of the Late Bronze Canaanite cities.

To this stage of Philistine settlement also belong two settlements, Tell Qasile (stratum XII) and Khirbet Muqannaʿ (Ekron?), which were towns first established by the Philistines on sites previously unoccupied.

The lack of external contacts helped the Philistines preserve their own singular culture. However, by the end of the initial phase of settlement, Philistine products had reached sites far from the main centers of Philistia, including Israelite settlements such as Tel Masos, ʿIzbet Ṣarṭah, Tel Dan, and Hazor. It should be noted, however, that this does not indicate settlement but rather contacts between the two cultures, probably resulting from sporadic trade or military contacts.

The later phase of Philistine settlement, from the end of the twelfth through the eleventh centuries and corresponding to the second and third phases of Philistine culture, witnessed the greatest expansion and consolidation of the Philistines. In addition to an increased number of settlements in Philistia proper, we also have evidence of Philistine control and influence, if not actual settlement, in the northern Negev and in much of the territory of the tribes of Simeon, Judah, and Dan.

During the second cultural phase, Philistine settlements such as Ashdod (stratum XI), Tell Qasile (stratum XI), and Tell el-Farʿah (S) (the Residency) continued to flourish. However, a slight decline in the quality of the material culture is evident.

At this same phase, if not earlier, the account of Wen Amun indicates that the Tjekker group of Sea Peoples settled at Dor. Until now pottery of the second and third phases of Philistine culture only has been found there. The evidence from nearby Tel Zeror shows not only pottery related to twelfth- and especially eleventh-century Philistine pottery, but also special features, such as metal objects and burial architecture, probably connected with the western Mediterranean. At Deir ʿAlla, a derivative of Philistine pottery has been associated with squatters who were probably a branch of one of the groups of Sea Peoples.

The decisive victory of the Philistines over the Israelites at Eben-ezer (ʿIzbet Ṣarṭah) ushered in the final phase of Philistine culture. Though not yet borne out by excavations, the Philistine encampments apparently extended to central Judah and Benjamin. Two settlements, Bethlehem and Gibeath-Elohim, are mentioned in the Bible as garrison towns. Neither of these has been excavated, and the latter has not even been definitely identified; but it is evident from biblical references that Philistines were the ruling element in these towns at this period.

The material culture of this phase is characterized by its many local variations. It should be stressed that it was during this period of greatest expansion that Philistine culture lost its uniqueness and vitality and slowly became assimilated into the surrounding Canaanite cultures, as is seen at Ashdod (stratum X), Tell Qasile (stratum X), Tell el-Farʿah (S) (pre-W), Tell Jemmeh (buildings H), Megiddo (stratum VIA), and Tell Beit Mirsim (final phase of stratum B₂). This period of expansion was brought to an end by the conquests of David; during the period of the United Monarchy, the Philistines were once again confined to the southern coast of Israel.

BIBLIOGRAPHY

Aharoni, Y. *The Land of the Bible*. London, 1974.

———. "New Aspects of the Israelite Occupation in the North." In *Near Eastern Archaeology in the Twentieth Century: Essays in Honor of Nelson Glueck*, edited by J. A. Sanders, pp. 254–62. New York, 1970.

Albright, W. F. "A Colony of Cretan Mercenaries on the Coast of the Negeb." *JPOS* 1 (1921): 187–94.

———. "The Excavations of Tell Beit Mirsim I," IA, II, III; *AASOR* 12 (1932): 53–75; IA, *AASOR* 13 (1933): 55–128; II, *AASOR* 17 (1938); III, *AASOR* 21–22 (1943).

———. "An Anthropoid Clay Coffin from Saḥâb in Transjordan." *AJA* 36 (1932): 295–306.

———. "Some Oriental Glosses on the Homeric Problem." *AJA* 54 (1950): 162–76.

———. "The Eastern Mediterranean about 1060 B.C." In *Studies Presented to David Moore Robinson*, vol. 1, edited by G. E. Mylonas, pp. 223–31. St. Louis, 1951.

———. "Northeast Mediterranean Dark Ages and the Early Iron Age Art of Syria." In *The Aegean and the Near East*, edited by S. S. Weinberg, pp. 144–64. New York, 1956.

———. *The Archeaology of Palestine*. The Pelican Archaeology Series. London, 1963.

———. "The Role of the Canaanites in the History of Civilization." In *The Bible and the Ancient Near East: Essays in Honor of W. F. Albright*, edited by G. E. Wright, pp. 438–87. New York, 1961.

———. "Syria, the Philistines and Phoenicia." In *CAH³*, vol. II, pt. 2, chap. 33, pp. 507–34.

Ålin, P. *Das Ende der mykenischen Fundstätten auf dem griechischen Festland*. SIMA, vol. 1. Lund, 1962.

Alt, A. *Kleine Schriften zur Geschichte des Volkes Israel*, vol. 1. Munich, 1959.

———. "Ägyptische Tempel in Palästina und die Landnahme der Philister." In *Kleine Schriften zur Geschichte des Volkes Israel*, vol. 1, pp. 216–30. Munich, 1959.

———. "Syrien und Palästina im Onomastikon des Amenope." In *Kleine Schriften zur Geschichte des Volkes Israel*, vol. 1, pp. 231–45. Munich, 1959.

———. "Zur Geschichte von Beth-Sean 1500–1000 v. Chr." In *Klein Schriften zur Geschichte des Volkes Israel*, vol. 1, pp. 246–55. Munich, 1959.

Amiran, R. "The Arm-shaped Vessel and Its Family." *JNES* 21 (1962): 161–74.

Astour, M. C. "New Evidence on the Last Days of Ugarit." *AJA* 69 (1965): 253–58.

———. *Hellenosemitica*. Leiden, 1965.

———. "Ugarit and the Aegean." In *Orient and Occident* (*Alter Orient* und Altes Testament 22), edited by H. A. Hoffner, Jr., pp. 17–28. Neukirchen-Vluyn, 1973.

Åström, L. "The Late Cypriote Bronze Age: Other Arts and Crafts." In *SCE*, IV, *Part 1D*, pp. 473–674.

Åström, P. "The Late Cypriote Bronze Age; Architecture and Pottery." In *SCE*, IV, *Part 1C*.

———. "Relative and Absolute Chronology, Foreign Relations, Historical Conclusions." In *SCE*, IV, *Part 1D*, pp. 675–781.

Barnett, R. D. "Mopsos." *JHS* 73 (1953): 140–43.

———. "The Sea Peoples." In *CAH³*, vol. II, chap. 28, pp. 359–78.

———. *A Catalogue of the Nimrud Ivories*. London, 1957.

Benson, J. L. "A Problem in Orientalizing Cretan Birds: Mycenaean or Philistine Prototypes?" *JNES* 20 (1961): 73–84.

———. *The Necropolis of Kaloriziki*. SIMA, vol. 36. Göteborg, 1973.

Berard, J. "Philistins et Préhèllenes." *Revue archéologique* 37 (1951): 129 ff.

Biran, A., and Negbi, O. "The Stratigraphical Sequence at Tel Sippor." *IEJ* 16 (1966): 160–73, pls. 18–23.

Biran, A. "Tel Dan." *BA* 37 (1974): 26–51.

Bliss, F. J., and Macalister, R. A. S. *Excavations in Palestine, 1898–1900*. London, 1902.

Blegen, C. W. *The Palace of Nestor at Pylos in Western Messenia*, vol. I. Princeton, 1966.

Bonfante, G. "Who Were the Philistines?" *AJA* 50 (1946): 251–62.

Breasted, J. H. *Ancient Records of Egypt*, vols. III–IV. Chicago, 1906.

Brock, J. K. *Fortetsa: Early Greek Tombs near Knossos*. Cambridge, 1957.

Brunton, G., and Engelbach, R. *Gurob*. London, 1927.

Burn, A. R. *Minoans, Philistines, and Greeks, B.C. 1400–900*. London, 1968.

Campbell, E. "In Search of the Philistines." *BA* 26 (1963): 30–32.

Casson, L. *Ships and Seamanship in the Ancient World*. Princeton, 1971.

Catling, H. W. *Cypriot Bronzework in the Mycenaean World*. Oxford, 1964.

———. "Patterns of Settlement in Bronze Age Cyprus." *Op.Ath.* 4 (1962): 129–69.

———. "Cyprus in the Late Bronze Age." In *CAH³*, vol. I, chap. 22(b).

———. "The Achaean Settlement of Cyprus." In *Mycenaeans in the Eastern Mediterranean*, pp. 34–39. Nicosia, 1973.

Černý, J. "Egypt from the Death of Ramesses III to the End of the Twenty-first Dynasty." In *CAH³*, vol. II, chap. 35.

Coche de la Ferté, E. *Essai de Classification de la Céramique Mycénienne d'Enkomi (Campagnes 1946 et 1947)*. Paris, 1951.

Cook, J. "Greek Settlements in the Eastern Aegean and Asia Minor." In *CAH³*, vol. II, chap. 38.

Courtois, J. C. "Sur Divers Groupes de Vases Mycéniens en Méditerranée Orientale (1250–1150 Av. J.-C.)." In *Mycenaeans in the Eastern Mediterranean*, pp. 137–65. Nicosia, 1973.

Cross, F. M. *Canaanite Myth and Hebrew Epic: Essays in the History of the Religion of Israel*. Cambridge, Mass., 1973.

Daniel, J. F. "Two Late Cypriote III Tombs at Kourion." *AJA* 41 (1937): 56–85.

Desborough, V. R. d'A. *Protogeometric Pottery*. Oxford, 1952.

———. *The Last Mycenaeans and Their Successors*. Oxford, 1964.

———. "The End of Mycenaean Civilization and the Dark Ages." In *CAH³*, vol. II, chap. 36(a).

———. *The Greek Dark Ages*. London, 1972.

———. "Mycenaeans in Cyprus in the 11th Century B.C." In *Mycenaeans in the Eastern Mediterranean*, pp. 79–87. Nicosia, 1973.

Dever, W. G., Lance, H. D., and Wright, G. E. *Gezer I (1964–1966)*.

Dever, W. G., Lance, H. D., Bullard, R. G., Cole, D. P., and Seger, J. D. *Gezer II (1967–1970)*.

Dikaios, P. "An Iron Age Painted Amphora in the Cyprus Museum." *BSA* 37 (1936–37): 56–72.

———. *A Guide to the Cyprus Museum* (3d rev. ed.). Nicosia, 1961.

———. "The Bronze Statue of a Horned God from Enkomi." *AA* 77 (1962): 1–39.

———. "The Context of the Enkomi Tablets." *Kadmos* 1 (1962): 39 ff.

———. *Enkomi Excavations*.

Dothan, M. "The Excavations at ʿAfula." *ʿAtiqot* I (1955): 19–70.

———. "Tel Mor (Tell Kheidar)." *IEJ* 9 (1959): 271–72; *IEJ* 10 (1960): 123–25.

———. "Excavations from Azor 1960." *IEJ* 11 (1961): 171–75.

———. "Relations between Cyprus and the Philistine Coast in the Late Bronze Age (Tel Mor, Ashdod)." *Praktika* 1 (1972): 51–56.

———. "The Foundations of Tel Mor and of Ashdod." *IEJ* 23 (1973): 1–17.

———. *Ashdod II–III*.

———. "Ashdod: A City of the Philistine Pentapolis." *Archaeology* 20 (1967): 178–86.

———. "Ashdod of the Philistines." In *New Directions in Biblical Archaeology*, edited by D. N. Freedman and J. C. Greenfield, pp. 17–27. New York, 1971.

———. "The Musicians of Ashdod." *Archaeology* 23 (1970): 310–11.

———. "A Stand with Musicians Motif from Ashdod." *Qadmoniot* 3 (1970): 94–95 (Hebrew).

Dothan, M., and Freedman, D. N. *Ashdod I*.

Dothan, M., Asaro, F., and Perlman, I. "An Introductory Study of Mycenaean IIIC:1 Ware from Tel Ashdod." *Archaeometry* 13 (1971): 169–75.

Dothan, T. "Archaeological Reflections on the Philistine Problem." *Antiquity and Survival* 2 (1957): 151–64.

———. "Philistine Civilization in the Light of Archaeological Finds in Palestine and Egypt." *Eretz-Israel* 5 (1958): 55–66 (Hebrew).

———. *The Philistines and Their Material Culture*. Jerusalem, 1967 (Hebrew).

———. "A Female Mourner Figurine from the Lachish Region." *Eretz-Israel* 9 (1969): 42–46 (Hebrew).

———. "Anthropoid Clay Coffins from a Late Bronze Age Cemetery near Deir el-Balah (Preliminary Report I)." *IEJ* 22 (1972): 65–72.

———. "Anthropoid Clay Coffins from a Late Bronze Age Cemetery near Deir el-Balah (Preliminary Report II)." *IEJ* 23 (1973): 129–46.

———. "The Cemetery near Deir el-Balah and Burial in Anthropoid Sarcophagi," *IEJ* 23 (1973): 129–46.

———. "Another Mourning-Woman Figurine from the Lachish Region," *Eretz-Israel* 11 (1973): 120–21 (Hebrew).

———. "Philistine Material Culture and its

Mycenaean Affinities." In *Mycenaeans in the Eastern Mediterranean*, pp. 187–88. Nicosia, 1973.

———. *Excavations at the Cemetery of Deir el-Balah.* Qedem 10. Jerusalem, 1979.

Drower, M. S. "Ugarit." In *CAH³*, vol. II, chap. 21(b).

Duncan, J. G. *Corpus of Dated Palestinian Pottery.* London, 1930.

Edel, E., and Mayrhofer, M. "Notizien zu Fremdnamen in ägyptischen Quellen." *Orientalia* 40 (1971): 1–10.

Edelstein, G., and Glass, Y. "The Origin of Philistine Pottery Based on Petrographic Analysis." In *Excavation and Studies: Essays in Honour of S. Yeivin*, edited by Y. Aharoni, pp. 125–31. Tel Aviv, 1973 (Hebrew).

Edgerton, W., and Wilson, J. *Historical Records of Rameses III: The Texts in Medinet Habu I–III.* Chicago, 1936.

Eissfeldt, O. *Philister und Phönizier.* Der Alte Orient Series 34. Leipzig, 1936.

Engelbach, R. *Riqqeh and Memphis VI.* London, 1915.

Erlenmeyer, M. L., and Erlenmeyer, H. "Uber Philister und Kreter." *Orientalia* 29 (1960): 121–50, 241–72; 30 (1961): 269–93; 33 (1964): 199–237.

———. "Einige syrische Siegel mit ägäischen Bildelementen (Philister)." *AfO* 21 (1966): 32–34.

Evans, A. *The Palace of Minos*, vols. I–IV. London, 1921–1964.

Faulkner, R. C. "Egypt: From the Inception of the Nineteenth Dynasty to the Death of Ramesses III." In *CAH³*, vol. II, chap. 23.

Fisher, C. S. *The Excavation of Armageddon.* Chicago, 1929.

Fitzgerald, G. M. *The Four Canaanite Temples of Beth-Shan*, vol. II, pt. 2: *The Pottery.* Philadelphia, 1930.

Forsdyke, E. J. *Catalogue of the Greek and Etruscan Vases in the British Museum*, vol. I, pt. I., *Prehistoric Aegean Pottery.* London, 1925.

Forsdyke, J. *Greece before Homer.* London, 1956.

Franken, H. J. "The Excavations at Deir ʿAlla in Jordan: 2nd Season." *VT* 11 (1961): 361–72.

———. "Clay Tablets from Deir ʿAlla, Jordan." *VT* 14 (1964): 377–79.

———. "Iron Age Jordan Village." *Illustrated London News* (1 May 1965): 27.

———. "Palestine in the Time of the Nineteenth Dynasty, Archaeological Evidence." In *CAH³*, vol. II, chap. 26(b).

———. *Excavations at Tell Deir ʿAlla.* Leiden, 1969.

French, E. "Pottery from Late Helladic III B 1 Destruction Contexts at Mycenae." *BSA* 62 (1967): 149–93.

———. "The First Phase of the LH IIIC." *AA* (1969): 133–36.

———. "The Development of Mycenaean Terracotta Figurines." *BSA* 66 (1971): 101–87.

Furumark, A. *The Chronology of Mycenaean Pottery.* Stockholm, 1941.

———. *The Mycenaean Pottery: Analysis and Classification.* Stockholm, 1941.

———. "The Mycenaean IIIC Pottery and its Relation to Cypriote Fabrics." *OA* 3 (1944): 194–265.

———. "The Settlement at Ialysos and Aegean History c. 1550–1400 B.C." *OA* 6 (1950): 150–271.

———. "The Excavations at Sinda. Some Historical Results." *Op.Ath.* 6 (1965): 99–116.

Galling, K. "Die Kopfzier der Philister in den Darstellungen von Medinet Habu." In *Ugaritica VI*, pp. 247–65.

Gardiner, A. H. *Ancient Egyptian Onomastica*, vols. I–III. Oxford, 1947.

———. *Egypt of the Pharaohs.* Oxford, 1961.

Garstang, J. A. "Tanturah (Dora)." *BBSAJ* 4 (1924): 35–45; 7 (1925): 80–98.

———. "Askalon Reports. The Philistine Problem." *PEFQSt* (1921): 162–63.

———. "Excavations at Askalon: A Summary." *PEFQSt* (1922): 112–19.

Gjerstad, E. "Initial Date of the Cypriote Iron Age." *OA* 3 (1944): 73–106.

———. *SCE IV, Part 2, The Cypro-Geometric, Cypro-Archaic and Cypro-Classical Periods.* Stockholm, 1948.

Goldman, H. *Excavations at Gözlü Kule: Tarsus*, vol. 2, *From the Neolithic through the Bronze Age.* Princeton, 1956.

Gophna, R. "Iron Age I Haserim in Southern Philistia." *ʿAtiqot* 3 (1966): 44–51 (Hebrew).

Gordon, C. H. "The Role of the Philistines." *Antiquity* 30 (1956): 22–26.

Grant, E. *Beth-Shemesh.* Haverford, Pa., 1929.

———. *Ain Shems Excavations, 1928–1931*, pts. I–II. Haverford, Pa., 1931–32.

———. *Rumeileh, being Ain Shems Excavations*, pt. III. Haverford, Pa., 1934.

———, and Wright, G. E. *Ain Shems Excavations*, pt. IV: *The Pottery*; pt. V: *The Text.* Haverford, Pa., 1938–39.

———. "The Philistine." *JBL* 55 (1936): 175–94.

Greenfield, J. C. "Philistine." In *Interpreter's Dictionary of the Bible III, K–Q*, pp. 791–95. New York, 1962.

Grosjean, R. "Recent Work in Corsica." *Antiquity* 40 (1966): 190–98.

Guido, M. *Sardinia.* London, 1963.

Gurney, O. *The Hittites.* London, 1952.

Guy, P. L. O. *Megiddo Tombs.* Chicago, 1938.

Hamilton, R. W. "Excavations at Tell Abu Hawām." *QDAP* 4 (1935): 1–69.

Hankey, V. "Late Mycenaean Pottery at Beth-Shan." *AJA* 70 (1966): 169–71.

———. "Mycenaean Pottery in the Middle East." *BSA* 62 (1967): 107–47.

———. "Turmoil in the Near East c. 1200 B.C." *Journal of the Royal Central Asian Society* 61 (1974): 51–60.

Helck, A. *Die Beziehungen Ägyptens zu Vorderasien in 3 und 2 Jahrtausend v. Chr.* Wiesbaden, 1962.

Hennequin, L. "Trois sarcophages anthropoides en poterie trouvés à Tell Douweir." In *Mélanges Syriens offerts à Monsieur René Dussaud*, vol. II, pp. 965–74. Paris, 1939.

Herbig, R. "Philister und Dorier." *JDAI* 55 (1940): 58–59.

Hestrin, R. *The Philistines and the Other Sea Peoples.* Catalogue 68, Israel Museum. Jerusalem, 1970.

———. "Two Anthropoid Coffins." *Bulletin of the Israel Museum* 9 (1972): 65–66.

Heurtley, W. A. "The Relationship between 'Philistine' and Mycenaean Pottery." *QDAP* 5 (1936): 90–110.

Higgins, R. A. *Catalogue of Terracottas in the Department of Greek and Roman Antiquities, British Museum*, vol. 1. London, 1954.

Hindson, E. W. *The Philistines and the Old Testament.* Grand Rapids, Mich., 1971.

Hrouda, B. "Die Einwanderung der Philister in Palastina." In *Vorderasiatische Archäologie Studien und aufsätze A. Moortgat*, pp. 126–35. Berlin, 1964.

Iakovidis, S. "A Mycenaean Mourning Custom." *AJA* 70 (1966): 43–50.

———. *Perati A–Γ, B.*

Jacopi, G. "Nuovi scavi nella necropoli micenea di Jalisso." *Annuario* 13–14 (1933–1940): 253–345.

James, F. W. *The Iron Age at Beth Shan.* Philadelphia, 1966.

Johansen, K. Friis. "Exochi, ein frührhodisches Gräberfeld." *Acta Archaeologica* 28 (1957): 1–192.

Jones, A. H. "Philistines and the Hearth: Their Journey to the Levant." *JNES* 31 (1972): 343–50.

Jones, F. F. "Three Mycenaean Figurines." In *Aegean and the Near East*, pp. 122–25. New York, 1956.

Jirku, A. "Zur Illyrischen Herkunft der Philister." *Wiener Zeitschrift für die Kunde des Morgenlandes* 49 (1943): 13–19.

Kantor, H. J. *The Aegean and the Orient in the Second Millennium B.C.* Bloomington, 1947.

———. "The Ivories from Floor 6 of Sounding IX." In *Soundings at Tell Fakhariyah*, by C. W. McEwan et al., pp. 63–64. Chicago, 1958.

Kaplan, Y. "Jaffa's History Revealed by the Spade." *Archaeology* 17 (1964): 270–76.

———. "The Archaeology and History of Tel-Aviv–Jaffa." *BA* 35 (1972): 66–95.

Karageorghis, V. *Treasures in the Cyprus Museum.* Nicosia, 1962.

———. *Corpus Vasorum Antiquorum:* Cyprus, vol. I: Nicosia, 1963; vol. II: Nicosia, 1965.

———. *Nouveaux Documents pour l'étude du Bronze Récent à Chypre.* Paris, 1965.

———. "An Early XIth Century B.C. Tomb from Palaepaphos." *RDAC* (1967): 1–24.

———. *Cyprus.* Archaeologia Mundi. Geneva, 1969.

———. *Mycenaean Art from Cyprus.* Picture Book No. 3. Nicosia, 1968.

———. "Contribution to the Religion of Cyprus in the 13th and 12th Centuries B.C." In *Mycenaeans in the Eastern Mediterranean*, pp. 105–09. Nicosia, 1973.

———. "Kition: Mycenaean and Phoenician." In Mortimer Wheeler Archaeological Lecture. *Proceedings of the British Academy* 59 (1973). (See this source for a full bibliography of the excavations at Kition.)

———. *Alaas. A Protogeometric Necropolis in Cyprus.* Nicosia, 1975.

Karageorghis, V., and Buchholz, H. G. *Altägäis und Altkypros.* Tübingen, 1971.

Kassis, H. "Gath and the Structure of the Philistine Society." *JBL* 84 (1965): 259–71.

Katzenstein, J. *The History of Tyre.* Jerusalem, 1973.

Kelso, J. L. et al. "The Excavations of Bethel (1934–1960)." *AASOR* 39 (1968).

Kenyon, K. M. *Archaeology in the Holy Land*, 2d ed. London, 1965.

Kinch, K. F. *Vroulia.* Berlin, 1914.

Kitchen, K. A. *The Third Intermediate Period in Egypt (1100–650 B.C.).* Warminster, England, 1973.

———. "The Philistines." In *Peoples of Old Testament Times*, edited by D. J. Wiseman, pp. 53–78. Oxford, 1973.

Krönig, W. "Ägyptische Fayence Schalen des Neuen Reiches." *MDIAA* 5 (1934): 144 ff.

Lamon, R., and Shipton, G. M. *Megiddo*, vol. I. Chicago, 1939.

Lapp, P. "Tell el-Fûl." *BA* 28 (1965): 2–10.

Lochner-Huttenbuch, F. *Die Pelasger.* Vienna, 1960.

Lorimer, H. *Homer and the Monuments.* London, 1950.

Loud, G. *The Megiddo Ivories.* Chicago, 1939.

———. *Megiddo*, vol. II. Chicago, 1948.

Macalister, R. A. S. *The Excavation of Gezer 1902–1905 and 1907–1909*, 3 vols. London, 1912.

———. *The Philistines: Their History and Civilization.* London, 1914; reprint, Chicago, 1965.

McCown, C. C. *Tell en-Nasbeh*, vol. I. Berkeley, 1947.

Macdonald, E., Starkey, J. L., and Harding, L. *Beth Pelet*, vol. II. London, 1932.

McEwan, C. W. et al. *Soundings at Tell Fakhariyah.* Chicago, 1958.

Mackenzie, D. "The Excavations at Ain Shems." *PEF Ann* 1 (1911): 41–94; *PEF Ann* 2 (1912–1913): 1–39.

Maier, F. G. "The Cemeteries of Old Paphos." *Archaeologia viva* 2 (1969): 116–30.

Maisler—*see* Mazar.

Maiuri, A. "Jalisos—Scavi della Missione Archeologica Italiana a Rodi (Parte I e II)," *Annuario* 6–7 (1926): 83–256.

Malamat, A. "Cushan Rishathaim and the Decline of the Near East around 1200 B.C." *JNES* 13 (1954): 231–42.

———. "The Kingdom of David and Solomon in Its Contact with Egypt and Aram Naharaim." *BA* 21 (1958): 96–102.

———. "The Struggle against the Philistines." In *The History of the Jewish People*, edited by H. H. Ben-Sasson, pp. 80–87. Cambridge, Mass., 1976.

———. "The Egyptian Decline in Canaan and the Sea-Peoples." In *The World History of the Jewish People*, vol. 3, *Judges*, edited by B. Mazar, pp. 23–38, 294–300. Tel Aviv, 1971.

———. "Campaigns to the Mediterranean by Iahdunlim and other early Mesopotamian Rulers." In *Studies in Honor of Benno Landsberger*, pp. 365–73. Chicago, 1965.

———. "Syro-Palestinian Destinations in a Mari Tin Inventory." *IEJ* 21 (1971): 29–38.

———. "Aspects of the Foreign Policies of David and Solomon." *JNES* 22 (1963): 1–17.

———. "Syrien-Palästina in der zweiten Hälfte des 2. Jahrtausends." In *Fischer Weltgeschichte*, vol. 2, pp. 200–21. Frankfurt, 1966.

———. "The Period of the Judges." In *The World History of the Jewish People*, vol. 3, *Judges*, edited by B. Mazar, pp. 129–63. New Brunswick, 1971.

———. "Western Asia Minor in the Time of 'Sea Peoples'." *BIES* 30 (1966): 195–208 (Hebrew).

Marquet-Krause, J. *Les Fouilles de ʿAy (et-Tell), 1933–35.* Paris, 1949.

May, G. *Material Remains of the Megiddo Cult.* Chicago, 1935.

Mazar, A. "Excavations at Tell Qasile, 1971–1972: Preliminary Report." *IEJ* 23 (1973): 65–71.

———. "Excavations at Tell Qasile, 1973–1974: Preliminary Report." *IEJ* 25 (1975): 77–88.

Mazar, B. "Ein ägäischer Bestattungsbrauch in Vorderasien." *AfO* 11 (1936–37): 239–40.

———. "The Excavations at Tell Qasile: Preliminary Report." *IEJ* 1 (1950–51): 61–76, 125–140, 194–218.

———. "The Stratification of Tell Abū Huwâm on the Bay of Acre." *BASOR* 124 (1951): 21–25.

———. "Yurza: The Identification of Tell Jemmeh." *PEQ* (1952): 48–51.

———. "Gath and Gittaim." *IEJ* 4 (1954): 227–35.

———. "The Philistines and the Rise of Israel and Tyre." *Proceedings of the Israel Academy of Sciences and Humanities* 1 (1964): 1–22.

———. "The Historical Background of the Book of Genesis. *JNES* 28 (1969): 73–83.

———. "The 'Orpheus' Jug from Megiddo." In *Canaan and Israel: Historical Essays*, pp. 174–82. Jerusalem, 1974 (Hebrew).

———. "The Philistines and Their Wars with Israel." In *The World History of the Jewish People*, vol. 3, *Judges*, edited by B. Mazar, pp. 164–79. New Brunswick, 1971.

———. *Canaan and Israel, Historical Essays.* Jerusalem, 1974 (Hebrew).

Mitchell, T. L. "Philistia." In *Archaeology and Old Testament Study*, edited by D. Winton Thomas, pp. 405–28. Oxford, 1967.

Müller, H., ed. *Jahresbericht des Instituts für Vorgeschichte der Universität Frankfurt A.M. 1976.* Munich, 1977.

Murray, A. S., and Walters, H. B. *Excavations in Cyprus.* London, 1900.

Mylonas, G. E. *Mycenae and the Mycenaean Age.* Princeton, 1967.

Myres, J. L. *Handbook of the Cesnola Collection of Antiquities from Cyprus.* New York: The Metropolitan Museum of Art, 1914.

Nagel, G. *La Céramique du Nouvel Empire à Deir el-Médineh*, tome I. Cairo, 1938.

Naveh, J. "Khirbat al-Muqannaʿ-Ekron." *IEJ* 8 (1958): 87–100.

Naville, E. *Ahnas el Medineh (Heracleopolis Magna).* London, 1894.

Naville, E., and Griffith, F. *The Mound of the Jew and the City of Onias, Antiquities of Tell el Yahudiyah.* London, 1887, 1890.

Negbi, O. "Origin and Distribution of Early Iron Age Palestinian Bronzeworks." *Tel Aviv* 1 (1974): 159–72.

Nelson, H. H. et al. *Medinet Habu.*

———. "The Naval Battle Pictured at Medinet Habu." *JNES* 2 (1943): 40–55.

Nibbi, A. *The Sea Peoples: A Re-examination of the Egyption Sources.* Oxford, 1972.

Nilsson, M. *The Minoan-Mycenaean Religion.* 2d ed. Lund, 1950.

Nylander, C. "Zur Moortgat Festschrift: Troja, Philister, Achämeniden." *Berliner Jahrbuch für Vor- und Frühgeschichte* 6 (1966): 203–17.

Ohata, K., ed. *Tel Zeror*, vols. I, II, III. Tokyo, 1966, 1967, 1970.

Oren, E. *The Northern Cemetery of Beth Shan.* Leiden, 1973.

———. "Tel Seraʿ (Tell esh-Shariʿa)." *IEJ* 23 (1973): 251–54.

———. "Tel Seraʿ (Tell esh-Shariʿa)." *RB* 80 (1973): 401–05.

Otten, H. "Neue Quellen zum Ausklang des Hethitischen Reiches." *MDOG* 94 (1963): 1–23.

Parr, P. J., Harding, G. L., and Dayton, J. E. "Preliminary Survey in N.W. Arabia, 1968." *BIAL* 8–9 (1968–69): 193–**242**.

Petrie, W. M. F. *Tanis II, Nebesheh and Defenneh*. London, 1888.

———. *Kahun, Gurob and Hawara*. London, 1890.

———. *Illahun, Kahun and Gurob*. London, 1891.

———. *Meydum Saft*. London, 1906.

———. *Gizeh and Rifeh*. London, 1907.

———. *Tools and Weapons*. London, 1917.

———. *Scarabs and Cylinders with Names*. London, 1917.

———. *Gerar*. London, 1928.

———. *Ancient Gaza*, vols. I–IV. London, 1931–1934.

———. *Anthedon Sinai*. London, 1937.

Petrie, W. M. F., and Duncan, J. G. *Hyksos and Israelite Cities*. London, 1906.

Petrie, W. M. F., Wainwright, G. A., and Mackay, E. J. H. *The Labyrinth, Gerzeh and Mazghuneh*. London, 1912.

Petrie, W. M. F., and Tufnell, O. *Beth Pelet*, vol. I. London, 1930.

Petrie, W. M. F., Mackay, E. J. H., and Murray, M. A. *Ancient Gaza*, vol. V, *City of Shepherd Kings*. London, 1952.

Phythian-Adams, W. J. "Askalon Reports. Stratigraphical Sections." *PEFQSt* (1921): 163–69.

———. "Report on the Stratification of Askalon." *PEFQSt* (1923): 60–84.

———. "Philistine Origins in the Light of Palestinian Archaeology." *BBSAJ* 3 (1923): 20–27.

Popham, M. R. *The Last Days of the Palace at Knossos—Complete Vases of the Late Minoan IIIB Period*. SIMA, vol. 5. Lund, 1964.

Popham, M. R., and Sackett, L. H. *Excavations at Lefkandi, Euboea, 1964–1966: A Preliminary Report*. London, 1968.

———. *The Destruction of the Palace at Knossos: Pottery of the Late Minoan IIIA Period*. SIMA, vol. 12. Göteborg, 1970.

Porada, E. "A Lyre Player from Tarsus and his Relations." In *Aegean and the Near East*, pp. 185–211.

Pritchard, J. B. *Palestinian Figurines in Relation to Certain Goddesses Known Through Literature*. New Haven, 1943.

———, ed. *ANET*.

———. *ANEP*.

———. "Two Tombs and a Tunnel in the Jordan Valley." *Expedition* 6 (1964): 3–9.

———. "The First Excavations at Tell es-Saʿidiyeh." *BA* 28 (1965): 10–17.

———. "New Evidence on the Role of the Sea Peoples in Canaan at the Beginning of the Iron Age." In *The Role of the Phoenicians in the Interaction of Mediterranean Civilizations*, edited by W. Ward, pp. 99–112.

American University of Beirut, Centennial Publications, 1968.

———. *Sarepta: A Preliminary Report on the Iron Age*. Philadelphia, 1975.

Rabin, C. "Hittite Words in Hebrew." In *Studies in the Bible Presented to M. Segal*, edited by M. Grintz and J. Liver, pp. 151–79. Jerusalem, 1964 (Hebrew).

———. "The Origin of the Hebrew Word *Pīlegeš*." *Journal of Jewish Studies* 25 (1974): 353–64.

Rahtjen, B. D. "Philistine and Hebrew Amphictyonies." *JNES* 24 (1965): 100–04.

Rainey, A. F. "Gath of the Philistines." *Christian News from Israel* 17 (1966): 23–37.

———. "The Identification of Philistine Gath." *Eretz-Israel* 12 (1975): 63*–76*.

Riis, P. J. *Hama. Fouilles et recherches 1931–38*, vol. II:3, *Les cimetières à crémation*. Copenhagen, 1948.

Rowe, A. *The Topography and History of Beth Shean*, vol. I. Philadelphia, 1930.

———. *A Catalogue of Egyptian Scarabs, Scaraboids, Seals and Amulets in the Palestine Archaeological Museum*. Cairo, 1936.

———. *The Four Canaanite Temples of Beth Shean*, vol. II, pt. I. Philadelphia, 1940.

Sandars, N. K. *The Sea Peoples, Warriors of the Mediterranean*. London, 1978.

Saussey, E. "La céramique philistine." *Syria* 5 (1924): 169 ff.

Schachermeyr, F. *Ägäis und Orient*. Vienna, 1967.

———. *Die ägäische Frühzeit*, band 2: *Die mykenische Zeit*. Vienna, 1976.

Schaeffer, C. F. A. *Ugaritica II*. Paris, 1949.

———. *Enkomi*.

———. "Götter der Nord- und Inselvölker in Zypern." *AFO* 21 (1966): 59–69.

———, et al. *Ugaritica VI*.

———. *Alasia I*. Paris, 1971.

Scherff, A., and Moortgat, A. *Ägypten und Vorderasien Altertum*. Munich, 1950.

Schumacher, G. *Tell et-Mutesellim*, vol. 1. Leipzig, 1908.

Seiradaki, M. "Pottery from Karphi." *BSA* 55 (1960): 1–37.

Sellers, O. R. *The Citadel of Beth-Zur*. Philadelphia, 1933.

Shiloh, Y. "The Four-Room House—Its Situation and Function in the Israelite City." *IEJ* 20 (1970): 180–90.

Shipton, G. M. "Notes on the Megiddo Pottery of Strata VI–XX." *Studies in Ancient Oriental Civilization*, no. 17. Chicago, 1939.

Sjöqvist, E. *Problems of the Late Cypriote Bronze Age*. Stockholm, 1940.

Smith, W. S. *Ancient Egypt as Represented in the Museum of Fine Arts*. Boston, 1960.

Snodgrass, A. M. *Early Greek Armour and Weapons.* Edinburgh, 1964.

———. *The Dark Age of Greece.* Edinburgh, 1971.

Starkey, J. L., and Harding, L. "Beth-Pelet Cemetery." In *BP II.*

Starr, C. G. *The Origin of Greek Civilization.* London, 1962.

Steindorff, G. et al. *Aniba I–II.*

Stiebing, W. H., Jr. "Another Look at the Origins of the Philistine Tombs at Tell el-Farʿah (S)." *AJA* 74 (1970): 139–93.

Strobel, A. *Der Spätbronzezeitliche Seevölkersturm.* Berlin, 1976.

Stubbings, F. H. *Mycenaean Pottery from the Levant.* Cambridge, 1951.

———. "The Recession of Mycenaean Civilization." In *CAH³,* vol. II, chap. 37.

Styrenius, C. G. "The Vases from the Submycenaean Cemetery of Salamis." *Op.Ath.* 4 (1962): 103–23.

Tadmor, H. "Philistia under Assyrian Rule." *BA* 29 (1966): 86–102.

———. "A Note on the Sabaʿa Stele of Adad-nirari III." *IEJ* 19 (1969): 46–48.

Taylor, J. du Plat. "Late Cypriot III in the Light of Recent Excavations." *PEQ* 88 (1956): 22–37.

Taylour, W. "New Light on Mycenaean Religion." *Antiquity* 44 (1970): 270–80.

Thiersch, H. "Die neueren Ausgrabungen in Palästina." *AA* 23 (1908): 344–413.

Tufnell, O. et al. *Lachish II, The Fosse Temple.* Oxford, 1940.

———. *Lachish III, The Iron Age.* London, 1953.

———. *Lachish IV, The Bronze Age.* London, 1958.

Tzori, N. "An Archaeological Survey of the Beth-Shan Valley." In *The Beth Shean Valley (the 17th Archaeological Convention),* pp. 135–98. Jerusalem, 1962 (Hebrew).

Van Beek, G. W. "Cypriote Chronology and the Dating of Iron I Sites in Palestine." *BASOR* 124 (1951): 26–29.

———. "The Date of Tell Abu Huwam, Stratum III." *BASOR* 138 (1955): 34–38.

Vercoutter, J. *L'Egypte et le Monde Egéen Préhellénique.* Cairo, 1956.

Vermeule, E. "The Fall of the Mycenaean Empire." *Archaeology* 13 (1960): 66–75.

———. *Greece in the Bronze Age.* Chicago, 1964.

———. "Painted Mycenaean Larnakes." *JHS* 85 (1965): 123–48.

Virolleaud, C. *Le palais royal d'Ugarit,* vol. V. Paris, 1965.

Wace, A. J. B. *Mycenae: An Archaeological History and Guide.* Princeton, 1949.

———. "The Last Days of Mycenae." In *Aegean and the Near East,* pp. 126–35.

Wace, A. J. B., and Stubbings, F. H., eds. *A Companion to Homer.* London, 1962.

Wainwright, G. A. "Caphtor, Keftiu and Cappadocia." *PEFQSt* (1931): 203–16.

———. "Keftiu." *JEA* 17 (1931): 26–43.

———. "Some Sea-Peoples and Others in the Hittite Archives." *JEA* 25 (1939): 148–53.

———. "Asiatic Keftiu." *AJA* 56 (1952): 196–212.

———. "Keftiu and Karamaina." *AS* 4 (1954): 33–48.

———. "Caphtor, Cappadocia." *VT* 6 (1956): 199–210.

———. "Some Early Philistine History." *VT* 9 (1959): 73–87.

———. "The Teresh, the Etruscans and Asia Minor." *AS* 9 (1959): 197–213.

———. "Some Sea-Peoples." *JEA* 47 (1961): 71–90.

———. "A Teucrian at Salamis in Cyprus." *JHS* 83 (1963): 146–51.

———. "Two Groups among the Sea Peoples." *JFK* 2 (1967): 482–89.

Waldbaum, J. "Philistine Tombs at Tell Fara and their Aegean Prototypes." *AJA* 70 (1966): 331–40.

———. "The Use of Iron in the Eastern Mediterranean: 1200–900 B.C." Ph.D. dissertation, Harvard University, 1968.

———. *From Bronze to Iron. SIMA,* vol. 54. Göteborg, 1978.

Wampler, J. C. *Nasbeh II.*

Watzinger, C. *Tell el-Mutesellim,* vol. II. Leipzig, 1929.

Weippert, M. Review of T. Dothan, *The Philistines and Their Material Culture. GGA* 223 (1971): 1–20.

Welch, F. B. "The Influence of the Aegean Civilization on South Palestine." *PEFQSt* (1900): 342–50.

Woolley, L. *Alalakh.* Oxford, 1955.

Wreszinski, W. *Atlas zur altägyptischen Kulturgeschichte,* vol. 2. Leipzig, 1935.

Wright, G. E. "Iron: The Date of its Introduction into Common Use in Palestine." *AJA* 43 (1939): 458–63.

———. "Philistine Coffins and Mercenaries." *BA* 22 (1959): 54–66.

———. "Fresh Evidence for the Philistine Story." *BA* 29 (1966): 70–86.

Yadin (Sukenik), Y. "Let the young men, I pray thee, arise and play before us." *JPOS* 21 (1948): 110–17.

———. "Goliath's Javelin and the *menor orgim.*" *PEQ* (1955): 58–69.

———. *The Art of Warfare in Biblical Lands in the Light of Archaeological Study.* New York, 1963.

———. "And Dan, Why Did He Remain in Ships?" *AJBA* 1 (1968): 9–23.

———. "Megiddo of the Kings of Israel." *BA* 33 (1970): 66–96.

Yon, M. *Salamine de Chypre II: La Tombe T. I. du XIᵉ, s.a.v.J-C.* Paris, 1971.

Yoyotte, J. "Un souvenir du 'Pharaon' Taousert en Jordanie." *VT* 12 (1962): 464–69.

INDEX

Abimelech, king of Philistines, 13

Tell Abu Hawam, 88, 160*n*125, 167, 291*n*5, 294

Achaeans, 292, 293

Achish, king of Gath, 16, 18, 22–23

Achzib, 57

Aegean influence on Philistine culture, 41, 58, 65, 66, 67, 185, 222. *See also* Philistines, Aegean background of

ʿAfula, 80–81, 105, 189, 295

Aharoni, Y., 15*n*53, 33*n*72

Ahiram, king of Byblos, 249*n*58

ʿAi, 189

Tell ʿAitun, 44, 106*n*24; cult objects, 237, 246; jugs, 153–54, 155, 172, 183, 198, 199, 203–04, 209

Akawasha (Sea People), 1, 293*n*9

Akerstrom, A., 151*n*80

Tel ʿAkko, 294

Alashya, king of, 293

Albright, W. F., 1*n*3, 24, 27*n*20, 28, 29*n*50, 30, 34*n*89, 84*n*332, 94*n*1, 252*n*2; anthropoid coffins, 260*n*9; Tell Beit Mirsim, 43, 44, 295; chronology of Philistine pottery, 94*n*1

Alon, D., 88*n*347

Alt, A., 4*n*17

Amarna letters, 1

Amenhotep II, 279

Amenhotep III, 21*n*78

Amenope, Onomasticon of, 3–4, 18, 35

Amiran, R., 172*n*148

Ammurapi, king of Ugarit, 293

Amphoriskoi, 125–31, 263–68

Anati, E., 292*n*5

Anatolia, 55*n*191, 159

Aniba (in Nubia), 118, 263, 279, 280, 284

Anthropoid clay coffins. *See* Coffins, anthropoid clay

Anthropomorphic vessels, 66

Antithetic tongue (motif), 198, 208, 209

Tel Aphek, 15, 89, 295

ʿAqir, 88*n*350

Architecture, 54, 58, 59, 80, 81, 87, 292; house, three-room, 59, 86; house, four-room, 59, 87; temple, 251. *See also* Temples; Tomb architecture

Argolid, 217; Close Style, 154, 155, 203; pottery tradition, 293

Asaro, F., 37*n*106, 254*n*4

Ashdod, 4, 17–18, 20, 24, 36–42, 90, 94*n*1, 96, 155, 209, 217; absolute

chronology, 294; "Ashdoda" (figurine), 41, 42, 215, 234–37, 251; bird motif, 198, 199, 200–04; bowls, 98, 212; cult vessels, 21, 219, 222, 227, 234, 237, 246, 251; kraters, 203, 205, 214, 215; mentioned in relation to other sites, 54, 59, 63, 82, 87, 115, 148; musicians stand, 42, 153, 249–51; Philistine settlement at, 295, 296; Type 1 bowls, 105–06; Type 2 kraters, 113; Type 3 stirrup jars, 123; Type 7 jugs, 157; Type 9 cylindrical bottles, 160, 166; Type 12 jugs, 172; Type 13 bowls, 188

Ashkelon (Tell el-Khadra), 4, 17, 24, 35–36, 94*n*1, 154, 294; Philistines settled in, 296; Type 1 bowls, 102; Type 2 kraters, 113; Type 16 juglets, 191

Asine (in Greece), 229

Astour, M. C., 17*n*61, 21, 292*n*6

Åstrom, P., 167*n*134, 234*n*38, 292*n*8

Tell Atchana-Alalakh, 159

Athens, 168

ʿAtlit, 57

Azor, 54–57, 172, 199; burial customs, 252*n*1; cult objects, 237, 246; mentioned in relation to other sites, 53, 149, 215; Type 1 bowls, 102–05; Type 2 kraters, 114–15; Type 3 stirrup jars, 123, 124–25; Type 5 amphoriskoi and pyxis, 130; Type 6 jugs, 149; Type 7 jugs, 157; Type 9 cylindrical bottles, 160, 166–67; Type 10 horn-shaped vessels, 171; Type 12 jugs, 172, 183; Type 13 bowls, 188; Type 16 juglets, 191

Baal-zebub (Baal-zebul) (deity), 20–21, 237

Bakry, H. S. K., 279*n*37

Balensi, J., 292*n*5

Barnett, R. D., 1*n*3, 168*n*139, 246*n*56

Beder, King of Tjekker, 69; prince of Dor, 4

Tel Beersheba, 87

Tell Beit Mirsim, 24, 43–44, 90–91, 295; mentioned in relation to other sites, 34, 35, 48, 50, 59, 86, 276, 294; Type 1 bowls, 102; Type 2 kraters, 113; Type 5 amphoriskoi, 130; Type 6 jugs, 149

Benson, J. L., 167*n*134, 200, 218

Ben-Tor, A., 90*n*356

Betancourt, P., 292*n*8

Beth-Dagon: temple, 20*n*72; town, 12, 20

Beth-Shean, 15, 16, 81–82, 189, 217; absolute chronology, 294; anthropoid coffin burials, 13, 29, 252, 255, 263, 268–86, 280, 284, 288; cult vessels, 222, 224, 227*n*27, 249; mentioned in relation to other sites, 70, 80, 86, 87, 125, 151*n*81, 154*n*98, 159; Philistine settlement in, 18, 295, 296; temple at, 21, 66, 251; Type 1 bowls, 105

Beth-Shemesh, 24, 50–51, 94*n*1, 199; absolute chronology, 294; mentioned in relation to other sites, 54, 59, 224; settlement of, 295; Type 1 bowls, 102; Type 2 kraters, 113–14; Type 3 stirrup jars, 123–24; Type 6 jugs, 148–49; Type 7 jugs, 157; Type 9 bottles, 160, 166; Type 10 horn-shaped vessels, 171; Type 12 jugs, 172; Type 14 jugs, 188–89; Type 15 juglets, 189

Beth-Zur (Khirbet eṭ-Ṭubeiqeh), 44–48

Bethel (Beitin), 54; settlement of, 295

Bible, 52, 218, 274, 289; accounts of Philistines in, 1, 4, 13–21, 295, 296; Philistine temples in, 251

Biran, A., 48*n*132, 113*n*26

Bird motif, 41, 44, 58, 96, 106, 151, 153, 198–203, 208, 214

Bird-shaped vessels, 224–27, 251

Birmingham, J., 59*n*203

Bittel, K., 159*n*119

Bliss, F. J., 48, 50*n*133, 88, 166*n*129, 227*n*27

Bonfante, G., 22*n*85

Bottles, 160–66, 198, 215, 222. *See also* Decoration; Philistine pottery; and under names of sites

Bouzek, J., 12*n*46

Bowls, 208, 224, 227; Type 1, 96–106, 197, 198; Type 13, 185–88. *See also* Decoration; Lekanai; Philistine pottery; and under names of sites

Brandl, B., 30*n*59, 43, 86*n*340, 152*n*88, 254*n*5

Briend, J., 159*n*118

Brock, J. K., 159*n*122

Brunkon, G., 183*n*160, 263*n*15

Bullard, R. G., 51*n*152, 102*n*13, 219*n*4

Burial caves (Beth Shemesh), 50–51, 81

Burial customs, 55–57, 246–49, 252–88; Crete, 244; Egypt, 279–88. *See also* Coffins, anthropoid clay; Tombs
Byblos, 4

Canaan, 13, 19, 91, 94, 224, 289; anthropoid burials in, 252–79, 288; chronology of Philistines in, 218, 289–96; cities of Late Bronze Age destroyed, 295–96; religion, deities, 20, 237; Sea Peoples in, 71; transition from Late Bronze to Iron Age, 289
Canaanite pottery, 125, 185, 200, 204, 224; influence on Philistine pottery, 96, 185–88, 215–17
Caphtor (Kephtiu; Kriti; Crete; Cappadocia), 21
Caphtorim (people), 13
Carpenter, R., 293*n*20
Caskey, L. D., 224*n*15
Casson, L., 7*n*30, 11
Catling, H. W., 11*n*36, 12*n*40, 67, 67*n*217, 189*n*178, 249*n*60, 292*n*9
Cemeteries, 35, 81, 252; Azor, 55–57; Tel Zeror, 70. *See also* Burial customs; Coffins, anthropoid clay; Tombs
Chapman, Susannah V., 59*n*203
Checkered patterns (motif), 198, 214, 215
Cherethites (people), 13
Chevrons (motif), 198, 200, 212–14
Chipiez, C., 11*n*34
Chronology, 217–18; absolute, 30, 33, 70–71, 76, 91, 218, 289–96; relative, 25–93. *See also* under names of Egyptian kings
Coche de la Ferté, E., 155*n*103
Coffins, anthropoid clay, 13, 27, 30, 185; in Canaan, 252–79, 288; in Egypt, 279–88; inscribed, 276; typology and iconography of, 254–60, 263, 268–74, 280
Coffins, mummiform, 279
Cohen, R., 88*n*348
Cole, D. P., 51*n*152, 102*n*13, 219*n*4
Concentric semicircles (motif), 198, 209–12
Courtois, J. C., 290*n*5
Cremation, 55–57, 252*n*1
Crete, 13, 21, 22, 198, 203, 231; burial customs, 244; cult objects, 237, 242–44, 246
Cross, F. M., 15*n*52, 289*n*2
Cult, 21, 41, 48, 219–51
Cult vessels, 53, 63, 65, 66, 67, 80, 219–51, 294
Cypriot prototypes of Philistine pottery, 53, 131, 160–72, 215
Cypro-Phoenician Black-on-Red ware, 27, 29, 34, 44*n*116, 48, 51, 53

Cyprus, 4, 7*n*34, 11, 12, 22, 23, 41, 125, 198*n*206, 292; cult objects, 234, 237, 246; "feeding bottle," 157; influence on Philistine culture, 65, 96, 203, 217; invasion of, by Aegeans, 292–94; Late Bronze Age culture disappeared in, 294–95; pottery finds, 130, 152, 154, 155, 159, 172, 191, 194, 224, 231; Rude Style, 154; Sea Peoples in, 218

Dagon (deity), 20, 237; temples of, 17, 18, 35
Tel Dan (Tell el-Qadi), 82–84, 296
Daniel, J. A., 171, 171*n*145
Danuna (Sea People), 57, 84
David, 51, 70, 86, 218, 276; and Goliath, 16, 18, 19; wars, campaigns, conquests, 25, 43, 52, 63, 67, 80, 169, 296
Dayton, J. E., 28*n*35
Decoration, 96, 184, 185, 198–217; cult vessels, 222, 229–31, 244, 246, 249, 251; evolution of, 217–18; Minoan prototypes, 200, 203–04, 205, 208–15, 231; Type 1 bowls, 98; Type 2 kraters, 105–15; Type 3 stirrup jars, 123–25; Type 6 jugs, 132, 148–55; Type 7 jugs, 155–57; Type 8 juglets, 157–60; Type 9 bottles, 160–66; Type 10 horn-shaped vessels, 168–72; Type 12 jugs, 172–85; Type 13 bowls, 185–88; Type 14 jugs, 189; Type 15 juglets, 189–91; Type 17 jugs, 191, 194; Type 18 kraters, 197. *See also* Motifs; Pottery, Philistine; and under names of sites
Decorative compositions, 152; Meggido jug, 148–52
Tell Deir 'Alla (Succoth?), 84–86, 218, 296; absolute chronology, 291–92, 294; mentioned in relation to other sites, 82, 224; Type 6 jugs, 153, 154, 155, 198
Deir el-Balah, 88*n*348, 172*n*150, 191*n*186; anthropoid coffin burials, 252–60, 263, 268, 276, 279–80, 288; Philistines in, 296
Deir el-Medineh, 227*n*27
Denyen (Sea People), 3, 11, 22; headdress, 5, 12, 274
Desborough, V. R. d'A., 12*n*43, 57*n*197, 94*n*1, 200, 218, 227, 227*n*25, 292*n*8, 293*n*9
Dever, W. G., 51*n*152, 102*n*13, 219*n*4
Dikaios, P., 11*n*39, 102*n*7, 155, 167*n*134, 218, 293*n*9
Djahi (in Phoenicia), 3, 5
Dor, 4, 16
Dor (Tell el-Burj), 69, 229
Dorians, 57, 65
Dothan, M., 17*n*61, 36*n*104, 55, 188*n*168, 219*n*2
Dothan, T., 94*n*1, 219*n*1, 252*n*3

Dots (motif), 199, 212
Dow, S., 13*n*51
Drower, M. S., 292*n*6
Druks, A., 55*n*191, 214*n*239
Dunayevsky, I., 70*n*232
Duncan, J. G., 28*n*33, 98*n*3, 254*n*6

Eben-ezer ('Izbet Ṣarṭah?), battle of, 15, 16, 17, 89, 90, 296
Edelstein, G., 44*n*119
Edwards, I. E. S., 279*n*32
Egypt, 13, 69, 81, 172; anthropoid burials in, 254–55, 279–88; decline of power, 1, 4, 289; historical sources on Philistines, 1–13, 218; influence in Canaan, 289, 295, 296; influence on Philistine culture, 41, 43, 70, 81, 82, 96, 148, 172–85, 203, 215, 217; New Kingdom period, 87, 279; Twelfth Dynasty, 19, 279; Eighteenth Dynasty, 184, 229, 231, 263, 279; Nineteenth Dynasty, 28, 55, 81, 86*n*340, 249*n*58, 254*n*6, 279, 289, 291; Twentieth Dynasty, 3*n*6, 4, 28, 55, 81, 279*n*34, 280, 295; Twenty-First Dynasty, 4, 52; Twenty-Third Dynasty, 254*n*6
Ekron (Khirbet Muqanna'?) (city), 17, 18, 20, 57, 88; Philistine settlement in, 296
Tell el-'Ajjul (Beth Eglayim?), 28, 35, 130, 171, 184
el-Amarna tablets, 21
Tell el-Batashi (Timnah?), 90
Tell el-Far'ah (Sharuhen?), 24, 27–33, 90, 242; absolute chronology, 294; anthropoid coffin burials, 185, 260–68, 276, 280, 284, 288; chalices, 184, 185; mentioned in relation to other sites, 34, 51, 57, 102, 149, 188, 189; Philistines in, 296; scarabs, 218, 295; Type 1 bowls, 98–102, 106; Type 2 kraters, 113; Type 3 jars, 123, 124; Type 5 jars, 132; Type 6 jugs, 132–48, 149; Type 7 jugs, 157; Type 8 juglets, 157, 159; Type 9 bottles, 160–66; Type 12 jugs, 172, 183; Type 15 juglets, 189–91; Type 17 jugs, 194
Tell el-Ḥesi (Eglon?), 86, 88
Tell el-Yahudiyeh, 28, 59*n*204, 254*n*6, 263; anthropoid coffin burials, 280–84
Elah Valley, 16
Tell en-Naṣbeh (Mizpah?), 54
Engelbach, R., 183*n*160, 263*n*15, 279
Enkomi, 7*n*34, 13, 22, 65, 102, 217, 218, 293; decorative elements, 203, 204, 274; Griffin Slayer (figure), 11, 12; mentioned in relation to other sites, 41, 115, 154, 188*n*170; pottery finds, 106*n*23, 132, 154–55, 167*n*134

Persson, A. W.; 229n28
Petrie, W. M. F., 24, 25, 27nn15, 20, 21, 28, 59n204, 98n3, 184, 254n6, 263; Tell el-Far'ah tombs, 29n50, 30, 32n65; Tell el-Hesi, 88; Tell Jemmeh, 33–34; Tell Nebesheh, 284
Phaestos Disk, 13, 22
Philistia (territory), 13, 15, 16–17, 24, 25, 41, 42, 52, 295, 296; cult objects, 246; Israelite ascendancy over, 218; royal office in, 19; Sea Peoples settled in, 251
Philistine (term), 23, 25
Philistine culture, 252, 295; assimilated into local, 96, 296; bird in, 227; diffusion of, 1, 24, 25, 217, 295, 296; eclectic nature of, 246–49, 251, 252; Egyptian elements in, 288; evolution of, 251; phases of, 296; relative chronology of, 25–93; term, 25
Philistine Pentapolis, 17–18, 35, 296
Philistine pottery, 25, 94–218; chronology of finds, 25–93; Aegean prototypes, 67; Cretan prototypes, 80; Cypriot prototypes, 53, 131, 160–72, 215; eclectic nature of, 185, 189, 191, 197–98, 200, 214, 217; Group I (Types 1–8), 6, 7, 96–160, 189, 194n194, 209, 215, 217; Group II (Types 9–11), 160–72, 209, 217; Group III (Type 12), 172–85, 189, 209, 215, 217; Group IV (Types 13–16), 184, 185–91, 209, 215, 217; Group V (Types 17–18), 191–98, 215; Group VI, 219; hallmark of Philistine culture, 217; human figures in, 150; hybrid, 63, 80; influence of Canaanite pottery on, 96, 185–88, 215–17; Mycenaean influence of, 36, 37–41, 96–160, 198–218; preceded by Mycenaean IIIC ceramics, 295; Phase 1, 27, 28, 29, 30, 32, 34, 36, 44, 52, 53, 87, 96, 113, 148–55, 159, 198, 214, 217; Phase 2, 27, 29, 32, 34, 44, 53, 80, 96, 148–55, 172, 183, 198, 217, 218; Phase 3, 29, 32, 34, 44, 48, 51, 54, 55, 70, 78, 80, 82, 96, 148–55, 191–98, 209, 214, 215, 217, 218; phases of, 27–28, 33, 90–91, 94–96; Syro-Palestinian prototypes, 154; uniqueness of, 218; workmanship, 115. See also Cult vessels; Decoration; and under names of sites
Philistines (Pelesti) (includes Peleset, Tjekker, and Denyen), 4, 5, 18; absolute chronology of coming to Canaan, 289–95; adopted Egyptian burial customs, 288; Aegean background of, 7–11, 13, 19–20, 21, 22, 24, 94, 203, 218, 237, 251; assimilation of, 1; at Beth-Shean, 274–76; in Canaan, 218,

252, 289–96; defeat of Israelites, 296; at Deir el-Balah, 255–60; deities, 237; dress, 19–20; under Egyptian rule, 4; expansion, 24, 35, 218, 296; feathered headdress, 5, 7, 11, 12–13, 22, 274; government, 18–19; historical sources, 1–24, 292; intercultural connections, 65; invasions, migrations, 1, 16, 218, 296; as mercenaries, 5, 13, 28, 288, 296; military organization, 5–7, 19–20; monopoly on iron, metalworking, 15, 20, 86, 91; origins, 21–23, 203, 217; process of settlement, 295–96; religion, 20–21; research on and archaeology, 23–24; social organization, 19
Phrygians, 65n211
Phylakopi (on Melos), 251; temple, 66
Phythian-Adams, W. J., 24, 35, 35n96, 94n1
Pichol (name), 23
Pieridou, A., 224n15
Pomegranate (vessel), 224
Porada, Edith, 11, 11n39, 150n78
Pottery: in anthropoid burials, 263–68; Dorian, 65; imported (Mycenaean and Cypriot), 33, 37, 50, 58, 72, 90, 125, 131, 255, 289, 294; local Canaanite, 28, 30–32, 37, 58, 59, 72; Midianite, 28. See also Philistine pottery
Pritchard, J. B., 1n4, 55n193, 168n139, 237n41, 252n2
Pylos, 217
Pyxis, 159, 168; and amphoriskos (Type 4), 96, 125–31

Tell Qasile, 24, 27, 48, 57–67, 90, 94n1, 204; cult objects, 208, 219, 224, 227, 229, 231, 249, 251; kraters, 208; mentioned in relation to other sites, 34, 35, 48, 53, 55, 57, 69, 76, 79, 80, 87, 98n3, 113, 115, 148, 268, 276, 284n45, 292n5; Philistine settlement in, 296; Type 1 bowls, 102; Type 2 kraters, 114; Type 5 pyxis, 130, 131; Type 6 jugs, 149; Type 7 jugs, 157; Type 8 juglets, 157, 159; Type 9 bottles, 160, 166; Type 10 horn-shaped vessel, 171; Type 12 jugs, 172, 183; Type 13 bowls, 188; Type 17 jug, 194; Type 18 kraters, 197
Qatra, 90
Tell Qiri (ha-Zore'a), 90
Qubur el-Walaida, 88
Tell Quneitra, 88
Qurayyah (in Arabia), 28

Raban, A., 90n357
Rabin, C., 17n64
Rainey, A. F., 50n133
Ramesses II, 1, 21, 27, 86n340, 89,

219n5, 242, 254, 293n16; scarabs, 29, 30n60, 260, 276n29, 279, 294
Ramesses III, 18, 21, 87, 279, 290, 292n6, 294, 295; and absolute chronology, 91, 289; cartouche, 17, 53, 70, 71, 81, 82, 219, 222, 229, 294; defeated Sea Peoples, 13, 288, 293, 296; palace at Tell el-Yahudiyeh, 28; scarabs, 29, 30, 35, 51, 71, 76, 276, 280, 293n11, 294, 295; statue of, 81, 294; temple at Medinet, 23; wall reliefs, 274 (see also Medinet Habu [Thebes] reliefs); wars with Sea Peoples, 1–3, 5–13
Ramesses IV, 28, 91, 276n29; scarabs, 29, 33, 260, 294, 295
Ramesses V, 91
Ramesses VI, 76, 89, 91, 280, 295
Ramesses VII, 91
Ramesses VIII, 29n50, 91, 260, 294
Ramesses IX, 91
Ramesses X, 30n59, 32, 33, 86n340, 91, 218
Ramesses XI, 30, 33
Ramesses-Weser-Khepesh, 81
Ranke, H., 274n21
Reed, W. L., 252n2
Religion. See Cult
Renfrew, Colin, 66n214
Rhodes, 125, 130, 172, 198n206, 217; cult objects, 234, 246; prototypes from, 131
Rhyta, 219, 224, 251; lion-headed, 205, 229–34
Richmond, E. T., 263n14
Riis, P. J., 57n197
Rimmer, J., 152n88
Ring kernoi, 219; Gezer cache, 222–24
Riqqeh, 279
Ritual stands, pottery, 249–51
Roberts, J. J. M., 15n52
Rothenberg, B., 28n34, 295n24
Rowe, A., 51n145, 151n81, 222n7, 254n7

St. Xanthudidis, 244n49
Salamis, Cyprus, 159, 160
Samson, 152, 251; cycle, 15, 17, 18
Sanders, J. A., 15n53
Saul, king of Israel, 15–16, 18, 19, 20, 81; death of, 57, 81, 274
Saussey, E., 94n1
Scale pattern (motif), 198, 212
Scarabs, 30, 32, 55, 65, 86n340, 254; in Tell el-Far'ah tombs, 29. See also under Ramesses
Schachermeyr, F., 13n49
Schaeffer, C. F. A., 7n31, 12, 65, 65n209, 67, 154–55, 154n101, 224n23, 234n37, 290n4
Schmid, H. E., 244n48
Schumacher, G., 249n60

Photo credits: Z. Radovan, chap. 2, pls. 1, 2, 4, 6, 8, 20; chap. 3, pls. 1–3, 9, 10 (detail), 11–14, 26, 28, 29, 32, 37, 39, 43, 62, 73–75, 81–84, 88, 89, 91, 92, 94; chap. 4, pls. 1, 3, 4, 6, 8, 9–13, 17, 18, 23:1,2, 24, 25, 31, 33, 35; chap. 5, pls. 1, 2, 3:2,3, 4, 5, 10, 12. J. Schweig, chap. 2, pl. 7; chap. 3, pls. 5, 6, 8, 10, 15, 17, 18, 20–23, 31, 48, 49, 51, 53, 61, 68, 69, 79, 86; chap. 4, pls. 15, 32. Pri-Or, chap. 2, pl. 13; chap. 3, pls. 16, 55. H. Berger, chap. 4, pl. 23:3. D. Harris, chap. 5, pl. 3:1,4. B. Rothenberg, chap. 5, pls. 8, 9. Z. Kluger, chap. 5, pl. 15.